To Catherine, Nicholas, and Peter,
my other contributions to the next generation

About the Author

N. Gregory Mankiw is professor of economics at Harvard University. As a student, he studied economics at Princeton University and MIT. As a teacher, he has taught macroeconomics, microeconomics, statistics, and principles of economics. He even spent one summer long ago as a sailing instructor on Long Beach Island.

Professor Mankiw is a prolific writer and a regular participant in academic and policy debates. His work has been published in scholarly journals, such as the *American Economic Review, Journal of Political Economy,* and *Quarterly Journal of Economics*, and in more popular forums, such as *The New York Times* and *The Wall Street Journal*. He is also author of the best-selling intermediate-level textbook *Macroeconomics* (Worth Publishers). In addition to his teaching, research, and writing, Professor Mankiw has been a research associate of the National Bureau of Economic Research, an adviser to the Federal Reserve Bank of Boston and the Congressional Budget Office, and a member of the ETS test development committee for the Advanced Placement exam in economics. From 2003 to 2005, he served as chairman of the President's Council of Economic Advisers.

Professor Mankiw lives in Wellesley, Massachusetts, with his wife, Deborah, three children, Catherine, Nicholas, and Peter, and their border terrier, Tobin.

PRINCIPLES OF
Microeconomics

FIFTH EDITION

N. GREGORY MANKIW
HARVARD UNIVERSITY

SOUTH-WESTERN
CENGAGE Learning™

Australia • Brazil • Japan • Korea • Mexico • Singapore • Spain • United Kingdom • United States

SOUTH-WESTERN
CENGAGE Learning

Principles of Microeconomics, 5e
N. Gregory Mankiw

Vice President of Editorial, Business:
Jack W. Calhoun

Vice President/Editor-in-Chief:
Alex von Rosenberg

Executive Editor: Mike Worls

Developmental Editor: Jane Tufts

Contributing Editors: Jennifer E. Thomas and
Katie Yanos

Executive Marketing Manager: Brian Joyner

Marketing Coordinator: Suellen Ruttkay

Senior Content Project Manager:
Colleen A. Farmer

Marketing Communications Manager:
Sarah Greber

Manager of Technology, Editorial: Pam Wallace

Media Editor: Deepak Kumar

Senior Frontlist Buyer, Manufacturing:
Sandee Milewski

Production Service: Lachina Publishing
Services

Senior Art Director: Michelle Kunkler

Internal and Cover Designer: Red Hangar
Design, LLC

Internal Paintings: © Michael Steirnagle/
Munro Campagna Artistic Representatives

Cover Painting: © Fine Art Photographic
Library/CORBIS

Photography Manager: Deanna Ettinger

Photo Researcher: Charlotte Goldman

For product information and technology assistance, contact us at
Cengage Learning Customer & Sales Support, 1-800-354-9706

For permission to use material from this text or product,
submit all requests online at **www.cengage.com/permissions**
Further permissions questions can be emailed to
permissionrequest@cengage.com

Library of Congress Control Number: 2008935332
ISBN-13: 978-0-324-58998-6
ISBN-10: 0-324-58998-0
Instructor's Edition ISBN 13: 978-0-324-59132-3
Instructor's Edition ISBN 10: 0-324-59132-2

South-Western Cengage Learning
5191 Natorp Boulevard
Mason, OH 45040
USA

Cengage Learning products are represented in Canada by
Nelson Education, Ltd.

For your course and learning solutions, visit **academic.cengage.com**

Purchase any of our products at your local college store or at our preferred online store **www.ichapters.com**

Printed in the United States of America
1 2 3 4 5 6 7 12 11 10 09 08

Brief Contents

Preface: To the Student

"Economics is a study of mankind in the ordinary business of life." So wrote Alfred Marshall, the great 19th-century economist, in his textbook, *Principles of Economics*. Although we have learned much about the economy since Marshall's time, this definition of economics is as true today as it was in 1890, when the first edition of his text was published.

Why should you, as a student at the beginning of the 21st century, embark on the study of economics? There are three reasons.

The first reason to study economics is that it will help you understand the world in which you live. There are many questions about the economy that might spark your curiosity. Why are apartments so hard to find in New York City? Why do airlines charge less for a round-trip ticket if the traveler stays over a Saturday night? Why is Johnny Depp paid so much to star in movies? Why are living standards so meager in many African countries? Why do some countries have high rates of inflation while others have stable prices? Why are jobs easy to find in some years and hard to find in others? These are just a few of the questions that a course in economics will help you answer.

The second reason to study economics is that it will make you a more astute participant in the economy. As you go about your life, you make many economic decisions. While you are a student, you decide how many years to stay in school. Once you take a job, you decide how much of your income to spend, how much to save, and how to invest your savings. Someday you may find yourself running a small business or a large corporation, and you will decide what prices to charge for your products. The insights developed in the coming chapters will give you a new perspective on how best to make these decisions. Studying economics will not by itself make you rich, but it will give you some tools that may help in that endeavor.

The third reason to study economics is that it will give you a better understanding of both the potential and the limits of economic policy. Economic questions are always on the minds of policymakers in mayors' offices, governors' mansions, and the White House. What are the burdens associated with alternative forms of taxation? What are the effects of free trade with other countries? What is the best way to protect the environment? How does a government budget deficit affect the economy? As a voter, you help choose the policies that guide the allocation of society's resources. An understanding of economics will help you carry out that responsibility. And who knows: Perhaps someday you will end up as one of those policymakers yourself.

Thus, the principles of economics can be applied in many of life's situations. Whether the future finds you reading the newspaper, running a business, or sitting in the Oval Office, you will be glad that you studied economics.

N. Gregory Mankiw
September 2008

Mankiw 5e. Experience It.

We know you are often short on time. But you can maximize your efforts — and results — when you Experience Mankiw Fifth Edition's engaging learning tools. With the product support website and EconCentral, you'll quickly reinforce chapter concepts and sharpen your skills with interactive, hands-on applications online.

If a printed Study Guide better suits your needs and study habits, the Mankiw 5e Study Guide is unsurpassed in its careful attention to accuracy, concise language, and practice that enhances your study time.

Product Support Website

www.cengage.com/economics/mankiw

The Mankiw product support website is an easy online stop. Here, you'll find access to free quizzing, Student Note Prompt handouts for the Premium PowerPoint® your instructor may use, and other resources.

Study Guide

Helping you achieve your personal best, the Mankiw Study Guide is based completely on the Fifth Edition, covering chapter material comprehensively — and accurately. Very hands-on, each chapter thoroughly covers the material in the corresponding chapter of Mankiw. Every key word and concept is addressed within the Study Guide chapter — meaning you'll feel confident that if you can do the study guide, you will understand all of the material in that chapter of Mankiw.

The "types" of questions used in the Study Guide reflect what you find most useful when studying. Our student surveys show that students like you felt that fill-in-the-blank questions, matching questions, and questions without specific single answers were an inefficient use of their time — and the Mankiw Study Guide avoids these kinds of questions.

To order the study guide, visit **www.ichapters.com**.

Self-Study Solutions

EconCentral

Multiple resources for learning and reinforcing principles concepts are now available in one place! EconCentral is your one-stop shop for the learning tools and activities to help you succeed.

At a minimal extra cost, EconCentral equips you with a portal to a wealth of resources that help you both study and apply economic concepts. As you read and study the chapters, you can access video tutorials with Greg Mankiw Answers Key Questions, 10 Principles Videos, and Ask the Instructor Videos. You can review with Flash Cards and the Graphing Workshop, check your understanding of the chapter with interactive quizzing, and print Student Note Prompt handouts for the Premium PowerPoint® to make note-taking in class much more efficient.

Ready to apply chapter concepts to the real world? EconCentral gives you ABC News videos, EconNews articles, Economic debates, Links to Economic Data, and more. All the study and application resources in EconCentral are organized by chapter to help you get the most from the Mankiw text and from your classes.

Visit **www.cengage.com/economics/mankiw/5e/ econcentral** to see the study options available!

Acknowledgments

In writing this book, I benefited from the input of many talented people. Indeed, the list of people who have contributed to this project is so long, and their contributions so valuable, that it seems an injustice that only a single name appears on the cover.

Let me begin with my colleagues in the economics profession. The four editions of this text and its supplemental materials have benefited enormously from their input. In reviews and surveys, they have offered suggestions, identified challenges, and shared ideas from their own classroom experience. I am indebted to them for the perspectives they have brought to the text. Unfortunately, the list has become too long to thank those who contributed to previous editions, even though students reading the current edition are still benefiting from their insights.

Most important in this process have been Ron Cronovich (Carthage College) and David Hakes (University of Northern Iowa). Ron and David, both dedicated teachers, have served as reliable sounding boards for ideas and hardworking partners with me in putting together the superb package of supplements.

For this new edition, the following diary reviewers recorded their day-to-day experience over the course of a semester, offering detailed suggestions about how to improve the text.

John Crooker, *University of Central Missouri*
Rachel Friedberg, *Brown University*
Greg Hunter, *California State University, Polytechnic, Pomona*
Lillian Kamal, *Northwestern University*

Francis Kemegue, *Bryant University*
Douglas Miller, *University of Missouri*
Babu Nahata, *University of Louisville*
Edward Skelton, *Southern Methodist University*

The following reviewers of the fourth edition provided suggestions for refining the content, organization, and approach in the fifth.

Syed Ahmed, *Cameron University*
Farhad Ameen, *State University of New York, Westchester Community College*
Mohammad Bajwa, *Northampton Community College*
Carl Bauer, *Oakton Community College*
Roberta Biby, *Grand Valley State University*
Stephen Billings, *University of Colorado at Boulder*

Bruce Brown, *California State University, Polytechnic, Pomona*
Lynn Burbridge, *Northern Kentucky University*
Mark Chester, *Reading Area Community College*
David Ching, *University of Hawaii, Manoa*
Sarah Cosgrove, *University of Massachusetts, Dartmouth*

Craig Depken, *University of North Carolina, Charlotte*
Angela Dzata, *Alabama State University*
Jose Esteban, *Palomar College*
Mark Frascatore, *Clarkson University*
Satyajit Ghosh, *University of Scranton*
Soma Ghosh, *Bridgewater State College*
Daniel Giedeman, *Grand Valley State University*
Robert L. Holland, *Purdue University*
Anisul Islam, *University of Houston, Downtown*
Nancy Jianakoplos, *Colorado State University*
Paul Johnson, *University of Alaska, Anchorage*
Robert Jones, *University of Massachusetts, Dartmouth*
Lillian Kamal, *Northwestern University*
Jongsung Kim, *Bryant University*
Marek Kolar, *Delta College*
Leonard Lardaro, *University of Rhode Island*
Nazma Latif-Zaman, *Providence College*

William Mertens, *University of Colorado*
Francis Mummery, *Fullerton College*
David Mushinski, *Colorado State University*
Christopher Mushrush, *Illinois State University*
Babu Nahata, *University of Louisville*
Laudo Ogura, *Grand Valley State University*
Michael Patrono, *Okaloosa-Walton College*
Jeff Rubin, *Rutgers University, New Brunswick*
Samuel Sarri, *College of Southern Nevada*
Harinder Singh, *Grand Valley State University*
David Spencer, *University of Michigan*
David Switzer, *Saint Cloud State University*
Henry Terrell, *University of Maryland*
Ngocbich Tran, *San Jacinto College*
Miao Wang, *Marquette University*
Elizabeth Wheaton, *Southern Methodist University*
Martin Zelder, *Northwestern University*

I received detailed feedback on specific elements in the text, including all end-of-chapter problems and applications, from the following instructors.

Casey R. Abington, *Kansas State University*
Seemi Ahmad, *Dutchess Community College*
Farhad Ameen, *State University of New York, Westchester Community College*
J. J. Arias, *Georgia College & State University*
James Bathgate, *Willamette University*
Scott Beaulier, *Mercer University*
Clive Belfield, *Queens College*
Calvin Blackwell, *College of Charleston*
Cecil E. Bohanon, *Ball State University*
Douglas Campbell, *University of Memphis*
Michael G. Carew, *Baruch College*
Sewin Chan, *New York University*

Joyce J. Chen, *The Ohio State University*
Edward A. Cohn, *Del Mar College*
Chad D. Cotti, *University of South Carolina*
Erik D. Craft, *University of Richmond*
Eleanor D. Craig, *University of Delaware*
Abdelmagead Elbiali, *Rio Hondo College*
Harold W. Elder, *University of Alabama*
Hadi Salehi Esfahani, *University of Illinois, Urbana-Champaign*
David Franck, *Francis Marion University*
Amanda S. Freeman, *Kansas State University*
J.P. Gilbert, *MiraCosta College*

Joanne Guo, *Dyson College of Pace University*

Charles E. Hegji, *Auburn University at Montgomery*

Andrew J. Hussey, *University of Memphis*

Hans R. Isakson, *University of Northern Iowa*

Simran Kahai, *John Carroll University*

David E. Kalist, *Shippensburg University*

Mark P. Karscig, *University of Central Missouri*

Theodore Kuhn, *Butler University*

Dong Li, *Kansas State University*

Daniel Lin, *George Mason University*

Nathaniel Manning, *Southern University*

Vince Marra, *University of Delaware*

Akbar Marvasti, *University of Southern Mississippi*

Heather Mattson, *University of Saint Thomas*

Charles C. Moul, *Washington University in St. Louis*

Albert A. Okunade, *University of Memphis*

J. Brian O'Roark, *Robert Morris University*

Anthony L. Ostrosky, *Illinois State University*

Nitin V. Paranjpe, *Wayne State University & Oakland University*

Sanela Porča, *University of South Carolina, Aiken*

Walter G. Park, *American University*

Reza M. Ramazani, *Saint Michael's College*

Rhonda Vonshay Sharpe, *University of Vermont*

Carolyn Fabian Stumph, *Indiana University–Purdue University Fort Wayne*

Rick Tannery, *Slippery Rock University*

Aditi Thapar, *New York University*

Michael H. Tew, *Troy University*

Jennifer A. Vincent, *Champlain College*

Milos Vulanovic, *Lehman College*

Bhavneet Walia, *Kansas State University*

Douglas M. Walker, *College of Charleston*

Patrick Walsh, *Saint Michael's College*

Larry Wolfenbarger, *Macon State College*

William C. Wood, *James Madison University*

Chiou-nan Yeh, *Alabama State University*

The accuracy of a textbook is critically important. I am responsible for any remaining errors, but I am grateful to the following professors for reading through the final manuscript and page proofs with me:

Joel Dalafave, *Bucks County Community College*

Greg Hunter, *California State University – Pomona*

Lillian Kamal, *Northwestern University*

Francis Kemegue, *Bryant University*

Douglas Miller, *University of Missouri*

Ed Skelton, *Southern Methodist University*

The team of editors who worked on this book improved it tremendously. Jane Tufts, developmental editor, provided truly spectacular editing—as she always does. Mike Worls, economics executive editor, did a splendid job of overseeing the many people involved in such a large project. Jennifer Thomas (senior developmental editor) and Katie Yanos (developmental editor) were crucial in assembling an extensive and thoughtful group of reviewers to give me feedback on the previous edition, while putting together an excellent team to revise the supplements. Colleen Farmer, senior content project manager, and Katherine Wilson, senior project manager, had the patience and dedication necessary to turn my manuscript into this book. Michelle Kunkler, senior art director, gave this book its clean, friendly look. Michael Steirnagle, the illustrator, helped make the book more visually appealing and the economics in it less abstract. Carolyn Crabtree, copyeditor, refined my prose, and Terry Casey, indexer, prepared a careful and thorough index. Brian Joyner, executive marketing manager, worked long hours getting the word out to potential users of this book. The rest of the Cengage team, including Jean Buttrom, Sandra Milewski and Deepak Kumar, was also consistently professional, enthusiastic, and dedicated.

I am grateful also to Josh Bookin, a former Advanced Placement economics teacher and recently an extraordinary section leader for Ec 10, the introductory course at Harvard. Josh helped me refine the manuscript and check the page proofs for this edition.

As always, I must thank my "in-house" editor Deborah Mankiw. As the first reader of almost everything I write, she continued to offer just the right mix of criticism and encouragement.

Finally, I would like to mention my three children Catherine, Nicholas, and Peter. Their contribution to this book was putting up with a father spending too many hours in his study. The four of us have much in common—not least of which is our love of ice cream (which becomes apparent in Chapter 4). Maybe sometime soon one of them will pick up my passion for economics as well.

N. Gregory Mankiw
September 2008

Table of Contents

PART II
HOW MARKETS WORK   63

PART III
MARKETS AND WELFARE   135

PART IV
THE ECONOMICS OF THE PUBLIC
SECTOR   201

PART V
FIRM BEHAVIOR AND THE ORGANIZATION OF INDUSTRY 265

PART VI
THE ECONOMICS OF LABOR
MARKETS   389

PART VII
TOPICS FOR FURTHER STUDY 455

PART I

Introduction

Ten Principles of Economics

The word *economy* comes from the Greek word *oikonomos*, which means "one who manages a household." At first, this origin might seem peculiar. But in fact, households and economies have much in common.

A household faces many decisions. It must decide which members of the household do which tasks and what each member gets in return: Who cooks dinner? Who does the laundry? Who gets the extra dessert at dinner? Who gets to choose what TV show to watch? In short, the household must allocate its scarce resources among its various members, taking into account each member's abilities, efforts, and desires.

Like a household, a society faces many decisions. A society must find some way to decide what jobs will be done and who will do them. It needs some people to grow food, other people to make clothing, and still others to design computer software. Once society has allocated people (as well as land, buildings, and machines) to various jobs, it must also allocate the output of goods and services they produce. It must decide who will eat caviar and who will eat potatoes. It must decide who will drive a Ferrari and who will take the bus.

The management of society's resources is important because resources are scarce. **Scarcity** means that society has limited resources and therefore cannot produce all the goods and services people wish to have. Just as each member of a household cannot get everything he or she wants, each individual in a society cannot attain the highest standard of living to which he or she might aspire.

scarcity
the limited nature of society's resources

economics
the study of how society manages its scarce resources

Economics is the study of how society manages its scarce resources. In most societies, resources are allocated not by an all-powerful dictator but through the combined actions of millions of households and firms. Economists therefore study how people make decisions: how much they work, what they buy, how much they save, and how they invest their savings. Economists also study how people interact with one another. For instance, they examine how the multitude of buyers and sellers of a good together determine the price at which the good is sold and the quantity that is sold. Finally, economists analyze forces and trends that affect the economy as a whole, including the growth in average income, the fraction of the population that cannot find work, and the rate at which prices are rising.

The study of economics has many facets, but it is unified by several central ideas. In this chapter, we look at *Ten Principles of Economics*. Don't worry if you don't understand them all at first or if you aren't completely convinced. We will explore these ideas more fully in later chapters. The ten principles are introduced here to give you an overview of what economics is all about. Consider this chapter a "preview of coming attractions."

HOW PEOPLE MAKE DECISIONS

There is no mystery to what an economy is. Whether we are talking about the economy of Los Angeles, the United States, or the whole world, an economy is just a group of people dealing with one another as they go about their lives. Because the behavior of an economy reflects the behavior of the individuals who make up the economy, we begin our study of economics with four principles of individual decision making.

PRINCIPLE 1: PEOPLE FACE TRADE-OFFS

You may have heard the old saying, "There ain't no such thing as a free lunch." Grammar aside, there is much truth to this adage. To get one thing that we like, we usually have to give up another thing that we like. Making decisions requires trading off one goal against another.

Consider a student who must decide how to allocate her most valuable resource—her time. She can spend all her time studying economics, spend all of it studying psychology, or divide it between the two fields. For every hour she studies one subject, she gives up an hour she could have used studying the other. And for every hour she spends studying, she gives up an hour that she could have spent napping, bike riding, watching TV, or working at her part-time job for some extra spending money.

Or consider parents deciding how to spend their family income. They can buy food, clothing, or a family vacation. Or they can save some of the family income for retirement or the children's college education. When they choose to spend an extra dollar on one of these goods, they have one less dollar to spend on some other good.

When people are grouped into societies, they face different kinds of trade-offs. The classic trade-off is between "guns and butter." The more a society spends on national defense (guns) to protect its shores from foreign aggressors, the less it can spend on consumer goods (butter) to raise the standard of living at home. Also important in modern society is the trade-off between a clean environment and a high level of income. Laws that require firms to reduce pollution raise the cost of producing goods and services. Because of the higher costs, these firms end up earning smaller profits, paying lower wages, charging higher prices, or some combination of these three. Thus, while pollution regulations yield the benefit of a cleaner environment and the improved health that comes with it, they have the cost of reducing the incomes of the firms' owners, workers, and customers.

Another trade-off society faces is between efficiency and equality. **Efficiency** means that society is getting the maximum benefits from its scarce resources. **Equality** means that those benefits are distributed uniformly among society's members. In other words, efficiency refers to the size of the economic pie, and equality refers to how the pie is divided into individual slices.

efficiency
the property of society getting the most it can from its scarce resources

equality
the property of distributing economic prosperity uniformly among the members of society

When government policies are designed, these two goals often conflict. Consider, for instance, policies aimed at equalizing the distribution of economic well-being. Some of these policies, such as the welfare system or unemployment insurance, try to help the members of society who are most in need. Others, such as the individual income tax, ask the financially successful to contribute more than others to support the government. While achieving greater equality, these policies reduce efficiency. When the government redistributes income from the rich to the poor, it reduces the reward for working hard; as a result, people work less and produce fewer goods and services. In other words, when the government tries to cut the economic pie into more equal slices, the pie gets smaller.

Recognizing that people face trade-offs does not by itself tell us what decisions they will or should make. A student should not abandon the study of psychology just because doing so would increase the time available for the study of economics. Society should not stop protecting the environment just because environmental regulations reduce our material standard of living. The poor should not be ignored just because helping them distorts work incentives. Nonetheless, people are likely to make good decisions only if they understand the options they have available. Our study of economics, therefore, starts by acknowledging life's trade-offs.

PRINCIPLE 2: THE COST OF SOMETHING IS WHAT YOU GIVE UP TO GET IT

Because people face trade-offs, making decisions requires comparing the costs and benefits of alternative courses of action. In many cases, however, the cost of an action is not as obvious as it might first appear.

Consider the decision to go to college. The main benefits are intellectual enrichment and a lifetime of better job opportunities. But what are the costs? To answer this question, you might be tempted to add up the money you spend on tuition, books, room, and board. Yet this total does not truly represent what you give up to spend a year in college.

There are two problems with this calculation. First, it includes some things that are not really costs of going to college. Even if you quit school, you need a place to sleep and food to eat. Room and board are costs of going to college only to the extent that they are more expensive at college than elsewhere. Second, this calculation ignores the largest cost of going to college—your time. When you spend a year listening to lectures, reading textbooks, and writing papers, you cannot spend that time working at a job. For most students, the earnings given up to attend school are the largest single cost of their education.

The **opportunity cost** of an item is what you give up to get that item. When making any decision, decision makers should be aware of the opportunity costs

opportunity cost
whatever must be given up to obtain some item

that accompany each possible action. In fact, they usually are. College athletes who can earn millions if they drop out of school and play professional sports are well aware that their opportunity cost of college is very high. It is not surprising that they often decide that the benefit is not worth the cost.

PRINCIPLE 3: RATIONAL PEOPLE THINK AT THE MARGIN

rational people
people who systematically and purposefully do the best they can to achieve their objectives

Economists normally assume that people are rational. **Rational people** systematically and purposefully do the best they can to achieve their objectives, given the available opportunities. As you study economics, you will encounter firms that decide how many workers to hire and how much of their product to manufacture and sell to maximize profits. You will also encounter individuals who decide how much time to spend working and what goods and services to buy with the resulting income to achieve the highest possible level of satisfaction.

Rational people know that decisions in life are rarely black and white but usually involve shades of gray. At dinnertime, the decision you face is not between fasting or eating like a pig but whether to take that extra spoonful of mashed potatoes. When exams roll around, your decision is not between blowing them off or studying 24 hours a day but whether to spend an extra hour reviewing your notes instead of watching TV. Economists use the term **marginal changes** to describe small incremental adjustments to an existing plan of action. Keep in mind that *margin* means "edge," so marginal changes are adjustments around the edges of what you are doing. Rational people often make decisions by comparing *marginal benefits* and *marginal costs*.

marginal changes
small incremental adjustments to a plan of action

For example, consider an airline deciding how much to charge passengers who fly standby. Suppose that flying a 200-seat plane across the United States costs the airline $100,000. In this case, the average cost of each seat is $100,000/200, which is $500. One might be tempted to conclude that the airline should never sell a ticket for less than $500. In fact, a rational airline can often find ways to raise its profits by thinking at the margin. Imagine that a plane is about to take off with ten empty seats, and a standby passenger waiting at the gate will pay $300 for a seat. Should the airline sell the ticket? Of course it should. If the plane has empty seats, the cost of adding one more passenger is tiny. Although the *average* cost of flying a passenger is $500, the *marginal* cost is merely the cost of the bag of peanuts and can of soda that the extra passenger will consume. As long as the standby passenger pays more than the marginal cost, selling the ticket is profitable.

Marginal decision making can help explain some otherwise puzzling economic phenomena. Here is a classic question: Why is water so cheap, while diamonds are so expensive? Humans need water to survive, while diamonds are unnecessary; but for some reason, people are willing to pay much more for a diamond than for a cup of water. The reason is that a person's willingness to pay for any good is based on the marginal benefit that an extra unit of the good would yield. The marginal benefit, in turn, depends on how many units a person already has. Water is essential, but the marginal benefit of an extra cup is small because water is plentiful. By contrast, no one needs diamonds to survive, but because diamonds are so rare, people consider the marginal benefit of an extra diamond to be large.

A rational decision maker takes an action if and only if the marginal benefit of the action exceeds the marginal cost. This principle can explain why airlines are willing to sell a ticket below average cost and why people are willing to pay more for diamonds than for water. It can take some time to get used to the logic of marginal thinking, but the study of economics will give you ample opportunity to practice.

PRINCIPLE 4: PEOPLE RESPOND TO INCENTIVES

An **incentive** is something that induces a person to act, such as the prospect of a punishment or a reward. Because rational people make decisions by comparing costs and benefits, they respond to incentives. You will see that incentives play a central role in the study of economics. One economist went so far as to suggest that the entire field could be simply summarized: "People respond to incentives. The rest is commentary."

Incentives are crucial to analyzing how markets work. For example, when the price of an apple rises, people decide to eat fewer apples. At the same time, apple orchards decide to hire more workers and harvest more apples. In other words, a higher price in a market provides an incentive for buyers to consume less and an incentive for sellers to produce more. As we will see, the influence of prices on the behavior of consumers and producers is crucial for how a market economy allocates scarce resources.

Public policymakers should never forget about incentives: Many policies change the costs or benefits that people face and, therefore, alter their behavior. A tax on gasoline, for instance, encourages people to drive smaller, more fuel-efficient cars. That is one reason people drive smaller cars in Europe, where gasoline taxes are high, than in the United States, where gasoline taxes are low. A gasoline tax also encourages people to carpool, take public transportation, and live closer to where they work. If the tax were larger, more people would be driving hybrid cars, and if it were large enough, they would switch to electric cars.

When policymakers fail to consider how their policies affect incentives, they often end up with unintended consequences. For example, consider public policy regarding auto safety. Today, all cars have seat belts, but this was not true 50 years ago. In the 1960s, Ralph Nader's book *Unsafe at Any Speed* generated much public concern over auto safety. Congress responded with laws requiring seat belts as standard equipment on new cars.

How does a seat belt law affect auto safety? The direct effect is obvious: When a person wears a seat belt, the probability of surviving an auto accident rises. But that's not the end of the story because the law also affects behavior by altering incentives. The relevant behavior here is the speed and care with which drivers operate their cars. Driving slowly and carefully is costly because it uses the driver's time and energy. When deciding how safely to drive, rational people compare, perhaps unconsciously, the marginal benefit from safer driving to the marginal cost. As result, they drive more slowly and carefully when the benefit of increased safety is high. For example, when road conditions are icy, people drive more attentively and at lower speeds than they do when road conditions are clear.

Consider how a seat belt law alters a driver's cost–benefit calculation. Seat belts make accidents less costly because they reduce the likelihood of injury or death. In other words, seat belts reduce the benefits of slow and careful driving. People respond to seat belts as they would to an improvement in road conditions—by driving faster and less carefully. The result of a seat belt law, therefore, is a larger number of accidents. The decline in safe driving has a clear, adverse impact on pedestrians, who are more likely to find themselves in an accident but (unlike the drivers) don't have the benefit of added protection.

At first, this discussion of incentives and seat belts might seem like idle speculation. Yet in a classic 1975 study, economist Sam Peltzman argued that auto-safety laws have had many of these effects. According to Peltzman's evidence, these laws produce both fewer deaths per accident and more accidents. He concluded

incentive
something that induces a person to act

©SHELLY LENNON/AI WIRE/LANDOV

BASKETBALL STAR LEBRON JAMES UNDERSTANDS OPPORTUNITY COST AND INCENTIVES. HE DECIDED TO SKIP COLLEGE AND GO STRAIGHT TO THE PROS, WHERE HE HAS EARNED MILLIONS OF DOLLARS AS ONE OF THE NBA'S TOP PLAYERS.

that the net result is little change in the number of driver deaths and an increase in the number of pedestrian deaths.

Peltzman's analysis of auto safety is an offbeat example of the general principle that people respond to incentives. When analyzing any policy, we must consider not only the direct effects but also the less obvious indirect effects that work through incentives. If the policy changes incentives, it will cause people to alter their behavior.

QUICK QUIZ Describe an important trade-off you recently faced. • Give an example of some action that has both a monetary and nonmonetary opportunity cost. • Describe an incentive your parents offered to you in an effort to influence your behavior.

HOW PEOPLE INTERACT

The first four principles discussed how individuals make decisions. As we go about our lives, many of our decisions affect not only ourselves but other people as well. The next three principles concern how people interact with one another.

PRINCIPLE 5: TRADE CAN MAKE EVERYONE BETTER OFF

You have probably heard on the news that the Japanese are our competitors in the world economy. In some ways, this is true because American and Japanese firms produce many of the same goods. Ford and Toyota compete for the same customers in the market for automobiles. Apple and Sony compete for the same customers in the market for digital music players.

Yet it is easy to be misled when thinking about competition among countries. Trade between the United States and Japan is not like a sports contest in which one side wins and the other side loses. In fact, the opposite is true: Trade between two countries can make each country better off.

To see why, consider how trade affects your family. When a member of your family looks for a job, he or she competes against members of other families who are looking for jobs. Families also compete against one another when they go shopping because each family wants to buy the best goods at the lowest prices. In a sense, each family in the economy is competing with all other families.

Despite this competition, your family would not be better off isolating itself from all other families. If it did, your family would need to grow its own food, make its own clothes, and build its own home. Clearly, your family gains much from its ability to trade with others. Trade allows each person to specialize in the activities he or she does best, whether it is farming, sewing, or home building. By trading with others, people can buy a greater variety of goods and services at lower cost.

Countries as well as families benefit from the ability to trade with one another. Trade allows countries to specialize in what they do best and to enjoy a greater variety of goods and services. The Japanese, as well as the French and the Egyptians and the Brazilians, are as much our partners in the world economy as they are our competitors.

PRINCIPLE 6: MARKETS ARE USUALLY A GOOD WAY TO ORGANIZE ECONOMIC ACTIVITY

The collapse of communism in the Soviet Union and Eastern Europe in the 1980s may be the most important change in the world during the past half century.

THE WALL STREET JOURNAL

"FOR $5 A WEEK YOU CAN WATCH BASEBALL WITHOUT BEING NAGGED TO CUT THE GRASS!"

In The News

Incentive Pay

How people are paid affects their incentives and the decisions they make.

Where the Buses Run on Time

By Austan Goolsbee

On a summer afternoon, the drive home from the University of Chicago to the north side of the city must be one of the most beautiful commutes in the world. On the left on Lake Shore Drive you pass Grant Park, some of the world's first skyscrapers, and the Sears Tower. On the right is the intense blue of Lake Michigan. But for all the beauty, the traffic can be hell. So, if you drive the route every day, you learn the shortcuts. You know that if it backs up from the Buckingham Fountain all the way to McCormick Place, you're better off taking the surface streets and getting back onto Lake Shore Drive a few miles north.

A lot of buses, however, wait in the traffic jams. I have always wondered about that: Why don't the bus drivers use the shortcuts? Surely they know about them—they drive the same route every day, and they probably avoid the traffic when they drive their own cars. Buses don't stop on Lake Shore Drive, so they wouldn't strand anyone by detour-

ing around the congestion. And when buses get delayed in heavy traffic, it wreaks havoc on the scheduled service. Instead of arriving once every 10 minutes, three buses come in at the same time after half an hour. That sort of bunching is the least efficient way to run a public transportation system. So, why not take the surface streets if that would keep the schedule properly spaced and on time?

You might think at first that the problem is that the drivers aren't paid enough to strategize. But Chicago bus drivers are the seventh-highest paid in the nation; full-timers earned more than $23 an hour, according to a November 2004 survey. The problem may have to do not with how much they are paid, but how they are paid. At least, that's the implication of a new study of Chilean bus drivers by Ryan Johnson and David Reiley of the University of Arizona and Juan Carlos Muñoz of Pontificia Universidad Católica de Chile.

Companies in Chile pay bus drivers one of two ways: either by the hour or by the passenger. Paying by the passenger leads to significantly shorter delays. Give them incentives, and drivers start acting like regu-

lar people do. They take shortcuts when the traffic is bad. They take shorter meal breaks and bathroom breaks. They want to get on the road and pick up more passengers as quickly as they can. In short, their productivity increases....

Not everything about incentive pay is perfect, of course. When bus drivers start moving from place to place more quickly, they get in more accidents (just like the rest of us). Some passengers also complain that the rides make them nauseated because the drivers stomp on the gas as soon as the last passenger gets on the bus. Yet when given the choice, people overwhelmingly choose the bus companies that get them where they're going on time. More than 95 percent of the routes in Santiago use incentive pay.

Perhaps we should have known that incentive pay could increase bus driver productivity. After all, the taxis in Chicago take the shortcuts on Lake Shore Drive to avoid the traffic that buses just sit in. Since taxi drivers earn money for every trip they make, they want to get you home as quickly as possible so they can pick up somebody else.

Source: Slate.com, March 16, 2006.

Communist countries worked on the premise that government officials were in the best position to allocate the economy's scarce resources. These central planners decided what goods and services were produced, how much was produced, and who produced and consumed these goods and services. The theory behind central planning was that only the government could organize economic activity in a way that promoted economic well-being for the country as a whole.

Most countries that once had centrally planned economies have abandoned the system and are instead developing market economies. In a **market economy**, the

market economy
an economy that allocates resources through the decentralized decisions of many firms and households as they interact in markets for goods and services

decisions of a central planner are replaced by the decisions of millions of firms and households. Firms decide whom to hire and what to make. Households decide which firms to work for and what to buy with their incomes. These firms and households interact in the marketplace, where prices and self-interest guide their decisions.

At first glance, the success of market economies is puzzling. In a market economy, no one is looking out for the economic well-being of society as a whole. Free markets contain many buyers and sellers of numerous goods and services, and all of them are interested primarily in their own well-being. Yet despite decentralized decision making and self-interested decision makers, market economies have proven remarkably successful in organizing economic activity to promote overall economic well-being.

In his 1776 book *An Inquiry into the Nature and Causes of the Wealth of Nations*, economist Adam Smith made the most famous observation in all of economics: Households and firms interacting in markets act as if they are guided by an "invisible hand" that leads them to desirable market outcomes. One of our goals in this book is to understand how this invisible hand works its magic.

As you study economics, you will learn that prices are the instrument with which the invisible hand directs economic activity. In any market, buyers look at the price when determining how much to demand, and sellers look at the price when deciding how much to supply. As a result of the decisions that buyers and sellers make, market prices reflect both the value of a good to society and the cost to society of making the good. Smith's great insight was that prices adjust to guide these individual buyers and sellers to reach outcomes that, in many cases, maximize the well-being of society as a whole.

Smith's insight has an important corollary: When the government prevents prices from adjusting naturally to supply and demand, it impedes the invisible hand's ability to coordinate the decisions of the households and firms that make up the economy. This corollary explains why taxes adversely affect the allocation of resources, for they distort prices and thus the decisions of households and firms. It also explains the great harm caused by policies that directly control prices, such as rent control. And it explains the failure of communism. In Communist countries, prices were not determined in the marketplace but were dictated by central planners. These planners lacked the necessary information about consumers' tastes and producers' costs, which in a market economy are reflected in prices. Central planners failed because they tried to run the economy with one hand tied behind their backs—the invisible hand of the marketplace.

PRINCIPLE 7: GOVERNMENTS CAN SOMETIMES IMPROVE MARKET OUTCOMES

If the invisible hand of the market is so great, why do we need government? One purpose of studying economics is to refine your view about the proper role and scope of government policy.

One reason we need government is that the invisible hand can work its magic only if the government enforces the rules and maintains the institutions that are key to a market economy. Most important, market economies need institutions to enforce **property rights** so individuals can own and control scarce resources. A farmer won't grow food if he expects his crop to be stolen; a restaurant won't serve meals unless it is assured that customers will pay before they leave; and a music company won't produce CDs if too many potential customers avoid paying

property rights
the ability of an individual to own and exercise control over scarce resources

by making illegal copies. We all rely on government-provided police and courts to enforce our rights over the things we produce—and the invisible hand counts on our ability to enforce our rights.

Yet there is another reason we need government: The invisible hand is powerful, but it is not omnipotent. There are two broad reasons for a government to intervene in the economy and change the allocation of resources that people would choose on their own: to promote efficiency or to promote equality. That is, most policies aim either to enlarge the economic pie or to change how the pie is divided.

Consider first the goal of efficiency. Although the invisible hand usually leads markets to allocate resources to maximize the size of the economic pie, this is not always the case. Economists use the term **market failure** to refer to a situation in which the market on its own fails to produce an efficient allocation of resources. As we will see, one possible cause of market failure is an **externality**, which is the impact of one person's actions on the well-being of a bystander. The classic example of an externality is pollution. Another possible cause of market failure

market failure
a situation in which a market left on its own fails to allocate resources efficiently

externality
the impact of one person's actions on the well-being of a bystander

FYI

Adam Smith and the Invisible Hand

It may be only a coincidence that Adam Smith's great book *The Wealth of Nations* was published in 1776, the exact year American revolutionaries signed the Declaration of Independence. But the two documents share a point of view that was prevalent at the time: Individuals are usually best left to their own devices, without the heavy hand of government guiding their actions. This political philosophy provides the intellectual basis for the market economy and for free society more generally.

Why do decentralized market economies work so well? Is it because people can be counted on to treat one another with love and kindness? Not at all. Here is Adam Smith's description of how people interact in a market economy:

Man has almost constant occasion for the help of his brethren, and it is in vain for him to expect it from their benevolence only. He will be more likely to prevail if he can interest their self-love in his favour, and show them that it is for their own advantage to do for him what he requires of them. . . . Give me that which I want, and you shall have this which you want, is the meaning of every such offer; and it is in this manner that we obtain from one another the far greater part of those good offices which we stand in need of.

Adam Smith

It is not from the benevolence of the butcher, the brewer, or the baker that we expect our dinner, but from their regard to their own interest. We address ourselves, not to their humanity but to their self-love, and never talk to them of our own necessities but of their advantages. Nobody but a beggar chooses to depend chiefly upon the benevolence of his fellow-citizens. . . .

Every individual . . . neither intends to promote the public interest, nor knows how much he is promoting it. . . . He intends only his own gain, and he is in this, as in many other cases, led by an invisible hand to promote an end which was no part of his intention. Nor is it always the worse for the society that it was no part of it. By pursuing his own interest he frequently promotes that of the society more effectually than when he really intends to promote it.

Smith is saying that participants in the economy are motivated by self-interest and that the "invisible hand" of the marketplace guides this self-interest into promoting general economic well-being.

Many of Smith's insights remain at the center of modern economics. Our analysis in the coming chapters will allow us to express Smith's conclusions more precisely and to analyze more fully the strengths and weaknesses of the market's invisible hand.

market power
the ability of a single economic actor (or small group of actors) to have a substantial influence on market prices

is **market power**, which refers to the ability of a single person (or small group) to unduly influence market prices. For example, if everyone in town needs water but there is only one well, the owner of the well is not subject to the rigorous competition with which the invisible hand normally keeps self-interest in check. In the presence of externalities or market power, well-designed public policy can enhance economic efficiency.

Now consider the goal of equality. Even when the invisible hand is yielding efficient outcomes, it can nonetheless leave sizable disparities in economic well-being. A market economy rewards people according to their ability to produce things that other people are willing to pay for. The world's best basketball player earns more than the world's best chess player simply because people are willing to pay more to watch basketball than chess. The invisible hand does not ensure that everyone has sufficient food, decent clothing, and adequate healthcare. This inequality may, depending on one's political philosophy, call for government intervention. In practice, many public policies, such as the income tax and the welfare system, aim to achieve a more equal distribution of economic well-being.

To say that the government *can* improve on market outcomes at times does not mean that it always *will*. Public policy is made not by angels but by a political process that is far from perfect. Sometimes policies are designed simply to reward the politically powerful. Sometimes they are made by well-intentioned leaders who are not fully informed. As you study economics, you will become a better judge of when a government policy is justifiable because it promotes efficiency or equality and when it is not.

QUICK QUIZ Why is a country better off not isolating itself from all other countries? • Why do we have markets and, according to economists, what roles should government play in them?

HOW THE ECONOMY AS A WHOLE WORKS

We started by discussing how individuals make decisions and then looked at how people interact with one another. All these decisions and interactions together make up "the economy." The last three principles concern the workings of the economy as a whole.

PRINCIPLE 8: A COUNTRY'S STANDARD OF LIVING DEPENDS ON ITS ABILITY TO PRODUCE GOODS AND SERVICES

The differences in living standards around the world are staggering. In 2006, the average American had an income of about $44,260. In the same year, the average Mexican earned $11,410, and the average Nigerian earned $1,050. Not surprisingly, this large variation in average income is reflected in various measures of the quality of life. Citizens of high-income countries have more TV sets, more cars, better nutrition, better healthcare, and a longer life expectancy than citizens of low-income countries.

Changes in living standards over time are also large. In the United States, incomes have historically grown about 2 percent per year (after adjusting for changes in the cost of living). At this rate, average income doubles every 35 years. Over the past century, average income has risen about eightfold.

What explains these large differences in living standards among countries and over time? The answer is surprisingly simple. Almost all variation in living standards is attributable to differences in countries' **productivity**—that is, the amount of goods and services produced from each unit of labor input. In nations where workers can produce a large quantity of goods and services per unit of time, most people enjoy a high standard of living; in nations where workers are less productive, most people endure a more meager existence. Similarly, the growth rate of a nation's productivity determines the growth rate of its average income.

The fundamental relationship between productivity and living standards is simple, but its implications are far-reaching. If productivity is the primary determinant of living standards, other explanations must be of secondary importance. For example, it might be tempting to credit labor unions or minimum-wage laws for the rise in living standards of American workers over the past century. Yet the real hero of American workers is their rising productivity. As another example, some commentators have claimed that increased competition from Japan and other countries explained the slow growth in U.S. incomes during the 1970s and 1980s. Yet the real villain was not competition from abroad but flagging productivity growth in the United States.

The relationship between productivity and living standards also has profound implications for public policy. When thinking about how any policy will affect living standards, the key question is how it will affect our ability to produce goods and services. To boost living standards, policymakers need to raise productivity by ensuring that workers are well educated, have the tools needed to produce goods and services, and have access to the best available technology.

productivity
the quantity of goods and services produced from each unit of labor input

PRINCIPLE 9: PRICES RISE WHEN THE GOVERNMENT PRINTS TOO MUCH MONEY

In January 1921, a daily newspaper in Germany cost 0.30 marks. Less than two years later, in November 1922, the same newspaper cost 70,000,000 marks. All other prices in the economy rose by similar amounts. This episode is one of history's most spectacular examples of **inflation**, an increase in the overall level of prices in the economy.

Although the United States has never experienced inflation even close to that in Germany in the 1920s, inflation has at times been an economic problem. During the 1970s, for instance, when the overall level of prices more than doubled, President Gerald Ford called inflation "public enemy number one." By contrast, inflation in the first decade of the 21st century has run about 2½ percent per year; at this rate, it would take almost 30 years for prices to double. Because high inflation imposes various costs on society, keeping inflation at a low level is a goal of economic policymakers around the world.

What causes inflation? In almost all cases of large or persistent inflation, the culprit is growth in the quantity of money. When a government creates large quantities of the nation's money, the value of the money falls. In Germany in the early 1920s, when prices were on average tripling every month, the quantity of money was also tripling every month. Although less dramatic, the economic history of the United States points to a similar conclusion: The high inflation of the 1970s was associated with rapid growth in the quantity of money, and the low

inflation
an increase in the overall level of prices in the economy

"WELL IT MAY HAVE BEEN 68 CENTS WHEN YOU GOT IN LINE, BUT IT'S 74 CENTS NOW!"

In The News

Why You Should Study Economics

In this excerpt from a commencement address, the former president of the Federal Reserve Bank of Dallas makes the case for studying economics.

The Dismal Science? Hardly!

By Robert D. McTeer, Jr.

My take on training in economics is that it becomes increasingly valuable as you move up the career ladder. I can't imagine a better major for corporate CEOs, congressmen, or American presidents. You've learned a systematic, disciplined way of thinking that will serve you well. By contrast, the economically challenged must be perplexed

about how it is that economies work better the fewer people they have in charge. Who does the planning? Who makes decisions? Who decides what to produce? For my money, Adam Smith's invisible hand is the most important thing you've learned by studying economics. You understand how we can each work for our own self-interest and still produce a desirable social outcome. You know how uncoordinated activity gets coordinated by the market to enhance the wealth of nations. You understand the

magic of markets and the dangers of tampering with them too much. You know better what you first learned in kindergarten: that you shouldn't kill or cripple the goose that lays the golden eggs. . . .

Economics training will help you understand fallacies and unintended consequences. In fact, I am inclined to define economics as the study of how to anticipate unintended consequences. . . .

Little in the literature seems more relevant to contemporary economic debates

inflation of more recent experience was associated with slow growth in the quantity of money.

PRINCIPLE 10: SOCIETY FACES A SHORT-RUN TRADE-OFF BETWEEN INFLATION AND UNEMPLOYMENT

Although a higher level of prices is, in the long run, the primary effect of increasing the quantity of money, the short-run story is more complex and controversial. Most economists describe the short-run effects of monetary injections as follows:

- Increasing the amount of money in the economy stimulates the overall level of spending and thus the demand for goods and services.
- Higher demand may over time cause firms to raise their prices, but in the meantime, it also encourages them to hire more workers and produce a larger quantity of goods and services.
- More hiring means lower unemployment.

This line of reasoning leads to one final economy-wide trade-off: a short-run trade-off between inflation and unemployment.

Although some economists still question these ideas, most accept that society faces a short-run trade-off between inflation and unemployment. This simply means that, over a period of a year or two, many economic policies push inflation and unemployment in opposite directions. Policymakers face this trade-off regardless of whether inflation and unemployment both start out at high levels (as they were in the early 1980s), at low levels (as they were in the late 1990s), than what usually is called the broken window fallacy. Whenever a government program is justified not on its merits but by the jobs it will create, remember the broken window: Some teenagers, being the little beasts that they are, toss a brick through a bakery window. A crowd gathers and laments, "What a shame." But before you know it, someone suggests a silver lining to the situation: Now the baker will have to spend money to have the window repaired. This will add to the income of the repairman, who will spend his additional income, which will add to another seller's income, and so on. You know the drill. The chain of spending will multiply and generate higher income and employment. If the broken window is large enough, it might produce an economic boom! . . .

Most voters fall for the broken window fallacy, but not economics majors. They will say, "Hey, wait a minute!" If the baker hadn't spent his money on window repair, he would have spent it on the new suit he was saving to buy. Then the tailor would have the new income to spend, and so on. The broken window didn't create net new spending; it just diverted spending from somewhere else. The broken window does not create new activity, just different activity. People see the activity that takes place. They don't see the activity that *would* have taken place.

The broken window fallacy is perpetuated in many forms. Whenever job creation or retention is the primary objective I call it the job-counting fallacy. Economics majors understand the non-intuitive reality that

real progress comes from job destruction. It once took 90 percent of our population to grow our food. Now it takes 3 percent. Pardon me, Willie, but are we worse off because of the job losses in agriculture? The would-have-been farmers are now college professors and computer gurus. . . .

So instead of counting jobs, we should make every job count. We will occasionally hit a soft spot when we have a mismatch of supply and demand in the labor market. But that is temporary. Don't become a Luddite and destroy the machinery, or become a protectionist and try to grow bananas in New York City.

Source: *The Wall Street Journal*, June 4, 2003.

or someplace in between. This short-run trade-off plays a key role in the analysis of the **business cycle**—the irregular and largely unpredictable fluctuations in economic activity, as measured by the production of goods and services or the number of people employed.

Policymakers can exploit the short-run trade-off between inflation and unemployment using various policy instruments. By changing the amount that the government spends, the amount it taxes, and the amount of money it prints, policymakers can influence the overall demand for goods and services. Changes in demand in turn influence the combination of inflation and unemployment that the economy experiences in the short-run. Because these instruments of economic policy are potentially so powerful, how policymakers should use these instruments to control the economy, if at all, is a subject of continuing debate.

business cycle
fluctuations in economic activity, such as employment and production

QUICK QUIZ   List and briefly explain the three principles that describe how the economy as a whole works.

CONCLUSION

You now have a taste of what economics is all about. In the coming chapters, we develop many specific insights about people, markets, and economies. Mastering these insights will take some effort, but it is not an overwhelming task. The field of economics is based on a few big ideas that can be applied in many different situations.

FYI

How to Read This Book

Economics is fun, but it can also be hard to learn. My aim in writing this text is to make it as enjoyable and easy as possible. But you, the student, also have a role to play. Experience shows that if you are actively involved as you study this book, you will enjoy a better outcome both on your exams and in the years that follow. Here are a few tips about how best to read this book.

1. *Read before class.* Students do better when they read the relevant textbook chapter before attending a lecture. You will understand the lecture better, and your questions will be better focused on where you need extra help.

2. *Summarize, don't highlight.* Running a yellow marker over the text is too passive an activity to keep your mind engaged. Instead, when you come to the end of a section, take a minute and summarize what you just learned in your own words, writing your summary in the wide margins we've provided. When you've finished the chapter, compare your summaries with the one at the end of the chapter. Did you pick up the main points?

3. *Test yourself.* Throughout the book, Quick Quizzes offer instant feedback to find out if you've learned what you are supposed to. Take the opportunity to write down your answer and then check it against the answers provided at this book's website. The quizzes are meant to test your basic comprehension. If your answer is incorrect, you probably need to review the section.

4. *Practice, practice, practice.* At the end of each chapter, Questions for Review test your understanding, and Problems and Applications ask you to apply and extend the material. Perhaps your instructor will assign some of these exercises as homework. If so, do them. If not, do them anyway. The more you use your new knowledge, the more solid it becomes.

5. *Go online.* The publisher of this book maintains an extensive website to help you in your study of economics. It includes additional examples, applications, and problems, as well as quizzes so you can test yourself. Check it out. The website is http://academic.cengage.com/economics/mankiw.

6. *Study in groups.* After you've read the book and worked problems on your own, get together with classmates to discuss the material. You will learn from each other—an example of the gains from trade.

7. *Teach someone.* As all teachers know, there is no better way to learn something than to teach it to someone else. Take the opportunity to teach new economic concepts to a study partner, a friend, a parent, or even a pet.

8. *Don't skip the real-world examples.* In the midst of all the numbers, graphs, and strange new words, it is easy to lose sight of what economics is all about. The Case Studies and In the News boxes sprinkled throughout this book should help remind you. They show how the theory is tied to events happening in all our lives.

9. *Apply economic thinking to your daily life.* Once you've read about how others apply economics to the real world, try it yourself! You can use economic analysis to better understand your own decisions, the economy around you, and the events you read about in the newspaper. The world may never look the same again.

Throughout this book, we will refer back to the *Ten Principles of Economics* highlighted in this chapter and summarized in Table 1. Keep these building blocks in mind: Even the most sophisticated economic analysis is founded on the ten principles introduced here.

TABLE **1**

Ten Principles of Economics

How People Make Decisions
  1: People Face Trade-offs
  2: The Cost of Something Is What You Give Up to Get It
  3: Rational People Think at the Margin
  4: People Respond to Incentives

How People Interact
  5: Trade Can Make Everyone Better Off
  6: Markets Are Usually a Good Way to Organize Economic Activity
  7: Governments Can Sometimes Improve Market Outcomes

How the Economy as a Whole Works
  8: A Country's Standard of Living Depends on Its Ability to Produce Goods and Services
  9: Prices Rise When the Government Prints Too Much Money
  10: Society Faces a Short-Run Trade-off between Inflation and Unemployment

SUMMARY

- The fundamental lessons about individual decision making are that people face trade-offs among alternative goals, that the cost of any action is measured in terms of forgone opportunities, that rational people make decisions by comparing marginal costs and marginal benefits, and that people change their behavior in response to the incentives they face.

- The fundamental lessons about interactions among people are that trade and interdependence can be mutually beneficial, that markets are usually a good way of coordinating economic activity among people, and that the government can potentially improve market outcomes by remedying a market failure or by promoting greater economic equality.

- The fundamental lessons about the economy as a whole are that productivity is the ultimate source of living standards, that growth in the quantity of money is the ultimate source of inflation, and that society faces a short-run trade-off between inflation and unemployment.

KEY CONCEPTS

scarcity, *p. 3*
economics, *p. 4*
efficiency, *p. 5*
equality, *p. 5*
opportunity cost, *p. 5*
rational people, *p. 6*

marginal changes, *p. 6*
incentive, *p. 7*
market economy, *p. 9*
property rights, *p. 10*
market failure, *p. 11*
externality, *p. 11*

market power, *p. 12*
productivity, *p. 13*
inflation, *p. 13*
business cycle, *p. 15*

QUESTIONS FOR REVIEW

1. Give three examples of important trade-offs that you face in your life.
2. What is the opportunity cost of seeing a movie?
3. Water is necessary for life. Is the marginal benefit of a glass of water large or small?
4. Why should policymakers think about incentives?
5. Why isn't trade among countries like a game with some winners and some losers?
6. What does the "invisible hand" of the marketplace do?
7. Explain the two main causes of market failure and give an example of each.
8. Why is productivity important?
9. What is inflation and what causes it?
10. How are inflation and unemployment related in the short run?

PROBLEMS AND APPLICATIONS

1. Describe some of the trade-offs faced by each of the following:
   a. a family deciding whether to buy a new car
   b. a member of Congress deciding how much to spend on national parks
   c. a company president deciding whether to open a new factory
   d. a professor deciding how much to prepare for class
   e. a recent college graduate deciding whether to go to graduate school
2. You are trying to decide whether to take a vacation. Most of the costs of the vacation (airfare, hotel, and forgone wages) are measured in dollars, but the benefits of the vacation are psychological. How can you compare the benefits to the costs?
3. You were planning to spend Saturday working at your part-time job, but a friend asks you to go skiing. What is the true cost of going skiing? Now suppose you had been planning to spend the day studying at the library. What is the cost of going skiing in this case? Explain.
4. You win $100 in a basketball pool. You have a choice between spending the money now or putting it away for a year in a bank account that pays 5 percent interest. What is the opportunity cost of spending the $100 now?
5. The company that you manage has invested $5 million in developing a new product, but the development is not quite finished. At a recent meeting, your salespeople report that the introduction of competing products has reduced the expected sales of your new product to $3 million. If it would cost $1 million to finish development and make the product, should you go ahead and do so? What is the most that you should pay to complete development?

6. Three managers of the Magic Potion Company are discussing a possible increase in production. Each suggests a way to make this decision.

   HARRY: We should examine whether our company's productivity—gallons of potion per worker—would rise or fall.

   RON: We should examine whether our average cost—cost per worker—would rise or fall.

   HERMIONE: We should examine whether the extra revenue from selling the additional potion would be greater or smaller than the extra costs.

   Who do you think is right? Why?

7. The Social Security system provides income for people over age 65. If a recipient of Social Security decides to work and earn some income, the amount he or she receives in Social Security benefits is typically reduced.
   a. How does the provision of Social Security affect people's incentive to save while working?
   b. How does the reduction in benefits associated with higher earnings affect people's incentive to work past age 65?

8. A recent bill reforming the government's anti-poverty programs limited many welfare recipients to only two years of benefits.
   a. How does this change affect the incentives for working?
   b. How might this change represent a trade-off between equality and efficiency?
9. Your roommate is a better cook than you are, but you can clean more quickly than your roommate can. If your roommate did all the cooking and you did all the cleaning, would your chores take you more or less time than if you divided each task evenly? Give a similar example of how specialization and trade can make two countries both better off.
10. Suppose the United States adopted central planning for its economy, and you became the chief planner. Among the millions of decisions that you need to make for next year are how many compact discs to produce, what artists to record, and which consumers should receive the discs. To make these decisions intelligently, what information would you need about the compact disc industry? What information would you need about each of the people in the United States? How well do you think you could do your job?
11. Explain whether each of the following government activities is motivated by a concern about equality or a concern about efficiency. In the case of efficiency, discuss the type of market failure involved.
    a. regulating cable TV prices
    b. providing some poor people with vouchers that can be used to buy food
    c. prohibiting smoking in public places
    d. breaking up Standard Oil (which once owned 90 percent of all oil refineries) into several smaller companies

   e. imposing higher personal income tax rates on people with higher incomes
   f. instituting laws against driving while intoxicated
12. Discuss each of the following statements from the standpoints of equality and efficiency.
    a. "Everyone in society should be guaranteed the best healthcare possible."
    b. "When workers are laid off, they should be able to collect unemployment benefits until they find a new job."
13. In what ways is your standard of living different from that of your parents or grandparents when they were your age? Why have these changes occurred?
14. Suppose Americans decide to save more of their incomes. If banks lend this extra savings to businesses, which use the funds to build new factories, how might this lead to faster growth in productivity? Who do you suppose benefits from the higher productivity? Is society getting a free lunch?
15. During the Revolutionary War, the American colonies could not raise enough tax revenue to fully fund the war effort; to make up this difference, the colonies decided to print more money. Printing money to cover expenditures is sometimes referred to as an "inflation tax." Who do you think is being "taxed" when more money is printed? Why?
16. Imagine that you are a policymaker trying to decide whether to reduce the rate of inflation. To make an intelligent decision, what would you need to know about inflation, unemployment, and the trade-off between them?

Thinking Like an Economist

Every field of study has its own language and its own way of thinking. Mathematicians talk about axioms, integrals, and vector spaces. Psychologists talk about ego, id, and cognitive dissonance. Lawyers talk about venue, torts, and promissory estoppel.

Economics is no different. Supply, demand, elasticity, comparative advantage, consumer surplus, deadweight loss—these terms are part of the economist's language. In the coming chapters, you will encounter many new terms and some familiar words that economists use in specialized ways. At first, this new language may seem needlessly arcane. But as you will see, its value lies in its ability to provide you with a new and useful way of thinking about the world in which you live.

The purpose of this book is to help you learn the economist's way of thinking. Just as you cannot become a mathematician, psychologist, or lawyer overnight, learning to think like an economist will take some time. Yet with a combination of theory, case studies, and examples of economics in the news, this book will give you ample opportunity to develop and practice this skill.

Before delving into the substance and details of economics, it is helpful to have an overview of how economists approach the world. This chapter discusses the field's methodology. What is distinctive about how economists confront a question? What does it mean to think like an economist?

THE ECONOMIST AS SCIENTIST

Economists try to address their subject with a scientist's objectivity. They approach the study of the economy in much the same way a physicist approaches the study of matter and a biologist approaches the study of life: They devise theories, collect data, and then analyze these data in an attempt to verify or refute their theories.

To beginners, it can seem odd to claim that economics is a science. After all, economists do not work with test tubes or telescopes. The essence of science, however, is the *scientific method*—the dispassionate development and testing of theories about how the world works. This method of inquiry is as applicable to studying a nation's economy as it is to studying the earth's gravity or a species' evolution. As Albert Einstein once put it, "The whole of science is nothing more than the refinement of everyday thinking."

Although Einstein's comment is as true for social sciences such as economics as it is for natural sciences such as physics, most people are not accustomed to looking at society through the eyes of a scientist. Let's discuss some of the ways in which economists apply the logic of science to examine how an economy works.

"I'M A SOCIAL SCIENTIST, MICHAEL. THAT MEANS I CAN'T EXPLAIN ELECTRICITY OR ANYTHING LIKE THAT, BUT IF YOU EVER WANT TO KNOW ABOUT PEOPLE, I'M YOUR MAN."

THE SCIENTIFIC METHOD: OBSERVATION, THEORY, AND MORE OBSERVATION

Isaac Newton, the famous 17th-century scientist and mathematician, allegedly became intrigued one day when he saw an apple fall from a tree. This observation motivated Newton to develop a theory of gravity that applies not only to an apple falling to the earth but to any two objects in the universe. Subsequent testing of Newton's theory has shown that it works well in many circumstances (although, as Einstein would later emphasize, not in all circumstances). Because Newton's theory has been so successful at explaining observation, it is still taught in undergraduate physics courses around the world.

This interplay between theory and observation also occurs in the field of economics. An economist might live in a country experiencing rapidly increasing prices and be moved by this observation to develop a theory of inflation. The theory might assert that high inflation arises when the government prints too much money. To test this theory, the economist could collect and analyze data on prices and money from many different countries. If growth in the quantity of money were not at all related to the rate at which prices are rising, the economist would start to doubt the validity of this theory of inflation. If money growth and inflation were strongly correlated in international data, as in fact they are, the economist would become more confident in the theory.

Although economists use theory and observation like other scientists, they face an obstacle that makes their task especially challenging: In economics, conducting experiments is often difficult and sometimes impossible. Physicists studying gravity can drop many objects in their laboratories to generate data to test their theories. By contrast, economists studying inflation are not allowed to manipulate a nation's monetary policy simply to generate useful data. Economists, like astronomers and evolutionary biologists, usually have to make do with whatever data the world happens to give them.

To find a substitute for laboratory experiments, economists pay close attention to the natural experiments offered by history. When a war in the Middle East interrupts the flow of crude oil, for instance, oil prices skyrocket around the world.

For consumers of oil and oil products, such an event depresses living standards. For economic policymakers, it poses a difficult choice about how best to respond. But for economic scientists, the event provides an opportunity to study the effects of a key natural resource on the world's economies. Throughout this book, therefore, we consider many historical episodes. These episodes are valuable to study because they give us insight into the economy of the past and, more important, because they allow us to illustrate and evaluate economic theories of the present.

THE ROLE OF ASSUMPTIONS

If you ask a physicist how long it would take a marble to fall from the top of a ten-story building, she will likely answer the question by assuming that the marble falls in a vacuum. Of course, this assumption is false. In fact, the building is surrounded by air, which exerts friction on the falling marble and slows it down. Yet the physicist will point out that friction on the marble is so small that its effect is negligible. Assuming the marble falls in a vacuum simplifies the problem without substantially affecting the answer.

Economists make assumptions for the same reason: Assumptions can simplify the complex world and make it easier to understand. To study the effects of international trade, for example, we might assume that the world consists of only two countries and that each country produces only two goods. In reality, there are numerous countries, each of which produces thousands of different types of goods. But by assuming two countries and two goods, we can focus our thinking on the essence of the problem. Once we understand international trade in this simplified imaginary world, we are in a better position to understand international trade in the more complex world in which we live.

The art in scientific thinking—whether in physics, biology, or economics—is deciding which assumptions to make. Suppose, for instance, that we were dropping a beachball rather than a marble from the top of the building. Our physicist would realize that the assumption of no friction is less accurate in this case: Friction exerts a greater force on a beachball than on a marble because a beachball is much larger. The assumption that gravity works in a vacuum is reasonable for studying a falling marble but not for studying a falling beachball.

Similarly, economists use different assumptions to answer different questions. Suppose that we want to study what happens to the economy when the government changes the number of dollars in circulation. An important piece of this analysis, it turns out, is how prices respond. Many prices in the economy change infrequently; the newsstand prices of magazines, for instance, change only every few years. Knowing this fact may lead us to make different assumptions when studying the effects of the policy change over different time horizons. For studying the short-run effects of the policy, we may assume that prices do not change much. We may even make the extreme and artificial assumption that all prices are completely fixed. For studying the long-run effects of the policy, however, we may assume that all prices are completely flexible. Just as a physicist uses different assumptions when studying falling marbles and falling beachballs, economists use different assumptions when studying the short-run and long-run effects of a change in the quantity of money.

ECONOMIC MODELS

High school biology teachers teach basic anatomy with plastic replicas of the human body. These models have all the major organs: the heart, the liver, the kidneys, and so on. The models allow teachers to show their students very simply how the important parts of the body fit together. Because these plastic models are stylized and omit many details, no one would mistake one of them for a real person. Despite this lack of realism—indeed, because of this lack of realism—studying these models is useful for learning how the human body works.

Economists also use models to learn about the world, but instead of being made of plastic, they are most often composed of diagrams and equations. Like a biology teacher's plastic model, economic models omit many details to allow us to see what is truly important. Just as the biology teacher's model does not include all the body's muscles and capillaries, an economist's model does not include every feature of the economy.

As we use models to examine various economic issues throughout this book, you will see that all the models are built with assumptions. Just as a physicist begins the analysis of a falling marble by assuming away the existence of friction, economists assume away many of the details of the economy that are irrelevant for studying the question at hand. All models—in physics, biology, and economics—simplify reality to improve our understanding of it.

Our First Model: The Circular-Flow Diagram

The economy consists of millions of people engaged in many activities—buying, selling, working, hiring, manufacturing, and so on. To understand how the economy works, we must find some way to simplify our thinking about all these activities. In other words, we need a model that explains, in general terms, how the economy is organized and how participants in the economy interact with one another.

Figure 1 presents a visual model of the economy called a **circular-flow diagram**. In this model, the economy is simplified to include only two types of decision makers—firms and households. Firms produce goods and services using inputs, such as labor, land, and capital (buildings and machines). These inputs are called the *factors of production*. Households own the factors of production and consume all the goods and services that the firms produce.

circular-flow diagram
a visual model of the economy that shows how dollars flow through markets among households and firms

Households and firms interact in two types of markets. In the *markets for goods and services,* households are buyers, and firms are sellers. In particular, households buy the output of goods and services that firms produce. In the *markets for the factors of production,* households are sellers, and firms are buyers. In these markets, households provide the inputs that firms use to produce goods and services. The circular-flow diagram offers a simple way of organizing the economic transactions that occur between households and firms in the economy.

The two loops of the circular-flow diagram are distinct but related. The inner loop represents the flows of inputs and outputs. The households sell the use of their labor, land, and capital to the firms in the markets for the factors of production. The firms then use these factors to produce goods and services, which in turn are sold to households in the markets for goods and services. The outer loop of the diagram represents the corresponding flow of dollars. The households spend money to buy goods and services from the firms. The firms use some of the revenue from these sales to pay for the factors of production, such as the wages of their workers. What's left is the profit of the firm owners, who themselves are members of households.

Let's take a tour of the circular flow by following a dollar bill as it makes its way from person to person through the economy. Imagine that the dollar begins at a household, say, in your wallet. If you want to buy a cup of coffee, you take the dollar to one of the economy's markets for goods and services, such as your local

FIGURE **1**

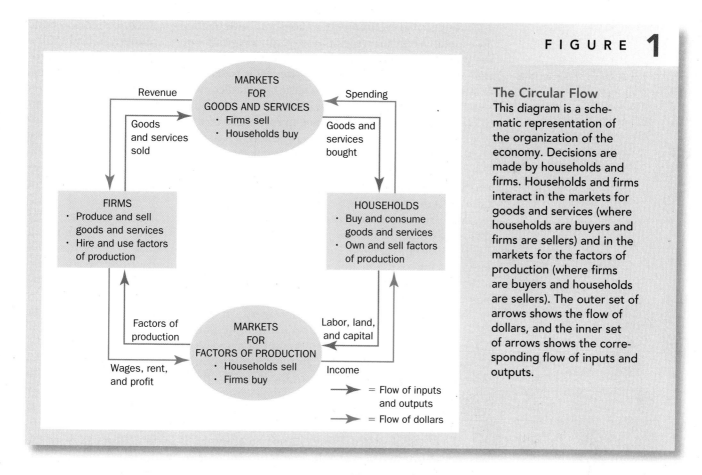

The Circular Flow
This diagram is a schematic representation of the organization of the economy. Decisions are made by households and firms. Households and firms interact in the markets for goods and services (where households are buyers and firms are sellers) and in the markets for the factors of production (where firms are buyers and households are sellers). The outer set of arrows shows the flow of dollars, and the inner set of arrows shows the corresponding flow of inputs and outputs.

Starbucks coffee shop. There you spend it on your favorite drink. When the dollar moves into the Starbucks cash register, it becomes revenue for the firm. The dollar doesn't stay at Starbucks for long, however, because the firm uses it to buy inputs in the markets for the factors of production. Starbucks might use the dollar to pay rent to its landlord for the space it occupies or to pay the wages of its workers. In either case, the dollar enters the income of some household and, once again, is back in someone's wallet. At that point, the story of the economy's circular flow starts once again.

The circular-flow diagram in Figure 1 is one simple model of the economy. It dispenses with details that, for some purposes, are significant. A more complex and realistic circular-flow model would include, for instance, the roles of government and international trade. (Some of that dollar you gave to Starbucks might be used to pay taxes and or to buy coffee beans from a farmer in Brazil.) Yet these details are not crucial for a basic understanding of how the economy is organized. Because of its simplicity, this circular-flow diagram is useful to keep in mind when thinking about how the pieces of the economy fit together.

OUR SECOND MODEL: THE PRODUCTION POSSIBILITIES FRONTIER

Most economic models, unlike the circular-flow diagram, are built using the tools of mathematics. Here we use one of the simplest such models, called the production possibilities frontier, to illustrate some basic economic ideas.

production possibilities frontier
a graph that shows the combinations of output that the economy can possibly produce given the available factors of production and the available production technology

Although real economies produce thousands of goods and services, let's assume an economy that produces only two goods—cars and computers. Together, the car industry and the computer industry use all of the economy's factors of production. The **production possibilities frontier** is a graph that shows the various combinations of output—in this case, cars and computers—that the economy can possibly produce given the available factors of production and the available production technology that firms use to turn these factors into output.

Figure 2 shows this economy's production possibilities frontier. If the economy uses all its resources in the car industry, it produces 1,000 cars and no computers. If it uses all its resources in the computer industry, it produces 3,000 computers and no cars. The two endpoints of the production possibilities frontier represent these extreme possibilities.

More likely, the economy divides its resources between the two industries, and this yields other points on the production possibilities frontier. For example, it can produce 600 cars and 2,200 computers, shown in the figure by point A. Or, by moving some of the factors of production to the car industry from the computer industry, the economy can produce 700 cars and 2,000 computers, represented by point B.

Because resources are scarce, not every conceivable outcome is feasible. For example, no matter how resources are allocated between the two industries, the economy cannot produce the amount of cars and computers represented by point C. Given the technology available for manufacturing cars and computers, the economy does not have enough of the factors of production to support that level of output. With the resources it has, the economy can produce at any point on or inside the production possibilities frontier, but it cannot produce at points outside the frontier.

An outcome is said to be *efficient* if the economy is getting all it can from the scarce resources it has available. Points on (rather than inside) the production possibilities frontier represent efficient levels of production. When the economy is producing at such a point, say point A, there is no way to produce more of one

2 **FIGURE**

The Production Possibilities Frontier
The production possibilities frontier shows the combinations of output—in this case, cars and computers—that the economy can possibly produce. The economy can produce any combination on or inside the frontier. Points outside the frontier are not feasible given the economy's resources.

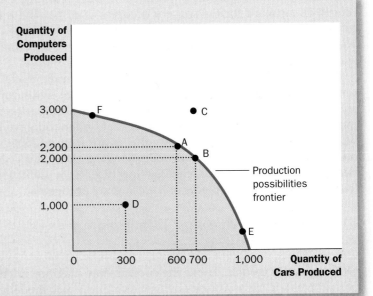

good without producing less of the other. Point D represents an *inefficient* outcome. For some reason, perhaps widespread unemployment, the economy is producing less than it could from the resources it has available: It is producing only 300 cars and 1,000 computers. If the source of the inefficiency is eliminated, the economy can increase its production of both goods. For example, if the economy moves from point D to point A, its production of cars increases from 300 to 600, and its production of computers increases from 1,000 to 2,200.

One of the *Ten Principles of Economics* discussed in Chapter 1 is that people face trade-offs. The production possibilities frontier shows one trade-off that society faces. Once we have reached the efficient points on the frontier, the only way of getting more of one good is to get less of the other. When the economy moves from point A to point B, for instance, society produces 100 more cars but at the expense of producing 200 fewer computers.

This trade-off helps us understand another of the *Ten Principles of Economics:* The cost of something is what you give up to get it. This is called the *opportunity cost.* The production possibilities frontier shows the opportunity cost of one good as measured in terms of the other good. When society moves from point A to point B, it gives up 200 computers to get 100 additional cars. That is, at point A, the opportunity cost of 100 cars is 200 computers. Put another way, the opportunity cost of each car is two computers. Notice that the opportunity cost of a car equals the slope of the production possibilities frontier. (If you don't recall what slope is, you can refresh your memory with the graphing appendix to this chapter.)

The opportunity cost of a car in terms of the number of computers is not constant in this economy but depends on how many cars and computers the economy is producing. This is reflected in the shape of the production possibilities frontier. Because the production possibilities frontier in Figure 2 is bowed outward, the opportunity cost of a car is highest when the economy is producing many cars and fewer computers, such as at point E, where the frontier is steep. When the economy is producing few cars and many computers, such as at point F, the frontier is flatter, and the opportunity cost of a car is lower.

Economists believe that production possibilities frontiers often have this bowed shape. When the economy is using most of its resources to make computers, such as at point F, the resources best suited to car production, such as skilled autoworkers, are being used in the computer industry. Because these workers probably aren't very good at making computers, the economy won't have to lose much computer production to increase car production by one unit. The opportunity cost of a car in terms of computers is small, and the frontier is relatively flat. By contrast, when the economy is using most of its resources to make cars, such as at point E, the resources best suited to making cars are already in the car industry. Producing an additional car means moving some of the best computer technicians out of the computer industry and making them autoworkers. As a result, producing an additional car will mean a substantial loss of computer output. The opportunity cost of a car is high, and the frontier is steep.

The production possibilities frontier shows the trade-off between the outputs of different goods at a given time, but the trade-off can change over time. For example, suppose a technological advance in the computer industry raises the number of computers that a worker can produce per week. This advance expands society's set of opportunities. For any given number of cars, the economy can make more computers. If the economy does not produce any computers, it can still produce 1,000 cars, so one endpoint of the frontier stays the same. But the rest of the production possibilities frontier shifts outward, as in Figure 3.

3 FIGURE

A Shift in the Production Possibilities Frontier
A technological advance in the computer industry enables the economy to produce more computers for any given number of cars. As a result, the production possibilities frontier shifts outward. If the economy moves from point A to point G, then the production of both cars and computers increases.

This figure illustrates economic growth. Society can move production from a point on the old frontier to a point on the new frontier. Which point it chooses depends on its preferences for the two goods. In this example, society moves from point A to point G, enjoying more computers (2,300 instead of 2,200) and more cars (650 instead of 600).

The production possibilities frontier simplifies a complex economy to highlight some basic but powerful ideas: scarcity, efficiency, trade-offs, opportunity cost, and economic growth. As you study economics, these ideas will recur in various forms. The production possibilities frontier offers one simple way of thinking about them.

MICROECONOMICS AND MACROECONOMICS

Many subjects are studied on various levels. Consider biology, for example. Molecular biologists study the chemical compounds that make up living things. Cellular biologists study cells, which are made up of many chemical compounds and, at the same time, are themselves the building blocks of living organisms. Evolutionary biologists study the many varieties of animals and plants and how species change gradually over the centuries.

Economics is also studied on various levels. We can study the decisions of individual households and firms. Or we can study the interaction of households and firms in markets for specific goods and services. Or we can study the operation of the economy as a whole, which is the sum of the activities of all these decision makers in all these markets.

The field of economics is traditionally divided into two broad subfields. **Microeconomics** is the study of how households and firms make decisions and how they interact in specific markets. **Macroeconomics** is the study of economy-wide phenomena. A microeconomist might study the effects of rent control on

microeconomics
the study of how households and firms make decisions and how they interact in markets

macroeconomics
the study of economy-wide phenomena, including inflation, unemployment, and economic growth

housing in New York City, the impact of foreign competition on the U.S. auto industry, or the effects of compulsory school attendance on workers' earnings. A macroeconomist might study the effects of borrowing by the federal government, the changes over time in the economy's rate of unemployment, or alternative policies to promote growth in national living standards.

Microeconomics and macroeconomics are closely intertwined. Because changes in the overall economy arise from the decisions of millions of individuals, it is impossible to understand macroeconomic developments without considering the associated microeconomic decisions. For example, a macroeconomist might study the effect of a federal income tax cut on the overall production of goods and services. But to analyze this issue, he or she must consider how the tax cut affects the decisions of households about how much to spend on goods and services.

FYI

Who Studies Economics?

As a college student, you might be asking yourself: How many economics classes should I take? How useful will this stuff be to me later in life? Economics can seem abstract at first, but the field is fundamentally very practical, and the study of economics is useful in many different career paths. Here is a small sampling of some well-known people who majored in economics when they were in college.

Meg Whitman	President and Chief Executive Officer, eBay
Ronald Reagan	Former President of the United States
William F. Buckley Jr.	Journalist
Danny Glover	Actor
Barbara Boxer	U.S. Senator
John Elway	NFL Quarterback
Kofi Annan	Former Secretary General, United Nations
Ted Turner	Founder of CNN and Owner of Atlanta Braves
Lionel Richie	Singer
Diane von Furstenberg	Fashion Designer
Michael Kinsley	Journalist
Ben Stein	Political Speechwriter, Actor, and Game Show Host
Cate Blanchett	Actor
Anthony Zinni	General (ret.), U.S. Marine Corps
Tiger Woods	Golfer
Steve Ballmer	Chief Executive Officer, Microsoft

Arnold Schwarzenegger	Governor of California
Sandra Day-O'Connor	Former Supreme Court Justice
Scott Adams	Cartoonist
Mick Jagger	Singer for The Rolling Stones

Having studied at the London School of Economics may not help Mick Jagger hit the high notes, but it has probably given him some insight about how to invest the substantial sums he has earned during his rock-'n'-roll career.

When asked in 2005 why The Rolling Stones were going on tour again, former economics major Mick Jagger replied, "Supply and demand." Keith Richards added, "If the demand's there, we'll supply."

Despite the inherent link between microeconomics and macroeconomics, the two fields are distinct. Because they address different questions, each field has its own set of models, which are often taught in separate courses.

QUICK QUIZ In what sense is economics like a science? ● Draw a production possibilities frontier for a society that produces food and clothing. Show an efficient point, an inefficient point, and an infeasible point. Show the effects of a drought. ● Define *microeconomics* and *macroeconomics*.

THE ECONOMIST AS POLICY ADVISER

Often, economists are asked to explain the causes of economic events. Why, for example, is unemployment higher for teenagers than for older workers? Sometimes, economists are asked to recommend policies to improve economic outcomes. What, for instance, should the government do to improve the economic well-being of teenagers? When economists are trying to explain the world, they are scientists. When they are trying to help improve it, they are policy advisers.

POSITIVE VERSUS NORMATIVE ANALYSIS

To help clarify the two roles that economists play, let's examine the use of language. Because scientists and policy advisers have different goals, they use language in different ways.

For example, suppose that two people are discussing minimum-wage laws. Here are two statements you might hear:

POLLY: Minimum-wage laws cause unemployment.
NORM: The government should raise the minimum wage.

Ignoring for now whether you agree with these statements, notice that Polly and Norm differ in what they are trying to do. Polly is speaking like a scientist: She is making a claim about how the world works. Norm is speaking like a policy adviser: He is making a claim about how he would like to change the world.

In general, statements about the world are of two types. One type, such as Polly's, is positive. **Positive statements** are descriptive. They make a claim about how the world *is*. A second type of statement, such as Norm's, is normative. **Normative statements** are prescriptive. They make a claim about how the world *ought to be*.

positive statements
claims that attempt to describe the world as it is

normative statements
claims that attempt to prescribe how the world should be

A key difference between positive and normative statements is how we judge their validity. We can, in principle, confirm or refute positive statements by examining evidence. An economist might evaluate Polly's statement by analyzing data on changes in minimum wages and changes in unemployment over time. By contrast, evaluating normative statements involves values as well as facts. Norm's statement cannot be judged using data alone. Deciding what is good or bad policy is not just a matter of science. It also involves our views on ethics, religion, and political philosophy.

Positive and normative statements are fundamentally different, but they are often intertwined in a person's set of beliefs. In particular, positive views about how the world works affect normative views about what policies are desirable. Polly's claim that the minimum wage causes unemployment, if true, might lead her to reject Norm's conclusion that the government should raise the minimum wage. Yet normative conclusions cannot come from positive analysis alone; they involve value judgments as well.

As you study economics, keep in mind the distinction between positive and normative statements because it will help you stay focused on the task at hand. Much of economics is positive: It just tries to explain how the economy works. Yet those who use economics often have normative goals: They want to learn how to improve the economy. When you hear economists making normative statements, you know they are speaking not as scientists but as policy advisers.

ECONOMISTS IN WASHINGTON

President Harry Truman once said that he wanted to find a one-armed economist. When he asked his economists for advice, they always answered, "On the one hand, . . . On the other hand, . . . "

Truman was right in realizing that economists' advice is not always straightforward. This tendency is rooted in one of the *Ten Principles of Economics:* People face trade-offs. Economists are aware that trade-offs are involved in most policy decisions. A policy might increase efficiency at the cost of equality. It might help future generations but hurt current generations. An economist who says that all policy decisions are easy is an economist not to be trusted.

Truman was also not alone among presidents in relying on the advice of economists. Since 1946, the president of the United States has received guidance from the Council of Economic Advisers, which consists of three members and a staff of several dozen economists. The council, whose offices are just a few steps from the White House, has no duty other than to advise the president and to write the annual *Economic Report of the President,* which discusses recent developments in the economy and presents the council's analysis of current policy issues.

The president also receives input from economists in many administrative departments. Economists at the Department of the Treasury help design tax policy. Economists at the Department of Labor analyze data on workers and those looking for work to help formulate labor-market policies. Economists at the Department of Justice help enforce the nation's antitrust laws.

Economists are also found outside the administrative branch of government. To obtain independent evaluations of policy proposals, Congress relies on the advice of the Congressional Budget Office, which is staffed by economists. The Federal Reserve, the institution that sets the nation's monetary policy, employs hundreds of economists to analyze economic developments in the United States and throughout the world.

The influence of economists on policy goes beyond their role as advisers: Their research and writings often affect policy indirectly. Economist John Maynard Keynes offered this observation:

> The ideas of economists and political philosophers, both when they are right and when they are wrong, are more powerful than is commonly understood. Indeed, the world is ruled by little else. Practical men, who believe themselves to be quite exempt from intellectual influences, are usually the slaves of some defunct economist. Madmen in authority, who hear voices in the air, are distilling their frenzy from some academic scribbler of a few years back.

Although these words were written in 1935, they remain true. Indeed, the "academic scribbler" now influencing public policy is often Keynes himself.

"LET'S SWITCH. I'LL MAKE THE POLICY, YOU IMPLEMENT IT, AND HE'LL EXPLAIN IT."

In The News

Football Economics

Economists often offer advice to policymakers. Sometimes those policymakers are coaches.

Go for It on Fourth Down, Coach? Maybe You Should Ask an Egghead.

By Shankar Vedantam

With just over five minutes to play in yesterday's game against the New York Jets, the Washington Redskins found themselves on their own 23-yard line facing a fourth and one. The team, which was ahead by just three points, elected to do what teams normally do in such situations: They played it safe and punted rather than try to keep the drive alive.

The Jets promptly came back to kick a field goal, tying the game and sending it into overtime. While this particular story had a happy ending for Washington, which won, 23–20, it illustrated the value of an analysis by David Romer, an economist at the Uni-

versity of California, who has concluded that football teams are far too conservative in play calling in fourth-down situations.

You don't have to be particularly interested in sports to find Romer's conclusion intriguing: His hunch about human behavior in general was that although people say they have a certain goal and are willing to do everything they can to achieve it, their

actual behavior regularly departs from the optimal path to reach that goal.

In his analysis of football teams, Romer specifically looked at a single question—whether teams should punt or kick the football on fourth down, or take a chance and run or throw the ball. Romer's calculations don't necessarily tell teams what to do in specific situations such as yesterday's game. But on average, teams that take the risk seem to win more often than lose.

Data from a large number of NFL games show that coaches rarely follow what Romer's calculations predict would give them the best chance of victory. While fans often suggest more aggressive play calling, even fans usually don't go as far as the economist does—his calculations show that teams should regularly be going for it on fourth down, even if it is early in the game,

WHY ECONOMISTS' ADVICE IS NOT ALWAYS FOLLOWED

Any economist who advises presidents or other elected leaders knows that his or her recommendations are not always heeded. Frustrating as this can be, it is easy to understand. The process by which economic policy is made differs in many ways from the idealized policy process assumed in economics textbooks.

Throughout this text, whenever we discuss economic policy, we often focus on one question: What is the best policy for the government to pursue? We act as if policy were set by a benevolent king. Once the king figures out the right policy, he has no trouble putting his ideas into action.

In the real world, figuring out the right policy is only part of a leader's job, sometimes the easiest part. After a president hears from his economic advisers about what policy is best from their perspective, he turns to other advisers for related input. His communications advisers will tell him how best to explain the proposed policy to the public, and they will try to anticipate any misunderstand-even if the score is tied, and even if the ball is on their own side of the field.

Romer's calculations have been backed up by independent analyses. Coaches have not raised a serious challenge to Romer's analysis, but they have simply ignored his finding.

New England Patriots coach Bill Belichick is among those who has said he agrees with Romer, and Belichick happens to be one of the more successful coaches in the league. Two Sundays ago, as the Patriots were piling up an astronomical score against Washington, Belichick took a chance on a fourth-down play and got his team seven points instead of the three he might have gotten had the team tried a field goal.

When asked by reporters why he took the chance, Belichick's response was the response of someone who really means what he says about maximizing points: "What do you want us to do, kick a field goal?"

Owners and fans have been receptive to Romer's ideas. However, in informal conversations Romer has had with the coaching staffs of various teams, the economist said he has been told to mind his own business in the ivory tower.

Indeed, since Romer wrote his paper a couple of years ago, NFL coaches seem to have gotten even more conservative in their play calling, which the economist attributes to their unwillingness to follow the advice of an academic, however useful it might be.

"It used to be that going for it on fourth down was the macho thing to do," Romer said. But after his findings were widely publicized in sports circles, he said: "Now going for it on fourth down is the egghead thing to do. Would you rather be macho or an egghead?"

The interesting question raised by Romer's research applies to a range of set-

David Romer

tings that have nothing to do with sports. Why do coaches persist in doing something that is less than optimal, when they say their only goal is to win? One theory that Romer has heard is that coaches—like generals, stock fund directors and managers in general—actually have different goals than the people they lead and the people they must answer to. Everyone wants to win, but managers are held to different standards than followers when they lose, especially when they lose after trying something that few others are doing.

Wayne Stewart, an associate professor of management at Clemson University, said his own research backs up the idea that owners and managers in general have different approaches to risk. While owners tend to be entrepreneurial and focused on outcomes, he said, managers are often principally focused on not screwing up.

Stewart said this might explain why coaches' approach to risk diverges from that of owners and fans, who are principally interested in outcomes. Stewart said successful managers understand that the fear of failure is itself often the principal cause of failure.

Source: *The Washington Post,* November 5, 2007.

ings that might arise to make the challenge more difficult. His press advisers will tell him how the news media will report on his proposal and what opinions will likely be expressed on the nation's editorial pages. His legislative affairs advisers will tell him how Congress will view the proposal, what amendments members of Congress will suggest, and the likelihood that Congress will pass some version of the president's proposal into law. His political advisers will tell him which groups will organize to support or oppose the proposed policy, how this proposal will affect his standing among different groups in the electorate, and whether it will affect support for any of the president's other policy initiatives. After hearing and weighing all this advice, the president then decides how to proceed.

Making economic policy in a representative democracy is a messy affair—and there are often good reasons presidents (and other politicians) do not advance the policies that economists advocate. Economists offer crucial input into the policy process, but their advice is only one ingredient of a complex recipe.

QUICK QUIZ Give an example of a positive statement and an example of a normative statement that somehow relates to your daily life. • Name three parts of government that regularly rely on advice from economists.

WHY ECONOMISTS DISAGREE

"If all economists were laid end to end, they would not reach a conclusion." This quip from George Bernard Shaw is revealing. Economists as a group are often criticized for giving conflicting advice to policymakers. President Ronald Reagan once joked that if the game Trivial Pursuit were designed for economists, it would have 100 questions and 3,000 answers.

Why do economists so often appear to give conflicting advice to policymakers? There are two basic reasons:

- Economists may disagree about the validity of alternative positive theories about how the world works.
- Economists may have different values and therefore different normative views about what policy should try to accomplish.

Let's discuss each of these reasons.

DIFFERENCES IN SCIENTIFIC JUDGMENTS

Several centuries ago, astronomers debated whether the earth or the sun was at the center of the solar system. More recently, meteorologists have debated whether the earth is experiencing global warming and, if so, why. Science is a search for understanding about the world around us. It is not surprising that as the search continues, scientists can disagree about the direction in which truth lies.

Economists often disagree for the same reason. Economics is a young science, and there is still much to be learned. Economists sometimes disagree because they have different hunches about the validity of alternative theories or about the size of important parameters that measure how economic variables are related.

For example, economists disagree about whether the government should tax a household's income or its consumption (spending). Advocates of a switch from the current income tax to a consumption tax believe that the change would encourage households to save more because income that is saved would not be taxed. Higher saving, in turn, would free resources for capital accumulation, leading to more rapid growth in productivity and living standards. Advocates of the current income tax system believe that household saving would not respond much to a change in the tax laws. These two groups of economists hold different normative views about the tax system because they have different positive views about the responsiveness of saving to tax incentives.

DIFFERENCES IN VALUES

Suppose that Peter and Paula both take the same amount of water from the town well. To pay for maintaining the well, the town taxes its residents. Peter has income of $50,000 and is taxed $5,000, or 10 percent of his income. Paula has income of $10,000 and is taxed $2,000, or 20 percent of her income.

Is this policy fair? If not, who pays too much and who pays too little? Does it matter whether Paula's low income is due to a medical disability or to her decision to pursue a career in acting? Does it matter whether Peter's high income is due to a large inheritance or to his willingness to work long hours at a dreary job?

These are difficult questions on which people are likely to disagree. If the town hired two experts to study how the town should tax its residents to pay for the well, we would not be surprised if they offered conflicting advice.

This simple example shows why economists sometimes disagree about public policy. As we learned earlier in our discussion of normative and positive analysis, policies cannot be judged on scientific grounds alone. Economists give conflicting advice sometimes because they have different values. Perfecting the science of economics will not tell us whether Peter or Paula pays too much.

PERCEPTION VERSUS REALITY

Because of differences in scientific judgments and differences in values, some disagreement among economists is inevitable. Yet one should not overstate the amount of disagreement. Economists agree with one another far more than is sometimes understood.

Table 1 contains 14 propositions about economic policy. In surveys of professional economists, these propositions were endorsed by an overwhelming majority of respondents. Most of these propositions would fail to command a similar consensus among the public.

TABLE 1

Propositions about Which Most Economists Agree

Proposition (and percentage of economists who agree)
1. A ceiling on rents reduces the quantity and quality of housing available. (93%)
2. Tariffs and import quotas usually reduce general economic welfare. (93%)
3. Flexible and floating exchange rates offer an effective international monetary arrangement. (90%)
4. Fiscal policy (e.g., tax cut and/or government expenditure increase) has a significant stimulative impact on a less than fully employed economy. (90%)
5. The United States should not restrict employers from outsourcing work to foreign countries. (90%)
6. The United States should eliminate agricultural subsidies. (85%)
7. Local and state governments should eliminate subsidies to professional sports franchises. (85%)
8. If the federal budget is to be balanced, it should be done over the business cycle rather than yearly. (85%)
9. The gap between Social Security funds and expenditures will become unsustainably large within the next 50 years if current policies remain unchanged. (85%)
10. Cash payments increase the welfare of recipients to a greater degree than do transfers-in-kind of equal cash value. (84%)
11. A large federal budget deficit has an adverse effect on the economy. (83%)
12. A minimum wage increases unemployment among young and unskilled workers. (79%)
13. The government should restructure the welfare system along the lines of a "negative income tax." (79%)
14. Effluent taxes and marketable pollution permits represent a better approach to pollution control than imposition of pollution ceilings. (78%)

Source: Richard M. Alston, J. R. Kearl, and Michael B. Vaughn, "Is There Consensus among Economists in the 1990s?" *American Economic Review* (May 1992): 203–209; Robert Whaples, "Do Economists Agree on Anything? Yes!" *Economists' Voice* (November 2006): 1–6.

The first proposition in the table is about rent control, a policy that sets a legal maximum on the amount landlords can charge for their apartments. Almost all economists believe that rent control adversely affects the availability and quality of housing and is a costly way of helping the neediest members of society. Nonetheless, many city governments ignore the advice of economists and place ceilings on the rents that landlords may charge their tenants.

The second proposition in the table concerns tariffs and import quotas, two policies that restrict trade among nations. For reasons we discuss more fully later in this text, almost all economists oppose such barriers to free trade. Nonetheless, over the years, presidents and Congress have chosen to restrict the import of certain goods.

Why do policies such as rent control and trade barriers persist if the experts are united in their opposition? It may be that the realities of the political process stand as immovable obstacles. But it also may be that economists have not yet convinced enough of the public that these policies are undesirable. One purpose of this book is to help you understand the economist's view of these and other subjects and, perhaps, to persuade you that it is the right one.

QUICK QUIZ Why might economic advisers to the president disagree about a question of policy?

LET'S GET GOING

The first two chapters of this book have introduced you to the ideas and methods of economics. We are now ready to get to work. In the next chapter, we start learning in more detail the principles of economic behavior and economic policy.

As you proceed through this book, you will be asked to draw on many of your intellectual skills. You might find it helpful to keep in mind some advice from the great economist John Maynard Keynes:

> The study of economics does not seem to require any specialized gifts of an unusually high order. Is it not . . . a very easy subject compared with the higher branches of philosophy or pure science? An easy subject, at which very few excel! The paradox finds its explanation, perhaps, in that the master-economist must possess a rare *combination* of gifts. He must be mathematician, historian, statesman, philosopher—in some degree. He must understand symbols and speak in words. He must contemplate the particular in terms of the general, and touch abstract and concrete in the same flight of thought. He must study the present in the light of the past for the purposes of the future. No part of man's nature or his institutions must lie entirely outside his regard. He must be purposeful and disinterested in a simultaneous mood; as aloof and incorruptible as an artist, yet sometimes as near the earth as a politician.

It is a tall order. But with practice, you will become more and more accustomed to thinking like an economist.

In The News

Environmental Economics

Some economists are helping to save the planet.

Green Groups See Potent Tool in Economics

By Jessica E. Vascellaro

Many economists dream of getting high-paying jobs on Wall Street, at prestigious think tanks and universities or at powerful government agencies like the Federal Reserve.

But a growing number are choosing to use their skills not to track inflation or interest rates but to rescue rivers and trees. These are the "green economists," more formally known as environmental economists, who use economic arguments and systems to persuade companies to clean up pollution and to help conserve natural areas.

Working at dozens of advocacy groups and a myriad of state and federal environmental agencies, they are helping to formulate the intellectual framework behind approaches to protecting endangered species, reducing pollution and preventing climate change. They also are becoming a link between left-leaning advocacy groups and the public and private sectors.

"In the past, many advocacy groups interpreted economics as how to make a profit or maximize income," says Lawrence Goulder, a professor of environmental and resource economics at Stanford University in Stanford, Calif. "More economists are realizing that it offers a framework for resource allocation where resources are not only labor and capital but natural resources as well."

Environmental economists are on the payroll of government agencies (the Environmental Protection Agency had about 164 on staff in 2004, up 36% from 1995) and groups like the Wilderness Society, a Washington-based conservation group, which has four of them to work on projects such as assessing the economic impact of building off-road driving trails. Environmental Defense, also based in Washington, was one of the first environmental-advocacy groups to hire economists and now has about eight, who do such things as develop market incentives to address environmental problems like climate change and water shortages. . . .

"There used to be this idea that we shouldn't have to monetize the environment because it is invaluable," says Caroline Alkire, who in 1991 joined the Wilderness Society, an advocacy group in Washington, D.C., as one of the group's first economists. "But if we are going to engage in debate on the Hill about drilling in the Arctic we need to be able to combat the financial arguments. We have to play that card or we are going to lose."

The field of environmental economics began to take form in the 1960s when academics started to apply the tools of economics to the nascent green movement. The discipline grew more popular throughout the 1980s when the Environmental Protection Agency adopted a system of tradable permits for phasing out leaded gasoline. It wasn't until the 1990 amendment to the Clean Air Act, however, that most environmentalists started to take economics seriously.

The amendment implemented a system of tradable allowances for acid rain, a program pushed by Environmental Defense. Under the law, plants that can reduce their emissions more cost-effectively may sell their allowances to more heavy polluters. Today, the program has exceeded its goal of reducing the amount of acid rain to half its 1980 level and is celebrated as evidence that markets can help achieve environmental goals.

Its success has convinced its former critics, who at the time contended that environmental regulation was a matter of ethics, not economics, and favored installing expensive acid rain removal technology in all power plants instead.

Greenpeace, the international environmental giant, was one of the leading opponents of the 1990 amendment. But Kert Davies, research director for Greenpeace USA, said its success and the lack of any significant action on climate policy throughout [the] early 1990s brought the organization around to the concept. "We now believe that [tradable permits] are the most straightforward system of reducing emissions and creating the incentives necessary for massive reductions."

Source: *The Wall Street Journal*, August 23, 2005.

SUMMARY

- Economists try to address their subject with a scientist's objectivity. Like all scientists, they make appropriate assumptions and build simplified models to understand the world around them. Two simple economic models are the circular-flow diagram and the production possibilities frontier.

- The field of economics is divided into two subfields: microeconomics and macroeconomics. Microeconomists study decision making by households and firms and the interaction among households and firms in the marketplace. Macroeconomists study the forces and trends that affect the economy as a whole.

- A positive statement is an assertion about how the world *is*. A normative statement is an assertion about how the world *ought to be*. When economists make normative statements, they are acting more as policy advisers than as scientists.

- Economists who advise policymakers offer conflicting advice either because of differences in scientific judgments or because of differences in values. At other times, economists are united in the advice they offer, but policymakers may choose to ignore it.

KEY CONCEPTS

circular-flow diagram, *p. 24*
production possibilities frontier,
   p. 26

microeconomics, *p. 28*
macroeconomics, *p. 28*
positive statements, *p. 30*

normative statements, *p. 30*

QUESTIONS FOR REVIEW

1. How is economics like a science?
2. Why do economists make assumptions?
3. Should an economic model describe reality exactly?
4. Name a way that your family interacts in the factor market, and a way that it interacts in the product market.
5. Name one economic interaction that isn't covered by the simplified circular-flow diagram.
6. Draw and explain a production possibilities frontier for an economy that produces milk and

cookies. What happens to this frontier if disease kills half of the economy's cows?
7. Use a production possibilities frontier to describe the idea of "efficiency."
8. What are the two subfields into which economics is divided? Explain what each subfield studies.
9. What is the difference between a positive and a normative statement? Give an example of each.
10. Why do economists sometimes offer conflicting advice to policymakers?

PROBLEMS AND APPLICATIONS

1. Draw a circular-flow diagram. Identify the parts of the model that correspond to the flow of goods and services and the flow of dollars for each of the following activities.

a. Selena pays a storekeeper $1 for a quart of milk.
b. Stuart earns $4.50 per hour working at a fast-food restaurant.

c. Shanna spends $30 to get a haircut.

d. Sally earns $10,000 from her 10 percent ownership of Acme Industrial.

2. Imagine a society that produces military goods and consumer goods, which we'll call "guns" and "butter."

a. Draw a production possibilities frontier for guns and butter. Using the concept of opportunity cost, explain why it most likely has a bowed-out shape.

b. Show a point that is impossible for the economy to achieve. Show a point that is feasible but inefficient.

c. Imagine that the society has two political parties, called the Hawks (who want a strong military) and the Doves (who want a smaller military). Show a point on your production possibilities frontier that the Hawks might choose and a point the Doves might choose.

d. Imagine that an aggressive neighboring country reduces the size of its military. As a result, both the Hawks and the Doves reduce their desired production of guns by the same amount. Which party would get the bigger "peace dividend," measured by the increase in butter production? Explain.

3. The first principle of economics discussed in Chapter 1 is that people face trade-offs. Use a production possibilities frontier to illustrate society's trade-off between two "goods"—a clean environment and the quantity of industrial output. What do you suppose determines the shape and position of the frontier? Show what happens to the frontier if engineers develop a new way of producing electricity that emits fewer pollutants.

4. An economy consists of three workers: Larry, Moe, and Curly. Each works ten hours a day and can produce two services: mowing lawns and washing cars. In an hour, Larry can either mow one lawn or wash one car; Moe can either mow one lawn or wash two cars; and Curly can either mow two lawns or wash one car.

a. Calculate how much of each service is produced under the following circumstances, which we label A, B, C, and D:

• All three spend all their time mowing lawns. (A)

• All three spend all their time washing cars. (B)

• All three spend half their time on each activity. (C)

• Larry spends half his time on each activity, while Moe only washes cars and Curly only mows lawns. (D)

b. Graph the production possibilities frontier for this economy. Using your answers to part (a), identify points A, B, C, and D on your graph.

c. Explain why the production possibilities frontier has the shape it does.

d. Are any of the allocations calculated in part (a) inefficient? Explain.

5. Classify the following topics as relating to microeconomics or macroeconomics.

a. a family's decision about how much income to save

b. the effect of government regulations on auto emissions

c. the impact of higher national saving on economic growth

d. a firm's decision about how many workers to hire

e. the relationship between the inflation rate and changes in the quantity of money

6. Classify each of the following statements as positive or normative. Explain.

a. Society faces a short-run trade-off between inflation and unemployment.

b. A reduction in the rate of money growth will reduce the rate of inflation.

c. The Federal Reserve should reduce the rate of money growth.

d. Society ought to require welfare recipients to look for jobs.

e. Lower tax rates encourage more work and more saving.

7. Classify each of the statements in Table 1 as positive, normative, or ambiguous. Explain.

8. If you were president, would you be more interested in your economic advisers' positive views or their normative views? Why?

9. Find a recent copy of the *Economic Report of the President* at your library or on the Internet (http://www.gpoaccess.gov/eop/index.html). Read a chapter about an issue that interests you. Summarize the economic problem at hand and describe the council's recommended policy.

APPENDIX

GRAPHING: A BRIEF REVIEW

Many of the concepts that economists study can be expressed with numbers—the price of bananas, the quantity of bananas sold, the cost of growing bananas, and so on. Often, these economic variables are related to one another. When the price of bananas rises, people buy fewer bananas. One way of expressing the relationships among variables is with graphs.

Graphs serve two purposes. First, when developing economic theories, graphs offer a way to visually express ideas that might be less clear if described with equations or words. Second, when analyzing economic data, graphs provide a powerful way of finding and interpreting patterns. Whether we are working with theory or with data, graphs provide a lens through which a recognizable forest emerges from a multitude of trees.

Numerical information can be expressed graphically in many ways, just as there are many ways to express a thought in words. A good writer chooses words that will make an argument clear, a description pleasing, or a scene dramatic. An effective economist chooses the type of graph that best suits the purpose at hand.

In this appendix, we discuss how economists use graphs to study the mathematical relationships among variables. We also discuss some of the pitfalls that can arise in the use of graphical methods.

GRAPHS OF A SINGLE VARIABLE

Three common graphs are shown in Figure A-1. The *pie chart* in panel (a) shows how total income in the United States is divided among the sources of income, including compensation of employees, corporate profits, and so on. A slice of the pie represents each source's share of the total. The *bar graph* in panel (b) compares

A-1 FIGURE

The pie chart in panel (a) shows how U.S. national income is derived from various sources. The bar graph in panel (b) compares the average income in four countries. The time-series graph in panel (c) shows the productivity of labor in U.S. businesses from 1950 to 2000.

Types of Graphs

income for four countries. The height of each bar represents the average income in each country. The *time-series graph* in panel (c) traces the rising productivity in the U.S. business sector over time. The height of the line shows output per hour in each year. You have probably seen similar graphs in newspapers and magazines.

GRAPHS OF TWO VARIABLES: THE COORDINATE SYSTEM

Although the three graphs in Figure A-1 are useful in showing how a variable changes over time or across individuals, such graphs are limited in how much they can tell us. These graphs display information only on a single variable. Economists are often concerned with the relationships between variables. Thus, they need to display two variables on a single graph. The *coordinate system* makes this possible.

Suppose you want to examine the relationship between study time and grade point average. For each student in your class, you could record a pair of numbers: hours per week spent studying and grade point average. These numbers could then be placed in parentheses as an *ordered pair* and appear as a single point on the graph. Albert E., for instance, is represented by the ordered pair (25 hours/week, 3.5 GPA), while his "what-me-worry?" classmate Alfred E. is represented by the ordered pair (5 hours/week, 2.0 GPA).

We can graph these ordered pairs on a two-dimensional grid. The first number in each ordered pair, called the *x-coordinate*, tells us the horizontal location of the point. The second number, called the *y-coordinate*, tells us the vertical location of the point. The point with both an *x*-coordinate and a *y*-coordinate of zero is known as the *origin*. The two coordinates in the ordered pair tell us where the point is located in relation to the origin: *x* units to the right of the origin and *y* units above it.

Figure A-2 graphs grade point average against study time for Albert E., Alfred E., and their classmates. This type of graph is called a *scatterplot* because it plots scattered points. Looking at this graph, we immediately notice that points farther to the right (indicating more study time) also tend to be higher (indicating a better

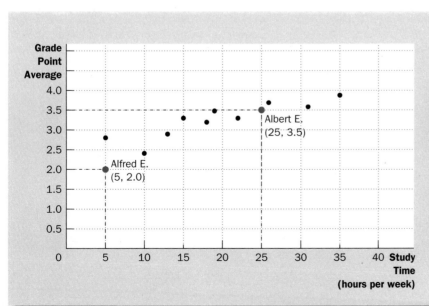

FIGURE A-2

Using the Coordinate System
Grade point average is measured on the vertical axis and study time on the horizontal axis. Albert E., Alfred E., and their classmates are represented by various points. We can see from the graph that students who study more tend to get higher grades.

grade point average). Because study time and grade point average typically move in the same direction, we say that these two variables have a *positive correlation*. By contrast, if we were to graph party time and grades, we would likely find that higher party time is associated with lower grades; because these variables typically move in opposite directions, we call this a *negative correlation*. In either case, the coordinate system makes the correlation between the two variables easy to see.

CURVES IN THE COORDINATE SYSTEM

Students who study more do tend to get higher grades, but other factors also influence a student's grade. Previous preparation is an important factor, for instance, as are talent, attention from teachers, even eating a good breakfast. A scatterplot like Figure A-2 does not attempt to isolate the effect that study has on grades from the effects of other variables. Often, however, economists prefer looking at how one variable affects another, holding everything else constant.

To see how this is done, let's consider one of the most important graphs in economics: the *demand curve*. The demand curve traces out the effect of a good's price on the quantity of the good consumers want to buy. Before showing a demand curve, however, consider Table A-1, which shows how the number of novels that Emma buys depends on her income and on the price of novels. When novels are cheap, Emma buys them in large quantities. As they become more expensive, she instead borrows books from the library or chooses to go to the movies rather than read. Similarly, at any given price, Emma buys more novels when she has a higher income. That is, when her income increases, she spends part of the additional income on novels and part on other goods.

We now have three variables—the price of novels, income, and the number of novels purchased—which are more than we can represent in two dimensions. To put the information from Table A-1 in graphical form, we need to hold one of the three variables constant and trace out the relationship between the other two. Because the demand curve represents the relationship between price and quantity demanded, we hold Emma's income constant and show how the number of novels she buys varies with the price of novels.

A-1 TABLE

Novels Purchased by Emma
This table shows the number of novels Emma buys at various incomes and prices. For any given level of income, the data on price and quantity demanded can be graphed to produce Emma's demand curve for novels, as shown in Figures A-3 and A-4.

		Income	
Price	$20,000	$30,000	$40,000
$10	2 novels	5 novels	8 novels
9	6	9	12
8	10	13	16
7	14	17	20
6	18	21	24
5	22	25	28
	Demand curve, D_3	Demand curve, D_1	Demand curve, D_2

Suppose that Emma's income is $30,000 per year. If we place the number of novels Emma purchases on the *x*-axis and the price of novels on the *y*-axis, we can graphically represent the middle column of Table A-1. When the points that represent these entries from the table—(5 novels, $10), (9 novels, $9), and so on—are connected, they form a line. This line, pictured in Figure A-3, is known as Emma's demand curve for novels; it tells us how many novels Emma purchases at any given price. The demand curve is downward sloping, indicating that a higher price reduces the quantity of novels demanded. Because the quantity of novels demanded and the price move in opposite directions, we say that the two variables are *negatively related*. (Conversely, when two variables move in the same direction, the curve relating them is upward sloping, and we say the variables are *positively related*.)

Now suppose that Emma's income rises to $40,000 per year. At any given price, Emma will purchase more novels than she did at her previous level of income. Just as earlier we drew Emma's demand curve for novels using the entries from the middle column of Table A-1, we now draw a new demand curve using the entries from the right column of the table. This new demand curve (curve D_2) is pictured alongside the old one (curve D_1) in Figure A-4; the new curve is a similar line drawn farther to the right. We therefore say that Emma's demand curve for novels *shifts* to the right when her income increases. Likewise, if Emma's income were to fall to $20,000 per year, she would buy fewer novels at any given price and her demand curve would shift to the left (to curve D_3).

In economics, it is important to distinguish between *movements along a curve* and *shifts of a curve*. As we can see from Figure A-3, if Emma earns $30,000 per year and novels cost $8 apiece, she will purchase 13 novels per year. If the price of

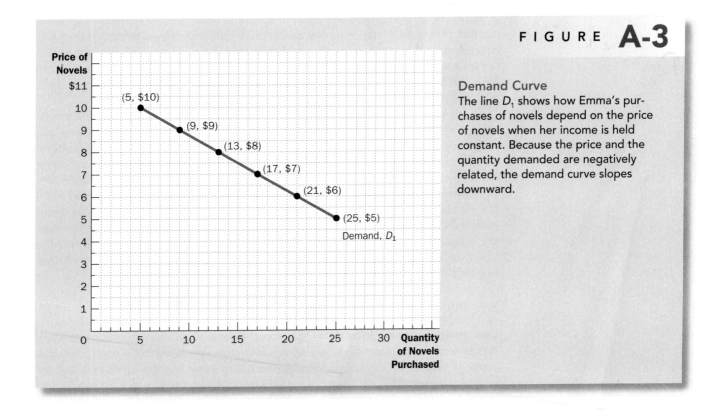

FIGURE **A-3**

Demand Curve
The line D_1 shows how Emma's purchases of novels depend on the price of novels when her income is held constant. Because the price and the quantity demanded are negatively related, the demand curve slopes downward.

A-4 FIGURE

Shifting Demand Curves
The location of Emma's demand curve for novels depends on how much income she earns. The more she earns, the more novels she will purchase at any given price, and the farther to the right her demand curve will lie. Curve D_1 represents Emma's original demand curve when her income is $30,000 per year. If her income rises to $40,000 per year, her demand curve shifts to D_2. If her income falls to $20,000 per year, her demand curve shifts to D_3.

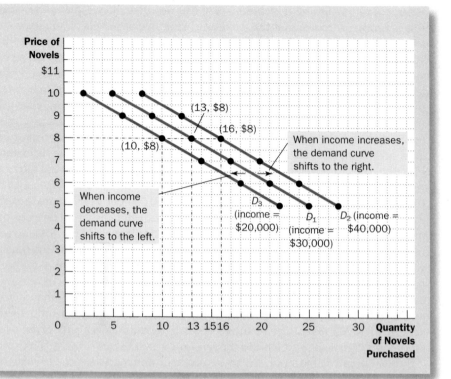

novels falls to $7, Emma will increase her purchases of novels to 17 per year. The demand curve, however, stays fixed in the same place. Emma still buys the same number of novels *at each price,* but as the price falls, she moves along her demand curve from left to right. By contrast, if the price of novels remains fixed at $8 but her income rises to $40,000, Emma increases her purchases of novels from 13 to 16 per year. Because Emma buys more novels *at each price,* her demand curve shifts out, as shown in Figure A-4.

There is a simple way to tell when it is necessary to shift a curve: *When a variable that is not named on either axis changes, the curve shifts.* Income is on neither the *x*-axis nor the *y*-axis of the graph, so when Emma's income changes, her demand curve must shift. The same is true for any change that affects Emma's purchasing habits besides a change in the price of novels. If, for instance, the public library closes and Emma must buy all the books she wants to read, she will demand more novels at each price, and her demand curve will shift to the right. Or if the price of movies falls and Emma spends more time at the movies and less time reading, she will demand fewer novels at each price, and her demand curve will shift to the left. By contrast, when a variable on an axis of the graph changes, the curve does not shift. We read the change as a movement along the curve.

SLOPE

One question we might want to ask about Emma is how much her purchasing habits respond to price. Look at the demand curve pictured in Figure A-5. If this curve is very steep, Emma purchases nearly the same number of novels regardless of whether they are cheap or expensive. If this curve is much flatter, Emma purchases many fewer novels when the price rises. To answer questions about how much one variable responds to changes in another variable, we can use the concept of slope.

The slope of a line is the ratio of the vertical distance covered to the horizontal distance covered as we move along the line. This definition is usually written out in mathematical symbols as follows:

$$\text{slope} = \frac{\Delta y}{\Delta x},$$

where the Greek letter Δ (delta) stands for the change in a variable. In other words, the slope of a line is equal to the "rise" (change in y) divided by the "run" (change in x). The slope will be a small positive number for a fairly flat upward-sloping line, a large positive number for a steep upward-sloping line, and a negative number for a downward-sloping line. A horizontal line has a slope of zero because in this case the y-variable never changes; a vertical line is said to have an infinite slope because the y-variable can take any value without the x-variable changing at all.

What is the slope of Emma's demand curve for novels? First of all, because the curve slopes down, we know the slope will be negative. To calculate a numerical value for the slope, we must choose two points on the line. With Emma's income at $30,000, she will purchase 21 novels at a price of $6 or 13 novels at a price of $8. When we apply the slope formula, we are concerned with the change between these two points; in other words, we are concerned with the difference between

I miss you -Trent

FIGURE **A-5**

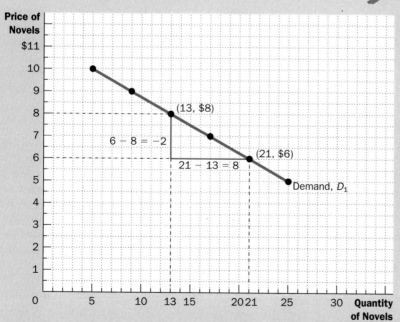

Calculating the Slope of a Line
To calculate the slope of the demand curve, we can look at the changes in the x- and y-coordinates as we move from the point (21 novels, $6) to the point (13 novels, $8). The slope of the line is the ratio of the change in the y-coordinate (−2) to the change in the x-coordinate (+8), which equals −¼.

them, which lets us know that we will have to subtract one set of values from the other, as follows:

$$\text{slope} = \frac{\Delta y}{\Delta x} = \frac{\text{first } y\text{-coordinate} - \text{second } y\text{-coordinate}}{\text{first } x\text{-coordinate} - \text{second } x\text{-coordinate}} = \frac{6-8}{21-13} = \frac{-2}{8} = \frac{-1}{4}$$

Figure A-5 shows graphically how this calculation works. Try computing the slope of Emma's demand curve using two different points. You should get exactly the same result, $-\frac{1}{4}$. One of the properties of a straight line is that it has the same slope everywhere. This is not true of other types of curves, which are steeper in some places than in others.

The slope of Emma's demand curve tells us something about how responsive her purchases are to changes in the price. A small slope (a number close to zero) means that Emma's demand curve is relatively flat; in this case, she adjusts the number of novels she buys substantially in response to a price change. A larger slope (a number farther from zero) means that Emma's demand curve is relatively steep; in this case, she adjusts the number of novels she buys only slightly in response to a price change.

Cause and Effect

Economists often use graphs to advance an argument about how the economy works. In other words, they use graphs to argue about how one set of events *causes* another set of events. With a graph like the demand curve, there is no doubt about cause and effect. Because we are varying price and holding all other variables constant, we know that changes in the price of novels cause changes in the quantity Emma demands. Remember, however, that our demand curve came from a hypothetical example. When graphing data from the real world, it is often more difficult to establish how one variable affects another.

The first problem is that it is difficult to hold everything else constant when studying the relationship between two variables. If we are not able to hold other variables constant, we might decide that one variable on our graph is causing changes in the other variable when actually those changes are caused by a third *omitted variable* not pictured on the graph. Even if we have identified the correct two variables to look at, we might run into a second problem—*reverse causality*. In other words, we might decide that A causes B when in fact B causes A. The omitted-variable and reverse-causality traps require us to proceed with caution when using graphs to draw conclusions about causes and effects.

"Do you think all these film crews brought on global warming or did global warming bring on all these film crews?"

Omitted Variables   To see how omitting a variable can lead to a deceptive graph, let's consider an example. Imagine that the government, spurred by public concern about the large number of deaths from cancer, commissions an exhaustive study from Big Brother Statistical Services, Inc. Big Brother examines many of the items found in people's homes to see which of them are associated with the risk of cancer. Big Brother reports a strong relationship between two variables: the number of cigarette lighters that a household owns and the probability that someone in the household will develop cancer. Figure A-6 shows this relationship.

What should we make of this result? Big Brother advises a quick policy response. It recommends that the government discourage the ownership of cigarette lighters by taxing their sale. It also recommends that the government require

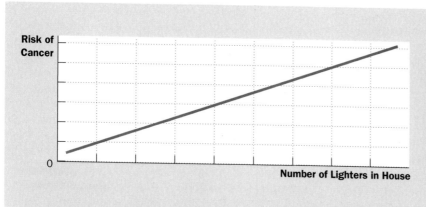

Graph with an Omitted Variable
The upward-sloping curve shows that members of households with more cigarette lighters are more likely to develop cancer. Yet we should not conclude that ownership of lighters causes cancer because the graph does not take into account the number of cigarettes smoked.

warning labels: "Big Brother has determined that this lighter is dangerous to your health."

In judging the validity of Big Brother's analysis, one question is paramount: Has Big Brother held constant every relevant variable except the one under consideration? If the answer is no, the results are suspect. An easy explanation for Figure A-6 is that people who own more cigarette lighters are more likely to smoke cigarettes and that cigarettes, not lighters, cause cancer. If Figure A-6 does not hold constant the amount of smoking, it does not tell us the true effect of owning a cigarette lighter.

This story illustrates an important principle: When you see a graph used to support an argument about cause and effect, it is important to ask whether the movements of an omitted variable could explain the results you see.

Reverse Causality Economists can also make mistakes about causality by misreading its direction. To see how this is possible, suppose the Association of American Anarchists commissions a study of crime in America and arrives at Figure A-7, which plots the number of violent crimes per thousand people in major cities against the number of police officers per thousand people. The anarchists note the curve's upward slope and argue that because police increase rather than decrease the amount of urban violence, law enforcement should be abolished.

If we could run a controlled experiment, we would avoid the danger of reverse causality. To run an experiment, we would set the number of police officers in different cities randomly and then examine the correlation between police and crime. Figure A-7, however, is not based on such an experiment. We simply observe that more dangerous cities have more police officers. The explanation for this may be that more dangerous cities hire more police. In other words, rather than police causing crime, crime may cause police. Nothing in the graph itself allows us to establish the direction of causality.

It might seem that an easy way to determine the direction of causality is to examine which variable moves first. If we see crime increase and then the police force expand, we reach one conclusion. If we see the police force expand and then crime increase, we reach the other. Yet there is also a flaw with this approach: Often, people change their behavior not in response to a change in their present conditions but in response to a change in their *expectations* of future conditions. A

A-7 FIGURE

Graph Suggesting Reverse Causality
The upward-sloping curve shows that cities with a higher concentration of police are more dangerous. Yet the graph does not tell us whether police cause crime or crime-plagued cities hire more police.

city that expects a major crime wave in the future, for instance, might hire more police now. This problem is even easier to see in the case of babies and minivans. Couples often buy a minivan in anticipation of the birth of a child. The minivan comes before the baby, but we wouldn't want to conclude that the sale of minivans causes the population to grow!

There is no complete set of rules that says when it is appropriate to draw causal conclusions from graphs. Yet just keeping in mind that cigarette lighters don't cause cancer (omitted variable) and minivans don't cause larger families (reverse causality) will keep you from falling for many faulty economic arguments.

Interdependence and the Gains from Trade

Consider your typical day. You wake up in the morning and pour yourself juice from oranges grown in Florida and coffee from beans grown in Brazil. Over breakfast, you watch a news program broadcast from New York on your television made in Japan. You get dressed in clothes made of cotton grown in Georgia and sewn in factories in Thailand. You drive to class in a car made of parts manufactured in more than a dozen countries around the world. Then you open up your economics textbook written by an author living in Massachusetts, published by a company located in Ohio, and printed on paper made from trees grown in Oregon.

Every day, you rely on many people, most of whom you have never met, to provide you with the goods and services that you enjoy. Such interdependence is possible because people trade with one another. Those people providing you goods and services are not acting out of generosity. Nor is some government agency directing them to satisfy your desires. Instead, people provide you and other consumers with the goods and services they produce because they get something in return.

In subsequent chapters, we examine how our economy coordinates the activities of millions of people with varying tastes and abilities. As a starting point for this analysis, here we consider the reasons for economic interdependence. One of the *Ten Principles of Economics* highlighted in Chapter 1 is that trade can make everyone better off. In this chapter, we examine this principle more closely. What exactly do people gain when they trade with one another? Why do people choose to become interdependent?

The answers to these questions are key to understanding the modern global economy. In most countries today, many goods and services consumed are imported from abroad, and many goods and services produced are exported to foreign customers. The analysis in this chapter explains interdependence not only among individuals but also among nations. As we will see, the gains from trade are much the same whether you are buying a haircut from your local barber or a T-shirt made by a worker on the other side of the globe.

A PARABLE FOR THE MODERN ECONOMY

To understand why people choose to depend on others for goods and services and how this choice improves their lives, let's look at a simple economy. Imagine that there are two goods in the world: meat and potatoes. And there are two people in the world—a cattle rancher and a potato farmer—each of whom would like to eat both meat and potatoes.

The gains from trade are most obvious if the rancher can produce only meat and the farmer can produce only potatoes. In one scenario, the rancher and the farmer could choose to have nothing to do with each other. But after several months of eating beef roasted, boiled, broiled, and grilled, the rancher might decide that self-sufficiency is not all it's cracked up to be. The farmer, who has been eating potatoes mashed, fried, baked, and scalloped, would likely agree. It is easy to see that trade would allow them to enjoy greater variety: Each could then have a steak with a baked potato or a burger with fries.

Although this scene illustrates most simply how everyone can benefit from trade, the gains would be similar if the rancher and the farmer were each capable of producing the other good, but only at great cost. Suppose, for example, that the potato farmer is able to raise cattle and produce meat, but that he is not very good at it. Similarly, suppose that the cattle rancher is able to grow potatoes but that her land is not very well suited for it. In this case, the farmer and the rancher can each benefit by specializing in what he or she does best and then trading with the other.

The gains from trade are less obvious, however, when one person is better at producing *every* good. For example, suppose that the rancher is better at raising cattle *and* better at growing potatoes than the farmer. In this case, should the rancher choose to remain self-sufficient? Or is there still reason for her to trade with the farmer? To answer this question, we need to look more closely at the factors that affect such a decision.

PRODUCTION POSSIBILITIES

Suppose that the farmer and the rancher each work 8 hours per day and can devote this time to growing potatoes, raising cattle, or a combination of the two. The table in Figure 1 shows the amount of time each person requires to produce 1 ounce of each good. The farmer can produce an ounce of potatoes in 15 minutes and an ounce of meat in 60 minutes. The rancher, who is more productive in both activities, can produce an ounce of potatoes in 10 minutes and an ounce of meat in 20 minutes. The last two columns in the table show the amounts of meat or potatoes the farmer and rancher can produce if they work an 8-hour day producing only that good.

Panel (b) of Figure 1 illustrates the amounts of meat and potatoes that the farmer can produce. If the farmer devotes all 8 hours of his time to potatoes, he produces 32 ounces of potatoes (measured on the horizontal axis) and no meat. If he devotes all his time to meat, he produces 8 ounces of meat (measured on the vertical axis) and no potatoes. If the farmer divides his time equally between the two activities, spending 4 hours on each, he produces 16 ounces of potatoes and 4 ounces of meat. The figure shows these three possible outcomes and all others in between.

This graph is the farmer's production possibilities frontier. As we discussed in Chapter 2, a production possibilities frontier shows the various mixes of output that an economy can produce. It illustrates one of the *Ten Principles of Economics* in Chapter 1: People face trade-offs. Here the farmer faces a trade-off between producing meat and producing potatoes.

Panel (a) shows the production opportunities available to the farmer and the rancher. Panel (b) shows the combinations of meat and potatoes that the farmer can produce. Panel (c) shows the combinations of meat and potatoes that the rancher can produce. Both production possibilities frontiers are derived assuming that the farmer and rancher each work 8 hours per day. If there is no trade, each person's production possibilities frontier is also his or her consumption possibilities frontier.

FIGURE 1

The Production Possibilities Frontier

(a) Production Opportunities

	Minutes Needed to Make 1 Ounce of:		Amount Produced in 8 Hours	
	Meat	Potatoes	Meat	Potatoes
Farmer	60 min/oz	15 min/oz	8 oz	32 oz
Rancher	20 min/oz	10 min/oz	24 oz	48 oz

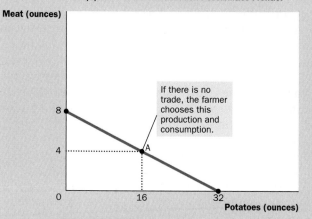

(b) The Farmer's Production Possibilities Frontier

If there is no trade, the farmer chooses this production and consumption.

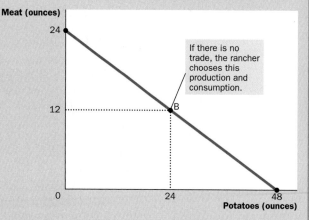

(c) The Rancher's Production Possibilities Frontier

If there is no trade, the rancher chooses this production and consumption.

You may recall that the production possibilities frontier in Chapter 2 was drawn bowed out. In that case, the rate at which society could trade one good for the other depended on the amounts that were being produced. Here, however, the farmer's technology for producing meat and potatoes (as summarized in Figure 1) allows him to switch between the two goods at a constant rate. Whenever the farmer spends 1 hour less producing meat and 1 hour more producing potatoes, he reduces his output of meat by 1 ounce and raises his output of potatoes by 4 ounces—and this is true regardless of how much he is already producing. As a result, the production possibilities frontier is a straight line.

Panel (c) of Figure 1 shows the production possibilities frontier for the rancher. If the rancher devotes all 8 hours of her time to potatoes, she produces 48 ounces of potatoes and no meat. If she devotes all her time to meat, she produces 24 ounces of meat and no potatoes. If the rancher divides her time equally, spending 4 hours on each activity, she produces 24 ounces of potatoes and 12 ounces of meat. Once again, the production possibilities frontier shows all the possible outcomes.

If the farmer and rancher choose to be self-sufficient rather than trade with each other, then each consumes exactly what he or she produces. In this case, the production possibilities frontier is also the consumption possibilities frontier. That is, without trade, Figure 1 shows the possible combinations of meat and potatoes that the farmer and rancher can each produce and then consume.

These production possibilities frontiers are useful in showing the trade-offs that the farmer and rancher face, but they do not tell us what the farmer and rancher will actually choose to do. To determine their choices, we need to know the tastes of the farmer and the rancher. Let's suppose they choose the combinations identified by points A and B in Figure 1: The farmer produces and consumes 16 ounces of potatoes and 4 ounces of meat, while the rancher produces and consumes 24 ounces of potatoes and 12 ounces of meat.

SPECIALIZATION AND TRADE

After several years of eating combination B, the rancher gets an idea and goes to talk to the farmer:

RANCHER: Farmer, my friend, have I got a deal for you! I know how to improve life for both of us. I think you should stop producing meat altogether and devote all your time to growing potatoes. According to my calculations, if you work 8 hours a day growing potatoes, you'll produce 32 ounces of potatoes. If you give me 15 of those 32 ounces, I'll give you 5 ounces of meat in return. In the end, you'll get to eat 17 ounces of potatoes and 5 ounces of meat every day, instead of the 16 ounces of potatoes and 4 ounces of meat you now get. If you go along with my plan, you'll have more of *both* foods. [To illustrate her point, the rancher shows the farmer panel (a) of Figure 2.]

FARMER: (sounding skeptical) That seems like a good deal for me. But I don't understand why you are offering it. If the deal is so good for me, it can't be good for you too.

RANCHER: Oh, but it is! Suppose I spend 6 hours a day raising cattle and 2 hours growing potatoes. Then I can produce 18 ounces of meat and 12 ounces of potatoes. After I give you 5 ounces of my meat in exchange for 15 ounces of your potatoes, I'll end up with 13 ounces of meat and 27 ounces of potatoes, instead of the 12 ounces of meat and

The proposed trade between the farmer and the rancher offers each of them a combination of meat and potatoes that would be impossible in the absence of trade. In panel (a), the farmer gets to consume at point A* rather than point A. In panel (b), the rancher gets to consume at point B* rather than point B. Trade allows each to consume more meat and more potatoes.

FIGURE 2

How Trade Expands the Set of Consumption Opportunities

(a) The Farmer's Production and Consumption

(b) The Rancher's Production and Consumption

(c) The Gains from Trade: A Summary

	Farmer		Rancher	
	Meat	Potatoes	Meat	Potatoes
Without Trade:				
Production and Consumption	4 oz	16 oz	12 oz	24 oz
With Trade:				
Production	0 oz	32 oz	18 oz	12 oz
Trade	Gets 5 oz	Gives 15 oz	Gives 5 oz	Gets 15 oz
Consumption	5 oz	17 oz	13 oz	27 oz
GAINS FROM TRADE:				
Increase in Consumption	+1 oz	+1 oz	+1 oz	+3 oz

24 ounces of potatoes that I now get. So I will also consume more of both foods than I do now. [She points out panel (b) of Figure 2.]

FARMER: I don't know. . . . This sounds too good to be true.

RANCHER: It's really not as complicated as it first seems. Here—I've summarized my proposal for you in a simple table. [The rancher shows the farmer a copy of the table at the bottom of Figure 2.]

FARMER: (after pausing to study the table) These calculations seem correct, but I am puzzled. How can this deal make us both better off?

RANCHER: We can both benefit because trade allows each of us to specialize in doing what we do best. You will spend more time growing potatoes and less time raising cattle. I will spend more time raising cattle and less time growing potatoes. As a result of specialization and trade, each of us can consume more meat and more potatoes without working any more hours.

QUICK QUIZ Draw an example of a production possibilities frontier for Robinson Crusoe, a shipwrecked sailor who spends his time gathering coconuts and catching fish. Does this frontier limit Crusoe's consumption of coconuts and fish if he lives by himself? Does he face the same limits if he can trade with natives on the island?

COMPARATIVE ADVANTAGE: THE DRIVING FORCE OF SPECIALIZATION

The rancher's explanation of the gains from trade, though correct, poses a puzzle: If the rancher is better at both raising cattle and growing potatoes, how can the farmer ever specialize in doing what he does best? The farmer doesn't seem to do anything best. To solve this puzzle, we need to look at the principle of *comparative advantage.*

As a first step in developing this principle, consider the following question: In our example, who can produce potatoes at a lower cost—the farmer or the rancher? There are two possible answers, and in these two answers lie the solution to our puzzle and the key to understanding the gains from trade.

ABSOLUTE ADVANTAGE

absolute advantage
the ability to produce a good using fewer inputs than another producer

One way to answer the question about the cost of producing potatoes is to compare the inputs required by the two producers. Economists use the term **absolute advantage** when comparing the productivity of one person, firm, or nation to that of another. The producer that requires a smaller quantity of inputs to produce a good is said to have an absolute advantage in producing that good.

In our example, time is the only input, so we can determine absolute advantage by looking at how much time each type of production takes. The rancher has an absolute advantage both in producing meat and in producing potatoes because she requires less time than the farmer to produce a unit of either good. The rancher needs to input only 20 minutes to produce an ounce of meat, whereas the farmer needs 60 minutes. Similarly, the rancher needs only 10 minutes to produce an ounce of potatoes, whereas the farmer needs 15 minutes. Based on this information, we can conclude that the rancher has the lower cost of producing potatoes, if we measure cost by the quantity of inputs.

OPPORTUNITY COST AND COMPARATIVE ADVANTAGE

opportunity cost
whatever must be given up to obtain some item

There is another way to look at the cost of producing potatoes. Rather than comparing inputs required, we can compare the opportunity costs. Recall from Chapter 1 that the **opportunity cost** of some item is what we give up to get that item. In our example, we assumed that the farmer and the rancher each spend 8 hours a day working. Time spent producing potatoes, therefore, takes away from time available for producing meat. When reallocating time between the two goods, the rancher and farmer give up units of one good to produce units of the other, thereby moving along the production possibilities frontier. The opportunity cost measures the trade-off between the two goods that each producer faces.

Let's first consider the rancher's opportunity cost. According to the table in panel (a) of Figure 1, producing 1 ounce of potatoes takes 10 minutes of work. When the rancher spends those 10 minutes producing potatoes, she spends 10 minutes less producing meat. Because the rancher needs 20 minutes to produce 1 ounce of meat, 10 minutes of work would yield ½ ounce of meat. Hence, the rancher's opportunity cost of producing 1 ounce of potatoes is ½ ounce of meat.

Now consider the farmer's opportunity cost. Producing 1 ounce of potatoes takes him 15 minutes. Because he needs 60 minutes to produce 1 ounce of meat, 15 minutes of work would yield ¼ ounce of meat. Hence, the farmer's opportunity cost of 1 ounce of potatoes is ¼ ounce of meat.

Table 1 shows the opportunity costs of meat and potatoes for the two producers. Notice that the opportunity cost of meat is the inverse of the opportunity cost of potatoes. Because 1 ounce of potatoes costs the rancher ½ ounce of meat, 1 ounce of meat costs the rancher 2 ounces of potatoes. Similarly, because 1 ounce of potatoes costs the farmer ¼ ounce of meat, 1 ounce of meat costs the farmer 4 ounces of potatoes.

Economists use the term **comparative advantage** when describing the opportunity cost of two producers. The producer who gives up less of other goods to produce Good X has the smaller opportunity cost of producing Good X and is said to have a comparative advantage in producing it. In our example, the farmer has a lower opportunity cost of producing potatoes than the rancher: An ounce of potatoes costs the farmer only ¼ ounce of meat, but it costs the rancher ½ ounce of meat. Conversely, the rancher has a lower opportunity cost of producing meat than the farmer: An ounce of meat costs the rancher 2 ounces of potatoes, but it costs the farmer 4 ounces of potatoes. Thus, the farmer has a comparative advantage in growing potatoes, and the rancher has a comparative advantage in producing meat.

Although it is possible for one person to have an absolute advantage in both goods (as the rancher does in our example), it is impossible for one person to have a comparative advantage in both goods. Because the opportunity cost of one good is the inverse of the opportunity cost of the other, if a person's opportunity cost of one good is relatively high, the opportunity cost of the other good must be relatively low. Comparative advantage reflects the relative opportunity cost. Unless two people have exactly the same opportunity cost, one person will have a comparative advantage in one good, and the other person will have a comparative advantage in the other good.

comparative advantage
the ability to produce a good at a lower opportunity cost than another producer

COMPARATIVE ADVANTAGE AND TRADE

The gains from specialization and trade are based not on absolute advantage but on comparative advantage. When each person specializes in producing the good

	Opportunity Cost of:	
	1 oz of Meat	1 oz of Potatoes
Farmer	4 oz potatoes	¼ oz meat
Rancher	2 oz potatoes	½ oz meat

TABLE 1

The Opportunity Cost of Meat and Potatoes

for which he or she has a comparative advantage, total production in the economy rises. This increase in the size of the economic pie can be used to make everyone better off.

In our example, the farmer spends more time growing potatoes, and the rancher spends more time producing meat. As a result, the total production of potatoes rises from 40 to 44 ounces, and the total production of meat rises from 16 to 18 ounces. The farmer and rancher share the benefits of this increased production.

We can also look at the gains from trade in terms of the price that each party pays the other. Because the farmer and rancher have different opportunity costs, they can both get a bargain. That is, each benefits from trade by obtaining a good at a price that is lower than his or her opportunity cost of that good.

Consider the proposed deal from the viewpoint of the farmer. The farmer gets 5 ounces of meat in exchange for 15 ounces of potatoes. In other words, the farmer buys each ounce of meat for a price of 3 ounces of potatoes. This price of meat is lower than his opportunity cost for an ounce of meat, which is 4 ounces of potatoes. Thus, the farmer benefits from the deal because he gets to buy meat at a good price.

Now consider the deal from the rancher's viewpoint. The rancher buys 15 ounces of potatoes for a price of 5 ounces of meat. That is, the price of potatoes is $\frac{1}{3}$ ounce of meat. This price of potatoes is lower than her opportunity cost of an ounce of potatoes, which is $\frac{1}{2}$ ounce of meat. The rancher benefits because she gets to buy potatoes at a good price.

The moral of the story of the farmer and the rancher should now be clear: *Trade can benefit everyone in society because it allows people to specialize in activities in which they have a comparative advantage.*

THE PRICE OF THE TRADE

The principle of comparative advantage establishes that there are gains from specialization and trade, but it leaves open a couple of related questions: What determines the price at which trade takes place? How are the gains from trade shared between the trading parties? The precise answer to these questions is beyond the scope of this chapter, but we can state one general rule: *For both parties to gain from trade, the price at which they trade must lie between the two opportunity costs.*

In our example, the farmer and rancher agreed to trade at a rate of 3 ounces of potatoes for each ounce of meat. This price is between the rancher's opportunity cost (2 ounces of potatoes per ounce of meat) and the farmer's opportunity cost (4 ounces of potatoes per ounce of meat). The price need not be exactly in the middle for both parties to gain, but it must be somewhere between 2 and 4.

To see why the price has to be in this range, consider what would happen if it were not. If the price of meat were below 2 ounces of potatoes, both the farmer and the rancher would want to buy meat, because the price would be below their opportunity costs. Similarly, if the price of meat were above 4 ounces of potatoes, both would want to sell meat, because the price would be above their opportunity costs. But there are only two members of this economy. They cannot both be buyers of meat, nor can they both be sellers. Someone has to take the other side of the deal.

A mutually advantageous trade can be struck at a price between 2 and 4. In this price range, the rancher wants to sell meat to buy potatoes, and the farmer wants to sell potatoes to buy meat. Each party can buy a good at a price that is lower

FYI

The Legacy of Adam Smith and David Ricardo

Economists have long understood the gains from trade. Here is how the great economist Adam Smith put the argument:

> It is a maxim of every prudent master of a family, never to attempt to make at home what it will cost him more to make than to buy. The tailor does not attempt to make his own shoes, but buys them of the shoemaker. The shoemaker does not attempt to make his own clothes but employs a tailor. The farmer attempts to make neither the one nor the other, but employs those different artificers. All of them find it for their interest to employ their whole industry in a way in which they have some advantage over their neighbors, and to purchase with a part of its produce, or what is the same thing, with the price of part of it, whatever else they have occasion for.

This quotation is from Smith's 1776 book *An Inquiry into the Nature and Causes of the Wealth of Nations*, which was a landmark in the analysis of trade and economic interdependence.

Smith's book inspired David Ricardo, a millionaire stockbroker, to become an economist. In his 1817 book

David Ricardo

Principles of Political Economy and Taxation, Ricardo developed the principle of comparative advantage as we know it today. He considered an example with two goods (wine and cloth) and two countries (England and Portugal). He showed that both countries can gain by opening up trade and specializing based on comparative advantage.

Ricardo's theory is the starting point of modern international economics, but his defense of free trade was not a mere academic exercise. Ricardo put his beliefs to work as a member of the British Parliament, where he opposed the Corn Laws, which restricted the import of grain.

The conclusions of Adam Smith and David Ricardo on the gains from trade have held up well over time. Although economists often disagree on questions of policy, they are united in their support of free trade. Moreover, the central argument for free trade has not changed much in the past two centuries. Even though the field of economics has broadened its scope and refined its theories since the time of Smith and Ricardo, economists' opposition to trade restrictions is still based largely on the principle of comparative advantage.

than his or her opportunity cost. In the end, both of them specialize in the good for which he or she has a comparative advantage and are, as a result, better off.

QUICK QUIZ   Robinson Crusoe can gather 10 coconuts or catch 1 fish per hour. His friend Friday can gather 30 coconuts or catch 2 fish per hour. What is Crusoe's opportunity cost of catching one fish? What is Friday's? Who has an absolute advantage in catching fish? Who has a comparative advantage in catching fish?

APPLICATIONS OF COMPARATIVE ADVANTAGE

The principle of comparative advantage explains interdependence and the gains from trade. Because interdependence is so prevalent in the modern world, the principle of comparative advantage has many applications. Here are two examples, one fanciful and one of great practical importance.

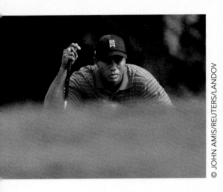

© JOHN AMIS/REUTERS/LANDOV

SHOULD TIGER WOODS MOW HIS OWN LAWN?

Tiger Woods spends a lot of time walking around on grass. One of the most talented golfers of all time, he can hit a drive and sink a putt in a way that most casual golfers only dream of doing. Most likely, he is talented at other activities too. For example, let's imagine that Woods can mow his lawn faster than anyone else. But just because he *can* mow his lawn fast, does this mean he *should*?

To answer this question, we can use the concepts of opportunity cost and comparative advantage. Let's say that Woods can mow his lawn in 2 hours. In that same 2 hours, he could film a television commercial for Nike and earn $10,000. By contrast, Forrest Gump, the boy next door, can mow Woods's lawn in 4 hours. In that same 4 hours, he could work at McDonald's and earn $20.

In this example, Woods has an absolute advantage in mowing lawns because he can do the work with a lower input of time. Yet because Woods's opportunity cost of mowing the lawn is $10,000 and Forrest's opportunity cost is only $20, Forrest has a comparative advantage in mowing lawns.

The gains from trade in this example are tremendous. Rather than mowing his own lawn, Woods should make the commercial and hire Forrest to mow the lawn. As long as Woods pays Forrest more than $20 and less than $10,000, both of them are better off.

SHOULD THE UNITED STATES TRADE WITH OTHER COUNTRIES?

Just as individuals can benefit from specialization and trade with one another, as the farmer and rancher did, so can populations of people in different countries. Many of the goods that Americans enjoy are produced abroad, and many of the goods produced in the United States are sold abroad. Goods produced abroad and sold domestically are called **imports**. Goods produced domestically and sold abroad are called **exports**.

imports
goods produced abroad and sold domestically

exports
goods produced domestically and sold abroad

To see how countries can benefit from trade, suppose there are two countries, the United States and Japan, and two goods, food and cars. Imagine that the two countries produce cars equally well: An American worker and a Japanese worker can each produce one car per month. By contrast, because the United States has more and better land, it is better at producing food: A U.S. worker can produce 2 tons of food per month, whereas a Japanese worker can produce only 1 ton of food per month.

The principle of comparative advantage states that each good should be produced by the country that has the smaller opportunity cost of producing that good. Because the opportunity cost of a car is 2 tons of food in the United States but only 1 ton of food in Japan, Japan has a comparative advantage in producing cars. Japan should produce more cars than it wants for its own use and export some of them to the United States. Similarly, because the opportunity cost of a ton of food is 1 car in Japan but only ½ car in the United States, the United States has a comparative advantage in producing food. The United States should produce more food than it wants to consume and export some to Japan. Through specialization and trade, both countries can have more food and more cars.

In reality, of course, the issues involved in trade among nations are more complex than this example suggests. Most important among these issues is that each country has many citizens with different interests. International trade can make some individuals worse off, even as it makes the country as a whole better off.

When the United States exports food and imports cars, the impact on an American farmer is not the same as the impact on an American autoworker. Yet, contrary to the opinions sometimes voiced by politicians and pundits, international trade is not like war, in which some countries win and others lose. Trade allows all countries to achieve greater prosperity.

QUICK QUIZ   Suppose that a skilled brain surgeon also happens to be the world's fastest typist. Should she do her own typing or hire a secretary? Explain.

In The News

The Changing Face of International Trade

A decade ago, no one would have asked which nation has a comparative advantage in slaying ogres. But technology is rapidly changing the goods and services that are traded across national borders.

Ogre to Slay? Outsource It to Chinese

By David Barboza

Fuzhou, China—One of China's newest factories operates here in the basement of an old warehouse. Posters of World of Warcraft and Magic Land hang above a corps of young people glued to their computer screens, pounding away at their keyboards in the latest hustle for money.

The people working at this clandestine locale are "gold farmers." Every day, in 12-hour shifts, they "play" computer games by killing onscreen monsters and winning battles, harvesting artificial gold coins and other virtual goods as rewards that, as it turns out, can be transformed into real cash.

That is because, from Seoul to San Francisco, affluent online gamers who lack the time and patience to work their way up to the higher levels of gamedom are willing to pay the young Chinese here to play the early rounds for them.

"For 12 hours a day, 7 days a week, my colleagues and I are killing monsters," said

a 23-year-old gamer who works here in this makeshift factory and goes by the online code name Wandering. "I make about $250 a month, which is pretty good compared with the other jobs I've had. And I can play games all day."

He and his comrades have created yet another new business out of cheap Chinese labor. They are tapping into the fast-growing world of "massively multiplayer online games," which involve role playing and often revolve around fantasy or warfare in medieval kingdoms or distant galaxies. . . .

For the Chinese in game-playing factories like these, though, it is not all fun and

games. These workers have strict quotas and are supervised by bosses who equip them with computers, software and Internet connections to thrash online trolls, gnomes and ogres.

As they grind through the games, they accumulate virtual currency that is valuable to game players around the world. The games allow players to trade currency to other players, who can then use it to buy better armor, amulets, magic spells and other accoutrements to climb to higher levels or create more powerful characters.

The Internet is now filled with classified advertisements from small companies—many of them here in China—auctioning for real money their powerful figures, called avatars. . . .

"It's unimaginable how big this is," says Chen Yu, 27, who employs 20 full-time gamers here in Fuzhou. "They say that in some of these popular games, 40 or 50 percent of the players are actually Chinese farmers."

Source: *New York Times*, December 9, 2005.

CONCLUSION

You should now understand more fully the benefits of living in an interdependent economy. When Americans buy tube socks from China, when residents of Maine drink orange juice from Florida, and when a homeowner hires the kid next door to mow the lawn, the same economic forces are at work. The principle of comparative advantage shows that trade can make everyone better off.

Having seen why interdependence is desirable, you might naturally ask how it is possible. How do free societies coordinate the diverse activities of all the people involved in their economies? What ensures that goods and services will get from those who should be producing them to those who should be consuming them? In a world with only two people, such as the rancher and the farmer, the answer is simple: These two people can bargain and allocate resources between themselves. In the real world with billions of people, the answer is less obvious. We take up this issue in the next chapter, where we see that free societies allocate resources through the market forces of supply and demand.

SUMMARY

- Each person consumes goods and services produced by many other people both in the United States and around the world. Interdependence and trade are desirable because they allow everyone to enjoy a greater quantity and variety of goods and services.

- There are two ways to compare the ability of two people in producing a good. The person who can produce the good with the smaller quantity of inputs is said to have an *absolute advantage* in producing the good. The person who has the smaller opportunity cost of producing the good is said

to have a *comparative advantage*. The gains from trade are based on comparative advantage, not absolute advantage.

- Trade makes everyone better off because it allows people to specialize in those activities in which they have a comparative advantage.

- The principle of comparative advantage applies to countries as well as to people. Economists use the principle of comparative advantage to advocate free trade among countries.

KEY CONCEPTS

absolute advantage, *p. 54*
opportunity cost, *p. 54*

comparative advantage, *p. 55*
imports, *p. 58*

exports, *p. 58*

QUESTIONS FOR REVIEW

1. Under what conditions is the production possibilities frontier linear rather than bowed out?
2. Explain how absolute advantage and comparative advantage differ.
3. Give an example in which one person has an absolute advantage in doing something but another person has a comparative advantage.
4. Is absolute advantage or comparative advantage more important for trade? Explain your reasoning using the example in your answer to Question 3.
5. Will a nation tend to export or import goods for which it has a comparative advantage? Explain.
6. Why do economists oppose policies that restrict trade among nations?

PROBLEMS AND APPLICATIONS

1. Maria can read 20 pages of economics in an hour. She can also read 50 pages of sociology in an hour. She spends 5 hours per day studying.
   a. Draw Maria's production possibilities frontier for reading economics and sociology.
   b. What is Maria's opportunity cost of reading 100 pages of sociology?
2. American and Japanese workers can each produce 4 cars a year. An American worker can produce 10 tons of grain a year, whereas a Japanese worker can produce 5 tons of grain a year. To keep things simple, assume that each country has 100 million workers.
   a. For this situation, construct a table analogous to the table in Figure 1.
   b. Graph the production possibilities frontier of the American and Japanese economies.
   c. For the United States, what is the opportunity cost of a car? Of grain? For Japan, what is the opportunity cost of a car? Of grain? Put this information in a table analogous to Table 1.
   d. Which country has an absolute advantage in producing cars? In producing grain?
   e. Which country has a comparative advantage in producing cars? In producing grain?
   f. Without trade, half of each country's workers produce cars and half produce grain. What quantities of cars and grain does each country produce?
   g. Starting from a position without trade, give an example in which trade makes each country better off.
3. Pat and Kris are roommates. They spend most of their time studying (of course), but they leave some time for their favorite activities: making pizza and brewing root beer. Pat takes 4 hours to brew a gallon of root beer and 2 hours to make a pizza. Kris takes 6 hours to brew a gallon of root beer and 4 hours to make a pizza.
   a. What is each roommate's opportunity cost of making a pizza? Who has the absolute advantage in making pizza? Who has the comparative advantage in making pizza?
   b. If Pat and Kris trade foods with each other, who will trade away pizza in exchange for root beer?
   c. The price of pizza can be expressed in terms of gallons of root beer. What is the highest price at which pizza can be traded that would make both roommates better off? What is the lowest price? Explain.
4. Suppose that there are 10 million workers in Canada and that each of these workers can produce either 2 cars or 30 bushels of wheat in a year.
   a. What is the opportunity cost of producing a car in Canada? What is the opportunity cost of producing a bushel of wheat in Canada? Explain the relationship between the opportunity costs of the two goods.
   b. Draw Canada's production possibilities frontier. If Canada chooses to consume 10 million cars, how much wheat can it consume without trade? Label this point on the production possibilities frontier.
   c. Now suppose that the United States offers to buy 10 million cars from Canada in exchange for 20 bushels of wheat per car. If Canada continues to consume 10 million cars, how

much wheat does this deal allow Canada to consume? Label this point on your diagram. Should Canada accept the deal?

5. England and Scotland both produce scones and sweaters. Suppose that an English worker can produce 50 scones per hour or 1 sweater per hour. Suppose that a Scottish worker can produce 40 scones per hour or 2 sweaters per hour.

   a. Which country has the absolute advantage in the production of each good? Which country has the comparative advantage?

   b. If England and Scotland decide to trade, which commodity will Scotland trade to England? Explain.

   c. If a Scottish worker could produce only 1 sweater per hour, would Scotland still gain from trade? Would England still gain from trade? Explain.

6. The following table describes the production possibilities of two cities in the country of Baseballia:

	Pairs of Red Socks per Worker per Hour	Pairs of White Socks per Worker per Hour
Boston	3	3
Chicago	2	1

   a. Without trade, what is the price of white socks (in terms of red socks) in Boston? What is the price in Chicago?

   b. Which city has an absolute advantage in the production of each color sock? Which city has a comparative advantage in the production of each color sock?

   c. If the cities trade with each other, which color sock will each export?

   d. What is the range of prices at which trade can occur?

7. Suppose that in a year an American worker can produce 100 shirts or 20 computers, while a Chinese worker can produce 100 shirts or 10 computers.

   a. Graph the production possibilities curve for the two countries. Suppose that without trade the workers in each country spend half their time producing each good. Identify this point in your graph.

   b. If these countries were open to trade, which country would export shirts? Give a specific numerical example and show it on your graph. Which country would benefit from trade? Explain.

   c. Explain at what price of computers (in terms of shirts) the two countries might trade.

   d. Suppose that China catches up with American productivity so that a Chinese worker can produce 100 shirts or 20 computers. What pattern of trade would you predict now? How does this advance in Chinese productivity affect the economic well-being of the citizens of the two countries?

8. An average worker in Brazil can produce an ounce of soybeans in 20 minutes and an ounce of coffee in 60 minutes, while an average worker in Peru can produce an ounce of soybeans in 50 minutes and an ounce of coffee in 75 minutes.

   a. Who has the absolute advantage in coffee? Explain.

   b. Who has the comparative advantage in coffee? Explain.

   c. If the two countries specialize and trade with each other, who will import coffee? Explain.

   d. Assume that the two countries trade and that the country importing coffee trades 2 ounces of soybeans for 1 ounce of coffee. Explain why both countries will benefit from this trade.

9. Are the following statements true or false? Explain in each case.

   a. "Two countries can achieve gains from trade even if one of the countries has an absolute advantage in the production of all goods."

   b. "Certain very talented people have a comparative advantage in everything they do."

   c. "If a certain trade is good for one person, it can't be good for the other one."

   d. "If a certain trade is good for one person, it is always good for the other one."

   e. "If trade is good for a country, it must be good for everyone in the country."

10. The United States exports corn and aircraft to the rest of the world, and it imports oil and clothing from the rest of the world. Do you think this pattern of trade is consistent with the principle of comparative advantage? Why or why not?

PART II

How Markets Work

The Market Forces of Supply and Demand

When a cold snap hits Florida, the price of orange juice rises in supermarkets throughout the country. When the weather turns warm in New England every summer, the price of hotel rooms in the Caribbean plummets. When a war breaks out in the Middle East, the price of gasoline in the United States rises, and the price of a used Cadillac falls. What do these events have in common? They all show the workings of supply and demand.

Supply and *demand* are the two words economists use most often—and for good reason. Supply and demand are the forces that make market economies work. They determine the quantity of each good produced and the price at which it is sold. If you want to know how any event or policy will affect the economy, you must think first about how it will affect supply and demand.

This chapter introduces the theory of supply and demand. It considers how buyers and sellers behave and how they interact with one another. It shows how supply and demand determine prices in a market economy and how prices, in turn, allocate the economy's scarce resources.

MARKETS AND COMPETITION

The terms *supply* and *demand* refer to the behavior of people as they interact with one another in competitive markets. Before discussing how buyers and sellers behave, let's first consider more fully what we mean by the terms *market* and *competition*.

WHAT IS A MARKET?

market
a group of buyers and sellers of a particular good or service

A **market** is a group of buyers and sellers of a particular good or service. The buyers as a group determine the demand for the product, and the sellers as a group determine the supply of the product.

Markets take many forms. Sometimes markets are highly organized, such as the markets for many agricultural commodities. In these markets, buyers and sellers meet at a specific time and place, where an auctioneer helps set prices and arrange sales.

More often, markets are less organized. For example, consider the market for ice cream in a particular town. Buyers of ice cream do not meet together at any one time. The sellers of ice cream are in different locations and offer somewhat different products. There is no auctioneer calling out the price of ice cream. Each seller posts a price for an ice-cream cone, and each buyer decides how much ice cream to buy at each store. Nonetheless, these consumers and producers of ice cream are closely connected. The ice-cream buyers are choosing from the various ice-cream sellers to satisfy their hunger, and the ice-cream sellers are all trying to appeal to the same ice-cream buyers to make their businesses successful. Even though it is not organized, the group of ice-cream buyers and ice-cream sellers forms a market.

WHAT IS COMPETITION?

The market for ice cream, like most markets in the economy, is highly competitive. Each buyer knows that there are several sellers from which to choose, and each seller is aware that his or her product is similar to that offered by other sellers. As a result, the price of ice cream and the quantity of ice cream sold are not determined by any single buyer or seller. Rather, price and quantity are determined by all buyers and sellers as they interact in the marketplace.

competitive market
a market in which there are many buyers and many sellers so that each has a negligible impact on the market price

Economists use the term **competitive market** to describe a market in which there are so many buyers and so many sellers that each has a negligible impact on the market price. Each seller of ice cream has limited control over the price because other sellers are offering similar products. A seller has little reason to charge less than the going price, and if he or she charges more, buyers will make their purchases elsewhere. Similarly, no single buyer of ice cream can influence the price of ice cream because each buyer purchases only a small amount.

In this chapter, we assume that markets are *perfectly competitive*. To reach this highest form of competition, a market must have two characteristics: (1) the goods offered for sale are all exactly the same, and (2) the buyers and sellers are so numerous that no single buyer or seller has any influence over the market price. Because buyers and sellers in perfectly competitive markets must accept the price the market determines, they are said to be *price takers*. At the market price, buyers can buy all they want, and sellers can sell all they want.

There are some markets in which the assumption of perfect competition applies perfectly. In the wheat market, for example, there are thousands of farmers who sell wheat and millions of consumers who use wheat and wheat products. Because no single buyer or seller can influence the price of wheat, each takes the price as given.

Not all goods and services, however, are sold in perfectly competitive markets. Some markets have only one seller, and this seller sets the price. Such a seller is called a *monopoly*. Your local cable television company, for instance, may be a monopoly. Residents of your town probably have only one cable company from which to buy this service. Still other markets fall between the extremes of perfect competition and monopoly.

Despite the diversity of market types we find in the world, assuming perfect competition is a useful simplification and, therefore, a natural place to start. Perfectly competitive markets are the easiest to analyze because everyone participating in the market takes the price as given by market conditions. Moreover, because some degree of competition is present in most markets, many of the lessons that we learn by studying supply and demand under perfect competition apply in more complicated markets as well. ↘

QUICK QUIZ   What is a market? • What are the characteristics of a perfectly competitive market?

DEMAND

We begin our study of markets by examining the behavior of buyers. To focus our thinking, let's keep in mind a particular good—ice cream.

THE DEMAND CURVE: THE RELATIONSHIP BETWEEN PRICE AND QUANTITY DEMANDED

The **quantity demanded** of any good is the amount of the good that buyers are willing and able to purchase. As we will see, many things determine the quantity demanded of any good, but when analyzing how markets work, one determinant plays a central role—the price of the good. If the price of ice cream rose to $20 per scoop, you would buy less ice cream. You might buy frozen yogurt instead. If the price of ice cream fell to $0.20 per scoop, you would buy more. This relationship between price and quantity demanded is true for most goods in the economy and, in fact, is so pervasive that economists call it the **law of demand**: Other things equal, when the price of a good rises, the quantity demanded of the good falls, and when the price falls, the quantity demanded rises.

The table in Figure 1 shows how many ice-cream cones Catherine buys each month at different prices of ice cream. If ice cream is free, Catherine eats 12 cones per month. At $0.50 per cone, Catherine buys 10 cones each month. As the price rises further, she buys fewer and fewer cones. When the price reaches $3.00, Catherine doesn't buy any ice cream at all. This table is a **demand schedule**, a table that shows the relationship between the price of a good and the quantity demanded, holding constant everything else that influences how much consumers of the good want to buy.

quantity demanded
the amount of a good that buyers are willing and able to purchase

law of demand
the claim that, other things equal, the quantity demanded of a good falls when the price of the good rises

demand schedule
a table that shows the relationship between the price of a good and the quantity demanded

1 FIGURE

The demand schedule is a table that shows the quantity demanded at each price. The demand curve, which graphs the demand schedule, illustrates how the quantity demanded of the good changes as its price varies. Because a lower price increases the quantity demanded, the demand curve slopes downward.

Catherine's Demand Schedule and Demand Curve

Price of Ice-Cream Cone	Quantity of Cones Demanded
$0.00	12 cones
0.50	10
1.00	8
1.50	6
2.00	4
2.50	2
3.00	0

1. A decrease in price . . .

2. . . . increases quantity of cones demanded.

Demand curve

The graph in Figure 1 uses the numbers from the table to illustrate the law of demand. By convention, the price of ice cream is on the vertical axis, and the quantity of ice cream demanded is on the horizontal axis. The downward-sloping line relating price and quantity demanded is called the **demand curve**.

demand curve
a graph of the relationship between the price of a good and the quantity demanded

MARKET DEMAND VERSUS INDIVIDUAL DEMAND

The demand curve in Figure 1 shows an individual's demand for a product. To analyze how markets work, we need to determine the *market demand*, the sum of all the individual demands for a particular good or service.

The table in Figure 2 shows the demand schedules for ice cream of the two individuals in this market—Catherine and Nicholas. At any price, Catherine's demand schedule tells us how much ice cream she buys, and Nicholas's demand schedule tells us how much ice cream he buys. The market demand at each price is the sum of the two individual demands.

The graph in Figure 2 shows the demand curves that correspond to these demand schedules. Notice that we sum the individual demand curves horizontally to obtain the market demand curve. That is, to find the total quantity demanded at any price, we add the individual quantities, which are found on the horizontal axis of the individual demand curves. Because we are interested in analyzing how markets function, we work most often with the market demand curve. The market demand curve shows how the total quantity demanded of a good varies as the

The quantity demanded in a market is the sum of the quantities demanded by all the buyers at each price. Thus, the market demand curve is found by adding horizontally the individual demand curves. At a price of $2.00, Catherine demands 4 ice-cream cones, and Nicholas demands 3 ice-cream cones. The quantity demanded in the market at this price is 7 cones.

FIGURE 2

Market Demand as the Sum of Individual Demands

Price of Ice-Cream Cone	Catherine		Nicholas		Market
$0.00	12	+	7	=	19 cones
0.50	10		6		16
1.00	8		5		13
1.50	6		4		10
2.00	4		3		7
2.50	2		2		4
3.00	0		1		1

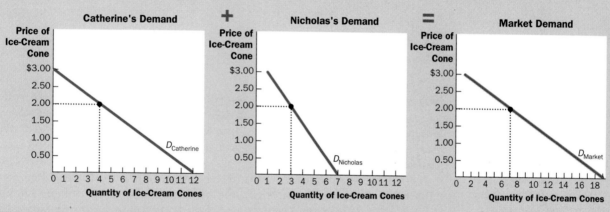

price of the good varies, while all the other factors that affect how much consumers want to buy are held constant.

SHIFTS IN THE DEMAND CURVE

Because the market demand curve holds other things constant, it need not be stable over time. If something happens to alter the quantity demanded at any given price, the demand curve shifts. For example, suppose the American Medical Association discovered that people who regularly eat ice cream live longer, healthier lives. The discovery would raise the demand for ice cream. At any given price, buyers would now want to purchase a larger quantity of ice cream, and the demand curve for ice cream would shift.

Figure 3 illustrates shifts in demand. Any change that increases the quantity demanded at every price, such as our imaginary discovery by the American Medical Association, shifts the demand curve to the right and is called an *increase in demand*. Any change that reduces the quantity demanded at every price shifts the demand curve to the left and is called a *decrease in demand*.

There are many variables that can shift the demand curve. Here are the most important.

3 FIGURE

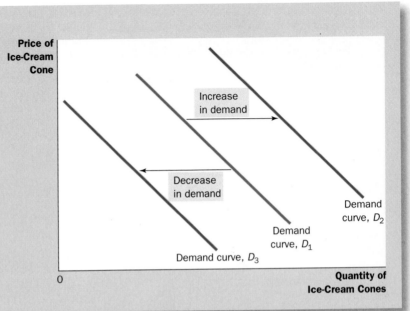

Shifts in the Demand Curve
Any change that raises the quantity that buyers wish to purchase at any given price shifts the demand curve to the right. Any change that lowers the quantity that buyers wish to purchase at any given price shifts the demand curve to the left.

Income   What would happen to your demand for ice cream if you lost your job one summer? Most likely, it would fall. A lower income means that you have less to spend in total, so you would have to spend less on some—and probably most—goods. If the demand for a good falls when income falls, the good is called a **normal good**.

Not all goods are normal goods. If the demand for a good rises when income falls, the good is called an **inferior good**. An example of an inferior good might be bus rides. As your income falls, you are less likely to buy a car or take a cab and more likely to ride a bus.

normal good
a good for which, other things equal, an increase in income leads to an increase in demand

inferior good
a good for which, other things equal, an increase in income leads to a decrease in demand

Prices of Related Goods   Suppose that the price of frozen yogurt falls. The law of demand says that you will buy more frozen yogurt. At the same time, you will probably buy less ice cream. Because ice cream and frozen yogurt are both cold, sweet, creamy desserts, they satisfy similar desires. When a fall in the price of one good reduces the demand for another good, the two goods are called **substitutes**. Substitutes are often pairs of goods that are used in place of each other, such as hot dogs and hamburgers, sweaters and sweatshirts, and movie tickets and video rentals.

Now suppose that the price of hot fudge falls. According to the law of demand, you will buy more hot fudge. Yet in this case, you will buy more ice cream as well because ice cream and hot fudge are often used together. When a fall in the price of one good raises the demand for another good, the two goods are called **complements**. Complements are often pairs of goods that are used together, such as gasoline and automobiles, computers and software, and peanut butter and jelly.

substitutes
two goods for which an increase in the price of one leads to an increase in the demand for the other

complements
two goods for which an increase in the price of one leads to a decrease in the demand for the other

Tastes   The most obvious determinant of your demand is your tastes. If you like ice cream, you buy more of it. Economists normally do not try to explain people's tastes because tastes are based on historical and psychological forces that are beyond the realm of economics. Economists do, however, examine what happens when tastes change.

T A B L E **1**

Variable	A Change in This Variable . . .
Price of the good itself	Represents a movement along the demand curve
Income	Shifts the demand curve
Prices of related goods	Shifts the demand curve
Tastes	Shifts the demand curve
Expectations	Shifts the demand curve
Number of buyers	Shifts the demand curve

Variables That Influence Buyers
This table lists the variables that affect how much consumers choose to buy of any good. Notice the special role that the price of the good plays: A change in the good's price represents a movement along the demand curve, whereas a change in one of the other variables shifts the demand curve.

Expectations   Your expectations about the future may affect your demand for a good or service today. For example, if you expect to earn a higher income next month, you may choose to save less now and spend more of your current income buying ice cream. As another example, if you expect the price of ice cream to fall tomorrow, you may be less willing to buy an ice-cream cone at today's price.

Number of Buyers   In addition to the preceding factors, which influence the behavior of individual buyers, market demand depends on the number of these buyers. If Peter were to join Catherine and Nicholas as another consumer of ice cream, the quantity demanded in the market would be higher at every price, and market demand would increase.

Summary   The demand curve shows what happens to the quantity demanded of a good when its price varies, holding constant all the other variables that influence buyers. When one of these other variables changes, the demand curve shifts. Table 1 lists the variables that influence how much consumers choose to buy of a good.

If you have trouble remembering whether you need to shift or move along the demand curve, it helps to recall a lesson from the appendix to Chapter 2. A curve shifts when there is a change in a relevant variable that is not measured on either axis. Because the price is on the vertical axis, a change in price represents a movement along the demand curve. By contrast, income, the prices of related goods, tastes, expectations, and the number of buyers are not measured on either axis, so a change in one of these variables shifts the demand curve.

CASE STUDY   TWO WAYS TO REDUCE THE QUANTITY OF SMOKING DEMANDED

Public policymakers often want to reduce the amount that people smoke. There are two ways that policy can attempt to achieve this goal.

One way to reduce smoking is to shift the demand curve for cigarettes and other tobacco products. Public service announcements, mandatory health warnings on cigarette packages, and the prohibition of cigarette advertising on television are all policies aimed at reducing the quantity of cigarettes demanded at any given price. If successful, these policies shift the demand curve for cigarettes to the left, as in panel (a) of Figure 4.

WHAT IS THE BEST WAY TO STOP THIS?

4 FIGURE

Shifts in the Demand Curve versus Movements along the Demand Curve

If warnings on cigarette packages convince smokers to smoke less, the demand curve for cigarettes shifts to the left. In panel (a), the demand curve shifts from D_1 to D_2. At a price of $2.00 per pack, the quantity demanded falls from 20 to 10 cigarettes per day, as reflected by the shift from point A to point B. By contrast, if a tax raises the price of cigarettes, the demand curve does not shift. Instead, we observe a movement to a different point on the demand curve. In panel (b), when the price rises from $2.00 to $4.00, the quantity demanded falls from 20 to 12 cigarettes per day, as reflected by the movement from point A to point C.

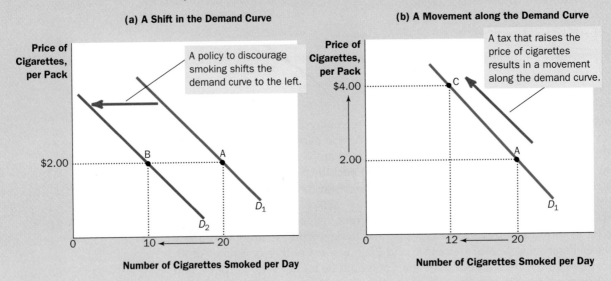

Alternatively, policymakers can try to raise the price of cigarettes. If the government taxes the manufacture of cigarettes, for example, cigarette companies pass much of this tax on to consumers in the form of higher prices. A higher price encourages smokers to reduce the numbers of cigarettes they smoke. In this case, the reduced amount of smoking does not represent a shift in the demand curve. Instead, it represents a movement along the same demand curve to a point with a higher price and lower quantity, as in panel (b) of Figure 4.

How much does the amount of smoking respond to changes in the price of cigarettes? Economists have attempted to answer this question by studying what happens when the tax on cigarettes changes. They have found that a 10 percent increase in the price causes a 4 percent reduction in the quantity demanded. Teenagers are found to be especially sensitive to the price of cigarettes: A 10 percent increase in the price causes a 12 percent drop in teenage smoking.

A related question is how the price of cigarettes affects the demand for illicit drugs, such as marijuana. Opponents of cigarette taxes often argue that tobacco and marijuana are substitutes so that high cigarette prices encourage marijuana use. By contrast, many experts on substance abuse view tobacco as a "gateway drug" leading the young to experiment with other harmful substances. Most studies of the data are consistent with this latter view: They find that lower cigarette prices are associated with greater use of marijuana. In other words, tobacco and marijuana appear to be complements rather than substitutes. ●

QUICK QUIZ   Make up an example of a monthly demand schedule for pizza and graph the implied demand curve. • Give an example of something that would shift this demand curve, and briefly explain your reasoning. • Would a change in the price of pizza shift this demand curve?

SUPPLY

We now turn to the other side of the market and examine the behavior of sellers. Once again, to focus our thinking, let's consider the market for ice cream.

THE SUPPLY CURVE: THE RELATIONSHIP BETWEEN PRICE AND QUANTITY SUPPLIED

The **quantity supplied** of any good or service is the amount that sellers are willing and able to sell. There are many determinants of quantity supplied, but once again, price plays a special role in our analysis. When the price of ice cream is high, selling ice cream is profitable, and so the quantity supplied is large. Sellers of ice cream work long hours, buy many ice-cream machines, and hire many workers. By contrast, when the price of ice cream is low, the business is less profitable, and so sellers produce less ice cream. At a low price, some sellers may even choose to shut down, and their quantity supplied falls to zero. This relationship between price and quantity supplied is called the **law of supply**: Other things equal, when the price of a good rises, the quantity supplied of the good also rises, and when the price falls, the quantity supplied falls as well.

The table in Figure 5 shows the quantity of ice-cream cones supplied each month by Ben, an ice-cream seller, at various prices of ice cream. At a price below $1.00, Ben does not supply any ice cream at all. As the price rises, he supplies a greater and greater quantity. This is the **supply schedule**, a table that shows the relationship between the price of a good and the quantity supplied, holding constant everything else that influences how much producers of the good want to sell.

The graph in Figure 5 uses the numbers from the table to illustrate the law of supply. The curve relating price and quantity supplied is called the **supply curve**. The supply curve slopes upward because, other things equal, a higher price means a greater quantity supplied.

MARKET SUPPLY VERSUS INDIVIDUAL SUPPLY

Just as market demand is the sum of the demands of all buyers, market supply is the sum of the supplies of all sellers. The table in Figure 6 shows the supply schedules for the two ice-cream producers in the market—Ben and Jerry. At any price, Ben's supply schedule tells us the quantity of ice cream Ben supplies, and Jerry's supply schedule tells us the quantity of ice cream Jerry supplies. The market supply is the sum of the two individual supplies.

The graph in Figure 6 shows the supply curves that correspond to the supply schedules. As with demand curves, we sum the individual supply curves *horizontally* to obtain the market supply curve. That is, to find the total quantity supplied at any price, we add the individual quantities, which are found on the horizontal axis of the individual supply curves. The market supply curve shows how the total quantity supplied varies as the price of the good varies, holding constant

quantity supplied
the amount of a good that sellers are willing and able to sell

law of supply
the claim that, other things equal, the quantity supplied of a good rises when the price of the good rises

supply schedule
a table that shows the relationship between the price of a good and the quantity supplied

supply curve
a graph of the relationship between the price of a good and the quantity supplied

5 F I G U R E

The supply schedule is a table that shows the quantity supplied at each price. This supply curve, which graphs the supply schedule, illustrates how the quantity supplied of the good changes as its price varies. Because a higher price increases the quantity supplied, the supply curve slopes upward.

Ben's Supply Schedule and Supply Curve

Price of Ice-Cream Cone	Quantity of Cones Supplied
$0.00	0 cones
0.50	0
1.00	1
1.50	2
2.00	3
2.50	4
3.00	5

all the other factors beyond price that influence producers' decisions about how much to sell.

SHIFTS IN THE SUPPLY CURVE

Because the market supply curve holds other things constant, the curve shifts when one of the factors changes. For example, suppose the price of sugar falls. Sugar is an input into producing ice cream, so the fall in the price of sugar makes selling ice cream more profitable. This raises the supply of ice cream: At any given price, sellers are now willing to produce a larger quantity. The supply curve for ice cream shifts to the right.

Figure 7 illustrates shifts in supply. Any change that raises quantity supplied at every price, such as a fall in the price of sugar, shifts the supply curve to the right and is called an *increase in supply*. Similarly, any change that reduces the quantity supplied at every price shifts the supply curve to the left and is called a *decrease in supply*.

There are many variables that can shift the supply curve. Here are some of the most important.

Input Prices   To produce their output of ice cream, sellers use various inputs: cream, sugar, flavoring, ice-cream machines, the buildings in which the ice cream is made, and the labor of workers to mix the ingredients and operate the machines.

Price of Ice-Cream Cone	Ben		Jerry		Market
$0.00	0	+	0	=	0 cones
0.50	0		0		0
1.00	1		0		1
1.50	2		2		4
2.00	3		4		7
2.50	4		6		10
3.00	5		8		13

Market Supply as the Sum of Individual Supplies

The quantity supplied in a market is the sum of the quantities supplied by all the sellers at each price. Thus, the market supply curve is found by adding horizontally the individual supply curves. At a price of $2.00, Ben supplies 3 ice-cream cones, and Jerry supplies 4 ice-cream cones. The quantity supplied in the market at this price is 7 cones.

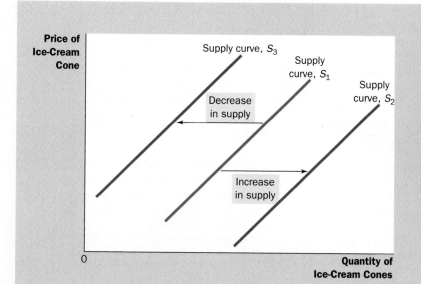

Shifts in the Supply Curve

Any change that raises the quantity that sellers wish to produce at any given price shifts the supply curve to the right. Any change that lowers the quantity that sellers wish to produce at any given price shifts the supply curve to the left.

When the price of one or more of these inputs rises, producing ice cream is less profitable, and firms supply less ice cream. If input prices rise substantially, a firm might shut down and supply no ice cream at all. Thus, the supply of a good is negatively related to the price of the inputs used to make the good.

Technology   The technology for turning inputs into ice cream is another determinant of supply. The invention of the mechanized ice-cream machine, for example, reduced the amount of labor necessary to make ice cream. By reducing firms' costs, the advance in technology raised the supply of ice cream.

Expectations   The amount of ice cream a firm supplies today may depend on its expectations about the future. For example, if a firm expects the price of ice cream to rise in the future, it will put some of its current production into storage and supply less to the market today.

Number of Sellers   In addition to the preceding factors, which influence the behavior of individual sellers, market supply depends on the number of these sellers. If Ben or Jerry were to retire from the ice-cream business, the supply in the market would fall.

Summary   The supply curve shows what happens to the quantity supplied of a good when its price varies, holding constant all the other variables that influence sellers. When one of these other variables changes, the supply curve shifts. Table 2 lists the variables that influence how much producers choose to sell of a good.

Once again, to remember whether you need to shift or move along the supply curve, keep in mind that a curve shifts only when there is a change in a relevant variable that is not named on either axis. The price is on the vertical axis, so a change in price represents a movement along the supply curve. By contrast, because input prices, technology, expectations, and the number of sellers are not measured on either axis, a change in one of these variables shifts the supply curve.

QUICK QUIZ   Make up an example of a monthly supply schedule for pizza and graph the implied supply curve. • Give an example of something that would shift this supply curve, and briefly explain your reasoning. • Would a change in the price of pizza shift this supply curve?

---

2 TABLE

Variables That Influence Sellers
This table lists the variables that affect how much producers choose to sell of any good. Notice the special role that the price of the good plays: A change in the good's price represents a movement along the supply curve, whereas a change in one of the other variables shifts the supply curve.

Variable	A Change in This Variable . . .
Price of the good itself	Represents a movement along the supply curve
Input prices	Shifts the supply curve
Technology	Shifts the supply curve
Expectations	Shifts the supply curve
Number of sellers	Shifts the supply curve

SUPPLY AND DEMAND TOGETHER

Having analyzed supply and demand separately, we now combine them to see how they determine the price and quantity of a good sold in a market.

EQUILIBRIUM

Figure 8 shows the market supply curve and market demand curve together. Notice that there is one point at which the supply and demand curves intersect. This point is called the market's **equilibrium**. The price at this intersection is called the **equilibrium price**, and the quantity is called the **equilibrium quantity**. Here the equilibrium price is $2.00 per cone, and the equilibrium quantity is 7 ice-cream cones.

The dictionary defines the word *equilibrium* as a situation in which various forces are in balance—and this also describes a market's equilibrium. *At the equilibrium price, the quantity of the good that buyers are willing and able to buy exactly balances the quantity that sellers are willing and able to sell.* The equilibrium price is sometimes called the market-clearing price because, at this price, everyone in the market has been satisfied: Buyers have bought all they want to buy, and sellers have sold all they want to sell.

The actions of buyers and sellers naturally move markets toward the equilibrium of supply and demand. To see why, consider what happens when the market price is not equal to the equilibrium price.

Suppose first that the market price is above the equilibrium price, as in panel (a) of Figure 9. At a price of $2.50 per cone, the quantity of the good supplied (10 cones) exceeds the quantity demanded (4 cones). There is a **surplus** of the good: Suppliers are unable to sell all they want at the going price. A surplus is sometimes called a situation of *excess supply*. When there is a surplus in the ice-cream market,

equilibrium
a situation in which the market price has reached the level at which quantity supplied equals quantity demanded

equilibrium price
the price that balances quantity supplied and quantity demanded

equilibrium quantity
the quantity supplied and the quantity demanded at the equilibrium price

surplus
a situation in which quantity supplied is greater than quantity demanded

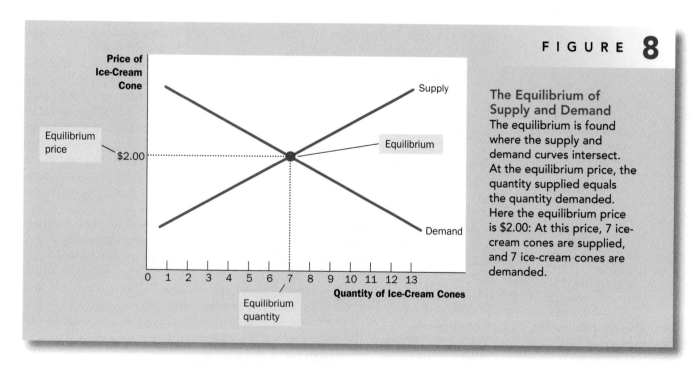

FIGURE 8

The Equilibrium of Supply and Demand
The equilibrium is found where the supply and demand curves intersect. At the equilibrium price, the quantity supplied equals the quantity demanded. Here the equilibrium price is $2.00: At this price, 7 ice-cream cones are supplied, and 7 ice-cream cones are demanded.

9 **FIGURE**

Markets Not in Equilibrium

In panel (a), there is a surplus. Because the market price of $2.50 is above the equilibrium price, the quantity supplied (10 cones) exceeds the quantity demanded (4 cones). Suppliers try to increase sales by cutting the price of a cone, and this moves the price toward its equilibrium level. In panel (b), there is a shortage. Because the market price of $1.50 is below the equilibrium price, the quantity demanded (10 cones) exceeds the quantity supplied (4 cones). With too many buyers chasing too few goods, suppliers can take advantage of the shortage by raising the price. Hence, in both cases, the price adjustment moves the market toward the equilibrium of supply and demand.

(a) Excess Supply

(b) Excess Demand

sellers of ice cream find their freezers increasingly full of ice cream they would like to sell but cannot. They respond to the surplus by cutting their prices. Falling prices, in turn, increase the quantity demanded and decrease the quantity supplied. Prices continue to fall until the market reaches the equilibrium.

Suppose now that the market price is below the equilibrium price, as in panel (b) of Figure 9. In this case, the price is $1.50 per cone, and the quantity of the good demanded exceeds the quantity supplied. There is a **shortage** of the good: Demanders are unable to buy all they want at the going price. A shortage is sometimes called a situation of *excess demand*. When a shortage occurs in the ice-cream market, buyers have to wait in long lines for a chance to buy one of the few cones available. With too many buyers chasing too few goods, sellers can respond to the shortage by raising their prices without losing sales. As the price rises, the quantity demanded falls, the quantity supplied rises, and the market once again moves toward the equilibrium.

Thus, the activities of the many buyers and sellers automatically push the market price toward the equilibrium price. Once the market reaches its equilibrium, all buyers and sellers are satisfied, and there is no upward or downward pressure on the price. How quickly equilibrium is reached varies from market to market depending on how quickly prices adjust. In most free markets, surpluses and shortages are only temporary because prices eventually move toward their equilibrium levels. Indeed, this phenomenon is so pervasive that it is called the **law of supply and demand**: The price of any good adjusts to bring the quantity supplied and quantity demanded for that good into balance.

shortage
a situation in which quantity demanded is greater than quantity supplied

law of supply and demand
the claim that the price of any good adjusts to bring the quantity supplied and the quantity demanded for that good into balance

THREE STEPS TO ANALYZING CHANGES IN EQUILIBRIUM

So far, we have seen how supply and demand together determine a market's equilibrium, which in turn determines the price and quantity of the good that buyers purchase and sellers produce. The equilibrium price and quantity depend on the position of the supply and demand curves. When some event shifts one of these curves, the equilibrium in the market changes, resulting in a new price and a new quantity exchanged between buyers and sellers.

When analyzing how some event affects the equilibrium in a market, we proceed in three steps. First, we decide whether the event shifts the supply curve, the demand curve, or, in some cases, both curves. Second, we decide whether the curve shifts to the right or to the left. Third, we use the supply-and-demand diagram to compare the initial and the new equilibrium, which shows how the shift affects the equilibrium price and quantity. Table 3 summarizes these three steps. To see how this recipe is used, let's consider various events that might affect the market for ice cream.

Example: A Change in Market Equilibrium Due to a Shift in Demand   Suppose that one summer the weather is very hot. How does this event affect the market for ice cream? To answer this question, let's follow our three steps.

1. The hot weather affects the demand curve by changing people's taste for ice cream. That is, the weather changes the amount of ice cream that people want to buy at any given price. The supply curve is unchanged because the weather does not directly affect the firms that sell ice cream.
2. Because hot weather makes people want to eat more ice cream, the demand curve shifts to the right. Figure 10 shows this increase in demand as the shift in the demand curve from D_1 to D_2. This shift indicates that the quantity of ice cream demanded is higher at every price.
3. As Figure 10 shows, the increase in demand raises the equilibrium price from $2.00 to $2.50 and the equilibrium quantity from 7 to 10 cones. In other words, the hot weather increases the price of ice cream and the quantity of ice cream sold.

Shifts in Curves versus Movements along Curves   Notice that when hot weather increases the demand for ice cream and drives up the price, the quantity of ice cream that firms supply rises, even though the supply curve remains the same. In this case, economists say there has been an increase in "quantity supplied" but no change in "supply."

3 T A B L E

Three Steps for Analyzing Changes in Equilibrium

1. Decide whether the event shifts the supply or demand curve (or perhaps both).
2. Decide in which direction the curve shifts.
3. Use the supply-and-demand diagram to see how the shift changes the equilibrium price and quantity.

10 FIGURE

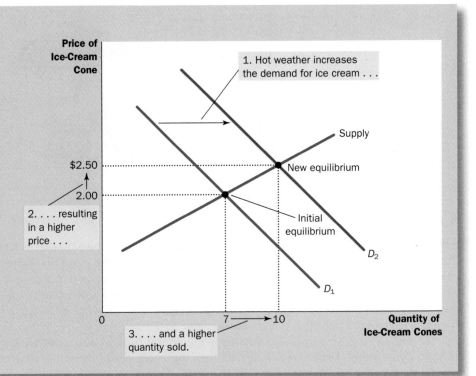

How an Increase in Demand Affects the Equilibrium
An event that raises quantity demanded at any given price shifts the demand curve to the right. The equilibrium price and the equilibrium quantity both rise. Here an abnormally hot summer causes buyers to demand more ice cream. The demand curve shifts from D_1 to D_2, which causes the equilibrium price to rise from $2.00 to $2.50 and the equilibrium quantity to rise from 7 to 10 cones.

Supply refers to the position of the supply curve, whereas the *quantity supplied* refers to the amount suppliers wish to sell. In this example, supply does not change because the weather does not alter firms' desire to sell at any given price. Instead, the hot weather alters consumers' desire to buy at any given price and thereby shifts the demand curve to the right. The increase in demand causes the equilibrium price to rise. When the price rises, the quantity supplied rises. This increase in quantity supplied is represented by the movement along the supply curve.

To summarize, a shift *in* the supply curve is called a "change in supply," and a shift *in* the demand curve is called a "change in demand." A movement *along* a fixed supply curve is called a "change in the quantity supplied," and a movement *along* a fixed demand curve is called a "change in the quantity demanded."

Example: A Change in Market Equilibrium Due to a Shift in Supply   Suppose that during another summer, a hurricane destroys part of the sugarcane crop and drives up the price of sugar. How does this event affect the market for ice cream? Once again, to answer this question, we follow our three steps.

1.   The change in the price of sugar, an input into making ice cream, affects the supply curve. By raising the costs of production, it reduces the amount of ice cream that firms produce and sell at any given price. The demand curve does not change because the higher cost of inputs does not directly affect the amount of ice cream households wish to buy.

2.   The supply curve shifts to the left because, at every price, the total amount that firms are willing and able to sell is reduced. Figure 11 illustrates this decrease in supply as a shift in the supply curve from S_1 to S_2.

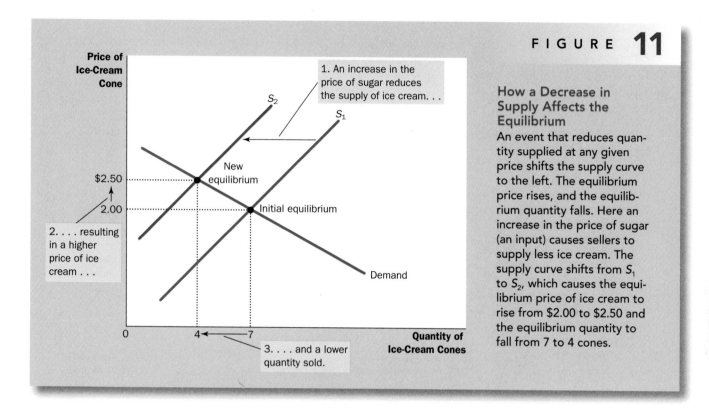

How a Decrease in Supply Affects the Equilibrium
An event that reduces quantity supplied at any given price shifts the supply curve to the left. The equilibrium price rises, and the equilibrium quantity falls. Here an increase in the price of sugar (an input) causes sellers to supply less ice cream. The supply curve shifts from S_1 to S_2, which causes the equilibrium price of ice cream to rise from $2.00 to $2.50 and the equilibrium quantity to fall from 7 to 4 cones.

*Figure labels:*
Price of Ice-Cream Cone

1. An increase in the price of sugar reduces the supply of ice cream. . .

S_2

S_1

New equilibrium

$2.50

2.00

Initial equilibrium

2. . . . resulting in a higher price of ice cream . . .

Demand

0   4   7

Quantity of Ice-Cream Cones

3. . . . and a lower quantity sold.

3. As Figure 11 shows, the shift in the supply curve raises the equilibrium price from $2.00 to $2.50 and lowers the equilibrium quantity from 7 to 4 cones. As a result of the sugar price increase, the price of ice cream rises, and the quantity of ice cream sold falls.

Example: Shifts in Both Supply and Demand   Now suppose that a heat wave and a hurricane occur during the same summer. To analyze this combination of events, we again follow our three steps.

1. We determine that both curves must shift. The hot weather affects the demand curve because it alters the amount of ice cream that households want to buy at any given price. At the same time, when the hurricane drives up sugar prices, it alters the supply curve for ice cream because it changes the amount of ice cream that firms want to sell at any given price.
2. The curves shift in the same directions as they did in our previous analysis: The demand curve shifts to the right, and the supply curve shifts to the left. Figure 12 illustrates these shifts.
3. As Figure 12 shows, two possible outcomes might result depending on the relative size of the demand and supply shifts. In both cases, the equilibrium price rises. In panel (a), where demand increases substantially while supply falls just a little, the equilibrium quantity also rises. By contrast, in panel (b), where supply falls substantially while demand rises just a little, the equilibrium quantity falls. Thus, these events certainly raise the price of ice cream, but their impact on the amount of ice cream sold is ambiguous (that is, it could go either way).

12 FIGURE

A Shift in Both Supply and Demand

Here we observe a simultaneous increase in demand and decrease in supply. Two outcomes are possible. In panel (a), the equilibrium price rises from P_1 to P_2, and the equilibrium quantity rises from Q_1 to Q_2. In panel (b), the equilibrium price again rises from P_1 to P_2, but the equilibrium quantity falls from Q_1 to Q_2.

(a) Price Rises, Quantity Rises

(b) Price Rises, Quantity Falls

Summary We have just seen three examples of how to use supply and demand curves to analyze a change in equilibrium. Whenever an event shifts the supply curve, the demand curve, or perhaps both curves, you can use these tools to predict how the event will alter the amount sold in equilibrium and the price at which the good is sold. Table 4 shows the predicted outcome for any combination of shifts in the two curves. To make sure you understand how to use the tools of supply and demand, pick a few entries in this table and make sure you can explain to yourself why the table contains the prediction it does.

QUICK QUIZ On the appropriate diagram, show what happens to the market for pizza if the price of tomatoes rises. ● On a separate diagram, show what happens to the market for pizza if the price of hamburgers falls.

4 TABLE

What Happens to Price and Quantity When Supply or Demand Shifts?
As a quick quiz, make sure you can explain at least a few of the entries in this table using a supply-and-demand diagram.

	No Change in Supply	An Increase in Supply	A Decrease in Supply
No Change in Demand	P same Q same	P down Q up	P up Q down
An Increase in Demand	P up Q up	P ambiguous Q up	P up Q ambiguous
A Decrease in Demand	P down Q down	P down Q ambiguous	P ambiguous Q down

In The News

The Helium Market

This analysis illustrates how supply and demand interact.

As Demand Balloons, Helium Is in Short Supply

By Ana Campoy

Syracuse University physicist Gianfranco Vidali spends most of his time studying how molecules are made in outer space, but a couple of months ago he abruptly dropped his interstellar research to address an earthly issue: the global shortage of helium.

The airy element best known for floating party balloons and the Goodyear blimp is also the lifeblood of a widening world of scientific research. Mr. Vidali uses the gas, which becomes the coldest liquid on earth when pressurized, to recreate conditions similar to outer space. Without it, he can't work. So when his helium supplier informed him it was cutting deliveries to his lab, Mr. Vidali said, "it sent us into a panic mode."

Helium is found in varying concentrations in the world's natural-gas deposits, and is separated out in a special refining process. As with oil and natural gas, the easiest-to-get helium supplies have been tapped and are declining. [*A leftward shift in the supply curve.*] Meanwhile, scientific research has rapidly multiplied the uses of helium in the past 50 years. [*A rightward shift*

in the demand curve.] It is needed to make computer microchips, flat-panel displays, fiber optics and to operate magnetic resonance imaging, or MRI, scans and welding machines. . . .

Glitches at some of the world's biggest helium-producing plants have put a further pinch on supplies in the past year. [*Another leftward shift in the supply curve.*] As supplies have tightened, prices have surged in recent months. For one New York laboratory, prices have increased to $8 a liquid liter, from close to $4 at the end of the summer. [*An increase in the equilibrium price.*]

The upshot: Helium users—from party planners to welding shops—are having to

do with less. [*A movement along the demand curve.*] Large industrial manufacturers are better able to weather the helium shortage, taking steps like installing equipment that can recycle the gas. So it is the nation's cash-strapped scientific community that is getting the worst of the crunch.

Soaring helium expenses could shut the doors of some independent labs, many [of] which have produced important research over the years, and slow down work at bigger research centers. Helium is used in research to find cures to deadly diseases, create new sources of energy and answer questions about how the universe was formed. . . .

Experts predict this situation will eventually price out many helium users, who will find substitutes or modify their technology. Some party balloon businesses are filling balloons with mixtures that contain less helium. Some welders are using argon. Industrial users are installing recovery systems. . . .

Reem Jaafar, a researcher at CUNY, says she will go into another area of physics if helium prices stay at their current levels. "If you have a fixed amount in a grant, and you have to spend it all on helium, you don't have anything left over," she says.

Source: *The Wall Street Journal,* December 5, 2007.

CONCLUSION: HOW PRICES ALLOCATE RESOURCES

This chapter has analyzed supply and demand in a single market. Although our discussion has centered on the market for ice cream, the lessons learned here apply in most other markets as well. Whenever you go to a store to buy something,

In The News

Price Increases after Natural Disasters

When a natural disaster such as a hurricane hits a region, basic commodities such as gasoline and bottled water experience increasing demand and shrinking supply. These shifts in demand and supply curves cause prices to rise, leading some people to complain about "price gouging." But, as journalist John Stossel argues in this opinion piece, there is an upside to higher prices after a disaster strikes.

In Praise of Price Gouging

By John Stossel

Politicians and the media are furious about price increases in the wake of Hurricane Katrina. They want gas stations and water sellers punished.

If you want to score points cracking down on mean, greedy profiteers, pushing anti-"gouging" rules is a very good thing. But if you're one of the people the law "protects" from "price gouging," you won't fare as well.

Consider this scenario: You are thirsty—worried that your baby is going to become dehydrated. You find a store that's open, and the storeowner thinks it's immoral to take advantage of your distress, so he won't charge you a dime more than he charged last week. But you can't buy water from him. It's sold out.

You continue on your quest, and finally find that dreaded monster, the price gouger. He offers a bottle of water that cost $1 last week at an "outrageous" price—say $20. You pay it to survive the disaster.

You resent the price gouger. But if he hadn't demanded $20, he'd have been out of water. It was the price gouger's "exploitation" that saved your child.

It saved her because people look out for their own interests. Before you got to the water seller, other people did. At $1 a bottle, they stocked up. At $20 a bottle, they bought more cautiously. By charging $20, the price gouger makes sure his water goes to those who really need it.

The people the softheaded politicians think are cruelest are doing the most to help. Assuming the demand for bottled water was going to go up, they bought a lot of it, planning to resell it at a steep profit. If they hadn't done that, that water would not have been available for the people who need it the most.

Might the water have been provided by volunteers? Certainly some people help others out of benevolence. But we can't count on benevolence. As Adam Smith wrote, "It is not from the benevolence of the butcher, the brewer or the baker, that we can expect our dinner, but from their regard to their own interest."

Consider the store owner's perspective: If he's not going to make a big profit, why open up the store at all? Staying in a disaster area is dangerous and means giving up the opportunity to be with family in order to take care of the needs of strangers. Why take the risk?

Any number of services—roofing, for example, carpentry, or tree removal—are in overwhelming demand after a disaster. When the time comes to rebuild New Orleans, it's safe to predict a shortage of local carpenters: The city's own population of carpenters won't be enough.

If this were a totalitarian country, the government might just order a bunch of tradesmen to go to New Orleans. But in a free society, those tradesmen must be persuaded to leave their homes and families, leave their employers and customers, and drive from say, Wisconsin, to take work in New Orleans. If they can't make more money in Louisiana than Wisconsin, why would they make the trip?

Some may be motivated by a desire to be heroic, but we can't expect enough heroes to fill the need, week after week; most will travel there for the same reason most Americans go to work: to make money. Any tradesman who treks to a disaster area must get higher pay than he would get in his hometown, or he won't do the trek. Limit him to what his New Orleans colleagues charged before the storm, and even a would-be hero may say, "the heck with it."

If he charges enough to justify his venture, he's likely to be condemned morally or legally by the very people he's trying to help. But they just don't understand basic economics. Force prices down, and you keep suppliers out. Let the market work, suppliers come—and competition brings prices as low as the challenges of the disaster allow. Goods that were in short supply become available, even to the poor.

It's the price "gougers" who bring the water, ship the gasoline, fix the roof, and rebuild the cities. The price "gougers" save lives.

Source: Townhall.com, September 7, 2005.

you are contributing to the demand for that item. Whenever you look for a job, you are contributing to the supply of labor services. Because supply and demand are such pervasive economic phenomena, the model of supply and demand is a powerful tool for analysis. We will be using this model repeatedly in the following chapters.

One of the *Ten Principles of Economics* discussed in Chapter 1 is that markets are usually a good way to organize economic activity. Although it is still too early to judge whether market outcomes are good or bad, in this chapter we have begun to see how markets work. In any economic system, scarce resources have to be allocated among competing uses. Market economies harness the forces of supply and demand to serve that end. Supply and demand together determine the prices of the economy's many different goods and services; prices in turn are the signals that guide the allocation of resources.

For example, consider the allocation of beachfront land. Because the amount of this land is limited, not everyone can enjoy the luxury of living by the beach. Who gets this resource? The answer is whoever is willing and able to pay the price. The price of beachfront land adjusts until the quantity of land demanded exactly balances the quantity supplied. Thus, in market economies, prices are the mechanism for rationing scarce resources.

Similarly, prices determine who produces each good and how much is produced. For instance, consider farming. Because we need food to survive, it is crucial that some people work on farms. What determines who is a farmer and who is not? In a free society, there is no government planning agency making this decision and ensuring an adequate supply of food. Instead, the allocation of workers to farms is based on the job decisions of millions of workers. This decentralized system works well because these decisions depend on prices. The prices of food and the wages of farmworkers (the price of their labor) adjust to ensure that enough people choose to be farmers.

If a person had never seen a market economy in action, the whole idea might seem preposterous. Economies are enormous groups of people engaged in a multitude of interdependent activities. What prevents decentralized decision making from degenerating into chaos? What coordinates the actions of the millions of people with their varying abilities and desires? What ensures that what needs to be done is in fact done? The answer, in a word, is *prices*. If an invisible hand guides market economies, as Adam Smith famously suggested, then the price system is the baton that the invisible hand uses to conduct the economic orchestra.

"Two dollars"

"—and seventy-five cents."

SUMMARY

- Economists use the model of supply and demand to analyze competitive markets. In a competitive market, there are many buyers and sellers, each of whom has little or no influence on the market price.

- The demand curve shows how the quantity of a good demanded depends on the price. According to the law of demand, as the price of a good

falls, the quantity demanded rises. Therefore, the demand curve slopes downward.

- In addition to price, other determinants of how much consumers want to buy include income, the prices of substitutes and complements, tastes, expectations, and the number of buyers. If one of these factors changes, the demand curve shifts.

- The supply curve shows how the quantity of a good supplied depends on the price. According to the law of supply, as the price of a good rises, the quantity supplied rises. Therefore, the supply curve slopes upward.

- In addition to price, other determinants of how much producers want to sell include input prices, technology, expectations, and the number of sellers. If one of these factors changes, the supply curve shifts.

- The intersection of the supply and demand curves determines the market equilibrium. At the equilibrium price, the quantity demanded equals the quantity supplied.

- The behavior of buyers and sellers naturally drives markets toward their equilibrium. When the market price is above the equilibrium price, there is a surplus of the good, which causes the market price to fall. When the market price is below the equilibrium price, there is a shortage, which causes the market price to rise.

- To analyze how any event influences a market, we use the supply-and-demand diagram to examine how the event affects the equilibrium price and quantity. To do this, we follow three steps. First, we decide whether the event shifts the supply curve or the demand curve (or both). Second, we decide in which direction the curve shifts. Third, we compare the new equilibrium with the initial equilibrium.

- In market economies, prices are the signals that guide economic decisions and thereby allocate scarce resources. For every good in the economy, the price ensures that supply and demand are in balance. The equilibrium price then determines how much of the good buyers choose to consume and how much sellers choose to produce.

KEY CONCEPTS

market, *p. 66*
competitive market, *p. 66*
quantity demanded, *p. 67*
law of demand, *p. 67*
demand schedule, *p. 67*
demand curve, *p. 68*
normal good, *p. 70*

inferior good, *p. 70*
substitutes, *p. 70*
complements, *p. 70*
quantity supplied, *p. 73*
law of supply, *p. 73*
supply schedule, *p. 73*
supply curve, *p. 73*

equilibrium, *p. 77*
equilibrium price, *p. 77*
equilibrium quantity, *p. 77*
surplus, *p. 77*
shortage, *p. 78*
law of supply and demand, *p. 78*

QUESTIONS FOR REVIEW

1. What is a competitive market? Briefly describe a type of market that is not perfectly competitive.
2. What are the demand schedule and the demand curve and how are they related? Why does the demand curve slope downward?
3. Does a change in consumers' tastes lead to a movement along the demand curve or a shift in the demand curve? Does a change in price lead to a movement along the demand curve or a shift in the demand curve?
4. Popeye's income declines, and as a result, he buys more spinach. Is spinach an inferior or a normal good? What happens to Popeye's demand curve for spinach?
5. What are the supply schedule and the supply curve and how are they related? Why does the supply curve slope upward?
6. Does a change in producers' technology lead to a movement along the supply curve or a shift in the supply curve? Does a change in price lead to a movement along the supply curve or a shift in the supply curve?
7. Define the equilibrium of a market. Describe the forces that move a market toward its equilibrium.

8. Beer and pizza are complements because they are often enjoyed together. When the price of beer rises, what happens to the supply, demand, quantity supplied, quantity demanded, and the price in the market for pizza?

9. Describe the role of prices in market economies.

PROBLEMS AND APPLICATIONS

1. Explain each of the following statements using supply-and-demand diagrams.
   a. "When a cold snap hits Florida, the price of orange juice rises in supermarkets throughout the country."
   b. "When the weather turns warm in New England every summer, the price of hotel rooms in Caribbean resorts plummets."
   c. "When a war breaks out in the Middle East, the price of gasoline rises, and the price of a used Cadillac falls."

2. "An increase in the demand for notebooks raises the quantity of notebooks demanded but not the quantity supplied." Is this statement true or false? Explain.

3. Consider the market for minivans. For each of the events listed here, identify which of the determinants of demand or supply are affected. Also indicate whether demand or supply increases or decreases. Then draw a diagram to show the effect on the price and quantity of minivans.
   a. People decide to have more children.
   b. A strike by steelworkers raises steel prices.
   c. Engineers develop new automated machinery for the production of minivans.
   d. The price of sports utility vehicles rises.
   e. A stock-market crash lowers people's wealth.

4. Identify the flaw in this analysis: "If more Americans go on a low-carb diet, the demand for bread will fall. The decrease in the demand for bread will cause the price of bread to fall. The lower price, however, will then increase the demand. In the new equilibrium, Americans might end up consuming more bread than they did initially."

5. Consider the markets for DVD movies, TV screens, and tickets at movie theaters.
   a. For each pair, identify whether they are complements or substitutes:
      • DVDs and TV screens
      • DVDs and movie tickets
      • TV screens and movie tickets
   b. Suppose a technological advance reduces the cost of manufacturing TV screens. Draw a diagram to show what happens in the market for TV screens.
   c. Draw two more diagrams to show how the change in the market for TV screens affects the markets for DVDs and movie tickets.

6. Over the past 20 years, technological advances have reduced the cost of computer chips. How do you think this affected the market for computers? For computer software? For typewriters?

7. Using supply-and-demand diagrams, show the effect of the following events on the market for sweatshirts.
   a. A hurricane in South Carolina damages the cotton crop.
   b. The price of leather jackets falls.
   c. All colleges require morning exercise in appropriate attire.
   d. New knitting machines are invented.

8. A survey shows an increase in drug use by young people. In the ensuing debate, two hypotheses are proposed:
   • Reduced police efforts have increased the availability of drugs on the street.
   • Cutbacks in education efforts have decreased awareness of the dangers of drug addiction.
   a. Use supply-and-demand diagrams to show how each of these hypotheses could lead to an increase in quantity of drugs consumed.
   b. How could information on what has happened to the price of drugs help us to distinguish between these explanations?

9. Suppose that in the year 2010 the number of births is temporarily high. How does this baby boom affect the price of babysitting services in 2015 and 2025? (Hint: 5-year-olds need babysitters, whereas 15-year-olds can be babysitters.)

10. Ketchup is a complement (as well as a condiment) for hot dogs. If the price of hot dogs rises, what happens to the market for ketchup? For tomatoes? For tomato juice? For orange juice?

11. The market for pizza has the following demand and supply schedules:

Price	Quantity Demanded	Quantity Supplied
$4	135 pizzas	26 pizzas
5	104	53
6	81	81
7	68	98
8	53	110
9	39	121

a. Graph the demand and supply curves. What is the equilibrium price and quantity in this market?

b. If the actual price in this market were *above* the equilibrium price, what would drive the market toward the equilibrium?

c. If the actual price in this market were *below* the equilibrium price, what would drive the market toward the equilibrium?

12. Consider the following events: Scientists reveal that consumption of oranges decreases the risk of diabetes and, at the same time, farmers use a new fertilizer that makes orange trees more productive. Illustrate and explain what effect these changes have on the equilibrium price and quantity of oranges.

13. Because bagels and cream cheese are often eaten together, they are complements.

a. We observe that both the equilibrium price of cream cheese and the equilibrium quantity of bagels have risen. What could be responsible for this pattern—a fall in the price of flour or a fall in the price of milk? Illustrate and explain your answer.

b. Suppose instead that the equilibrium price of cream cheese has risen but the equilibrium quantity of bagels has fallen. What could be responsible for this pattern—a rise in the price of flour or a rise in the price of milk? Illustrate and explain your answer.

14. Suppose that the price of basketball tickets at your college is determined by market forces.

Currently, the demand and supply schedules are as follows:

Price	Quantity Demanded	Quantity Supplied
$ 4	10,000 tickets	8,000 tickets
8	8,000	8,000
12	6,000	8,000
16	4,000	8,000
20	2,000	8,000

a. Draw the demand and supply curves. What is unusual about this supply curve? Why might this be true?

b. What are the equilibrium price and quantity of tickets?

c. Your college plans to increase total enrollment next year by 5,000 students. The additional students will have the following demand schedule:

Price	Quantity Demanded
$ 4	4,000 tickets
8	3,000
12	2,000
16	1,000
20	0

Now add the old demand schedule and the demand schedule for the new students to calculate the new demand schedule for the entire college. What will be the new equilibrium price and quantity?

15. Market research has revealed the following information about the market for chocolate bars: The demand schedule can be represented by the equation $Q^D = 1,600 - 300P$, where Q^D is the quantity demanded and P is the price. The supply schedule can be represented by the equation $Q^S = 1,400 + 700P$, where Q^S is the quantity supplied. Calculate the equilibrium price and quantity in the market for chocolate bars.

Elasticity and Its Application

Imagine that some event drives up the price of gasoline in the United States. It could be a war in the Middle East that disrupts the world supply of oil, a booming Chinese economy that boosts the world demand for oil, or a new tax on gasoline passed by Congress. How would U.S. consumers respond to the higher price?

It is easy to answer this question in broad fashion: Consumers would buy less. That is simply the law of demand we learned in the previous chapter. But you might want a precise answer. By how much would consumption of gasoline fall? This question can be answered using a concept called *elasticity*, which we develop in this chapter.

Elasticity is a measure of how much buyers and sellers respond to changes in market conditions. When studying how some event or policy affects a market, we can discuss not only the direction of the effects but their magnitude as well. Elasticity is useful in many applications, as we will see toward the end of this chapter.

Before proceeding, however, you might be curious about the answer to the gasoline question. Many studies have examined consumers' response to gasoline prices, and they typically find that the quantity demanded responds more in the long run than it does in the short run. A 10 percent increase in gasoline prices reduces gasoline consumption by about 2.5 percent after a year and about 6 percent after five years. About half of the long-run reduction in quantity demanded arises because people drive less and half because they switch to more fuel-efficient cars. Both responses are reflected in the demand curve and its elasticity.

THE ELASTICITY OF DEMAND

When we introduced demand in Chapter 4, we noted that consumers usually buy more of a good when its price is lower, when their incomes are higher, when the prices of substitutes for the good are higher, or when the prices of complements of the good are lower. Our discussion of demand was qualitative, not quantitative. That is, we discussed the direction in which quantity demanded moves but not the size of the change. To measure how much consumers respond to changes in these variables, economists use the concept of **elasticity**.

elasticity
a measure of the responsiveness of quantity demanded or quantity supplied to one of its determinants

price elasticity of demand
a measure of how much the quantity demanded of a good responds to a change in the price of that good, computed as the percentage change in quantity demanded divided by the percentage change in price

THE PRICE ELASTICITY OF DEMAND AND ITS DETERMINANTS

The law of demand states that a fall in the price of a good raises the quantity demanded. The **price elasticity of demand** measures how much the quantity demanded responds to a change in price. Demand for a good is said to be *elastic* if the quantity demanded responds substantially to changes in the price. Demand is said to be *inelastic* if the quantity demanded responds only slightly to changes in the price.

The price elasticity of demand for any good measures how willing consumers are to buy less of the good as its price rises. Thus, the elasticity reflects the many economic, social, and psychological forces that shape consumer preferences. Based on experience, however, we can state some general rules about what determines the price elasticity of demand.

Availability of Close Substitutes   Goods with close substitutes tend to have more elastic demand because it is easier for consumers to switch from that good to others. For example, butter and margarine are easily substitutable. A small increase in the price of butter, assuming the price of margarine is held fixed, causes the quantity of butter sold to fall by a large amount. By contrast, because eggs are a food without a close substitute, the demand for eggs is less elastic than the demand for butter.

Necessities versus Luxuries   Necessities tend to have inelastic demands, whereas luxuries have elastic demands. When the price of a doctor's visit rises, people will not dramatically reduce the number of times they go to the doctor, although they might go somewhat less often. By contrast, when the price of sailboats rises, the quantity of sailboats demanded falls substantially. The reason is that most people view doctor visits as a necessity and sailboats as a luxury. Of course, whether a good is a necessity or a luxury depends not on the intrinsic properties of the good but on the preferences of the buyer. For avid sailors with little concern over their health, sailboats might be a necessity with inelastic demand and doctor visits a luxury with elastic demand.

Definition of the Market   The elasticity of demand in any market depends on how we draw the boundaries of the market. Narrowly defined markets tend to have more elastic demand than broadly defined markets because it is easier to find close substitutes for narrowly defined goods. For example, food, a broad category, has a fairly inelastic demand because there are no good substitutes for food. Ice cream, a narrower category, has a more elastic demand because it is easy to substitute other desserts for ice cream. Vanilla ice cream, a very narrow category, has a very elastic demand because other flavors of ice cream are almost perfect substitutes for vanilla.

Time Horizon   Goods tend to have more elastic demand over longer time horizons. When the price of gasoline rises, the quantity of gasoline demanded falls only slightly in the first few months. Over time, however, people buy more fuel-efficient cars, switch to public transportation, and move closer to where they work. Within several years, the quantity of gasoline demanded falls more substantially.

COMPUTING THE PRICE ELASTICITY OF DEMAND

Now that we have discussed the price elasticity of demand in general terms, let's be more precise about how it is measured. Economists compute the price elasticity of demand as the percentage change in the quantity demanded divided by the percentage change in the price. That is,

$$\text{Price elasticity of demand} = \frac{\text{Percentage change in quantity demanded}}{\text{Percentage change in price}}.$$

For example, suppose that a 10 percent increase in the price of an ice-cream cone causes the amount of ice cream you buy to fall by 20 percent. We calculate your elasticity of demand as

$$\text{Price elasticity of demand} = \frac{20 \text{ percent}}{10 \text{ percent}} = 2.$$

In this example, the elasticity is 2, reflecting that the change in the quantity demanded is proportionately twice as large as the change in the price.

   Because the quantity demanded of a good is negatively related to its price, the percentage change in quantity will always have the opposite sign as the percentage change in price. In this example, the percentage change in price is a *positive* 10 percent (reflecting an increase), and the percentage change in quantity demanded is a *negative* 20 percent (reflecting a decrease). For this reason, price elasticities of demand are sometimes reported as negative numbers. In this book, we follow the common practice of dropping the minus sign and reporting all price elasticities of demand as positive numbers. (Mathematicians call this the *absolute value*.) With this convention, a larger price elasticity implies a greater responsiveness of quantity demanded to price.

THE MIDPOINT METHOD: A BETTER WAY TO CALCULATE PERCENTAGE CHANGES AND ELASTICITIES

If you try calculating the price elasticity of demand between two points on a demand curve, you will quickly notice an annoying problem: The elasticity from point A to point B seems different from the elasticity from point B to point A. For example, consider these numbers:

Point A:	Price = $4	Quantity = 120
Point B:	Price = $6	Quantity = 80

Going from point A to point B, the price rises by 50 percent, and the quantity falls by 33 percent, indicating that the price elasticity of demand is 33/50, or 0.66. By contrast, going from point B to point A, the price falls by 33 percent, and the quantity rises by 50 percent, indicating that the price elasticity of demand is 50/33, or 1.5. This difference arises because the percentage changes are calculated from a different base.

One way to avoid this problem is to use the *midpoint method* for calculating elasticities. The standard procedure for computing a percentage change is to divide the change by the initial level. By contrast, the midpoint method computes a percentage change by dividing the change by the midpoint (or average) of the initial and final levels. For instance, $5 is the midpoint between $4 and $6. Therefore, according to the midpoint method, a change from $4 to $6 is considered a 40 percent rise because $(6 - 4) / 5 \times 100 = 40$. Similarly, a change from $6 to $4 is considered a 40 percent fall.

Because the midpoint method gives the same answer regardless of the direction of change, it is often used when calculating the price elasticity of demand between two points. In our example, the midpoint between point A and point B is:

Midpoint:	Price = $5	Quantity = 100

According to the midpoint method, when going from point A to point B, the price rises by 40 percent, and the quantity falls by 40 percent. Similarly, when going from point B to point A, the price falls by 40 percent, and the quantity rises by 40 percent. In both directions, the price elasticity of demand equals 1.

The following formula expresses the midpoint method for calculating the price elasticity of demand between two points, denoted (Q_1, P_1) and (Q_2, P_2):

$$\text{Price elasticity of demand} = \frac{(Q_2 - Q_1) / [(Q_2 + Q_1) / 2]}{(P_2 - P_1) / [(P_2 + P_1) / 2]}.$$

The numerator is the percentage change in quantity computed using the midpoint method, and the denominator is the percentage change in price computed using the midpoint method. If you ever need to calculate elasticities, you should use this formula.

In this book, however, we rarely perform such calculations. For most of our purposes, what elasticity represents—the responsiveness of quantity demanded to a change in price—is more important than how it is calculated.

THE VARIETY OF DEMAND CURVES

Economists classify demand curves according to their elasticity. Demand is considered *elastic* when the elasticity is greater than 1, which means the quantity moves proportionately more than the price. Demand is considered *inelastic* when the elasticity is less than 1, which means the quantity moves proportionately less

The price elasticity of demand determines whether the demand curve is steep or flat. Note that all percentage changes are calculated using the midpoint method.

F I G U R E   **1**

The Price Elasticity of Demand

(a) Perfectly Inelastic Demand: Elasticity Equals 0

Price

Demand

$5
4

1. An increase in price . . .

0   100   **Quantity**

2. . . . leaves the quantity demanded unchanged.

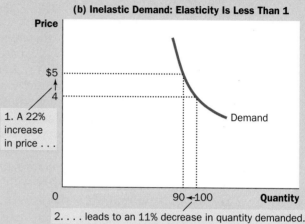

(b) Inelastic Demand: Elasticity Is Less Than 1

Price

$5
4

Demand

1. A 22% increase in price . . .

0   90 ←100   **Quantity**

2. . . . leads to an 11% decrease in quantity demanded.

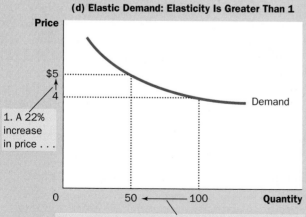

(c) Unit Elastic Demand: Elasticity Equals 1

Price

$5
4

Demand

1. A 22% increase in price . . .

0   80 ←100   **Quantity**

2. . . . leads to a 22% decrease in quantity demanded.

(d) Elastic Demand: Elasticity Is Greater Than 1

Price

$5
4

Demand

1. A 22% increase in price . . .

0   50 ←——— 100   **Quantity**

2. . . . leads to a 67% decrease in quantity demanded.

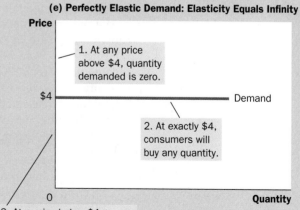

(e) Perfectly Elastic Demand: Elasticity Equals Infinity

Price

1. At any price above $4, quantity demanded is zero.

$4   Demand

2. At exactly $4, consumers will buy any quantity.

0   **Quantity**

3. At a price below $4, quantity demanded is infinite.

than the price. If the elasticity is exactly 1, the quantity moves the same amount proportionately as the price, and demand is said to have *unit elasticity*.

Because the price elasticity of demand measures how much quantity demanded responds to changes in the price, it is closely related to the slope of the demand curve. The following rule of thumb is a useful guide: The flatter the demand curve that passes through a given point, the greater the price elasticity of demand. The steeper the demand curve that passes through a given point, the smaller the price elasticity of demand.

Figure 1 on the previous page shows five cases. In the extreme case of a zero elasticity, shown in panel (a), demand is *perfectly inelastic*, and the demand curve is vertical. In this case, regardless of the price, the quantity demanded stays the same. As the elasticity rises, the demand curve gets flatter and flatter, as shown in panels (b), (c), and (d). At the opposite extreme, shown in panel (e), demand is *perfectly elastic*. This occurs as the price elasticity of demand approaches infinity and the demand curve becomes horizontal, reflecting the fact that very small changes in the price lead to huge changes in the quantity demanded.

Finally, if you have trouble keeping straight the terms *elastic* and *inelastic*, here's a memory trick for you: *I*nelastic curves, such as in panel (a) of Figure 1, look like the letter I. This is not a deep insight, but it might help on your next exam.

TOTAL REVENUE AND THE PRICE ELASTICITY OF DEMAND

total revenue
the amount paid by buyers and received by sellers of a good, computed as the price of the good times the quantity sold

When studying changes in supply or demand in a market, one variable we often want to study is **total revenue**, the amount paid by buyers and received by sellers of the good. In any market, total revenue is $P \times Q$, the price of the good times the quantity of the good sold. We can show total revenue graphically, as in Figure 2. The height of the box under the demand curve is P, and the width is Q. The area of this box, $P \times Q$, equals the total revenue in this market. In Figure 2, where $P = \$4$ and $Q = 100$, total revenue is $\$4 \times 100$, or $\$400$.

How does total revenue change as one moves along the demand curve? The answer depends on the price elasticity of demand. If demand is inelastic, as in panel (a) of Figure 3, then an increase in the price causes an increase in total revenue. Here an increase in price from $1 to $3 causes the quantity demanded to fall from 100 to 80, so total revenue rises from $100 to $240. An increase in price raises $P \times Q$ because the fall in Q is proportionately smaller than the rise in P.

We obtain the opposite result if demand is elastic: An increase in the price causes a decrease in total revenue. In panel (b) of Figure 3, for instance, when the price rises from $4 to $5, the quantity demanded falls from 50 to 20, so total revenue falls from $200 to $100. Because demand is elastic, the reduction in the quantity demanded is so great that it more than offsets the increase in the price. That is, an increase in price reduces $P \times Q$ because the fall in Q is proportionately greater than the rise in P.

Although the examples in this figure are extreme, they illustrate some general rules:

- When demand is inelastic (a price elasticity less than 1), price and total revenue move in the same direction.
- When demand is elastic (a price elasticity greater than 1), price and total revenue move in opposite directions.

FIGURE 2

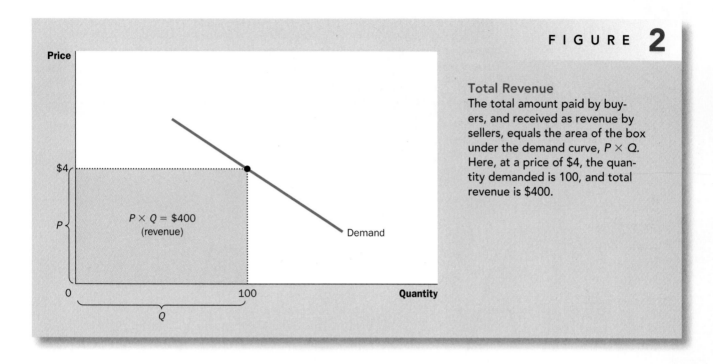

Price

$4

P

$P \times Q = \$400$
(revenue)

Demand

0   100   **Quantity**

Q

Total Revenue
The total amount paid by buyers, and received as revenue by sellers, equals the area of the box under the demand curve, $P \times Q$. Here, at a price of $4, the quantity demanded is 100, and total revenue is $400.

- If demand is unit elastic (a price elasticity exactly equal to 1), total revenue remains constant when the price changes.

Elasticity and Total Revenue along a Linear Demand Curve

Let's examine how elasticity varies along a linear demand curve, as shown in Figure 4. We know that a straight line has a constant slope. Slope is defined as "rise over run," which here is the ratio of the change in price ("rise") to the change in quantity ("run"). This particular demand curve's slope is constant because each $1 increase in price causes the same two-unit decrease in the quantity demanded.

Even though the slope of a linear demand curve is constant, the elasticity is not. This is true because the slope is the ratio of *changes* in the two variables, whereas the elasticity is the ratio of *percentage changes* in the two variables. You can see this by looking at the table in Figure 4, which shows the demand schedule for the linear demand curve in the graph. The table uses the midpoint method to calculate the price elasticity of demand. At points with a low price and high quantity, the demand curve is inelastic. At points with a high price and low quantity, the demand curve is elastic.

The table also presents total revenue at each point on the demand curve. These numbers illustrate the relationship between total revenue and elasticity. When the price is $1, for instance, demand is inelastic, and a price increase to $2 raises total revenue. When the price is $5, demand is elastic, and a price increase to $6 reduces total revenue. Between $3 and $4, demand is exactly unit elastic, and total revenue is the same at these two prices.

The linear demand curve illustrates that the price elasticity of demand need not be the same at all points on a demand curve. A constant elasticity is possible, but it is not always the case.

3 FIGURE

How Total Revenue
Changes When Price
Changes

The impact of a price change on total revenue (the product of price and quantity) depends on the elasticity of demand. In panel (a), the demand curve is inelastic. In this case, an increase in the price leads to a decrease in quantity demanded that is proportionately smaller, so total revenue increases. Here an increase in the price from $1 to $3 causes the quantity demanded to fall from 100 to 80. Total revenue rises from $100 to $240. In panel (b), the demand curve is elastic. In this case, an increase in the price leads to a decrease in quantity demanded that is proportionately larger, so total revenue decreases. Here an increase in the price from $4 to $5 causes the quantity demanded to fall from 50 to 20. Total revenue falls from $200 to $100.

(a) The Case of Inelastic Demand

 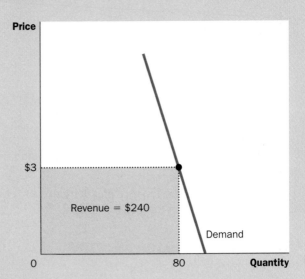

(b) The Case of Elastic Demand

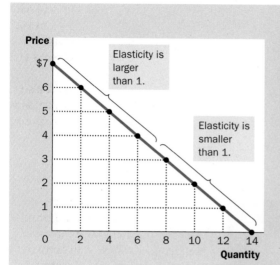

FIGURE **4**

Elasticity of a Linear Demand Curve
The slope of a linear demand curve is constant, but its elasticity is not. The demand schedule in the table was used to calculate the price elasticity of demand by the midpoint method. At points with a low price and high quantity, the demand curve is inelastic. At points with a high price and low quantity, the demand curve is elastic.

Price	Quantity	Total Revenue (Price × Quantity)	Percentage Change in Price	Percentage Change in Quantity	Elasticity	Description
$7	0	$ 0				
6	2	12	15	200	13.0	Elastic
5	4	20	18	67	3.7	Elastic
4	6	24	22	40	1.8	Elastic
3	8	24	29	29	1.0	Unit elastic
2	10	20	40	22	0.6	Inelastic
1	12	12	67	18	0.3	Inelastic
0	14	0	200	15	0.1	Inelastic

OTHER DEMAND ELASTICITIES

In addition to the price elasticity of demand, economists use other elasticities to describe the behavior of buyers in a market.

The Income Elasticity of Demand   The **income elasticity of demand** measures how the quantity demanded changes as consumer income changes. It is calculated as the percentage change in quantity demanded divided by the percentage change in income. That is,

$$\text{Income elasticity of demand} = \frac{\text{Percentage change in quantity demanded}}{\text{Percentage change in income}}.$$

As we discussed in Chapter 4, most goods are *normal goods:* Higher income raises the quantity demanded. Because quantity demanded and income move in the same direction, normal goods have positive income elasticities. A few goods, such as bus rides, are *inferior goods:* Higher income lowers the quantity demanded. Because quantity demanded and income move in opposite directions, inferior goods have negative income elasticities.

income elasticity of demand
a measure of how much the quantity demanded of a good responds to a change in consumers' income, computed as the percentage change in quantity demanded divided by the percentage change in income

In The News

Energy Demand

What would induce consumers to use less gasoline and electricity?

Real Energy Savers Don't Wear Cardigans. Or Do They?

By Anna Bernasek

When oil and gas prices surged after Hurricanes Katrina and Rita, President Bush appealed to Americans to conserve energy. He asked people to cut back on nonessential travel, for example, and to carpool to work. Then, in October, the White House started a campaign for energy conservation in American homes, dusting off some old ideas like switching to fluorescent light bulbs and installing better insulation in attics.

Some critics derided the program as a bizarre flashback from the 1970's—a collection of worn-out ideas that evoked feelings of deprivation and gloom. It will be a pity, though, if an effective energy policy never gets off the ground. Much has been learned since the 70's about what works and what doesn't. . . .

There are reasons for optimism. One is that market forces can help provide solutions: higher prices, on their own, can make people cut back. Just how responsive consumers are to price changes—what economists call the elasticity of demand—has been the focus of much research. Today, economists believe that they have developed a pretty good rule of thumb for energy use. In the case of electricity, which is relatively easy to measure, they have found that

when the price rises 10 percent, electricity use falls roughly 3 percent. At the gas pump, a 10 percent increase in price leads to a decline of around 2 percent in demand. [*Author's note:* It would be more precise to say that the price increase leads to a 2 percent decline in quantity demanded, because the change represents a movement along the demand curve.]

Consumer behavior can change quickly in a crisis. A study by Peter C. Reiss, a professor of economics at Stanford, and Matthew W. White, a professor of business and public policy at the Wharton School of the University of Pennsylvania, provides some recent evidence. In examining San Diego households during the California electricity crisis of 2000 and 2001, they found that use of electricity dropped surprisingly fast. In the summer of 2000, within 60 days of seeing monthly electric bills rise by about $60—an increase of 130 percent—the average household cut its use of electricity by 12 percent.

That kind of drop requires a big change in behavior. The authors found that households had turned off air-conditioners in the middle of summer and had invested in new energy-efficient appliances, among other things.

High costs aren't the only force that will influence consumers to cut back. Although public appeals to save energy may be ridiculed by comedians on late-night television—recall President Jimmy Carter's cardigan sweater—the efforts can have a substantial impact.

Professors Reiss and White found that to be true in San Diego. In February 2001, with electricity prices capped, the state of California began a campaign to have households conserve electricity. It worked. "It was clear by about six months into 2001 that public appeals were having a big impact," Professor White said. Such campaigns can have significant effects on consumer behavior, he said, if they offer a clear explanation of what people can do and how it will make a difference.

Perhaps the most important reason for optimism is technology's role in promoting energy savings. From 1979 to 1985, in the aftermath of energy shortages, Americans reduced their oil consumption by 15 percent. The single biggest factor was a shift in car-buying habits. Americans found that driving fuel-efficient cars, instead of gas guzzlers, didn't stop them from going where they wanted to go.

Source: *New York Times,* November 13, 2005.

Even among normal goods, income elasticities vary substantially in size. Necessities, such as food and clothing, tend to have small income elasticities because consumers choose to buy some of these goods even when their incomes are low. Luxuries, such as caviar and diamonds, tend to have large income elasticities because consumers feel that they can do without these goods altogether if their incomes are too low.

The Cross-Price Elasticity of Demand   The **cross-price elasticity of demand** measures how the quantity demanded of one good responds to a change in the price of another good. It is calculated as the percentage change in quantity demanded of good 1 divided by the percentage change in the price of good 2. That is,

$$\text{Cross-price elasticity of demand} = \frac{\text{Percentage change in quantity demanded of good 1}}{\text{Percentage change in the price of good 2}}.$$

Whether the cross-price elasticity is a positive or negative number depends on whether the two goods are substitutes or complements. As we discussed in Chapter 4, substitutes are goods that are typically used in place of one another, such as hamburgers and hot dogs. An increase in hot dog prices induces people to grill hamburgers instead. Because the price of hot dogs and the quantity of hamburgers demanded move in the same direction, the cross-price elasticity is positive. Conversely, complements are goods that are typically used together, such as computers and software. In this case, the cross-price elasticity is negative, indicating that an increase in the price of computers reduces the quantity of software demanded.

cross-price elasticity of demand
a measure of how much the quantity demanded of one good responds to a change in the price of another good, computed as the percentage change in quantity demanded of the first good divided by the percentage change in the price of the second good

QUICK QUIZ   Define the price elasticity of demand. • Explain the relationship between total revenue and the price elasticity of demand.

THE ELASTICITY OF SUPPLY

When we introduced supply in Chapter 4, we noted that producers of a good offer to sell more of it when the price of the good rises. To turn from qualitative to quantitative statements about quantity supplied, we once again use the concept of elasticity.

THE PRICE ELASTICITY OF SUPPLY AND ITS DETERMINANTS

The law of supply states that higher prices raise the quantity supplied. The **price elasticity of supply** measures how much the quantity supplied responds to changes in the price. Supply of a good is said to be *elastic* if the quantity supplied responds substantially to changes in the price. Supply is said to be *inelastic* if the quantity supplied responds only slightly to changes in the price.

The price elasticity of supply depends on the flexibility of sellers to change the amount of the good they produce. For example, beachfront land has an inelastic supply because it is almost impossible to produce more of it. By contrast, manufactured goods, such as books, cars, and televisions, have elastic supplies because

price elasticity of supply
a measure of how much the quantity supplied of a good responds to a change in the price of that good, computed as the percentage change in quantity supplied divided by the percentage change in price

firms that produce them can run their factories longer in response to a higher price.

In most markets, a key determinant of the price elasticity of supply is the time period being considered. Supply is usually more elastic in the long run than in the short run. Over short periods of time, firms cannot easily change the size of their factories to make more or less of a good. Thus, in the short run, the quantity supplied is not very responsive to the price. By contrast, over longer periods, firms can build new factories or close old ones. In addition, new firms can enter a market, and old firms can shut down. Thus, in the long run, the quantity supplied can respond substantially to price changes.

Computing the Price Elasticity of Supply

Now that we have a general understanding about the price elasticity of supply, let's be more precise. Economists compute the price elasticity of supply as the percentage change in the quantity supplied divided by the percentage change in the price. That is,

$$\text{Price elasticity of supply} = \frac{\text{Percentage change in quantity supplied}}{\text{Percentage change in price}}.$$

For example, suppose that an increase in the price of milk from \$2.85 to \$3.15 a gallon raises the amount that dairy farmers produce from 9,000 to 11,000 gallons per month. Using the midpoint method, we calculate the percentage change in price as

$$\text{Percentage change in price} = (3.15 - 2.85) / 3.00 \times 100 = 10 \text{ percent}.$$

Similarly, we calculate the percentage change in quantity supplied as

$$\text{Percentage change in quantity supplied} = (11{,}000 - 9{,}000) / 10{,}000 \times 100 = 20 \text{ percent}.$$

In this case, the price elasticity of supply is

$$\text{Price elasticity of supply} = \frac{20 \text{ percent}}{10 \text{ percent}} = 2.0.$$

In this example, the elasticity of 2 indicates that the quantity supplied changes proportionately twice as much as the price.

The Variety of Supply Curves

Because the price elasticity of supply measures the responsiveness of quantity supplied to the price, it is reflected in the appearance of the supply curve. Figure 5 shows five cases. In the extreme case of a zero elasticity, as shown in panel (a), supply is *perfectly inelastic*, and the supply curve is vertical. In this case, the quantity supplied is the same regardless of the price. As the elasticity rises, the supply curve gets flatter, which shows that the quantity supplied responds more to changes in the price. At the opposite extreme, shown in panel (e), supply is *perfectly elastic*. This occurs as the price elasticity of supply approaches infinity and the supply curve becomes horizontal, meaning that very small changes in the price lead to very large changes in the quantity supplied.

The price elasticity of supply determines whether the supply curve is steep or flat. Note that all percentage changes are calculated using the midpoint method.

FIGURE 5

The Price Elasticity of Supply

(a) Perfectly Inelastic Supply: Elasticity Equals 0

1. An increase in price . . .

2. . . . leaves the quantity supplied unchanged.

(b) Inelastic Supply: Elasticity Is Less Than 1

1. A 22% increase in price . . .

2. . . . leads to a 10% increase in quantity supplied.

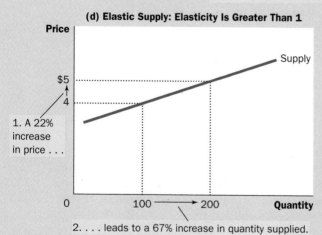

(c) Unit Elastic Supply: Elasticity Equals 1

1. A 22% increase in price . . .

2. . . . leads to a 22% increase in quantity supplied.

(d) Elastic Supply: Elasticity Is Greater Than 1

1. A 22% increase in price . . .

2. . . . leads to a 67% increase in quantity supplied.

(e) Perfectly Elastic Supply: Elasticity Equals Infinity

1. At any price above $4, quantity supplied is infinite.

2. At exactly $4, producers will supply any quantity.

3. At a price below $4, quantity supplied is zero.

In some markets, the elasticity of supply is not constant but varies over the supply curve. Figure 6 shows a typical case for an industry in which firms have factories with a limited capacity for production. For low levels of quantity supplied, the elasticity of supply is high, indicating that firms respond substantially to changes in the price. In this region, firms have capacity for production that is not being used, such as plants and equipment idle for all or part of the day. Small increases in price make it profitable for firms to begin using this idle capacity. As the quantity supplied rises, firms begin to reach capacity. Once capacity is fully used, increasing production further requires the construction of new plants. To induce firms to incur this extra expense, the price must rise substantially, so supply becomes less elastic.

Figure 6 presents a numerical example of this phenomenon. When the price rises from $3 to $4 (a 29 percent increase, according to the midpoint method), the quantity supplied rises from 100 to 200 (a 67 percent increase). Because quantity supplied changes proportionately more than the price, the supply curve has elasticity greater than 1. By contrast, when the price rises from $12 to $15 (a 22 percent increase), the quantity supplied rises from 500 to 525 (a 5 percent increase). In this case, quantity supplied moves proportionately less than the price, so the elasticity is less than 1.

QUICK QUIZ Define the price elasticity of supply. • Explain why the price elasticity of supply might be different in the long run and in the short run.

THREE APPLICATIONS OF SUPPLY, DEMAND, AND ELASTICITY

Can good news for farming be bad news for farmers? Why did OPEC fail to keep the price of oil high? Does drug interdiction increase or decrease drug-related crime? At first, these questions might seem to have little in common. Yet all three

6 FIGURE

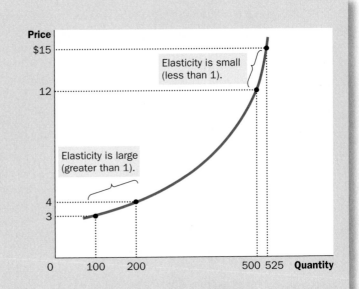

How the Price Elasticity of Supply Can Vary
Because firms often have a maximum capacity for production, the elasticity of supply may be very high at low levels of quantity supplied and very low at high levels of quantity supplied. Here an increase in price from $3 to $4 increases the quantity supplied from 100 to 200. Because the 67 percent increase in quantity supplied (computed using the midpoint method) is larger than the 29 percent increase in price, the supply curve is elastic in this range. By contrast, when the price rises from $12 to $15, the quantity supplied rises only from 500 to 525. Because the 5 percent increase in quantity supplied is smaller than the 22 percent increase in price, the supply curve is inelastic in this range.

questions are about markets, and all markets are subject to the forces of supply and demand. Here we apply the versatile tools of supply, demand, and elasticity to answer these seemingly complex questions.

CAN GOOD NEWS FOR FARMING BE BAD NEWS FOR FARMERS?

Imagine yourself as a Kansas wheat farmer. Because you earn all your income from selling wheat, you devote much effort to making your land as productive as possible. You monitor weather and soil conditions, check your fields for pests and disease, and study the latest advances in farm technology. You know that the more wheat you grow, the more you will have to sell after the harvest, and the higher will be your income and your standard of living.

One day, Kansas State University announces a major discovery. Researchers in its agronomy department have devised a new hybrid of wheat that raises the amount farmers can produce from each acre of land by 20 percent. How should you react to this news? Does this discovery make you better off or worse off than you were before?

Recall from Chapter 4 that we answer such questions in three steps. First, we examine whether the supply or demand curve shifts. Second, we consider in which direction the curve shifts. Third, we use the supply-and-demand diagram to see how the market equilibrium changes.

In this case, the discovery of the new hybrid affects the supply curve. Because the hybrid increases the amount of wheat that can be produced on each acre of land, farmers are now willing to supply more wheat at any given price. In other words, the supply curve shifts to the right. The demand curve remains the same because consumers' desire to buy wheat products at any given price is not affected by the introduction of a new hybrid. Figure 7 shows an example of such a change. When the supply curve shifts from S_1 to S_2, the quantity of wheat sold increases from 100 to 110, and the price of wheat falls from $3 to $2.

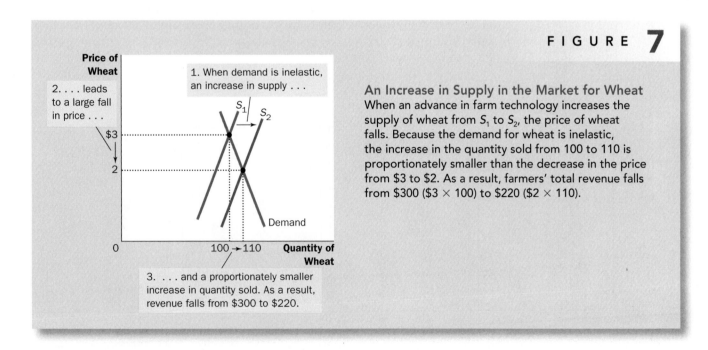

FIGURE **7**

An Increase in Supply in the Market for Wheat When an advance in farm technology increases the supply of wheat from S_1 to S_2, the price of wheat falls. Because the demand for wheat is inelastic, the increase in the quantity sold from 100 to 110 is proportionately smaller than the decrease in the price from $3 to $2. As a result, farmers' total revenue falls from $300 ($3 × 100) to $220 ($2 × 110).

Price of Wheat

2. . . . leads to a large fall in price . . .

1. When demand is inelastic, an increase in supply . . .

S_1 S_2

$3

2

Demand

0

100 → 110 Quantity of Wheat

3. . . . and a proportionately smaller increase in quantity sold. As a result, revenue falls from $300 to $220.

Does this discovery make farmers better off? As a first cut to answering this question, consider what happens to the total revenue received by farmers. Farmers' total revenue is $P \times Q$, the price of the wheat times the quantity sold. The discovery affects farmers in two conflicting ways. The hybrid allows farmers to produce more wheat (Q rises), but now each bushel of wheat sells for less (P falls).

Whether total revenue rises or falls depends on the elasticity of demand. In practice, the demand for basic foodstuffs such as wheat is usually inelastic because these items are relatively inexpensive and have few good substitutes. When the demand curve is inelastic, as it is in Figure 7, a decrease in price causes total revenue to fall. You can see this in the figure: The price of wheat falls substantially, whereas the quantity of wheat sold rises only slightly. Total revenue falls from $300 to $220. Thus, the discovery of the new hybrid lowers the total revenue that farmers receive from the sale of their crops.

If farmers are made worse off by the discovery of this new hybrid, one might wonder why they adopt it. The answer goes to the heart of how competitive markets work. Because each farmer is only a small part of the market for wheat, he or she takes the price of wheat as given. For any given price of wheat, it is better to use the new hybrid to produce and sell more wheat. Yet when all farmers do this, the supply of wheat increases, the price falls, and farmers are worse off.

Although this example may at first seem hypothetical, it helps to explain a major change in the U.S. economy over the past century. Two hundred years ago, most Americans lived on farms. Knowledge about farm methods was sufficiently primitive that most Americans had to be farmers to produce enough food to feed the nation's population. Yet over time, advances in farm technology increased the amount of food that each farmer could produce. This increase in food supply, together with inelastic food demand, caused farm revenues to fall, which in turn encouraged people to leave farming.

A few numbers show the magnitude of this historic change. As recently as 1950, there were 10 million people working on farms in the United States, representing 17 percent of the labor force. Today, fewer than 3 million people work on farms, or 2 percent of the labor force. This change coincided with tremendous advances in farm productivity: Despite the 70 percent drop in the number of farmers, U.S. farms now produce more than twice the output of crops and livestock that they did in 1950.

This analysis of the market for farm products also helps to explain a seeming paradox of public policy: Certain farm programs try to help farmers by inducing them *not* to plant crops on all of their land. The purpose of these programs is to reduce the supply of farm products and thereby raise prices. With inelastic demand for their products, farmers as a group receive greater total revenue if they supply a smaller crop to the market. No single farmer would choose to leave his land fallow on his own because each takes the market price as given. But if all farmers do so together, each of them can be better off.

When analyzing the effects of farm technology or farm policy, it is important to keep in mind that what is good for farmers is not necessarily good for society as a whole. Improvement in farm technology can be bad for farmers because it makes farmers increasingly unnecessary, but it is surely good for consumers who pay less for food. Similarly, a policy aimed at reducing the supply of farm products may raise the incomes of farmers, but it does so at the expense of consumers.

WHY DID OPEC FAIL TO KEEP THE PRICE OF OIL HIGH?

Many of the most disruptive events for the world's economies over the past several decades have originated in the world market for oil. In the 1970s, members of the Organization of Petroleum Exporting Countries (OPEC) decided to raise the world price of oil to increase their incomes. These countries accomplished this goal by jointly reducing the amount of oil they supplied. From 1973 to 1974, the price of oil (adjusted for overall inflation) rose more than 50 percent. Then, a few years later, OPEC did the same thing again. From 1979 to 1981, the price of oil approximately doubled.

Yet OPEC found it difficult to maintain a high price. From 1982 to 1985, the price of oil steadily declined about 10 percent per year. Dissatisfaction and disarray soon prevailed among the OPEC countries. In 1986, cooperation among OPEC members completely broke down, and the price of oil plunged 45 percent. In 1990, the price of oil (adjusted for overall inflation) was back to where it began in 1970, and it stayed at that low level throughout most of the 1990s. (In the first decade of the 21st century, the price of oil rose again, but the main driving force was not OPEC supply restrictions but, rather, increased world demand, in part from a large and rapidly growing Chinese economy.)

This OPEC episode of the 1970s and 1980s shows how supply and demand can behave differently in the short run and in the long run. In the short run, both the supply and demand for oil are relatively inelastic. Supply is inelastic because the quantity of known oil reserves and the capacity for oil extraction cannot be changed quickly. Demand is inelastic because buying habits do not respond immediately to changes in price. Thus, as panel (a) of Figure 8 shows, the short-run supply and demand curves are steep. When the supply of oil shifts from S_1 to S_2, the price increase from P_1 to P_2 is large.

The situation is very different in the long run. Over long periods of time, producers of oil outside OPEC respond to high prices by increasing oil exploration and by building new extraction capacity. Consumers respond with greater conservation, for instance by replacing old inefficient cars with newer efficient ones. Thus, as panel (b) of Figure 8 shows, the long-run supply and demand curves are more elastic. In the long run, the shift in the supply curve from S_1 to S_2 causes a much smaller increase in the price.

8 FIGURE

A Reduction in Supply in the World Market for Oil

When the supply of oil falls, the response depends on the time horizon. In the short run, supply and demand are relatively inelastic, as in panel (a). Thus, when the supply curve shifts from S_1 to S_2, the price rises substantially. By contrast, in the long run, supply and demand are relatively elastic, as in panel (b). In this case, the same size shift in the supply curve (S_1 to S_2) causes a smaller increase in the price.

(a) The Oil Market in the Short Run

Price of Oil

1. In the short run, when supply and demand are inelastic, a shift in supply . . .

S_2 S_1

P_2

2. . . . leads to a large increase in price.

P_1

Demand

0   Quantity of Oil

(b) The Oil Market in the Long Run

Price of Oil

1. In the long run, when supply and demand are elastic, a shift in supply . . .

S_2 S_1

2. . . . leads to a small increase in price.

P_2 P_1

Demand

0   Quantity of Oil

This analysis shows why OPEC succeeded in maintaining a high price of oil only in the short run. When OPEC countries agreed to reduce their production of oil, they shifted the supply curve to the left. Even though each OPEC member sold less oil, the price rose by so much in the short run that OPEC incomes rose. By contrast, in the long run, when supply and demand are more elastic, the same reduction in supply, measured by the horizontal shift in the supply curve, caused a smaller increase in the price. Thus, OPEC's coordinated reduction in supply proved less profitable in the long run. The cartel learned that raising prices is easier in the short run than in the long run.

DOES DRUG INTERDICTION INCREASE OR DECREASE DRUG-RELATED CRIME?

A persistent problem facing our society is the use of illegal drugs, such as heroin, cocaine, ecstasy, and crack. Drug use has several adverse effects. One is that drug dependence can ruin the lives of drug users and their families. Another is that drug addicts often turn to robbery and other violent crimes to obtain the money needed to support their habit. To discourage the use of illegal drugs, the U.S. government devotes billions of dollars each year to reduce the flow of drugs into the country. Let's use the tools of supply and demand to examine this policy of drug interdiction.

Suppose the government increases the number of federal agents devoted to the war on drugs. What happens in the market for illegal drugs? As is usual, we answer this question in three steps. First, we consider whether the supply or demand curve shifts. Second, we consider the direction of the shift. Third, we see how the shift affects the equilibrium price and quantity.

Although the purpose of drug interdiction is to reduce drug use, its direct impact is on the sellers of drugs rather than the buyers. When the government stops some drugs from entering the country and arrests more smugglers, it raises the cost of selling drugs and, therefore, reduces the quantity of drugs supplied at any given price. The demand for drugs—the amount buyers want at any given price—is not changed. As panel (a) of Figure 9 shows, interdiction shifts the supply curve to the left from S_1 to S_2 and leaves the demand curve the same. The equilibrium price of drugs rises from P_1 to P_2, and the equilibrium quantity falls from Q_1 to Q_2. The fall in the equilibrium quantity shows that drug interdiction does reduce drug use.

But what about the amount of drug-related crime? To answer this question, consider the total amount that drug users pay for the drugs they buy. Because few drug addicts are likely to break their destructive habits in response to a higher price, it is likely that the demand for drugs is inelastic, as it is drawn in the figure.

Drug interdiction reduces the supply of drugs from S_1 to S_2 as in panel (a). If the demand for drugs is inelastic, then the total amount paid by drug users rises, even as the amount of drug use falls. By contrast, drug education reduces the demand for drugs from D_1 to D_2 as in panel (b). Because both price and quantity fall, the amount paid by drug users falls.

FIGURE 9

Policies to Reduce the Use of Illegal Drugs

If demand is inelastic, then an increase in price raises total revenue in the drug market. That is, because drug interdiction raises the price of drugs proportionately more than it reduces drug use, it raises the total amount of money that drug users pay for drugs. Addicts who already had to steal to support their habits would have an even greater need for quick cash. Thus, drug interdiction could increase drug-related crime.

Because of this adverse effect of drug interdiction, some analysts argue for alternative approaches to the drug problem. Rather than trying to reduce the supply of drugs, policymakers might try to reduce the demand by pursuing a policy of drug education. Successful drug education has the effects shown in panel (b) of Figure 9. The demand curve shifts to the left from D_1 to D_2. As a result, the equilibrium quantity falls from Q_1 to Q_2, and the equilibrium price falls from P_1 to P_2. Total revenue, which is price times quantity, also falls. Thus, in contrast to drug interdiction, drug education can reduce both drug use and drug-related crime.

Advocates of drug interdiction might argue that the long-run effects of this policy are different from the short-run effects because the elasticity of demand depends on the time horizon. The demand for drugs is probably inelastic over short periods because higher prices do not substantially affect drug use by established addicts. But demand may be more elastic over longer periods because higher prices would discourage experimentation with drugs among the young and, over time, lead to fewer drug addicts. In this case, drug interdiction would increase drug-related crime in the short run while decreasing it in the long run.

QUICK QUIZ How might a drought that destroys half of all farm crops be good for farmers? If such a drought is good for farmers, why don't farmers destroy their own crops in the absence of a drought?

CONCLUSION

According to an old quip, even a parrot can become an economist simply by learning to say "supply and demand." These last two chapters should have convinced you that there is much truth in this statement. The tools of supply and demand allow you to analyze many of the most important events and policies that shape the economy. You are now well on your way to becoming an economist (or at least a well-educated parrot).

SUMMARY

- The price elasticity of demand measures how much the quantity demanded responds to changes in the price. Demand tends to be more elastic if close substitutes are available, if the good is a luxury rather than a necessity, if the market is narrowly defined, or if buyers have substantial time to react to a price change.

- The price elasticity of demand is calculated as the percentage change in quantity demanded divided by the percentage change in price. If quantity demanded moves proportionately less than the price, then the elasticity is less than 1, and demand is said to be inelastic. If quantity demanded moves proportionately more than the price, then the elasticity is greater than 1, and demand is said to be elastic.

- Total revenue, the total amount paid for a good, equals the price of the good times the quantity sold. For inelastic demand curves, total revenue rises as price rises. For elastic demand curves, total revenue falls as price rises.

- The income elasticity of demand measures how much the quantity demanded responds to changes in consumers' income. The cross-price elasticity of demand measures how much the quantity demanded of one good responds to changes in the price of another good.

- The price elasticity of supply measures how much the quantity supplied responds to changes in the price. This elasticity often depends on the time horizon under consideration. In most markets, supply is more elastic in the long run than in the short run.

- The price elasticity of supply is calculated as the percentage change in quantity supplied divided by the percentage change in price. If quantity supplied moves proportionately less than the price, then the elasticity is less than 1, and supply is said to be inelastic. If quantity supplied moves proportionately more than the price, then the elasticity is greater than 1, and supply is said to be elastic.

- The tools of supply and demand can be applied in many different kinds of markets. This chapter uses them to analyze the market for wheat, the market for oil, and the market for illegal drugs.

KEY CONCEPTS

elasticity, *p. 90*
price elasticity of demand, *p. 90*
total revenue, *p. 93*

income elasticity of
  demand, *p. 97*
cross-price elasticity of
  demand, *p. 99*

price elasticity of supply, *p. 99*

QUESTIONS FOR REVIEW

1. Define the price elasticity of demand and the income elasticity of demand.
2. List and explain the four determinants of the price elasticity of demand discussed in the chapter.
3. What is the main advantage of using the midpoint method for calculating elasticity?
4. If the elasticity is greater than 1, is demand elastic or inelastic? If the elasticity equals 0, is demand perfectly elastic or perfectly inelastic?
5. On a supply-and-demand diagram, show equilibrium price, equilibrium quantity, and the total revenue received by producers.
6. If demand is elastic, how will an increase in price change total revenue? Explain.
7. What do we call a good whose income elasticity is less than 0?
8. How is the price elasticity of supply calculated? Explain what it measures.
9. What is the price elasticity of supply of Picasso paintings?
10. Is the price elasticity of supply usually larger in the short run or in the long run? Why?
11. How did elasticity help explain why drug interdiction could reduce the supply of drugs, yet possibly increase drug-related crime?

PROBLEMS AND APPLICATIONS

1. For each of the following pairs of goods, which good would you expect to have more elastic demand and why?
   a. required textbooks or mystery novels
   b. Beethoven recordings or classical music recordings in general
   c. subway rides during the next 6 months or subway rides during the next 5 years
   d. root beer or water
2. Suppose that business travelers and vacationers have the following demand for airline tickets from New York to Boston:

Price	Quantity Demanded (business travelers)	Quantity Demanded (vacationers)
$150	2,100 tickets	1,000 tickets
200	2,000	800
250	1,900	600
300	1,800	400

   a. As the price of tickets rises from $200 to $250, what is the price elasticity of demand for (i) business travelers and (ii) vacationers? (Use the midpoint method in your calculations.)
   b. Why might vacationers have a different elasticity from business travelers?
3. Suppose the price elasticity of demand for heating oil is 0.2 in the short run and 0.7 in the long run.
   a. If the price of heating oil rises from $1.80 to $2.20 per gallon, what happens to the quantity of heating oil demanded in the short run? In the long run? (Use the midpoint method in your calculations.)
   b. Why might this elasticity depend on the time horizon?
4. A price change causes the quantity demanded of a good to decrease by 30 percent, while the total revenue of that good increases by 15 percent. Is the demand curve elastic or inelastic? Explain.
5. The equilibrium price of coffee mugs rose sharply last month, but the equilibrium quantity was the same as ever. Three people tried to explain the situation. Which explanations could be right? Explain your logic.

   BILLY: Demand increased, but supply was totally inelastic.
   MARIAN: Supply increased, but so did demand.
   VALERIE: Supply decreased, but demand was totally inelastic.

6. Suppose that your demand schedule for compact discs is as follows:

Price	Quantity Demanded (income = $10,000)	Quantity Demanded (income = $12,000)
$ 8	40 CDs	50 CDs
10	32	45
12	24	30
14	16	20
16	8	12

   a. Use the midpoint method to calculate your price elasticity of demand as the price of compact discs increases from $8 to $10 if (i) your income is $10,000 and (ii) your income is $12,000.
   b. Calculate your income elasticity of demand as your income increases from $10,000 to $12,000 if (i) the price is $12 and (ii) the price is $16.
7. You have the following information about good X and good Y:
   • Income elasticity of demand for good X: −3
   • Cross-price elasticity of demand for good X with respect to the price of good Y: 2
   Would an increase in income and a decrease in the price of good Y unambiguously decrease the demand for good X? Why or why not?
8. Maria has decided always to spend one-third of her income on clothing.
   a. What is her income elasticity of clothing demand?
   b. What is her price elasticity of clothing demand?
   c. If Maria's tastes change and she decides to spend only one-fourth of her income on clothing, how does her demand curve change? What is her income elasticity and price elasticity now?

9. The *New York Times* reported (Feb. 17, 1996, p. 25) that subway ridership declined after a fare increase: "There were nearly four million fewer riders in December 1995, the first full month after the price of a token increased 25 cents to $1.50, than in the previous December, a 4.3 percent decline."
   a. Use these data to estimate the price elasticity of demand for subway rides.
   b. According to your estimate, what happens to the Transit Authority's revenue when the fare rises?
   c. Why might your estimate of the elasticity be unreliable?
10. Two drivers—Tom and Jerry—each drive up to a gas station. Before looking at the price, each places an order. Tom says, "I'd like 10 gallons of gas." Jerry says, "I'd like $10 worth of gas." What is each driver's price elasticity of demand?
11. Consider public policy aimed at smoking.
   a. Studies indicate that the price elasticity of demand for cigarettes is about 0.4. If a pack of cigarettes currently costs $2 and the government wants to reduce smoking by 20 percent, by how much should it increase the price?
   b. If the government permanently increases the price of cigarettes, will the policy have a larger effect on smoking 1 year from now or 5 years from now?
   c. Studies also find that teenagers have a higher price elasticity than do adults. Why might this be true?
12. You are the curator of a museum. The museum is running short of funds, so you decide to increase revenue. Should you increase or decrease the price of admission? Explain.
13. Pharmaceutical drugs have an inelastic demand, and computers have an elastic demand. Suppose that technological advance doubles the supply of both products (that is, the quantity supplied at each price is twice what it was).
   a. What happens to the equilibrium price and quantity in each market?
   b. Which product experiences a larger change in price?
   c. Which product experiences a larger change in quantity?
   d. What happens to total consumer spending on each product?
14. Beachfront resorts have an inelastic supply, and automobiles have an elastic supply. Suppose that a rise in population doubles the demand for both products (that is, the quantity demanded at each price is twice what it was).
   a. What happens to the equilibrium price and quantity in each market?
   b. Which product experiences a larger change in price?
   c. Which product experiences a larger change in quantity?
   d. What happens to total consumer spending on each product?
15. Several years ago, flooding along the Missouri and the Mississippi rivers destroyed thousands of acres of wheat.
   a. Farmers whose crops were destroyed by the floods were much worse off, but farmers whose crops were not destroyed benefited from the floods. Why?
   b. What information would you need about the market for wheat to assess whether farmers as a group were hurt or helped by the floods?
16. Explain why the following might be true: A drought around the world raises the total revenue that farmers receive from the sale of grain, but a drought only in Kansas reduces the total revenue that Kansas farmers receive.
17. Suppose the demand curve for a product is $Q = 60/P$. Compute the quantity demanded at prices of $1, $2, $3, $4, $5, and $6. Graph the demand curve. Use the midpoint method to calculate the price elasticity of demand between $1 and $2 and between $5 and $6. How does this demand curve compare to the linear demand curve?

Supply, Demand, and Government Policies

Economists have two roles. As scientists, they develop and test theories to explain the world around them. As policy advisers, they use their theories to help change the world for the better. The focus of the preceding two chapters has been scientific. We have seen how supply and demand determine the price of a good and the quantity of the good sold. We have also seen how various events shift supply and demand and thereby change the equilibrium price and quantity.

This chapter offers our first look at policy. Here we analyze various types of government policy using only the tools of supply and demand. As you will see, the analysis yields some surprising insights. Policies often have effects that their architects did not intend or anticipate.

We begin by considering policies that directly control prices. For example, rent-control laws dictate a maximum rent that landlords may charge tenants. Minimum-wage laws dictate the lowest wage that firms may pay workers. Price controls are usually enacted when policymakers believe that the market price of a good or service is unfair to buyers or sellers. Yet, as we will see, these policies can generate inequities of their own.

After discussing price controls, we consider the impact of taxes. Policymakers use taxes to raise revenue for public purposes and to influence market outcomes. Although the prevalence of taxes in our economy is obvious, their effects are not. For example, when the government levies a tax on the amount that firms pay their workers, do the firms or the workers bear the burden of the tax? The answer is not at all clear—until we apply the powerful tools of supply and demand.

CONTROLS ON PRICES

To see how price controls affect market outcomes, let's look once again at the market for ice cream. As we saw in Chapter 4, if ice cream is sold in a competitive market free of government regulation, the price of ice cream adjusts to balance supply and demand: At the equilibrium price, the quantity of ice cream that buyers want to buy exactly equals the quantity that sellers want to sell. To be concrete, suppose the equilibrium price is $3 per cone.

Not everyone may be happy with the outcome of this free-market process. Let's say the American Association of Ice-Cream Eaters complains that the $3 price is too high for everyone to enjoy a cone a day (their recommended diet). Meanwhile, the National Organization of Ice-Cream Makers complains that the $3 price—the result of "cutthroat competition"—is too low and is depressing the incomes of its members. Each of these groups lobbies the government to pass laws that alter the market outcome by directly controlling the price of an ice-cream cone.

Because buyers of any good always want a lower price while sellers want a higher price, the interests of the two groups conflict. If the Ice-Cream Eaters are successful in their lobbying, the government imposes a legal maximum on the price at which ice cream can be sold. Because the price is not allowed to rise above this level, the legislated maximum is called a **price ceiling**. By contrast, if the Ice-Cream Makers are successful, the government imposes a legal minimum on the price. Because the price cannot fall below this level, the legislated minimum is called a **price floor**. Let us consider the effects of these policies in turn.

price ceiling
a legal maximum on the price at which a good can be sold

price floor
a legal minimum on the price at which a good can be sold

How Price Ceilings Affect Market Outcomes

When the government, moved by the complaints and campaign contributions of the Ice-Cream Eaters, imposes a price ceiling on the market for ice cream, two outcomes are possible. In panel (a) of Figure 1, the government imposes a price ceiling of $4 per cone. In this case, because the price that balances supply and demand ($3) is below the ceiling, the price ceiling is *not binding*. Market forces naturally move the economy to the equilibrium, and the price ceiling has no effect on the price or the quantity sold.

Panel (b) of Figure 1 shows the other, more interesting, possibility. In this case, the government imposes a price ceiling of $2 per cone. Because the equilibrium price of $3 is above the price ceiling, the ceiling is a *binding constraint* on the market. The forces of supply and demand tend to move the price toward the equilibrium price, but when the market price hits the ceiling, it can, by law, rise no further. Thus, the market price equals the price ceiling. At this price, the quantity of ice cream demanded (125 cones in the figure) exceeds the quantity supplied (75 cones). There is a shortage of ice cream: 50 people who want to buy ice cream at the going price are unable to do so.

FIGURE 1

A Market with a
Price Ceiling

In panel (a), the government imposes a price ceiling of $4. Because the price ceiling is above the equilibrium price of $3, the price ceiling has no effect, and the market can reach the equilibrium of supply and demand. In this equilibrium, quantity supplied and quantity demanded both equal 100 cones. In panel (b), the government imposes a price ceiling of $2. Because the price ceiling is below the equilibrium price of $3, the market price equals $2. At this price, 125 cones are demanded and only 75 are supplied, so there is a shortage of 50 cones.

(a) A Price Ceiling That Is Not Binding

(b) A Price Ceiling That Is Binding

When a shortage of ice cream develops because of this price ceiling, some mechanism for rationing ice cream will naturally develop. The mechanism could be long lines: Buyers who are willing to arrive early and wait in line get a cone, but those unwilling to wait do not. Alternatively, sellers could ration ice cream according to their own personal biases, selling it only to friends, relatives, or members of their own racial or ethnic group. Notice that even though the price ceiling was motivated by a desire to help buyers of ice cream, not all buyers benefit from the policy. Some buyers do get to pay a lower price, although they may have to wait in line to do so, but other buyers cannot get any ice cream at all.

This example in the market for ice cream shows a general result: *When the government imposes a binding price ceiling on a competitive market, a shortage of the good arises, and sellers must ration the scarce goods among the large number of potential buyers.* The rationing mechanisms that develop under price ceilings are rarely desirable. Long lines are inefficient because they waste buyers' time. Discrimination according to seller bias is both inefficient (because the good does not necessarily go to the buyer who values it most highly) and potentially unfair. By contrast, the rationing mechanism in a free, competitive market is both efficient and impersonal. When the market for ice cream reaches its equilibrium, anyone who wants to pay the market price can get a cone. Free markets ration goods with prices.

CASE STUDY LINES AT THE GAS PUMP

As we discussed in the preceding chapter, in 1973 the Organization of Petroleum Exporting Countries (OPEC) raised the price of crude oil in world oil markets. Because crude oil is the major input used to make gasoline, the higher oil prices reduced the supply of gasoline. Long lines at gas stations became commonplace, and motorists often had to wait for hours to buy only a few gallons of gas.

What was responsible for the long gas lines? Most people blame OPEC. Surely, if OPEC had not raised the price of crude oil, the shortage of gasoline would not have occurred. Yet economists blame U.S. government regulations that limited the price oil companies could charge for gasoline.

Figure 2 shows what happened. As shown in panel (a), before OPEC raised the price of crude oil, the equilibrium price of gasoline, P_1, was below the price ceiling. The price regulation, therefore, had no effect. When the price of crude oil rose, however, the situation changed. The increase in the price of crude oil raised the cost of producing gasoline, and this reduced the supply of gasoline. As panel (b) shows, the supply curve shifted to the left from S_1 to S_2. In an unregulated market, this shift in supply would have raised the equilibrium price of gasoline from P_1 to P_2, and no shortage would have resulted. Instead, the price ceiling prevented the price from rising to the equilibrium level. At the price ceiling, producers were willing to sell Q_S, and consumers were willing to buy Q_D. Thus, the shift in supply caused a severe shortage at the regulated price.

2 **FIGURE**

The Market for Gasoline with a Price Ceiling

Panel (a) shows the gasoline market when the price ceiling is not binding because the equilibrium price, P_1, is below the ceiling. Panel (b) shows the gasoline market after an increase in the price of crude oil (an input into making gasoline) shifts the supply curve to the left from S_1 to S_2. In an unregulated market, the price would have risen from P_1 to P_2. The price ceiling, however, prevents this from happening. At the binding price ceiling, consumers are willing to buy Q_D, but producers of gasoline are willing to sell only Q_S. The difference between quantity demanded and quantity supplied, $Q_D - Q_S$, measures the gasoline shortage.

Eventually, the laws regulating the price of gasoline were repealed. Lawmakers came to understand that they were partly responsible for the many hours Americans lost waiting in line to buy gasoline. Today, when the price of crude oil changes, the price of gasoline can adjust to bring supply and demand into equilibrium. ●

CASE STUDY RENT CONTROL IN THE SHORT RUN AND THE LONG RUN

One common example of a price ceiling is rent control. In many cities, the local government places a ceiling on rents that landlords may charge their tenants. The goal of this policy is to help the poor by making housing more affordable. Economists often criticize rent control, arguing that it is a highly inefficient way to help the poor raise their standard of living. One economist called rent control "the best way to destroy a city, other than bombing."

The adverse effects of rent control are less apparent to the general population because these effects occur over many years. In the short run, landlords have a fixed number of apartments to rent, and they cannot adjust this number quickly as market conditions change. Moreover, the number of people searching for housing in a city may not be highly responsive to rents in the short run because people take time to adjust their housing arrangements. Therefore, the short-run supply and demand for housing are relatively inelastic.

Panel (a) of Figure 3 shows the short-run effects of rent control on the housing market. As with any binding price ceiling, rent control causes a shortage. Yet

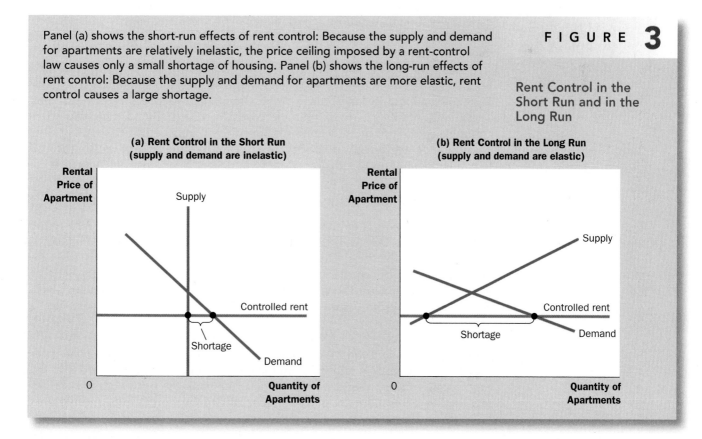

Panel (a) shows the short-run effects of rent control: Because the supply and demand for apartments are relatively inelastic, the price ceiling imposed by a rent-control law causes only a small shortage of housing. Panel (b) shows the long-run effects of rent control: Because the supply and demand for apartments are more elastic, rent control causes a large shortage.

FIGURE **3**

Rent Control in the Short Run and in the Long Run

(a) Rent Control in the Short Run (supply and demand are inelastic)

Rental Price of Apartment

Supply

Controlled rent

Shortage

Demand

0

Quantity of Apartments

(b) Rent Control in the Long Run (supply and demand are elastic)

Rental Price of Apartment

Supply

Controlled rent

Shortage

Demand

0

Quantity of Apartments

because supply and demand are inelastic in the short run, the initial shortage caused by rent control is small. The primary effect in the short run is to reduce rents.

The long-run story is very different because the buyers and sellers of rental housing respond more to market conditions as time passes. On the supply side, landlords respond to low rents by not building new apartments and by failing to maintain existing ones. On the demand side, low rents encourage people to find their own apartments (rather than living with their parents or sharing apartments with roommates) and induce more people to move into a city. Therefore, both supply and demand are more elastic in the long run.

Panel (b) of Figure 3 illustrates the housing market in the long run. When rent control depresses rents below the equilibrium level, the quantity of apartments supplied falls substantially, and the quantity of apartments demanded rises substantially. The result is a large shortage of housing.

In cities with rent control, landlords use various mechanisms to ration housing. Some landlords keep long waiting lists. Others give a preference to tenants without children. Still others discriminate on the basis of race. Sometimes apartments are allocated to those willing to offer under-the-table payments to building superintendents. In essence, these bribes bring the total price of an apartment (including the bribe) closer to the equilibrium price.

To understand fully the effects of rent control, we have to remember one of the *Ten Principles of Economics* from Chapter 1: People respond to incentives. In free markets, landlords try to keep their buildings clean and safe because desirable apartments command higher prices. By contrast, when rent control creates shortages and waiting lists, landlords lose their incentive to respond to tenants' concerns. Why should a landlord spend money to maintain and improve the property when people are waiting to get in as it is? In the end, tenants get lower rents, but they also get lower-quality housing.

Policymakers often react to the effects of rent control by imposing additional regulations. For example, there are laws that make racial discrimination in housing illegal and require landlords to provide minimally adequate living conditions. These laws, however, are difficult and costly to enforce. By contrast, when rent control is eliminated and a market for housing is regulated by the forces of competition, such laws are less necessary. In a free market, the price of housing adjusts to eliminate the shortages that give rise to undesirable landlord behavior. ●

HOW PRICE FLOORS AFFECT MARKET OUTCOMES

To examine the effects of another kind of government price control, let's return to the market for ice cream. Imagine now that the government is persuaded by the pleas of the National Organization of Ice-Cream Makers. In this case, the government might institute a price floor. Price floors, like price ceilings, are an attempt by the government to maintain prices at other than equilibrium levels. Whereas a price ceiling places a legal maximum on prices, a price floor places a legal minimum.

When the government imposes a price floor on the ice-cream market, two outcomes are possible. If the government imposes a price floor of $2 per cone when the equilibrium price is $3, we obtain the outcome in panel (a) of Figure 4. In this case, because the equilibrium price is above the floor, the price floor is not binding. Market forces naturally move the economy to the equilibrium, and the price floor has no effect.

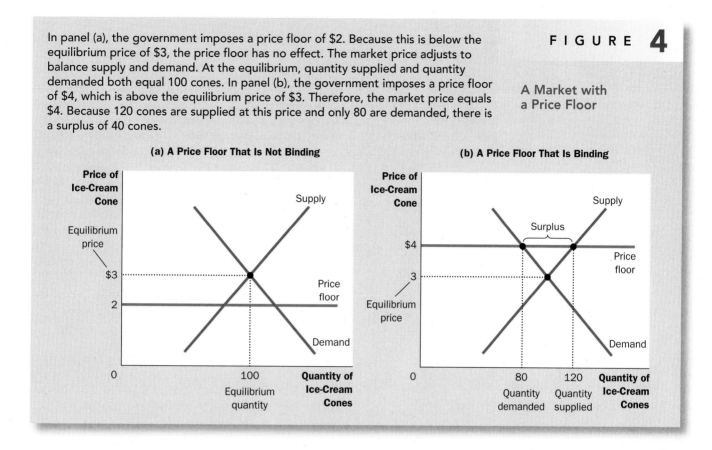

In panel (a), the government imposes a price floor of $2. Because this is below the equilibrium price of $3, the price floor has no effect. The market price adjusts to balance supply and demand. At the equilibrium, quantity supplied and quantity demanded both equal 100 cones. In panel (b), the government imposes a price floor of $4, which is above the equilibrium price of $3. Therefore, the market price equals $4. Because 120 cones are supplied at this price and only 80 are demanded, there is a surplus of 40 cones.

FIGURE 4

A Market with a Price Floor

(a) A Price Floor That Is Not Binding

(b) A Price Floor That Is Binding

Panel (b) of Figure 4 shows what happens when the government imposes a price floor of $4 per cone. In this case, because the equilibrium price of $3 is below the floor, the price floor is a binding constraint on the market. The forces of supply and demand tend to move the price toward the equilibrium price, but when the market price hits the floor, it can fall no further. The market price equals the price floor. At this floor, the quantity of ice cream supplied (120 cones) exceeds the quantity demanded (80 cones). Some people who want to sell ice cream at the going price are unable to. *Thus, a binding price floor causes a surplus.*

Just as the shortages resulting from price ceilings can lead to undesirable rationing mechanisms, so can the surpluses resulting from price floors. In the case of a price floor, some sellers are unable to sell all they want at the market price. The sellers who appeal to the personal biases of the buyers, perhaps due to racial or familial ties, are better able to sell their goods than those who do not. By contrast, in a free market, the price serves as the rationing mechanism, and sellers can sell all they want at the equilibrium price.

THE MINIMUM WAGE

An important example of a price floor is the minimum wage. Minimum-wage laws dictate the lowest price for labor that any employer may pay. The U.S. Congress first instituted a minimum wage with the Fair Labor Standards Act of 1938 to ensure workers a minimally adequate standard of living. In 2007, the minimum wage according to federal law was $5.15 per hour, and it was scheduled to increase to $7.25 by 2010. (Some states mandate minimum wages above the federal level.) Most European nations have minimum-wage laws as well; some, such as France and the United Kingdom, have significantly higher minimums than the United States.

To examine the effects of a minimum wage, we must consider the market for labor. Panel (a) of Figure 5 shows the labor market, which, like all markets, is subject to the forces of supply and demand. Workers determine the supply of labor, and firms determine the demand. If the government doesn't intervene, the wage normally adjusts to balance labor supply and labor demand.

Panel (b) of Figure 5 shows the labor market with a minimum wage. If the minimum wage is above the equilibrium level, as it is here, the quantity of labor supplied exceeds the quantity demanded. The result is unemployment. Thus, the minimum wage raises the incomes of those workers who have jobs, but it lowers the incomes of workers who cannot find jobs.

To fully understand the minimum wage, keep in mind that the economy contains not a single labor market but many labor markets for different types of workers. The impact of the minimum wage depends on the skill and experience of the worker. Workers with high skills and much experience are not affected because their equilibrium wages are well above the minimum. For these workers, the minimum wage is not binding.

The minimum wage has its greatest impact on the market for teenage labor. The equilibrium wages of teenagers are low because teenagers are among the least skilled and least experienced members of the labor force. In addition, teenagers are often willing to accept a lower wage in exchange for on-the-job training. (Some

5 F I G U R E

How the Minimum
Wage Affects the
Labor Market

Panel (a) shows a labor market in which the wage adjusts to balance labor supply and labor demand. Panel (b) shows the impact of a binding minimum wage. Because the minimum wage is a price floor, it causes a surplus: The quantity of labor supplied exceeds the quantity demanded. The result is unemployment.

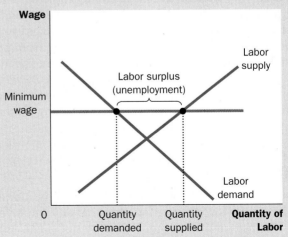

teenagers are willing to work as "interns" for no pay at all. Because internships pay nothing, however, the minimum wage does not apply to them. If it did, these jobs might not exist.) As a result, the minimum wage is more often binding for teenagers than for other members of the labor force.

Many economists have studied how minimum-wage laws affect the teenage labor market. These researchers compare the changes in the minimum wage over time with the changes in teenage employment. Although there is some debate about how much the minimum wage affects employment, the typical study finds that a 10 percent increase in the minimum wage depresses teenage employment between 1 and 3 percent. In interpreting this estimate, note that a 10 percent increase in the minimum wage does not raise the average wage of teenagers by 10 percent. A change in the law does not directly affect those teenagers who are already paid well above the minimum, and enforcement of minimum-wage laws is not perfect. Thus, the estimated drop in employment of 1 to 3 percent is significant.

In addition to altering the quantity of labor demanded, the minimum wage alters the quantity supplied. Because the minimum wage raises the wage that teenagers can earn, it increases the number of teenagers who choose to look for jobs. Studies have found that a higher minimum wage influences which teenagers are employed. When the minimum wage rises, some teenagers who are still attending school choose to drop out and take jobs. These new dropouts displace other teenagers who had already dropped out of school and who now become unemployed.

The minimum wage is a frequent topic of debate. Economists are about evenly divided on the issue. In a 2006 survey of PhD economists, 47 percent favored eliminating the minimum wage, while 14 percent would maintain it at its current level and 38 percent would increase it.

Advocates of the minimum wage view the policy as one way to raise the income of the working poor. They correctly point out that workers who earn the minimum wage can afford only a meager standard of living. In 2007, for instance, when the minimum wage was $5.15 per hour, two adults working 40 hours a week for every week of the year at minimum-wage jobs had a total annual income of only $21,424, which was less than half of the median family income. Many advocates of the minimum wage admit that it has some adverse effects, including unemployment, but they believe that these effects are small and that, all things considered, a higher minimum wage makes the poor better off.

Opponents of the minimum wage contend that it is not the best way to combat poverty. They note that a high minimum wage causes unemployment, encourages teenagers to drop out of school, and prevents some unskilled workers from getting the on-the-job training they need. Moreover, opponents of the minimum wage point out that it is a poorly targeted policy. Not all minimum-wage workers are heads of households trying to help their families escape poverty. In fact, fewer than a third of minimum-wage earners are in families with incomes below the poverty line. Many are teenagers from middle-class homes working at part-time jobs for extra spending money. ●

EVALUATING PRICE CONTROLS

One of the *Ten Principles of Economics* discussed in Chapter 1 is that markets are usually a good way to organize economic activity. This principle explains why economists usually oppose price ceilings and price floors. To economists, prices

In The News

President Chavez versus the Market

Venezuela's president has tried to replace market prices with his own.

Price Caps Ail Venezuelan Economy

By Peter Millard and Raul Gallegos

CARACAS, VENEZUELA—After 21 years in the milk business, Ismael Cárdenas Gil is throwing in the towel.

Mr. Cárdenas, who heads Alimentaria Internacional, can no longer make a profit selling imported powdered milk under government-imposed price controls. As a result, he has cut back his imports to "practically zero."

"The controls have been very harsh. The numbers don't work out to import milk and sell it here," Mr. Cárdenas says.

His plight is becoming more common in Venezuela, with President Hugo Chávez meddling in the economy to advance his populist-leftist agenda as companies selling price-regulated products watch their profits disappear. While government controls have slowed the growth of inflation, Venezuela's rate is still the highest in Latin America. The controls also have led to frequent product shortages and the emergence of a thriving black market. Some farmers and retailers are skirting the rules or have stopped selling certain goods altogether rather than sell them at a loss.

The problems facing Venezuelan businesses and consumers serve as a cautionary tale for the growing ranks of Latin American populists pushing for a heavy government hand in the economy.... Mr. Chávez is taking advantage of the country's massive oil-revenue windfall to fund a governing philosophy he has dubbed "socialism for the 21st century." His goal is to increase social spending and curb inflation through a mix of price caps, a fixed exchange rate and fixed interest rates.

But some Venezuelan businesses hurt by the price controls are beginning to balk. Last week, corn growers marched outside the presidential palace, protesting government controls they say have dried up demand for their corn. While the farmers are getting a

are not the outcome of some haphazard process. Prices, they contend, are the result of the millions of business and consumer decisions that lie behind the supply and demand curves. Prices have the crucial job of balancing supply and demand and, thereby, coordinating economic activity. When policymakers set prices by legal decree, they obscure the signals that normally guide the allocation of society's resources.

Another one of the *Ten Principles of Economics* is that governments can sometimes improve market outcomes. Indeed, policymakers are led to control prices because they view the market's outcome as unfair. Price controls are often aimed at helping the poor. For instance, rent-control laws try to make housing affordable for everyone, and minimum-wage laws try to help people escape poverty.

Yet price controls often hurt those they are trying to help. Rent control may keep rents low, but it also discourages landlords from maintaining their buildings and makes housing hard to find. Minimum-wage laws may raise the incomes of some workers, but they also cause other workers to be unemployed.

Helping those in need can be accomplished in ways other than controlling prices. For instance, the government can make housing more affordable by paying a fraction of the rent for poor families. Unlike rent control, such rent subsidies do not reduce the quantity of housing supplied and, therefore, do not lead to housing decent price, processors are refusing to buy the corn because they can't sell it at what they consider an acceptable markup. The country's largest food company, Alimentos Polar, has warned it may have to halt production of corn flour for such reasons. In early December, coffee producers challenged the new price ceilings, paralyzing deliveries and causing an acute coffee shortage for weeks.

As the world's fifth-largest oil exporter—the state-run oil company supplies about 15% of U.S. petroleum imports—Venezuela has amassed a hoard of cash that has allowed it to import goods and sell them at a loss through the state-run Mercal supermarket chain, subsidizing Mr. Chávez's pricing policies. Enforcement of price controls is being stepped up as Mr. Chávez readies a December re-election bid. [*Author's note:* Chavez was reelected to a new six-year term that began January 2007.]

The predominance of the state, Mr. Chávez says, aims to protect the poor majority from "greedy capitalists" and "speculators." He has threatened to expropriate plants of those who shut down operations, while government troops have seized stockpiled grain to stop shortages.

Mr. Cárdenas, the milk importer, has responded to the regulations by cutting his staff to a dozen employees, from 280 in 2001. He is using his office space to start a construction company and is looking to produce agricultural goods not included in the long list of price regulations. "We're not idle," he says. . . .

The coffee strike in December has been the most vocal so far. Roasters shut their plants after the government raised the price of green coffee that farmers sell to roasters by 100% while leaving processed-coffee prices unchanged. After weeks of protests, the government agreed to raise retail coffee prices by 60%. But Pedro Obediente, a retired university professor living in Caracas's hilly suburbs, says he is still looking for his favorite brand. "I haven't found Café El Peñón, which is what I like," he says, referring to one of the country's largest roasting companies.

Businesses increasingly are finding ways to get around the price caps, and some stores violate the price controls outright. Top cuts of beef can sell for 30% more than the government-set price in Caracas supermarkets. Some businesses have turned to selling more-expensive imported meat instead of the regulated local cuts; others refocus their efforts on producing goods that fall outside the regulations. Milk producers, for instance, have boosted their output of unregulated goods, such as yogurts and cheeses.

Source: *The Wall Street Journal*, February 15, 2006.

shortages. Similarly, wage subsidies raise the living standards of the working poor without discouraging firms from hiring them. An example of a wage subsidy is the *earned income tax credit*, a government program that supplements the incomes of low-wage workers.

Although these alternative policies are often better than price controls, they are not perfect. Rent and wage subsidies cost the government money and, therefore, require higher taxes. As we see in the next section, taxation has costs of its own.

QUICK QUIZ Define *price ceiling* and *price floor* and give an example of each. Which leads to a shortage? Which leads to a surplus? Why?

TAXES

All governments—from the federal government in Washington, D.C., to the local governments in small towns—use taxes to raise revenue for public projects, such as roads, schools, and national defense. Because taxes are such an important policy instrument, and because they affect our lives in many ways, we return to the study of taxes several times throughout this book. In this section, we begin our study of how taxes affect the economy.

To set the stage for our analysis, imagine that a local government decides to hold an annual ice-cream celebration—with a parade, fireworks, and speeches by town officials. To raise revenue to pay for the event, the town decides to place a $0.50 tax on the sale of ice-cream cones. When the plan is announced, our two lob-bying groups swing into action. The American Association of Ice-Cream Eaters claims that consumers of ice cream are having trouble making ends meet, and it argues that *sellers* of ice cream should pay the tax. The National Organization of Ice-Cream Makers claims that its members are struggling to survive in a competi-tive market, and it argues that *buyers* of ice cream should pay the tax. The town mayor, hoping to reach a compromise, suggests that half the tax be paid by the buyers and half be paid by the sellers.

To analyze these proposals, we need to address a simple but subtle question: When the government levies a tax on a good, who actually bears the burden of the tax? The people buying the good? The people selling the good? Or if buyers and sellers share the tax burden, what determines how the burden is divided? Can the government simply legislate the division of the burden, as the mayor is suggest-ing, or is the division determined by more fundamental market forces? The term **tax incidence** refers to how the burden of a tax is distributed among the various people who make up the economy. As we will see, some surprising lessons about tax incidence can be learned by applying the tools of supply and demand.

tax incidence
the manner in which the burden of a tax is shared among participants in a market

HOW TAXES ON SELLERS AFFECT MARKET OUTCOMES

We begin by considering a tax levied on sellers of a good. Suppose the local gov-ernment passes a law requiring sellers of ice-cream cones to send $0.50 to the gov-ernment for each cone they sell. How does this law affect the buyers and sellers of ice cream? To answer this question, we can follow the three steps in Chapter 4 for analyzing supply and demand: (1) We decide whether the law affects the supply curve or demand curve. (2) We decide which way the curve shifts. (3) We examine how the shift affects the equilibrium price and quantity.

Step One   The immediate impact of the tax is on the sellers of ice cream. Because the tax is not levied on buyers, the quantity of ice cream demanded at any given price is the same; thus, the demand curve does not change. By contrast, the tax on sellers makes the ice-cream business less profitable at any given price, so it shifts the supply curve.

Step Two   Because the tax on sellers raises the cost of producing and selling ice cream, it reduces the quantity supplied at every price. The supply curve shifts to the left (or, equivalently, upward).

We can, in this case, be precise about how much the curve shifts. For any mar-ket price of ice cream, the effective price to sellers—the amount they get to keep after paying the tax—is $0.50 lower. For example, if the market price of a cone happened to be $2.00, the effective price received by sellers would be $1.50. What-ever the market price, sellers will supply a quantity of ice cream as if the price were $0.50 lower than it is. Put differently, to induce sellers to supply any given quantity, the market price must now be $0.50 higher to compensate for the effect of the tax. Thus, as shown in Figure 6, the supply curve shifts *upward* from S_1 to S_2 by the exact size of the tax ($0.50).

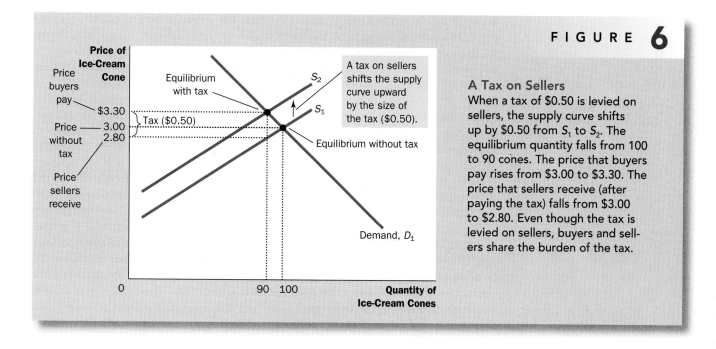

FIGURE **6**

A Tax on Sellers
When a tax of $0.50 is levied on sellers, the supply curve shifts up by $0.50 from S_1 to S_2. The equilibrium quantity falls from 100 to 90 cones. The price that buyers pay rises from $3.00 to $3.30. The price that sellers receive (after paying the tax) falls from $3.00 to $2.80. Even though the tax is levied on sellers, buyers and sellers share the burden of the tax.

Step Three   Having determined how the supply curve shifts, we can now compare the initial and the new equilibriums. The figure shows that the equilibrium price of ice cream rises from $3.00 to $3.30, and the equilibrium quantity falls from 100 to 90 cones. Because sellers sell less and buyers buy less in the new equilibrium, the tax reduces the size of the ice-cream market.

Implications   We can now return to the question of tax incidence: Who pays the tax? Although sellers send the entire tax to the government, buyers and sellers share the burden. Because the market price rises from $3.00 to $3.30 when the tax is introduced, buyers pay $0.30 more for each ice-cream cone than they did without the tax. Thus, the tax makes buyers worse off. Sellers get a higher price ($3.30) from buyers than they did previously, but the effective price after paying the tax falls from $3.00 before the tax to $2.80 with the tax ($3.30 − $0.50 = $2.80). Thus, the tax also makes sellers worse off.

To sum up, the analysis yields two lessons:

- Taxes discourage market activity. When a good is taxed, the quantity of the good sold is smaller in the new equilibrium.
- Buyers and sellers share the burden of taxes. In the new equilibrium, buyers pay more for the good, and sellers receive less.

How Taxes on Buyers Affect Market Outcomes

Now consider a tax levied on buyers of a good. Suppose that our local government passes a law requiring buyers of ice-cream cones to send $0.50 to the government for each ice-cream cone they buy. What are the effects of this law? Again, we apply our three steps.

Step One   The initial impact of the tax is on the demand for ice cream. The supply curve is not affected because, for any given price of ice cream, sellers have the same incentive to provide ice cream to the market. By contrast, buyers now have to pay a tax to the government (as well as the price to the sellers) whenever they buy ice cream. Thus, the tax shifts the demand curve for ice cream.

Step Two   We next determine the direction of the shift. Because the tax on buyers makes buying ice cream less attractive, buyers demand a smaller quantity of ice cream at every price. As a result, the demand curve shifts to the left (or, equivalently, downward), as shown in Figure 7.

Once again, we can be precise about the magnitude of the shift. Because of the $0.50 tax levied on buyers, the effective price to buyers is now $0.50 higher than the market price (whatever the market price happens to be). For example, if the market price of a cone happened to be $2.00, the effective price to buyers would be $2.50. Because buyers look at their total cost including the tax, they demand a quantity of ice cream as if the market price were $0.50 higher than it actually is. In other words, to induce buyers to demand any given quantity, the market price must now be $0.50 lower to make up for the effect of the tax. Thus, the tax shifts the demand curve *downward* from D_1 to D_2 by the exact size of the tax ($0.50).

Step Three   Having determined how the demand curve shifts, we can now see the effect of the tax by comparing the initial equilibrium and the new equilibrium. You can see in the figure that the equilibrium price of ice cream falls from $3.00 to $2.80 and the equilibrium quantity falls from 100 to 90 cones. Once again, the tax on ice cream reduces the size of the ice-cream market. And once again, buyers and sellers share the burden of the tax. Sellers get a lower price for their product; buyers pay a lower market price to sellers than they did previously, but the effective price (including the tax buyers have to pay) rises from $3.00 to $3.30.

7 **FIGURE**

A Tax on Buyers
When a tax of $0.50 is levied on buyers, the demand curve shifts down by $0.50 from D_1 to D_2. The equilibrium quantity falls from 100 to 90 cones. The price that sellers receive falls from $3.00 to $2.80. The price that buyers pay (including the tax) rises from $3.00 to $3.30. Even though the tax is levied on buyers, buyers and sellers share the burden of the tax.

Implications   If you compare Figures 6 and 7, you will notice a surprising conclusion: *Taxes levied on sellers and taxes levied on buyers are equivalent.* In both cases, the tax places a wedge between the price that buyers pay and the price that sellers receive. The wedge between the buyers' price and the sellers' price is the same, regardless of whether the tax is levied on buyers or sellers. In either case, the wedge shifts the relative position of the supply and demand curves. In the new equilibrium, buyers and sellers share the burden of the tax. The only difference between taxes on sellers and taxes on buyers is who sends the money to the government.

   The equivalence of these two taxes is easy to understand if we imagine that the government collects the $0.50 ice-cream tax in a bowl on the counter of each ice-cream store. When the government levies the tax on sellers, the seller is required to place $0.50 in the bowl after the sale of each cone. When the government levies the tax on buyers, the buyer is required to place $0.50 in the bowl every time a cone is bought. Whether the $0.50 goes directly from the buyer's pocket into the bowl, or indirectly from the buyer's pocket into the seller's hand and then into the bowl, does not matter. Once the market reaches its new equilibrium, buyers and sellers share the burden, regardless of how the tax is levied.

CASE STUDY   CAN CONGRESS DISTRIBUTE THE BURDEN OF A PAYROLL TAX?

If you have ever received a paycheck, you probably noticed that taxes were deducted from the amount you earned. One of these taxes is called FICA, an acronym for the Federal Insurance Contributions Act. The federal government uses the revenue from the FICA tax to pay for Social Security and Medicare, the income support and healthcare programs for the elderly. FICA is an example of a *payroll tax*, which is a tax on the wages that firms pay their workers. In 2008, the total FICA tax for the typical worker was 15.3 percent of earnings.

   Who do you think bears the burden of this payroll tax—firms or workers? When Congress passed this legislation, it tried to mandate a division of the tax burden. According to the law, half of the tax is paid by firms, and half is paid by workers. That is, half of the tax is paid out of firms' revenues, and half is deducted from workers' paychecks. The amount that shows up as a deduction on your pay stub is the worker contribution.

   Our analysis of tax incidence, however, shows that lawmakers cannot so easily dictate the distribution of a tax burden. To illustrate, we can analyze a payroll tax as merely a tax on a good, where the good is labor and the price is the wage. The key feature of the payroll tax is that it places a wedge between the wage that firms pay and the wage that workers receive. Figure 8 shows the outcome. When a payroll tax is enacted, the wage received by workers falls, and the wage paid by firms rises. In the end, workers and firms share the burden of the tax, much as the legislation requires. Yet this division of the tax burden between workers and firms has nothing to do with the legislated division: The division of the burden in Figure 8 is not necessarily fifty-fifty, and the same outcome would prevail if the law levied the entire tax on workers or if it levied the entire tax on firms.

   This example shows that the most basic lesson of tax incidence is often overlooked in public debate. Lawmakers can decide whether a tax comes from the buyer's pocket or from the seller's, but they cannot legislate the true burden of a tax. Rather, tax incidence depends on the forces of supply and demand. ●

8 F I G U R E

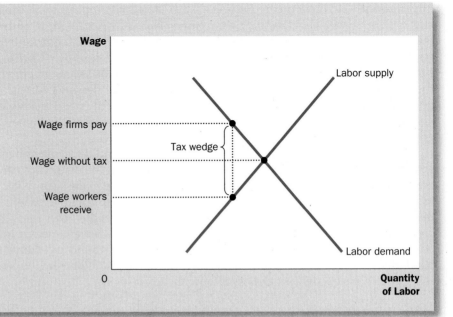

A Payroll Tax
A payroll tax places a wedge between the wage that workers receive and the wage that firms pay. Comparing wages with and without the tax, you can see that workers and firms share the tax burden. This division of the tax burden between workers and firms does not depend on whether the government levies the tax on workers, levies the tax on firms, or divides the tax equally between the two groups.

ELASTICITY AND TAX INCIDENCE

When a good is taxed, buyers and sellers of the good share the burden of the tax. But how exactly is the tax burden divided? Only rarely will it be shared equally. To see how the burden is divided, consider the impact of taxation in the two markets in Figure 9. In both cases, the figure shows the initial demand curve, the initial supply curve, and a tax that drives a wedge between the amount paid by buyers and the amount received by sellers. (Not drawn in either panel of the figure is the new supply or demand curve. Which curve shifts depends on whether the tax is levied on buyers or sellers. As we have seen, this is irrelevant for the incidence of the tax.) The difference in the two panels is the relative elasticity of supply and demand.

Panel (a) of Figure 9 shows a tax in a market with very elastic supply and relatively inelastic demand. That is, sellers are very responsive to changes in the price of the good (so the supply curve is relatively flat), whereas buyers are not very responsive (so the demand curve is relatively steep). When a tax is imposed on a market with these elasticities, the price received by sellers does not fall much, so sellers bear only a small burden. By contrast, the price paid by buyers rises substantially, indicating that buyers bear most of the burden of the tax.

Panel (b) of Figure 9 shows a tax in a market with relatively inelastic supply and very elastic demand. In this case, sellers are not very responsive to changes in the price (so the supply curve is steeper), whereas buyers are very responsive (so the demand curve is flatter). The figure shows that when a tax is imposed, the price paid by buyers does not rise much, but the price received by sellers falls substantially. Thus, sellers bear most of the burden of the tax.

The two panels of Figure 9 show a general lesson about how the burden of a tax is divided: *A tax burden falls more heavily on the side of the market that is less elastic.* Why is this true? In essence, the elasticity measures the willingness of buyers or

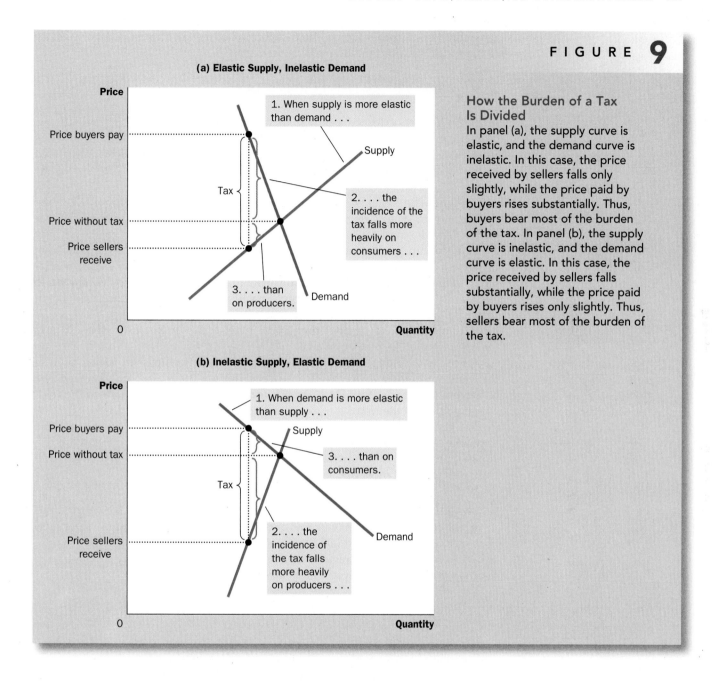

FIGURE 9

(a) Elastic Supply, Inelastic Demand

Price

1. When supply is more elastic than demand . . .

Supply

Price buyers pay

Tax

2. . . . the incidence of the tax falls more heavily on consumers . . .

Price without tax

Price sellers receive

3. . . . than on producers.

Demand

0   Quantity

(b) Inelastic Supply, Elastic Demand

Price

1. When demand is more elastic than supply . . .

Supply

Price buyers pay

Price without tax

3. . . . than on consumers.

Tax

Price sellers receive

2. . . . the incidence of the tax falls more heavily on producers . . .

Demand

0   Quantity

How the Burden of a Tax Is Divided

In panel (a), the supply curve is elastic, and the demand curve is inelastic. In this case, the price received by sellers falls only slightly, while the price paid by buyers rises substantially. Thus, buyers bear most of the burden of the tax. In panel (b), the supply curve is inelastic, and the demand curve is elastic. In this case, the price received by sellers falls substantially, while the price paid by buyers rises only slightly. Thus, sellers bear most of the burden of the tax.

sellers to leave the market when conditions become unfavorable. A small elasticity of demand means that buyers do not have good alternatives to consuming this particular good. A small elasticity of supply means that sellers do not have good alternatives to producing this particular good. When the good is taxed, the side of the market with fewer good alternatives is less willing to leave the market and must, therefore, bear more of the burden of the tax.

We can apply this logic to the payroll tax discussed in the previous case study. Most labor economists believe that the supply of labor is much less elastic than the demand. This means that workers, rather than firms, bear most of the burden of the payroll tax. In other words, the distribution of the tax burden is not at all close to the fifty-fifty split that lawmakers intended.

 WHO PAYS THE LUXURY TAX?

In 1990, Congress adopted a new luxury tax on items such as yachts, private airplanes, furs, jewelry, and expensive cars. The goal of the tax was to raise revenue from those who could most easily afford to pay. Because only the rich could afford to buy such extravagances, taxing luxuries seemed a logical way of taxing the rich.

Yet, when the forces of supply and demand took over, the outcome was quite different from what Congress intended. Consider, for example, the market for yachts. The demand for yachts is quite elastic. A millionaire can easily not buy a yacht; she can use the money to buy a bigger house, take a European vacation, or leave a larger bequest to her heirs. By contrast, the supply of yachts is relatively inelastic, at least in the short run. Yacht factories are not easily converted to alternative uses, and workers who build yachts are not eager to change careers in response to changing market conditions.

Our analysis makes a clear prediction in this case. With elastic demand and inelastic supply, the burden of a tax falls largely on the suppliers. That is, a tax on yachts places a burden largely on the firms and workers who build yachts because they end up getting a significantly lower price for their product. The workers, however, are not wealthy. Thus, the burden of a luxury tax falls more on the middle class than on the rich.

The mistaken assumptions about the incidence of the luxury tax quickly became apparent after the tax went into effect. Suppliers of luxuries made their congressional representatives well aware of the economic hardship they experienced, and Congress repealed most of the luxury tax in 1993. ●

"IF THIS BOAT WERE ANY MORE EXPENSIVE, WE'D BE PLAYING GOLF."

QUICK QUIZ In a supply-and-demand diagram, show how a tax on car buyers of $1,000 per car affects the quantity of cars sold and the price of cars. In another diagram, show how a tax on car sellers of $1,000 per car affects the quantity of cars sold and the price of cars. In both of your diagrams, show the change in the price paid by car buyers and the change in the price received by car sellers.

CONCLUSION

The economy is governed by two kinds of laws: the laws of supply and demand and the laws enacted by governments. In this chapter, we have begun to see how these laws interact. Price controls and taxes are common in various markets in the economy, and their effects are frequently debated in the press and among policymakers. Even a little bit of economic knowledge can go a long way toward understanding and evaluating these policies.

In subsequent chapters, we analyze many government policies in greater detail. We will examine the effects of taxation more fully, and we will consider a broader range of policies than we considered here. Yet the basic lessons of this chapter will not change: When analyzing government policies, supply and demand are the first and most useful tools of analysis.

SUMMARY

- A price ceiling is a legal maximum on the price of a good or service. An example is rent control. If the price ceiling is below the equilibrium price, the quantity demanded exceeds the quantity supplied. Because of the resulting shortage, sellers must in some way ration the good or service among buyers.

- A price floor is a legal minimum on the price of a good or service. An example is the minimum wage. If the price floor is above the equilibrium price, the quantity supplied exceeds the quantity demanded. Because of the resulting surplus, buyers' demands for the good or service must in some way be rationed among sellers.

- When the government levies a tax on a good, the equilibrium quantity of the good falls. That is, a tax on a market shrinks the size of the market.

- A tax on a good places a wedge between the price paid by buyers and the price received by sellers. When the market moves to the new equilibrium, buyers pay more for the good and sellers receive less for it. In this sense, buyers and sellers share the tax burden. The incidence of a tax (that is, the division of the tax burden) does not depend on whether the tax is levied on buyers or sellers.

- The incidence of a tax depends on the price elasticities of supply and demand. Most of the burden falls on the side of the market that is less elastic because that side of the market can respond less easily to the tax by changing the quantity bought or sold.

KEY CONCEPTS

price ceiling, *p. 114*   price floor, *p. 114*   tax incidence, *p. 124*

QUESTIONS FOR REVIEW

1. Give an example of a price ceiling and an example of a price floor.
2. Which causes a shortage of a good—a price ceiling or a price floor? Justify your answer with a graph.
3. What mechanisms allocate resources when the price of a good is not allowed to bring supply and demand into equilibrium?
4. Explain why economists usually oppose controls on prices.
5. Suppose the government removes a tax on buyers of a good and levies a tax of the same size on sellers of the good. How does this change in tax policy affect the price that buyers pay sellers for this good, the amount buyers are out of pocket including the tax, the amount sellers receive net of the tax, and the quantity of the good sold?
6. How does a tax on a good affect the price paid by buyers, the price received by sellers, and the quantity sold?
7. What determines how the burden of a tax is divided between buyers and sellers? Why?

PROBLEMS AND APPLICATIONS

1. Lovers of classical music persuade Congress to impose a price ceiling of $40 per concert ticket. As a result of this policy, do more or fewer people attend classical music concerts?

2. The government has decided that the free-market price of cheese is too low.
   a. Suppose the government imposes a binding price floor in the cheese market. Draw a supply-and-demand diagram to show the effect of this policy on the price of cheese and the quantity of cheese sold. Is there a shortage or surplus of cheese?
   b. Farmers complain that the price floor has reduced their total revenue. Is this possible? Explain.
   c. In response to farmers' complaints, the government agrees to purchase all the surplus cheese at the price floor. Compared to the basic price floor, who benefits from this new policy? Who loses?

3. A recent study found that the demand and supply schedules for Frisbees are as follows:

Price per Frisbee	Quantity Demanded	Quantity Supplied
$11	1 million Frisbees	15 million Frisbees
10	2	12
9	4	9
8	6	6
7	8	3
6	10	1

   a. What are the equilibrium price and quantity of Frisbees?
   b. Frisbee manufacturers persuade the government that Frisbee production improves scientists' understanding of aerodynamics and thus is important for national security. A concerned Congress votes to impose a price floor $2 above the equilibrium price. What is the new market price? How many Frisbees are sold?
   c. Irate college students march on Washington and demand a reduction in the price of Frisbees. An even more concerned Congress votes to repeal the price floor and impose a price ceiling $1 below the former price floor. What is the new market price? How many Frisbees are sold?

4. Suppose the federal government requires beer drinkers to pay a $2 tax on each case of beer purchased. (In fact, both the federal and state governments impose beer taxes of some sort.)
   a. Draw a supply-and-demand diagram of the market for beer without the tax. Show the price paid by consumers, the price received by producers, and the quantity of beer sold. What is the difference between the price paid by consumers and the price received by producers?
   b. Now draw a supply-and-demand diagram for the beer market with the tax. Show the price paid by consumers, the price received by producers, and the quantity of beer sold. What is the difference between the price paid by consumers and the price received by producers? Has the quantity of beer sold increased or decreased?

5. A senator wants to raise tax revenue and make workers better off. A staff member proposes raising the payroll tax paid by firms and using part of the extra revenue to reduce the payroll tax paid by workers. Would this accomplish the senator's goal? Explain.

6. If the government places a $500 tax on luxury cars, will the price paid by consumers rise by more than $500, less than $500, or exactly $500? Explain.

7. Congress and the president decide that the United States should reduce air pollution by reducing its use of gasoline. They impose a $0.50 tax for each gallon of gasoline sold.
   a. Should they impose this tax on producers or consumers? Explain carefully using a supply-and-demand diagram.
   b. If the demand for gasoline were more elastic, would this tax be more effective or less effective in reducing the quantity of gasoline consumed? Explain with both words and a diagram.
   c. Are consumers of gasoline helped or hurt by this tax? Why?
   d. Are workers in the oil industry helped or hurt by this tax? Why?

8. A case study in this chapter discusses the federal minimum-wage law.

a. Suppose the minimum wage is above the equilibrium wage in the market for unskilled labor. Using a supply-and-demand diagram of the market for unskilled labor, show the market wage, the number of workers who are employed, and the number of workers who are unemployed. Also show the total wage payments to unskilled workers.

b. Now suppose the secretary of labor proposes an increase in the minimum wage. What effect would this increase have on employment? Does the change in employment depend on the elasticity of demand, the elasticity of supply, both elasticities, or neither?

c. What effect would this increase in the minimum wage have on unemployment? Does the change in unemployment depend on the elasticity of demand, the elasticity of supply, both elasticities, or neither?

d. If the demand for unskilled labor were inelastic, would the proposed increase in the minimum wage raise or lower total wage payments to unskilled workers? Would your answer change if the demand for unskilled labor were elastic?

9. Consider the following policies, each of which is aimed at reducing violent crime by reducing the use of guns. Illustrate each of these proposed policies in a supply-and-demand diagram of the gun market.
   a. a tax on gun buyers
   b. a tax on gun sellers
   c. a price floor on guns
   d. a tax on ammunition

10. In 2007, Rod Blagojevich, the governor of Illinois, proposed a 3 percent payroll tax to finance some state health programs. The proposed legislation provided that the payroll tax "shall not be withheld from wages paid to employees or otherwise be collected from employees or reduce the compensation paid to employees." What do you think was the intent of this language? Would the bill in fact have accomplished this objective?

11. The U.S. government administers two programs that affect the market for cigarettes. Media campaigns and labeling requirements are aimed at making the public aware of the dangers of cigarette smoking. At the same time, the Department of Agriculture maintains a price-support program for tobacco farmers, which raises the price of tobacco above the equilibrium price.
   a. How do these two programs affect cigarette consumption? Use a graph of the cigarette market in your answer.
   b. What is the combined effect of these two programs on the price of cigarettes?
   c. Cigarettes are also heavily taxed. What effect does this tax have on cigarette consumption?

12. At Fenway Park, home of the Boston Red Sox, seating is limited to 34,000. Hence, the number of tickets issued is fixed at that figure. (Assume that all seats are equally desirable and are sold at the same price.) Seeing a golden opportunity to raise revenue, the City of Boston levies a per ticket tax of $5 to be paid by the ticket buyer. Boston sports fans, a famously civic-minded lot, dutifully send in the $5 per ticket. Draw a well-labeled graph showing the impact of the tax. On whom does the tax burden fall—the team's owners, the fans, or both? Why?

13. A subsidy is the opposite of a tax. With a $0.50 tax on the buyers of ice-cream cones, the government collects $0.50 for each cone purchased; with a $0.50 subsidy for the buyers of ice-cream cones, the government pays buyers $0.50 for each cone purchased.
   a. Show the effect of a $0.50 per cone subsidy on the demand curve for ice-cream cones, the effective price paid by consumers, the effective price received by sellers, and the quantity of cones sold.
   b. Do consumers gain or lose from this policy? Do producers gain or lose? Does the government gain or lose?

14. In the spring of 2008, Senators John McCain and Hillary Clinton (who were then running for President) proposed a temporary elimination of the federal gasoline tax, effective only during the summer of 2008, in order to help consumers deal with high gasoline prices.
   a. During the summer, when gasoline demand is high because of vacation driving, gasoline refiners are operating near full capacity. What does this fact suggest about the price elasticity of supply?
   b. In light of your answer to (a), who do you predict would benefit from the temporary gas tax holiday?

PART III

Markets and Welfare

Consumers, Producers, and the Efficiency of Markets

When consumers go to grocery stores to buy their turkeys for Thanksgiving dinner, they may be disappointed that the price of turkey is as high as it is. At the same time, when farmers bring to market the turkeys they have raised, they wish the price of turkey were even higher. These views are not surprising: Buyers always want to pay less, and sellers always want to be paid more. But is there a "right price" for turkey from the standpoint of society as a whole?

In previous chapters, we saw how, in market economies, the forces of supply and demand determine the prices of goods and services and the quantities sold. So far, however, we have described the way markets allocate scarce resources without directly addressing the question of whether these market allocations are desirable. In other words, our analysis has been *positive* (what is) rather than *normative* (what should be). We know that the price of turkey adjusts to ensure that the quantity of turkey supplied equals the quantity of turkey demanded. But at this equilibrium, is the quantity of turkey produced and consumed too small, too large, or just right?

In this chapter, we take up the topic of **welfare economics**, the study of how the allocation of resources affects economic well-being. We begin by examining

welfare economics
the study of how the allocation of resources affects economic well-being

the benefits that buyers and sellers receive from taking part in a market. We then examine how society can make these benefits as large as possible. This analysis leads to a profound conclusion: The equilibrium of supply and demand in a market maximizes the total benefits received by buyers and sellers.

As you may recall from Chapter 1, one of the *Ten Principles of Economics* is that markets are usually a good way to organize economic activity. The study of welfare economics explains this principle more fully. It also answers our question about the right price of turkey: The price that balances the supply and demand for turkey is, in a particular sense, the best one because it maximizes the total welfare of turkey consumers and turkey producers. No consumer or producer of turkeys aims to achieve this goal, but their joint action directed by market prices moves them toward a welfare-maximizing outcome, as if led by an invisible hand.

CONSUMER SURPLUS

We begin our study of welfare economics by looking at the benefits buyers receive from participating in a market.

WILLINGNESS TO PAY

willingness to pay
the maximum amount that a buyer will pay for a good

Imagine that you own a mint-condition recording of Elvis Presley's first album. Because you are not an Elvis Presley fan, you decide to sell it. One way to do so is to hold an auction.

Four Elvis fans show up for your auction: John, Paul, George, and Ringo. Each of them would like to own the album, but there is a limit to the amount that each is willing to pay for it. Table 1 shows the maximum price that each of the four possible buyers would pay. Each buyer's maximum is called his **willingness to pay**, and it measures how much that buyer values the good. Each buyer would be eager to buy the album at a price less than his willingness to pay, and he would refuse to buy the album at a price greater than his willingness to pay. At a price equal to his willingness to pay, the buyer would be indifferent about buying the good: If the price is exactly the same as the value he places on the album, he would be equally happy buying it or keeping his money.

To sell your album, you begin the bidding at a low price, say, $10. Because all four buyers are willing to pay much more, the price rises quickly. The bidding stops when John bids $80 (or slightly more). At this point, Paul, George, and Ringo have dropped out of the bidding because they are unwilling to bid any more than $80. John pays you $80 and gets the album. Note that the album has gone to the buyer who values the album most highly.

1 TABLE

Four Possible Buyers' Willingness to Pay

Buyer	Willingness to Pay
John	$100
Paul	80
George	70
Ringo	50

What benefit does John receive from buying the Elvis Presley album? In a sense, John has found a real bargain: He is willing to pay $100 for the album but pays only $80 for it. We say that John receives *consumer surplus* of $20. **Consumer surplus** is the amount a buyer is willing to pay for a good minus the amount the buyer actually pays for it.

Consumer surplus measures the benefit buyers receive from participating in a market. In this example, John receives a $20 benefit from participating in the auction because he pays only $80 for a good he values at $100. Paul, George, and Ringo get no consumer surplus from participating in the auction because they left without the album and without paying anything.

Now consider a somewhat different example. Suppose that you had two identical Elvis Presley albums to sell. Again, you auction them off to the four possible buyers. To keep things simple, we assume that both albums are to be sold for the same price and that no buyer is interested in buying more than one album. Therefore, the price rises until two buyers are left.

In this case, the bidding stops when John and Paul bid $70 (or slightly higher). At this price, John and Paul are each happy to buy an album, and George and Ringo are not willing to bid any higher. John and Paul each receive consumer surplus equal to his willingness to pay minus the price. John's consumer surplus is $30, and Paul's is $10. John's consumer surplus is higher now than in the previous example because he gets the same album but pays less for it. The total consumer surplus in the market is $40.

> **consumer surplus**
> the amount a buyer is willing to pay for a good minus the amount the buyer actually pays for it

USING THE DEMAND CURVE TO MEASURE CONSUMER SURPLUS

Consumer surplus is closely related to the demand curve for a product. To see how they are related, let's continue our example and consider the demand curve for this rare Elvis Presley album.

We begin by using the willingness to pay of the four possible buyers to find the demand schedule for the album. The table in Figure 1 shows the demand schedule that corresponds to Table 1. If the price is above $100, the quantity demanded in the market is 0 because no buyer is willing to pay that much. If the price is between $80 and $100, the quantity demanded is 1 because only John is willing to pay such a high price. If the price is between $70 and $80, the quantity demanded is 2 because both John and Paul are willing to pay the price. We can continue this analysis for other prices as well. In this way, the demand schedule is derived from the willingness to pay of the four possible buyers.

The graph in Figure 1 shows the demand curve that corresponds to this demand schedule. Note the relationship between the height of the demand curve and the buyers' willingness to pay. At any quantity, the price given by the demand curve shows the willingness to pay of the *marginal* buyer, the buyer who would leave the market first if the price were any higher. At a quantity of 4 albums, for instance, the demand curve has a height of $50, the price that Ringo (the marginal buyer) is willing to pay for an album. At a quantity of 3 albums, the demand curve has a height of $70, the price that George (who is now the marginal buyer) is willing to pay.

Because the demand curve reflects buyers' willingness to pay, we can also use it to measure consumer surplus. Figure 2 uses the demand curve to compute consumer surplus in our two examples. In panel (a), the price is $80 (or slightly

1 FIGURE

The table shows the demand schedule for the buyers in Table 1. The graph shows the corresponding demand curve. Note that the height of the demand curve reflects buyers' willingness to pay.

The Demand Schedule and the Demand Curve

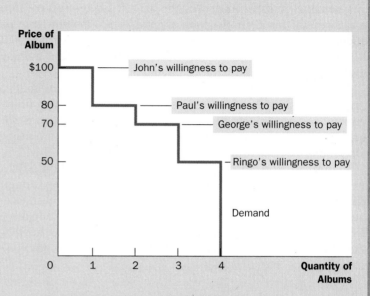

Price	Buyers	Quantity Demanded
More than $100	None	0
$80 to $100	John	1
$70 to $80	John, Paul	2
$50 to $70	John, Paul, George	3
$50 or less	John, Paul, George, Ringo	4

above), and the quantity demanded is 1. Note that the area above the price and below the demand curve equals $20. This amount is exactly the consumer surplus we computed earlier when only 1 album is sold.

Panel (b) of Figure 2 shows consumer surplus when the price is $70 (or slightly above). In this case, the area above the price and below the demand curve equals the total area of the two rectangles: John's consumer surplus at this price is $30 and Paul's is $10. This area equals a total of $40. Once again, this amount is the consumer surplus we computed earlier.

The lesson from this example holds for all demand curves: *The area below the demand curve and above the price measures the consumer surplus in a market.* This is true because the height of the demand curve measures the value buyers place on the good, as measured by their willingness to pay for it. The difference between this willingness to pay and the market price is each buyer's consumer surplus. Thus, the total area below the demand curve and above the price is the sum of the consumer surplus of all buyers in the market for a good or service.

HOW A LOWER PRICE RAISES CONSUMER SURPLUS

Because buyers always want to pay less for the goods they buy, a lower price makes buyers of a good better off. But how much does buyers' well-being rise in response to a lower price? We can use the concept of consumer surplus to answer this question precisely.

Figure 3 shows a typical demand curve. You may notice that this curve gradually slopes downward instead of taking discrete steps as in the previous two

In panel (a), the price of the good is $80, and the consumer surplus is $20. In panel (b), the price of the good is $70, and the consumer surplus is $40.

FIGURE **2**

Measuring Consumer Surplus with the Demand Curve

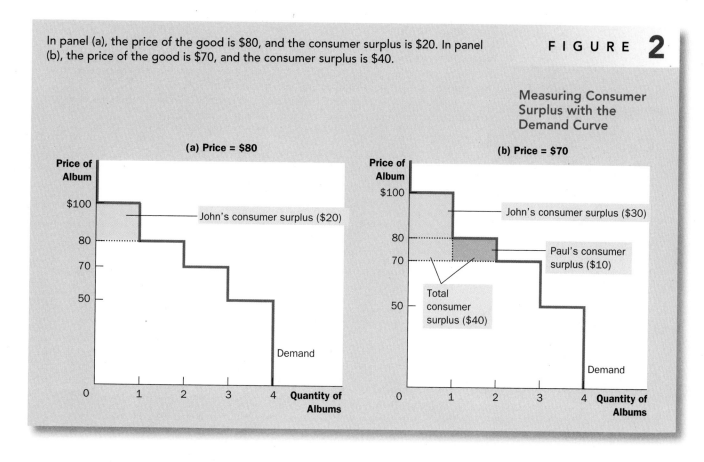

figures. In a market with many buyers, the resulting steps from each buyer dropping out are so small that they form, in essence, a smooth curve. Although this curve has a different shape, the ideas we have just developed still apply: Consumer surplus is the area above the price and below the demand curve. In panel (a), consumer surplus at a price of P_1 is the area of triangle ABC.

Now suppose that the price falls from P_1 to P_2, as shown in panel (b). The consumer surplus now equals area ADF. The increase in consumer surplus attributable to the lower price is the area BCFD.

This increase in consumer surplus is composed of two parts. First, those buyers who were already buying Q_1 of the good at the higher price P_1 are better off because they now pay less. The increase in consumer surplus of existing buyers is the reduction in the amount they pay; it equals the area of the rectangle BCED. Second, some new buyers enter the market because they are willing to buy the good at the lower price. As a result, the quantity demanded in the market increases from Q_1 to Q_2. The consumer surplus these newcomers receive is the area of the triangle CEF.

WHAT DOES CONSUMER SURPLUS MEASURE?

Our goal in developing the concept of consumer surplus is to make judgments about the desirability of market outcomes. Now that you have seen what consumer surplus is, let's consider whether it is a good measure of economic well-being.

3 F I G U R E

How the Price Affects Consumer Surplus

In panel (a), the price is P_1, the quantity demanded is Q_1, and consumer surplus equals the area of the triangle ABC. When the price falls from P_1 to P_2, as in panel (b), the quantity demanded rises from Q_1 to Q_2, and the consumer surplus rises to the area of the triangle ADF. The increase in consumer surplus (area BCFD) occurs in part because existing consumers now pay less (area BCED) and in part because new consumers enter the market at the lower price (area CEF).

(a) Consumer Surplus at Price P_1

(b) Consumer Surplus at Price P_2

Imagine that you are a policymaker trying to design a good economic system. Would you care about the amount of consumer surplus? Consumer surplus, the amount that buyers are willing to pay for a good minus the amount they actually pay for it, measures the benefit that buyers receive from a good *as the buyers themselves perceive it*. Thus, consumer surplus is a good measure of economic well-being if policymakers want to respect the preferences of buyers.

In some circumstances, policymakers might choose not to care about consumer surplus because they do not respect the preferences that drive buyer behavior. For example, drug addicts are willing to pay a high price for heroin. Yet we would not say that addicts get a large benefit from being able to buy heroin at a low price (even though addicts might say they do). From the standpoint of society, willingness to pay in this instance is not a good measure of the buyers' benefit, and consumer surplus is not a good measure of economic well-being, because addicts are not looking after their own best interests.

In most markets, however, consumer surplus does reflect economic well-being. Economists normally assume that buyers are rational when they make decisions. Rational people do the best they can to achieve their objectives, given their opportunities. Economists also normally assume that people's preferences should be respected. In this case, consumers are the best judges of how much benefit they receive from the goods they buy.

QUICK QUIZ Draw a demand curve for turkey. In your diagram, show a price of turkey and the consumer surplus at that price. Explain in words what this consumer surplus measures.

PRODUCER SURPLUS

We now turn to the other side of the market and consider the benefits sellers receive from participating in a market. As you will see, our analysis of sellers' welfare is similar to our analysis of buyers' welfare.

Cost and the Willingness to Sell

Imagine now that you are a homeowner and you want to get your house painted. You turn to four sellers of painting services: Mary, Frida, Georgia, and Grandma. Each painter is willing to do the work for you if the price is right. You decide to take bids from the four painters and auction off the job to the painter who will do the work for the lowest price.

Each painter is willing to take the job if the price she would receive exceeds her cost of doing the work. Here the term **cost** should be interpreted as the painters' opportunity cost: It includes the painters' out-of-pocket expenses (for paint, brushes, and so on) as well as the value that the painters place on their own time. Table 2 shows each painter's cost. Because a painter's cost is the lowest price she would accept for her work, cost is a measure of her willingness to sell her services. Each painter would be eager to sell her services at a price greater than her cost, and she would refuse to sell her services at a price less than her cost. At a price exactly equal to her cost, she would be indifferent about selling her services: She would be equally happy getting the job or using her time and energy for another purpose.

When you take bids from the painters, the price might start high, but it quickly falls as the painters compete for the job. Once Grandma has bid $600 (or slightly less), she is the sole remaining bidder. Grandma is happy to do the job for this price because her cost is only $500. Mary, Frida, and Georgia are unwilling to do the job for less than $600. Note that the job goes to the painter who can do the work at the lowest cost.

What benefit does Grandma receive from getting the job? Because she is willing to do the work for $500 but gets $600 for doing it, we say that she receives *producer surplus* of $100. **Producer surplus** is the amount a seller is paid minus the cost of production. Producer surplus measures the benefit sellers receive from participating in a market.

Now consider a somewhat different example. Suppose that you have two houses that need painting. Again, you auction off the jobs to the four painters. To keep things simple, let's assume that no painter is able to paint both houses and that you will pay the same amount to paint each house. Therefore, the price falls until two painters are left.

cost
the value of everything a seller must give up to produce a good

producer surplus
the amount a seller is paid for a good minus the seller's cost of providing it

Seller	Cost
Mary	$900
Frida	800
Georgia	600
Grandma	500

TABLE **2**

The Costs of Four Possible Sellers

In this case, the bidding stops when Georgia and Grandma each offer to do the job for a price of $800 (or slightly less). Georgia and Grandma are willing to do the work at this price, while Mary and Frida are not willing to bid a lower price. At a price of $800, Grandma receives producer surplus of $300, and Georgia receives producer surplus of $200. The total producer surplus in the market is $500.

USING THE SUPPLY CURVE TO MEASURE PRODUCER SURPLUS

Just as consumer surplus is closely related to the demand curve, producer surplus is closely related to the supply curve. To see how, let's continue our example.

We begin by using the costs of the four painters to find the supply schedule for painting services. The table in Figure 4 shows the supply schedule that corresponds to the costs in Table 2. If the price is below $500, none of the four painters is willing to do the job, so the quantity supplied is zero. If the price is between $500 and $600, only Grandma is willing to do the job, so the quantity supplied is 1. If the price is between $600 and $800, Grandma and Georgia are willing to do the job, so the quantity supplied is 2, and so on. Thus, the supply schedule is derived from the costs of the four painters.

The graph in Figure 4 shows the supply curve that corresponds to this supply schedule. Note that the height of the supply curve is related to the sellers' costs. At any quantity, the price given by the supply curve shows the cost of the *marginal seller*, the seller who would leave the market first if the price were any lower. At a quantity of 4 houses, for instance, the supply curve has a height of $900, the cost that Mary (the marginal seller) incurs to provide her painting services. At a quan-

4 FIGURE

The table shows the supply schedule for the sellers in Table 2. The graph shows the corresponding supply curve. Note that the height of the supply curve reflects sellers' costs.

The Supply Schedule and the Supply Curve

Price	Sellers	Quantity Supplied
$900 or more	Mary, Frida, Georgia, Grandma	4
$800 to $900	Frida, Georgia, Grandma	3
$600 to $800	Georgia, Grandma	2
$500 to $600	Grandma	1
Less than $500	None	0

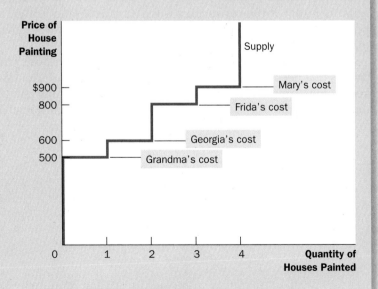

tity of 3 houses, the supply curve has a height of $800, the cost that Frida (who is now the marginal seller) incurs.

Because the supply curve reflects sellers' costs, we can use it to measure producer surplus. Figure 5 uses the supply curve to compute producer surplus in our two examples. In panel (a), we assume that the price is $600. In this case, the quantity supplied is 1. Note that the area below the price and above the supply curve equals $100. This amount is exactly the producer surplus we computed earlier for Grandma.

Panel (b) of Figure 5 shows producer surplus at a price of $800. In this case, the area below the price and above the supply curve equals the total area of the two rectangles. This area equals $500, the producer surplus we computed earlier for Georgia and Grandma when two houses needed painting.

The lesson from this example applies to all supply curves: *The area below the price and above the supply curve measures the producer surplus in a market.* The logic is straightforward: The height of the supply curve measures sellers' costs, and the difference between the price and the cost of production is each seller's producer surplus. Thus, the total area is the sum of the producer surplus of all sellers.

HOW A HIGHER PRICE RAISES PRODUCER SURPLUS

You will not be surprised to hear that sellers always want to receive a higher price for the goods they sell. But how much does sellers' well-being rise in response to

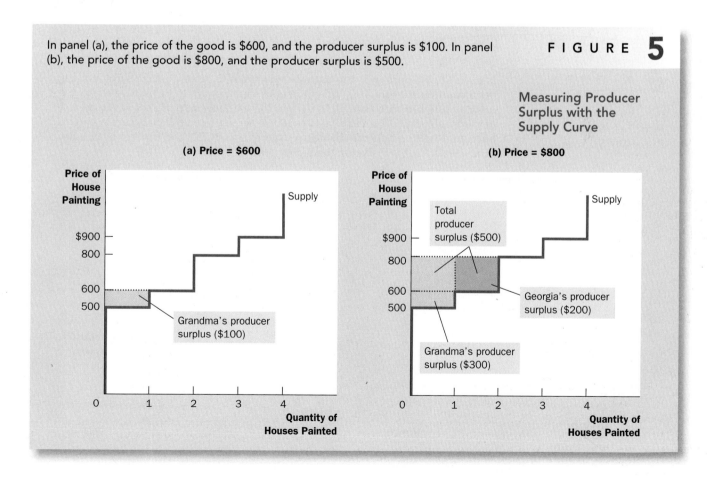

In panel (a), the price of the good is $600, and the producer surplus is $100. In panel (b), the price of the good is $800, and the producer surplus is $500.

FIGURE 5

Measuring Producer Surplus with the Supply Curve

a higher price? The concept of producer surplus offers a precise answer to this question.

Figure 6 shows a typical upward-sloping supply curve that would arise in a market with many sellers. Although this supply curve differs in shape from the previous figure, we measure producer surplus in the same way: Producer surplus is the area below the price and above the supply curve. In panel (a), the price is P_1, and producer surplus is the area of triangle ABC.

Panel (b) shows what happens when the price rises from P_1 to P_2. Producer surplus now equals area ADF. This increase in producer surplus has two parts. First, those sellers who were already selling Q_1 of the good at the lower price P_1 are better off because they now get more for what they sell. The increase in producer surplus for existing sellers equals the area of the rectangle BCED. Second, some new sellers enter the market because they are willing to produce the good at the higher price, resulting in an increase in the quantity supplied from Q_1 to Q_2. The producer surplus of these newcomers is the area of the triangle CEF.

As this analysis shows, we use producer surplus to measure the well-being of sellers in much the same way as we use consumer surplus to measure the well-being of buyers. Because these two measures of economic welfare are so similar, it is natural to use them together. And indeed, that is exactly what we do in the next section.

QUICK QUIZ   Draw a supply curve for turkey. In your diagram, show a price of turkey and the producer surplus at that price. Explain in words what this producer surplus measures.

6 **F I G U R E**

How the Price Affects Producer Surplus

In panel (a), the price is P_1, the quantity supplied is Q_1, and producer surplus equals the area of the triangle ABC. When the price rises from P_1 to P_2, as in panel (b), the quantity supplied rises from Q_1 to Q_2, and the producer surplus rises to the area of the triangle ADF. The increase in producer surplus (area BCFD) occurs in part because existing producers now receive more (area BCED) and in part because new producers enter the market at the higher price (area CEF).

(a) Producer Surplus at Price P_1

(b) Producer Surplus at Price P_2

MARKET EFFICIENCY

Consumer surplus and producer surplus are the basic tools that economists use to study the welfare of buyers and sellers in a market. These tools can help us address a fundamental economic question: Is the allocation of resources determined by free markets desirable?

THE BENEVOLENT SOCIAL PLANNER

To evaluate market outcomes, we introduce into our analysis a new, hypothetical character called the benevolent social planner. The benevolent social planner is an all-knowing, all-powerful, well-intentioned dictator. The planner wants to maximize the economic well-being of everyone in society. What should this planner do? Should he just leave buyers and sellers at the equilibrium that they reach naturally on their own? Or can he increase economic well-being by altering the market outcome in some way?

To answer this question, the planner must first decide how to measure the economic well-being of a society. One possible measure is the sum of consumer and producer surplus, which we call *total surplus*. Consumer surplus is the benefit that buyers receive from participating in a market, and producer surplus is the benefit that sellers receive. It is therefore natural to use total surplus as a measure of society's economic well-being.

To better understand this measure of economic well-being, recall how we measure consumer and producer surplus. We define consumer surplus as

Consumer surplus = Value to buyers − Amount paid by buyers.

Similarly, we define producer surplus as

Producer surplus = Amount received by sellers − Cost to sellers.

When we add consumer and producer surplus together, we obtain

Total surplus = (Value to buyers − Amount paid by buyers)
+ (Amount received by sellers − Cost to sellers).

The amount paid by buyers equals the amount received by sellers, so the middle two terms in this expression cancel each other. As a result, we can write total surplus as

Total surplus = Value to buyers − Cost to sellers.

Total surplus in a market is the total value to buyers of the goods, as measured by their willingness to pay, minus the total cost to sellers of providing those goods.

If an allocation of resources maximizes total surplus, we say that the allocation exhibits **efficiency**. If an allocation is not efficient, then some of the potential gains from trade among buyers and sellers are not being realized. For example, an allocation is inefficient if a good is not being produced by the sellers with lowest cost. In this case, moving production from a high-cost producer to a low-cost producer will lower the total cost to sellers and raise total surplus. Similarly, an

efficiency
the property of a resource allocation of maximizing the total surplus received by all members of society

allocation is inefficient if a good is not being consumed by the buyers who value it most highly. In this case, moving consumption of the good from a buyer with a low valuation to a buyer with a high valuation will raise total surplus.

In addition to efficiency, the social planner might also care about **equality**—that is, whether the various buyers and sellers in the market have a similar level of economic well-being. In essence, the gains from trade in a market are like a pie to be shared among the market participants. The question of efficiency concerns whether the pie is as big as possible. The question of equality concerns how the pie is sliced and how the portions are distributed among members of society. In this chapter, we concentrate on efficiency as the social planner's goal. Keep in mind, however, that real policymakers often care about equality as well.

equality
the property of distributing economic prosperity uniformly among the members of society

EVALUATING THE MARKET EQUILIBRIUM

Figure 7 shows consumer and producer surplus when a market reaches the equilibrium of supply and demand. Recall that consumer surplus equals the area above the price and under the demand curve and producer surplus equals the area below the price and above the supply curve. Thus, the total area between the supply and demand curves up to the point of equilibrium represents the total surplus in this market.

Is this equilibrium allocation of resources efficient? That is, does it maximize total surplus? To answer this question, recall that when a market is in equilibrium, the price determines which buyers and sellers participate in the market. Those buyers who value the good more than the price (represented by the segment AE on the demand curve) choose to buy the good; buyers who value it less than the price (represented by the segment EB) do not. Similarly, those sellers whose

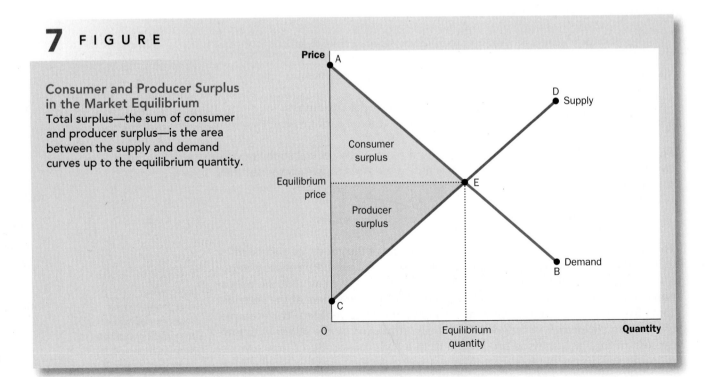

7 FIGURE

Consumer and Producer Surplus in the Market Equilibrium
Total surplus—the sum of consumer and producer surplus—is the area between the supply and demand curves up to the equilibrium quantity.

In The News

The Miracle of the Market

An opinion columnist suggests that the next time you sit down for Thanksgiving dinner, you should give thanks not only for the turkey on your plate but also for the economic system in which you live.

Giving Thanks for the "Invisible Hand"

By Jeff Jacoby

Gratitude to the Almighty is the theme of Thanksgiving, and has been ever since the Pilgrims of Plymouth brought in their first good harvest.... Today, in millions of homes across the nation, God will be thanked for many gifts—for the feast on the table and the company of loved ones, for health and good fortune in the year gone by, for peace at home in a time of war, for the incalculable privilege of having been born—or having become—American.

But it probably won't occur to too many of us to give thanks for the fact that the local supermarket had plenty of turkey for sale this week. Even the devout aren't likely to thank God for airline schedules that made it possible for some of those loved ones to fly home for Thanksgiving. Or for the arrival of "Master and Commander" at the local movie theater in time for the holiday weekend. Or for that great cranberry-apple pie recipe in the food section of the newspaper.

Those things we take more or less for granted. It hardly takes a miracle to explain why grocery stores stock up on turkey before Thanksgiving, or why Hollywood releases big movies in time for big holidays. That's what they do. Where is God in that?

And yet, isn't there something wondrous—something almost inexplicable—in the way your Thanksgiving weekend is made possible by the skill and labor of vast numbers of total strangers?

To bring that turkey to the dining room table, for example, required the efforts of thousands of people—the poultry farmers who raised the birds, of course, but also the feed distributors who supplied their nourishment and the truckers who brought it to the farm, not to mention the architect who designed the hatchery, the workmen who built it, and the technicians who keep it running. The bird had to be slaughtered and defeathered and inspected and transported and unloaded and wrapped and priced and displayed. The people who accomplished those tasks were supported in turn by armies of other people accomplishing other tasks—from refining the gasoline that fueled the trucks to manufacturing the plastic in which the meat was packaged.

The activities of countless far-flung men and women over the course of many months had to be intricately choreographed and precisely timed, so that when you showed up to buy a fresh Thanksgiving turkey, there would be one—or more likely, a few dozen—waiting. The level of coordination that was required to pull it off is mind-boggling. But

what is even more mind-boggling is this: No one coordinated it.

No turkey czar sat in a command post somewhere, consulting a master plan and issuing orders. No one rode herd on all those people, forcing them to cooperate for your benefit. And yet they did cooperate. When you arrived at the supermarket, your turkey was there. You didn't have to do anything but show up to buy it. If that isn't a miracle, what should we call it?

Adam Smith called it "the invisible hand"—the mysterious power that leads innumerable people, each working for his own gain, to promote ends that benefit many. Out of the seeming chaos of millions of uncoordinated private transactions emerges the spontaneous order of the market. Free human beings freely interact, and the result is an array of goods and services more immense than the human mind can comprehend. No dictator, no bureaucracy, no supercomputer plans it in advance. Indeed, the more an economy is planned, the more it is plagued by shortages, dislocation, and failure....

The social order of freedom, like the wealth and the progress it makes possible, is an extraordinary gift from above. On this Thanksgiving Day and every day, may we be grateful.

Source: *The Boston Globe*, November 27, 2003.

ers and sellers do not consider these side effects when deciding how much to consume and produce, the equilibrium in a market can be inefficient from the standpoint of society as a whole.

Market power and externalities are examples of a general phenomenon called *market failure*—the inability of some unregulated markets to allocate resources efficiently. When markets fail, public policy can potentially remedy the problem and increase economic efficiency. Microeconomists devote much effort to studying when market failure is likely and what sorts of policies are best at correcting market failures. As you continue your study of economics, you will see that the tools of welfare economics developed here are readily adapted to that endeavor.

Despite the possibility of market failure, the invisible hand of the marketplace is extraordinarily important. In many markets, the assumptions we made in this chapter work well, and the conclusion of market efficiency applies directly. Moreover, we can use our analysis of welfare economics and market efficiency to shed light on the effects of various government policies. In the next two chapters, we apply the tools we have just developed to study two important policy issues—the welfare effects of taxation and of international trade.

SUMMARY

- Consumer surplus equals buyers' willingness to pay for a good minus the amount they actually pay, and it measures the benefit buyers get from participating in a market. Consumer surplus can be computed by finding the area below the demand curve and above the price.

- Producer surplus equals the amount sellers receive for their goods minus their costs of production, and it measures the benefit sellers get from participating in a market. Producer surplus can be computed by finding the area below the price and above the supply curve.

- An allocation of resources that maximizes the sum of consumer and producer surplus is said

to be efficient. Policymakers are often concerned with the efficiency, as well as the equality, of economic outcomes.

- The equilibrium of supply and demand maximizes the sum of consumer and producer surplus. That is, the invisible hand of the marketplace leads buyers and sellers to allocate resources efficiently.

- Markets do not allocate resources efficiently in the presence of market failures such as market power or externalities.

KEY CONCEPTS

welfare economics, *p. 137*
willingness to pay, *p. 138*
consumer surplus, *p. 139*

cost, *p. 143*
producer surplus, *p. 143*
efficiency, *p. 147*

equality, *p. 148*

QUESTIONS FOR REVIEW

1. Explain how buyers' willingness to pay, consumer surplus, and the demand curve are related.
2. Explain how sellers' costs, producer surplus, and the supply curve are related.
3. In a supply-and-demand diagram, show producer and consumer surplus in the market equilibrium.

4. What is efficiency? Is it the only goal of economic policymakers?
5. What does the invisible hand do?
6. Name two types of market failure. Explain why each may cause market outcomes to be inefficient.

PROBLEMS AND APPLICATIONS

1. Melissa buys an iPod for $120 and gets consumer surplus of $80.
   a. What is her willingness to pay?
   b. If she had bought the iPod on sale for $90, what would her consumer surplus have been?
   c. If the price of an iPod were $250, what would her consumer surplus have been?
2. An early freeze in California sours the lemon crop. Explain what happens to consumer surplus in the market for lemons. Explain what happens to consumer surplus in the market for lemonade. Illustrate your answers with diagrams.
3. Suppose the demand for French bread rises. Explain what happens to producer surplus in the market for French bread. Explain what happens to producer surplus in the market for flour. Illustrate your answers with diagrams.
4. It is a hot day, and Bert is thirsty. Here is the value he places on a bottle of water:

Value of first bottle	$7
Value of second bottle	$5
Value of third bottle	$3
Value of fourth bottle	$1

   a. From this information, derive Bert's demand schedule. Graph his demand curve for bottled water.
   b. If the price of a bottle of water is $4, how many bottles does Bert buy? How much consumer surplus does Bert get from his purchases? Show Bert's consumer surplus in your graph.
   c. If the price falls to $2, how does quantity demanded change? How does Bert's consumer surplus change? Show these changes in your graph.
5. Ernie owns a water pump. Because pumping large amounts of water is harder than pumping small amounts, the cost of producing a bottle of water rises as he pumps more. Here is the cost he incurs to produce each bottle of water:

Cost of first bottle	$1
Cost of second bottle	$3
Cost of third bottle	$5
Cost of fourth bottle	$7

   a. From this information, derive Ernie's supply schedule. Graph his supply curve for bottled water.

b. If the price of a bottle of water is $4, how many bottles does Ernie produce and sell? How much producer surplus does Ernie get from these sales? Show Ernie's producer surplus in your graph.

c. If the price rises to $6, how does quantity supplied change? How does Ernie's producer surplus change? Show these changes in your graph.

6. Consider a market in which Bert from Problem 4 is the buyer and Ernie from Problem 5 is the seller.

a. Use Ernie's supply schedule and Bert's demand schedule to find the quantity supplied and quantity demanded at prices of $2, $4, and $6. Which of these prices brings supply and demand into equilibrium?

b. What are consumer surplus, producer surplus, and total surplus in this equilibrium?

c. If Ernie produced and Bert consumed one fewer bottle of water, what would happen to total surplus?

d. If Ernie produced and Bert consumed one additional bottle of water, what would happen to total surplus?

7. The cost of producing flat-screen TVs has fallen over the past several decades. Let's consider some implications of this fact.

a. Draw a supply-and-demand diagram to show the effect of falling production costs on the price and quantity of flat-screen TVs sold.

b. In your diagram, show what happens to consumer surplus and producer surplus.

c. Suppose the supply of flat-screen TVs is very elastic. Who benefits most from falling production costs—consumers or producers of these TVs?

8. There are four consumers willing to pay the following amounts for haircuts:

Jerry: $7   Oprah: $2   Ellen: $8   Phil: $5

There are four haircutting businesses with the following costs:

Firm A: $3   Firm B: $6   Firm C: $4   Firm D: $2

Each firm has the capacity to produce only one haircut. For efficiency, how many haircuts should be given? Which businesses should cut hair and which consumers should have their hair cut? How large is the maximum possible total surplus?

9. Suppose a technological advance reduces the cost of making computers.

a. Draw a supply-and-demand diagram to show what happens to price, quantity, consumer surplus, and producer surplus in the market for computers.

b. Computers and adding machines are substitutes. Use a supply-and-demand diagram to show what happens to price, quantity, consumer surplus, and producer surplus in the market for adding machines. Should adding machine producers be happy or sad about the technological advance in computers?

c. Computers and software are complements. Draw a supply-and-demand diagram to show what happens to price, quantity, consumer surplus, and producer surplus in the market for software. Should software producers be happy or sad about the technological advance in computers?

d. Does this analysis help explain why software producer Bill Gates is one of the world's richest men?

10. Consider how health insurance affects the quantity of healthcare services performed. Suppose that the typical medical procedure has a cost of $100, yet a person with health insurance pays only $20 out of pocket. Her insurance company pays the remaining $80. (The insurance company recoups the $80

through premiums, but the premium a person pays does not depend on how many procedures that person chooses to undertake.)

a. Draw the demand curve in the market for medical care. (In your diagram, the horizontal axis should represent the number of medical procedures.) Show the quantity of procedures demanded if each procedure has a price of $100.

b. On your diagram, show the quantity of procedures demanded if consumers pay only $20 per procedure. If the cost of each procedure to society is truly $100, and if individuals have health insurance as just described, will the number of procedures performed maximize total surplus? Explain.

c. Economists often blame the health insurance system for excessive use of medical care.

Given your analysis, why might the use of care be viewed as "excessive"?

d. What sort of policies might prevent this excessive use?

11. The supply and demand for broccoli are described by the following equations:

Supply: $Q^S = 4P - 80$
Demand: $Q^D = 100 - 2P$.

Q is in bushels, and P is in dollars per bushel.

a. Graph the supply curve and the demand curve. What is the equilibrium price and quantity?

b. Calculate consumer surplus, producer surplus, and total surplus at the equilibrium.

c. If a dictator who hated broccoli were to ban the vegetable, who would bear the larger burden—the buyers or sellers of broccoli?

C H A P T E R

8

Application: The Costs of Taxation

Taxes are often a source of heated political debate. In 1776, the anger of the American colonists over British taxes sparked the American Revolution. More than two centuries later, the American political parties continue to debate the proper size and shape of the tax system. Yet no one would deny that some level of taxation is necessary. As Oliver Wendell Holmes Jr. once said, "Taxes are what we pay for civilized society."

Because taxation has such a major impact on the modern economy, we return to the topic several times throughout this book as we expand the set of tools we have at our disposal. We began our study of taxes in Chapter 6. There we saw how a tax on a good affects its price and the quantity sold and how the forces of supply and demand divide the burden of a tax between buyers and sellers. In this chapter, we extend this analysis and look at how taxes affect welfare, the economic well-being of participants in a market. In other words, we see how high the price of civilized society can be.

The effects of taxes on welfare might at first seem obvious. The government enacts taxes to raise revenue, and that revenue must come out of someone's pocket. As we saw in Chapter 6, both buyers and sellers are worse off when a good is taxed: A tax raises the price buyers pay and lowers the price sellers receive. Yet to

159

understand more fully how taxes affect economic well-being, we must compare the reduced welfare of buyers and sellers to the amount of revenue the government raises. The tools of consumer and producer surplus allow us to make this comparison. The analysis will show that the cost of taxes to buyers and sellers exceeds the revenue raised by the government.

THE DEADWEIGHT LOSS OF TAXATION

We begin by recalling one of the surprising lessons from Chapter 6: The outcome is the same whether a tax on a good is levied on buyers or sellers of the good. When a tax is levied on buyers, the demand curve shifts downward by the size of the tax; when it is levied on sellers, the supply curve shifts upward by that amount. In either case, when the tax is enacted, the price paid by buyers rises, and the price received by sellers falls. In the end, the elasticities of supply and demand determine how the tax burden is distributed between producers and consumers. This distribution is the same regardless of how it is levied.

Figure 1 shows these effects. To simplify our discussion, this figure does not show a shift in either the supply or demand curve, although one curve must shift. Which curve shifts depends on whether the tax is levied on sellers (the supply curve shifts) or buyers (the demand curve shifts). In this chapter, we can keep the analysis general and simplify the graphs by not bothering to show the shift. The key result for our purposes here is that the tax places a wedge between the price buyers pay and the price sellers receive. Because of this tax wedge, the quantity sold falls below the level that would be sold without a tax. In other words, a tax on a good causes the size of the market for the good to shrink. These results should be familiar from Chapter 6.

1 FIGURE

The Effects of a Tax
A tax on a good places a wedge between the price that buyers pay and the price that sellers receive. The quantity of the good sold falls.

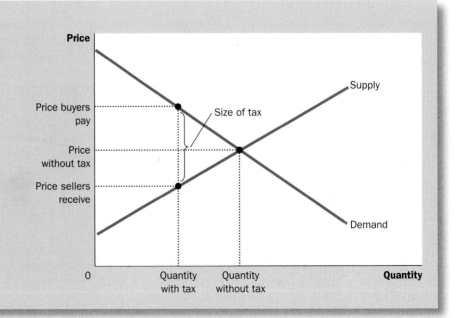

How a Tax Affects Market Participants

Let's use the tools of welfare economics to measure the gains and losses from a tax on a good. To do this, we must take into account how the tax affects buyers, sellers, and the government. The benefit received by buyers in a market is measured by consumer surplus—the amount buyers are willing to pay for the good minus the amount they actually pay for it. The benefit received by sellers in a market is measured by producer surplus—the amount sellers receive for the good minus their costs. These are precisely the measures of economic welfare we used in Chapter 7.

What about the third interested party, the government? If T is the size of the tax and Q is the quantity of the good sold, then the government gets total tax revenue of $T \times Q$. It can use this tax revenue to provide services, such as roads, police, and public education, or to help the needy. Therefore, to analyze how taxes affect economic well-being, we use the government's tax revenue to measure the public benefit from the tax. Keep in mind, however, that this benefit actually accrues not to government but to those on whom the revenue is spent.

Figure 2 shows that the government's tax revenue is represented by the rectangle between the supply and demand curves. The height of this rectangle is the size of the tax, T, and the width of the rectangle is the quantity of the good sold, Q. Because a rectangle's area is its height times its width, this rectangle's area is $T \times Q$, which equals the tax revenue.

Welfare without a Tax To see how a tax affects welfare, we begin by considering welfare before the government imposes a tax. Figure 3 shows the supply-and-demand diagram and marks the key areas with the letters A through F.

Without a tax, the equilibrium price and quantity are found at the intersection of the supply and demand curves. The price is P_1, and the quantity sold is Q_1.

"You know, the idea of taxation *with* representation doesn't appeal to me very much, either."

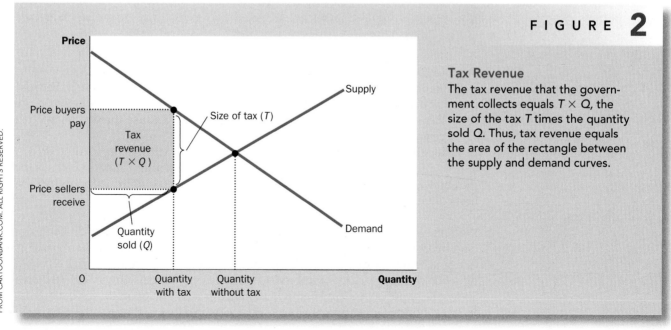

FIGURE **2**

Tax Revenue
The tax revenue that the government collects equals $T \times Q$, the size of the tax T times the quantity sold Q. Thus, tax revenue equals the area of the rectangle between the supply and demand curves.

3 FIGURE

How a Tax Affects Welfare

A tax on a good reduces consumer surplus (by the area B + C) and producer surplus (by the area D + E). Because the fall in producer and consumer surplus exceeds tax revenue (area B + D), the tax is said to impose a deadweight loss (area C + E).

	Without Tax	With Tax	Change
Consumer Surplus	A + B + C	A	−(B + C)
Producer Surplus	D + E + F	F	−(D + E)
Tax Revenue	None	B + D	+(B + D)
Total Surplus	A + B + C + D + E + F	A + B + D + F	−(C + E)

The area C + E shows the fall in total surplus and is the deadweight loss of the tax.

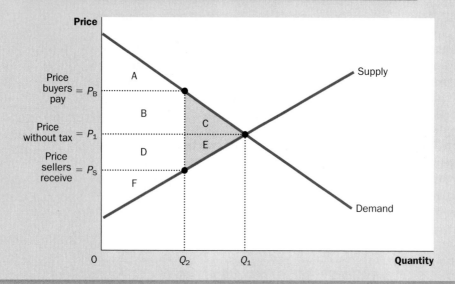

Because the demand curve reflects buyers' willingness to pay, consumer surplus is the area between the demand curve and the price, A + B + C. Similarly, because the supply curve reflects sellers' costs, producer surplus is the area between the supply curve and the price, D + E + F. In this case, because there is no tax, tax revenue equals zero.

Total surplus, the sum of consumer and producer surplus, equals the area A + B + C + D + E + F. In other words, as we saw in Chapter 7, total surplus is the area between the supply and demand curves up to the equilibrium quantity. The first column of the table in Figure 3 summarizes these conclusions.

Welfare with a Tax Now consider welfare after the tax is enacted. The price paid by buyers rises from P_1 to P_B, so consumer surplus now equals only area A (the area below the demand curve and above the buyer's price). The price received by sellers falls from P_1 to P_S, so producer surplus now equals only area F (the area above the supply curve and below the seller's price). The quantity sold falls from Q_1 to Q_2, and the government collects tax revenue equal to the area B + D.

To compute total surplus with the tax, we add consumer surplus, producer surplus, and tax revenue. Thus, we find that total surplus is area A + B + D + F. The second column of the table summarizes these results.

Changes in Welfare   We can now see the effects of the tax by comparing welfare before and after the tax is enacted. The third column of the table in Figure 3 shows the changes. The tax causes consumer surplus to fall by the area B + C and producer surplus to fall by the area D + E. Tax revenue rises by the area B + D. Not surprisingly, the tax makes buyers and sellers worse off and the government better off.

The change in total welfare includes the change in consumer surplus (which is negative), the change in producer surplus (which is also negative), and the change in tax revenue (which is positive). When we add these three pieces together, we find that total surplus in the market falls by the area C + E. *Thus, the losses to buyers and sellers from a tax exceed the revenue raised by the government.* The fall in total surplus that results when a tax (or some other policy) distorts a market outcome is called the **deadweight loss**. The area C + E measures the size of the deadweight loss.

deadweight loss
the fall in total surplus that results from a market distortion, such as a tax

To understand why taxes impose deadweight losses, recall one of the *Ten Principles of Economics* in Chapter 1: People respond to incentives. In Chapter 7, we saw that free markets normally allocate scarce resources efficiently. That is, the equilibrium of supply and demand maximizes the total surplus of buyers and sellers in a market. When a tax raises the price to buyers and lowers the price to sellers, however, it gives buyers an incentive to consume less and sellers an incentive to produce less than they would in the absence of the tax. As buyers and sellers respond to these incentives, the size of the market shrinks below its optimum (as shown in the figure by the movement from Q_1 to Q_2). Thus, because taxes distort incentives, they cause markets to allocate resources inefficiently.

DEADWEIGHT LOSSES AND THE GAINS FROM TRADE

To gain some intuition for why taxes result in deadweight losses, consider an example. Imagine that Joe cleans Jane's house each week for $100. The opportunity cost of Joe's time is $80, and the value of a clean house to Jane is $120. Thus, Joe and Jane each receive a $20 benefit from their deal. The total surplus of $40 measures the gains from trade in this particular transaction.

Now suppose that the government levies a $50 tax on the providers of cleaning services. There is now no price that Jane can pay Joe that will leave both of them better off after paying the tax. The most Jane would be willing to pay is $120, but then Joe would be left with only $70 after paying the tax, which is less than his $80 opportunity cost. Conversely, for Joe to receive his opportunity cost of $80, Jane would need to pay $130, which is above the $120 value she places on a clean house. As a result, Jane and Joe cancel their arrangement. Joe goes without the income, and Jane lives in a dirtier house.

The tax has made Joe and Jane worse off by a total of $40 because they have each lost $20 of surplus. But note that the government collects no revenue from Joe and Jane because they decide to cancel their arrangement. The $40 is pure deadweight loss: It is a loss to buyers and sellers in a market that is not offset by an increase in government revenue. From this example, we can see the ultimate source of deadweight losses: *Taxes cause deadweight losses because they prevent buyers and sellers from realizing some of the gains from trade.*

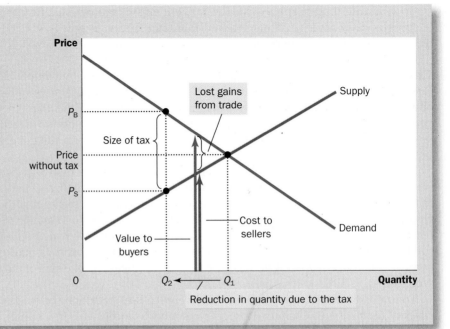

4 FIGURE

The Deadweight Loss
When the government imposes a tax on a good, the quantity sold falls from Q_1 to Q_2. At every quantity between Q_1 and Q_2, the potential gains from trade among buyers and sellers are not realized. These lost gains from trade create the deadweight loss.

The area of the triangle between the supply and demand curves (area C + E in Figure 3) measures these losses. This conclusion can be seen more easily in Figure 4 by recalling that the demand curve reflects the value of the good to consumers and that the supply curve reflects the costs of producers. When the tax raises the price to buyers to P_B and lowers the price to sellers to P_S, the marginal buyers and sellers leave the market, so the quantity sold falls from Q_1 to Q_2. Yet as the figure shows, the value of the good to these buyers still exceeds the cost to these sellers. At every quantity between Q_1 and Q_2, the situation is the same as in our example with Joe and Jane. The gains from trade—the difference between buyers' value and sellers' cost—are less than the tax. As a result, these trades are not made once the tax is imposed. The deadweight loss is the surplus lost because the tax discourages these mutually advantageous trades.

QUICK QUIZ   Draw the supply and demand curves for cookies. If the government imposes a tax on cookies, show what happens to the price paid by buyers, the price received by sellers, and the quantity sold. In your diagram, show the deadweight loss from the tax. Explain the meaning of the deadweight loss.

THE DETERMINANTS OF THE DEADWEIGHT LOSS

What determines whether the deadweight loss from a tax is large or small? The answer is the price elasticities of supply and demand, which measure how much the quantity supplied and quantity demanded respond to changes in the price.

Let's consider first how the elasticity of supply affects the size of the deadweight loss. In the top two panels of Figure 5, the demand curve and the size of the tax are the same. The only difference in these figures is the elasticity of the supply curve. In panel (a), the supply curve is relatively inelastic: Quantity supplied responds only slightly to changes in the price. In panel (b), the supply curve is relatively elastic: Quantity supplied responds substantially to changes in the price. Notice that the deadweight loss, the area of the triangle between the supply and demand curves, is larger when the supply curve is more elastic.

Similarly, the bottom two panels of Figure 5 show how the elasticity of demand affects the size of the deadweight loss. Here the supply curve and the size of the

In panels (a) and (b), the demand curve and the size of the tax are the same, but the price elasticity of supply is different. Notice that the more elastic the supply curve, the larger the deadweight loss of the tax. In panels (c) and (d), the supply curve and the size of the tax are the same, but the price elasticity of demand is different. Notice that the more elastic the demand curve, the larger the deadweight loss of the tax.

FIGURE **5**

Tax Distortions and Elasticities

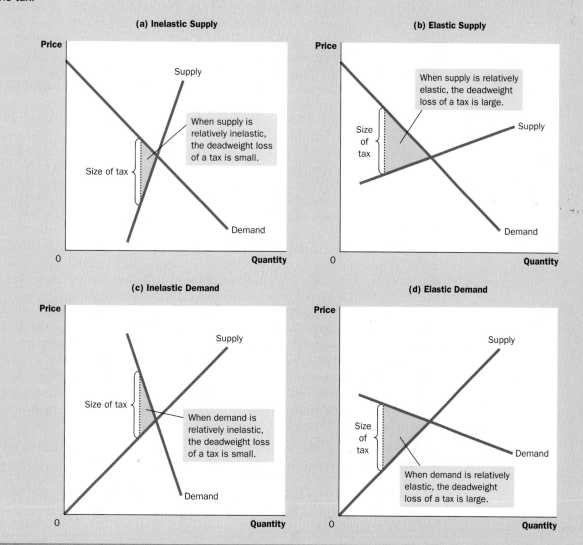

tax are held constant. In panel (c), the demand curve is relatively inelastic, and the deadweight loss is small. In panel (d), the demand curve is more elastic, and the deadweight loss from the tax is larger.

The lesson from this figure is easy to explain. A tax has a deadweight loss because it induces buyers and sellers to change their behavior. The tax raises the price paid by buyers, so they consume less. At the same time, the tax lowers the price received by sellers, so they produce less. Because of these changes in behavior, the size of the market shrinks below the optimum. The elasticities of supply and demand measure how much sellers and buyers respond to the changes in the price and, therefore, determine how much the tax distorts the market outcome. Hence, *the greater the elasticities of supply and demand, the greater the deadweight loss of a tax.*

 ## THE DEADWEIGHT LOSS DEBATE

Supply, demand, elasticity, deadweight loss—all this economic theory is enough to make your head spin. But believe it or not, these ideas go to the heart of a profound political question: How big should the government be? The debate hinges on these concepts because the larger the deadweight loss of taxation, the larger the cost of any government program. If taxation entails large deadweight losses, then these losses are a strong argument for a leaner government that does less and taxes less. But if taxes impose small deadweight losses, then government programs are less costly than they otherwise might be.

So how big are the deadweight losses of taxation? Economists disagree on the answer to this question. To see the nature of this disagreement, consider the most important tax in the U.S. economy: the tax on labor. The Social Security tax, the Medicare tax, and, to a large extent, the federal income tax are labor taxes. Many state governments also tax labor earnings. A labor tax places a wedge between the wage that firms pay and the wage that workers receive. For a typical worker, if all forms of labor taxes are added together, the *marginal tax rate* on labor income—the tax on the last dollar of earnings—is about 40 percent.

Although the size of the labor tax is easy to determine, the deadweight loss of this tax is less straightforward. Economists disagree about whether this 40 percent labor tax has a small or a large deadweight loss. This disagreement arises because economists hold different views about the elasticity of labor supply.

Economists who argue that labor taxes do not greatly distort market outcomes believe that labor supply is fairly inelastic. Most people, they claim, would work full time regardless of the wage. If so, the labor supply curve is almost vertical, and a tax on labor has a small deadweight loss.

Economists who argue that labor taxes are highly distorting believe that labor supply is more elastic. While admitting that some groups of workers may supply their labor inelastically, these economists claim that many other groups respond more to incentives. Here are some examples:

- Many workers can adjust the number of hours they work—for instance, by working overtime. The higher the wage, the more hours they choose to work.
- Some families have second earners—often married women with children—with some discretion over whether to do unpaid work at home or paid work in the marketplace. When deciding whether to take a job, these second earn-

ers compare the benefits of being at home (including savings on the cost of child care) with the wages they could earn.

- Many of the elderly can choose when to retire, and their decisions are partly based on the wage. Once they are retired, the wage determines their incentive to work part time.
- Some people consider engaging in illegal economic activity, such as the drug trade, or working at jobs that pay "under the table" to evade taxes. Economists call this the *underground* economy. In deciding whether to work in the underground economy or at a legitimate job, these potential criminals compare what they can earn by breaking the law with the wage they can earn legally.

"WHAT'S YOUR POSITION ON THE ELASTICITY OF LABOR SUPPLY?"

In each of these cases, the quantity of labor supplied responds to the wage (the price of labor). Thus, the decisions of these workers are distorted when their labor earnings are taxed. Labor taxes encourage workers to work fewer hours, second earners to stay at home, the elderly to retire early, and the unscrupulous to enter the underground economy.

These two views of labor taxation persist to this day. Indeed, whenever you see two political candidates debating whether the government should provide more services or reduce the tax burden, keep in mind that part of the disagreement may rest on different views about the elasticity of labor supply and the deadweight loss of taxation. ●

QUICK QUIZ   The demand for beer is more elastic than the demand for milk. Would a tax on beer or a tax on milk have a larger deadweight loss? Why?

DEADWEIGHT LOSS AND TAX REVENUE AS TAXES VARY

Taxes rarely stay the same for long periods of time. Policymakers in local, state, and federal governments are always considering raising one tax or lowering another. Here we consider what happens to the deadweight loss and tax revenue when the size of a tax changes.

Figure 6 shows the effects of a small, medium, and large tax, holding constant the market's supply and demand curves. The deadweight loss—the reduction in total surplus that results when the tax reduces the size of a market below the optimum—equals the area of the triangle between the supply and demand curves. For the small tax in panel (a), the area of the deadweight loss triangle is quite small. But as the size of a tax rises in panels (b) and (c), the deadweight loss grows larger and larger.

Indeed, the deadweight loss of a tax rises even more rapidly than the size of the tax. This occurs because the deadweight loss is an area of a triangle, and the area of a triangle depends on the *square* of its size. If we double the size of a tax, for instance, the base and height of the triangle double, so the deadweight loss rises by a factor of 4. If we triple the size of a tax, the base and height triple, so the deadweight loss rises by a factor of 9.

The government's tax revenue is the size of the tax times the amount of the good sold. As the first three panels of Figure 6 show, tax revenue equals the area

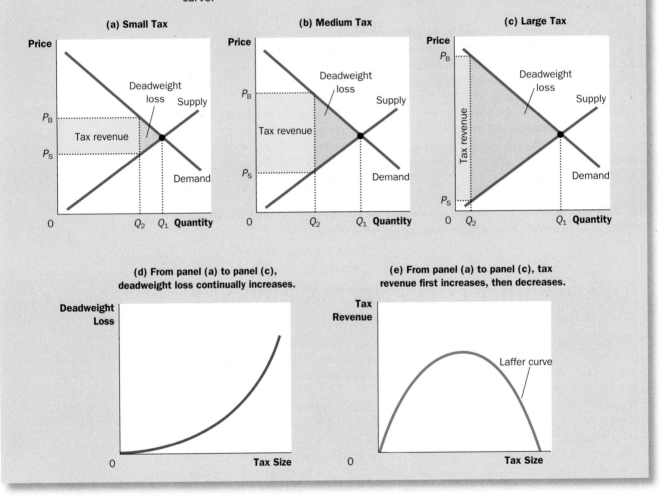

6 FIGURE

How Deadweight Loss and Tax Revenue Vary with the Size of a Tax

The deadweight loss is the reduction in total surplus due to the tax. Tax revenue is the amount of the tax times the amount of the good sold. In panel (a), a small tax has a small deadweight loss and raises a small amount of revenue. In panel (b), a somewhat larger tax has a larger deadweight loss and raises a larger amount of revenue. In panel (c), a very large tax has a very large deadweight loss, but because it has reduced the size of the market so much, the tax raises only a small amount of revenue. Panels (d) and (e) summarize these conclusions. Panel (d) shows that as the size of a tax grows larger, the deadweight loss grows larger. Panel (e) shows that tax revenue first rises and then falls. This relationship is sometimes called the Laffer curve.

of the rectangle between the supply and demand curves. For the small tax in panel (a), tax revenue is small. As the size of a tax increases from panel (a) to panel (b), tax revenue grows. But as the size of the tax increases further from panel (b) to panel (c), tax revenue falls because the higher tax drastically reduces the size of the market. For a very large tax, no revenue would be raised because people would stop buying and selling the good altogether.

The last two panels of Figure 6 summarize these results. In panel (d), we see that as the size of a tax increases, its deadweight loss quickly gets larger. By con-

FYI

Henry George and the Land Tax

Is there an ideal tax? Henry George, the 19th-century American economist and social philosopher, thought so. In his 1879 book *Progress and Poverty*, George argued that the government should raise all its revenue from a tax on land. This "single tax" was, he claimed, both equitable and efficient. George's ideas won him a large political following, and in 1886, he lost a close race for mayor of New York City (although he finished well ahead of Republican candidate Theodore Roosevelt).

George's proposal to tax land was motivated largely by a concern over the distribution of economic well-being. He deplored the "shocking contrast between monstrous wealth and debasing want" and thought landowners benefited more than they should from the rapid growth in the overall economy.

George's arguments for the land tax can be understood using the tools of modern economics. Consider first supply and demand in the market for renting land. As immigration causes the population to rise and technological progress causes incomes to grow, the demand for land rises over time. Yet because the amount of land is fixed, the supply is perfectly inelastic. Rapid increases in demand together with inelastic supply lead to large increases in the equilibrium rents on land so that economic growth makes rich landowners even richer.

Now consider the incidence of a tax on land. As we first saw in Chapter 6, the burden of a tax falls more heavily on the side of the market that is less elastic. A tax on land takes this principle to an

Henry George

extreme. Because the elasticity of supply is zero, the landowners bear the entire burden of the tax.

Consider next the question of efficiency. As we just discussed, the deadweight loss of a tax depends on the elasticities of supply and demand. Again, a tax on land is an extreme case. Because supply is perfectly inelastic, a tax on land does not alter the market allocation. There is no deadweight loss, and the government's tax revenue exactly equals the loss of the landowners.

Although taxing land may look attractive in theory, it is not as straightforward in practice as it may appear. For a tax on land not to distort economic incentives, it must be a tax on raw land. Yet the value of land often comes from improvements, such as clearing trees, providing sewers, and building roads. Unlike the supply of raw land, the supply of improvements has an elasticity greater than zero. If a land tax were imposed on improvements, it would distort incentives. Landowners would respond by devoting fewer resources to improving their land.

Today, few economists support George's proposal for a single tax on land. Not only is taxing improvements a potential problem, but the tax would not raise enough revenue to pay for the much larger government we have today. Yet many of George's arguments remain valid. Here is the assessment of the eminent economist Milton Friedman a century after George's book: "In my opinion, the least bad tax is the property tax on the unimproved value of land, the Henry George argument of many, many years ago."

trast, panel (e) shows that tax revenue first rises with the size of the tax, but as the tax gets larger, the market shrinks so much that tax revenue starts to fall.

CASE STUDY THE LAFFER CURVE AND SUPPLY-SIDE ECONOMICS

One day in 1974, economist Arthur Laffer sat in a Washington restaurant with some prominent journalists and politicians. He took out a napkin and drew a figure on it to show how tax rates affect tax revenue. It looked much like panel (e) of our Figure 6. Laffer then suggested that the United States was on the

In The News

On the Way to France

Tax rates affect work effort. This proposition helps explain why the U.S. economy differs from many others around the world.

U.S. Could Follow Europe's High-Tax Path

Americans owe their economic edge over Europeans in part to the fact that they work more, a distinction often attributed to cultural differences: Americans want to consume more, while Europeans enjoy their leisure more.

As late as the 1970s, though, the French actually worked longer than Americans. The reason they now work one-third fewer hours has less to do with a yearning for the good life than it does with escalating taxes, including payroll taxes, in Europe. But Americans can't afford to be smug: The U.S. may be headed in the same high-tax direction if it doesn't tackle the looming crisis in Social Security and Medicare. . . .

Edward Prescott of the University of Minnesota says Europe's higher taxes made it more expensive to hire labor, even though take-home pay may not have increased much. The bigger the burden, the harder it is for employers to pay a salary that will entice someone to take a job rather than stay on public assistance, go to school, or retire early. Between the early 1970s and

mid-1990s, he says, the French tax rate rose to 59 percent from 49 percent, while the U.S. tax rate held at 40 percent.

The result: The average French person of working age logged 24.4 hours a week in the early 1970s, one hour more than an American. By the mid-1990s, the French workweek had shrunk to 17.5 hours, while the U.S. workweek had grown to 25.9 hours.

Who Works Hardest?

In countries with higher taxes, people tend to work less.

Country	Tax Rate	Workweek
Italy	64%	16.5 hours
France	59	17.5
Germany	59	19.3
Canada	52	22.8
U.K.	44	22.9
U.S.	40	25.9
Japan	37	27.0

The relationship between work and tax rates was similar for the seven major industrial countries. The Japanese, with even

lower taxes than the U.S., work more, and the Italians, with the highest taxes, work the least. The difference in hours was narrower in the 1970s, when the difference in tax rates was smaller. . . .

Europe's larger lesson for the U.S. may be about the costs of failing to prepare for the expense of the baby boomers' retirement. The White House budget office says Social Security and Medicare have promised to pay out $18 trillion more than they will receive in revenue in coming decades. . . . Closing that gap without any cuts in benefits would require a 7.1 percentage point increase in the combined Social Security–Medicare payroll tax, now at 15.3 percent. . . .

"People would just stop working," says Arthur Rolnick, research director of the Minneapolis Fed. As the work force shrank, taxes would have to go up even more for the remaining workers. . . .

Alan Auerbach of the University of California at Berkeley says the system's generosity will have to be curtailed and "the sooner, the better." Otherwise, American work habits again could look like those of the French.

Source: *The Wall Street Journal*, October 20, 2003.

downward-sloping side of this curve. Tax rates were so high, he argued, that reducing them would actually raise tax revenue.

Most economists were skeptical of Laffer's suggestion. The idea that a cut in tax rates could raise tax revenue was correct as a matter of economic theory, but there was more doubt about whether it would do so in practice. There was little evidence for Laffer's view that U.S. tax rates had in fact reached such extreme levels.

Nonetheless, the *Laffer curve* (as it became known) captured the imagination of Ronald Reagan. David Stockman, budget director in the first Reagan administration, offers the following story:

> [Reagan] had once been on the Laffer curve himself. "I came into the Big Money making pictures during World War II," he would always say. At that time the wartime income surtax hit 90 percent. "You could only make four pictures and then you were in the top bracket," he would continue. "So we all quit working after four pictures and went off to the country." High tax rates caused less work. Low tax rates caused more. His experience proved it.

When Reagan ran for president in 1980, he made cutting taxes part of his platform. Reagan argued that taxes were so high that they were discouraging hard work. He argued that lower taxes would give people the proper incentive to work, which would raise economic well-being and perhaps even tax revenue. Because the cut in tax rates was intended to encourage people to increase the quantity of labor they supplied, the views of Laffer and Reagan became known as *supply-side economics.*

Economists continue to debate Laffer's argument. Many believe that subsequent history refuted Laffer's conjecture that lower tax rates would raise tax revenue. Yet because history is open to alternative interpretations, other economists view the events of the 1980s as more favorable to the supply-siders. To evaluate Laffer's hypothesis definitively, we would need to rerun history without the Reagan tax cuts and see if tax revenues were higher or lower. Unfortunately, that experiment is impossible.

Some economists take an intermediate position on this issue. They believe that while an overall cut in tax rates normally reduces revenue, some taxpayers at some times may find themselves on the wrong side of the Laffer curve. Other things equal, a tax cut is more likely to raise tax revenue if the cut applies to those taxpayers facing the highest tax rates. In addition, Laffer's argument may be more compelling when considering countries with much higher tax rates than the United States. In Sweden in the early 1980s, for instance, the typical worker faced a marginal tax rate of about 80 percent. Such a high tax rate provides a substantial disincentive to work. Studies have suggested that Sweden would indeed have raised more tax revenue if it had lowered its tax rates.

Economists disagree about these issues in part because there is no consensus about the size of the relevant elasticities. The more elastic that supply and demand are in any market, the more taxes in that market distort behavior, and the more likely it is that a tax cut will raise tax revenue. There is no debate, however, about the general lesson: How much revenue the government gains or loses from a tax change cannot be computed just by looking at tax rates. It also depends on how the tax change affects people's behavior. ●

QUICK QUIZ If the government doubles the tax on gasoline, can you be sure that revenue from the gasoline tax will rise? Can you be sure that the deadweight loss from the gasoline tax will rise? Explain.

CONCLUSION

In this chapter we have used the tools developed in the previous chapter to further our understanding of taxes. One of the *Ten Principles of Economics* discussed in Chapter 1 is that markets are usually a good way to organize economic activity. In Chapter 7, we used the concepts of producer and consumer surplus to make this principle more precise. Here we have seen that when the government imposes taxes on buyers or sellers of a good, society loses some of the benefits of market efficiency. Taxes are costly to market participants not only because taxes transfer resources from those participants to the government but also because they alter incentives and distort market outcomes.

The analysis presented here and in Chapter 6 should give you a good basis for understanding the economic impact of taxes, but this is not the end of the story. Microeconomists study how best to design a tax system, including how to strike the right balance between equality and efficiency. Macroeconomists study how taxes influence the overall economy and how policymakers can use the tax system to stabilize economic activity and to achieve more rapid economic growth. So don't be surprised that, as you continue your study of economics, the subject of taxation comes up yet again.

SUMMARY

- A tax on a good reduces the welfare of buyers and sellers of the good, and the reduction in consumer and producer surplus usually exceeds the revenue raised by the government. The fall in total surplus—the sum of consumer surplus, producer surplus, and tax revenue—is called the deadweight loss of the tax.

- Taxes have deadweight losses because they cause buyers to consume less and sellers to produce less, and these changes in behavior shrink the size of the market below the level that maxi-

mizes total surplus. Because the elasticities of supply and demand measure how much market participants respond to market conditions, larger elasticities imply larger deadweight losses.

- As a tax grows larger, it distorts incentives more, and its deadweight loss grows larger. Because a tax reduces the size of the market, however, tax revenue does not continually increase. It first rises with the size of a tax, but if a tax gets large enough, tax revenue starts to fall.

KEY CONCEPT

deadweight loss, *p. 163*

QUESTIONS FOR REVIEW

1. What happens to consumer and producer surplus when the sale of a good is taxed? How does the change in consumer and producer surplus compare to the tax revenue? Explain.
2. Draw a supply-and-demand diagram with a tax on the sale of the good. Show the deadweight loss. Show the tax revenue.
3. How do the elasticities of supply and demand affect the deadweight loss of a tax? Why do they have this effect?
4. Why do experts disagree about whether labor taxes have small or large deadweight losses?
5. What happens to the deadweight loss and tax revenue when a tax is increased?

PROBLEMS AND APPLICATIONS

1. The market for pizza is characterized by a downward-sloping demand curve and an upward-sloping supply curve.
   a. Draw the competitive market equilibrium. Label the price, quantity, consumer surplus, and producer surplus. Is there any deadweight loss? Explain.
   b. Suppose that the government forces each pizzeria to pay a $1 tax on each pizza sold. Illustrate the effect of this tax on the pizza market, being sure to label the consumer surplus, producer surplus, government revenue, and deadweight loss. How does each area compare to the pre-tax case?
   c. If the tax were removed, pizza eaters and sellers would be better off, but the government would lose tax revenue. Suppose that consumers and producers voluntarily transferred some of their gains to the government. Could all parties (including the government) be better off than they were with a tax? Explain using the labeled areas in your graph.
2. Evaluate the following two statements. Do you agree? Why or why not?
   a. "A tax that has no deadweight loss cannot raise any revenue for the government."
   b. "A tax that raises no revenue for the government cannot have any deadweight loss."
3. Consider the market for rubber bands.
   a. If this market has very elastic supply and very inelastic demand, how would the burden of a tax on rubber bands be shared between consumers and producers? Use the tools of consumer surplus and producer surplus in your answer.
   b. If this market has very inelastic supply and very elastic demand, how would the burden of a tax on rubber bands be shared between consumers and producers? Contrast your answer with your answer to part (a).
4. The 19th-century economist Henry George argued that the government should levy a sizable tax on land, the supply of which he took to be completely inelastic.
   a. George believed that economic growth increased the demand for land and made rich landowners richer at the expense of the tenants who made up the demand side of the market. Show this argument on an appropriately labeled diagram.
   b. Who bears the burden of a tax on land—the owners of land or the tenants on the land? Explain.

c. Is the deadweight loss of this tax large or small? Explain.

d. Many cities and towns today levy taxes on the value of real estate. Why might the above analysis of George's land tax not apply to this modern tax?

5. Suppose that the government imposes a tax on heating oil.

a. Would the deadweight loss from this tax likely be greater in the first year after it is imposed or in the fifth year? Explain.

b. Would the revenue collected from this tax likely be greater in the first year after it is imposed or in the fifth year? Explain.

6. After economics class one day, your friend suggests that taxing food would be a good way to raise revenue because the demand for food is quite inelastic. In what sense is taxing food a "good" way to raise revenue? In what sense is it not a "good" way to raise revenue?

7. Daniel Patrick Moynihan, the late senator from New York, once introduced a bill that would levy a 10,000 percent tax on certain hollow-tipped bullets.

a. Do you expect that this tax would raise much revenue? Why or why not?

b. Even if the tax would raise no revenue, why might Senator Moynihan have proposed it?

8. The government places a tax on the purchase of socks.

a. Illustrate the effect of this tax on equilibrium price and quantity in the sock market. Identify the following areas both before and after the imposition of the tax: total spending by consumers, total revenue for producers, and government tax revenue.

b. Does the price received by producers rise or fall? Can you tell whether total receipts for producers rise or fall? Explain.

c. Does the price paid by consumers rise or fall? Can you tell whether total spending by consumers rises or falls? Explain carefully. (Hint: Think about elasticity.) If total consumer spending falls, does consumer surplus rise? Explain.

9. Suppose the government currently raises $100 million through a 1-cent tax on widgets, and another $100 million through a 10-cent tax on gadgets. If the government doubled the tax rate on widgets and eliminated the tax on gadgets, would it raise more money than today, less money, or the same amount of money? Explain.

10. This chapter analyzed the welfare effects of a tax on a good. Consider now the opposite policy. Suppose that the government *subsidizes* a good: For each unit of the good sold, the government pays $2 to the buyer. How does the subsidy affect consumer surplus, producer surplus, tax revenue, and total surplus? Does a subsidy lead to a deadweight loss? Explain.

11. Hotel rooms in Smalltown go for $100, and 1,000 rooms are rented on a typical day.

a. To raise revenue, the mayor decides to charge hotels a tax of $10 per rented room. After the tax is imposed, the going rate for hotel rooms rises to $108, and the number of rooms rented falls to 900. Calculate the amount of revenue this tax raises for Smalltown and the deadweight loss of the tax. (Hint: The area of a triangle is ½ × base × height.)

b. The mayor now doubles the tax to $20. The price rises to $116, and the number of rooms rented falls to 800. Calculate tax revenue and deadweight loss with this larger tax. Do they double, more than double, or less than double? Explain.

12. Suppose that a market is described by the following supply and demand equations:

$$Q^S = 2P$$
$$Q^D = 300 - P$$

a. Solve for the equilibrium price and the equilibrium quantity.

b. Suppose that a tax of T is placed on buyers, so the new demand equation is

$$Q^D = 300 - (P + T).$$

Solve for the new equilibrium. What happens to the price received by sellers, the price paid by buyers, and the quantity sold?

c. Tax revenue is $T \times Q$. Use your answer to part (b) to solve for tax revenue as a function of T. Graph this relationship for T between 0 and 300.

d. The deadweight loss of a tax is the area of the triangle between the supply and demand curves. Recalling that the area of a triangle is $\frac{1}{2} \times$ base $\times$ height, solve for deadweight loss as a function of T. Graph this relation-ship for T between 0 and 300. (Hint: Looking sideways, the base of the deadweight loss triangle is T, and the height is the difference between the quantity sold with the tax and the quantity sold without the tax.)

e. The government now levies a tax on this good of $200 per unit. Is this a good policy? Why or why not? Can you propose a better policy?

Application: International Trade

If you check the labels on the clothes you are now wearing, you will probably find that some of your clothes were made in another country. A century ago, the textile and clothing industry was a major part of the U.S. economy, but that is no longer the case. Faced with foreign competitors that can produce quality goods at low cost, many U.S. firms have found it increasingly difficult to produce and sell textiles and clothing at a profit. As a result, they have laid off their workers and shut down their factories. Today, much of the textiles and clothing that Americans consume are imported.

The story of the textile industry raises important questions for economic policy: How does international trade affect economic well-being? Who gains and who loses from free trade among countries, and how do the gains compare to the losses?

Chapter 3 introduced the study of international trade by applying the principle of comparative advantage. According to this principle, all countries can benefit from trading with one another because trade allows each country to specialize in doing what it does best. But the analysis in Chapter 3 was incomplete. It did not explain how the international marketplace achieves these gains from trade or how the gains are distributed among various economic participants.

We now return to the study of international trade and take up these questions. Over the past several chapters, we have developed many tools for analyzing how markets work: supply, demand, equilibrium, consumer surplus, producer surplus, and so on. With these tools, we can learn more about how international trade affects economic well-being.

THE DETERMINANTS OF TRADE

Consider the market for textiles. The textile market is well suited to examining the gains and losses from international trade: Textiles are made in many countries around the world, and there is much world trade in textiles. Moreover, the textile market is one in which policymakers often consider (and sometimes implement) trade restrictions to protect domestic producers from foreign competitors. We examine here the textile market in the imaginary country of Isoland.

THE EQUILIBRIUM WITHOUT TRADE

As our story begins, the Isolandian textile market is isolated from the rest of the world. By government decree, no one in Isoland is allowed to import or export textiles, and the penalty for violating the decree is so large that no one dares try.

Because there is no international trade, the market for textiles in Isoland consists solely of Isolandian buyers and sellers. As Figure 1 shows, the domestic price adjusts to balance the quantity supplied by domestic sellers and the quantity demanded by domestic buyers. The figure shows the consumer and producer surplus in the equilibrium without trade. The sum of consumer and producer surplus

1 FIGURE

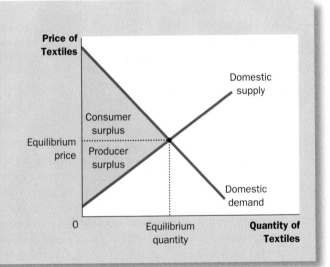

The Equilibrium without International Trade
When an economy cannot trade in world markets, the price adjusts to balance domestic supply and demand. This figure shows consumer and producer surplus in an equilibrium without international trade for the textile market in the imaginary country of Isoland.

measures the total benefits that buyers and sellers receive from participating in the textile market.

Now suppose that, in an election upset, Isoland elects a new president. The president campaigned on a platform of "change" and promised the voters bold new ideas. Her first act is to assemble a team of economists to evaluate Isolandian trade policy. She asks them to report on three questions:

- If the government allows Isolandians to import and export textiles, what will happen to the price of textiles and the quantity of textiles sold in the domestic textile market?
- Who will gain from free trade in textiles and who will lose, and will the gains exceed the losses?
- Should a tariff (a tax on textile imports) be part of the new trade policy?

After reviewing supply and demand in their favorite textbook (this one, of course), the Isolandian economics team begins its analysis.

THE WORLD PRICE AND COMPARATIVE ADVANTAGE

The first issue our economists take up is whether Isoland is likely to become a textile importer or a textile exporter. In other words, if free trade is allowed, will Isolandians end up buying or selling textiles in world markets?

To answer this question, the economists compare the current Isolandian price of textiles to the price of textiles in other countries. We call the price prevailing in world markets the **world price**. If the world price of textiles is higher than the domestic price, then Isoland will export textiles once trade is permitted. Isolandian textile producers will be eager to receive the higher prices available abroad and will start selling their textiles to buyers in other countries. Conversely, if the world price of textiles is lower than the domestic price, then Isoland will import textiles. Because foreign sellers offer a better price, Isolandian textile consumers will quickly start buying textiles from other countries.

world price
the price of a good that prevails in the world market for that good

In essence, comparing the world price and the domestic price before trade indicates whether Isoland has a comparative advantage in producing textiles. The domestic price reflects the opportunity cost of textiles: It tells us how much an Isolandian must give up to obtain one unit of textiles. If the domestic price is low, the cost of producing textiles in Isoland is low, suggesting that Isoland has a comparative advantage in producing textiles relative to the rest of the world. If the domestic price is high, then the cost of producing textiles in Isoland is high, suggesting that foreign countries have a comparative advantage in producing textiles.

As we saw in Chapter 3, trade among nations is ultimately based on comparative advantage. That is, trade is beneficial because it allows each nation to specialize in doing what it does best. By comparing the world price and the domestic price before trade, we can determine whether Isoland is better or worse at producing textiles than the rest of the world.

QUICK QUIZ   The country Autarka does not allow international trade. In Autarka, you can buy a wool suit for 3 ounces of gold. Meanwhile, in neighboring countries, you can buy the same suit for 2 ounces of gold. If Autarka were to allow free trade, would it import or export wool suits? Why?

THE WINNERS AND LOSERS FROM TRADE

To analyze the welfare effects of free trade, the Isolandian economists begin with the assumption that Isoland is a small economy compared to the rest of the world. This small-economy assumption means that Isoland's actions have little effect on world markets. Specifically, any change in Isoland's trade policy will not affect the world price of textiles. The Isolandians are said to be *price takers* in the world economy. That is, they take the world price of textiles as given. Isoland can be an exporting country by selling textiles at this price or an importing country by buying textiles at this price.

The small-economy assumption is not necessary to analyze the gains and losses from international trade. But the Isolandian economists know from experience (and from reading Chapter 2 of this book) that making simplifying assumptions is a key part of building a useful economic model. The assumption that Isoland is a small economy simplifies the analysis, and the basic lessons do not change in the more complicated case of a large economy.

THE GAINS AND LOSSES OF AN EXPORTING COUNTRY

Figure 2 shows the Isolandian textile market when the domestic equilibrium price before trade is below the world price. Once trade is allowed, the domestic price rises to equal the world price. No seller of textiles would accept less than the world price, and no buyer would pay more than the world price.

2 FIGURE

International Trade in an Exporting Country
Once trade is allowed, the domestic price rises to equal the world price. The supply curve shows the quantity of textiles produced domestically, and the demand curve shows the quantity consumed domestically. Exports from Isoland equal the difference between the domestic quantity supplied and the domestic quantity demanded at the world price. Sellers are better off (producer surplus rises from C to B + C + D), and buyers are worse off (consumer surplus falls from A + B to A). Total surplus rises by an amount equal to area D, indicating that trade raises the economic well-being of the country as a whole.

	Before Trade	After Trade	Change
Consumer Surplus	A + B	A	−B
Producer Surplus	C	B + C + D	+(B + D)
Total Surplus	A + B + C	A + B + C + D	+D

The area D shows the increase in total surplus and represents the gains from trade.

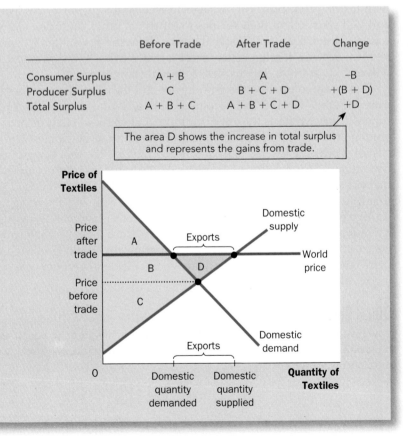

After the domestic price has risen to equal the world price, the domestic quantity supplied differs from the domestic quantity demanded. The supply curve shows the quantity of textiles supplied by Isolandian sellers. The demand curve shows the quantity of textiles demanded by Isolandian buyers. Because the domestic quantity supplied is greater than the domestic quantity demanded, Isoland sells textiles to other countries. Thus, Isoland becomes a textile exporter.

Although domestic quantity supplied and domestic quantity demanded differ, the textile market is still in equilibrium because there is now another participant in the market: the rest of the world. One can view the horizontal line at the world price as representing the rest of the world's demand for textiles. This demand curve is perfectly elastic because Isoland, as a small economy, can sell as many textiles as it wants at the world price.

Now consider the gains and losses from opening up trade. Clearly, not everyone benefits. Trade forces the domestic price to rise to the world price. Domestic producers of textiles are better off because they can now sell textiles at a higher price, but domestic consumers of textiles are worse off because they have to buy textiles at a higher price.

To measure these gains and losses, we look at the changes in consumer and producer surplus. Before trade is allowed, the price of textiles adjusts to balance domestic supply and domestic demand. Consumer surplus, the area between the demand curve and the before-trade price, is area A + B. Producer surplus, the area between the supply curve and the before-trade price, is area C. Total surplus before trade, the sum of consumer and producer surplus, is area A + B + C.

After trade is allowed, the domestic price rises to the world price. Consumer surplus is reduced to area A (the area between the demand curve and the world price). Producer surplus is increased to area B + C + D (the area between the supply curve and the world price). Thus, total surplus with trade is area A + B + C + D.

These welfare calculations show who wins and who loses from trade in an exporting country. Sellers benefit because producer surplus increases by the area B + D. Buyers are worse off because consumer surplus decreases by the area B. Because the gains of sellers exceed the losses of buyers by the area D, total surplus in Isoland increases.

This analysis of an exporting country yields two conclusions:

- When a country allows trade and becomes an exporter of a good, domestic producers of the good are better off, and domestic consumers of the good are worse off.
- Trade raises the economic well-being of a nation in the sense that the gains of the winners exceed the losses of the losers.

THE GAINS AND LOSSES OF AN IMPORTING COUNTRY

Now suppose that the domestic price before trade is above the world price. Once again, after trade is allowed, the domestic price must equal the world price. As Figure 3 shows, the domestic quantity supplied is less than the domestic quantity demanded. The difference between the domestic quantity demanded and the domestic quantity supplied is bought from other countries, and Isoland becomes a textile importer.

In this case, the horizontal line at the world price represents the supply of the rest of the world. This supply curve is perfectly elastic because Isoland is a small economy and, therefore, can buy as many textiles as it wants at the world price.

3 F I G U R E

International Trade in an Importing Country
Once trade is allowed, the domestic price falls to equal the world price. The supply curve shows the amount produced domestically, and the demand curve shows the amount consumed domestically. Imports equal the difference between the domestic quantity demanded and the domestic quantity supplied at the world price. Buyers are better off (consumer surplus rises from A to A + B + D), and sellers are worse off (producer surplus falls from B + C to C). Total surplus rises by an amount equal to area D, indicating that trade raises the economic well-being of the country as a whole.

	Before Trade	After Trade	Change
Consumer Surplus	A	A + B + D	+(B + D)
Producer Surplus	B + C	C	−B
Total Surplus	A + B + C	A + B + C + D	+D

The area D shows the increase in total surplus and represents the gains from trade.

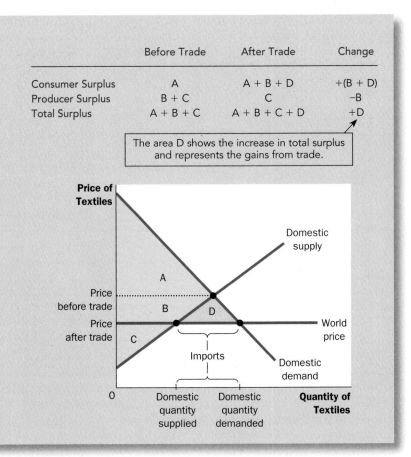

Now consider the gains and losses from trade. Once again, not everyone benefits. When trade forces the domestic price to fall, domestic consumers are better off (they can now buy textiles at a lower price), and domestic producers are worse off (they now have to sell textiles at a lower price). Changes in consumer and producer surplus measure the size of the gains and losses. Before trade, consumer surplus is area A, producer surplus is area B + C, and total surplus is area A + B + C. After trade is allowed, consumer surplus is area A + B + D, producer surplus is area C, and total surplus is area A + B + C + D.

These welfare calculations show who wins and who loses from trade in an importing country. Buyers benefit because consumer surplus increases by the area B + D. Sellers are worse off because producer surplus falls by the area B. The gains of buyers exceed the losses of sellers, and total surplus increases by the area D.

This analysis of an importing country yields two conclusions parallel to those for an exporting country:

- When a country allows trade and becomes an importer of a good, domestic consumers of the good are better off, and domestic producers of the good are worse off.
- Trade raises the economic well-being of a nation in the sense that the gains of the winners exceed the losses of the losers.

Having completed our analysis of trade, we can better understand one of the *Ten Principles of Economics* in Chapter 1: Trade can make everyone better off. If Isoland opens its textile market to international trade, the change will create winners and losers, regardless of whether Isoland ends up exporting or importing textiles. In either case, however, the gains of the winners exceed the losses of the losers, so the winners could compensate the losers and still be better off. In this sense, trade *can* make everyone better off. But *will* trade make everyone better off? Probably not. In practice, compensation for the losers from international trade is rare. Without such compensation, opening an economy to international trade is a policy that expands the size of the economic pie, while perhaps leaving some participants in the economy with a smaller slice.

We can now see why the debate over trade policy is often contentious. Whenever a policy creates winners and losers, the stage is set for a political battle. Nations sometimes fail to enjoy the gains from trade because the losers from free trade are better organized than the winners. The losers may turn their cohesiveness into political clout, lobbying for trade restrictions such as tariffs or import quotas.

The Effects of a Tariff

The Isolandian economists next consider the effects of a **tariff**—a tax on imported goods. The economists quickly realize that a tariff on textiles will have no effect if Isoland becomes a textile exporter. If no one in Isoland is interested in importing textiles, a tax on textile imports is irrelevant. The tariff matters only if Isoland becomes a textile importer. Concentrating their attention on this case, the economists compare welfare with and without the tariff.

tariff
a tax on goods produced abroad and sold domestically

Figure 4 shows the Isolandian market for textiles. Under free trade, the domestic price equals the world price. A tariff raises the price of imported textiles above the world price by the amount of the tariff. Domestic suppliers of textiles, who compete with suppliers of imported textiles, can now sell their textiles for the world price plus the amount of the tariff. Thus, the price of textiles—both imported and domestic—rises by the amount of the tariff and is, therefore, closer to the price that would prevail without trade.

The change in price affects the behavior of domestic buyers and sellers. Because the tariff raises the price of textiles, it reduces the domestic quantity demanded from Q_1^D to Q_2^D and raises the domestic quantity supplied from Q_1^S to Q_2^S. *Thus, the tariff reduces the quantity of imports and moves the domestic market closer to its equilibrium without trade.*

Now consider the gains and losses from the tariff. Because the tariff raises the domestic price, domestic sellers are better off, and domestic buyers are worse off. In addition, the government raises revenue. To measure these gains and losses, we look at the changes in consumer surplus, producer surplus, and government revenue. These changes are summarized in the table in Figure 4.

Before the tariff, the domestic price equals the world price. Consumer surplus, the area between the demand curve and the world price, is area A + B + C + D + E + F. Producer surplus, the area between the supply curve and the world price, is area G. Government revenue equals zero. Total surplus, the sum of consumer surplus, producer surplus, and government revenue, is area A + B + C + D + E + F + G.

Once the government imposes a tariff, the domestic price exceeds the world price by the amount of the tariff. Consumer surplus is now area A + B. Producer

4 FIGURE

A tariff reduces the quantity of imports and moves a market closer to the equilibrium that would exist without trade. Total surplus falls by an amount equal to area D + F. These two triangles represent the deadweight loss from the tariff.

The Effects of a Tariff

	Before Tariff	After Tariff	Change
Consumer Surplus	A + B + C + D + E + F	A + B	−(C + D + E + F)
Producer Surplus	G	C + G	+C
Government Revenue	None	E	+E
Total Surplus	A + B + C + D + E + F + G	A + B + C + E + G	−(D + F)

The area D + F shows the fall in total surplus and represents the deadweight loss of the tariff.

surplus is area C + G. Government revenue, which is the quantity of after-tariff imports times the size of the tariff, is the area E. Thus, total surplus with the tariff is area A + B + C + E + G.

To determine the total welfare effects of the tariff, we add the change in consumer surplus (which is negative), the change in producer surplus (positive), and the change in government revenue (positive). We find that total surplus in the market decreases by the area D + F. This fall in total surplus is called the *deadweight loss* of the tariff.

A tariff causes a deadweight loss simply because a tariff is a type of tax. Like most taxes, it distorts incentives and pushes the allocation of scarce resources

FYI

Import Quotas: Another Way to Restrict Trade

Beyond tariffs, another way that nations sometimes restrict international trade is by putting limits on how much of a good can be imported. In this book, we will not analyze such a policy, other than to point out the conclusion: Import quotas are much like tariffs. Both tariffs and import quotas reduce the quantity of imports, raise the domestic price of the good, decrease the welfare of domestic consumers, increase the welfare of domestic producers, and cause deadweight losses.

There is only one difference between these two types of trade restriction: A tariff raises revenue for the government, whereas an import quota creates surplus for those who obtain the licenses to import. The profit for the holder of an import license is the difference between the domestic price (at which he sells the imported good) and the world price (at which he buys it).

Tariffs and import quotas are even more similar if the government charges a fee for the import licenses. Suppose the government sets the license fee equal to the difference between the domestic price and the world price. In this case, all the profit of license holders is paid to the government in license fees, and the import quota works exactly like a tariff. Consumer surplus, producer surplus, and government revenue are precisely the same under the two policies.

In practice, however, countries that restrict trade with import quotas rarely do so by selling the import licenses. For example, the U.S. government has at times pressured Japan to "voluntarily" limit the sale of Japanese cars in the United States. In this case, the Japanese government allocates the import licenses to Japanese firms, and the surplus from these licenses accrues to those firms. From the standpoint of U.S. welfare, this kind of import quota is worse than a U.S. tariff on imported cars. Both a tariff and an import quota raise prices, restrict trade, and cause deadweight losses, but at least the tariff produces revenue for the U.S. government rather than profit for foreign producers.

---

away from the optimum. In this case, we can identify two effects. First, when the tariff raises the domestic price of textiles above the world price, it encourages domestic producers to increase production from Q_1^S to Q_2^S. Even though the cost of making these incremental units exceeds the cost of buying them at the world price, the tariff makes it profitable for domestic producers to manufacture them nonetheless. Second, when the tariff raises the price that domestic textile consumers have to pay, it encourages them to reduce consumption of textiles from Q_1^D to Q_2^D. Even though domestic consumers value these incremental units at more than the world price, the tariff induces them to cut back their purchases. Area D represents the deadweight loss from the overproduction of textiles, and area F represents the deadweight loss from the underconsumption. The total deadweight loss of the tariff is the sum of these two triangles.

THE LESSONS FOR TRADE POLICY

The team of Isolandian economists can now write to the new president:

Dear Madame President,

You asked us three questions about opening up trade. After much hard work, we have the answers.

Question: If the government allows Isolandians to import and export textiles, what will happen to the price of textiles and the quantity of textiles sold in the domestic textile market?

Answer: Once trade is allowed, the Isolandian price of textiles will be driven to equal the price prevailing around the world.

If the world price is now higher than the Isolandian price, our price will rise. The higher price will reduce the amount of textiles Isolandians consume and raise the amount of textiles that Isolandians produce. Isoland will, therefore, become a textile exporter. This occurs because, in this case, Isoland has a comparative advantage in producing textiles.

Conversely, if the world price is now lower than the Isolandian price, our price will fall. The lower price will raise the amount of textiles that Isolandians consume and lower the amount of textiles that Isolandians produce. Isoland will, therefore, become a textile importer. This occurs because, in this case, other countries have a comparative advantage in producing textiles.

Question: Who will gain from free trade in textiles and who will lose, and will the gains exceed the losses?

Answer: The answer depends on whether the price rises or falls when trade is allowed. If the price rises, producers of textiles gain, and consumers of textiles lose. If the price falls, consumers gain, and producers lose. In both cases, the gains are larger than the losses. Thus, free trade raises the total welfare of Isolandians.

Question: Should a tariff be part of the new trade policy?

Answer: A tariff has an impact only if Isoland becomes a textile importer. In this case, a tariff moves the economy closer to the no-trade equilibrium and, like most taxes, has deadweight losses. Although a tariff improves the welfare of domestic producers and raises revenue for the government, these gains are more than offset by the losses suffered by consumers. The best policy, from the standpoint of economic efficiency, would be to allow trade without a tariff.

We hope you find these answers helpful as you decide on your new policy.

Your faithful servants,
Isolandian economics team

OTHER BENEFITS OF INTERNATIONAL TRADE

The conclusions of the Isolandian economics team are based on the standard analysis of international trade. Their analysis uses the most fundamental tools in the economist's toolbox: supply, demand, and producer and consumer surplus. It shows that there are winners and losers when a nation opens itself up to trade, but the gains to the winners exceed the losses of the losers.

The case for free trade can be made even stronger, however, because there are several other economic benefits of trade beyond those emphasized in the standard analysis. Here, in a nutshell, are some of these other benefits:

- **Increased variety of goods.** Goods produced in different countries are not exactly the same. German beer, for instance, is not the same as American beer. Free trade gives consumers in all countries greater variety from which to choose.

In The News

Should the Winners from Free Trade Compensate the Losers?

Political candidates often say that the government should help those made worse off by international trade. In this opinion piece, an economist makes the opposite case.

What to Expect When You're Free Trading

By Steven E. Landsburg

In the days before Tuesday's Republican presidential primary in Michigan, Mitt Romney and John McCain battled over what the government owes to workers who lose their jobs because of the foreign competition unleashed by free trade. Their rhetoric differed—Mr. Romney said he would "fight for every single job," while Mr. McCain said some jobs "are not coming back"—but their proposed policies were remarkably similar: educate and retrain the workers for new jobs.

All economists know that when American jobs are outsourced, Americans as a group are net winners. What we lose through lower wages is more than offset by what we gain through lower prices. In other words, the winners can more than afford to compensate the losers. Does that mean they ought to? Does it create a moral mandate for the taxpayer-subsidized retraining programs proposed by Mr. McCain and Mr. Romney?

Um, no. Even if you've just lost your job, there's something fundamentally churlish about blaming the very phenomenon that's elevated you above the subsistence level since the day you were born. If the world owes you compensation for enduring the downside of trade, what do you owe the world for enjoying the upside?

I doubt there's a human being on earth who hasn't benefited from the opportunity to trade freely with his neighbors. Imagine what your life would be like if you had to grow your own food, make your own clothes and rely on your grandmother's home remedies for health care. Access to a trained physician might reduce the demand for grandma's home remedies, but—especially at her age—she's still got plenty of reason to be thankful for having a doctor.

Some people suggest, however, that it makes sense to isolate the moral effects of a single new trading opportunity or free trade agreement. Surely we have fellow citizens who are hurt by those agreements, at least in the limited sense that they'd be better off in a world where trade flourishes, except in this one instance. What do we owe those fellow citizens?

One way to think about that is to ask what your moral instincts tell you in analogous situations. Suppose, after years of buying shampoo at your local pharmacy, you discover you can order the same shampoo for less money on the Web. Do you have an obligation to compensate your pharmacist? If you move to a cheaper apartment, should you compensate your landlord? When you eat at McDonald's, should you compensate the owners of the diner next door? Public policy should not be designed to advance moral instincts that we all reject every day of our lives.

In what morally relevant way, then, might displaced workers differ from displaced pharmacists or displaced landlords? You might argue that pharmacists and landlords have always faced cutthroat competition and therefore knew what they were getting into, while decades of tariffs and quotas have led manufacturing workers to expect a modicum of protection. That expectation led them to develop certain skills, and now it's unfair to pull the rug out from under them.

Once again, that argument does not mesh with our everyday instincts. For many decades, schoolyard bullying has been a profitable occupation. All across America, bullies have built up skills so they can take advantage of that opportunity. If we toughen the rules to make bullying unprofitable, must we compensate the bullies?

Bullying and protectionism have a lot in common. They both use force (either directly or through the power of the law) to enrich someone else at your involuntary expense. If you're forced to pay $20 an hour to an American for goods you could have bought from a Mexican for $5 an hour, you're being extorted. When a free trade agreement allows you to buy from the Mexican after all, rejoice in your liberation—even if Mr. McCain, Mr. Romney and the rest of the presidential candidates don't want you to.

Source: *New York Times*, January 16, 2008.

- **Lower costs through economies of scale.** Some goods can be produced at low cost only if they are produced in large quantities—a phenomenon called *economies of scale*. A firm in a small country cannot take full advantage of economies of scale if it can sell only in a small domestic market. Free trade gives firms access to larger world markets and allows them to realize economies of scale more fully.

- **Increased competition.** A company shielded from foreign competitors is more likely to have market power, which in turn gives it the ability to raise prices above competitive levels. This is a type of market failure. Opening up trade fosters competition and gives the invisible hand a better chance to work its magic.

- **Enhanced flow of ideas.** The transfer of technological advances around the world is often thought to be linked to the trading of the goods that embody those advances. The best way for a poor agricultural nation to learn about the computer revolution, for instance, is to buy some computers from abroad rather than trying to make them domestically.

Thus, free international trade increases variety for consumers, allows firms to take advantage of economies of scale, makes markets more competitive, and facilitates the spread of technology. If the Isolandian economists also took these effects into account, their advice to their president would be even more forceful.

QUICK QUIZ   Draw a supply and demand diagram for wool suits in the country of Autarka. When trade is allowed, the price of a suit falls from 3 to 2 ounces of gold. In your diagram, show the change in consumer surplus, the change in producer surplus, and the change in total surplus. How would a tariff on suit imports alter these effects?

THE ARGUMENTS FOR RESTRICTING TRADE

The letter from the economics team starts to persuade the new president of Isoland to consider allowing trade in textiles. She notes that the domestic price is now high compared to the world price. Free trade would, therefore, cause the price of textiles to fall and hurt domestic textiles producers. Before implementing the new policy, she asks Isolandian textile companies to comment on the economists' advice.

Not surprisingly, the textile companies oppose free trade in textiles. They believe that the government should protect the domestic textile industry from foreign competition. Let's consider some of the arguments they might give to support their position and how the economics team would respond.

THE JOBS ARGUMENT

Opponents of free trade often argue that trade with other countries destroys domestic jobs. In our example, free trade in textiles would cause the price of textiles to fall, reducing the quantity of textiles produced in Isoland and thus reducing employment in the Isolandian textile industry. Some Isolandian textile workers would lose their jobs.

Berry's World

"YOU LIKE PROTECTIONISM AS A 'WORKING MAN.' HOW ABOUT AS A CONSUMER?"

In The News

Offshore Outsourcing

If you buy a new computer and call the company for tech support, you shouldn't be surprised if you end up talking to someone in Bangalore, India. In 2004, the author of this textbook, while an adviser to President Bush, was asked about the movement of such jobs overseas. I replied that the trend was "probably a plus for the economy in the long run." Most economists agreed, but some elected officials responded differently.

The Economics of Progress
By George F. Will

It is difficult to say something perfectly, precisely false. But House Speaker Dennis Hastert did when participating in the bipartisan piling-on against the president's economic adviser, who imprudently said something sensible.

John Kerry and John Edwards, who are not speaking under oath and who know that economic illiteracy has never been a disqualification for high office, have led the scrum against the chairman of the president's Council of Economic Advisers, N. Gregory Mankiw, who said the arguments for free trade apply to trade in services as well as manufactured goods. But the prize for the pithiest nonsense went to Hastert: "An economy suffers when jobs disappear."

So the economy suffered when automobiles caused the disappearance of the jobs of most blacksmiths, buggy makers, operators of livery stables, etc.? The economy did not seem to be suffering in 1999, when 33 million jobs were wiped out—by an economic dynamism that created 35.7 million jobs. How many of the 4,500 U.S. jobs that IBM is planning to create this year will be made possible by sending 3,000 jobs overseas?

Hastert's ideal economy, where jobs do not disappear, existed almost everywhere for almost everyone through almost all of human history. In, say, 12th-century France, the ox behind which a man plowed a field changed, but otherwise the plowman was doing what generations of his ancestors had done and what generations of his descendants were to do. Those were the good old days, before economic growth. . . .

For the highly competent workforce of this wealthy nation, the loss of jobs is not a zero-sum game: It is a trading up in social rewards. When the presidential candidates were recently in South Carolina, histrionically lamenting the loss of textile jobs, they surely noticed the huge BMW presence. It is the "offshoring" of German jobs because Germany's irrational labor laws, among other things, give America a comparative advantage. Such economic calculation explains the manufacture of Mercedes-Benzes in Alabama, Hondas in Ohio, Toyotas in California.

As long as the American jobs going offshore were blue-collar jobs, the political issue did not attain the heat it has now that white-collar job losses frighten a more articulate, assertive social class. . . .

Kerry says offshoring is done by "Benedict Arnold CEOs." But if he wants to improve the health of U.S. airlines, and the security of the jobs and pensions of most airline employees, should he not applaud Delta for saving $25 million a year by sending some reservation services to India?

Does Kerry really want to restrain the rise of health care costs? Does he oppose having X-rays analyzed in India at a fraction of the U.S. cost?

In November, Indiana Gov. Joseph Kernan canceled a $15 million contract with a firm in India to process state unemployment claims. The contract was given to a U.S. firm that will charge $23 million. Because of this 53 percent price increase, there will be 8 million fewer state dollars for schools, hospitals, law enforcement, etc. And the benefit to Indiana is . . . what?

When Kernan made this gesture he probably was wearing something that was wholly or partly imported and that at one time, before offshoring, would have been entirely made here. Such potential embarrassments are among the perils of making moral grandstanding into an economic policy.

Source: *The Washington Post*, Friday, February 20, 2004. Page A25. Copyright © 2004, The Washington Post Writers Group. Reprinted with permission.

Yet free trade creates jobs at the same time that it destroys them. When Isolandians buy textiles from other countries, those countries obtain the resources to buy other goods from Isoland. Isolandian workers would move from the textile industry to those industries in which Isoland has a comparative advantage. The transition may impose hardship on some workers in the short run, but it allows Isolandians as a whole to enjoy a higher standard of living.

Opponents of trade are often skeptical that trade creates jobs. They might respond that *everything* can be produced more cheaply abroad. Under free trade, they might argue, Isolandians could not be profitably employed in any industry. As Chapter 3 explains, however, the gains from trade are based on comparative advantage, not absolute advantage. Even if one country is better than another country at producing everything, each country can still gain from trading with the other. Workers in each country will eventually find jobs in an industry in which that country has a comparative advantage.

THE NATIONAL-SECURITY ARGUMENT

When an industry is threatened with competition from other countries, opponents of free trade often argue that the industry is vital for national security. For example, if Isoland were considering free trade in steel, domestic steel companies might point out that steel is used to make guns and tanks. Free trade would allow Isoland to become dependent on foreign countries to supply steel. If a war later broke out and the foreign supply was interrupted, Isoland might be unable to produce enough steel and weapons to defend itself.

Economists acknowledge that protecting key industries may be appropriate when there are legitimate concerns over national security. Yet they fear that this argument may be used too quickly by producers eager to gain at consumers' expense.

One should be wary of the national-security argument when it is made by representatives of industry rather than the defense establishment. Companies have an incentive to exaggerate their role in national defense to obtain protection from foreign competition. A nation's generals may see things very differently. Indeed, when the military is a consumer of an industry's output, it would benefit from imports. Cheaper steel in Isoland, for example, would allow the Isolandian military to accumulate a stockpile of weapons at lower cost.

THE INFANT-INDUSTRY ARGUMENT

New industries sometimes argue for temporary trade restrictions to help them get started. After a period of protection, the argument goes, these industries will mature and be able to compete with foreign firms.

Similarly, older industries sometimes argue that they need temporary protection to help them adjust to new conditions. For example, in 2002, President Bush imposed temporary tariffs on imported steel. He said, "I decided that imports were severely affecting our industry, an important industry." The tariff, which lasted 20 months, offered "temporary relief so that the industry could restructure itself."

Economists are often skeptical about such claims, largely because the infant-industry argument is difficult to implement in practice. To apply protection successfully, the government would need to decide which industries will eventually be profitable and decide whether the benefits of establishing these industries exceed the costs of this protection to consumers. Yet "picking winners" is extraordinarily difficult. It is made even more difficult by the political process, which often awards protection to those industries that are politically powerful. And once a powerful industry is protected from foreign competition, the "temporary" policy is sometimes hard to remove.

In addition, many economists are skeptical about the infant-industry argument in principle. Suppose, for instance, that an industry is young and unable to compete profitably against foreign rivals, but there is reason to believe that the industry can be profitable in the long run. In this case, firm owners should be willing to incur temporary losses to obtain the eventual profits. Protection is not necessary for an infant industry to grow. History shows that start-up firms often incur temporary losses and succeed in the long run, even without protection from competition.

THE UNFAIR-COMPETITION ARGUMENT

A common argument is that free trade is desirable only if all countries play by the same rules. If firms in different countries are subject to different laws and regulations, then it is unfair (the argument goes) to expect the firms to compete in the international marketplace. For instance, suppose that the government of Neighborland subsidizes its textile industry by giving textile companies large tax breaks. The Isolandian textile industry might argue that it should be protected from this foreign competition because Neighborland is not competing fairly.

Would it, in fact, hurt Isoland to buy textiles from another country at a subsidized price? Certainly, Isolandian textile producers would suffer, but Isolandian textile consumers would benefit from the low price. The case for free trade is no different: The gains of the consumers from buying at the low price would exceed the losses of the producers. Neighborland's subsidy to its textile industry may be a bad policy, but it is the taxpayers of Neighborland who bear the burden. Isoland can benefit from the opportunity to buy textiles at a subsidized price.

THE PROTECTION-AS-A-BARGAINING-CHIP ARGUMENT

Another argument for trade restrictions concerns the strategy of bargaining. Many policymakers claim to support free trade but, at the same time, argue that trade restrictions can be useful when we bargain with our trading partners. They claim that the threat of a trade restriction can help remove a trade restriction already imposed by a foreign government. For example, Isoland might threaten to impose a tariff on textiles unless Neighborland removes its tariff on wheat. If Neighborland responds to this threat by removing its tariff, the result can be freer trade.

The problem with this bargaining strategy is that the threat may not work. If it doesn't work, the country faces a choice between two bad options. It can carry out its threat and implement the trade restriction, which would reduce its own economic welfare. Or it can back down from its threat, which would cause it to lose prestige in international affairs. Faced with this choice, the country would probably wish that it had never made the threat in the first place.

In The News

Second Thoughts about Free Trade

Some economists worry about the impact of trade on the distribution of income. Even if free trade enhances efficiency, it may reduce equality.

Trouble with Trade

By Paul Krugman

While the United States has long imported oil and other raw materials from the third world, we used to import manufactured goods mainly from other rich countries like Canada, European nations and Japan.

But recently we crossed an important watershed: we now import more manufactured goods from the third world than from other advanced economies. That is, a majority of our industrial trade is now with countries that are much poorer than we are and that pay their workers much lower wages.

For the world economy as a whole—and especially for poorer nations—growing trade between high-wage and low-wage countries is a very good thing. Above all, it offers backward economies their best hope of moving up the income ladder.

But for American workers the story is much less positive. In fact, it's hard to avoid the conclusion that growing U.S. trade with third-world countries reduces the real wages of many and perhaps most workers in this country. And that reality makes the politics of trade very difficult.

Let's talk for a moment about the economics.

Trade between high-wage countries tends to be a modest win for all, or almost all, concerned. When a free-trade pact made it possible to integrate the U.S. and Canadian auto industries in the 1960s, each country's industry concentrated on producing a nar-rower range of products at larger scale. The result was an all-round, broadly shared rise in productivity and wages.

By contrast, trade between countries at very different levels of economic development tends to create large classes of losers as well as winners.

Although the outsourcing of some high-tech jobs to India has made headlines, on balance, highly educated workers in the United States benefit from higher wages and expanded job opportunities because of trade. For example, ThinkPad notebook computers are now made by a Chinese company, Lenovo, but a lot of Lenovo's research and development is conducted in North Carolina.

But workers with less formal education either see their jobs shipped overseas or

---

CASE STUDY

TRADE AGREEMENTS AND THE WORLD TRADE ORGANIZATION

A country can take one of two approaches to achieving free trade. It can take a *unilateral* approach and remove its trade restrictions on its own. This is the approach that Great Britain took in the 19th century and that Chile and South Korea have taken in recent years. Alternatively, a country can take a *multilateral* approach and reduce its trade restrictions while other countries do the same. In other words, it can bargain with its trading partners in an attempt to reduce trade restrictions around the world.

One important example of the multilateral approach is the North American Free Trade Agreement (NAFTA), which in 1993 lowered trade barriers among the United States, Mexico, and Canada. Another is the General Agreement on Tariffs and Trade (GATT), which is a continuing series of negotiations among many of the world's countries with the goal of promoting free trade. The United States find their wages driven down by the ripple effect as other workers with similar qualifications crowd into their industries and look for employment to replace the jobs they lost to foreign competition. And lower prices at Wal-Mart aren't sufficient compensation.

All this is textbook international economics: contrary to what people sometimes assert, economic theory says that free trade normally makes a country richer, but it doesn't say that it's normally good for everyone. Still, when the effects of third-world exports on U.S. wages first became an issue in the 1990s, a number of economists—myself included—looked at the data and concluded that any negative effects on U.S. wages were modest.

The trouble now is that these effects may no longer be as modest as they were, because imports of manufactured goods from the third world have grown dramatically—from just 2.5 percent of G.D.P. in 1990 to 6 percent in 2006.

And the biggest growth in imports has come from countries with very low wages.

The original "newly industrializing economies" exporting manufactured goods—South Korea, Taiwan, Hong Kong and Singapore—paid wages that were about 25 percent of U.S. levels in 1990. Since then, however, the sources of our imports have shifted to Mexico, where wages are only 11 percent of the U.S. level, and China, where they're only about 3 percent or 4 percent.

There are some qualifying aspects to this story. For example, many of those made-in-China goods contain components made in Japan and other high-wage economies. Still, there's little doubt that the pressure of globalization on American wages has increased.

So am I arguing for protectionism? No. Those who think that globalization is always and everywhere a bad thing are wrong. On the contrary, keeping world markets relatively open is crucial to the hopes of billions of people.

But I am arguing for an end to the finger-wagging, the accusation either of not understanding economics or of kowtow-ing to special interests that tends to be the editorial response to politicians who express skepticism about the benefits of free-trade agreements.

It's often claimed that limits on trade benefit only a small number of Americans, while hurting the vast majority. That's still true of things like the import quota on sugar. But when it comes to manufactured goods, it's at least arguable that the reverse is true. The highly educated workers who clearly benefit from growing trade with third-world economies are a minority, greatly outnumbered by those who probably lose.

As I said, I'm not a protectionist. For the sake of the world as a whole, I hope that we respond to the trouble with trade not by shutting trade down, but by doing things like strengthening the social safety net. But those who are worried about trade have a point, and deserve some respect.

Source: *New York Times,* December 28, 2007.

helped to found GATT after World War II in response to the high tariffs imposed during the Great Depression of the 1930s. Many economists believe that the high tariffs contributed to the worldwide economic hardship of that period. GATT has successfully reduced the average tariff among member countries from about 40 percent after World War II to about 5 percent today.

The rules established under GATT are now enforced by an international institution called the World Trade Organization (WTO). The WTO was established in 1995 and has its headquarters in Geneva, Switzerland. As of July 2007, 151 countries have joined the organization, accounting for more than 97 percent of world trade. The functions of the WTO are to administer trade agreements, provide a forum for negotiations, and handle disputes among member countries.

What are the pros and cons of the multilateral approach to free trade? One advantage is that the multilateral approach has the potential to result in freer trade than a unilateral approach because it can reduce trade restrictions abroad as well as at home. If international negotiations fail, however, the result could be more restricted trade than under a unilateral approach.

In addition, the multilateral approach may have a political advantage. In most markets, producers are fewer and better organized than consumers—and thus wield greater political influence. Reducing the Isolandian tariff on textiles, for example, may be politically difficult if considered by itself. The textile companies would oppose free trade, and the buyers of textiles who would benefit are so numerous that organizing their support would be difficult. Yet suppose that Neighborland promises to reduce its tariff on wheat at the same time that Isoland reduces its tariff on textiles. In this case, the Isolandian wheat farmers, who are also politically powerful, would back the agreement. Thus, the multilateral approach to free trade can sometimes win political support when a unilateral approach cannot. ●

QUICK QUIZ The textile industry of Autarka advocates a ban on the import of wool suits. Describe five arguments its lobbyists might make. Give a response to each of these arguments.

CONCLUSION

Economists and the public often disagree about free trade. In December 2007, the *Los Angeles Times* asked the American public, "Generally speaking, do you believe that free international trade has helped or hurt the economy, or hasn't it made a difference to the economy one way or the other?" Only 27 percent of those polled said free international trade helped, whereas 44 percent thought it hurt. (The rest thought it made no difference or were unsure.) By contrast, most economists support free international trade. They view free trade as a way of allocating production efficiently and raising living standards both at home and abroad.

Economists view the United States as an ongoing experiment that confirms the virtues of free trade. Throughout its history, the United States has allowed unrestricted trade among the states, and the country as a whole has benefited from the specialization that trade allows. Florida grows oranges, Texas pumps oil, California makes wine, and so on. Americans would not enjoy the high standard of living they do today if people could consume only those goods and services produced in their own states. The world could similarly benefit from free trade among countries.

To better understand economists' view of trade, let's continue our parable. Suppose that the president of Isoland, after reading the latest poll results, ignores the advice of her economics team and decides not to allow free trade in textiles. The country remains in the equilibrium without international trade.

Then, one day, some Isolandian inventor discovers a new way to make textiles at very low cost. The process is quite mysterious, however, and the inventor insists on keeping it a secret. What is odd is that the inventor doesn't need traditional inputs such as cotton or wool. The only material input he needs is wheat. And even more oddly, to manufacture textiles from wheat, he hardly needs any labor input at all.

The inventor is hailed as a genius. Because everyone buys clothing, the lower cost of textiles allows all Isolandians to enjoy a higher standard of living. Workers who had previously produced textiles experience some hardship when their factories close, but eventually, they find work in other industries. Some become farmers and grow the wheat that the inventor turns into textiles. Others enter new industries that emerge as a result of higher Isolandian living standards. Everyone understands that the displacement of workers in outmoded industries is an inevitable part of technological progress and economic growth.

After several years, a newspaper reporter decides to investigate this mysterious new textiles process. She sneaks into the inventor's factory and learns that the inventor is a fraud. The inventor has not been making textiles at all. Instead, he has been smuggling wheat abroad in exchange for textiles from other countries. The only thing that the inventor had discovered was the gains from international trade.

When the truth is revealed, the government shuts down the inventor's operation. The price of textiles rises, and workers return to jobs in textile factories. Living standards in Isoland fall back to their former levels. The inventor is jailed and held up to public ridicule. After all, he was no inventor. He was just an economist.

SUMMARY

- The effects of free trade can be determined by comparing the domestic price without trade to the world price. A low domestic price indicates that the country has a comparative advantage in producing the good and that the country will become an exporter. A high domestic price indicates that the rest of the world has a comparative advantage in producing the good and that the country will become an importer.

- When a country allows trade and becomes an exporter of a good, producers of the good are better off, and consumers of the good are worse off. When a country allows trade and becomes an importer of a good, consumers are better off, and producers are worse off. In both cases, the gains from trade exceed the losses.

- A tariff—a tax on imports—moves a market closer to the equilibrium that would exist without trade and, therefore, reduces the gains from trade. Although domestic producers are better off and the government raises revenue, the losses to consumers exceed these gains.

- There are various arguments for restricting trade: protecting jobs, defending national security, helping infant industries, preventing unfair competition, and responding to foreign trade restrictions. Although some of these arguments have some merit in some cases, economists believe that free trade is usually the better policy.

KEY CONCEPTS

world price, *p. 179*   tariff, *p. 183*

QUESTIONS FOR REVIEW

1. What does the domestic price that prevails without international trade tell us about a nation's comparative advantage?
2. When does a country become an exporter of a good? An importer?
3. Draw the supply-and-demand diagram for an importing country. What is consumer surplus and producer surplus before trade is allowed? What is consumer surplus and producer surplus with free trade? What is the change in total surplus?
4. Describe what a tariff is and its economic effects.
5. List five arguments often given to support trade restrictions. How do economists respond to these arguments?
6. What is the difference between the unilateral and multilateral approaches to achieving free trade? Give an example of each.

PROBLEMS AND APPLICATIONS

1. Mexico represents a small part of the world orange market.
   a. Draw a diagram depicting the equilibrium in the Mexican orange market without international trade. Identify the equilibrium price, equilibrium quantity, consumer surplus, and producer surplus.
   b. Suppose that the world orange price is below the Mexican price before trade and that the Mexican orange market is now opened to trade. Identify the new equilibrium price, quantity consumed, quantity produced domestically, and quantity imported. Also show the change in the surplus of domestic consumers and producers. Has total surplus increased or decreased?

2. The world price of wine is below the price that would prevail in Canada in the absence of trade.
   a. Assuming that Canadian imports of wine are a small part of total world wine production, draw a graph for the Canadian market for wine under free trade. Identify consumer surplus, producer surplus, and total surplus in an appropriate table.
   b. Now suppose that an unusual shift of the Gulf Stream leads to an unseasonably cold summer in Europe, destroying much of the grape harvest there. What effect does this shock have on the world price of wine? Using your graph and table from part (a), show the effect on consumer surplus, producer sur-

plus, and total surplus in Canada. Who are the winners and losers? Is Canada as a whole better or worse off?

3. Suppose that Congress imposes a tariff on imported autos to protect the U.S. auto industry from foreign competition. Assuming that the United States is a price taker in the world auto market, show on a diagram: the change in the quantity of imports, the loss to U.S. consumers, the gain to U.S. manufacturers, government revenue, and the deadweight loss associated with the tariff. The loss to consumers can be decomposed into three pieces: a gain to domestic producers, revenue for the government, and a deadweight loss. Use your diagram to identify these three pieces.

4. When China's clothing industry expands, the increase in world supply lowers the world price of clothing.
   a. Draw an appropriate diagram to analyze how this change in price affects consumer surplus, producer surplus, and total surplus in a nation that imports clothing, such as the United States.
   b. Now draw an appropriate diagram to show how this change in price affects consumer surplus, producer surplus, and total surplus in a nation that exports clothing, such as the Dominican Republic.
   c. Compare your answers to parts (a) and (b). What are the similarities and what are the differences? Which country should be concerned about the expansion of the Chinese textile industry? Which country should be applauding it? Explain.

5. Imagine that winemakers in the state of Washington petitioned the state government to tax wines imported from California. They argue that this tax would both raise tax revenue for the state government and raise employment in the Washington State wine industry. Do you agree with these claims? Is it a good policy?

6. Consider the arguments for restricting trade.
   a. Assume you are a lobbyist for timber, an established industry suffering from low-priced foreign competition. Which two or three of the five arguments do you think would be most persuasive to the average member of Congress as to why he or she should support trade restrictions? Explain your reasoning.
   b. Now assume you are an astute student of economics (hopefully not a hard assumption). Although all the arguments for restricting trade have their shortcomings, name the two or three arguments that seem to make the most economic sense to you. For each, describe the economic rationale for and against these arguments for trade restrictions.

7. Senator Ernest Hollings once wrote that "consumers *do not* benefit from lower-priced imports. Glance through some mail-order catalogs and you'll see that consumers pay exactly the same price for clothing whether it is U.S.-made or imported." Comment.

8. The nation of Textilia does not allow imports of clothing. In its equilibrium without trade, a T-shirt costs $20, and the equilibrium quantity is 3 million T-shirts. One day, after reading Adam Smith's *The Wealth of Nations* while on vacation, the president decides to open the Textilian market to international trade. The market price of a T-shirt falls to the world price of $16. The number of T-shirts consumed in Textilia rises to 4 million, while the number of T-shirts produced declines to 1 million.
   a. Illustrate the situation just described in a graph. Your graph should show all the numbers.
   b. Calculate the change in consumer surplus, producer surplus, and total surplus that results from opening up trade. (Hint: Recall that the area of a triangle is ½ × base × height.)

9. China is a major producer of grains, such as wheat, corn, and rice. In 2008 the Chinese government, concerned that grain exports were driving up food prices for domestic consumers, imposed a tax on grain exports.
   a. Draw the graph that describes the market for grain in an exporting country. Use this graph as the starting point to answer the following questions.
   b. How does an export tax affect domestic grain prices?
   c. How does it affect the welfare of domestic consumers, the welfare of domestic producers, and government revenue?
   d. What happens to total welfare in China, as measured by the sum of consumer surplus, producer surplus, and tax revenue?

10. Consider a country that imports a good from abroad. For each of following statements, say whether it is true or false. Explain your answer.
    a. "The greater the elasticity of demand, the greater the gains from trade."
    b. "If demand is perfectly inelastic, there are no gains from trade."
    c. "If demand is perfectly inelastic, consumers do not benefit from trade."

11. Kawmin is a small country that produces and consumes jelly beans. The world price of jelly beans is $1 per bag, and Kawmin's domestic demand and supply for jelly beans are governed by the following equations:

    Demand: $Q^D = 8 - P$
    Supply: $Q^S = P$,

    where P is in dollars per bag and Q is in bags of jelly beans.
    a. Draw a well-labeled graph of the situation in Kawmin if the nation does not allow trade. Calculate the following (recalling that the area of a triangle is ½ × base × height): the equilibrium price and quantity, consumer surplus, producer surplus, and total surplus.

    b. Kawmin then opens the market to trade. Draw another graph to describe the new situation in the jelly bean market. Calculate the equilibrium price, quantities of consumption and production, imports, consumer surplus, producer surplus, and total surplus.
    c. After awhile, the Czar of Kawmin responds to the pleas of jelly bean producers by placing a $1 per bag tariff on jelly bean imports. On a graph, show the effects of this tariff. Calculate the equilibrium price, quantities of consumption and production, imports, consumer surplus, producer surplus, government revenue, and total surplus.
    d. What are the gains from opening up trade? What are the deadweight losses from restricting trade with the tariff? Give numerical answers.

12. Assume the United States is an importer of televisions and there are no trade restrictions. U.S. consumers buy 1 million televisions per year, of which 400,000 are produced domestically and 600,000 are imported.
    a. Suppose that a technological advance among Japanese television manufacturers causes the world price of televisions to fall by $100. Draw a graph to show how this change affects the welfare of U.S. consumers and U.S. producers and how it affects total surplus in the United States.
    b. After the fall in price, consumers buy 1.2 million televisions, of which 200,000 are produced domestically and 1 million are imported. Calculate the change in consumer surplus, producer surplus, and total surplus from the price reduction.
    c. If the government responded by putting a $100 tariff on imported televisions, what would this do? Calculate the revenue that would be raised and the deadweight loss. Would it be a good policy from the standpoint of U.S. welfare? Who might support the policy?

d. Suppose that the fall in price is attributable not to technological advance but to a $100 per television subsidy from the Japanese government to Japanese industry. How would this affect your analysis?

13. Consider a small country that exports steel. Suppose that a "pro-trade" government decides to subsidize the export of steel by paying a certain amount for each ton sold abroad. How does this export subsidy affect the domestic price of steel, the quantity of steel produced, the quantity of steel consumed, and the quantity of steel exported? How does it affect consumer surplus, producer surplus, government revenue, and total surplus? Is it a good policy from the standpoint of economic efficiency? (Hint: The analysis of an export subsidy is similar to the analysis of a tariff.)

PART IV

The Economics of the Public Sector

Externalities

Firms that make and sell paper also create, as a by-product of the manufacturing process, a chemical called dioxin. Scientists believe that once dioxin enters the environment, it raises the population's risk of cancer, birth defects, and other health problems.

Is the production and release of dioxin a problem for society? In Chapters 4 through 9, we examined how markets allocate scarce resources with the forces of supply and demand, and we saw that the equilibrium of supply and demand is typically an efficient allocation of resources. To use Adam Smith's famous metaphor, the "invisible hand" of the marketplace leads self-interested buyers and sellers in a market to maximize the total benefit that society derives from that market. This insight is the basis for one of the *Ten Principles of Economics* in Chapter 1: Markets are usually a good way to organize economic activity. Should we conclude, therefore, that the invisible hand prevents firms in the paper market from emitting too much dioxin?

Markets do many things well, but they do not do everything well. In this chapter, we begin our study of another of the *Ten Principles of Economics:* Government action can sometimes improve upon market outcomes. We examine why markets sometimes fail to allocate resources efficiently, how government policies can potentially improve the market's allocation, and what kinds of policies are likely to work best.

externality
the uncompensated
impact of one person's
actions on the well-being
of a bystander

The market failures examined in this chapter fall under a general category called *externalities*. An **externality** arises when a person engages in an activity that influences the well-being of a bystander and yet neither pays nor receives any compensation for that effect. If the impact on the bystander is adverse, it is called a *negative externality*. If it is beneficial, it is called a *positive externality*. In the presence of externalities, society's interest in a market outcome extends beyond the well-being of buyers and sellers who participate in the market to include the well-being of bystanders who are affected indirectly. Because buyers and sellers neglect the external effects of their actions when deciding how much to demand or supply, the market equilibrium is not efficient when there are externalities. That is, the equilibrium fails to maximize the total benefit to society as a whole. The release of dioxin into the environment, for instance, is a negative externality. Self-interested paper firms will not consider the full cost of the pollution they create in their production process, and consumers of paper will not consider the full cost of the pollution they contribute from their purchasing decisions. Therefore, the firms will emit too much pollution unless the government prevents or discourages them from doing so.

Externalities come in many varieties, as do the policy responses that try to deal with the market failure. Here are some examples:

- The exhaust from automobiles is a negative externality because it creates smog that other people have to breathe. As a result of this externality, drivers tend to pollute too much. The federal government attempts to solve this problem by setting emission standards for cars. It also taxes gasoline to reduce the amount that people drive.
- Restored historic buildings convey a positive externality because people who walk or ride by them can enjoy the beauty and the sense of history that these buildings provide. Building owners do not get the full benefit of restoration and, therefore, tend to discard older buildings too quickly. Many local governments respond to this problem by regulating the destruction of historic buildings and by providing tax breaks to owners who restore them.
- Barking dogs create a negative externality because neighbors are disturbed by the noise. Dog owners do not bear the full cost of the noise and, therefore, tend to take too few precautions to prevent their dogs from barking. Local governments address this problem by making it illegal to "disturb the peace."
- Research into new technologies provides a positive externality because it creates knowledge that other people can use. Because inventors cannot capture the full benefits of their inventions, they tend to devote too few resources to research. The federal government addresses this problem partially through the patent system, which gives inventors exclusive use of their inventions for a limited time.

In each of these cases, some decision maker fails to take account of the external effects of his or her behavior. The government responds by trying to influence this behavior to protect the interests of bystanders.

EXTERNALITIES AND MARKET INEFFICIENCY

In this section, we use the tools of welfare economics developed in Chapter 7 to examine how externalities affect economic well-being. The analysis shows precisely why externalities cause markets to allocate resources inefficiently. Later in the chapter, we examine various ways in which private individuals and public policymakers may remedy this type of market failure.

WELFARE ECONOMICS: A RECAP

We begin by recalling the key lessons of welfare economics from Chapter 7. To make our analysis concrete, we consider a specific market—the market for aluminum. Figure 1 shows the supply and demand curves in the market for aluminum.

As you should recall from Chapter 7, the supply and demand curves contain important information about costs and benefits. The demand curve for aluminum reflects the value of aluminum to consumers, as measured by the prices they are willing to pay. At any given quantity, the height of the demand curve shows the willingness to pay of the marginal buyer. In other words, it shows the value to the consumer of the last unit of aluminum bought. Similarly, the supply curve reflects the costs of producing aluminum. At any given quantity, the height of the supply curve shows the cost of the marginal seller. In other words, it shows the cost to the producer of the last unit of aluminum sold.

In the absence of government intervention, the price adjusts to balance the supply and demand for aluminum. The quantity produced and consumed in the market equilibrium, shown as Q_{MARKET} in Figure 1, is efficient in the sense that it maximizes the sum of producer and consumer surplus. That is, the market allocates resources in a way that maximizes the total value to the consumers who buy and use aluminum minus the total costs to the producers who make and sell aluminum.

NEGATIVE EXTERNALITIES

Now let's suppose that aluminum factories emit pollution: For each unit of aluminum produced, a certain amount of smoke enters the atmosphere. Because this

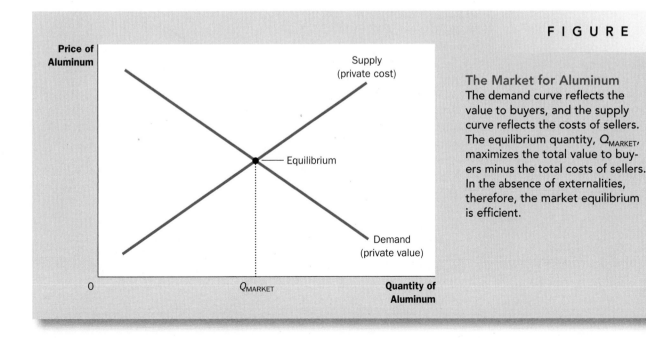

FIGURE 1

The Market for Aluminum
The demand curve reflects the value to buyers, and the supply curve reflects the costs of sellers. The equilibrium quantity, Q_{MARKET}, maximizes the total value to buyers minus the total costs of sellers. In the absence of externalities, therefore, the market equilibrium is efficient.

"ALL I CAN SAY IS THAT IF BEING A LEADING MANUFACTURER MEANS BEING A LEADING POLLUTER, SO BE IT."

smoke creates a health risk for those who breathe the air, it is a negative externality. How does this externality affect the efficiency of the market outcome?

Because of the externality, the cost to *society* of producing aluminum is larger than the cost to the aluminum producers. For each unit of aluminum produced, the *social cost* includes the private costs of the aluminum producers plus the costs to those bystanders affected adversely by the pollution. Figure 2 shows the social cost of producing aluminum. The social-cost curve is above the supply curve because it takes into account the external costs imposed on society by aluminum producers. The difference between these two curves reflects the cost of the pollution emitted.

What quantity of aluminum should be produced? To answer this question, we once again consider what a benevolent social planner would do. The planner wants to maximize the total surplus derived from the market—the value to consumers of aluminum minus the cost of producing aluminum. The planner understands, however, that the cost of producing aluminum includes the external costs of the pollution.

The planner would choose the level of aluminum production at which the demand curve crosses the social-cost curve. This intersection determines the optimal amount of aluminum from the standpoint of society as a whole. Below this level of production, the value of the aluminum to consumers (as measured by the height of the demand curve) exceeds the social cost of producing it (as measured by the height of the social-cost curve). The planner does not produce more than this level because the social cost of producing additional aluminum exceeds the value to consumers.

Note that the equilibrium quantity of aluminum, Q_{MARKET}, is larger than the socially optimal quantity, $Q_{OPTIMUM}$. This inefficiency occurs because the market equilibrium reflects only the private costs of production. In the market equilib-

---

2 F I G U R E

Pollution and the Social Optimum
In the presence of a negative externality, such as pollution, the social cost of the good exceeds the private cost. The optimal quantity, $Q_{OPTIMUM}$, is therefore smaller than the equilibrium quantity, Q_{MARKET}.

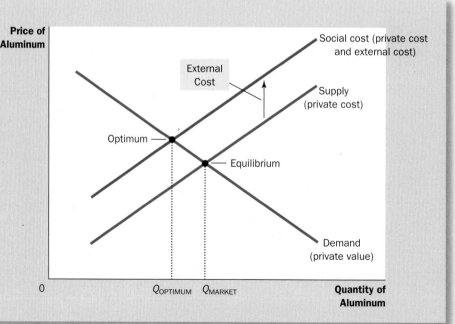

rium, the marginal consumer values aluminum at less than the social cost of producing it. That is, at Q_{MARKET}, the demand curve lies below the social-cost curve. Thus, reducing aluminum production and consumption below the market equilibrium level raises total economic well-being.

How can the social planner achieve the optimal outcome? One way would be to tax aluminum producers for each ton of aluminum sold. The tax would shift the supply curve for aluminum upward by the size of the tax. If the tax accurately reflected the external cost of smoke released into the atmosphere, the new supply curve would coincide with the social-cost curve. In the new market equilibrium, aluminum producers would produce the socially optimal quantity of aluminum.

The use of such a tax is called **internalizing the externality** because it gives buyers and sellers in the market an incentive to take into account the external effects of their actions. Aluminum producers would, in essence, take the costs of pollution into account when deciding how much aluminum to supply because the tax would make them pay for these external costs. And, because the market price would reflect the tax on producers, consumers of aluminum would have an incentive to use a smaller quantity. The policy is based on one of the *Ten Principles of Economics:* People respond to incentives. Later in this chapter, we consider in more detail how policymakers can deal with externalities.

internalizing the externality
altering incentives so that people take account of the external effects of their actions

POSITIVE EXTERNALITIES

Although some activities impose costs on third parties, others yield benefits. For example, consider education. To a large extent, the benefit of education is private: The consumer of education becomes a more productive worker and thus reaps much of the benefit in the form of higher wages. Beyond these private benefits, however, education also yields positive externalities. One externality is that a more educated population leads to more informed voters, which means better government for everyone. Another externality is that a more educated population tends to mean lower crime rates. A third externality is that a more educated population may encourage the development and dissemination of technological advances, leading to higher productivity and wages for everyone. Because of these three positive externalities, a person may prefer to have neighbors who are well educated.

The analysis of positive externalities is similar to the analysis of negative externalities. As Figure 3 shows, the demand curve does not reflect the value to society of the good. Because the social value is greater than the private value, the social-value curve lies above the demand curve. The optimal quantity is found where the social-value curve and the supply curve (which represents costs) intersect. Hence, the socially optimal quantity is greater than the quantity determined by the private market.

Once again, the government can correct the market failure by inducing market participants to internalize the externality. The appropriate response in the case of positive externalities is exactly the opposite to the case of negative externalities. To move the market equilibrium closer to the social optimum, a positive externality requires a subsidy. In fact, that is exactly the policy the government follows: Education is heavily subsidized through public schools and government scholarships.

To summarize: *Negative externalities lead markets to produce a larger quantity than is socially desirable. Positive externalities lead markets to produce a smaller quantity than*

3 FIGURE

Education and the Social Optimum
In the presence of a positive externality, the social value of the good exceeds the private value. The optimal quantity, $Q_{OPTIMUM}$, is therefore larger than the equilibrium quantity, Q_{MARKET}.

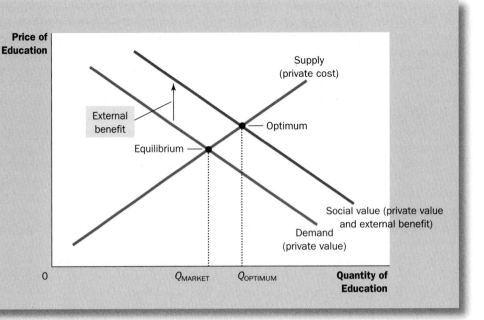

is socially desirable. To remedy the problem, the government can internalize the externality by taxing goods that have negative externalities and subsidizing goods that have positive externalities.

CASE STUDY   TECHNOLOGY SPILLOVERS, INDUSTRIAL POLICY, AND PATENT PROTECTION

A potentially important type of positive externality is called a *technology spillover*—the impact of one firm's research and production efforts on other firms' access to technological advance. For example, consider the market for industrial robots. Robots are at the frontier of a rapidly changing technology. Whenever a firm builds a robot, there is some chance that it will discover a new and better design. This new design may benefit not only this firm but society as a whole because the design will enter society's pool of technological knowledge. That is, the new design may have positive externalities for other producers in the economy.

In this case, the government can internalize the externality by subsidizing the production of robots. If the government paid firms a subsidy for each robot produced, the supply curve would shift down by the amount of the subsidy, and this shift would increase the equilibrium quantity of robots. To ensure that the market equilibrium equals the social optimum, the subsidy should equal the value of the technology spillover.

How large are technology spillovers, and what do they imply for public policy? This is an important question because technological progress is the key to why living standards rise over time. Yet it is also a difficult question on which economists often disagree.

Some economists believe that technology spillovers are pervasive and that the government should encourage those industries that yield the largest spillovers.

For instance, these economists argue that if making computer chips yields greater spillovers than making potato chips, then the government should encourage the production of computer chips relative to the production of potato chips. The U.S. tax code does this in a limited way by offering special tax breaks for expenditures on research and development. Some other nations go further by subsidizing specific industries that supposedly offer large technology spillovers. Government intervention in the economy that aims to promote technology-enhancing industries is sometimes called *industrial policy*.

Other economists are skeptical about industrial policy. Even if technology spillovers are common, the success of an industrial policy requires that the government be able to measure the size of the spillovers from different markets. This measurement problem is difficult at best. Moreover, without precise measurements, the political system may end up subsidizing industries with the most political clout rather than those that yield the largest positive externalities.

Another way to deal with technology spillovers is patent protection. The patent laws protect the rights of inventors by giving them exclusive use of their inventions for a period of time. When a firm makes a technological breakthrough, it can patent the idea and capture much of the economic benefit for itself. The patent internalizes the externality by giving the firm a *property right* over its invention. If other firms want to use the new technology, they would have to obtain permission from the inventing firm and pay it some royalty. Thus, the patent system gives firms a greater incentive to engage in research and other activities that advance technology.   ●

QUICK QUIZ   Give an example of a negative externality and a positive externality. Explain why market outcomes are inefficient in the presence of these externalities.

PUBLIC POLICIES TOWARD EXTERNALITIES

We have discussed why externalities lead markets to allocate resources inefficiently but have mentioned only briefly how this inefficiency can be remedied. In practice, both public policymakers and private individuals respond to externalities in various ways. All of the remedies share the goal of moving the allocation of resources closer to the social optimum.

This section considers governmental solutions. As a general matter, the government can respond to externalities in one of two ways. *Command-and-control policies* regulate behavior directly. *Market-based policies* provide incentives so that private decision makers will choose to solve the problem on their own.

COMMAND-AND-CONTROL POLICIES: REGULATION

The government can remedy an externality by making certain behaviors either required or forbidden. For example, it is a crime to dump poisonous chemicals into the water supply. In this case, the external costs to society far exceed the benefits to the polluter. The government therefore institutes a command-and-control policy that prohibits this act altogether.

In most cases of pollution, however, the situation is not this simple. Despite the stated goals of some environmentalists, it would be impossible to prohibit all polluting activity. For example, virtually all forms of transportation—even the horse—produce some undesirable polluting by-products. But it would not be sensible for the government to ban all transportation. Thus, instead of trying to eradicate pollution entirely, society has to weigh the costs and benefits to decide the kinds and quantities of pollution it will allow. In the United States, the Environmental Protection Agency (EPA) is the government agency with the task of developing and enforcing regulations aimed at protecting the environment.

Environmental regulations can take many forms. Sometimes the EPA dictates a maximum level of pollution that a factory may emit. Other times the EPA requires that firms adopt a particular technology to reduce emissions. In all cases, to design good rules, the government regulators need to know the details about specific industries and about the alternative technologies that those industries could adopt. This information is often difficult for government regulators to obtain.

MARKET-BASED POLICY 1: CORRECTIVE TAXES AND SUBSIDIES

corrective tax
a tax designed to induce private decision makers to take account of the social costs that arise from a negative externality

Instead of regulating behavior in response to an externality, the government can use market-based policies to align private incentives with social efficiency. For instance, as we saw earlier, the government can internalize the externality by taxing activities that have negative externalities and subsidizing activities that have positive externalities. Taxes enacted to deal with the effects of negative externalities are called **corrective taxes**. They are also called *Pigovian taxes* after economist Arthur Pigou (1877–1959), an early advocate of their use. An ideal corrective tax would equal the external cost from an activity with negative externalities, and an ideal corrective subsidy would equal the external benefit from an activity with positive externalities.

Economists usually prefer corrective taxes to regulations as a way to deal with pollution because they can reduce pollution at a lower cost to society. To see why, let us consider an example.

Suppose that two factories—a paper mill and a steel mill—are each dumping 500 tons of glop into a river each year. The EPA decides that it wants to reduce the amount of pollution. It considers two solutions:

- Regulation: The EPA could tell each factory to reduce its pollution to 300 tons of glop per year.
- Corrective tax: The EPA could levy a tax on each factory of $50,000 for each ton of glop it emits.

The regulation would dictate a level of pollution, whereas the tax would give factory owners an economic incentive to reduce pollution. Which solution do you think is better?

Most economists prefer the tax. To explain this preference, they would first point out that a tax is just as effective as a regulation in reducing the overall level of pollution. The EPA can achieve whatever level of pollution it wants by setting the tax at the appropriate level. The higher the tax, the larger the reduction in pollution. If the tax is high enough, the factories will close down altogether, reducing pollution to zero.

Although regulation and corrective taxes are both capable of reducing pollution, the tax accomplishes this goal more efficiently. The regulation requires each factory to reduce pollution by the same amount. An equal reduction, however, is not necessarily the least expensive way to clean up the water. It is possible that the paper mill can reduce pollution at lower cost than the steel mill. If so, the paper mill would respond to the tax by reducing pollution substantially to avoid the tax, whereas the steel mill would respond by reducing pollution less and paying the tax.

In essence, the corrective tax places a price on the right to pollute. Just as markets allocate goods to those buyers who value them most highly, a corrective tax allocates pollution to those factories that face the highest cost of reducing it. Whatever the level of pollution the EPA chooses, it can achieve this goal at the lowest total cost using a tax.

Economists also argue that corrective taxes are better for the environment. Under the command-and-control policy of regulation, the factories have no reason to reduce emission further once they have reached the target of 300 tons of glop. By contrast, the tax gives the factories an incentive to develop cleaner technologies because a cleaner technology would reduce the amount of tax the factory has to pay.

Corrective taxes are unlike most other taxes. As we discussed in Chapter 8, most taxes distort incentives and move the allocation of resources away from the social optimum. The reduction in economic well-being—that is, in consumer and producer surplus—exceeds the amount of revenue the government raises, resulting in a deadweight loss. By contrast, when externalities are present, society also cares about the well-being of the bystanders who are affected. Corrective taxes alter incentives to account for the presence of externalities and thereby move the allocation of resources closer to the social optimum. Thus, while corrective taxes raise revenue for the government, they also enhance economic efficiency.

 ## WHY IS GASOLINE TAXED SO HEAVILY?

In many nations, gasoline is among the most heavily taxed goods. The gas tax can be viewed as a corrective tax aimed at three negative externalities associated with driving:

- *Congestion:* If you have ever been stuck in bumper-to-bumper traffic, you have probably wished that there were fewer cars on the road. A gasoline tax keeps congestion down by encouraging people to take public transportation, carpool more often, and live closer to work.
- *Accidents:* Whenever people buy large cars or sport-utility vehicles, they may make themselves safer but they certainly put their neighbors at risk. According to the National Highway Traffic Safety Administration, a person driving a typical car is five times as likely to die if hit by a sport-utility vehicle than if hit by another car. The gas tax is an indirect way of making people pay when their large, gas-guzzling vehicles impose risk on others, which in turn makes them take this risk into account when choosing what vehicle to purchase.
- *Pollution:* The burning of fossil fuels such as gasoline is widely believed to be the cause of global warming. Experts disagree about how dangerous this threat is, but there is no doubt that the gas tax reduces the threat by reducing the use of gasoline.

So the gas tax, rather than causing deadweight losses like most taxes, actually makes the economy work better. It means less traffic congestion, safer roads, and a cleaner environment.

How high should the tax on gasoline be? Most European countries impose gasoline taxes that are much higher than those in the United States. Many observers have suggested that the United States also should tax gasoline more heavily. A 2007 study published in the *Journal of Economic Literature* summarized the research on the size of the various externalities associated with driving. It concluded that the optimal corrective tax on gasoline was $2.10 per gallon, compared to the actual tax in the United States of 40 cents.

The tax revenue from a gasoline tax could be used to lower taxes that distort incentives and cause deadweight losses. In addition, some of the burdensome government regulations that require automakers to produce more fuel-efficient cars would prove unnecessary. This idea, however, has never proven politically popular. ●

MARKET-BASED POLICY 2: TRADABLE POLLUTION PERMITS

Returning to our example of the paper mill and the steel mill, let us suppose that, despite the advice of its economists, the EPA adopts the regulation and requires each factory to reduce its pollution to 300 tons of glop per year. Then one day, after the regulation is in place and both mills have complied, the two firms go to the EPA with a proposal. The steel mill wants to increase its emission of glop by 100 tons. The paper mill has agreed to reduce its emission by the same amount if the steel mill pays it $5 million. Should the EPA allow the two factories to make this deal?

From the standpoint of economic efficiency, allowing the deal is good policy. The deal must make the owners of the two factories better off because they are voluntarily agreeing to it. Moreover, the deal does not have any external effects because the total amount of pollution remains the same. Thus, social welfare is enhanced by allowing the paper mill to sell its pollution rights to the steel mill.

The same logic applies to any voluntary transfer of the right to pollute from one firm to another. If the EPA allows firms to make these deals, it will, in essence, have created a new scarce resource: pollution permits. A market to trade these permits will eventually develop, and that market will be governed by the forces of supply and demand. The invisible hand will ensure that this new market allocates the right to pollute efficiently. That is, the permits will end up in the hands of those firms that value them most highly, as judged by their willingness to pay. A firm's willingness to pay, in turn, will depend on its cost of reducing pollution: The more costly it is for a firm to cut back on pollution, the more it will be willing to pay for a permit.

An advantage of allowing a market for pollution permits is that the initial allocation of pollution permits among firms does not matter from the standpoint of economic efficiency. Those firms that can reduce pollution at a low cost will sell whatever permits they get, and firms that can reduce pollution only at a high cost will buy whatever permits they need. As long as there is a free market for the pollution rights, the final allocation will be efficient regardless of the initial allocation.

Although reducing pollution using pollution permits may seem very different from using corrective taxes, the two policies have much in common. In both cases, firms pay for their pollution. With corrective taxes, polluting firms must pay a tax to the government. With pollution permits, polluting firms must pay to buy the permit. (Even firms that already own permits must pay to pollute: The opportunity cost of polluting is what they could have received by selling their permits on the open market.) Both corrective taxes and pollution permits internalize the externality of pollution by making it costly for firms to pollute.

The similarity of the two policies can be seen by considering the market for pollution. Both panels in Figure 4 show the demand curve for the right to pollute. This curve shows that the lower the price of polluting, the more firms will choose to pollute. In panel (a), the EPA uses a corrective tax to set a price for pollution. In this case, the supply curve for pollution rights is perfectly elastic (because firms can pollute as much as they want by paying the tax), and the position of the demand curve determines the quantity of pollution. In panel (b), the EPA sets a quantity of pollution by issuing pollution permits. In this case, the supply curve for pollution rights is perfectly inelastic (because the quantity of pollution is fixed by the number of permits), and the position of the demand curve determines the price of pollution. Hence, the EPA can achieve any point on a given demand curve either by setting a price with a corrective tax or by setting a quantity with pollution permits.

In some circumstances, however, selling pollution permits may be better than levying a corrective tax. Suppose the EPA wants no more than 600 tons of glop dumped into the river. But because the EPA does not know the demand curve for pollution, it is not sure what size tax would achieve that goal. In this case, it can simply auction off 600 pollution permits. The auction price would yield the appropriate size of the corrective tax.

The idea of the government auctioning off the right to pollute may at first sound like a creature of some economist's imagination. And in fact, that is how the idea began. But increasingly, the EPA has used the system as a way to control pollution. A notable success story has been the case of sulfur dioxide (SO_2)—a

4 **FIGURE**

In panel (a), the EPA sets a price on pollution by levying a corrective tax, and the demand curve determines the quantity of pollution. In panel (b), the EPA limits the quantity of pollution by limiting the number of pollution permits, and the demand curve determines the price of pollution. The price and quantity of pollution are the same in the two cases.

The Equivalence of Corrective Taxes and Pollution Permits

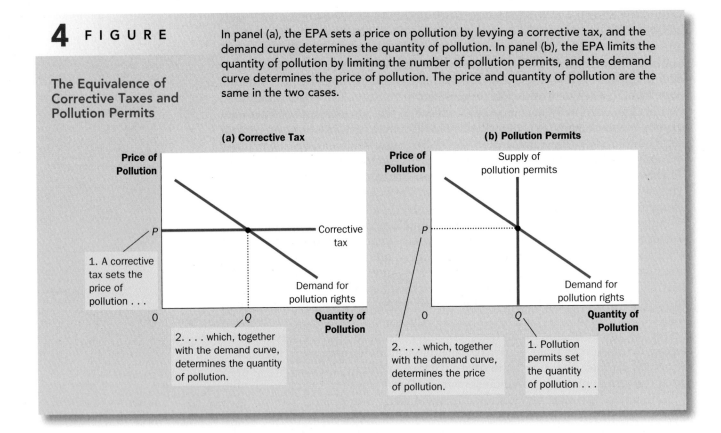

leading cause of acid rain. In 1990, amendments to the Clean Air Act required power plants to reduce SO_2 emissions substantially. At the same time, the amendments set up a system that allowed plants to trade their SO_2 allowances. Although initially both industry representatives and environmentalists were skeptical of the proposal, over time the system has proved that it can reduce pollution with minimal disruption. Pollution permits, like corrective taxes, are now widely viewed as a cost-effective way to keep the environment clean.

OBJECTIONS TO THE ECONOMIC ANALYSIS OF POLLUTION

"We cannot give anyone the option of polluting for a fee." This comment by former Senator Edmund Muskie reflects the view of some environmentalists. Clean air and clean water, they argue, are fundamental human rights that should not be debased by considering them in economic terms. How can you put a price on clean air and clean water? The environment is so important, they claim, that we should protect it as much as possible, regardless of the cost.

Economists have little sympathy for this type of argument. To economists, good environmental policy begins by acknowledging the first of the *Ten Principles of Economics* in Chapter 1: People face trade-offs. Certainly, clean air and clean water have value. But their value must be compared to their opportunity cost—that is, to what one must give up to obtain them. Eliminating all pollution is impossible. Trying to eliminate all pollution would reverse many of the technological advances that allow us to enjoy a high standard of living. Few people would be willing to accept poor nutrition, inadequate medical care, or shoddy housing to make the environment as clean as possible.

Economists argue that some environmental activists hurt their own cause by not thinking in economic terms. A clean environment is a good like other goods. Like all normal goods, it has a positive income elasticity: Rich countries can afford a cleaner environment than poor ones and, therefore, usually have more rigorous environmental protection. In addition, like most other goods, clean air and clean water obey the law of demand: The lower the price of environmental protection, the more the public will want. The economic approach of using pollution permits and corrective taxes reduces the cost of environmental protection and should, therefore, increase the public's demand for a clean environment.

QUICK QUIZ A glue factory and a steel mill emit smoke containing a chemical that is harmful if inhaled in large amounts. Describe three ways the town government might respond to this externality. What are the pros and cons of each solution?

PRIVATE SOLUTIONS TO EXTERNALITIES

Although externalities tend to cause markets to be inefficient, government action is not always needed to solve the problem. In some circumstances, people can develop private solutions.

THE TYPES OF PRIVATE SOLUTIONS

Sometimes the problem of externalities is solved with moral codes and social sanctions. Consider, for instance, why most people do not litter. Although there are laws against littering, these laws are not vigorously enforced. Most people do not litter just because it is the wrong thing to do. The Golden Rule taught to most children says, "Do unto others as you would have them do unto you." This moral injunction tells us to take account of how our actions affect other people. In economic terms, it tells us to internalize externalities.

Another private solution to externalities is charities, many of which are established to deal with externalities. For example, the Sierra Club, whose goal is to protect the environment, is a nonprofit organization funded with private donations. As another example, colleges and universities receive gifts from alumni, corporations, and foundations in part because education has positive externalities for society. The government encourages this private solution to externalities through the tax system by allowing an income tax deduction for charitable donations.

The private market can often solve the problem of externalities by relying on the self-interest of the relevant parties. Sometimes the solution takes the form of integrating different types of businesses. For example, consider an apple grower and a beekeeper who are located next to each other. Each business confers a positive externality on the other: By pollinating the flowers on the trees, the bees help the orchard produce apples. At the same time, the bees use the nectar they get from the apple trees to produce honey. Nonetheless, when the apple grower is deciding how many trees to plant and the beekeeper is deciding how many bees to keep, they neglect the positive externality. As a result, the apple grower plants too few trees and the beekeeper keeps too few bees. These externalities could be internalized if the beekeeper bought the apple orchard or if the apple grower

In The News

The Case for Taxing Carbon

An obscure economist proposes a way to deal with global climate change.

One Answer to Global Warming: A New Tax

By N. Gregory Mankiw

In the debate over global climate change, there is a yawning gap that needs to be bridged. The gap is not between environmentalists and industrialists, or between Democrats and Republicans. It is between policy wonks and political consultants.

Among policy wonks like me, there is a broad consensus. The scientists tell us that world temperatures are rising because humans are emitting carbon into the atmosphere. Basic economics tells us that when you tax something, you normally get less of it. So if we want to reduce global emissions of carbon, we need a global carbon tax. QED.

The idea of using taxes to fix problems, rather than merely raise government revenue, has a long history. The British economist Arthur Pigou advocated such corrective taxes to deal with pollution in the early 20th

century. In his honor, economics textbooks now call them "Pigovian taxes."

Using a Pigovian tax to address global warming is also an old idea. It was proposed as far back as 1992 by Martin S. Feldstein on the editorial page of *The Wall Street Journal.* Once chief economist to Ronald Reagan, Mr. Feldstein has devoted much of his career to studying how high tax rates distort incentives and impede economic growth. But like most other policy wonks, he appreciates that some taxes align private incentives with social costs and move us toward better outcomes.

Those vying for elected office, however, are reluctant to sign on to this agenda. Their political consultants are no fans of taxes, Pigovian or otherwise. Republican consultants advise using the word "tax" only if followed immediately by the word "cut." Democratic consultants recommend the word "tax" be followed by "on the rich."

Yet this natural aversion to carbon taxes can be overcome if the revenue from the tax is used to reduce other taxes. By itself,

a carbon tax would raise the tax burden on anyone who drives a car or uses electricity produced with fossil fuels, which means just about everybody. Some might fear this would be particularly hard on the poor and middle class.

But Gilbert Metcalf, a professor of economics at Tufts, has shown how revenue from a carbon tax could be used to reduce payroll taxes in a way that would leave the distribution of total tax burden approximately unchanged. He proposes a tax of $15 per metric ton of carbon dioxide, together with a rebate of the federal payroll tax on the first $3,660 of earnings for each worker.

The case for a carbon tax looks even stronger after an examination of the other options on the table. Lawmakers in both political parties want to require carmakers to increase the fuel efficiency of the cars they sell. Passing the buck to auto companies has a lot of popular appeal.

Increased fuel efficiency, however, is not free. Like a tax, the cost of complying with

bought the beehives: Both activities would then take place within the same firm, and this single firm could choose the optimal number of trees and bees. Internalizing externalities is one reason that some firms are involved in different types of businesses.

Another way for the private market to deal with external effects is for the interested parties to enter into a contract. In the foregoing example, a contract between the apple grower and the beekeeper can solve the problem of too few trees and too few bees. The contract can specify the number of trees, the number of bees, and perhaps a payment from one party to the other. By setting the right number of trees and bees, the contract can solve the inefficiency that normally arises from these externalities and make both parties better off.

more stringent regulation will be passed on to consumers in the form of higher car prices. But the government will not raise any revenue that it can use to cut other taxes to compensate for these higher prices. (And don't expect savings on gas to compensate consumers in a meaningful way: Any truly cost-effective increase in fuel efficiency would already have been made.)

More important, enhancing fuel efficiency by itself is not the best way to reduce energy consumption. Fuel use depends not only on the efficiency of the car fleet but also on the daily decisions that people make—how far from work they choose to live and how often they carpool or use public transportation.

A carbon tax would provide incentives for people to use less fuel in a multitude of ways. By contrast, merely having more efficient cars encourages more driving. Increased driving not only produces more carbon but also exacerbates other problems, like accidents and road congestion.

Another popular proposal to limit carbon emissions is a cap-and-trade system, under which carbon emissions are limited and allowances are bought and sold in the marketplace. The effect of such a system depends on how the carbon allowances are allocated. If the government auctions them off, then the price of a carbon allowance is effectively a carbon tax.

But the history of cap-and-trade systems suggests that the allowances would probably be handed out to power companies and other carbon emitters, which would then be free to use them or sell them at market prices. In this case, the prices of energy products would rise as they would under a carbon tax, but the government would collect no revenue to reduce other taxes and compensate consumers.

The international dimension of the problem also suggests the superiority of a carbon tax over cap-and-trade. Any long-term approach to global climate change will have to deal with the emerging economies of China and India. By some reports, China is now the world's leading emitter of carbon, in large part simply because it has so many people. The failure of the Kyoto treaty to include these emerging economies is one reason that, in 1997, the United States Senate passed a resolution rejecting the Kyoto approach by a vote of 95 to zero.

Agreement on a truly global cap-and-trade system, however, is hard to imagine. China is unlikely to be persuaded to accept fewer carbon allowances per person than the United States. Using a historical baseline to allocate allowances, as is often proposed, would reward the United States for having been a leading cause of the problem.

But allocating carbon allowances based on population alone would create a system in which the United States, with its higher standard of living, would buy allowances from China. American voters are not going to embrace a system of higher energy prices, coupled with a large transfer of national income to the Chinese. It would amount to a massive foreign aid program to one of the world's most rapidly growing economies.

A global carbon tax would be easier to negotiate. All governments require revenue for public purposes. The world's nations could agree to use a carbon tax as one instrument to raise some of that revenue. No money needs to change hands across national borders. Each government could keep the revenue from its tax and use it to finance spending or whatever form of tax relief it considered best.

Convincing China of the virtues of a carbon tax, however, may prove to be the easy part. The first and more difficult step is to convince American voters, and therefore political consultants, that "tax" is not a four-letter word.

Source: *New York Times*, September 16, 2007.

THE COASE THEOREM

How effective is the private market in dealing with externalities? A famous result, called the **Coase theorem** after economist Ronald Coase, suggests that it can be very effective in some circumstances. According to the Coase theorem, if private parties can bargain over the allocation of resources at no cost, then the private market will always solve the problem of externalities and allocate resources efficiently.

To see how the Coase theorem works, consider an example. Suppose that Dick owns a dog named Spot. Spot barks and disturbs Jane, Dick's neighbor. Dick gets a benefit from owning the dog, but the dog confers a negative externality on Jane.

Coase theorem
the proposition that if private parties can bargain without cost over the allocation of resources, they can solve the problem of externalities on their own

Should Dick be forced to send Spot to the pound, or should Jane have to suffer sleepless nights because of Spot's barking?

Consider first what outcome is socially efficient. A social planner, considering the two alternatives, would compare the benefit that Dick gets from the dog to the cost that Jane bears from the barking. If the benefit exceeds the cost, it is efficient for Dick to keep the dog and for Jane to live with the barking. Yet if the cost exceeds the benefit, then Dick should get rid of the dog.

According to the Coase theorem, the private market will reach the efficient outcome on its own. How? Jane can simply offer to pay Dick to get rid of the dog. Dick will accept the deal if the amount of money Jane offers is greater than the benefit of keeping the dog.

By bargaining over the price, Dick and Jane can always reach the efficient outcome. For instance, suppose that Dick gets a $500 benefit from the dog and Jane bears an $800 cost from the barking. In this case, Jane can offer Dick $600 to get rid of the dog, and Dick will gladly accept. Both parties are better off than they were before, and the efficient outcome is reached.

It is possible, of course, that Jane would not be willing to offer any price that Dick would accept. For instance, suppose that Dick gets a $1,000 benefit from the dog and Jane bears an $800 cost from the barking. In this case, Dick would turn down any offer below $1,000, while Jane would not offer any amount above $800. Therefore, Dick ends up keeping the dog. Given these costs and benefits, however, this outcome is efficient.

So far, we have assumed that Dick has the legal right to keep a barking dog. In other words, we have assumed that Dick can keep Spot unless Jane pays him enough to induce him to give up the dog voluntarily. But how different would the outcome be if Jane had the legal right to peace and quiet?

According to the Coase theorem, the initial distribution of rights does not matter for the market's ability to reach the efficient outcome. For instance, suppose that Jane can legally compel Dick to get rid of the dog. Although having this right works to Jane's advantage, it probably will not change the outcome. In this case, Dick can offer to pay Jane to allow him to keep the dog. If the benefit of the dog to Dick exceeds the cost of the barking to Jane, then Dick and Jane will strike a bargain in which Dick keeps the dog.

Although Dick and Jane can reach the efficient outcome regardless of how rights are initially distributed, the distribution of rights is not irrelevant: It determines the distribution of economic well-being. Whether Dick has the right to a barking dog or Jane the right to peace and quiet determines who pays whom in the final bargain. But in either case, the two parties can bargain with each other and solve the externality problem. Dick will end up keeping the dog only if the benefit exceeds the cost.

To sum up: *The Coase theorem says that private economic actors can solve the problem of externalities among themselves. Whatever the initial distribution of rights, the interested parties can always reach a bargain in which everyone is better off and the outcome is efficient.*

WHY PRIVATE SOLUTIONS DO NOT ALWAYS WORK

Despite the appealing logic of the Coase theorem, private individuals on their own often fail to resolve the problems caused by externalities. The Coase theorem applies only when the interested parties have no trouble reaching and enforcing an agreement. In the real world, however, bargaining does not always work, even when a mutually beneficial agreement is possible.

Sometimes the interested parties fail to solve an externality problem because of **transaction costs**, the costs that parties incur in the process of agreeing to and following through on a bargain. In our example, imagine that Dick and Jane speak different languages so that, to reach an agreement, they need to hire a translator. If the benefit of solving the barking problem is less than the cost of the translator, Dick and Jane might choose to leave the problem unsolved. In more realistic examples, the transaction costs are the expenses not of translators but of the lawyers required to draft and enforce contracts.

At other times, bargaining simply breaks down. The recurrence of wars and labor strikes shows that reaching agreement can be difficult and that failing to reach agreement can be costly. The problem is often that each party tries to hold out for a better deal. For example, suppose that Dick gets a $500 benefit from the dog, and Jane bears an $800 cost from the barking. Although it is efficient for Jane to pay Dick to get rid of the dog, there are many prices that could lead to this outcome. Dick might demand $750, and Jane might offer only $550. As they haggle over the price, the inefficient outcome with the barking dog persists.

Reaching an efficient bargain is especially difficult when the number of interested parties is large because coordinating everyone is costly. For example, consider a factory that pollutes the water of a nearby lake. The pollution confers a negative externality on the local fishermen. According to the Coase theorem, if the pollution is inefficient, then the factory and the fishermen could reach a bargain in which the fishermen pay the factory not to pollute. If there are many fishermen, however, trying to coordinate them all to bargain with the factory may be almost impossible.

When private bargaining does not work, the government can sometimes play a role. The government is an institution designed for collective action. In this example, the government can act on behalf of the fishermen, even when it is impractical for the fishermen to act for themselves.

transaction costs
the costs that parties incur in the process of agreeing to and following through on a bargain

QUICK QUIZ   Give an example of a private solution to an externality. • What is the Coase theorem? • Why are private economic participants sometimes unable to solve the problems caused by an externality?

CONCLUSION

The invisible hand is powerful but not omnipotent. A market's equilibrium maximizes the sum of producer and consumer surplus. When the buyers and sellers in the market are the only interested parties, this outcome is efficient from the standpoint of society as a whole. But when there are external effects, such as pollution, evaluating a market outcome requires taking into account the well-being of third parties as well. In this case, the invisible hand of the marketplace may fail to allocate resources efficiently.

In some cases, people can solve the problem of externalities on their own. The Coase theorem suggests that the interested parties can bargain among themselves and agree on an efficient solution. Sometimes, however, an efficient outcome cannot be reached, perhaps because the large number of interested parties makes bargaining difficult.

When people cannot solve the problem of externalities privately, the government often steps in. Yet even with government intervention, society should not abandon market forces entirely. Rather, the government can address the problem by requiring decision makers to bear the full costs of their actions. Corrective taxes on emissions and pollution permits, for instance, are designed to internalize the externality of pollution. More and more, these are the policies of choice for those interested in protecting the environment. Market forces, properly redirected, are often the best remedy for market failure.

SUMMARY

- When a transaction between a buyer and seller directly affects a third party, the effect is called an externality. If an activity yields negative externalities, such as pollution, the socially optimal quantity in a market is less than the equilibrium quantity. If an activity yields positive externalities, such as technology spillovers, the socially optimal quantity is greater than the equilibrium quantity.

- Governments pursue various policies to remedy the inefficiencies caused by externalities. Sometimes the government prevents socially inefficient activity by regulating behavior. Other times it internalizes an externality using corrective taxes. Another public policy is to issue permits. For example, the government could protect the environment by issuing a limited number of pollution permits. The result of this policy is largely the same as imposing corrective taxes on polluters.

- Those affected by externalities can sometimes solve the problem privately. For instance, when one business imposes an externality on another business, the two businesses can internalize the externality by merging. Alternatively, the interested parties can solve the problem by negotiating a contract. According to the Coase theorem, if people can bargain without cost, then they can always reach an agreement in which resources are allocated efficiently. In many cases, however, reaching a bargain among the many interested parties is difficult, so the Coase theorem does not apply.

KEY CONCEPTS

externality, *p. 204*
internalizing the
   externality, *p. 207*

corrective tax, *p. 210*
Coase theorem, *p. 217*
transaction costs, *p. 219*

QUESTIONS FOR REVIEW

1. Give an example of a negative externality and an example of a positive externality.
2. Draw a supply-and-demand diagram to explain the effect of a negative externality that occurs as a result of a firm's production process.
3. In what way does the patent system help society solve an externality problem?
4. What are corrective taxes? Why do economists prefer them to regulations as a way to protect the environment from pollution?
5. List some of the ways that the problems caused by externalities can be solved without government intervention.
6. Imagine that you are a nonsmoker sharing a room with a smoker. According to the Coase theorem, what determines whether your roommate smokes in the room? Is this outcome efficient? How do you and your roommate reach this solution?

PROBLEMS AND APPLICATIONS

1. There are two ways to protect your car from theft. The Club makes it difficult for a car thief to take your car. Lojack makes it easier for the police to catch the car thief who has stolen it. Which of these types of protection conveys a negative externality on other car owners? Which conveys a positive externality? Do you think there are any policy implications of your analysis?
2. Do you agree with the following statements? Why or why not?
   a. "The benefits of corrective taxes as a way to reduce pollution have to be weighed against the deadweight losses that these taxes cause."
   b. "When deciding whether to levy a corrective tax on consumers or producers, the government should be careful to levy the tax on the side of the market generating the externality."
3. Consider the market for fire extinguishers.
   a. Why might fire extinguishers exhibit positive externalities?
   b. Draw a graph of the market for fire extinguishers, labeling the demand curve, the social-value curve, the supply curve, and the social-cost curve.
   c. Indicate the market equilibrium level of output and the efficient level of output. Give an intuitive explanation for why these quantities differ.
   d. If the external benefit is $10 per extinguisher, describe a government policy that would yield the efficient outcome.
4. It is rumored that the Swiss government subsidizes cattle farming and that the subsidy is larger in areas with more tourist attractions. Can you think of a reason this policy might be efficient?
5. A local drama company proposes a new neighborhood theater in San Francisco. Before approving the permit, the city planner completes a study of the theater's impact on the surrounding community.
   a. One finding of the study is that theaters attract traffic, which adversely affects the community. The city planner estimates that the cost to the community from the extra traffic is $5 per ticket. What kind of an externality is this? Why?
   b. Graph the market for theater tickets, labeling the demand curve, the social-value curve, the supply curve, the social-cost curve, the market equilibrium level of output, and the efficient level of output. Also show the per-unit amount of the externality.
   c. Upon further review, the city planner uncovers a second externality. Rehearsals for the plays tend to run until late at night, with actors, stagehands, and other theater members coming and going at various hours. The planner has found that the increased foot traffic improves the safety of the surrounding streets, an estimated benefit to the community of $2 per ticket. What kind of externality is this? Why?

d. On a new graph, illustrate the market for theater tickets in the case of these two externalities. Again, label the demand curve, the social-value curve, the supply curve, the social-cost curve, the market equilibrium level of output, the efficient level of output, and the per-unit amount of both externalities.

e. Describe a government policy that would result in an efficient outcome.

6. Greater consumption of alcohol leads to more motor vehicle accidents and, thus, imposes costs on people who do not drink and drive.

a. Illustrate the market for alcohol, labeling the demand curve, the social-value curve, the supply curve, the social-cost curve, the market equilibrium level of output, and the efficient level of output.

b. On your graph, shade the area corresponding to the deadweight loss of the market equilibrium. (Hint: The deadweight loss occurs because some units of alcohol are consumed for which the social cost exceeds the social value.) Explain.

7. Many observers believe that the levels of pollution in our society are too high.

a. If society wishes to reduce overall pollution by a certain amount, why is it efficient to have different amounts of reduction at different firms?

b. Command-and-control approaches often rely on uniform reductions among firms. Why are these approaches generally unable to target the firms that should undertake bigger reductions?

c. Economists argue that appropriate corrective taxes or tradable pollution rights will result in efficient pollution reduction. How do these approaches target the firms that should undertake bigger reductions?

8. Ringo loves playing rock-'n'-roll music at high volume. Luciano loves opera and hates rock-'n'-roll. Unfortunately, they are next-door neighbors in an apartment building with paper-thin walls.

a. What is the externality here?

b. What command-and-control policy might the landlord impose? Could such a policy lead to an inefficient outcome?

c. Suppose the landlord lets the tenants do whatever they want. According to the Coase theorem, how might Ringo and Luciano reach an efficient outcome on their own? What might prevent them from reaching an efficient outcome?

9. The Pristine River has two polluting firms on its banks. Acme Industrial and Creative Chemicals each dump 100 tons of glop into the river each year. The cost of reducing glop emissions per ton equals $10 for Acme and $100 for Creative. The local government wants to reduce overall pollution from 200 tons to 50 tons.

a. If the government knows the cost of reduction for each firm, what reductions will it impose to reach its overall goal? What will be the cost to each firm and the total cost to the firms together?

b. In a more typical situation, the government does not know the cost of pollution reduction for each firm. If the government decides to reach its overall goal by imposing uniform reductions on the firms, calculate the reduction made by each firm, the cost to each firm, and the total cost to the firms together.

c. Compare the total cost of pollution reduction in parts (a) and (b). If the government does not know the cost of reduction for each firm, is there still some way for it to reduce pollution to 50 tons at the total cost you calculated in part (a)? Explain.

10. Figure 4 shows that for any given demand curve for the right to pollute, the government can achieve the same outcome either by setting a price with a corrective tax or by setting a quantity with pollution permits. Suppose there is a sharp improvement in the technology for controlling pollution.

a. Using graphs similar to those in Figure 4, illustrate the effect of this development on the demand for pollution rights.

b. What is the effect on the price and quantity of pollution under each regulatory system? Explain.

11. Suppose that the government decides to issue tradable permits for a certain form of pollution.

a. Does it matter for economic efficiency whether the government distributes or auctions the permits?

b. If the government chooses to distribute the permits, does the allocation of permits among firms matter for efficiency?

12. There are three industrial firms in Happy Valley.

Firm	Initial Pollution Level	Cost of Reducing Pollution by 1 Unit
A	70 units	$20
B	80 units	$25
C	50 units	$10

The government wants to reduce pollution to 120 units, so it gives each firm 40 tradable pollution permits.

a. Who sells permits and how many do they sell? Who buys permits and how many do they buy? Briefly explain why the sellers and buyers are each willing to do so. What is the total cost of pollution reduction in this situation?

b. How much higher would the costs of pollution reduction be if the permits could not be traded?

13. The market for a particular chemical, called Negext, is described by the following equations.

Demand is given by:
$$Q^D = 100 - 5P$$

Supply is given by:
$$Q^S = 5P$$

where Q is measured as units of Negext and P is price in dollars per unit.

a. Find the equilibrium price and quantity. Compute consumer surplus, producer surplus, and total surplus in the market equilibrium.

b. For each unit of Negext produced, 4 units of pollution are emitted, and each unit of pollution imposes a cost on society of $1. Compute the total cost of pollution when the market for Negext is in equilibrium. What is total surplus from this market after taking into account the cost of pollution?

c. Would banning Negext increase or decrease welfare? Why?

d. Suppose that the government restricts emissions to 100 units of pollution. Graph the Negext market under this constraint. Find the new equilibrium price and quantity and show them on your graph. Compute how this policy affects consumer surplus, producer surplus, and the cost of pollution. Would you recommend this policy? Why?

e. Suppose that instead of restricting pollution, the government imposes a tax on producers equal to $4 for each unit of chemical produced. Calculate the new equilibrium price and quantity, as well as consumer surplus, producer surplus, tax revenue, and the cost of pollution. What is total surplus now? Would you recommend this policy? Why?

f. New research finds the social cost of pollution is really higher than $1. How would that change the optimal policy response? Is there some cost of pollution that would make it sensible to ban Negext? If so, what is it?

Public Goods and Common Resources

An old song lyric maintains that "the best things in life are free." A moment's thought reveals a long list of goods that the songwriter could have had in mind. Nature provides some of them, such as rivers, mountains, beaches, lakes, and oceans. The government provides others, such as playgrounds, parks, and parades. In each case, people do not pay a fee when they choose to enjoy the benefit of the good.

Goods without prices provide a special challenge for economic analysis. Most goods in our economy are allocated in markets, where buyers pay for what they receive and sellers are paid for what they provide. For these goods, prices are the signals that guide the decisions of buyers and sellers, and these decisions lead to an efficient allocation of resources. When goods are available free of charge, however, the market forces that normally allocate resources in our economy are absent.

In this chapter, we examine the problems that arise for the allocation of resources when there are goods without market prices. Our analysis will shed light on one of the *Ten Principles of Economics* in Chapter 1: Governments can sometimes improve market outcomes. When a good does not have a price attached to it, private markets cannot ensure that the good is produced and consumed in the proper amounts. In such cases, government policy can potentially remedy the market failure and raise economic well-being.

THE DIFFERENT KINDS OF GOODS

How well do markets work in providing the goods that people want? The answer to this question depends on the good being considered. As we discussed in Chapter 7, a market can provide the efficient number of ice-cream cones: The price of ice-cream cones adjusts to balance supply and demand, and this equilibrium maximizes the sum of producer and consumer surplus. Yet as we discussed in Chapter 10, the market cannot be counted on to prevent aluminum manufacturers from polluting the air we breathe: Buyers and sellers in a market typically do not take into account the external effects of their decisions. Thus, markets work well when the good is ice cream, but they work badly when the good is clean air.

In thinking about the various goods in the economy, it is useful to group them according to two characteristics:

excludability
the property of a good whereby a person can be prevented from using it

- Is the good **excludable**? That is, can people be prevented from using the good?

rivalry in consumption
the property of a good whereby one person's use diminishes other people's use

- Is the good **rival in consumption**? That is, does one person's use of the good reduce another person's ability to use it?

Using these two characteristics, Figure 1 divides goods into four categories:

private goods
goods that are both excludable and rival in consumption

1. **Private goods** are both excludable and rival in consumption. Consider an ice-cream cone, for example. An ice-cream cone is excludable because it is possible to prevent someone from eating an ice-cream cone—you just don't give it to him. An ice-cream cone is rival in consumption because if one person eats an ice-cream cone, another person cannot eat the same cone. Most goods in the economy are private goods like ice-cream cones: You don't get one unless you pay, and once you have it, you are the only person who benefits. When we analyzed supply and demand in Chapters 4, 5, and 6 and the efficiency of markets in Chapters 7, 8, and 9, we implicitly assumed that goods were both excludable and rival in consumption.

public goods
goods that are neither excludable nor rival in consumption

2. **Public goods** are neither excludable nor rival in consumption. That is, people cannot be prevented from using a public good, and one person's use of a public good does not reduce another person's ability to use it. For example,

1 FIGURE

Four Types of Goods
Goods can be grouped into four categories according to two characteristics: (1) A good is *excludable* if people can be prevented from using it. (2) A good is *rival in consumption* if one person's use of the good diminishes other people's use of it. This diagram gives examples of goods in each category.

	Rival in consumption?	
	Yes	**No**
Excludable? Yes	Private Goods • Ice-cream cones • Clothing • Congested toll roads	Natural Monopolies • Fire protection • Cable TV • Uncongested toll roads
Excludable? No	Common Resources • Fish in the ocean • The environment • Congested nontoll roads	Public Goods • Tornado siren • National defense • Uncongested nontoll roads

a tornado siren in a small town is a public good. Once the siren sounds, it is impossible to prevent any single person from hearing it (so it is not excludable). Moreover, when one person gets the benefit of the warning, she does not reduce the benefit to anyone else (so it is not rival in consumption).

3. **Common resources** are rival in consumption but not excludable. For example, fish in the ocean are rival in consumption: When one person catches fish, there are fewer fish for the next person to catch. Yet these fish are not an excludable good because, given the vast size of an ocean, it is difficult to stop fishermen from taking fish out of it.

common resources
goods that are rival in consumption but not excludable

4. When a good is excludable but not rival in consumption, it is an example of a good produced by a *natural monopoly.* For instance, consider fire protection in a small town. It is easy to exclude someone from using this good: The fire department can just let his house burn down. Yet fire protection is not rival in consumption: Once a town has paid for the fire department, the additional cost of protecting one more house is small. (In Chapter 15, we give a more complete definition of natural monopolies and study them in some detail.)

Although Figure 1 offers a clean separation of goods into four categories, the boundary between the categories is sometimes fuzzy. Whether goods are excludable or rival in consumption is often a matter of degree. Fish in an ocean may not be excludable because monitoring fishing is so difficult, but a large enough coast guard could make fish at least partly excludable. Similarly, although fish are generally rival in consumption, this would be less true if the population of fishermen were small relative to the population of fish. (Think of North American fishing waters before the arrival of European settlers.) For purposes of our analysis, however, it will be helpful to group goods into these four categories.

In this chapter, we examine goods that are not excludable: public goods and common resources. Because people cannot be prevented from using these goods, they are available to everyone free of charge. The study of public goods and common resources is closely related to the study of externalities. For both of these types of goods, externalities arise because something of value has no price attached to it. If one person were to provide a public good, such as a tornado siren, other people would be better off. They would receive a benefit without paying for it—a positive externality. Similarly, when one person uses a common resource such as the fish in the ocean, other people are worse off because there are fewer fish to catch. They suffer a loss but are not compensated for it—a negative externality. Because of these external effects, private decisions about consumption and production can lead to an inefficient allocation of resources, and government intervention can potentially raise economic well-being.

QUICK QUIZ Define *public goods* and *common resources* and give an example of each.

PUBLIC GOODS

To understand how public goods differ from other goods and the problems they present for society, let's consider an example: a fireworks display. This good is not excludable because it is impossible to prevent someone from seeing fireworks, and it is not rival in consumption because one person's enjoyment of fireworks does not reduce anyone else's enjoyment of them.

THE FREE-RIDER PROBLEM

The citizens of Smalltown, U.S.A., like seeing fireworks on the Fourth of July. Each of the town's 500 residents places a $10 value on the experience for a total benefit of $5,000. The cost of putting on a fireworks display is $1,000. Because the $5,000 benefit exceeds the $1,000 cost, it is efficient for Smalltown to have a fireworks display on the Fourth of July.

Would the private market produce the efficient outcome? Probably not. Imagine that Ellen, a Smalltown entrepreneur, decided to put on a fireworks display. Ellen would surely have trouble selling tickets to the event because her potential customers would quickly figure out that they could see the fireworks even without a ticket. Because fireworks are not excludable, people have an incentive to be free riders. A **free rider** is a person who receives the benefit of a good but does not pay for it. Because people would have an incentive to be free riders rather than ticket buyers, the market would fail to provide the efficient outcome.

One way to view this market failure is that it arises because of an externality. If Ellen puts on the fireworks display, she confers an external benefit on those who see the display without paying for it. When deciding whether to put on the display, however, Ellen does not take the external benefits into account. Even though the fireworks display is socially desirable, it is not profitable. As a result, Ellen makes the privately rational but socially inefficient decision not to put on the display.

Although the private market fails to supply the fireworks display demanded by Smalltown residents, the solution to Smalltown's problem is obvious: The local government can sponsor a Fourth of July celebration. The town council can raise everyone's taxes by $2 and use the revenue to hire Ellen to produce the fireworks. Everyone in Smalltown is better off by $8—the $10 in value from the fireworks minus the $2 tax bill. Ellen can help Smalltown reach the efficient outcome as a public employee even though she could not do so as a private entrepreneur.

The story of Smalltown is simplified but realistic. In fact, many local governments in the United States pay for fireworks on the Fourth of July. Moreover, the story shows a general lesson about public goods: Because public goods are not excludable, the free-rider problem prevents the private market from supplying them. The government, however, can potentially remedy the problem. If the government decides that the total benefits of a public good exceed its costs, it can provide the public good, pay for it with tax revenue, and make everyone better off.

SOME IMPORTANT PUBLIC GOODS

There are many examples of public goods. Here we consider three of the most important.

National Defense The defense of a country from foreign aggressors is a classic example of a public good. Once the country is defended, it is impossible to prevent any single person from enjoying the benefit of this defense. Moreover, when one person enjoys the benefit of national defense, he does not reduce the benefit to anyone else. Thus, national defense is neither excludable nor rival in consumption.

National defense is also one of the most expensive public goods. In 2007, the U.S. federal government spent a total of $553 billion on national defense, more than $1,800 per person. People disagree about whether this amount is too small or

---

free rider
a person who receives the benefit of a good but avoids paying for it

too large, but almost no one doubts that some government spending for national defense is necessary. Even economists who advocate small government agree that the national defense is a public good the government should provide.

"I LIKE THE CONCEPT IF WE CAN DO IT WITH NO NEW TAXES."

Basic Research   Knowledge is created through research. In evaluating the appropriate public policy toward knowledge creation, it is important to distinguish general knowledge from specific technological knowledge. Specific technological knowledge, such as the invention of a longer-lasting battery, a smaller microchip, or a better digital music player, can be patented. The patent gives the inventor the exclusive right to the knowledge he or she has created for a period of time. Anyone else who wants to use the patented information must pay the inventor for the right to do so. In other words, the patent makes the knowledge created by the inventor excludable.

By contrast, general knowledge is a public good. For example, a mathematician cannot patent a theorem. Once a theorem is proved, the knowledge is not excludable: The theorem enters society's general pool of knowledge that anyone can use without charge. The theorem is also not rival in consumption: One person's use of the theorem does not prevent any other person from using the theorem.

Profit-seeking firms spend a lot on research trying to develop new products that they can patent and sell, but they do not spend much on basic research. Their incentive, instead, is to free ride on the general knowledge created by others. As a result, in the absence of any public policy, society would devote too few resources to creating new knowledge.

The government tries to provide the public good of general knowledge in various ways. Government agencies, such as the National Institutes of Health and the National Science Foundation, subsidize basic research in medicine, mathematics, physics, chemistry, biology, and even economics. Some people justify government funding of the space program on the grounds that it adds to society's pool of knowledge (although many scientists are skeptical of the scientific value of manned space travel). Determining the appropriate level of government support for these endeavors is difficult because the benefits are hard to measure. Moreover, the members of Congress who appropriate funds for research usually have little expertise in science and, therefore, are not in the best position to judge what lines of research will produce the largest benefits. So, while basic research is surely a public good, we should not be surprised if the public sector fails to pay for the right amount and the right kinds.

Fighting Poverty   Many government programs are aimed at helping the poor. The welfare system (officially called Temporary Assistance for Needy Families) provides a small income for some poor families. Similarly, the Food Stamp program subsidizes the purchase of food for those with low incomes, and various government housing programs make shelter more affordable. These antipoverty programs are financed by taxes paid by families that are financially more successful.

Economists disagree among themselves about what role the government should play in fighting poverty. Although we discuss this debate more fully in Chapter 20, here we note one important argument: Advocates of antipoverty programs claim that fighting poverty is a public good. Even if everyone prefers living in a society without poverty, fighting poverty is not a "good" that private actions will adequately provide.

To see why, suppose someone tried to organize a group of wealthy individuals to try to eliminate poverty. They would be providing a public good. This good would not be rival in consumption: One person's enjoyment of living in a society without poverty would not reduce anyone else's enjoyment of it. The good would not be excludable: Once poverty is eliminated, no one can be prevented from taking pleasure in this fact. As a result, there would be a tendency for people to free ride on the generosity of others, enjoying the benefits of poverty elimination without contributing to the cause.

Because of the free-rider problem, eliminating poverty through private charity will probably not work. Yet government action can solve this problem. Taxing the wealthy to raise the living standards of the poor can potentially make everyone better off. The poor are better off because they now enjoy a higher standard of living, and those paying the taxes are better off because they enjoy living in a society with less poverty.

ARE LIGHTHOUSES PUBLIC GOODS?

Some goods can switch between being public goods and being private goods depending on the circumstances. For example, a fireworks display is a public good if performed in a town with many residents. Yet if performed at a private amusement park, such as Walt Disney World, a fireworks display is more like a private good because visitors to the park pay for admission.

Another example is a lighthouse. Economists have long used lighthouses as an example of a public good. Lighthouses mark specific locations so that passing ships can avoid treacherous waters. The benefit that the lighthouse provides to the ship captain is neither excludable nor rival in consumption, so each captain has an incentive to free ride by using the lighthouse to navigate without paying for the service. Because of this free-rider problem, private markets usually fail to provide the lighthouses that ship captains need. As a result, most lighthouses today are operated by the government.

In some cases, however, lighthouses have been closer to private goods. On the coast of England in the 19th century, for example, some lighthouses were privately owned and operated. Instead of trying to charge ship captains for the service, however, the owner of the lighthouse charged the owner of the nearby port. If the port owner did not pay, the lighthouse owner turned off the light, and ships avoided that port.

In deciding whether something is a public good, one must determine who the beneficiaries are and whether these beneficiaries can be excluded from using the good. A free-rider problem arises when the number of beneficiaries is large and exclusion of any one of them is impossible. If a lighthouse benefits many ship captains, it is a public good. Yet if it primarily benefits a single port owner, it is more like a private good. ●

WHAT KIND OF GOOD IS THIS?

THE DIFFICULT JOB OF COST–BENEFIT ANALYSIS

So far we have seen that the government provides public goods because the private market on its own will not produce an efficient quantity. Yet deciding that the government must play a role is only the first step. The government must then determine what kinds of public goods to provide and in what quantities.

Suppose that the government is considering a public project, such as building a new highway. To judge whether to build the highway, it must compare the total benefits of all those who would use it to the costs of building and maintaining it. To make this decision, the government might hire a team of economists and engineers to conduct a study, called a **cost–benefit analysis**, the goal of which is to estimate the total costs and benefits of the project to society as a whole.

Cost–benefit analysts have a tough job. Because the highway will be available to everyone free of charge, there is no price with which to judge the value of the highway. Simply asking people how much they would value the highway is not reliable: Quantifying benefits is difficult using the results from a questionnaire, and respondents have little incentive to tell the truth. Those who would use the highway have an incentive to exaggerate the benefit they receive to get the highway built. Those who would be harmed by the highway have an incentive to exaggerate the costs to them to prevent the highway from being built.

The efficient provision of public goods is, therefore, intrinsically more difficult than the efficient provision of private goods. When buyers of a private good enter a market, they reveal the value they place on it through the prices they are willing to pay. At the same time, sellers reveal their costs with the prices they are willing to accept. The equilibrium is an efficient allocation of resources because it reflects all this information. By contrast, cost–benefit analysts do not have any price signals to observe when evaluating whether the government should provide a public good and how much to provide. Their findings on the costs and benefits of public projects are rough approximations at best.

cost–benefit analysis
a study that compares the costs and benefits to society of providing a public good

CASE STUDY   HOW MUCH IS A LIFE WORTH?

Imagine that you have been elected to serve as a member of your local town council. The town engineer comes to you with a proposal: The town can spend $10,000 to build and operate a traffic light at a town intersection that now has only a stop sign. The benefit of the traffic light is increased safety. The engineer estimates, based on data from similar intersections, that the traffic light would reduce the risk of a fatal traffic accident over the lifetime of the traffic light from 1.6 to 1.1 percent. Should you spend the money for the new light?

To answer this question, you turn to cost–benefit analysis. But you quickly run into an obstacle: The costs and benefits must be measured in the same units if you are to compare them meaningfully. The cost is measured in dollars, but the benefit—the possibility of saving a person's life—is not directly monetary. To make your decision, you have to put a dollar value on a human life.

At first, you may be tempted to conclude that a human life is priceless. After all, there is probably no amount of money that you could be paid to voluntarily give up your life or that of a loved one. This suggests that a human life has an infinite dollar value.

For the purposes of cost–benefit analysis, however, this answer leads to nonsensical results. If we truly placed an infinite value on human life, we should place traffic lights on every street corner, and we should all drive large cars loaded with all the latest safety features. Yet traffic lights are not at every corner, and people sometimes choose to pay less for smaller cars without safety options such as side-impact air bags or antilock brakes. In both our public and private decisions, we are at times willing to risk our lives to save some money.

Once we have accepted the idea that a person's life has an implicit dollar value, how can we determine what that value is? One approach, sometimes used by courts to award damages in wrongful-death suits, is to look at the total amount of money a person would have earned if he or she had lived. Economists are often critical of this approach because it ignores other opportunity costs of losing one's life. It thus has the bizarre implication that the life of a retired or disabled person has no value.

A better way to value human life is to look at the risks that people are voluntarily willing to take and how much they must be paid for taking them. Mortality risk varies across jobs, for example. Construction workers in high-rise buildings face greater risk of death on the job than office workers do. By comparing wages in risky and less risky occupations, controlling for education, experience, and other determinants of wages, economists can get some sense about what value people put on their own lives. Studies using this approach conclude that the value of a human life is about $10 million.

We can now return to our original example and respond to the town engineer. The traffic light reduces the risk of fatality by 0.5 percentage points. Thus, the expected benefit from installing the traffic light is 0.005 × $10 million, or $50,000. This estimate of the benefit well exceeds the cost of $10,000, so you should approve the project. ●

QUICK QUIZ What is the *free-rider problem*? Why does the free-rider problem induce the government to provide public goods? ● How should the government decide whether to provide a public good?

COMMON RESOURCES

Tragedy of the Commons
a parable that illustrates why common resources are used more than is desirable from the standpoint of society as a whole

Common resources, like public goods, are not excludable: They are available free of charge to anyone who wants to use them. Common resources are, however, rival in consumption: One person's use of the common resource reduces other people's ability to use it. Thus, common resources give rise to a new problem. Once the good is provided, policymakers need to be concerned about how much it is used. This problem is best understood from the classic parable called the **Tragedy of the Commons**.

THE TRAGEDY OF THE COMMONS

Consider life in a small medieval town. Of the many economic activities that take place in the town, one of the most important is raising sheep. Many of the town's families own flocks of sheep and support themselves by selling the sheep's wool, which is used to make clothing.

As our story begins, the sheep spend much of their time grazing on the land surrounding the town, called the Town Common. No family owns the land. Instead, the town residents own the land collectively, and all the residents are allowed to graze their sheep on it. Collective ownership works well because land is plentiful. As long as everyone can get all the good grazing land they want, the Town Common is not rival in consumption, and allowing residents' sheep to graze for free causes no problems. Everyone in town is happy.

As the years pass, the population of the town grows, and so does the number of sheep grazing on the Town Common. With a growing number of sheep and a fixed amount of land, the land starts to lose its ability to replenish itself. Eventually, the land is grazed so heavily that it becomes barren. With no grass left on the Town Common, raising sheep is impossible, and the town's once prosperous wool industry disappears. Many families lose their source of livelihood.

What causes the tragedy? Why do the shepherds allow the sheep population to grow so large that it destroys the Town Common? The reason is that social and private incentives differ. Avoiding the destruction of the grazing land depends on the collective action of the shepherds. If the shepherds acted together, they could reduce the sheep population to a size that the Town Common can support. Yet no single family has an incentive to reduce the size of its own flock because each flock represents only a small part of the problem.

In essence, the Tragedy of the Commons arises because of an externality. When one family's flock grazes on the common land, it reduces the quality of the land available for other families. Because people neglect this negative externality when deciding how many sheep to own, the result is an excessive number of sheep.

If the tragedy had been foreseen, the town could have solved the problem in various ways. It could have regulated the number of sheep in each family's flock, internalized the externality by taxing sheep, or auctioned off a limited number of sheep-grazing permits. That is, the medieval town could have dealt with the problem of overgrazing in the way that modern society deals with the problem of pollution.

In the case of land, however, there is a simpler solution. The town can divide the land among town families. Each family can enclose its parcel of land with a fence and then protect it from excessive grazing. In this way, the land becomes a private good rather than a common resource. This outcome in fact occurred during the enclosure movement in England in the 17th century.

The Tragedy of the Commons is a story with a general lesson: When one person uses a common resource, he or she diminishes other people's enjoyment of it. Because of this negative externality, common resources tend to be used excessively. The government can solve the problem by using regulation or taxes to reduce consumption of the common resource. Alternatively, the government can sometimes turn the common resource into a private good.

This lesson has been known for thousands of years. The ancient Greek philosopher Aristotle pointed out the problem with common resources: "What is common to many is taken least care of, for all men have greater regard for what is their own than for what they possess in common with others."

SOME IMPORTANT COMMON RESOURCES

There are many examples of common resources. In almost all cases, the same problem arises as in the Tragedy of the Commons: Private decision makers use the common resource too much. Governments often regulate behavior or impose fees to mitigate the problem of overuse.

Clean Air and Water As we discussed in Chapter 10, markets do not adequately protect the environment. Pollution is a negative externality that can be remedied with regulations or with corrective taxes on polluting activities. One can view this market failure as an example of a common-resource problem. Clean air and clean

In The News

The Bloomberg Plan

Many economists have advocated road pricing as a mechanism to control traffic. Recently, they have convinced the mayor of New York City.

Don't Drive, He Said
By Elizabeth Kolbert

Michael Bloomberg has always favored grand schemes. Last week, on Earth Day, the Mayor stood in the American Museum of Natural History's Hall of Ocean Life, beneath the blue whale, to lay out his vision for the city's future. In an expansive speech, Bloomberg described a New York that would, in 2030, be both "greater" and "greener," a city with nearly a million more residents, as well as cleaner water, new open space, and zippier transportation. This bigger, better metropolis would be a leader in combatting global warming; despite its increased population, the New York of the future would produce thirty percent less CO_2, resulting, as the Mayor put it, in "the most dramatic reduction in greenhouse gases ever achieved by any American city."

The printed version of Bloomberg's plan ran to a hundred and fifty-five full-color pages and contained a hundred and twenty-seven new initiatives. Just one of them—congestion pricing—got almost all the attention, much of it negative. The Mayor anticipated this—he referred to the pricing proposal as "the elephant in the room"—and his decision to include it anyway is perhaps the best reason to take the plan seriously.

The basic idea behind congestion pricing is simple: make motorists pay to use the busiest streets. Under the Mayor's proposal, an invisible line would be drawn around Manhattan from Eighty-sixth Street south to the Battery. Vehicles crossing this line on weekdays between 6 A.M. and 6 P.M. would be charged a fee—eight dollars for cars, twenty-one dollars for trucks. (Those travelling only within the congestion zone would pay half price, while taxis and livery cabs would be exempt.) The fees would be assessed electronically and could be paid either with a toll pass or over the phone or the Internet.

Driving crosstown for lunch is an easy, if maddening, way to appreciate the scheme's logic. The impression that one could walk—or at least trot—just as quickly is borne out by the numbers; according to data collected by the New York Metropolitan Transportation Council and analyzed by Bruce Schaller, a Brooklyn-based consultant, the average speed achieved by a vehicle travelling along Forty-second Street between the hours of 10 A.M. and 4 P.M. is 4.7 miles per hour. On Thirty-fourth Street approaching the entrance to the Queens Midtown Tunnel, the average speed drops to 2.5 miles per hour.

A few cities have tried congestion pricing, most notably Stockholm and London, and in most cases it has been a success. Stockholm imposed congestion pricing on a trial basis last year; the program worked so well that voters opted to reinstitute it. Since the London plan was introduced, in 2003, vehicle speeds in the city's central business district have increased by thirty-seven percent and carbon-dioxide emissions from cars and trucks have dropped by fifteen percent. The plan, which the newspapers initially derided as "Kengestion"—after its main supporter,

---

water are common resources like open grazing land, and excessive pollution is like excessive grazing. Environmental degradation is a modern Tragedy of the Commons.

Congested Roads   Roads can be either public goods or common resources. If a road is not congested, then one person's use does not affect anyone else. In this case, use is not rival in consumption, and the road is a public good. Yet if a road is congested, then use of that road yields a negative externality. When one person drives on the road, it becomes more crowded, and other people must drive more slowly. In this case, the road is a common resource.

London's mayor, Ken Livingstone—has grown increasingly popular; in 2004, Livingstone was easily reelected, and now nearly two-thirds of Londoners say that they back the scheme. Just three months ago, the congestion zone was expanded westward to include most of the boroughs of Kensington and Chelsea and Westminster.

The case against congestion pricing is often posed in egalitarian terms. "The middle class and the poor will not be able to pay these fees and the rich will," State Assemblyman Richard Brodsky, of Westchester County, declared after listening to the Mayor's speech. In fact, the poor don't, as a rule, drive in and out of Manhattan: compare the cost of buying, insuring, and parking a car with the seventy-six dollars a month the M.T.A. charges for an unlimited-ride MetroCard. For those who do use cars to commute, eight dollars a day would, it's true, quickly add up. And that is precisely the point. Congestion pricing works only to the extent that it makes other choices—changing the hours of one's daily drive or, better yet, using mass transit—more attractive. One of the Mayor's proposals is to put the money raised by congestion pricing—an estimated four hundred million dollars a year—toward improving subway and bus service.

Mayor Bloomberg

Meanwhile, it's naïve to suppose that congestion isn't itself costly. Sitting in traffic, a plumber can't plumb and a deliveryman can't deliver. The value of time lost to congestion delays in the city has been put at five billion dollars annually. When expenses like wasted fuel, lost revenue, and the increased cost of doing business are added in, that figure rises to thirteen billion dollars. The question, Bloomberg observed, is "not whether we want to pay but how do we want to pay?"

Many elements of the Mayor's plan, including congestion pricing, will require approval by the state legislature, which is too bad, since, as a recent *Times* editorial put it, Albany is a place where good policies generally "go to die." Even Governor Eliot Spitzer, who, as state attorney general,

sued the country's largest carbon emitters, offered what can only be described as a tepid endorsement of the Mayor's proposal, saying, "We look forward to reviewing the plan."

As a matter of city planning, congestion pricing is a compelling idea; in the context of climate change, it is much more than that. Any meaningful effort to address the problem will have to include incentives for low-emitting activities (walking, biking, riding the subway) and costs for high-emitting ones (flying, driving, sitting at home and cranking up the A.C.). These costs will inconvenience some people—perhaps most people—and the burden will not always be distributed with perfect fairness. But, as the Mayor pointed out, New York, a flood-prone coastal city, is vulnerable to one of global warming's most destructive—and most certain—consequences: rising sea levels. If New Yorkers won't change their behavior, then it's hard to see why anyone in the rest of the country or, for that matter, the world should, either. The congestion problem will, in that case, find a different resolution. Who, after all, wants to drive into a city that's under water?

Source: *New Yorker*, May 7, 2007.

One way for the government to address the problem of road congestion is to charge drivers a toll. A toll is, in essence, a corrective tax on the externality of congestion. Sometimes, as in the case of local roads, tolls are not a practical solution because the cost of collecting them is too high. But the city of London has found increasing tolls to be a very effective way to reduce congestion, and as the accompanying In The News box discusses, a similar plan is being considered for New York City.

Sometimes congestion is a problem only at certain times of day. If a bridge is heavily traveled only during rush hour, for instance, the congestion externality is largest during this time. The efficient way to deal with these externalities is to charge higher tolls during rush hour. This toll would provide an incentive for drivers to alter their schedules, reducing traffic when congestion is greatest.

Another policy that responds to the problem of road congestion, discussed in a case study in the previous chapter, is the tax on gasoline. Gasoline is a complementary good to driving: An increase in the price of gasoline tends to reduce the quantity of driving demanded. Therefore, a gasoline tax reduces road congestion. A gasoline tax, however, is an imperfect solution, because it affects other decisions besides the amount of driving on congested roads. For example, the gasoline tax discourages driving on uncongested roads, even though there is no congestion externality for these roads.

Fish, Whales, and Other Wildlife   Many species of animals are common resources. Fish and whales, for instance, have commercial value, and anyone can go to the ocean and catch whatever is available. Each person has little incentive to maintain the species for the next year. Just as excessive grazing can destroy the Town Common, excessive fishing and whaling can destroy commercially valuable marine populations.

The ocean remains one of the least regulated common resources. Two problems prevent an easy solution. First, many countries have access to the oceans, so any solution would require international cooperation among countries that hold different values. Second, because the oceans are so vast, enforcing any agreement is difficult. As a result, fishing rights have been a frequent source of international tension among normally friendly countries.

Within the United States, various laws aim to protect fish and other wildlife. For example, the government charges for fishing and hunting licenses, and it restricts the lengths of the fishing and hunting seasons. Fishermen are often required to throw back small fish, and hunters can kill only a limited number of animals. All these laws reduce the use of a common resource and help maintain animal populations.

"WILL THE MARKET PROTECT ME?"

 WHY THE COW IS NOT EXTINCT

Throughout history, many species of animals have been threatened with extinction. When Europeans first arrived in North America, more than 60 million buffalo roamed the continent. Yet hunting the buffalo was so popular during the 19th century that by 1900 the animal's population had fallen to about 400 before the government stepped in to protect the species. In some African countries today, the elephant faces a similar challenge, as poachers kill the animals for the ivory in their tusks.

Yet not all animals with commercial value face this threat. The cow, for example, is a valuable source of food, but no one worries that the cow will soon be extinct. Indeed, the great demand for beef seems to ensure that the species will continue to thrive.

Why is the commercial value of ivory a threat to the elephant, while the commercial value of beef is a guardian of the cow? The reason is that elephants are a common resource, whereas cows are a private good. Elephants roam freely without any owners. Each poacher has a strong incentive to kill as many elephants as he can find. Because poachers are numerous, each poacher has only a slight incentive to preserve the elephant population. By contrast, cattle live on ranches that are privately owned. Each rancher makes great effort to maintain the cattle population on his ranch because he reaps the benefit of these efforts.

Governments have tried to solve the elephant's problem in two ways. Some countries, such as Kenya, Tanzania, and Uganda, have made it illegal to kill elephants and sell their ivory. Yet these laws have been hard to enforce, and elephant populations have continued to dwindle. By contrast, other countries, such as Botswana, Malawi, Namibia, and Zimbabwe, have made elephants a private good by allowing people to kill elephants, but only those on their own property. Landowners now have an incentive to preserve the species on their own land, and as a result, elephant populations have started to rise. With private ownership and the profit motive now on its side, the African elephant might someday be as safe from extinction as the cow.   ●

QUICK QUIZ   Why do governments try to limit the use of common resources?

CONCLUSION: THE IMPORTANCE OF PROPERTY RIGHTS

In this and the previous chapter, we have seen there are some "goods" that the market does not provide adequately. Markets do not ensure that the air we breathe is clean or that our country is defended from foreign aggressors. Instead, societies rely on the government to protect the environment and to provide for the national defense.

Although the problems we considered in these chapters arise in many different markets, they share a common theme. In all cases, the market fails to allocate resources efficiently because *property rights* are not well established. That is, some item of value does not have an owner with the legal authority to control it. For example, although no one doubts that the "good" of clean air or national defense is valuable, no one has the right to attach a price to it and profit from its use. A factory pollutes too much because no one charges the factory for the pollution it emits. The market does not provide for national defense because no one can charge those who are defended for the benefit they receive.

When the absence of property rights causes a market failure, the government can potentially solve the problem. Sometimes, as in the sale of pollution permits, the solution is for the government to help define property rights and thereby unleash market forces. Other times, as in restricted hunting seasons, the solution is for the government to regulate private behavior. Still other times, as in the provision of national defense, the solution is for the government to use tax revenue to supply a good that the market fails to supply. In all cases, if the policy is well planned and well run, it can make the allocation of resources more efficient and thus raise economic well-being.

SUMMARY

- Goods differ in whether they are excludable and whether they are rival in consumption. A good is excludable if it is possible to prevent someone from using it. A good is rival in consumption if one person's use of the good reduces other people's ability to use the same unit of the good. Markets work best for private goods, which are both excludable and rival in consumption. Markets do not work as well for other types of goods.

- Public goods are neither rival in consumption nor excludable. Examples of public goods include fireworks displays, national defense, and the creation of fundamental knowledge. Because people are not charged for their use of the public good, they have an incentive to free ride when the good is provided privately. Therefore, governments provide public goods, making their decision about the quantity of each good based on cost–benefit analysis.

- Common resources are rival in consumption but not excludable. Examples include common grazing land, clean air, and congested roads. Because people are not charged for their use of common resources, they tend to use them excessively. Therefore, governments use various methods to limit the use of common resources.

KEY CONCEPTS

excludability, *p. 226*
rivalry in consumption, *p. 226*
private goods, *p. 226*

public goods, *p. 226*
common resources, *p. 227*
free rider, *p. 228*

cost–benefit analysis, *p. 231*
Tragedy of the Commons, *p. 232*

QUESTIONS FOR REVIEW

1. Explain what is meant by a good being "excludable." Explain what is meant by a good being "rival in consumption." Is a slice of pizza excludable? Is it rival in consumption?
2. Define and give an example of a public good. Can the private market provide this good on its own? Explain.
3. What is cost–benefit analysis of public goods? Why is it important? Why is it hard?
4. Define and give an example of a common resource. Without government intervention, will people use this good too much or too little? Why?

PROBLEMS AND APPLICATIONS

1. Think about the goods and services provided by your local government.
   a. Using the classification in Figure 1, explain which category each of the following goods falls into:
      - police protection
      - snow plowing
      - education
      - rural roads
      - city streets
   b. Why do you think the government provides items that are not public goods?
2. Both public goods and common resources involve externalities.

a. Are the externalities associated with public goods generally positive or negative? Use examples in your answer. Is the free-market quantity of public goods generally greater or less than the efficient quantity?

b. Are the externalities associated with common resources generally positive or negative? Use examples in your answer. Is the free-market use of common resources generally greater or less than the efficient use?

3. Charlie loves watching *Teletubbies* on his local public TV station, but he never sends any money to support the station during its fund-raising drives.

a. What name do economists have for Charlie?

b. How can the government solve the problem caused by people like Charlie?

c. Can you think of ways the private market can solve this problem? How does the existence of cable TV alter the situation?

4. Four roommates are planning to spend the weekend in their dorm room watching old movies, and they are debating how many to watch. Here is their willingness to pay for each film:

	Orson	Alfred	Woody	Ingmar
First film	$7	$5	$3	$2
Second film	6	4	2	1
Third film	5	3	1	0
Fourth film	4	2	0	0
Fifth film	3	1	0	0

a. Within the dorm room, is the showing of a movie a public good? Why or why not?

b. If it costs $8 to rent a movie, how many movies should the roommates rent to maximize total surplus?

c. If they choose the optimal number from part (b) and then split the cost of renting the movies equally, how much surplus does each person obtain from watching the movies?

d. Is there any way to split the cost to ensure that everyone benefits? What practical problems does this solution raise?

e. Suppose they agree in advance to choose the efficient number and to split the cost of the movies equally. When Orson is asked his willingness to pay, will he have an incentive to tell the truth? If so, why? If not, what will he be tempted to say?

f. What does this example teach you about the optimal provision of public goods?

5. Some economists argue that private firms will not undertake the efficient amount of basic scientific research.

a. Explain why this might be so. In your answer, classify basic research in one of the categories shown in Figure 1.

b. What sort of policy has the United States adopted in response to this problem?

c. It is often argued that this policy increases the technological capability of American producers relative to that of foreign firms. Is this argument consistent with your classification of basic research in part (a)? (Hint: Can excludability apply to some potential beneficiaries of a public good and not others?)

6. There is often litter along highways but rarely in people's yards. Provide an economic explanation for this fact.

7. The village of Ectenia has ten residents. Villagers can earn income by either weaving baskets or fishing. Because the lake has a limited number of fish, the more villagers fish, the less each catches. In particular, if n households fish in the lake, then each fishing household makes an amount:

$$I_f = 12 - 2n$$

where I_f is daily income measured in dollars. The income that a household makes by weaving baskets is $2 a day.

a. Assume that each household makes the decision of whether to weave baskets or fish in the lake independently. How many households do you expect to see fishing each day? How many households do you expect to see weaving baskets? (Hint: Think about opportunity cost.) Calculate the total income of the village in this equilibrium.

b. Show that, when 3 households fish in the lake, the total income of the village is larger than the one you found in part (a). What prevented the villagers from reaching this higher-income allocation of resources when they acted independently?

c. If the villagers together decided to achieve the allocation in part (b), what kinds of rules would they need to institute? If they wanted everyone to benefit equally in the new system, what kind of tax and transfer system would they need?

d. What type of good is the fishery? What characteristics make it that type of good?

8. The Washington, D.C., Metro (subway) system charges higher fares during rush hours than during the rest of the day. Why might it do this?

9. Timber companies in the United States cut down many trees on publicly owned land and many trees on privately owned land. Discuss the likely efficiency of logging on each type of land in the absence of government regulation. How do you think the government should regulate logging on publicly owned lands? Should similar regulations apply to privately owned land?

10. The federal government tests the safety of car models and provides the test results free of charge to the public. Do you think this information qualifies as a public good? Why or why not?

11. High-income people are willing to pay more than lower-income people to avoid the risk of death. For example, they are more likely to pay for safety features on cars. Do you think cost–benefit analysts should take this fact into account when evaluating public projects? Consider, for instance, a rich town and a poor town, both of which are considering the installation of a traffic light. Should the rich town use a higher dollar value for a human life in making this decision? Why or why not?

The Design of the Tax System

Al "Scarface" Capone, the notorious 1920s gangster and crime boss, was never convicted for his many violent crimes. Yet eventually, he did go to jail—for tax evasion. He had neglected to heed Ben Franklin's observation that "in this world nothing is certain but death and taxes."

When Franklin made this claim in 1789, the average American paid less than 5 percent of his income in taxes, and that remained true for the next hundred years. Over the course of the 20th century, however, taxes became ever more important in the life of the typical U.S. citizen. Today, all taxes taken together—including personal income taxes, corporate income taxes, payroll taxes, sales taxes, and property taxes—use up about a third of the average American's income. In many European countries, the tax bite is even larger.

Taxes are inevitable because we as citizens expect the government to provide us with various goods and services. The previous two chapters shed light on one of the *Ten Principles of Economics* from Chapter 1: The government can sometimes improve market outcomes. When the government remedies an externality (such as air pollution), provides a public good (such as national defense), or regulates the use of a common resource (such as fish in a public lake), it can raise economic well-being. Yet these activities are costly. For the government to perform these and its many other functions, it needs to raise revenue through taxation.

We began our study of taxation in earlier chapters, where we saw how a tax on a good affects supply and demand for that good. In Chapter 6, we saw that a tax reduces the quantity sold in a market, and we examined how the burden of a tax is shared by buyers and sellers depending on the elasticities of supply and demand. In Chapter 8, we examined how taxes affect economic well-being. We learned that taxes cause *deadweight losses:* The reduction in consumer and producer surplus resulting from a tax exceeds the revenue raised by the government.

In this chapter, we build on these lessons to discuss the design of a tax system. We begin with a financial overview of the U.S. government. When thinking about the tax system, it is useful to know some basic facts about how the U.S. government raises and spends money. We then consider the fundamental principles of taxation. Most people agree that taxes should impose as small a cost on society as possible and that the burden of taxes should be distributed fairly. That is, the tax system should be both *efficient* and *equitable*. As we will see, however, stating these goals is easier than achieving them.

A FINANCIAL OVERVIEW OF THE U.S. GOVERNMENT

How much of the nation's income does the government take as taxes? Figure 1 shows government revenue, including federal, state, and local governments, as a percentage of total income for the U.S. economy. It shows that the role of government has grown substantially over the past century. In 1902, the government

1 FIGURE

This figure shows revenue of the federal government and of state and local governments as a percentage of gross domestic product (GDP), which measures total income in the economy. It shows that the government plays a large role in the U.S. economy and that its role has grown over time.

Government Revenue as a Percentage of GDP

Source: *Historical Statistics of the United States*; Bureau of Economic Analysis; and author's calculations.

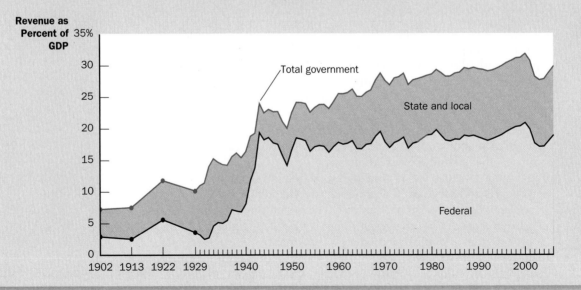

Sweden	50%	United States	28%	
France	45	Japan	27	
United Kingdom	37	Mexico	20	
Germany	36	Chile	19	
Canada	36	China	15	
Brazil	30	India	14	
Russia	32			

TABLE 1

Total Government Tax Revenue as a Percentage of GDP

Source: OECD, United Nations. Data are for most recent year available.

collected 7 percent of total income; in recent years, government has collected about 30 percent. In other words, as the economy's income has grown, the government's revenue from taxation has grown even more.

Table 1 compares the tax burden for several major countries, as measured by the government's tax revenue as a percentage of the nation's total income. The United States is in the middle of the pack. The U.S. tax burden is low compared to many European countries, but it is high compared to some other nations around the world. Less economically developed countries, such as India, often have relatively low tax burdens. This fact is consistent with the evidence in Figure 1 of a growing tax burden over time: As a nation gets richer, the government typically takes a larger share of income in taxes.

The overall size of government tells only part of the story. Behind the total dollar figures lie thousands of individual decisions about taxes and spending. To understand the government's finances more fully, let's look at how the total breaks down into some broad categories.

THE FEDERAL GOVERNMENT

The U.S. federal government collects about two-thirds of the taxes in our economy. It raises this money in a number of ways, and it finds even more ways to spend it.

Receipts   Table 2 shows the receipts of the federal government in 2007. Total receipts that year were $2,568 billion, a number so large that it is hard to

Tax	Amount (billions)	Amount per Person	Percent of Receipts
Individual income taxes	$1,163	$3,851	45%
Social insurance taxes	870	2,881	34
Corporate income taxes	370	1,225	14
Other	165	546	7
Total	$2,568	$8,503	100%

TABLE 2

Receipts of the Federal Government: 2007

Source: *Economic Report of the President*, 2008, Table B-81.

comprehend. To bring this astronomical number down to earth, we can divide it by the size of the U.S. population, which was about 302 million in 2007. We then find that the average American paid $8,503 to the federal government.

The largest source of revenue for the federal government is the individual income tax. As April 15 approaches each year, almost every American family fills out a tax form to determine how much income tax it owes the government. Each family is required to report its income from all sources: wages from working, interest on savings, dividends from corporations in which it owns shares, profits from any small businesses it operates, and so on. The family's *tax liability* (how much it owes) is then based on its total income.

A family's income tax liability is not simply proportional to its income. Instead, the law requires a more complicated calculation. Taxable income is computed as total income minus an amount based on the number of dependents (primarily children) and minus certain expenses that policymakers have deemed "deductible" (such as mortgage interest payments, state and local tax payments, and charitable giving). Then the tax liability is calculated from taxable income using a schedule such as the one shown in Table 3.

This table presents the *marginal tax rate*—the tax rate applied to each additional dollar of income. Because the marginal tax rate rises as income rises, higher-income families pay a larger percentage of their income in taxes. Note that each tax rate in the table applies only to income within the associated range, not to a person's entire income. For example, a person with an income of $1 million still pays only 10 percent of the first $7,825. (Later in this chapter we discuss the concept of marginal tax rate more fully.)

Almost as important to the federal government as the individual income tax are payroll taxes. A *payroll tax* is a tax on the wages that a firm pays its workers. Table 2 calls this revenue *social insurance taxes* because the revenue from these taxes is earmarked to pay for Social Security and Medicare. Social Security is an income-support program designed primarily to maintain the living standards of the elderly. Medicare is the government health program for the elderly. Table 2 shows that the average American paid $2,881 in social insurance taxes in 2007.

Next in magnitude, but much smaller than either individual income taxes or social insurance taxes, is the corporate income tax. A *corporation* is a business that is set up as a separate legal entity. The government taxes each corporation based on its profit—the amount the corporation receives for the goods or services it sells minus the costs of producing those goods or services. Notice that corporate profits

3 TABLE

The Federal Income Tax Rates: 2007
This table shows the marginal tax rates for an unmarried taxpayer. The taxes owed by a taxpayer depend on all the marginal tax rates up to his or her income level. For example, a taxpayer with income of $25,000 pays 10 percent of the first $7,825 of income, and then 15 percent of the rest.

On Taxable Income . . .	The Tax Rate Is . . .
Up to $7,825	10%
From $7,825 to $31,850	15%
From $31,850 to $77,100	25%
From $77,100 to $160,850	28%
From $160,850 to $349,700	33%
Over $349,700	35%

are, in essence, taxed twice. They are taxed once by the corporate income tax when the corporation earns the profits; they are taxed a second time by the individual income tax when the corporation uses its profits to pay dividends to its shareholders. In 2003, the tax rate on dividend income was reduced to 15 percent, in part to compensate for this double taxation.

The last category, labeled "other" in Table 2, makes up 7 percent of receipts. This category includes *excise taxes*, which are taxes on specific goods like gasoline, cigarettes, and alcoholic beverages. It also includes various small items, such as estate taxes and customs duties.

Spending   Table 4 shows the spending of the federal government in 2007. Total spending was $2,730 billion, or $9,040 per person. This table also shows how the federal government's spending was divided among major categories.

The largest category in Table 4 is Social Security, which represents mostly transfer payments to the elderly. A *transfer payment* is a government payment not made in exchange for a good or service. This category made up 21 percent of spending by the federal government in 2007.

The second largest category of spending is national defense. This includes both the salaries of military personnel and the purchases of military equipment such as guns, fighter jets, and warships. Spending on national defense fluctuates over time as international tensions and the political climate change. Not surprisingly, spending on national defense rises substantially during wars. In part because of the war in Iraq, defense spending rose from 17 to 20 percent of total federal spending from 2001 to 2007.

Health spending looms large in the federal budget. Medicare, the third category in Table 4, is the government's health plan for the elderly. The fifth category in the table is other health spending, which includes Medicaid, the federal health program for the poor, and spending on medical research, such as through the National Institutes of Health. Total health spending makes up about a quarter of the federal budget.

The fourth category in Table 4 is spending on income security, which includes transfer payments to poor families. One program is Temporary Assistance for Needy Families (TANF), often simply called "welfare." Another is the Food

TABLE 4

Category	Amount (billions)	Amount per Person	Percent of Spending
Social Security	$ 586	$1,940	21%
National defense	553	1,831	20
Medicare	375	1,242	14
Income security	366	1,212	13
Health	266	881	10
Net interest	237	785	9
Other	347	1,149	13
Total	$2,730	$9,040	100%

Spending of the Federal Government: 2007

Source: *Economic Report of the President, 2008, Table B-81.*

Stamp program, which gives poor families vouchers that they can use to buy food. The federal government pays some of this money to state and local governments, which administer the programs under federal guidelines.

Next on the list is net interest. When a person borrows from a bank, the bank requires the borrower to pay interest for the loan. The same is true when the government borrows from the public. The more indebted the government, the larger the amount it must spend in interest payments.

The "other" category in Table 4 consists of many less expensive functions of government. It includes, for example, the federal court system, the space program, and farm-support programs, as well as the salaries of members of Congress and the president.

budget deficit
an excess of government spending over government receipts

budget surplus
an excess of government receipts over government spending

You might have noticed that total receipts of the federal government shown in Table 2 fall short of total spending shown in Table 4 by $162 billion. In such a situation, the government is said to run a **budget deficit**. When receipts exceed spending, the government is said to run a **budget surplus**. The government finances a budget deficit by borrowing from the public. That is, it sells government debt to the private sector, including both investors in the United States and those abroad. When the government runs a budget surplus, it uses the excess receipts to reduce its outstanding debts.

 THE FISCAL CHALLENGE AHEAD

In 2007, the federal government ran a budget deficit of $162 billion. This excess of government spending over government revenue is only the tip of an iceberg: Long-term projections of the government's budget show that, under current law, the government will spend vastly more than it will receive in tax revenue in the decades ahead. As a percentage of gross domestic product (the total income in the economy), taxes are projected to be about constant. But government spending as a percentage of GDP is projected to rise gradually but substantially over the next several decades.

One reason for the rise in government spending is that Social Security and Medicare provide significant benefits for the elderly, who are a growing percentage of the overall population. Over the past half century, medical advances and lifestyle improvements have greatly increased life expectancy. In 1950, a man age 65 could expect to live for another 13 years; now he can expect to live another 17 years. The life expectancy of a 65-year-old woman has risen from 16 years in 1950 to 20 years today. At the same time, people are having fewer children. In 1950, the typical woman had three children. Today, the number is about two. As a result of smaller families, the labor force is growing more slowly now than it has in the past.

Panel (a) of Figure 2 shows the demographic shift that is arising from the combination of longer life expectancy and lower fertility. In 1950, the elderly population equaled about 14 percent of the working-age population. Now the elderly are about 21 percent of the working-age population, and that figure will rise to about 40 percent over the next 50 years. This means that there will be fewer workers paying taxes to support the government benefits that each elderly person receives.

A second, related trend that will affect government spending in the decades ahead is the rising cost of healthcare. The government provides healthcare to the elderly through the Medicare system and to the poor through Medicaid. As the cost of healthcare increases, government spending on these programs will increase as well.

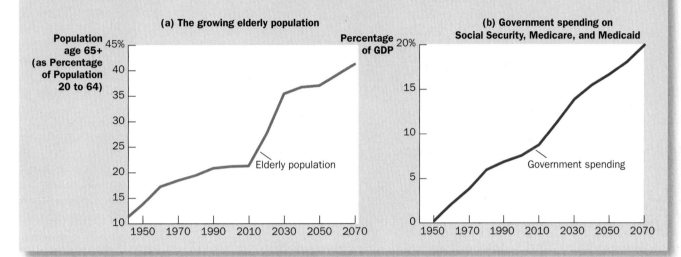

Panel (a) shows the U.S. population age 65 and older as a percentage of the population age 20 to 64. The growing elderly population will put increasing pressure on the government budget. Panel (b) shows government spending on Social Security, Medicare, and Medicaid as a percentage of GDP. The projection for future years assumes no change in current law. Unless changes in benefits are enacted, government spending on these programs will rise significantly and will require large tax increases to pay for them.

FIGURE **2**

The Demographic and Fiscal Challenge

Source: Congressional Budget Office.

Policymakers have proposed various ways to stem the rise in healthcare costs, such as reducing the burden of lawsuits on the healthcare system, encouraging more competition among healthcare providers, and promoting greater use of information technology. Most health economists, however, believe that such measures will have only a limited impact. The main reason for rising healthcare costs is medical advances that provide new, better, but often expensive ways to extend and improve our lives.

Panel (b) of Figure 2 shows government spending on Social Security, Medicare, and Medicaid as a percentage of GDP. Spending on these programs has risen from less than 1 percent in 1950 to about 8 percent today. The combination of a growing elderly population and rising healthcare costs is expected to continue and even accelerate the trend.

How our society will handle these spending increases is an open question. Simply increasing the budget deficit is not feasible. A budget deficit just pushes the cost of government spending onto a future generation of taxpayers, who will inherit a government with greater debts. In the long run, the government needs to pay for what it spends.

Some economists believe that to pay for these commitments, we will need to raise taxes substantially as a percentage of GDP. If so, the long-term trend we saw in Figure 1 will continue. Spending on Social Security, Medicare, and Medicaid is expected to rise by about 10 percentage points of GDP. Because taxes are now 30 percent of GDP, paying for these benefits would require approximately a one-third increase in all taxes.

Other economists believe that such high tax rates would impose too great a cost on younger workers. They believe that policymakers should reduce the promises now being made to the elderly of the future and that, at the same time, people should be encouraged to take a greater role caring for themselves as they age. This might entail raising the normal retirement age, while giving people more incentive to save during their working years to prepare for their own retirement and health costs.

It is likely that the final resolution will involve a combination of measures. No one can dispute that resolving this debate is one of the great challenges ahead. ●

STATE AND LOCAL GOVERNMENT

State and local governments collect about 40 percent of all taxes paid. Let's look at how they obtain tax revenue and how they spend it.

Receipts   Table 5 shows the receipts of U.S. state and local governments. Total receipts for 2005 were $2,021 billion, or $6,827 per person. The table also shows how this total is broken down into different kinds of taxes.

The two most important taxes for state and local governments are sales taxes and property taxes. Sales taxes are levied as a percentage of the total amount spent at retail stores. Every time a customer buys something, he or she pays the storekeeper an extra amount that the storekeeper remits to the government. (Some states exclude certain items that are considered necessities, such as food and clothing.) Property taxes are levied as a percentage of the estimated value of land and structures and are paid by property owners. Together, these two taxes make up more than a third of all receipts of state and local governments.

State and local governments also levy individual and corporate income taxes. In many cases, state and local income taxes are similar to federal income taxes. In other cases, they are quite different. For example, some states tax income from wages less heavily than income earned in the form of interest and dividends. Some states do not tax income at all.

State and local governments also receive substantial funds from the federal government. To some extent, the federal government's policy of sharing its revenue

5 TABLE

Receipts of State and Local Governments: 2005

Source: *Economic Report of the President*, 2008, Table B-86.

Tax	Amount (billions)	Amount per Person	Percent of Spending
Sales taxes	$ 383	$1,294	19%
Property taxes	336	1,135	17
Individual income taxes	241	814	12
Corporate income taxes	43	145	2
From federal government	438	1,480	22
Other	580	1,959	28
Total	$2,021	6,827	100%

TABLE 6

Category	Amount (billions)	Amount per Person	Percent of Spending
Education	$ 689	$2,328	34%
Public welfare	367	1,240	18
Highways	124	419	6
Other	834	2,817	42
Total	$2,014	$6,804	100%

Spending of State and Local Governments: 2005

Source: *Economic Report of the President*, 2008, Table B-86.

with state governments redistributes funds from high-income states (who pay more taxes) to low-income states (who receive more benefits). Often, these funds are tied to specific programs that the federal government wants to subsidize.

Finally, state and local governments receive much of their receipts from various sources included in the "other" category in Table 5. These include fees for fishing and hunting licenses, tolls from roads and bridges, and fares for public buses and subways.

Spending   Table 6 shows the total spending of state and local governments in 2005 and its breakdown among the major categories.

By far the biggest single expenditure for state and local governments is education. Local governments pay for the public schools, which educate most students from kindergarten through high school. State governments contribute to the support of public universities. In 2005, education accounted for about a third of the spending of state and local governments.

The second largest category of spending is for public welfare, which includes transfer payments to the poor. This category includes some federal programs that are administered by state and local governments. The next category is highways, which includes the building of new roads and the maintenance of existing ones. The large "other" category in Table 6 includes the many additional services provided by state and local governments, such as libraries, police, garbage removal, fire protection, park maintenance, and snow removal.

QUICK QUIZ   What are the two most important sources of tax revenue for the federal government? • What are the two most important sources of tax revenue for state and local governments?

TAXES AND EFFICIENCY

Now that we have seen how various levels of the U.S. government raise and spend money, let's consider how one might evaluate its tax policy and design a tax system. The primary aim of a tax system is to raise revenue for the government, but there are many ways to raise any given amount of money. When choosing among the many alternative tax systems, policymakers have two objectives: efficiency and equity.

One tax system is more efficient than another if it raises the same amount of revenue at a smaller cost to taxpayers. What are the costs of taxes to taxpayers? The most obvious cost is the tax payment itself. This transfer of money from the taxpayer to the government is an inevitable feature of any tax system. Yet taxes also impose two other costs, which a well-designed tax policy tries to avoid or, at least, minimize:

- The deadweight losses that result when taxes distort the decisions that people make
- The administrative burdens that taxpayers bear as they comply with the tax laws

An efficient tax system is one that imposes small deadweight losses and small administrative burdens.

DEADWEIGHT LOSSES

One of the *Ten Principles of Economics* is that people respond to incentives, and this includes incentives provided by the tax system. If the government taxes ice cream, people eat less ice cream and more frozen yogurt. If the government taxes housing, people live in smaller houses and spend more of their income on other things. If the government taxes labor earnings, people work less and enjoy more leisure.

Because taxes distort incentives, they entail deadweight losses. As we first discussed in Chapter 8, the deadweight loss of a tax is the reduction in economic well-being of taxpayers in excess of the amount of revenue raised by the government. The deadweight loss is the inefficiency that a tax creates as people allocate resources according to the tax incentive rather than the true costs and benefits of the goods and services that they buy and sell.

To recall how taxes cause deadweight losses, consider an example. Suppose that Joe places an $8 value on a pizza, and Jane places a $6 value on it. If there is no tax on pizza, the price of pizza will reflect the cost of making it. Let's suppose that the price of pizza is $5, so both Joe and Jane choose to buy one. Both consumers get some surplus of value over the amount paid. Joe gets consumer surplus of $3, and Jane gets consumer surplus of $1. Total surplus is $4.

Now suppose that the government levies a $2 tax on pizza and the price of pizza rises to $7. Joe still buys a pizza, but now he has consumer surplus of only $1. Jane now decides not to buy a pizza because its price is higher than its value to her. The government collects tax revenue of $2 on Joe's pizza. Total consumer surplus has fallen by $3 (from $4 to $1). Because total surplus has fallen by more than the tax revenue, the tax has a deadweight loss. In this case, the deadweight loss is $1.

Notice that the deadweight loss comes not from Joe, the person who pays the tax, but from Jane, the person who doesn't. The reduction of $2 in Joe's surplus exactly offsets the amount of revenue the government collects. The deadweight loss arises because the tax causes Jane to alter her behavior. When the tax raises the price of pizza, Jane is worse off, and yet there is no offsetting revenue to the government. This reduction in Jane's welfare is the deadweight loss of the tax.

"I WAS GONNA FIX THE PLACE UP, BUT IF I DID THE CITY WOULD JUST RAISE MY TAXES!"

SHOULD INCOME OR CONSUMPTION BE TAXED?

When taxes induce people to change their behavior—such as inducing Jane to buy less pizza—the taxes cause deadweight losses and make the allocation of resources less efficient. As we have already seen, much government revenue comes from the individual income tax. In a case study in Chapter 8, we discussed how this tax discourages people from working as hard as they otherwise might. Another inefficiency caused by this tax is that it discourages people from saving.

Consider a person 25 years old who is considering saving $100. If he puts this money in a savings account that earns 8 percent and leaves it there, he would have $2,172 when he retires at age 65. Yet if the government taxes one-fourth of his interest income each year, the effective interest rate is only 6 percent. After 40 years of earning 6 percent, the $100 grows to only $1,029, less than half of what it would have been without taxation. Thus, because interest income is taxed, saving is much less attractive.

Some economists advocate eliminating the current tax system's disincentive toward saving by changing the basis of taxation. Rather than taxing the amount of income that people earn, the government could tax the amount that people spend. Under this proposal, all income that is saved would not be taxed until the saving is later spent. This alternative system, called a *consumption tax*, would not distort people's saving decisions.

Various provisions of the current tax code already make the tax system a bit like a consumption tax. Taxpayers can put a limited amount of their saving into special accounts—such as Individual Retirement Accounts and 401(k) plans—that escape taxation until the money is withdrawn at retirement. For people who do most of their saving through these retirement accounts, their tax bill is, in effect, based on their consumption rather than their income.

European countries tend to rely more on consumption taxes than does the United States. Most of them raise a significant amount of government revenue through a value-added tax, or a VAT. A VAT is like the retail sales tax that many U.S. states use, but rather than collecting all of the tax at the retail level when the consumer buys the final good, the government collects the tax in stages as the good is being produced (that is, as value is added by firms along the chain of production).

Various U.S. policymakers have proposed that the tax code move further in the direction of taxing consumption rather than income. In 2005, economist Alan Greenspan, then Chairman of the Federal Reserve, offered this advice to a presidential commission on tax reform: "As you know, many economists believe that a consumption tax would be best from the perspective of promoting economic growth—particularly if one were designing a tax system from scratch—because a consumption tax is likely to encourage saving and capital formation. However, getting from the current tax system to a consumption tax raises a challenging set of transition issues." ●

ADMINISTRATIVE BURDEN

If you ask the typical person on April 15 for an opinion about the tax system, you might get an earful (perhaps peppered with expletives) about the headache of filling out tax forms. The administrative burden of any tax system is part of the inefficiency it creates. This burden includes not only the time spent in early April filling out forms but also the time spent throughout the year keeping records for tax purposes and the resources the government has to use to enforce the tax laws.

Many taxpayers—especially those in higher tax brackets—hire tax lawyers and accountants to help them with their taxes. These experts in the complex tax laws fill out the tax forms for their clients and help them arrange their affairs in a way that reduces the amount of taxes owed. This behavior is legal tax avoidance, which is different from illegal tax evasion.

Critics of our tax system say that these advisers help their clients avoid taxes by abusing some of the detailed provisions of the tax code, often dubbed "loopholes." In some cases, loopholes are congressional mistakes: They arise from ambiguities or omissions in the tax laws. More often, they arise because Congress has chosen to give special treatment to specific types of behavior. For example, the U.S. federal tax code gives preferential treatment to investors in municipal bonds because Congress wanted to make it easier for state and local governments to borrow money. To some extent, this provision benefits states and localities, and to some extent, it benefits high-income taxpayers. Most loopholes are well known by those in Congress who make tax policy, but what looks like a loophole to one taxpayer may look like a justifiable tax deduction to another.

The resources devoted to complying with the tax laws are a type of deadweight loss. The government gets only the amount of taxes paid. By contrast, the taxpayer loses not only this amount but also the time and money spent documenting, computing, and avoiding taxes.

The administrative burden of the tax system could be reduced by simplifying the tax laws. Yet simplification is often politically difficult. Most people are ready to simplify the tax code by eliminating the loopholes that benefit others, but few are eager to give up the loopholes that benefit them. In the end, the complexity of the tax law results from the political process as various taxpayers with their own special interests lobby for their causes.

MARGINAL TAX RATES VERSUS AVERAGE TAX RATES

average tax rate
total taxes paid divided by total income

marginal tax rate
the extra taxes paid on an additional dollar of income

When discussing the efficiency and equity of income taxes, economists distinguish between two notions of the tax rate: the average and the marginal. The **average tax rate** is total taxes paid divided by total income. The **marginal tax rate** is the extra taxes paid on an additional dollar of income.

For example, suppose that the government taxes 20 percent of the first $50,000 of income and 50 percent of all income above $50,000. Under this tax, a person who makes $60,000 pays a tax of $15,000: 20 percent of the first $50,000 (0.20 × $50,000 = $10,000) plus 50 percent of the next $10,000 (0.50 × $10,000 = $5,000). For this person, the average tax rate is $15,000 / $60,000, or 25 percent. But the marginal tax rate is 50 percent. If the taxpayer earned an additional dollar of income, that dollar would be subject to the 50 percent tax rate, so the amount the taxpayer would owe to the government would rise by $0.50.

The marginal and average tax rates each contain a useful piece of information. If we are trying to gauge the sacrifice made by a taxpayer, the average tax rate is more appropriate because it measures the fraction of income paid in taxes. By contrast, if we are trying to gauge how much the tax system distorts incentives, the marginal tax rate is more meaningful. One of the *Ten Principles of Economics* in Chapter 1 is that rational people think at the margin. A corollary to this principle is that the marginal tax rate measures how much the tax system discourages people from working. If you are thinking of working an extra few hours, the marginal tax rate determines how much the government takes of your additional earnings. It is the marginal tax rate, therefore, that determines the deadweight loss of an income tax.

LUMP–SUM TAXES

Suppose the government imposes a tax of $4,000 on everyone. That is, everyone owes the same amount, regardless of earnings or any actions that a person might take. Such a tax is called a **lump-sum tax**.

A lump-sum tax shows clearly the difference between average and marginal tax rates. For a taxpayer with income of $20,000, the average tax rate of a $4,000 lump-sum tax is 20 percent; for a taxpayer with income of $40,000, the average tax rate is 10 percent. For both taxpayers, the marginal tax rate is zero because no tax is owed on an additional dollar of income.

A lump-sum tax is the most efficient tax possible. Because a person's decisions do not alter the amount owed, the tax does not distort incentives and, therefore, does not cause deadweight losses. Because everyone can easily compute the amount owed and because there is no benefit to hiring tax lawyers and accountants, the lump-sum tax imposes a minimal administrative burden on taxpayers.

If lump-sum taxes are so efficient, why do we rarely observe them in the real world? The reason is that efficiency is only one goal of the tax system. A lump-sum tax would take the same amount from the poor and the rich, an outcome most people would view as unfair. To understand the tax systems that we observe, we must therefore consider the other major goal of tax policy: equity.

lump-sum tax
a tax that is the same amount for every person

QUICK QUIZ   What is meant by the *efficiency* of a tax system? ● What can make a tax system inefficient?

TAXES AND EQUITY

Ever since American colonists dumped imported tea into Boston harbor to protest high British taxes, tax policy has generated some of the most heated debates in American politics. The heat is rarely fueled by questions of efficiency. Instead, it arises from disagreements over how the tax burden should be distributed. Senator Russell Long once mimicked the public debate with this ditty:

Don't tax you.
Don't tax me.
Tax that fella behind the tree.

Of course, if we are to rely on the government to provide some of the goods and services we want, taxes must fall on someone. In this section, we consider the equity of a tax system. How should the burden of taxes be divided among the population? How do we evaluate whether a tax system is fair? Everyone agrees that the tax system should be equitable, but there is much disagreement about what equity means and how the equity of a tax system can be judged.

THE BENEFITS PRINCIPLE

benefits principle
the idea that people should pay taxes based on the benefits they receive from government services

One principle of taxation, called the **benefits principle**, states that people should pay taxes based on the benefits they receive from government services. This principle tries to make public goods similar to private goods. It seems fair that a person who often goes to the movies pays more in total for movie tickets than a person who rarely goes. Similarly, a person who gets great benefit from a public good should pay more for it than a person who gets little benefit.

The gasoline tax, for instance, is sometimes justified using the benefits principle. In some states, revenues from the gasoline tax are used to build and maintain roads. Because those who buy gasoline are the same people who use the roads, the gasoline tax might be viewed as a fair way to pay for this government service.

The benefits principle can also be used to argue that wealthy citizens should pay higher taxes than poorer ones. Why? Simply because the wealthy benefit more from public services. Consider, for example, the benefits of police protection from theft. Citizens with much to protect benefit more from police than do those with less to protect. Therefore, according to the benefits principle, the wealthy should contribute more than the poor to the cost of maintaining the police force. The same argument can be used for many other public services, such as fire protection, national defense, and the court system.

It is even possible to use the benefits principle to argue for antipoverty programs funded by taxes on the wealthy. As we discussed in Chapter 11, people prefer living in a society without poverty, suggesting that antipoverty programs are a public good. If the wealthy place a greater dollar value on this public good than members of the middle class do, perhaps just because the wealthy have more to spend, then according to the benefits principle, they should be taxed more heavily to pay for these programs.

THE ABILITY-TO-PAY PRINCIPLE

ability-to-pay principle
the idea that taxes should be levied on a person according to how well that person can shoulder the burden

Another way to evaluate the equity of a tax system is called the **ability-to-pay principle**, which states that taxes should be levied on a person according to how well that person can shoulder the burden. This principle is sometimes justified by the claim that all citizens should make an "equal sacrifice" to support the government. The magnitude of a person's sacrifice, however, depends not only on the size of his tax payment but also on his income and other circumstances. A $1,000 tax paid by a poor person may require a larger sacrifice than a $10,000 tax paid by a rich one.

The ability-to-pay principle leads to two corollary notions of equity: vertical equity and horizontal equity. **Vertical equity** states that taxpayers with a greater ability to pay taxes should contribute a larger amount. **Horizontal equity** states that taxpayers with similar abilities to pay should contribute the same amount. These notions of equity are widely accepted, but applying them to evaluate a tax system is rarely straightforward.

vertical equity
the idea that taxpayers with a greater ability to pay taxes should pay larger amounts

horizontal equity
the idea that taxpayers with similar abilities to pay taxes should pay the same amount

Vertical Equity   If taxes are based on ability to pay, then richer taxpayers should pay more than poorer taxpayers. But how much more should the rich pay? Much of the debate over tax policy concerns this question.

	Proportional Tax		Regressive Tax		Progressive Tax		TABLE **7**
Income	Amount of Tax	Percent of Income	Amount of Tax	Percent of Income	Amount of Tax	Percent of Income	Three Tax Systems
$ 50,000	$12,500	25%	$15,000	30%	$10,000	20%	
100,000	25,000	25	25,000	25	25,000	25	
200,000	50,000	25	40,000	20	60,000	30	

Consider the three tax systems in Table 7. In each case, taxpayers with higher incomes pay more. Yet the systems differ in how quickly taxes rise with income. The first system is called **proportional** because all taxpayers pay the same fraction of income. The second system is called **regressive** because high-income taxpayers pay a smaller fraction of their income, even though they pay a larger amount. The third system is called **progressive** because high-income taxpayers pay a larger fraction of their income.

Which of these three tax systems is most fair? There is no obvious answer, and economic theory does not offer any help in trying to find one. Equity, like beauty, is in the eye of the beholder.

 ### HOW THE TAX BURDEN IS DISTRIBUTED

Much debate over tax policy concerns whether the wealthy pay their fair share. There is no objective way to make this judgment. In evaluating the issue for yourself, however, it is useful to know how much families with different incomes pay under the current tax system.

Table 8 presents some data on how all federal taxes are distributed among income classes. To construct this table, families are ranked according to their income and placed into five groups of equal size, called *quintiles*. The table also presents data on the richest 1 percent of Americans.

The second column of the table shows the average income of each group. The poorest one-fifth of families had average income of $15,900, and the richest one-fifth had average income of $231,300. The richest 1 percent had average income of over $1 million.

The next column of the table shows total taxes as a percentage of income. As you can see, the U.S. federal tax system is progressive. The poorest fifth of families paid 4.3 percent of their incomes in taxes, and the richest fifth paid 25.5 percent. The top 1 percent paid 31.2 percent of their incomes.

The fourth and fifth columns compare the distribution of income and the distribution of taxes. The poorest quintile earns 4.0 percent of all income and pays 0.8 percent of all taxes. The richest quintile earns 55.1 percent of all income and pays 68.7 percent of all taxes. The richest 1 percent (which, remember, is ⅟₂₀ the size of each quintile) earns 18.1 percent of all income and pays 27.6 percent of all taxes.

This table on taxes is a good starting point for understanding the burden of government, but the picture it offers is incomplete. Although it includes all the

proportional tax
a tax for which high-income and low-income taxpayers pay the same fraction of income

regressive tax
a tax for which high-income taxpayers pay a smaller fraction of their income than do low-income taxpayers

progressive tax
a tax for which high-income taxpayers pay a larger fraction of their income than do low-income taxpayers

8 T A B L E

The Burden of Federal Taxes

Source: Congressional Budget Office. Figures are for 2005.

Quintile	Average Income	Taxes as a Percentage of Income	Percentage of All Income	Percentage of All Taxes
Lowest	$15,900	4.3%	4.0%	0.8%
Second	37,400	9.9	8.5	4.1
Middle	58,500	14.2	13.3	9.3
Fourth	85,200	17.4	19.8	16.9
Highest	231,300	25.5	55.1	68.7
Top 1%	1,558,500	31.2	18.1	27.6

taxes that flow from households to the federal government, it fails to include the transfer payments, such as Social Security and welfare, that flow from the federal government back to households.

Studies that include both taxes and transfers show even greater progressivity. The richest group of families still pays about one-quarter of its income to the government, even after transfers are subtracted. By contrast, poor families typically receive more in transfers than they pay in taxes. The average tax rate of the poorest quintile, rather than being 4.3 percent as in the table, is approximately *negative* 30 percent. In other words, their income is about 30 percent higher than it would be without government taxes and transfers. The lesson is clear: To understand fully the progressivity of government policies, one must take account of both what people pay and what they receive. ●

Horizontal Equity If taxes are based on ability to pay, then similar taxpayers should pay similar amounts of taxes. But what determines if two taxpayers are similar? Families differ in many ways. To evaluate whether a tax code is horizontally equitable, one must determine which differences are relevant for a family's ability to pay and which differences are not.

Suppose the Smith and Jones families each have income of $80,000. The Smiths have no children, but Mr. Smith has an illness that causes medical expenses of $30,000. The Joneses are in good health, but they have four children. Two of the Jones children are in college, generating tuition bills of $40,000. Would it be fair for these two families to pay the same tax because they have the same income? Would it be fair to give the Smiths a tax break to help them offset their high medical expenses? Would it be fair to give the Joneses a tax break to help them with their tuition expenses?

There are no easy answers to these questions. In practice, the U.S. income tax is filled with special provisions that alter a family's tax based on its specific circumstances.

TAX INCIDENCE AND TAX EQUITY

Tax incidence—the study of who bears the burden of taxes—is central to evaluating tax equity. As we first saw in Chapter 6, the person who bears the burden of a tax is not always the person who gets the tax bill from the government. Because taxes alter supply and demand, they alter equilibrium prices. As a result, they affect people beyond those who, according to statute, actually pay the tax. When evaluating the vertical and horizontal equity of any tax, it is important to take these indirect effects into account.

Many discussions of tax equity ignore the indirect effects of taxes and are based on what economists mockingly call the *flypaper theory* of tax incidence. According to this theory, the burden of a tax, like a fly on flypaper, sticks wherever it first lands. This assumption, however, is rarely valid.

For example, a person not trained in economics might argue that a tax on expensive fur coats is vertically equitable because most buyers of furs are wealthy. Yet if these buyers can easily substitute other luxuries for furs, then a tax on furs might only reduce the sale of furs. In the end, the burden of the tax will fall more on those who make and sell furs than on those who buy them. Because most workers who make furs are not wealthy, the equity of a fur tax could be quite different from what the flypaper theory indicates.

 WHO PAYS THE CORPORATE INCOME TAX?

The corporate income tax provides a good example of the importance of tax incidence for tax policy. The corporate tax is popular among voters. After all, corporations are not people. Voters are always eager to have their taxes reduced and have some impersonal corporation pick up the tab.

But before deciding that the corporate income tax is a good way for the government to raise revenue, we should consider who bears the burden of the corporate tax. This is a difficult question on which economists disagree, but one thing is certain: *People pay all taxes.* When the government levies a tax on a corporation, the corporation is more like a tax collector than a taxpayer. The burden of the tax ultimately falls on people—the owners, customers, or workers of the corporation.

Many economists believe that workers and customers bear much of the burden of the corporate income tax. To see why, consider an example. Suppose that the U.S. government decides to raise the tax on the income earned by car companies. At first, this tax hurts the owners of the car companies, who receive less profit. But over time, these owners will respond to the tax. Because producing cars is less profitable, they invest less in building new car factories. Instead, they invest their wealth in other ways—for example, by buying larger houses or by building factories in other industries or other countries. With fewer car factories, the supply of cars declines, as does the demand for autoworkers. Thus, a tax on corporations making cars causes the price of cars to rise and the wages of autoworkers to fall.

The corporate income tax shows how dangerous the flypaper theory of tax incidence can be. The corporate income tax is popular in part because it appears to be paid by rich corporations. Yet those who bear the ultimate burden of the tax—the customers and workers of corporations—are often not rich. If the true incidence of the corporate tax were more widely known, this tax might be less popular among voters. ●

© BRIAN KERSEY/UPI/LANDOV

THIS WORKER PAYS PART OF THE CORPORATE INCOME TAX.

QUICK QUIZ Explain the *benefits principle* and the *ability-to-pay principle*. ● What are *vertical equity* and *horizontal equity*? ● Why is studying tax incidence important for determining the equity of a tax system?

In The News

Questions and Answers about Tax Reform

The most recent attempt at major tax reform was in 2005, when President Bush appointed a bipartisan advisory panel to study the issue. This Q&A explains what the panel tried to achieve. Answers are from Edward Lazear and James Poterba, the two economists on the panel. Because Congress failed to adopt the panel's recommendations, the tax code is much the same now as it was in 2005, and the issues the panel raised remain relevant.

Q: *What should the goal of a tax system be?*

A: A tax system should generate the government's required revenue with as little economic distortion as possible, while distributing tax burdens fairly. It should not discourage work, saving or entrepreneurship more than is necessary, and it should not discourage individuals from acquiring the skills and education that will increase their productivity. It should not discourage investment, or favor investments in one asset over those in another. In short, an efficient tax system alters economic decision-making as little as possible.

Q: *What is wrong with the current system?*

A: The more than 15,000 changes to the tax code in the last 19 years have undermined many achievements of the 1986 tax reform. They have created a tax code that is riddled with targeted incentives, phase-out rules, phantom tax rates, and complex and sometimes inconsistent provisions that leave most taxpayers unable to understand the rules under which they are taxed, let alone able to complete their own tax return.

Q: *What should reform try to accomplish?*

A: Although many see simplification as the primary goal of tax reform, promoting economic growth is a more important objective. Even in the relatively short run, the economic costs of a tax system that slows growth are likely to exceed compliance costs. U.S. households spend roughly 1% of GDP in complying with the income tax system. Halving the costs of compliance would be equivalent to raising GDP by one half of one percent—no minor accomplishment. The increase in GDP that might result from a tax reform that reduces tax burdens on investment and shifts the tax system toward a consumption tax are much larger.

Q: *How might tax reform promote economic growth?*

A: A substantial body of economic research suggests that tax wedges between the before-tax and the after-tax return on saving and investment are particularly detrimental to long-term economic growth. The current tax system taxes corporate income once at the corporate level and again at the investor level. The Treasury Department estimates that, on average, the total tax burden on a new corporate investment project is 24%. By comparison, investments in the non-corporate sector, which are taxed only once, face a 17% tax burden. Investments in owner-occupied housing, which yield untaxed returns in the form of implicit rental income, are untaxed. Taxing different invest-

CONCLUSION: THE TRADE-OFF BETWEEN EQUITY AND EFFICIENCY

Almost everyone agrees that equity and efficiency are the two most important goals of the tax system. But often, these two goals conflict, especially when equity is judged by the progressivity of the tax system. People disagree about tax policy often because they attach different weights to these goals.

The recent history of tax policy shows how political leaders differ in their views on equity and efficiency. When Ronald Reagan was elected president in 1980, the marginal tax rate on the earnings of the richest Americans was 50 percent. On interest income, the marginal tax rate was 70 percent. Reagan argued that such ments differently distorts capital formation and slows growth.

The Treasury Department estimates that eliminating the tax burden on new investment, for example by adopting a consumption tax, would eventually raise GDP by between 5% and 7%. GDP growth is essential to improving the standard of living for all Americans, and it is closely tied to productivity growth. The surest way to raise wages is to raise productivity.

Q: *What specifically do you propose?*

A: The Tax Panel endorses two reform proposals that would improve economic growth, simplify the tax code, and roughly preserve the current distribution of tax burdens. Both would repeal the individual and corporate Alternative Minimum Tax. The first is the Simplified Income Tax. It preserves the income tax framework but cuts marginal rates to 15%, 25% and 33%. It provides for a large amount of tax-free saving, consolidates credits, and rationalizes the system of business taxation. The second reform proposal, the Growth and Investment Tax, builds on the Simplified Income Tax system, and by allowing full expensing of capital, shifts the tax system toward a consumption tax base.

Productivity growth depends on investment in human and physical capital. Investment in human capital means acquiring skills through formal education and learning on the job. Investment in physical capital means adding to the stock of plant, equipment, technological know-how and other intangibles that make workers productive. Both proposals encourage investment in skills by reducing marginal tax rates on labor supply for most earners. They encourage investment in physical capital by reducing taxes on business investment. Treasury estimates that moving from the current structure to the Growth and Investment Tax would lower the average tax burden on all investment from 17% to 6%. This would encourage new investment and significantly increase productivity and wage growth.

Q: *How do these proposals reduce tax rates without reducing tax revenue?*

A: Both proposals trim many of the deductions that currently narrow the income tax base, while retaining incentives for charitable giving, homeownership and the purchase of health insurance. Both proposals allow taxpayers a deduction for charitable contributions in excess of 1%

of taxable income. Both proposals replace the current itemized deduction for interest on a mortgage of up to $1 million, plus a $100,000 home equity loan, with a 15% tax credit on interest for loans up to 125% of an area's median home price.

Employer-provided health insurance is currently untaxed regardless of its cost. This encourages the purchase of excessively generous insurance policies. To preserve incentives for employers to provide families with basic insurance coverage, both plans tax employer-provided health insurance, but only on the amount of insurance valued at more than $11,500 for a married couple and $5,000 for a single individual.

Both plans eliminate the federal tax deduction for payments of state and local income and property taxes.

Q: *How about vertical equity?*

A: The plans leave the burden of paying for the work of government virtually unchanged. There is a very slight increase in the burden carried by the rich, but the standard of living of this group would still rise in the long run, as a result of the plans' favorable effects on long-term economic growth.

Source: Answers are excerpts from "A Golden Opportunity," by Edward P. Lazear and James M. Poterba, *The Wall Street Journal*, November 1, 2005. More information on the tax reform advisory panel can be found at http://www.taxreformpanel.gov/.

high tax rates greatly distorted economic incentives to work and save. In other words, he claimed that these high tax rates cost too much in terms of economic efficiency. Tax reform was, therefore, a high priority of his administration. Reagan signed into law large cuts in tax rates in 1981 and then again in 1986. When Reagan left office in 1989, the richest Americans faced a marginal tax rate of only 28 percent.

The pendulum of political debate swings both ways. When Bill Clinton ran for president in 1992, he argued that the rich were not paying their fair share of taxes. In other words, the low tax rates on the rich violated his view of vertical equity. In 1993, President Clinton signed into law a bill that raised the tax rates on the richest Americans to about 40 percent. When George W. Bush ran for president, he reprised many of Reagan's themes, and as president he reversed part of the

Clinton tax increase, reducing the highest tax rate to 35 percent. During the 2008 presidential campaign, Republican John McCain advocated making the Bush tax cuts permanent, while Democrat Barack Obama proposed increasing the top marginal tax rate.

Economics alone cannot determine the best way to balance the goals of efficiency and equity. This issue involves political philosophy as well as economics. But economists do have an important role in this debate: They can shed light on the trade-offs that society inevitably faces when designing the tax system and can help us avoid policies that sacrifice efficiency without any benefit in terms of equity.

SUMMARY

- The U.S. government raises revenue using various taxes. The most important taxes for the federal government are individual income taxes and payroll taxes for social insurance. The most important taxes for state and local governments are sales taxes and property taxes.

- The efficiency of a tax system refers to the costs it imposes on taxpayers. There are two costs of taxes beyond the transfer of resources from the taxpayer to the government. The first is the deadweight loss that arises as taxes alter incentives and distort the allocation of resources. The second is the administrative burden of complying with the tax laws.

- The equity of a tax system concerns whether the tax burden is distributed fairly among the popu-

lation. According to the benefits principle, it is fair for people to pay taxes based on the benefits they receive from the government. According to the ability-to-pay principle, it is fair for people to pay taxes based on their capability to handle the financial burden. When evaluating the equity of a tax system, it is important to remember a lesson from the study of tax incidence: The distribution of tax burdens is not the same as the distribution of tax bills.

- When considering changes in the tax laws, policymakers often face a trade-off between efficiency and equity. Much of the debate over tax policy arises because people give different weights to these two goals.

KEY CONCEPTS

budget deficit, *p. 246*
budget surplus, *p. 246*
average tax rate, *p. 252*
marginal tax rate, *p. 252*

lump-sum tax, *p. 253*
benefits principle, *p. 254*
ability-to-pay principle, *p. 254*
vertical equity, *p. 254*

horizontal equity, *p. 254*
proportional tax, *p. 255*
regressive tax, *p. 255*
progressive tax, *p. 255*

QUESTIONS FOR REVIEW

1. Over the past century, has the government's tax revenue grown more or less slowly than the rest of the economy?
2. What are the two most important sources of revenue for the U.S. federal government?
3. Explain how corporate profits are taxed twice.
4. Why is the burden of a tax to taxpayers greater than the revenue received by the government?
5. Why do some economists advocate taxing consumption rather than income?
6. What is the marginal tax rate on a lump-sum tax? How is this related to the efficiency of the tax?
7. Give two arguments why wealthy taxpayers should pay more taxes than poor taxpayers.
8. What is the concept of horizontal equity and why is it hard to apply?

PROBLEMS AND APPLICATIONS

1. In a published source or on the Internet, find out whether the U.S. federal government had a budget deficit or surplus last year. What do policymakers expect to happen over the next few years? (Hint: The website of the Congressional Budget Office is http://www.cbo.gov.)
2. The information in many of the tables in this chapter can be found in the *Economic Report of the President*, which appears annually. Using a recent issue of the report at your library or on the Internet, answer the following questions and provide some numbers to support your answers. (Hint: The website of the Government Printing Office is http://www.gpo.gov.)
   a. Figure 1 shows that government revenue as a percentage of total income has increased over time. Is this increase primarily attributable to changes in federal government revenue or in state and local government revenue?
   b. Looking at the combined revenue of the federal government and state and local governments, how has the composition of total revenue changed over time? Are personal income taxes more or less important? Social insurance taxes? Corporate profits taxes?
   c. Looking at the combined expenditures of the federal government and state and local governments, how have the relative shares of transfer payments and purchases of goods and services changed over time?
3. The chapter states that the elderly population in the United States is growing more rapidly than the total population. In particular, the number of workers is rising slowly, while the number of retirees is rising quickly. Concerned about the future of Social Security, some members of Congress propose a "freeze" on the program.
   a. If total expenditures were frozen, what would happen to benefits per retiree? To tax payments per worker? (Assume that Social Security taxes and receipts are balanced in each year.)
   b. If benefits per retiree were frozen, what would happen to total expenditures? To tax payments per worker?
   c. If tax payments per worker were frozen, what would happen to total expenditures? To benefits per retiree?
   d. What do your answers to parts (a), (b), and (c) imply about the difficult decisions faced by policymakers?

4. Suppose you are a typical person in the U.S. economy. You pay 4 percent of your income in a state income tax and 15.3 percent of your labor earnings in federal payroll taxes (employer and employee shares combined). You also pay federal income taxes as in Table 3. How much tax of each type do you pay if you earn $20,000 a year? Taking all taxes into account, what are your average and marginal tax rates? What happens to your tax bill and to your average and marginal tax rates if your income rises to $40,000?

5. Some states exclude necessities, such as food and clothing, from their sales tax. Other states do not. Discuss the merits of this exclusion. Consider both efficiency and equity.

6. When someone owns an asset (such as a share of stock) that rises in value, he has an "accrued" capital gain. If he sells the asset, he "realizes" the gains that have previously accrued. Under the U.S. income tax, realized capital gains are taxed, but accrued gains are not.
   a. Explain how individuals' behavior is affected by this rule.
   b. Some economists believe that cuts in capital gains tax rates, especially temporary ones, can raise tax revenue. How might this be so?
   c. Do you think it is a good rule to tax realized but not accrued capital gains? Why or why not?

7. Suppose that your state raises its sales tax from 5 percent to 6 percent. The state revenue commissioner forecasts a 20 percent increase in sales tax revenue. Is this plausible? Explain.

8. The Tax Reform Act of 1986 eliminated the deductibility of interest payments on consumer debt (mostly credit cards and auto loans) but maintained the deductibility of interest payments on mortgages and home equity loans. What do you think happened to the relative amounts of borrowing through consumer debt and home equity debt?

9. Categorize each of the following funding schemes as examples of the benefits principle or the ability-to-pay principle.
   a. Visitors to many national parks pay an entrance fee.
   b. Local property taxes support elementary and secondary schools.
   c. An airport trust fund collects a tax on each plane ticket sold and uses the money to improve airports and the air traffic control system.

10. Any income tax schedule embodies two types of tax rates: average tax rates and marginal tax rates.
    a. The average tax rate is defined as total taxes paid divided by income. For the proportional tax system presented in Table 7, what are the average tax rates for people earning $50,000, $100,000, and $200,000? What are the corresponding average tax rates in the regressive and progressive tax systems?
    b. The marginal tax rate is defined as the extra taxes paid on additional income divided by the increase in income. Calculate the marginal tax rate for the proportional tax system as income rises from $50,000 to $100,000. Calculate the marginal tax rate as income rises from $100,000 to $200,000. Calculate the corresponding marginal tax rates for the regressive and progressive tax systems.
    c. Describe the relationship between average tax rates and marginal tax rates for each of these three systems. In general, which rate is relevant for someone deciding whether to accept a job that pays slightly more than her current job? Which rate is relevant for judging the vertical equity of a tax system?

11. Use the data in Table 8 to answer these questions about the U.S. tax system:
    a. For each quintile, compute the federal taxes paid by the typical taxpayer.
    b. As a taxpayer moves from each quintile to the next higher quintile, compute the change in income and the change in taxes.

c. Use the information in part (b) to compute the marginal tax rate as a person moves from one quintile to the next.

d. For any given taxpayer, which is higher—the marginal tax rate or the average tax rate?

e. What happens to the average tax rate and the marginal tax rate as income rises? Which changes more?

12. Each of the following expenditures is a deduction for the purposes of calculating a person's federal income tax liability:

a. Mortgage interest

b. State and local taxes

c. Charitable contributions

If the income tax base were broadened by eliminating these deductions, tax rates could be lowered, while raising the same amount of tax revenue.

For each of these deductions, what would you expect the likely effect on taxpayer behavior to be? Discuss the pros and cons of each deduction from the standpoint of efficiency, vertical equity, and horizontal equity. Would you keep or eliminate the deduction?

PART V

Firm Behavior and the Organization of Industry

The Costs of Production

The economy is made up of thousands of firms that produce the goods and services you enjoy every day: General Motors produces automobiles, General Electric produces lightbulbs, and General Mills produces breakfast cereals. Some firms, such as these three, are large; they employ thousands of workers and have thousands of stockholders who share in the firms' profits. Other firms, such as the local barbershop or candy store, are small; they employ only a few workers and are owned by a single person or family.

In previous chapters, we used the supply curve to summarize firms' production decisions. According to the law of supply, firms are willing to produce and sell a greater quantity of a good when the price of the good is higher, and this response leads to a supply curve that slopes upward. For analyzing many questions, the law of supply is all you need to know about firm behavior.

In this chapter and the ones that follow, we examine firm behavior in more detail. This topic will give you a better understanding of the decisions behind the supply curve. In addition, it will introduce you to a part of economics called *industrial organization*—the study of how firms' decisions about prices and quantities depend on the market conditions they face. The town in which you live, for instance, may have several pizzerias but only one cable television company. This raises a key question: How does the number of firms affect the prices in a market and the efficiency of the market outcome? The field of industrial organization addresses exactly this question.

Before turning to these issues, we need to discuss the costs of production. All firms, from Delta Air Lines to your local deli, incur costs as they make the goods and services that they sell. As we will see in the coming chapters, a firm's costs are a key determinant of its production and pricing decisions. In this chapter, we define some of the variables that economists use to measure a firm's costs, and we consider the relationships among these variables.

A word of warning: This topic is dry and technical. To be honest, one might even call it boring. But this material provides a crucial foundation for the fascinating topics that follow.

WHAT ARE COSTS?

We begin our discussion of costs at Caroline's Cookie Factory. Caroline, the owner of the firm, buys flour, sugar, chocolate chips, and other cookie ingredients. She also buys the mixers and ovens and hires workers to run this equipment. She then sells the cookies to consumers. By examining some of the issues that Caroline faces in her business, we can learn some lessons about costs that apply to all firms in an economy.

TOTAL REVENUE, TOTAL COST, AND PROFIT

We begin with the firm's objective. To understand the decisions a firm makes, we must understand what it is trying to do. It is conceivable that Caroline started her firm because of an altruistic desire to provide the world with cookies or, perhaps, out of love for the cookie business. More likely, Caroline started her business to make money. Economists normally assume that the goal of a firm is to maximize profit, and they find that this assumption works well in most cases.

total revenue
the amount a firm receives for the sale of its output

total cost
the market value of the inputs a firm uses in production

profit
total revenue minus total cost

What is a firm's profit? The amount that the firm receives for the sale of its output (cookies) is called its **total revenue**. The amount that the firm pays to buy inputs (flour, sugar, workers, ovens, and so forth) is called its **total cost**. Caroline gets to keep any revenue that is not needed to cover costs. **Profit** is a firm's total revenue minus its total cost:

$$\text{Profit} = \text{Total revenue} - \text{Total cost}.$$

Caroline's objective is to make her firm's profit as large as possible.

To see how a firm goes about maximizing profit, we must consider fully how to measure its total revenue and its total cost. Total revenue is the easy part: It equals the quantity of output the firm produces times the price at which it sells its output. If Caroline produces 10,000 cookies and sells them at $2 a cookie, her total revenue is $20,000. By contrast, the measurement of a firm's total cost is more subtle.

COSTS AS OPPORTUNITY COSTS

When measuring costs at Caroline's Cookie Factory or any other firm, it is important to keep in mind one of the *Ten Principles of Economics* from Chapter 1: The cost of something is what you give up to get it. Recall that the *opportunity cost* of an item refers to all those things that must be forgone to acquire that item. When economists speak of a firm's cost of production, they include all the opportunity costs of making its output of goods and services.

While some of a firm's opportunity costs of production are obvious, others are less so. When Caroline pays $1,000 for flour, that $1,000 is an opportunity cost because Caroline can no longer use that $1,000 to buy something else. Similarly, when Caroline hires workers to make the cookies, the wages she pays are part of the firm's costs. Because these opportunity costs require the firm to pay out some money, they are called **explicit costs**. By contrast, some of a firm's opportunity costs, called **implicit costs**, do not require a cash outlay. Imagine that Caroline is skilled with computers and could earn $100 per hour working as a programmer. For every hour that Caroline works at her cookie factory, she gives up $100 in income, and this forgone income is also part of her costs. The total cost of Caroline's business is the sum of the explicit costs and the implicit costs.

The distinction between explicit and implicit costs highlights an important difference between how economists and accountants analyze a business. Economists are interested in studying how firms make production and pricing decisions. Because these decisions are based on both explicit and implicit costs, economists include both when measuring a firm's costs. By contrast, accountants have the job of keeping track of the money that flows into and out of firms. As a result, they measure the explicit costs but usually ignore the implicit costs.

The difference between economists and accountants is easy to see in the case of Caroline's Cookie Factory. When Caroline gives up the opportunity to earn money as a computer programmer, her accountant will not count this as a cost of her cookie business. Because no money flows out of the business to pay for this cost, it never shows up on the accountant's financial statements. An economist, however, will count the forgone income as a cost because it will affect the decisions that Caroline makes in her cookie business. For example, if Caroline's wage as a computer programmer rises from $100 to $500 per hour, she might decide that running her cookie business is too costly and choose to shut down the factory to become a full-time computer programmer.

explicit costs
input costs that require an outlay of money by the firm

implicit costs
input costs that do not require an outlay of money by the firm

The Cost of Capital as an Opportunity Cost

An important implicit cost of almost every business is the opportunity cost of the financial capital that has been invested in the business. Suppose, for instance, that Caroline used $300,000 of her savings to buy her cookie factory from its previous owner. If Caroline had instead left this money deposited in a savings account that pays an interest rate of 5 percent, she would have earned $15,000 per year. To own her cookie factory, therefore, Caroline has given up $15,000 a year in interest income. This forgone $15,000 is one of the implicit opportunity costs of Caroline's business.

As we have already noted, economists and accountants treat costs differently, and this is especially true in their treatment of the cost of capital. An economist views the $15,000 in interest income that Caroline gives up every year as a cost of her business, even though it is an implicit cost. Caroline's accountant, however, will not show this $15,000 as a cost because no money flows out of the business to pay for it.

To further explore the difference between economists and accountants, let's change the example slightly. Suppose now that Caroline did not have the entire $300,000 to buy the factory but, instead, used $100,000 of her own savings and borrowed $200,000 from a bank at an interest rate of 5 percent. Caroline's accountant, who only measures explicit costs, will now count the $10,000 interest paid on the bank loan every year as a cost because this amount of money now flows out of the firm. By contrast, according to an economist, the opportunity cost of owning the business is still $15,000. The opportunity cost equals the interest on the bank loan (an explicit cost of $10,000) plus the forgone interest on savings (an implicit cost of $5,000).

ECONOMIC PROFIT VERSUS ACCOUNTING PROFIT

economic profit
total revenue minus total cost, including both explicit and implicit costs

accounting profit
total revenue minus total explicit cost

Now let's return to the firm's objective: profit. Because economists and accountants measure costs differently, they also measure profit differently. An economist measures a firm's **economic profit** as the firm's total revenue minus all the opportunity costs (explicit and implicit) of producing the goods and services sold. An accountant measures the firm's **accounting profit** as the firm's total revenue minus only the firm's explicit costs.

Figure 1 summarizes this difference. Notice that because the accountant ignores the implicit costs, accounting profit is usually larger than economic profit. For a business to be profitable from an economist's standpoint, total revenue must cover all the opportunity costs, both explicit and implicit.

Economic profit is an important concept because it is what motivates the firms that supply goods and services. As we will see, a firm making positive economic profit will stay in business. It is covering all its opportunity costs and has some revenue left to reward the firm owners. When a firm is making economic losses (that is, when economic profits are negative), the business owners are failing to earn enough revenue to cover all the costs of production. Unless conditions change, the firm owners will eventually close down the business and exit the industry. To understand business decisions, we need to keep an eye on economic profit.

QUICK QUIZ Farmer McDonald gives banjo lessons for $20 an hour. One day, he spends 10 hours planting $100 worth of seeds on his farm. What opportunity cost has he incurred? What cost would his accountant measure? If these seeds yield $200 worth of crops, does McDonald earn an accounting profit? Does he earn an economic profit?

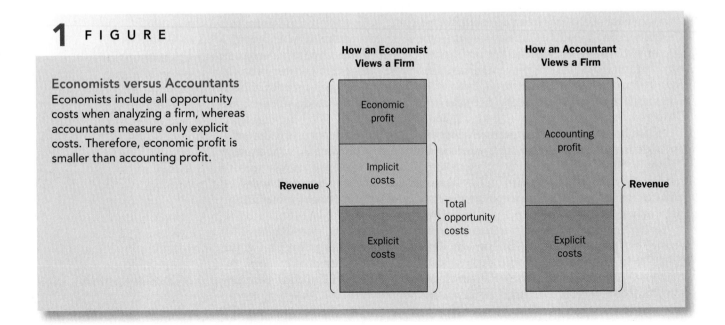

1 FIGURE

Economists versus Accountants
Economists include all opportunity costs when analyzing a firm, whereas accountants measure only explicit costs. Therefore, economic profit is smaller than accounting profit.

How an Economist Views a Firm

How an Accountant Views a Firm

PRODUCTION AND COSTS

Firms incur costs when they buy inputs to produce the goods and services that they plan to sell. In this section, we examine the link between a firm's production process and its total cost. Once again, we consider Caroline's Cookie Factory.

In the analysis that follows, we make an important simplifying assumption: We assume that the size of Caroline's factory is fixed and that Caroline can vary the quantity of cookies produced only by changing the number of workers she employs. This assumption is realistic in the short run but not in the long run. That is, Caroline cannot build a larger factory overnight, but she can do so over the next year or two. This analysis, therefore, describes the production decisions that Caroline faces in the short run. We examine the relationship between costs and time horizon more fully later in the chapter.

THE PRODUCTION FUNCTION

Table 1 shows how the quantity of cookies produced per hour at Caroline's factory depends on the number of workers. As you can see in the first two columns, if there are no workers in the factory, Caroline produces no cookies. When there is 1 worker, she produces 50 cookies. When there are 2 workers, she produces 90 cookies and so on. Panel (a) of Figure 2 presents a graph of these two columns of numbers. The number of workers is on the horizontal axis, and the number of cookies produced is on the vertical axis. This relationship between the quantity of inputs (workers) and quantity of output (cookies) is called the **production function**.

production function
the relationship between quantity of inputs used to make a good and the quantity of output of that good

TABLE **1**

A Production Function and Total Cost: Caroline's Cookie Factory

Number of Workers	Output (quantity of cookies produced per hour)	Marginal Product of Labor	Cost of Factory	Cost of Workers	Total Cost of Inputs (cost of factory + cost of workers)
0	0		$30	$0	$30
		50			
1	50		30	10	40
		40			
2	90		30	20	50
		30			
3	120		30	30	60
		20			
4	140		30	40	70
		10			
5	150		30	50	80
		5			
6	155		30	60	90

2 FIGURE

Caroline's Production Function and Total-Cost Curve

The production function in panel (a) shows the relationship between the number of workers hired and the quantity of output produced. Here the number of workers hired (on the horizontal axis) is from the first column in Table 1, and the quantity of output produced (on the vertical axis) is from the second column. The production function gets flatter as the number of workers increases, which reflects diminishing marginal product. The total-cost curve in panel (b) shows the relationship between the quantity of output produced and total cost of production. Here the quantity of output produced (on the horizontal axis) is from the second column in Table 1, and the total cost (on the vertical axis) is from the sixth column. The total-cost curve gets steeper as the quantity of output increases because of diminishing marginal product.

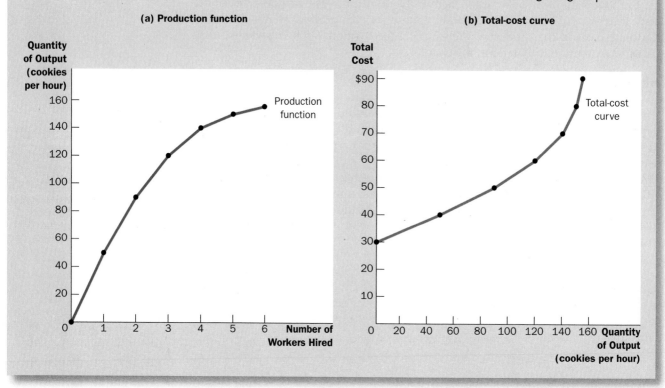

(a) Production function

(b) Total-cost curve

One of the *Ten Principles of Economics* introduced in Chapter 1 is that rational people think at the margin. As we will see in future chapters, this idea is the key to understanding the decisions a firm makes about how many workers to hire and how much output to produce. To take a step toward understanding these decisions, the third column in the table gives the marginal product of a worker. The **marginal product** of any input in the production process is the increase in the quantity of output obtained from one additional unit of that input. When the number of workers goes from 1 to 2, cookie production increases from 50 to 90, so the marginal product of the second worker is 40 cookies. And when the number of workers goes from 2 to 3, cookie production increases from 90 to 120, so the marginal product of the third worker is 30 cookies. In the table, the marginal product is shown halfway between two rows because it represents the change in output as the number of workers increases from one level to another.

marginal product
the increase in output that arises from an additional unit of input

Notice that as the number of workers increases, the marginal product declines. The second worker has a marginal product of 40 cookies, the third worker has a marginal product of 30 cookies, and the fourth worker has a marginal product of 20 cookies. This property is called **diminishing marginal product**. At first, when only a few workers are hired, they have easy access to Caroline's kitchen equipment. As the number of workers increases, additional workers have to share equipment and work in more crowded conditions. Eventually, the kitchen is so crowded that the workers start getting in each other's way. Hence, as more and more workers are hired, each additional worker contributes fewer additional cookies to total production.

Diminishing marginal product is also apparent in Figure 2. The production function's slope ("rise over run") tells us the change in Caroline's output of cookies ("rise") for each additional input of labor ("run"). That is, the slope of the production function measures the marginal product of a worker. As the number of workers increases, the marginal product declines, and the production function becomes flatter.

diminishing marginal product
the property whereby the marginal product of an input declines as the quantity of the input increases

FROM THE PRODUCTION FUNCTION TO THE TOTAL-COST CURVE

The last three columns of Table 1 show Caroline's cost of producing cookies. In this example, the cost of Caroline's factory is $30 per hour, and the cost of a worker is $10 per hour. If she hires 1 worker, her total cost is $40 per hour. If she hires 2 workers, her total cost is $50 per hour, and so on. With this information, the table now shows how the number of workers Caroline hires is related to the quantity of cookies she produces and to her total cost of production.

Our goal in the next several chapters is to study firms' production and pricing decisions. For this purpose, the most important relationship in Table 1 is between quantity produced (in the second column) and total costs (in the sixth column). Panel (b) of Figure 2 graphs these two columns of data with the quantity produced on the horizontal axis and total cost on the vertical axis. This graph is called the *total-cost curve.*

Now compare the total-cost curve in panel (b) with the production function in panel (a). These two curves are opposite sides of the same coin. The total-cost curve gets steeper as the amount produced rises, whereas the production function gets flatter as production rises. These changes in slope occur for the same reason. High production of cookies means that Caroline's kitchen is crowded with many workers. Because the kitchen is crowded, each additional worker adds less to production, reflecting diminishing marginal product. Therefore, the production function is relatively flat. But now turn this logic around: When the kitchen is crowded, producing an additional cookie requires a lot of additional labor and is thus very costly. Therefore, when the quantity produced is large, the total-cost curve is relatively steep.

QUICK QUIZ If Farmer Jones plants no seeds on his farm, he gets no harvest. If he plants 1 bag of seeds, he gets 3 bushels of wheat. If he plants 2 bags, he gets 5 bushels. If he plants 3 bags, he gets 6 bushels. A bag of seeds costs $100, and seeds are his only cost. Use these data to graph the farmer's production function and total-cost curve. Explain their shapes.

THE VARIOUS MEASURES OF COST

Our analysis of Caroline's Cookie Factory demonstrated how a firm's total cost reflects its production function. From data on a firm's total cost, we can derive several related measures of cost, which will turn out to be useful when we analyze production and pricing decisions in future chapters. To see how these related measures are derived, we consider the example in Table 2. This table presents cost data on Caroline's neighbor—Conrad's Coffee Shop.

The first column of the table shows the number of cups of coffee that Conrad might produce, ranging from 0 to 10 cups per hour. The second column shows Conrad's total cost of producing coffee. Figure 3 plots Conrad's total-cost curve. The quantity of coffee (from the first column) is on the horizontal axis, and total cost (from the second column) is on the vertical axis. Conrad's total-cost curve has a shape similar to Caroline's. In particular, it becomes steeper as the quantity produced rises, which (as we have discussed) reflects diminishing marginal product.

fixed costs
costs that do not vary with the quantity of output produced

FIXED AND VARIABLE COSTS

Conrad's total cost can be divided into two types. Some costs, called **fixed costs**, do not vary with the quantity of output produced. They are incurred even if the

2 TABLE

The Various Measures of Cost: Conrad's Coffee Shop

Quantity of Coffee (cups per hour)	Total Cost	Fixed Cost	Variable Cost	Average Fixed Cost	Average Variable Cost	Average Total Cost	Marginal Cost
0	$ 3.00	$3.00	$ 0.00	—	—	—	
							$0.30
1	3.30	3.00	0.30	$3.00	$0.30	$3.30	
							0.50
2	3.80	3.00	0.80	1.50	0.40	1.90	
							0.70
3	4.50	3.00	1.50	1.00	0.50	1.50	
							0.90
4	5.40	3.00	2.40	0.75	0.60	1.35	
							1.10
5	6.50	3.00	3.50	0.60	0.70	1.30	
							1.30
6	7.80	3.00	4.80	0.50	0.80	1.30	
							1.50
7	9.30	3.00	6.30	0.43	0.90	1.33	
							1.70
8	11.00	3.00	8.00	0.38	1.00	1.38	
							1.90
9	12.90	3.00	9.90	0.33	1.10	1.43	
							2.10
10	15.00	3.00	12.00	0.30	1.20	1.50	

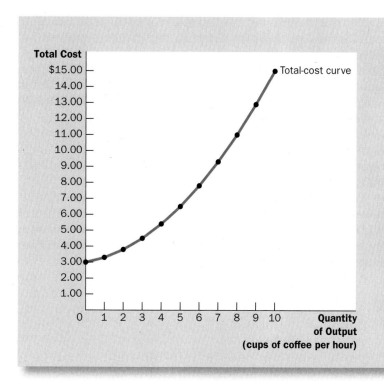

FIGURE **3**

Conrad's Total-Cost Curve
Here the quantity of output produced (on the horizontal axis) is from the first column in Table 2, and the total cost (on the vertical axis) is from the second column. As in Figure 2, the total-cost curve gets steeper as the quantity of output increases because of diminishing marginal product.

firm produces nothing at all. Conrad's fixed costs include any rent he pays because this cost is the same regardless of how much coffee he produces. Similarly, if Conrad needs to hire a full-time bookkeeper to pay bills, regardless of the quantity of coffee produced, the bookkeeper's salary is a fixed cost. The third column in Table 2 shows Conrad's fixed cost, which in this example is $3.00.

Some of the firm's costs, called **variable costs**, change as the firm alters the quantity of output produced. Conrad's variable costs include the cost of coffee beans, milk, sugar, and paper cups: The more cups of coffee Conrad makes, the more of these items he needs to buy. Similarly, if Conrad has to hire more workers to make more cups of coffee, the salaries of these workers are variable costs. The fourth column of the table shows Conrad's variable cost. The variable cost is 0 if he produces nothing, $0.30 if he produces 1 cup of coffee, $0.80 if he produces 2 cups, and so on.

variable costs
costs that vary with the quantity of output produced

A firm's total cost is the sum of fixed and variable costs. In Table 2, total cost in the second column equals fixed cost in the third column plus variable cost in the fourth column.

AVERAGE AND MARGINAL COST

As the owner of his firm, Conrad has to decide how much to produce. A key part of this decision is how his costs will vary as he changes the level of production. In making this decision, Conrad might ask his production supervisor the following two questions about the cost of producing coffee:

- How much does it cost to make the typical cup of coffee?
- How much does it cost to increase production of coffee by 1 cup?

Although at first these two questions might seem to have the same answer, they do not. Both answers will turn out to be important for understanding how firms make production decisions.

To find the cost of the typical unit produced, we would divide the firm's costs by the quantity of output it produces. For example, if the firm produces 2 cups of coffee per hour, its total cost is $3.80, and the cost of the typical cup is $3.80/2, or $1.90. Total cost divided by the quantity of output is called **average total cost**. Because total cost is the sum of fixed and variable costs, average total cost can be expressed as the sum of average fixed cost and average variable cost. **Average fixed cost** is the fixed cost divided by the quantity of output, and **average variable cost** is the variable cost divided by the quantity of output.

Although average total cost tells us the cost of the typical unit, it does not tell us how much total cost will change as the firm alters its level of production. The last column in Table 2 shows the amount that total cost rises when the firm increases production by 1 unit of output. This number is called **marginal cost**. For example, if Conrad increases production from 2 to 3 cups, total cost rises from $3.80 to $4.50, so the marginal cost of the third cup of coffee is $4.50 minus $3.80, or $0.70. In the table, the marginal cost appears halfway between two rows because it represents the change in total cost as quantity of output increases from one level to another.

It may be helpful to express these definitions mathematically:

$$\text{Average total cost} = \text{Total cost}/\text{Quantity}$$

$$ATC = TC/Q$$

and

$$\text{Marginal cost} = \text{Change in total cost}/\text{Change in quantity}$$

$$MC = \Delta TC/\Delta Q.$$

Here Δ, the Greek letter delta, represents the change in a variable. These equations show how average total cost and marginal cost are derived from total cost. *Average total cost tells us the cost of a typical unit of output if total cost is divided evenly over all the units produced. Marginal cost tells us the increase in total cost that arises from producing an additional unit of output.* As we will see more fully in the next chapter, business managers like Conrad need to keep in mind the concepts of average total cost and marginal cost when deciding how much of their product to supply to the market.

Cost Curves and Their Shapes

Just as in previous chapters we found graphs of supply and demand useful when analyzing the behavior of markets, we will find graphs of average and marginal cost useful when analyzing the behavior of firms. Figure 4 graphs Conrad's costs using the data from Table 2. The horizontal axis measures the quantity the firm produces, and the vertical axis measures marginal and average costs. The graph shows four curves: average total cost (*ATC*), average fixed cost (*AFC*), average variable cost (*AVC*), and marginal cost (*MC*).

The cost curves shown here for Conrad's Coffee Shop have some features that are common to the cost curves of many firms in the economy. Let's examine

---

average total cost
total cost divided by the quantity of output

average fixed cost
fixed cost divided by the quantity of output

average variable cost
variable cost divided by the quantity of output

marginal cost
the increase in total cost that arises from an extra unit of production

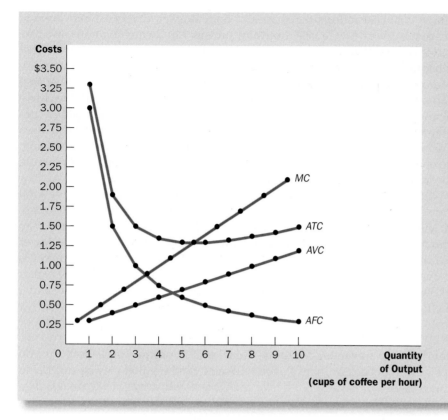

Conrad's Average-Cost and Marginal-Cost Curves
This figure shows the average total cost (*ATC*), average fixed cost (*AFC*), average variable cost (*AVC*), and marginal cost (*MC*) for Conrad's Coffee Shop. All of these curves are obtained by graphing the data in Table 2. These cost curves show three features that are typical of many firms: (1) Marginal cost rises with the quantity of output. (2) The average-total-cost curve is U-shaped. (3) The marginal-cost curve crosses the average-total-cost curve at the minimum of average total cost.

three features in particular: the shape of the marginal-cost curve, the shape of the average-total-cost curve, and the relationship between marginal and average total cost.

Rising Marginal Cost Conrad's marginal cost rises with the quantity of output produced. This reflects the property of diminishing marginal product. When Conrad produces a small quantity of coffee, he has few workers, and much of his equipment is not used. Because he can easily put these idle resources to use, the marginal product of an extra worker is large, and the marginal cost of an extra cup of coffee is small. By contrast, when Conrad produces a large quantity of coffee, his shop is crowded with workers, and most of his equipment is fully utilized. Conrad can produce more coffee by adding workers, but these new workers have to work in crowded conditions and may have to wait to use the equipment. Therefore, when the quantity of coffee produced is already high, the marginal product of an extra worker is low, and the marginal cost of an extra cup of coffee is large.

U-Shaped Average Total Cost Conrad's average-total-cost curve is U-shaped, as shown in Figure 4. To understand why, remember that average total cost is the sum of average fixed cost and average variable cost. Average fixed cost always declines as output rises because the fixed cost is spread over a larger number of units. Average variable cost typically rises as output increases because of diminishing marginal product.

Average total cost reflects the shapes of both average fixed cost and average variable cost. At very low levels of output, such as 1 or 2 cups per hour, average total cost is very high. Even though average variable cost is low, average fixed cost is high because the fixed cost is spread over only a few units. As output increases, the fixed cost is spread more widely. Average fixed cost declines, rapidly at first and then more slowly. As a result, average total cost also declines until the firm's output reaches 5 cups of coffee per hour, when average total cost is $1.30 per cup. When the firm produces more than 6 cups per hour, however, the increase in average variable cost becomes the dominant force, and average total cost starts rising. The tug of war between average fixed cost and average variable cost generates the U-shape in average total cost.

The bottom of the U-shape occurs at the quantity that minimizes average total cost. This quantity is sometimes called the **efficient scale** of the firm. For Conrad, the efficient scale is 5 or 6 cups of coffee per hour. If he produces more or less than this amount, his average total cost rises above the minimum of $1.30. At lower levels of output, average total cost is higher than $1.30 because the fixed cost is spread over so few units. At higher levels of output, average total cost is higher than $1.30 because the marginal product of inputs has diminished significantly. At the efficient scale, these two forces are balanced to yield the lowest average total cost.

efficient scale
the quantity of output that minimizes average total cost

The Relationship between Marginal Cost and Average Total Cost If you look at Figure 4 (or back at Table 2), you will see something that may be surprising at first. *Whenever marginal cost is less than average total cost, average total cost is falling. Whenever marginal cost is greater than average total cost, average total cost is rising.* This feature of Conrad's cost curves is not a coincidence from the particular numbers used in the example: It is true for all firms.

To see why, consider an analogy. Average total cost is like your cumulative grade point average. Marginal cost is like the grade in the next course you will take. If your grade in your next course is less than your grade point average, your grade point average will fall. If your grade in your next course is higher than your grade point average, your grade point average will rise. The mathematics of average and marginal costs is exactly the same as the mathematics of average and marginal grades.

This relationship between average total cost and marginal cost has an important corollary: *The marginal-cost curve crosses the average-total-cost curve at its minimum.* Why? At low levels of output, marginal cost is below average total cost, so average total cost is falling. But after the two curves cross, marginal cost rises above average total cost. For the reason we have just discussed, average total cost must start to rise at this level of output. Hence, this point of intersection is the minimum of average total cost. As you will see in the next chapter, minimum average total cost plays a key role in the analysis of competitive firms.

TYPICAL COST CURVES

In the examples we have studied so far, the firms exhibit diminishing marginal product and, therefore, rising marginal cost at all levels of output. This simplifying assumption was useful because it allowed us to focus on the key features of cost curves that will prove useful in analyzing firm behavior. Yet actual firms are usually more complicated than this. In many firms, marginal product does not start to fall immediately after the first worker is hired. Depending on the production process, the second or third worker might have a higher marginal product than the first because a team of workers can divide tasks and work more productively than a single worker. Firms exhibiting this pattern would experience increasing marginal product for a while before diminishing marginal product set in.

Figure 5 shows the cost curves for such a firm, including average total cost (*ATC*), average fixed cost (*AFC*), average variable cost (*AVC*), and marginal cost (*MC*). At low levels of output, the firm experiences increasing marginal product, and the marginal-cost curve falls. Eventually, the firm starts to experience diminishing marginal product, and the marginal-cost curve starts to rise. This combination of increasing then diminishing marginal product also makes the average-variable-cost curve U-shaped.

Despite these differences from our previous example, the cost curves shown here share the three properties that are most important to remember:

- Marginal cost eventually rises with the quantity of output.
- The average-total-cost curve is U-shaped.
- The marginal-cost curve crosses the average-total-cost curve at the minimum of average total cost.

QUICK QUIZ Suppose Honda's total cost of producing 4 cars is $225,000 and its total cost of producing 5 cars is $250,000. What is the average total cost of producing 5 cars? What is the marginal cost of the fifth car? ● Draw the marginal-cost curve and the average-total-cost curve for a typical firm, and explain why these curves cross where they do.

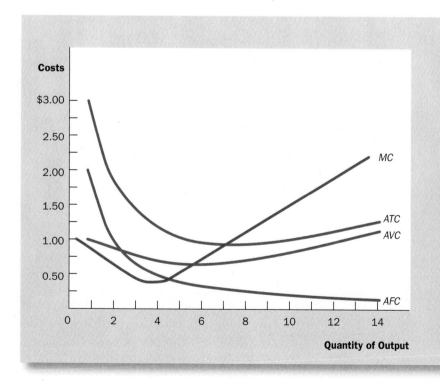

FIGURE **5**

Cost Curves for a Typical Firm
Many firms experience increasing marginal product before diminishing marginal product. As a result, they have cost curves shaped like those in this figure. Notice that marginal cost and average variable cost fall for a while before starting to rise.

COSTS IN THE SHORT RUN AND IN THE LONG RUN

We noted earlier in this chapter that a firm's costs might depend on the time horizon under consideration. Let's examine more precisely why this might be the case.

THE RELATIONSHIP BETWEEN SHORT-RUN AND LONG-RUN AVERAGE TOTAL COST

For many firms, the division of total costs between fixed and variable costs depends on the time horizon. Consider, for instance, a car manufacturer such as Ford Motor Company. Over a period of only a few months, Ford cannot adjust the number or sizes of its car factories. The only way it can produce additional cars is to hire more workers at the factories it already has. The cost of these factories is, therefore, a fixed cost in the short run. By contrast, over a period of several years, Ford can expand the size of its factories, build new factories, or close old ones. Thus, the cost of its factories is a variable cost in the long run.

Because many decisions are fixed in the short run but variable in the long run, a firm's long-run cost curves differ from its short-run cost curves. Figure 6 shows an example. The figure presents three short-run average-total-cost curves—for a small, medium, and large factory. It also presents the long-run average-total-cost curve. As the firm moves along the long-run curve, it is adjusting the size of the factory to the quantity of production.

This graph shows how short-run and long-run costs are related. The long-run average-total-cost curve is a much flatter U-shape than the short-run average-total-cost curve. In addition, all the short-run curves lie on or above the long-run

6 FIGURE

Average Total Cost in the Short and Long Runs
Because fixed costs are variable in the long run, the average-total-cost curve in the short run differs from the average-total-cost curve in the long run.

curve. These properties arise because firms have greater flexibility in the long run. In essence, in the long run, the firm gets to choose which short-run curve it wants to use. But in the short run, it has to use whatever short-run curve it has chosen in the past.

The figure shows an example of how a change in production alters costs over different time horizons. When Ford wants to increase production from 1,000 to 1,200 cars per day, it has no choice in the short run but to hire more workers at its existing medium-sized factory. Because of diminishing marginal product, average total cost rises from $10,000 to $12,000 per car. In the long run, however, Ford can expand both the size of the factory and its workforce, and average total cost returns to $10,000.

How long does it take a firm to get to the long run? The answer depends on the firm. It can take a year or longer for a major manufacturing firm, such as a car company, to build a larger factory. By contrast, a person running a coffee shop can buy another coffee maker within a few hours. There is, therefore, no single answer to how long it takes a firm to adjust its production facilities.

ECONOMIES AND DISECONOMIES OF SCALE

The shape of the long-run average-total-cost curve conveys important information about the production processes that a firm has available for manufacturing a good. In particular, it tells us how costs vary with the scale—that is, the size—of a firm's operations. When long-run average total cost declines as output increases, there are said to be **economies of scale**. When long-run average total cost rises as output increases, there are said to be **diseconomies of scale**. When long-run average total cost does not vary with the level of output, there are said to be **constant returns to scale**. In this example, Ford has economies of scale at low levels of output, constant returns to scale at intermediate levels of output, and diseconomies of scale at high levels of output.

What might cause economies or diseconomies of scale? Economies of scale often arise because higher production levels allow *specialization* among workers, which permits each worker to become better at a specific task. For instance, if Ford hires a large number of workers and produces a large number of cars, it can reduce costs with modern assembly-line production. Diseconomies of scale can arise because of *coordination problems* that are inherent in any large organization. The more cars Ford produces, the more stretched the management team becomes, and the less effective the managers become at keeping costs down.

This analysis shows why long-run average-total-cost curves are often U-shaped. At low levels of production, the firm benefits from increased size because it can take advantage of greater specialization. Coordination problems, meanwhile, are not yet acute. By contrast, at high levels of production, the benefits of specialization have already been realized, and coordination problems become more severe as the firm grows larger. Thus, long-run average total cost is falling at low levels of production because of increasing specialization and rising at high levels of production because of increasing coordination problems.

economies of scale
the property whereby long-run average total cost falls as the quantity of output increases

diseconomies of scale
the property whereby long-run average total cost rises as the quantity of output increases

constant returns to scale
the property whereby long-run average total cost stays the same as the quantity of output changes

QUICK QUIZ If Boeing produces 9 jets per month, its long-run total cost is $9.0 million per month. If it produces 10 jets per month, its long-run total cost is $9.5 million per month. Does Boeing exhibit economies or diseconomies of scale?

FYI

Lessons from a Pin Factory

"Jack of all trades, master of none." This well-known adage helps explain why firms sometimes experience economies of scale. A person who tries to do everything usually ends up doing nothing very well. If a firm wants its workers to be as productive as they can be, it is often best to give each worker a limited task that he or she can master. But this is possible only if a firm employs many workers and produces a large quantity of output.

In his celebrated book *An Inquiry into the Nature and Causes of the Wealth of Nations,* Adam Smith described a visit he made to a pin factory. Smith was impressed by the specialization among the workers and the resulting economies of scale. He wrote,

One man draws out the wire, another straightens it, a third cuts it, a fourth points it, a fifth grinds it at the top for receiving the head; to make the head requires two or three distinct operations; to put it on is a peculiar business; to whiten it is another; it is even a trade by itself to put them into paper.

Smith reported that because of this specialization, the pin factory produced thousands of pins per worker every day. He conjectured that if the workers had chosen to work separately, rather than as a team of specialists, "they certainly could not each of them make twenty, perhaps not one pin a day." In other words, because of specialization, a large pin factory could achieve higher output per worker and lower average cost per pin than a small pin factory.

The specialization that Smith observed in the pin factory is prevalent in the modern economy. If you want to build a house, for instance, you could try to do all the work yourself. But most people turn to a builder, who in turn hires carpenters, plumbers, electricians, painters, and many other types of workers. These workers specialize in particular jobs, and this allows them to become better at their jobs than if they were generalists. Indeed, the use of specialization to achieve economies of scale is one reason modern societies are as prosperous as they are.

CONCLUSION

The purpose of this chapter has been to develop some tools that we can use to study how firms make production and pricing decisions. You should now understand what economists mean by the term *costs* and how costs vary with the quantity of output a firm produces. To refresh your memory, Table 3 summarizes some of the definitions we have encountered.

By themselves, a firm's cost curves do not tell us what decisions the firm will make. But they are an important component of that decision, as we will begin to see in the next chapter.

TABLE 3

The Many Types of Cost: A Summary

Term	Definition	Mathematical Description
Explicit costs	Costs that require an outlay of money by the firm	
Implicit costs	Costs that do not require an outlay of money by the firm	
Fixed costs	Costs that do not vary with the quantity of output produced	FC
Variable costs	Costs that vary with the quantity of output produced	VC
Total cost	The market value of all the inputs that a firm uses in production	$TC = FC + VC$
Average fixed cost	Fixed cost divided by the quantity of output	$AFC = FC / Q$
Average variable cost	Variable cost divided by the quantity of output	$AVC = VC / Q$
Average total cost	Total cost divided by the quantity of output	$ATC = TC / Q$
Marginal cost	The increase in total cost that arises from an extra unit of production	$MC = \Delta TC / \Delta Q$

SUMMARY

- The goal of firms is to maximize profit, which equals total revenue minus total cost.

- When analyzing a firm's behavior, it is important to include all the opportunity costs of production. Some of the opportunity costs, such as the wages a firm pays its workers, are explicit. Other opportunity costs, such as the wages the firm owner gives up by working in the firm rather than taking another job, are implicit.

- A firm's costs reflect its production process. A typical firm's production function gets flatter as the quantity of an input increases, displaying the property of diminishing marginal product. As a result, a firm's total-cost curve gets steeper as the quantity produced rises.

- A firm's total costs can be divided between fixed costs and variable costs. Fixed costs are costs that do not change when the firm alters the quantity of output produced. Variable costs are costs that change when the firm alters the quantity of output produced.

- From a firm's total cost, two related measures of cost are derived. Average total cost is total cost divided by the quantity of output. Marginal cost is the amount by which total cost rises if output increases by 1 unit.

- When analyzing firm behavior, it is often useful to graph average total cost and marginal cost. For a typical firm, marginal cost rises with the quantity of output. Average total cost first falls as output increases and then rises as output increases further. The marginal-cost curve always crosses the average-total-cost curve at the minimum of average total cost.

- A firm's costs often depend on the time horizon considered. In particular, many costs are fixed in the short run but variable in the long run. As a result, when the firm changes its level of production, average total cost may rise more in the short run than in the long run.

KEY CONCEPTS

total revenue, *p. 268*
total cost, *p. 268*
profit, *p. 268*
explicit costs, *p. 269*
implicit costs, *p. 269*
economic profit, *p. 270*
accounting profit, *p. 270*

production function, *p. 271*
marginal product, *p. 272*
diminishing marginal product, *p. 273*
fixed costs, *p. 274*
variable costs, *p. 275*
average total cost, *p. 276*

average fixed cost, *p. 276*
average variable cost, *p. 276*
marginal cost, *p. 276*
efficient scale, *p. 278*
economies of scale, *p. 281*
diseconomies of scale, *p. 281*
constant returns to scale, *p. 281*

QUESTIONS FOR REVIEW

1. What is the relationship between a firm's total revenue, profit, and total cost?
2. Give an example of an opportunity cost that an accountant might not count as a cost. Why would the accountant ignore this cost?
3. What is marginal product, and what does it mean if it is diminishing?
4. Draw a production function that exhibits diminishing marginal product of labor. Draw the associated total-cost curve. (In both cases, be sure to label the axes.) Explain the shapes of the two curves you have drawn.

5. Define *total cost, average total cost,* and *marginal cost.* How are they related?
6. Draw the marginal-cost and average-total-cost curves for a typical firm. Explain why the curves have the shapes that they do and why they cross where they do.
7. How and why does a firm's average-total-cost curve differ in the short run and in the long run?
8. Define *economies of scale* and explain why they might arise. Define *diseconomies of scale* and explain why they might arise.

PROBLEMS AND APPLICATIONS

1. This chapter discusses many types of costs: opportunity cost, total cost, fixed cost, variable cost, average total cost, and marginal cost. Fill in the type of cost that best completes each sentence:
   a. What you give up for taking some action is called the _____.
   b. _____ is falling when marginal cost is below it and rising when marginal cost is above it.
   c. A cost that does not depend on the quantity produced is a _____.
   d. In the ice-cream industry in the short run, _____ includes the cost of cream and sugar but not the cost of the factory.
   e. Profits equal total revenue less _____.
   f. The cost of producing an extra unit of output is the _____.

2. Your aunt is thinking about opening a hardware store. She estimates that it would cost $500,000 per year to rent the location and buy the stock. In addition, she would have to quit her $50,000 per year job as an accountant.
   a. Define *opportunity cost*.
   b. What is your aunt's opportunity cost of running a hardware store for a year? If your aunt thought she could sell $510,000 worth of merchandise in a year, should she open the store? Explain.

3. A commercial fisherman notices the following relationship between hours spent fishing and the quantity of fish caught:

Hours	Quantity of Fish (in pounds)
0 hours	0 lb.
1	10
2	18
3	24
4	28
5	30

   a. What is the marginal product of each hour spent fishing?
   b. Use these data to graph the fisherman's production function. Explain its shape.
   c. The fisherman has a fixed cost of $10 (his pole). The opportunity cost of his time is $5 per hour. Graph the fisherman's total-cost curve. Explain its shape.

4. Nimbus, Inc., makes brooms and then sells them door-to-door. Here is the relationship between the number of workers and Nimbus's output in a given day:

Workers	Output	Marginal Product	Total Cost	Average Total Cost	Marginal Cost
0	0		—	—	
1	20	—	—	—	—
2	50	—	—	—	—
3	90	—	—	—	—
4	120	—	·	—	—
5	140	—	—	—	—
6	150	—	—	—	—
7	155	—	—	—	—

   a. Fill in the column of marginal products. What pattern do you see? How might you explain it?
   b. A worker costs $100 a day, and the firm has fixed costs of $200. Use this information to fill in the column for total cost.
   c. Fill in the column for average total cost. (Recall that $ATC = TC/Q$.) What pattern do you see?

d. Now fill in the column for marginal cost. (Recall that $MC = \Delta TC / \Delta Q$.) What pattern do you see?

e. Compare the column for marginal product and the column for marginal cost. Explain the relationship.

f. Compare the column for average total cost and the column for marginal cost. Explain the relationship.

5. You are the Chief Financial Officer for a firm that sells digital music players. Your firm has the following average total cost schedule:

Quantity	Average Total Cost
600 players	$300
601	301

Your current level of production is 600 devices, all of which have been sold. Someone calls, desperate to buy one of your music players. The caller offers you $550 for it. Should you accept the offer? Why or why not?

6. Consider the following cost information for a pizzeria:

Quantity	Total Cost	Variable Cost
0 dozen pizzas	$300	$ 0
1	350	50
2	390	90
3	420	120
4	450	150
5	490	190
6	540	240

a. What is the pizzeria's fixed cost?

b. Construct a table in which you calculate the marginal cost per dozen pizzas using the information on total cost. Also, calculate the marginal cost per dozen pizzas using the information on variable cost. What is the relationship between these sets of numbers? Comment.

7. You are thinking about setting up a lemonade stand. The stand itself costs $200. The ingredients for each cup of lemonade cost $0.50.

a. What is your fixed cost of doing business? What is your variable cost per cup?

b. Construct a table showing your total cost, average total cost, and marginal cost for output levels varying from 0 to 10 gallons. (Hint: There are 16 cups in a gallon.) Draw the three cost curves.

8. Your cousin Vinnie owns a painting company with fixed costs of $200 and the following schedule for variable costs:

Quantity of Houses Painted per Month	1	2	3	4	5	6	7
Variable Costs	$10	$20	$40	$80	$160	$320	$640

Calculate average fixed cost, average variable cost, and average total cost for each quantity. What is the efficient scale of the painting company?

9. The city government is considering two tax proposals:

- A lump-sum tax of $300 on each producer of hamburgers.
- A tax of $1 per burger, paid by producers of hamburgers.

a. Which of the following curves—average fixed cost, average variable cost, average total cost, and marginal cost—would shift as a result of the lump-sum tax? Why? Show this in a graph. Label the graph as precisely as possible.

b. Which of these same four curves would shift as a result of the per-burger tax? Why? Show this in a new graph. Label the graph as precisely as possible.

10. Jane's Juice Bar has the following cost schedules:

Quantity	Variable Cost	Total Cost
0 vats of juice	$ 0	$ 30
1	10	40
2	25	55
3	45	75
4	70	100
5	100	130
6	135	165

a. Calculate average variable cost, average total cost, and marginal cost for each quantity.

b. Graph all three curves. What is the relationship between the marginal-cost curve and the average-total-cost curve? Between the marginal-cost curve and the average-variable-cost curve? Explain.

11. A firm has fixed cost of $100 and average variable cost of $5 \times Q$, where Q is the number of units produced.

a. Construct a table showing total cost for Q from 0 to 10.

b. Graph the firm's curves for marginal cost and average total cost.

c. How does marginal cost change with Q? What does this suggest about the firm's production process?

12. Consider the following table of long-run total costs for three different firms:

Quantity	1	2	3	4	5	6	7
Firm A	$60	$70	$80	$90	$100	$110	$120
Firm B	11	24	39	56	75	96	119
Firm C	21	34	49	66	85	106	129

Does each of these firms experience economies of scale or diseconomies of scale?

Firms in Competitive Markets

I f your local gas station raised its price for gasoline by 20 percent, it would see a large drop in the amount of gasoline it sold. Its customers would quickly switch to buying their gasoline at other gas stations. By contrast, if your local water company raised the price of water by 20 percent, it would see only a small decrease in the amount of water it sold. People might water their lawns less often and buy more water-efficient showerheads, but they would be hard-pressed to reduce water consumption greatly and would be unlikely to find another supplier. The difference between the gasoline market and the water market is obvious: Many firms supply gasoline to the local market, but only one firm supplies water. As you might expect, this difference in market structure shapes the pricing and production decisions of the firms that operate in these markets.

In this chapter, we examine the behavior of competitive firms, such as your local gas station. You may recall that a market is competitive if each buyer and seller is small compared to the size of the market and, therefore, has little ability to influence market prices. By contrast, if a firm can influence the market price of the good it sells, it is said to have *market power*. Later in the book, we examine the behavior of firms with market power, such as your local water company.

Our analysis of competitive firms in this chapter sheds light on the decisions that lie behind the supply curve in a competitive market. Not surprisingly, we will find that a market supply curve is tightly linked to firms' costs of production. Less obvious, however, is the question of which among a firm's many types of cost—fixed, variable, average, and marginal—are most relevant for its supply decisions. We will see that all these measures of cost play important and interrelated roles.

WHAT IS A COMPETITIVE MARKET?

Our goal in this chapter is to examine how firms make production decisions in competitive markets. As a background for this analysis, we begin by reviewing what a competitive market is.

THE MEANING OF COMPETITION

competitive market
a market with many buyers and sellers trading identical products so that each buyer and seller is a price taker

A **competitive market**, sometimes called a *perfectly competitive market*, has two characteristics:

- There are many buyers and many sellers in the market.
- The goods offered by the various sellers are largely the same.

As a result of these conditions, the actions of any single buyer or seller in the market have a negligible impact on the market price. Each buyer and seller takes the market price as given.

As an example, consider the market for milk. No single consumer of milk can influence the price of milk because each buyer purchases a small amount relative to the size of the market. Similarly, each dairy farmer has limited control over the price because many other sellers are offering milk that is essentially identical. Because each seller can sell all he wants at the going price, he has little reason to charge less, and if he charges more, buyers will go elsewhere. Buyers and sellers in competitive markets must accept the price the market determines and, therefore, are said to be *price takers*.

In addition to the foregoing two conditions for competition, there is a third condition sometimes thought to characterize perfectly competitive markets:

- Firms can freely enter or exit the market.

If, for instance, anyone can decide to start a dairy farm, and if any existing dairy farmer can decide to leave the dairy business, then the dairy industry would satisfy this condition. Much of the analysis of competitive firms does not need the assumption of free entry and exit because this condition is not necessary for firms to be price takers. Yet, as we will see later in this chapter, if there is free entry and exit in a competitive market, it is a powerful force shaping the long-run equilibrium.

THE REVENUE OF A COMPETITIVE FIRM

A firm in a competitive market, like most other firms in the economy, tries to maximize profit (total revenue minus total cost). To see how it does this, we first consider the revenue of a competitive firm. To keep matters concrete, let's consider a specific firm: the Vaca Family Dairy Farm.

The Vaca Farm produces a quantity of milk, Q, and sells each unit at the market price, P. The farm's total revenue is $P \times Q$. For example, if a gallon of milk sells for $6 and the farm sells 1,000 gallons, its total revenue is $6,000.

Because the Vaca Farm is small compared to the world market for milk, it takes the price as given by market conditions. This means, in particular, that the price of milk does not depend on the number of gallons that the Vaca Farm produces and sells. If the Vacas double the amount of milk they produce to 2,000 gallons, the price of milk remains the same, and their total revenue doubles to $12,000. As a result, total revenue is proportional to the amount of output.

Table 1 shows the revenue for the Vaca Family Dairy Farm. The first two columns show the amount of output the farm produces and the price at which it sells its output. The third column is the farm's total revenue. The table assumes that the price of milk is $6 a gallon, so total revenue is $6 times the number of gallons.

Just as the concepts of average and marginal were useful in the preceding chapter when analyzing costs, they are also useful when analyzing revenue. To see what these concepts tell us, consider these two questions:

- How much revenue does the farm receive for the typical gallon of milk?
- How much additional revenue does the farm receive if it increases production of milk by 1 gallon?

The last two columns in Table 1 answer these questions.

The fourth column in the table shows **average revenue**, which is total revenue (from the third column) divided by the amount of output (from the first column). Average revenue tells us how much revenue a firm receives for the typical unit sold. In Table 1, you can see that average revenue equals $6, the price of a gallon of milk. This illustrates a general lesson that applies not only to competitive firms but to other firms as well. Average revenue is total revenue ($P \times Q$) divided by the quantity (Q). Therefore, *for all firms, average revenue equals the price of the good.*

average revenue
total revenue divided by the quantity sold

TABLE 1

Total, Average, and Marginal Revenue for a Competitive Firm

Quantity (Q)	Price (P)	Total Revenue ($TR = P \times Q$)	Average Revenue ($AR = TR / Q$)	Marginal Revenue ($MR = \Delta TR / \Delta Q$)
1 gallon	$6	$ 6	$6	
				$6
2	6	12	6	
				6
3	6	18	6	
				6
4	6	24	6	
				6
5	6	30	6	
				6
6	6	36	6	
				6
7	6	42	6	
				6
8	6	48	6	

marginal revenue
the change in total revenue from an additional unit sold

The fifth column shows **marginal revenue**, which is the change in total revenue from the sale of each additional unit of output. In Table 1, marginal revenue equals $6, the price of a gallon of milk. This result illustrates a lesson that applies only to competitive firms. Total revenue is $P \times Q$, and P is fixed for a competitive firm. Therefore, when Q rises by 1 unit, total revenue rises by P dollars. *For competitive firms, marginal revenue equals the price of the good.*

QUICK QUIZ When a competitive firm doubles the amount it sells, what happens to the price of its output and its total revenue?

PROFIT MAXIMIZATION AND THE COMPETITIVE FIRM'S SUPPLY CURVE

The goal of a competitive firm is to maximize profit, which equals total revenue minus total cost. We have just discussed the firm's revenue, and in the preceding chapter, we discussed the firm's costs. We are now ready to examine how a competitive firm maximizes profit and how that decision determines its supply curve.

A SIMPLE EXAMPLE OF PROFIT MAXIMIZATION

Let's begin our analysis of the firm's supply decision with the example in Table 2. In the first column of the table is the number of gallons of milk the Vaca Family Dairy Farm produces. The second column shows the farm's total revenue, which is $6 times the number of gallons. The third column shows the farm's total cost. Total cost includes fixed costs, which are $3 in this example, and variable costs, which depend on the quantity produced.

The fourth column shows the farm's profit, which is computed by subtracting total cost from total revenue. If the farm produces nothing, it has a loss of $3 (its fixed cost). If it produces 1 gallon, it has a profit of $1. If it produces 2 gallons, it has a profit of $4 and so on. Because the Vaca family's goal is to maximize profit, it chooses to produce the quantity of milk that makes profit as large as possible. In this example, profit is maximized when the farm produces 4 or 5 gallons of milk, for a profit of $7.

There is another way to look at the Vaca Farm's decision: The Vacas can find the profit-maximizing quantity by comparing the marginal revenue and marginal cost from each unit produced. The fifth and sixth columns in Table 2 compute marginal revenue and marginal cost from the changes in total revenue and total cost, and the last column shows the change in profit for each additional gallon produced. The first gallon of milk the farm produces has a marginal revenue of $6 and a marginal cost of $2; hence, producing that gallon increases profit by $4 (from −$3 to $1). The second gallon produced has a marginal revenue of $6 and a marginal cost of $3, so that gallon increases profit by $3 (from $1 to $4). As long as marginal revenue exceeds marginal cost, increasing the quantity produced raises profit. Once the Vaca Farm has reached 5 gallons of milk, however, the situation changes. The sixth gallon would have a marginal revenue of $6 and a marginal cost of $7, so producing it would reduce profit by $1 (from $7 to $6). As a result, the Vacas would not produce beyond 5 gallons.

One of the *Ten Principles of Economics* in Chapter 1 is that rational people think at the margin. We now see how the Vaca Family Dairy Farm can apply this

Quantity (Q)	Total Revenue (TR)	Total Cost (TC)	Profit (TR − TC)	Marginal Revenue (MR = ΔTR / ΔQ)	Marginal Cost (MC = ΔTC /ΔQ)	Change in Profit (MR − MC)
0 gallons	$ 0	$ 3	−$3			
				$6	$2	$ 4
1	6	5	1			
				6	3	3
2	12	8	4			
				6	4	2
3	18	12	6			
				6	5	1
4	24	17	7			
				6	6	0
5	30	23	7			
				6	7	−1
6	36	30	6			
				6	8	−2
7	42	38	4			
				6	9	−3
8	48	47	1			

TABLE **2**

Profit Maximization: A Numerical Example

principle. If marginal revenue is greater than marginal cost—as it is at 1, 2, or 3 gallons—the Vacas should increase the production of milk because it will put more money in their pockets (marginal revenue) than it takes out (marginal cost). If marginal revenue is less than marginal cost—as it is at 6, 7, or 8 gallons—the Vacas should decrease production. If the Vacas think at the margin and make incremental adjustments to the level of production, they are naturally led to produce the profit-maximizing quantity.

THE MARGINAL–COST CURVE AND THE FIRM'S SUPPLY DECISION

To extend this analysis of profit maximization, consider the cost curves in Figure 1. These cost curves have the three features that, as we discussed in the previous chapter, are thought to describe most firms: The marginal-cost curve (MC) is upward sloping. The average-total-cost curve (ATC) is U-shaped. And the marginal-cost curve crosses the average-total-cost curve at the minimum of average total cost. The figure also shows a horizontal line at the market price (P). The price line is horizontal because the firm is a price taker: The price of the firm's output is the same regardless of the quantity that the firm decides to produce. Keep in mind that, for a competitive firm, the firm's price equals both its average revenue (AR) and its marginal revenue (MR).

We can use Figure 1 to find the quantity of output that maximizes profit. Imagine that the firm is producing at Q_1. At this level of output, marginal revenue is greater than marginal cost. That is, if the firm raised its level of production and sales by 1 unit, the additional revenue (MR_1) would exceed the additional cost (MC_1). Profit, which equals total revenue minus total cost, would increase.

1 FIGURE

Profit Maximization for
a Competitive Firm

This figure shows the marginal-cost curve (*MC*), the average-total-cost curve (*ATC*), and the average-variable-cost curve (*AVC*). It also shows the market price (*P*), which equals marginal revenue (*MR*) and average revenue (*AR*). At the quantity Q_1, marginal revenue MR_1 exceeds marginal cost MC_1, so raising production increases profit. At the quantity Q_2, marginal cost MC_2 is above marginal revenue MR_2, so reducing production increases profit. The profit-maximizing quantity Q_{MAX} is found where the horizontal price line intersects the marginal-cost curve.

Hence, if marginal revenue is greater than marginal cost, as it is at Q_1, the firm can increase profit by increasing production.

A similar argument applies when output is at Q_2. In this case, marginal cost is greater than marginal revenue. If the firm reduced production by 1 unit, the costs saved (MC_2) would exceed the revenue lost (MR_2). Therefore, if marginal revenue is less than marginal cost, as it is at Q_2, the firm can increase profit by reducing production.

Where do these marginal adjustments to production end? Regardless of whether the firm begins with production at a low level (such as Q_1) or at a high level (such as Q_2), the firm will eventually adjust production until the quantity produced reaches Q_{MAX}. This analysis yields three general rules for profit maximization:

- If marginal revenue is greater than marginal cost, the firm should increase its output.
- If marginal cost is greater than marginal revenue, the firm should decrease its output.
- At the profit-maximizing level of output, marginal revenue and marginal cost are exactly equal.

These rules are the key to rational decision making by a profit-maximizing firm. They apply not only to competitive firms but, as we will see in the next chapter, to other types of firms as well.

We can now see how the competitive firm decides the quantity of its good to supply to the market. Because a competitive firm is a price taker, its marginal revenue equals the market price. For any given price, the competitive firm's profit-maximizing quantity of output is found by looking at the intersection of the price with the marginal-cost curve. In Figure 1, that quantity of output is Q_{MAX}.

Suppose that the price prevailing in this market rises, perhaps because of an increase in market demand. Figure 2 shows how a competitive firm responds to the price increase. When the price is P_1, the firm produces quantity Q_1, the quantity that equates marginal cost to the price. When the price rises to P_2, the firm finds that marginal revenue is now higher than marginal cost at the previous level of output, so the firm increases production. The new profit-maximizing quantity is Q_2, at which marginal cost equals the new higher price. *In essence, because the firm's marginal-cost curve determines the quantity of the good the firm is willing to supply at any price, the marginal-cost curve is also the competitive firm's supply curve.* There are, however, some caveats to that conclusion, which we examine next.

THE FIRM'S SHORT-RUN DECISION TO SHUT DOWN

So far, we have been analyzing the question of how much a competitive firm will produce. In certain circumstances, however, the firm will decide to shut down and not produce anything at all.

Here we should distinguish between a temporary shutdown of a firm and the permanent exit of a firm from the market. A *shutdown* refers to a short-run decision not to produce anything during a specific period of time because of current market conditions. *Exit* refers to a long-run decision to leave the market. The short-run and long-run decisions differ because most firms cannot avoid their fixed costs in the short run but can do so in the long run. That is, a firm that shuts down temporarily still has to pay its fixed costs, whereas a firm that exits the market does not have to pay any costs at all, fixed or variable.

FIGURE **2**

Marginal Cost as the Competitive Firm's Supply Curve
An increase in the price from P_1 to P_2 leads to an increase in the firm's profit-maximizing quantity from Q_1 to Q_2. Because the marginal-cost curve shows the quantity supplied by the firm at any given price, it is the firm's supply curve.

For example, consider the production decision that a farmer faces. The cost of the land is one of the farmer's fixed costs. If the farmer decides not to produce any crops one season, the land lies fallow, and he cannot recover this cost. When making the short-run decision whether to shut down for a season, the fixed cost of land is said to be a *sunk cost*. By contrast, if the farmer decides to leave farming altogether, he can sell the land. When making the long-run decision whether to exit the market, the cost of land is not sunk. (We return to the issue of sunk costs shortly.)

Now let's consider what determines a firm's shutdown decision. If the firm shuts down, it loses all revenue from the sale of its product. At the same time, it saves the variable costs of making its product (but must still pay the fixed costs). Thus, *the firm shuts down if the revenue that it would get from producing is less than its variable costs of production.*

A small bit of mathematics can make this shutdown criterion more useful. If TR stands for total revenue and VC stands for variable costs, then the firm's decision can be written as

$$\text{Shut down if } TR < VC.$$

The firm shuts down if total revenue is less than variable cost. By dividing both sides of this inequality by the quantity Q, we can write it as

$$\text{Shut down if } TR \,/\, Q < VC \,/\, Q.$$

The left side of the inequality, $TR \,/\, Q$, is total revenue $P \times Q$ divided by quantity Q, which is average revenue, most simply expressed as the good's price, P. The right side of the inequality, $VC \,/\, Q$, is average variable cost, AVC. Therefore, the firm's shutdown criterion can be restated as

$$\text{Shut down if } P < AVC.$$

That is, a firm chooses to shut down if the price of the good is less than the average variable cost of production. This criterion is intuitive: When choosing to produce, the firm compares the price it receives for the typical unit to the average variable cost that it must incur to produce the typical unit. If the price doesn't cover the average variable cost, the firm is better off stopping production altogether. The firm will be losing money (since it still has to pay fixed costs), but it would lose even more money staying open. The firm can reopen in the future if conditions change so that price exceeds average variable cost.

We now have a full description of a competitive firm's profit-maximizing strategy. If the firm produces anything, it produces the quantity at which marginal cost equals the price of the good. Yet if the price is less than average variable cost at that quantity, the firm is better off shutting down and not producing anything. These results are illustrated in Figure 3. *The competitive firm's short-run supply curve is the portion of its marginal-cost curve that lies above average variable cost.*

SPILT MILK AND OTHER SUNK COSTS

sunk cost
a cost that has already been committed and cannot be recovered

Sometime in your life you may have been told, "Don't cry over spilt milk," or "Let bygones be bygones." These adages hold a deep truth about rational decision making. Economists say that a cost is a **sunk cost** when it has already been com-

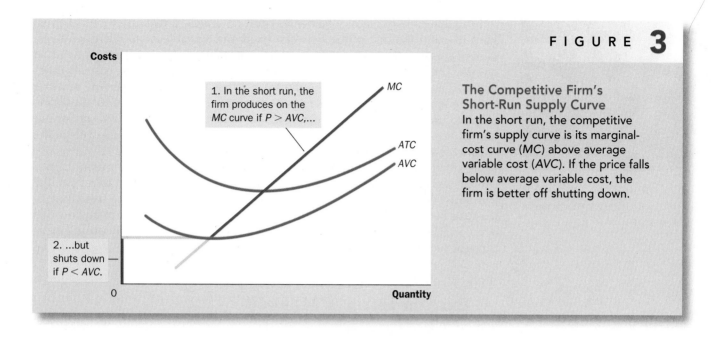

FIGURE **3**

Costs

1. In the short run, the firm produces on the *MC* curve if *P* > *AVC*,...

MC

ATC

AVC

2. ...but shuts down — if *P* < *AVC*.

0

Quantity

The Competitive Firm's Short-Run Supply Curve
In the short run, the competitive firm's supply curve is its marginal-cost curve (*MC*) above average variable cost (*AVC*). If the price falls below average variable cost, the firm is better off shutting down.

mitted and cannot be recovered. Because nothing can be done about sunk costs, you can ignore them when making decisions about various aspects of life, including business strategy.

Our analysis of the firm's shutdown decision is one example of the irrelevance of sunk costs. We assume that the firm cannot recover its fixed costs by temporarily stopping production. That is, regardless of the quantity of output supplied, and even if it is zero, the firm still has to pay its fixed costs. As a result, the fixed costs are sunk in the short run, and the firm can ignore them when deciding how much to produce. The firm's short-run supply curve is the part of the marginal-cost curve that lies above average variable cost, and the size of the fixed cost does not matter for this supply decision.

The irrelevance of sunk costs is also important when making personal decisions. Imagine, for instance, that you place a $15 value on seeing a newly released movie. You buy a ticket for $10, but before entering the theater, you lose the ticket. Should you buy another ticket? Or should you now go home and refuse to pay a total of $20 to see the movie? The answer is that you should buy another ticket. The benefit of seeing the movie ($15) still exceeds the opportunity cost (the $10 for the second ticket). The $10 you paid for the lost ticket is a sunk cost. As with spilt milk, there is no point in crying about it.

CASE STUDY NEAR-EMPTY RESTAURANTS AND OFF-SEASON MINIATURE GOLF

Have you ever walked into a restaurant for lunch and found it almost empty? Why, you might have asked, does the restaurant even bother to stay open? It might seem that the revenue from the few customers could not possibly cover the cost of running the restaurant.

STAYING OPEN CAN BE PROFIT-
ABLE, EVEN WITH MANY TABLES
EMPTY.

In making the decision whether to open for lunch, a restaurant owner must keep in mind the distinction between fixed and variable costs. Many of a restaurant's costs—the rent, kitchen equipment, tables, plates, silverware, and so on—are fixed. Shutting down during lunch would not reduce these costs. In other words, these costs are sunk in the short run. When the owner is deciding whether to serve lunch, only the variable costs—the price of the additional food and the wages of the extra staff—are relevant. The owner shuts down the restaurant at lunchtime only if the revenue from the few lunchtime customers fails to cover the restaurant's variable costs.

An operator of a miniature-golf course in a summer resort community faces a similar decision. Because revenue varies substantially from season to season, the firm must decide when to open and when to close. Once again, the fixed costs—the costs of buying the land and building the course—are irrelevant in making this decision. The miniature-golf course should be open for business only during those times of year when its revenue exceeds its variable costs.   ●

THE FIRM'S LONG-RUN DECISION TO EXIT OR ENTER A MARKET

A firm's long-run decision to exit a market is similar to its shutdown decision. If the firm exits, it will again lose all revenue from the sale of its product, but now it will save not only its variable costs of production but also its fixed costs. Thus, *the firm exits the market if the revenue it would get from producing is less than its total costs.*

We can again make this criterion more useful by writing it mathematically. If TR stands for total revenue, and TC stands for total cost, then the firm's exit criterion can be written as

$$\text{Exit if } TR < TC.$$

The firm exits if total revenue is less than total cost. By dividing both sides of this inequality by quantity Q, we can write it as

$$\text{Exit if } TR/Q < TC/Q.$$

We can simplify this further by noting that TR/Q is average revenue, which equals the price P, and that TC/Q is average total cost, ATC. Therefore, the firm's exit criterion is

$$\text{Exit if } P < ATC.$$

That is, a firm chooses to exit if the price of its good is less than the average total cost of production.

A parallel analysis applies to an entrepreneur who is considering starting a firm. The firm will enter the market if such an action would be profitable, which occurs if the price of the good exceeds the average total cost of production. The entry criterion is

$$\text{Enter if } P > ATC.$$

The criterion for entry is exactly the opposite of the criterion for exit.

We can now describe a competitive firm's long-run profit-maximizing strategy. If the firm is in the market, it produces the quantity at which marginal cost equals the price of the good. Yet if the price is less than average total cost at that quantity, the firm chooses to exit (or not enter) the market. These results are illustrated in Figure 4. *The competitive firm's long-run supply curve is the portion of its marginal-cost curve that lies above average total cost.*

MEASURING PROFIT IN OUR GRAPH FOR THE COMPETITIVE FIRM

As we analyze exit and entry, it is useful to be able to analyze the firm's profit in more detail. Recall that profit equals total revenue (*TR*) minus total cost (*TC*):

$$\text{Profit} = TR - TC.$$

We can rewrite this definition by multiplying and dividing the right side by *Q*:

$$\text{Profit} = (TR/Q - TC/Q) \times Q.$$

But note that TR/Q is average revenue, which is the price, P, and TC/Q is average total cost, ATC. Therefore,

$$\text{Profit} = (P - ATC) \times Q.$$

This way of expressing the firm's profit allows us to measure profit in our graphs.

Panel (a) of Figure 5 shows a firm earning positive profit. As we have already discussed, the firm maximizes profit by producing the quantity at which price equals marginal cost. Now look at the shaded rectangle. The height of the rectangle

FIGURE 4

The Competitive Firm's Long-Run Supply Curve
In the long run, the competitive firm's supply curve is its marginal-cost curve (*MC*) above average total cost (*ATC*). If the price falls below average total cost, the firm is better off exiting the market.

Costs

1. In the long run, the firm produces on the *MC* curve if *P* > *ATC*,...

MC

ATC

2. ...but exits if *P* < *ATC*.

0   Quantity

5 **FIGURE**

Profit as the Area
between Price and
Average Total Cost

The area of the shaded box between price and average total cost represents the firm's profit. The height of this box is price minus average total cost ($P - ATC$), and the width of the box is the quantity of output (Q). In panel (a), price is above average total cost, so the firm has positive profit. In panel (b), price is less than average total cost, so the firm has losses.

(a) A Firm with Profits

(b) A Firm with Losses

is $P - ATC$, the difference between price and average total cost. The width of the rectangle is Q, the quantity produced. Therefore, the area of the rectangle is $(P - ATC) \times Q$, which is the firm's profit.

Similarly, panel (b) of this figure shows a firm with losses (negative profit). In this case, maximizing profit means minimizing losses, a task accomplished once again by producing the quantity at which price equals marginal cost. Now consider the shaded rectangle. The height of the rectangle is $ATC - P$, and the width is Q. The area is $(ATC - P) \times Q$, which is the firm's loss. Because a firm in this situation is not making enough revenue to cover its average total cost, the firm would choose in the long run to exit the market.

QUICK QUIZ How does a competitive firm determine its profit-maximizing level of output? Explain. • When does a profit-maximizing competitive firm decide to shut down? When does a profit-maximizing competitive firm decide to exit a market?

THE SUPPLY CURVE IN A COMPETITIVE MARKET

Now that we have examined the supply decision of a single firm, we can discuss the supply curve for a market. There are two cases to consider. First, we examine a market with a fixed number of firms. Second, we examine a market in which the number of firms can change as old firms exit the market and new firms enter. Both cases are important, for each applies over a specific time horizon. Over short periods of time, it is often difficult for firms to enter and exit, so the assumption of a fixed number of firms is appropriate. But over long periods of time, the number of firms can adjust to changing market conditions.

THE SHORT RUN: MARKET SUPPLY WITH A FIXED NUMBER OF FIRMS

Consider first a market with 1,000 identical firms. For any given price, each firm supplies a quantity of output so that its marginal cost equals the price, as shown in panel (a) of Figure 6. That is, as long as price is above average variable cost, each firm's marginal-cost curve is its supply curve. The quantity of output supplied to the market equals the sum of the quantities supplied by each of the 1,000 individual firms. Thus, to derive the market supply curve, we add the quantity supplied by each firm in the market. As panel (b) of Figure 6 shows, because the firms are identical, the quantity supplied to the market is 1,000 times the quantity supplied by each firm.

THE LONG RUN: MARKET SUPPLY WITH ENTRY AND EXIT

Now consider what happens if firms are able to enter or exit the market. Let's suppose that everyone has access to the same technology for producing the good and access to the same markets to buy the inputs into production. Therefore, all firms and all potential firms have the same cost curves.

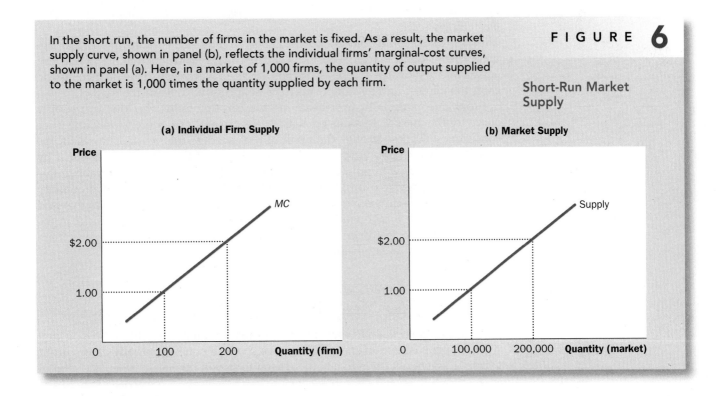

In the short run, the number of firms in the market is fixed. As a result, the market supply curve, shown in panel (b), reflects the individual firms' marginal-cost curves, shown in panel (a). Here, in a market of 1,000 firms, the quantity of output supplied to the market is 1,000 times the quantity supplied by each firm.

FIGURE **6**

Short-Run Market Supply

(a) Individual Firm Supply

(b) Market Supply

Decisions about entry and exit in a market of this type depend on the incentives facing the owners of existing firms and the entrepreneurs who could start new firms. If firms already in the market are profitable, then new firms will have an incentive to enter the market. This entry will expand the number of firms, increase the quantity of the good supplied, and drive down prices and profits. Conversely, if firms in the market are making losses, then some existing firms will exit the market. Their exit will reduce the number of firms, decrease the quantity of the good supplied, and drive up prices and profits. *At the end of this process of entry and exit, firms that remain in the market must be making zero economic profit.*

Recall that we can write a firm's profit as

$$\text{Profit} = (P - ATC) \times Q.$$

This equation shows that an operating firm has zero profit if and only if the price of the good equals the average total cost of producing that good. If price is above average total cost, profit is positive, which encourages new firms to enter. If price is less than average total cost, profit is negative, which encourages some firms to exit. *The process of entry and exit ends only when price and average total cost are driven to equality.*

This analysis has a surprising implication. We noted earlier in the chapter that competitive firms maximize profits by choosing a quantity at which price equals marginal cost. We just noted that free entry and exit force price to equal average total cost. But if price is to equal both marginal cost and average total cost, these two measures of cost must equal each other. Marginal cost and average total cost are equal, however, only when the firm is operating at the minimum of average total cost. Recall from the preceding chapter that the level of production with lowest average total cost is called the firm's *efficient scale*. Therefore, *in the long-run equilibrium of a competitive market with free entry and exit, firms must be operating at their efficient scale.*

Panel (a) of Figure 7 shows a firm in such a long-run equilibrium. In this figure, price P equals marginal cost MC, so the firm is profit-maximizing. Price also equals average total cost ATC, so profits are zero. New firms have no incentive to enter the market, and existing firms have no incentive to leave the market.

From this analysis of firm behavior, we can determine the long-run supply curve for the market. In a market with free entry and exit, there is only one price consistent with zero profit—the minimum of average total cost. As a result, the long-run market supply curve must be horizontal at this price, as illustrated by the perfectly elastic supply curve in panel (b) of Figure 7. Any price above this level would generate profit, leading to entry and an increase in the total quantity supplied. Any price below this level would generate losses, leading to exit and a decrease in the total quantity supplied. Eventually, the number of firms in the market adjusts so that price equals the minimum of average total cost, and there are enough firms to satisfy all the demand at this price.

WHY DO COMPETITIVE FIRMS STAY IN BUSINESS IF THEY MAKE ZERO PROFIT?

At first, it might seem odd that competitive firms earn zero profit in the long run. After all, people start businesses to make a profit. If entry eventually drives profit to zero, there might seem to be little reason to stay in business.

In the long run, firms will enter or exit the market until profit is driven to zero. As a result, price equals the minimum of average total cost, as shown in panel (a). The number of firms adjusts to ensure that all demand is satisfied at this price. The long-run market supply curve is horizontal at this price, as shown in panel (b).

FIGURE **7**

Long-Run Market Supply

(a) Firm's Zero-Profit Condition

Price

MC

ATC

$P = $ minimum ATC

0

Quantity (firm)

(b) Market Supply

Price

Supply

0

Quantity (market)

To understand the zero-profit condition more fully, recall that profit equals total revenue minus total cost and that total cost includes all the opportunity costs of the firm. In particular, total cost includes the time and money that the firm owners devote to the business. In the zero-profit equilibrium, the firm's revenue must compensate the owners for these opportunity costs.

Consider an example. Suppose that, to start his farm, a farmer had to invest $1 million, which otherwise he could have deposited in a bank to earn $50,000 a year in interest. In addition, he had to give up another job that would have paid him $30,000 a year. Then the farmer's opportunity cost of farming includes both the interest he could have earned and the forgone wages—a total of $80,000. Even if his profit is driven to zero, his revenue from farming compensates him for these opportunity costs.

Keep in mind that accountants and economists measure costs differently. As we discussed in the previous chapter, accountants keep track of explicit costs but not implicit costs. That is, they measure costs that require an outflow of money from the firm, but they do not include the opportunity costs of production that do not involve an outflow of money. As a result, in the zero-profit equilibrium, economic profit is zero, but accounting profit is positive. Our farmer's accountant, for instance, would conclude that the farmer earned an accounting profit of $80,000, which is enough to keep the farmer in business.

A SHIFT IN DEMAND IN THE SHORT RUN AND LONG RUN

Now that we have a more complete understanding of how firms make supply decisions, we can better explain how markets respond to changes in demand.

"WE'RE A NONPROFIT ORGANIZATION—WE DON'T INTEND TO BE, BUT WE ARE!"

Because firms can enter and exit in the long run but not in the short run, the response of a market to a change in demand depends on the time horizon. To see this, let's trace the effects of a shift in demand over time.

Suppose the market for milk begins in a long-run equilibrium. Firms are earning zero profit, so price equals the minimum of average total cost. Panel (a) of Figure 8 shows the situation. The long-run equilibrium is point A, the quantity sold in the market is Q_1, and the price is P_1.

Now suppose scientists discover that milk has miraculous health benefits. As a result, the demand curve for milk shifts outward from D_1 to D_2, as in panel (b). The short-run equilibrium moves from point A to point B; as a result, the quantity rises from Q_1 to Q_2, and the price rises from P_1 to P_2. All of the existing firms respond to the higher price by raising the amount produced. Because each firm's supply curve reflects its marginal-cost curve, how much they each increase production is determined by the marginal-cost curve. In the new short-run equilibrium, the price of milk exceeds average total cost, so the firms are making positive profit.

Over time, the profit in this market encourages new firms to enter. Some farmers may switch to milk from other farm products, for example. As the number of firms grows, the short-run supply curve shifts to the right from S_1 to S_2, as in panel (c), and this shift causes the price of milk to fall. Eventually, the price is driven back down to the minimum of average total cost, profits are zero, and firms stop entering. Thus, the market reaches a new long-run equilibrium, point C. The price of milk has returned to P_1, but the quantity produced has risen to Q_3. Each firm is again producing at its efficient scale, but because more firms are in the dairy business, the quantity of milk produced and sold is higher.

WHY THE LONG–RUN SUPPLY CURVE MIGHT SLOPE UPWARD

So far, we have seen that entry and exit can cause the long-run market supply curve to be perfectly elastic. The essence of our analysis is that there are a large number of potential entrants, each of which faces the same costs. As a result, the long-run market supply curve is horizontal at the minimum of average total cost. When the demand for the good increases, the long-run result is an increase in the number of firms and in the total quantity supplied, without any change in the price.

There are, however, two reasons that the long-run market supply curve might slope upward. The first is that some resource used in production may be available only in limited quantities. For example, consider the market for farm products. Anyone can choose to buy land and start a farm, but the quantity of land is limited. As more people become farmers, the price of farmland is bid up, which raises the costs of all farmers in the market. Thus, an increase in demand for farm products cannot induce an increase in quantity supplied without also inducing a rise in farmers' costs, which in turn means a rise in price. The result is a long-run market supply curve that is upward sloping, even with free entry into farming.

A second reason for an upward-sloping supply curve is that firms may have different costs. For example, consider the market for painters. Anyone can enter the market for painting services, but not everyone has the same costs. Costs vary in part because some people work faster than others and in part because some people have better alternative uses of their time than others. For any given price, those with lower costs are more likely to enter than those with higher costs. To increase the quantity of painting services supplied, additional entrants must be encouraged to enter the market. Because these new entrants have higher costs,

The market starts in a long-run equilibrium, shown as point A in panel (a). In this equilibrium, each firm makes zero profit, and the price equals the minimum average total cost. Panel (b) shows what happens in the short run when demand rises from D_1 to D_2. The equilibrium goes from point A to point B, price rises from P_1 to P_2, and the quantity sold in the market rises from Q_1 to Q_2. Because price now exceeds average total cost, firms make profits, which over time encourage new firms to enter the market. This entry shifts the short-run supply curve to the right from S_1 to S_2, as shown in panel (c). In the new long-run equilibrium, point C, price has returned to P_1 but the quantity sold has increased to Q_3. Profits are again zero, price is back to the minimum of average total cost, but the market has more firms to satisfy the greater demand.

FIGURE 8

An Increase in Demand in the Short Run and Long Run

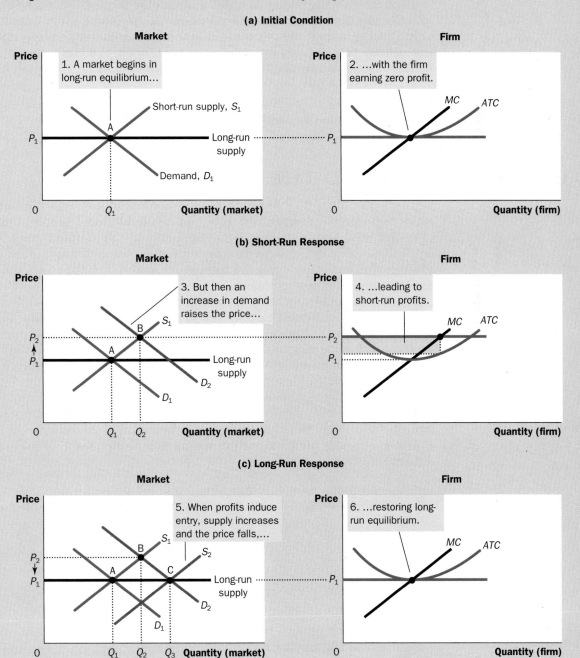

the price must rise to make entry profitable for them. Thus, the long-run market supply curve for painting services slopes upward even with free entry into the market.

Notice that if firms have different costs, some firms earn profit even in the long run. In this case, the price in the market reflects the average total cost of the *marginal firm*—the firm that would exit the market if the price were any lower. This firm earns zero profit, but firms with lower costs earn positive profit. Entry does not eliminate this profit because would-be entrants have higher costs than firms already in the market. Higher-cost firms will enter only if the price rises, making the market profitable for them.

Thus, for these two reasons, a higher price may be necessary to induce a larger quantity supplied, in which case the long-run supply curve is upward sloping rather than horizontal. Nonetheless, the basic lesson about entry and exit remains true. *Because firms can enter and exit more easily in the long run than in the short run, the long-run supply curve is typically more elastic than the short-run supply curve.*

QUICK QUIZ In the long run with free entry and exit, is the price in a market equal to marginal cost, average total cost, both, or neither? Explain with a diagram.

CONCLUSION: BEHIND THE SUPPLY CURVE

We have been discussing the behavior of profit-maximizing firms that supply goods in perfectly competitive markets. You may recall from Chapter 1 that one of the *Ten Principles of Economics* is that rational people think at the margin. This chapter has applied this idea to the competitive firm. Marginal analysis has given us a theory of the supply curve in a competitive market and, as a result, a deeper understanding of market outcomes.

We have learned that when you buy a good from a firm in a competitive market, you can be assured that the price you pay is close to the cost of producing that good. In particular, if firms are competitive and profit maximizing, the price of a good equals the marginal cost of making that good. In addition, if firms can freely enter and exit the market, the price also equals the lowest possible average total cost of production.

Although we have assumed throughout this chapter that firms are price takers, many of the tools developed here are also useful for studying firms in less competitive markets. We now turn to an examination of the behavior of firms with market power. Marginal analysis will again be useful, but it will have quite different implications.

SUMMARY

- Because a competitive firm is a price taker, its revenue is proportional to the amount of output it produces. The price of the good equals both the firm's average revenue and its marginal revenue.

- To maximize profit, a firm chooses a quantity of output such that marginal revenue equals marginal cost. Because marginal revenue for a competitive firm equals the market price, the firm chooses quantity so that price equals marginal cost. Thus, the firm's marginal-cost curve is its supply curve.

- In the short run when a firm cannot recover its fixed costs, the firm will choose to shut down temporarily if the price of the good is less than average variable cost. In the long run when the firm can recover both fixed and variable costs, it

will choose to exit if the price is less than average total cost.

- In a market with free entry and exit, profits are driven to zero in the long run. In this long-run equilibrium, all firms produce at the efficient scale, price equals the minimum of average total cost, and the number of firms adjusts to satisfy the quantity demanded at this price.

- Changes in demand have different effects over different time horizons. In the short run, an increase in demand raises prices and leads to profits, and a decrease in demand lowers prices and leads to losses. But if firms can freely enter and exit the market, then in the long run, the number of firms adjusts to drive the market back to the zero-profit equilibrium.

KEY CONCEPTS

competitive market, *p. 290*
average revenue, *p. 291*

marginal revenue, *p. 292*

sunk cost, *p. 296*

QUESTIONS FOR REVIEW

1. What is meant by a competitive firm?
2. Explain the difference between a firm's revenue and its profit. Which do firms maximize?
3. Draw the cost curves for a typical firm. For a given price, explain how the firm chooses the level of output that maximizes profit. At that level of output, show on your graph the total revenue of the firm. Show its total costs.
4. Under what conditions will a firm shut down temporarily? Explain.
5. Under what conditions will a firm exit a market? Explain.
6. Does a firm's price equal marginal cost in the short run, in the long run, or both? Explain.
7. Does a firm's price equal the minimum of average total cost in the short run, in the long run, or both? Explain.
8. Are market supply curves typically more elastic in the short run or in the long run? Explain.

PROBLEMS AND APPLICATIONS

1. Many small boats are made of fiberglass, which is derived from crude oil. Suppose that the price of oil rises.
   a. Using diagrams, show what happens to the cost curves of an individual boat-making firm and to the market supply curve.
   b. What happens to the profits of boat makers in the short run? What happens to the number of boat makers in the long run?

2. You go out to the best restaurant in town and order a lobster dinner for $40. After eating half of the lobster, you realize that you are quite full. Your date wants you to finish your dinner because you can't take it home and because "you've already paid for it." What should you do? Relate your answer to the material in this chapter.

3. Bob's lawn-mowing service is a profit-maximizing, competitive firm. Bob mows lawns for $27 each. His total cost each day is $280, of which $30 is a fixed cost. He mows 10 lawns a day. What can you say about Bob's short-run decision regarding shutdown and his long-run decision regarding exit?

4. Consider total cost and total revenue given in the following table:

Quantity	0	1	2	3	4	5	6	7
Total cost	$8	9	10	11	13	19	27	37
Total revenue	$0	8	16	24	32	40	48	56

   a. Calculate profit for each quantity. How much should the firm produce to maximize profit?
   b. Calculate marginal revenue and marginal cost for each quantity. Graph them. (Hint: Put the points between whole numbers. For example, the marginal cost between 2 and 3 should be graphed at 2½.) At what quantity do these curves cross? How does this relate to your answer to part (a)?
   c. Can you tell whether this firm is in a competitive industry? If so, can you tell whether the industry is in a long-run equilibrium?

5. Ball Bearings Inc. faces costs of production as follows:

Quantity	Total Fixed Costs	Total Variable Costs
0	$100	$ 0
1	100	50
2	100	70
3	100	90
4	100	140
5	100	200
6	100	360

   a. Calculate the company's average fixed costs, average variable costs, average total costs, and marginal costs.
   b. The price of a case of ball bearings is $50. Seeing that she can't make a profit, the Chief Executive Officer (CEO) decides to shut down operations. What are the firm's profits/losses? Was this a wise decision? Explain.
   c. Vaguely remembering his introductory economics course, the Chief Financial Officer tells the CEO it is better to produce 1 case of ball bearings, because marginal revenue equals marginal cost at that quantity. What are the firm's profits/losses at that level of production? Was this the best decision? Explain.

6. Suppose the book-printing industry is competitive and begins in a long-run equilibrium.
   a. Draw a diagram describing the typical firm in the industry.
   b. Hi-Tech Printing Company invents a new process that sharply reduces the cost of printing books. What happens to Hi-Tech's profits and the price of books in the short run when Hi-Tech's patent prevents other firms from using the new technology?
   c. What happens in the long run when the patent expires and other firms are free to use the technology?

7. A firm in a competitive market receives $500 in total revenue and has marginal revenue of $10. What is the average revenue, and how many units were sold?

8. A profit-maximizing firm in a competitive market is currently producing 100 units of output. It has average revenue of $10, average total cost of $8, and fixed costs of $200.
   a. What is profit?
   b. What is marginal cost?
   c. What is average variable cost?
   d. Is the efficient scale of the firm more than, less than, or exactly 100 units?

9. The market for fertilizer is perfectly competitive. Firms in the market are producing output, but are currently making economic losses.
   a. How does the price of fertilizer compare to the average total cost, the average variable cost, and the marginal cost of producing fertilizer?
   b. Draw two graphs, side by side, illustrating the present situation for the typical firm and in the market.
   c. Assuming there is no change in demand or the firms' cost curves, explain what will happen in the long run to the price of fertilizer, marginal cost, average total cost, the quantity supplied by each firm, and the total quantity supplied to the market.

10. Suppose that the U.S. textile industry is competitive, and there is no international trade in textiles. In long-run equilibrium, the price per unit of cloth is $30.
    a. Describe the equilibrium using graphs for the entire market and for an individual producer. Now suppose that textile producers in other countries are willing to sell large quantities of cloth in the United States for only $25 per unit.
    b. Assuming that U.S. textile producers have large fixed costs, what is the short-run effect of these imports on the quantity produced by an individual producer? What is the short-run effect on profits? Illustrate your answer with a graph.
    c. What is the long-run effect on the number of U.S. firms in the industry?

11. An industry currently has 100 firms, all of which have fixed costs of $16 and average variable cost as follows:

Quantity	Average Variable Cost
1	$1
2	2
3	3
4	4
5	5
6	6

   a. Compute marginal cost and average total cost.
   b. The price is currently $10. What is the total quantity supplied in the market?
   c. As this market makes the transition to its long-run equilibrium, will the price rise or fall? Will the quantity demanded rise or fall? Will the quantity supplied by each firm rise or fall?
   d. Graph the long-run supply curve for this market.

12. Suppose there are 1,000 hot pretzel stands operating in New York City. Each stand has the usual U-shaped average-total-cost curve. The market demand curve for pretzels slopes downward, and the market for pretzels is in long-run competitive equilibrium.
    a. Draw the current equilibrium, using graphs for the entire market and for an individual pretzel stand.
    b. The city decides to restrict the number of pretzel-stand licenses, reducing the number of stands to only 800. What effect will this action have on the market and on an individual stand that is still operating? Draw graphs to illustrate your answer.
    c. Suppose that the city decides to charge a fee for the 800 licenses, all of which are quickly sold. How will the size of the fee affect the number of pretzels sold by an individual stand? How will it affect the price of pretzels in the city?
    d. The city wants to raise as much revenue as possible, while ensuring that all 800 licenses are sold. How high should the city set the license fee? Show the answer on your graph.

13. Assume that the gold-mining industry is competitive.
    a. Illustrate a long-run equilibrium using diagrams for the gold market and for a representative gold mine.
    b. Suppose that an increase in jewelry demand induces a surge in the demand for gold. Using your diagrams from part (a), show what happens in the short run to the gold market and to each existing gold mine.
    c. If the demand for gold remains high, what would happen to the price over time? Specifically, would the new long-run equilibrium price be above, below, or equal to the short-run equilibrium price in part (b)? Is it possible for the new long-run equilibrium price to be above the original long-run equilibrium price? Explain.

14. Analyze the two following situations for firms in competitive markets:
    a. Suppose that $TC = 100 + 15q$, where TC is total cost and q is the quantity produced. What is the minimum price necessary for this firm to produce any output in the short run?
    b. Suppose that $MC = 4q$, where MC is marginal cost. The perfectly competitive firm maximizes profits by producing 10 units of output. At what price does it sell these units?

Monopoly

I f you own a personal computer, it probably uses some version of Windows, the operating system sold by the Microsoft Corporation. When Microsoft first designed Windows many years ago, it applied for and received a copyright from the government. The copyright gives Microsoft the exclusive right to make and sell copies of the Windows operating system. If a person wants to buy a copy of Windows, he or she has little choice but to give Microsoft the approximately $100 that the firm has decided to charge for its product. Microsoft is said to have a *monopoly* in the market for Windows.

Microsoft's business decisions are not well described by the model of firm behavior we developed in the previous chapter. In that chapter, we analyzed competitive markets, in which there are many firms offering essentially identical products, so each firm has little influence over the price it receives. By contrast, a monopoly such as Microsoft has no close competitors and, therefore, has the power to influence the market price of its product. While a competitive firm is a *price taker*, a monopoly firm is a *price maker*.

In this chapter, we examine the implications of this market power. We will see that market power alters the relationship between a firm's costs and the price at which it sells its product. A competitive firm takes the price of its output as given by the market and then chooses the quantity it will supply so that price equals marginal cost. By contrast, a monopoly charges a price that exceeds marginal cost.

This result is clearly true in the case of Microsoft's Windows. The marginal cost of Windows—the extra cost that Microsoft incurs by printing one more copy of the program onto a CD—is only a few dollars. The market price of Windows is many times marginal cost.

It is not surprising that monopolies charge high prices for their products. Customers of monopolies might seem to have little choice but to pay whatever the monopoly charges. But if so, why does a copy of Windows not cost $1,000? Or $10,000? The reason is that if Microsoft sets the price that high, fewer people would buy the product. People would buy fewer computers, switch to other operating systems, or make illegal copies. A monopoly firm can control the price of the good it sells, but because a high price reduces the quantity that its customers buy, the monopoly's profits are not unlimited.

As we examine the production and pricing decisions of monopolies, we also consider the implications of monopoly for society as a whole. Monopoly firms, like competitive firms, aim to maximize profit. But this goal has very different ramifications for competitive and monopoly firms. In competitive markets, self-interested consumers and producers behave as if they are guided by an invisible hand to promote general economic well-being. By contrast, because monopoly firms are unchecked by competition, the outcome in a market with a monopoly is often not in the best interest of society.

One of the *Ten Principles of Economics* in Chapter 1 is that governments can sometimes improve market outcomes. The analysis in this chapter sheds more light on this principle. As we examine the problems that monopolies raise for society, we discuss the various ways in which government policymakers might respond to these problems. The U.S. government, for example, keeps a close eye on Microsoft's business decisions. In 1994, it blocked Microsoft from buying Intuit, a leading seller of personal finance software, on the grounds that combining the two firms would concentrate too much market power. Similarly, in 1998, the U.S. Department of Justice objected when Microsoft started integrating its Internet browser into its Windows operating system, claiming that this addition would extend the firm's market power into new areas. To this day, Microsoft continues to wrangle with antitrust regulators in the United States and abroad.

WHY MONOPOLIES ARISE

monopoly
a firm that is the sole seller of a product without close substitutes

A firm is a **monopoly** if it is the sole seller of its product and if its product does not have close substitutes. The fundamental cause of monopoly is *barriers to entry*: A monopoly remains the only seller in its market because other firms cannot enter the market and compete with it. Barriers to entry, in turn, have three main sources:

- *Monopoly resources:* A key resource required for production is owned by a single firm.
- *Government regulation:* The government gives a single firm the exclusive right to produce some good or service.
- *The production process:* A single firm can produce output at a lower cost than can a larger number of producers.

Let's briefly discuss each of these.

Monopoly Resources

The simplest way for a monopoly to arise is for a single firm to own a key resource. For example, consider the market for water in a small town in the Old West. If dozens of town residents have working wells, the competitive model discussed in the preceding chapter describes the behavior of sellers. As a result of the competition among water suppliers, the price of a gallon is driven to equal the marginal cost of pumping an extra gallon. But if there is only one well in town and it is impossible to get water from anywhere else, then the owner of the well has a monopoly on water. Not surprisingly, the monopolist has much greater market power than any single firm in a competitive market. In the case of a necessity like water, the monopolist could command quite a high price, even if the marginal cost of pumping an extra gallon is low.

A classic example of market power arising from the ownership of a key resource is DeBeers, the South African diamond company. Founded in 1888 by Cecil Rhodes, an English businessman (and benefactor for the Rhodes scholarship), DeBeers has at times controlled up to 80 percent of the production from the world's diamond mines. Because its market share is less than 100 percent, DeBeers is not exactly a monopoly, but the company has nonetheless exerted substantial influence over the market price of diamonds.

Although exclusive ownership of a key resource is a potential cause of monopoly, in practice monopolies rarely arise for this reason. Economies are large, and resources are owned by many people. Indeed, because many goods are traded internationally, the natural scope of their markets is often worldwide. There are, therefore, few examples of firms that own a resource for which there are no close substitutes.

"RATHER THAN A MONOPOLY, WE LIKE TO CONSIDER OURSELVES 'THE ONLY GAME IN TOWN.'"

Government-Created Monopolies

In many cases, monopolies arise because the government has given one person or firm the exclusive right to sell some good or service. Sometimes the monopoly arises from the sheer political clout of the would-be monopolist. Kings, for example, once granted exclusive business licenses to their friends and allies. At other times, the government grants a monopoly because doing so is viewed to be in the public interest.

The patent and copyright laws are two important examples. When a pharmaceutical company discovers a new drug, it can apply to the government for a patent. If the government deems the drug to be truly original, it approves the patent, which gives the company the exclusive right to manufacture and sell the drug for 20 years. Similarly, when a novelist finishes a book, she can copyright it. The copyright is a government guarantee that no one can print and sell the work without the author's permission. The copyright makes the novelist a monopolist in the sale of her novel.

The effects of patent and copyright laws are easy to see. Because these laws give one producer a monopoly, they lead to higher prices than would occur under competition. But by allowing these monopoly producers to charge higher prices and earn higher profits, the laws also encourage some desirable behavior. Drug companies are allowed to be monopolists in the drugs they discover to encourage research. Authors are allowed to be monopolists in the sale of their books to encourage them to write more and better books.

Thus, the laws governing patents and copyrights have benefits and costs. The benefits of the patent and copyright laws are the increased incentives for creative activity. These benefits are offset, to some extent, by the costs of monopoly pricing, which we examine fully later in this chapter.

NATURAL MONOPOLIES

natural monopoly
a monopoly that arises because a single firm can supply a good or service to an entire market at a smaller cost than could two or more firms

An industry is a **natural monopoly** when a single firm can supply a good or service to an entire market at a lower cost than could two or more firms. A natural monopoly arises when there are economies of scale over the relevant range of output. Figure 1 shows the average total costs of a firm with economies of scale. In this case, a single firm can produce any amount of output at least cost. That is, for any given amount of output, a larger number of firms leads to less output per firm and higher average total cost.

An example of a natural monopoly is the distribution of water. To provide water to residents of a town, a firm must build a network of pipes throughout the town. If two or more firms were to compete in the provision of this service, each firm would have to pay the fixed cost of building a network. Thus, the average total cost of water is lowest if a single firm serves the entire market.

We saw other examples of natural monopolies when we discussed public goods and common resources in Chapter 11. We noted in passing that some goods are excludable but not rival in consumption. An example is a bridge used so infrequently that it is never congested. The bridge is excludable because a toll collector can prevent someone from using it. The bridge is not rival in consumption because use of the bridge by one person does not diminish the ability of others to use it. Because there is a fixed cost of building the bridge and a negligible marginal cost of additional users, the average total cost of a trip across the bridge (the total cost divided by the number of trips) falls as the number of trips rises. Hence, the bridge is a natural monopoly.

1 FIGURE

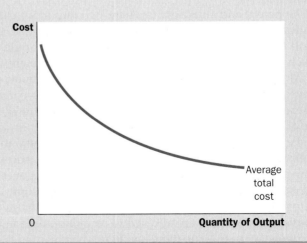

Economies of Scale as a Cause of Monopoly
When a firm's average-total-cost curve continually declines, the firm has what is called a natural monopoly. In this case, when production is divided among more firms, each firm produces less, and average total cost rises. As a result, a single firm can produce any given amount at the smallest cost.

When a firm is a natural monopoly, it is less concerned about new entrants eroding its monopoly power. Normally, a firm has trouble maintaining a monopoly position without ownership of a key resource or protection from the government. The monopolist's profit attracts entrants into the market, and these entrants make the market more competitive. By contrast, entering a market in which another firm has a natural monopoly is unattractive. Would-be entrants know that they cannot achieve the same low costs that the monopolist enjoys because, after entry, each firm would have a smaller piece of the market.

In some cases, the size of the market is one determinant of whether an industry is a natural monopoly. Again, consider a bridge across a river. When the population is small, the bridge may be a natural monopoly. A single bridge can satisfy the entire demand for trips across the river at lowest cost. Yet as the population grows and the bridge becomes congested, satisfying the entire demand may require two or more bridges across the same river. Thus, as a market expands, a natural monopoly can evolve into a more competitive market.

QUICK QUIZ What are the three reasons that a market might have a monopoly? • Give two examples of monopolies and explain the reason for each.

HOW MONOPOLIES MAKE PRODUCTION AND PRICING DECISIONS

Now that we know how monopolies arise, we can consider how a monopoly firm decides how much of its product to make and what price to charge for it. The analysis of monopoly behavior in this section is the starting point for evaluating whether monopolies are desirable and what policies the government might pursue in monopoly markets.

MONOPOLY VERSUS COMPETITION

The key difference between a competitive firm and a monopoly is the monopoly's ability to influence the price of its output. A competitive firm is small relative to the market in which it operates and, therefore, has no power to influence the price of its output. It takes the price as given by market conditions. By contrast, because a monopoly is the sole producer in its market, it can alter the price of its good by adjusting the quantity it supplies to the market.

One way to view this difference between a competitive firm and a monopoly is to consider the demand curve that each firm faces. When we analyzed profit maximization by competitive firms in the preceding chapter, we drew the market price as a horizontal line. Because a competitive firm can sell as much or as little as it wants at this price, the competitive firm faces a horizontal demand curve, as in panel (a) of Figure 2. In effect, because the competitive firm sells a product with many perfect substitutes (the products of all the other firms in its market), the demand curve that any one firm faces is perfectly elastic.

By contrast, because a monopoly is the sole producer in its market, its demand curve is the market demand curve. Thus, the monopolist's demand curve slopes downward for all the usual reasons, as in panel (b) of Figure 2. If the monopolist raises the price of its good, consumers buy less of it. Looked at another way, if the

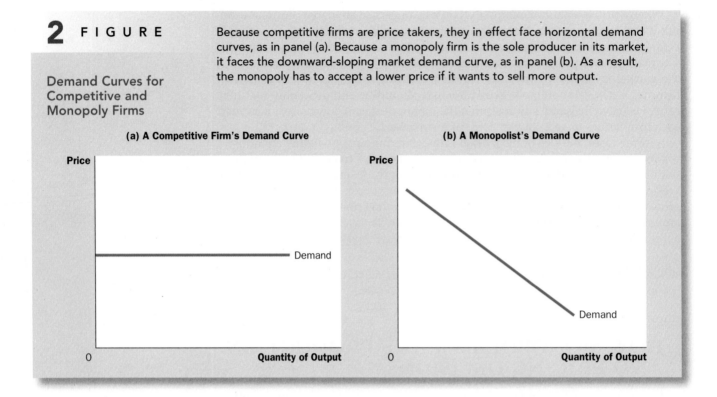

2 **FIGURE**

Demand Curves for Competitive and Monopoly Firms

Because competitive firms are price takers, they in effect face horizontal demand curves, as in panel (a). Because a monopoly firm is the sole producer in its market, it faces the downward-sloping market demand curve, as in panel (b). As a result, the monopoly has to accept a lower price if it wants to sell more output.

(a) A Competitive Firm's Demand Curve

Price

Demand

0   Quantity of Output

(b) A Monopolist's Demand Curve

Price

Demand

0   Quantity of Output

monopolist reduces the quantity of output it produces and sells, the price of its output increases.

The market demand curve provides a constraint on a monopoly's ability to profit from its market power. A monopolist would prefer, if it were possible, to charge a high price and sell a large quantity at that high price. The market demand curve makes that outcome impossible. In particular, the market demand curve describes the combinations of price and quantity that are available to a monopoly firm. By adjusting the quantity produced (or equivalently, the price charged), the monopolist can choose any point on the demand curve, but it cannot choose a point off the demand curve.

What price and quantity of output will the monopolist choose? As with competitive firms, we assume that the monopolist's goal is to maximize profit. Because the firm's profit is total revenue minus total costs, our next task in explaining monopoly behavior is to examine a monopolist's revenue.

A MONOPOLY'S REVENUE

Consider a town with a single producer of water. Table 1 shows how the monopoly's revenue might depend on the amount of water produced.

The first two columns show the monopolist's demand schedule. If the monopolist produces 1 gallon of water, it can sell that gallon for $10. If it produces 2 gallons, it must lower the price to $9 to sell both gallons. If it produces 3 gallons, it must lower the price to $8. And so on. If you graphed these two columns of numbers, you would get a typical downward-sloping demand curve.

TABLE **1**

Quantity of Water (Q)	Price (P)	Total Revenue (TR = P × Q)	Average Revenue (AR = TR / Q)	Marginal Revenue (MR = ΔTR / ΔQ)
0 gallons	$11	$ 0	—	
				$10
1	10	10	$10	
				8
2	9	18	9	
				6
3	8	24	8	
				4
4	7	28	7	
				2
5	6	30	6	
				0
6	5	30	5	
				−2
7	4	28	4	
				−4
8	3	24	3	

A Monopoly's Total, Average, and Marginal Revenue

The third column of the table presents the monopolist's *total revenue*. It equals the quantity sold (from the first column) times the price (from the second column). The fourth column computes the firm's *average revenue*, the amount of revenue the firm receives per unit sold. We compute average revenue by taking the number for total revenue in the third column and dividing it by the quantity of output in the first column. As we discussed in the previous chapter, average revenue always equals the price of the good. This is true for monopolists as well as for competitive firms.

The last column of Table 1 computes the firm's *marginal revenue*, the amount of revenue that the firm receives for each additional unit of output. We compute marginal revenue by taking the change in total revenue when output increases by 1 unit. For example, when the firm is producing 3 gallons of water, it receives total revenue of $24. Raising production to 4 gallons increases total revenue to $28. Thus, marginal revenue from the sale of the fourth gallon is $28 minus $24, or $4.

Table 1 shows a result that is important for understanding monopoly behavior: *A monopolist's marginal revenue is always less than the price of its good.* For example, if the firm raises production of water from 3 to 4 gallons, it will increase total revenue by only $4, even though it will be able to sell each gallon for $7. For a monopoly, marginal revenue is lower than price because a monopoly faces a downward-sloping demand curve. To increase the amount sold, a monopoly firm must lower the price it charges to all customers. Hence, to sell the fourth gallon of water, the monopolist will get $1 less revenue for each of the first three gallons. This $3 loss accounts for the difference between the price of the fourth gallon ($7) and the marginal revenue of that fourth gallon ($4).

Marginal revenue for monopolies is very different from marginal revenue for competitive firms. When a monopoly increases the amount it sells, this action has two effects on total revenue ($P \times Q$):

- *The output effect:* More output is sold, so Q is higher, which tends to increase total revenue.
- *The price effect:* The price falls, so P is lower, which tends to decrease total revenue.

Because a competitive firm can sell all it wants at the market price, there is no price effect. When it increases production by 1 unit, it receives the market price for that unit, and it does not receive any less for the units it was already selling. That is, because the competitive firm is a price taker, its marginal revenue equals the price of its good. By contrast, when a monopoly increases production by 1 unit, it must reduce the price it charges for every unit it sells, and this cut in price reduces revenue on the units it was already selling. As a result, a monopoly's marginal revenue is less than its price.

Figure 3 graphs the demand curve and the marginal-revenue curve for a monopoly firm. (Because the firm's price equals its average revenue, the demand curve is also the average-revenue curve.) These two curves always start at the same point on the vertical axis because the marginal revenue of the first unit sold equals the price of the good. But for the reason we just discussed, the monopolist's marginal revenue on all units after the first is less than the price of the good. Thus, a monopoly's marginal-revenue curve lies below its demand curve.

You can see in the figure (as well as in Table 1) that marginal revenue can even become negative. Marginal revenue is negative when the price effect on revenue is greater than the output effect. In this case, when the firm produces an extra unit of output, the price falls by enough to cause the firm's total revenue to decline, even though the firm is selling more units.

3 FIGURE

Demand and Marginal-Revenue Curves for a Monopoly
The demand curve shows how the quantity affects the price of the good. The marginal-revenue curve shows how the firm's revenue changes when the quantity increases by 1 unit. Because the price on *all* units sold must fall if the monopoly increases production, marginal revenue is always less than the price.

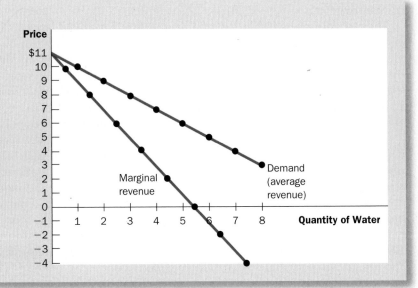

PROFIT MAXIMIZATION

Now that we have considered the revenue of a monopoly firm, we are ready to examine how such a firm maximizes profit. Recall from Chapter 1 that one of the *Ten Principles of Economics* is that rational people think at the margin. This lesson is as true for monopolists as it is for competitive firms. Here we apply the logic of marginal analysis to the monopolist's decision about how much to produce.

Figure 4 graphs the demand curve, the marginal-revenue curve, and the cost curves for a monopoly firm. All these curves should seem familiar: The demand and marginal-revenue curves are like those in Figure 3, and the cost curves are like those we encountered in the last two chapters. These curves contain all the information we need to determine the level of output that a profit-maximizing monopolist will choose.

Suppose, first, that the firm is producing at a low level of output, such as Q_1. In this case, marginal cost is less than marginal revenue. If the firm increased production by 1 unit, the additional revenue would exceed the additional costs, and profit would rise. Thus, when marginal cost is less than marginal revenue, the firm can increase profit by producing more units.

A similar argument applies at high levels of output, such as Q_2. In this case, marginal cost is greater than marginal revenue. If the firm reduced production by 1 unit, the costs saved would exceed the revenue lost. Thus, if marginal cost is greater than marginal revenue, the firm can raise profit by reducing production.

In the end, the firm adjusts its level of production until the quantity reaches Q_{MAX}, at which marginal revenue equals marginal cost. *Thus, the monopolist's profit-maximizing quantity of output is determined by the intersection of the marginal-revenue curve and the marginal-cost curve.* In Figure 4, this intersection occurs at point A.

You might recall from the previous chapter that competitive firms also choose the quantity of output at which marginal revenue equals marginal cost. In

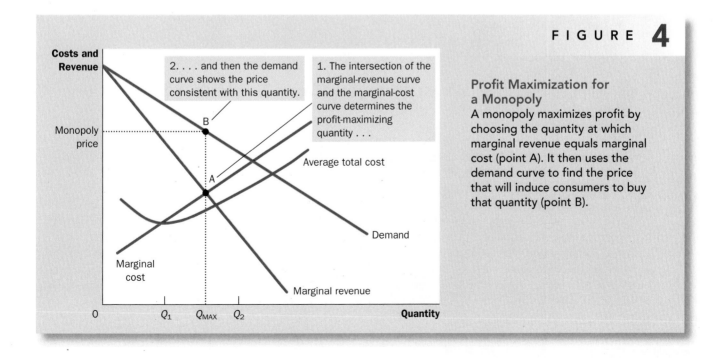

FIGURE 4

Profit Maximization for a Monopoly
A monopoly maximizes profit by choosing the quantity at which marginal revenue equals marginal cost (point A). It then uses the demand curve to find the price that will induce consumers to buy that quantity (point B).

following this rule for profit maximization, competitive firms and monopolies are alike. But there is also an important difference between these types of firms: The marginal revenue of a competitive firm equals its price, whereas the marginal revenue of a monopoly is less than its price. That is,

For a competitive firm: $P = MR = MC.$
For a monopoly firm: $P > MR = MC.$

The equality of marginal revenue and marginal cost at the profit-maximizing quantity is the same for both types of firms. What differs is the relationship of the price to marginal revenue and marginal cost.

How does the monopoly find the profit-maximizing price for its product? The demand curve answers this question because the demand curve relates the amount that customers are willing to pay to the quantity sold. Thus, after the monopoly firm chooses the quantity of output that equates marginal revenue and marginal cost, it uses the demand curve to find the highest price it can charge and sell that quantity. In Figure 4, the profit-maximizing price is found at point B.

We can now see a key difference between markets with competitive firms and markets with a monopoly firm: *In competitive markets, price equals marginal cost. In monopolized markets, price exceeds marginal cost.* As we will see in a moment, this finding is crucial to understanding the social cost of monopoly.

A Monopoly's Profit

How much profit does a monopoly make? To see a monopoly firm's profit in a graph, recall that profit equals total revenue (*TR*) minus total costs (*TC*):

$$\text{Profit} = TR - TC.$$

FYI

Why a Monopoly Does Not Have a Supply Curve

You may have noticed that we have analyzed the price in a monopoly market using the market demand curve and the firm's cost curves. We have not made any mention of the market supply curve. By contrast, when we analyzed prices in competitive markets beginning in Chapter 4, the two most important words were always *supply* and *demand*.

What happened to the supply curve? Although monopoly firms make decisions about what quantity to supply (in the way described in this chapter), a monopoly does not have a supply curve. A supply curve tells us the quantity that firms choose to supply at any given price. This concept makes sense when we are analyzing competitive firms, which are price takers. But a monopoly firm is a price maker,

not a price taker. It is not meaningful to ask what such a firm would produce at any price because the firm sets the price at the same time it chooses the quantity to supply.

Indeed, the monopolist's decision about how much to supply is impossible to separate from the demand curve it faces. The shape of the demand curve determines the shape of the marginal-revenue curve, which in turn determines the monopolist's profit-maximizing quantity. In a competitive market, supply decisions can be analyzed without knowing the demand curve, but that is not true in a monopoly market. Therefore, we never talk about a monopoly's supply curve.

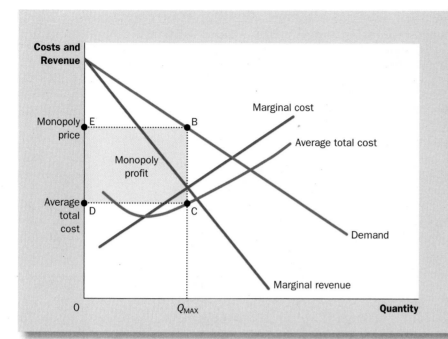

FIGURE **5**

The Monopolist's Profit
The area of the box BCDE equals the profit of the monopoly firm. The height of the box (BC) is price minus average total cost, which equals profit per unit sold. The width of the box (DC) is the number of units sold.

We can rewrite this as

$$\text{Profit} = (TR/Q - TC/Q) \times Q.$$

TR/Q is average revenue, which equals the price, P, and TC/Q is average total cost, ATC. Therefore,

$$\text{Profit} = (P - ATC) \times Q.$$

This equation for profit (which also holds for competitive firms) allows us to measure the monopolist's profit in our graph.

Consider the shaded box in Figure 5. The height of the box (the segment BC) is price minus average total cost, $P - ATC$, which is the profit on the typical unit sold. The width of the box (the segment DC) is the quantity sold, Q_{MAX}. Therefore, the area of this box is the monopoly firm's total profit.

MONOPOLY DRUGS VERSUS GENERIC DRUGS

According to our analysis, prices are determined differently in monopolized markets and competitive markets. A natural place to test this theory is the market for pharmaceutical drugs because this market takes on both market structures. When a firm discovers a new drug, patent laws give the firm a monopoly on the sale of that drug. But eventually, the firm's patent runs out, and any company can make and sell the drug. At that time, the market switches from being monopolistic to being competitive.

What should happen to the price of a drug when the patent runs out? Figure 6 shows the market for a typical drug. In this figure, the marginal cost of producing

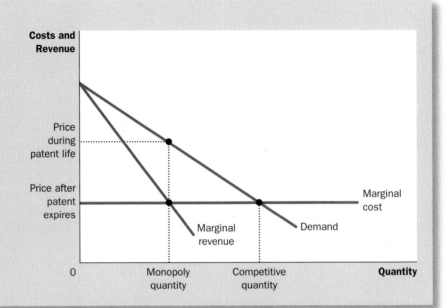

6 FIGURE

The Market for Drugs
When a patent gives a firm a monopoly over the sale of a drug, the firm charges the monopoly price, which is well above the marginal cost of making the drug. When the patent on a drug runs out, new firms enter the market, making it more competitive. As a result, the price falls from the monopoly price to marginal cost.

the drug is constant. (This is approximately true for many drugs.) During the life of the patent, the monopoly firm maximizes profit by producing the quantity at which marginal revenue equals marginal cost and charging a price well above marginal cost. But when the patent runs out, the profit from making the drug should encourage new firms to enter the market. As the market becomes more competitive, the price should fall to equal marginal cost.

Experience is, in fact, consistent with our theory. When the patent on a drug expires, other companies quickly enter and begin selling so-called generic products that are chemically identical to the former monopolist's brand-name product. And just as our analysis predicts, the price of the competitively produced generic drug is well below the price that the monopolist was charging.

The expiration of a patent, however, does not cause the monopolist to lose all its market power. Some consumers remain loyal to the brand-name drug, perhaps out of fear that the new generic drugs are not actually the same as the drug they have been using for years. As a result, the former monopolist can continue to charge a price at least somewhat above the price charged by its new competitors.   ●

QUICK QUIZ   Explain how a monopolist chooses the quantity of output to produce and the price to charge.

THE WELFARE COST OF MONOPOLIES

Is monopoly a good way to organize a market? We have seen that a monopoly, in contrast to a competitive firm, charges a price above marginal cost. From the standpoint of consumers, this high price makes monopoly undesirable. At the same time, however, the monopoly is earning profit from charging this high price.

From the standpoint of the owners of the firm, the high price makes monopoly very desirable. Is it possible that the benefits to the firm's owners exceed the costs imposed on consumers, making monopoly desirable from the standpoint of society as a whole?

We can answer this question using the tools of welfare economics. Recall from Chapter 7 that total surplus measures the economic well-being of buyers and sellers in a market. Total surplus is the sum of consumer surplus and producer surplus. Consumer surplus is consumers' willingness to pay for a good minus the amount they actually pay for it. Producer surplus is the amount producers receive for a good minus their costs of producing it. In this case, there is a single producer—the monopolist.

You can probably guess the result of this analysis. In Chapter 7, we concluded that the equilibrium of supply and demand in a competitive market is not only a natural outcome but also a desirable one. The invisible hand of the market leads to an allocation of resources that makes total surplus as large as it can be. Because a monopoly leads to an allocation of resources different from that in a competitive market, the outcome must, in some way, fail to maximize total economic well-being.

The Deadweight Loss

We begin by considering what the monopoly firm would do if it were run by a benevolent social planner. The social planner cares not only about the profit earned by the firm's owners but also about the benefits received by the firm's consumers. The planner tries to maximize total surplus, which equals producer surplus (profit) plus consumer surplus. Keep in mind that total surplus equals the value of the good to consumers minus the costs of making the good incurred by the monopoly producer.

Figure 7 analyzes how a benevolent social planner would choose the monopoly's level of output. The demand curve reflects the value of the good to consumers, as measured by their willingness to pay for it. The marginal-cost curve reflects the costs of the monopolist. Thus, the socially efficient quantity is found where the demand curve and the marginal-cost curve intersect. Below this quantity, the value of an extra unit to consumers exceeds the cost of providing it, so increasing output would raise total surplus. Above this quantity, the cost of producing an extra unit exceeds the value of that unit to consumers, so decreasing output would raise total surplus. At the optimal quantity, the value of an extra unit to consumers exactly equals the marginal cost of production.

If the social planner were running the monopoly, the firm could achieve this efficient outcome by charging the price found at the intersection of the demand and marginal-cost curves. Thus, like a competitive firm and unlike a profit-maximizing monopoly, a social planner would charge a price equal to marginal cost. Because this price would give consumers an accurate signal about the cost of producing the good, consumers would buy the efficient quantity.

We can evaluate the welfare effects of monopoly by comparing the level of output that the monopolist chooses to the level of output that a social planner would choose. As we have seen, the monopolist chooses to produce and sell the quantity of output at which the marginal-revenue and marginal-cost curves intersect; the social planner would choose the quantity at which the demand and marginal-cost curves intersect. Figure 8 shows the comparison. The monopolist produces less than the socially efficient quantity of output.

7 FIGURE

The Efficient Level of Output
A benevolent social planner who wanted to maximize total surplus in the market would choose the level of output where the demand curve and marginal-cost curve intersect. Below this level, the value of the good to the marginal buyer (as reflected in the demand curve) exceeds the marginal cost of making the good. Above this level, the value to the marginal buyer is less than marginal cost.

We can also view the inefficiency of monopoly in terms of the monopolist's price. Because the market demand curve describes a negative relationship between the price and quantity of the good, a quantity that is inefficiently low is equivalent to a price that is inefficiently high. When a monopolist charges a price above marginal cost, some potential consumers value the good at more than its marginal cost but less than the monopolist's price. These consumers do not buy the good. Because the value these consumers place on the good is greater than the cost of providing it to them, this result is inefficient. Thus, monopoly pricing prevents some mutually beneficial trades from taking place.

The inefficiency of monopoly can be measured with a deadweight loss triangle, as illustrated in Figure 8. Because the demand curve reflects the value to consumers and the marginal-cost curve reflects the costs to the monopoly producer, the area of the deadweight loss triangle between the demand curve and the marginal-cost curve equals the total surplus lost because of monopoly pricing. It is the reduction in economic well-being that results from the monopoly's use of its market power.

The deadweight loss caused by monopoly is similar to the deadweight loss caused by a tax. Indeed, a monopolist is like a private tax collector. As we saw in Chapter 8, a tax on a good places a wedge between consumers' willingness to pay (as reflected in the demand curve) and producers' costs (as reflected in the supply curve). Because a monopoly exerts its market power by charging a price above marginal cost, it places a similar wedge. In both cases, the wedge causes the quantity sold to fall short of the social optimum. The difference between the two

FIGURE 8

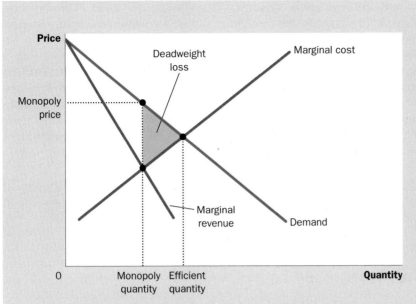

The Inefficiency of Monopoly
Because a monopoly charges a price above marginal cost, not all consumers who value the good at more than its cost buy it. Thus, the quantity produced and sold by a monopoly is below the socially efficient level. The deadweight loss is represented by the area of the triangle between the demand curve (which reflects the value of the good to consumers) and the marginal-cost curve (which reflects the costs of the monopoly producer).

cases is that the government gets the revenue from a tax, whereas a private firm gets the monopoly profit.

THE MONOPOLY'S PROFIT: A SOCIAL COST?

It is tempting to decry monopolies for "profiteering" at the expense of the public. And indeed, a monopoly firm does earn a higher profit by virtue of its market power. According to the economic analysis of monopoly, however, the firm's profit is not in itself necessarily a problem for society.

Welfare in a monopolized market, like all markets, includes the welfare of both consumers and producers. Whenever a consumer pays an extra dollar to a producer because of a monopoly price, the consumer is worse off by a dollar, and the producer is better off by the same amount. This transfer from the consumers of the good to the owners of the monopoly does not affect the market's total surplus—the sum of consumer and producer surplus. In other words, the monopoly profit itself represents not a reduction in the size of the economic pie but merely a bigger slice for producers and a smaller slice for consumers. Unless consumers are for some reason more deserving than producers—a normative judgment about equity that goes beyond the realm of economic efficiency—the monopoly profit is not a social problem.

The problem in a monopolized market arises because the firm produces and sells a quantity of output below the level that maximizes total surplus. The deadweight loss measures how much the economic pie shrinks as a result. This inefficiency is connected to the monopoly's high price: Consumers buy fewer units when the firm raises its price above marginal cost. But keep in mind that the profit earned on the units that continue to be sold is not the problem. The problem stems from the inefficiently low quantity of output. Put differently, if the high monopoly price did not discourage some consumers from buying the good, it would raise producer surplus by exactly the amount it reduced consumer surplus, leaving total surplus the same as could be achieved by a benevolent social planner.

There is, however, a possible exception to this conclusion. Suppose that a monopoly firm has to incur additional costs to maintain its monopoly position. For example, a firm with a government-created monopoly might need to hire lobbyists to convince lawmakers to continue its monopoly. In this case, the monopoly may use up some of its monopoly profits paying for these additional costs. If so, the social loss from monopoly includes both these costs and the deadweight loss resulting from a price above marginal cost.

QUICK QUIZ How does a monopolist's quantity of output compare to the quantity of output that maximizes total surplus? How does this difference relate to the concept of deadweight loss?

PRICE DISCRIMINATION

price discrimination
the business practice of selling the same good at different prices to different customers

So far, we have been assuming that the monopoly firm charges the same price to all customers. Yet in many cases, firms sell the same good to different customers for different prices, even though the costs of producing for the two customers are the same. This practice is called **price discrimination**.

Before discussing the behavior of a price-discriminating monopolist, we should note that price discrimination is not possible when a good is sold in a competitive market. In a competitive market, many firms are selling the same good at the market price. No firm is willing to charge a lower price to any customer because the firm can sell all it wants at the market price. And if any firm tried to charge a higher price to a customer, that customer would buy from another firm. For a firm to price discriminate, it must have some market power.

A PARABLE ABOUT PRICING

To understand why a monopolist would price discriminate, let's consider an example. Imagine that you are the president of Readalot Publishing Company. Readalot's best-selling author has just written a new novel. To keep things simple, let's imagine that you pay the author a flat $2 million for the exclusive rights to publish the book. Let's also assume that the cost of printing the book is zero. Readalot's profit, therefore, is the revenue from selling the book minus the $2 million it has paid to the author. Given these assumptions, how would you, as Readalot's president, decide the book's price?

Your first step is to estimate the demand for the book. Readalot's marketing department tells you that the book will attract two types of readers. The book will appeal to the author's 100,000 die-hard fans who are willing to pay as much as $30. In addition, the book will appeal to about 400,000 less enthusiastic readers who will pay up to $5.

If Readalot charges a single price to all customers, what price maximizes profit? There are two natural prices to consider: $30 is the highest price Readalot can charge and still get the 100,000 die-hard fans, and $5 is the highest price it can charge and still get the entire market of 500,000 potential readers. Solving Readalot's problem is a matter of simple arithmetic. At a price of $30, Readalot sells 100,000 copies, has revenue of $3 million, and makes profit of $1 million. At a price of $5, it sells 500,000 copies, has revenue of $2.5 million, and makes profit of $500,000. Thus, Readalot maximizes profit by charging $30 and forgoing the opportunity to sell to the 400,000 less enthusiastic readers.

Notice that Readalot's decision causes a deadweight loss. There are 400,000 readers willing to pay $5 for the book, and the marginal cost of providing it to them is zero. Thus, $2 million of total surplus is lost when Readalot charges the higher price. This deadweight loss is the inefficiency that arises whenever a monopolist charges a price above marginal cost.

Now suppose that Readalot's marketing department makes a discovery: These two groups of readers are in separate markets. The die-hard fans live in Australia, and the other readers live in the United States. Moreover, it is hard for readers in one country to buy books in the other.

In response to this discovery, Readalot can change its marketing strategy and increase profits. To the 100,000 Australian readers, it can charge $30 for the book. To the 400,000 American readers, it can charge $5 for the book. In this case, revenue is $3 million in Australia and $2 million in the United States, for a total of $5 million. Profit is then $3 million, which is substantially greater than the $1 million the company could earn charging the same $30 price to all customers. Not surprisingly, Readalot chooses to follow this strategy of price discrimination.

The story of Readalot Publishing is hypothetical, but it describes accurately the business practice of many publishing companies. Textbooks, for example, are often sold at a lower price in Europe than in the United States. Even more important is the price differential between hardcover books and paperbacks. When a publisher has a new novel, it initially releases an expensive hardcover edition and later releases a cheaper paperback edition. The difference in price between these two editions far exceeds the difference in printing costs. The publisher's goal is just as in our example. By selling the hardcover to die-hard fans and the paperback to less enthusiastic readers, the publisher price discriminates and raises its profit.

THE MORAL OF THE STORY

Like any parable, the story of Readalot Publishing is stylized. Yet also like any parable, it teaches some general lessons. In this case, there are three lessons to be learned about price discrimination.

The first and most obvious lesson is that price discrimination is a rational strategy for a profit-maximizing monopolist. That is, by charging different prices to different customers, a monopolist can increase its profit. In essence, a price-discriminating monopolist charges each customer a price closer to his or her willingness to pay, therefore selling more than is possible with a single price.

The second lesson is that price discrimination requires the ability to separate customers according to their willingness to pay. In our example, customers were separated geographically. But sometimes monopolists choose other differences, such as age or income, to distinguish among customers.

A corollary to this second lesson is that certain market forces can prevent firms from price discriminating. In particular, one such force is *arbitrage*, the process of buying a good in one market at a low price and selling it in another market at a higher price to profit from the price difference. In our example, if Australian bookstores could buy the book in the United States and resell it to Australian readers, the arbitrage would prevent Readalot from price discriminating, because no Australian would buy the book at the higher price.

The third lesson from our parable is the most surprising: Price discrimination can raise economic welfare. Recall that a deadweight loss arises when Readalot charges a single $30 price because the 400,000 less enthusiastic readers do not end up with the book, even though they value it at more than its marginal cost of production. By contrast, when Readalot price discriminates, all readers get the book, and the outcome is efficient. Thus, price discrimination can eliminate the inefficiency inherent in monopoly pricing.

Note that in this example the increase in welfare from price discrimination shows up as higher producer surplus rather than higher consumer surplus. Consumers are no better off for having bought the book: The price they pay exactly equals the value they place on the book, so they receive no consumer surplus. The entire increase in total surplus from price discrimination accrues to Readalot Publishing in the form of higher profit.

THE ANALYTICS OF PRICE DISCRIMINATION

Let's consider a bit more formally how price discrimination affects economic welfare. We begin by assuming that the monopolist can price discriminate perfectly. *Perfect price discrimination* describes a situation in which the monopolist knows exactly the willingness to pay of each customer and can charge each customer a different price. In this case, the monopolist charges each customer exactly his or her willingness to pay, and the monopolist gets the entire surplus in every transaction.

Figure 9 shows producer and consumer surplus with and without price discrimination. Without price discrimination, the firm charges a single price above marginal cost, as shown in panel (a). Because some potential customers who value the good at more than marginal cost do not buy it at this high price, the monopoly causes a deadweight loss. Yet when a firm can perfectly price discriminate, as shown in panel (b), each customer who values the good at more than marginal cost buys the good and is charged his or her willingness to pay. All mutually beneficial trades take place, there is no deadweight loss, and the entire surplus derived from the market goes to the monopoly producer in the form of profit.

In reality, of course, price discrimination is not perfect. Customers do not walk into stores with signs displaying their willingness to pay. Instead, firms price discriminate by dividing customers into groups: young versus old, weekday versus weekend shoppers, Americans versus Australians, and so on. Unlike those in our parable of Readalot Publishing, customers within each group differ in their willingness to pay for the product, making perfect price discrimination impossible.

How does this imperfect price discrimination affect welfare? The analysis of these pricing schemes is quite complicated, and it turns out that there is no general answer to this question. Compared to the monopoly outcome with a single price, imperfect price discrimination can raise, lower, or leave unchanged total surplus in a market. The only certain conclusion is that price discrimination raises the monopoly's profit; otherwise, the firm would choose to charge all customers the same price.

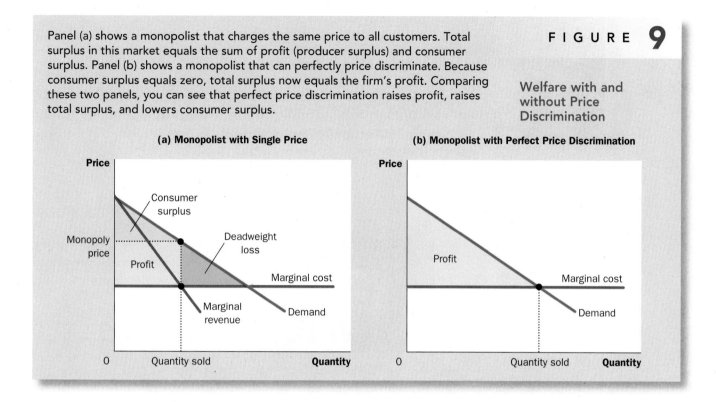

Panel (a) shows a monopolist that charges the same price to all customers. Total surplus in this market equals the sum of profit (producer surplus) and consumer surplus. Panel (b) shows a monopolist that can perfectly price discriminate. Because consumer surplus equals zero, total surplus now equals the firm's profit. Comparing these two panels, you can see that perfect price discrimination raises profit, raises total surplus, and lowers consumer surplus.

FIGURE **9**

Welfare with and without Price Discrimination

(a) Monopolist with Single Price

(b) Monopolist with Perfect Price Discrimination

EXAMPLES OF PRICE DISCRIMINATION

Firms in our economy use various business strategies aimed at charging different prices to different customers. Now that we understand the economics of price discrimination, let's consider some examples.

Movie Tickets   Many movie theaters charge a lower price for children and senior citizens than for other patrons. This fact is hard to explain in a competitive market. In a competitive market, price equals marginal cost, and the marginal cost of providing a seat for a child or senior citizen is the same as the marginal cost of providing a seat for anyone else. Yet the differential pricing is easily explained if movie theaters have some local monopoly power and if children and senior citizens have a lower willingness to pay for a ticket. In this case, movie theaters raise their profit by price discriminating.

Airline Prices   Seats on airplanes are sold at many different prices. Most airlines charge a lower price for a round-trip ticket between two cities if the traveler stays over a Saturday night. At first, this seems odd. Why should it matter to the airline whether a passenger stays over a Saturday night? The reason is that this rule provides a way to separate business travelers and leisure travelers. A passenger on a business trip has a high willingness to pay and, most likely, does not want to stay over a Saturday night. By contrast, a passenger traveling for personal reasons has

"WOULD IT BOTHER YOU TO HEAR HOW LITTLE I PAID FOR THIS FLIGHT?"

In The News

TKTS and Other Schemes

Economist Hal Varian discusses a dramatic example of price discrimination.

The Dynamics of Pricing Tickets for Broadway Shows

By Hal R. Varian

Every night in New York, about 25,000 people, on average, attend Broadway shows.

As avid theatergoers know, ticket prices have been rising inexorably. The top ticket price for Broadway shows has risen 31 percent since 1998. But the actual price paid has gone up by only 24 percent.

The difference is a result of discounting. Savvy fans know that there are deals available for even the most popular shows, with the most popular discounts being offered through coupons, two-for-one deals, special

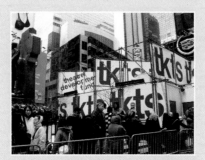

BARGAIN HUNTERS

prices for students, and through the TKTS booth in Times Square.

Why so much discounting? The value of a seat in a theater, like a seat on an airplane, is highly perishable. Once the show starts or

the plane takes off, a seat is worth next to nothing.

In both industries, sellers use a variety of strategies to try to ensure that the seats are sold to those who are willing to pay the most.

This phenomenon was examined recently by a Stanford economist, Phillip Leslie, in an article, "Price Discrimination in Broadway Theater," published in the autumn 2004 issue of the *RAND Journal of Economics*.

Mr. Leslie was able to collect detailed data on a 1996 Broadway play, "Seven Guitars." Over 140,000 people saw this play, and they bought tickets in 17 price categories. Some price variation was due to the qual-

a lower willingness to pay and is more likely to be willing to stay over a Saturday night. Thus, the airlines can successfully price discriminate by charging a lower price for passengers who stay over a Saturday night.

Discount Coupons   Many companies offer discount coupons to the public in newspapers and magazines. A buyer simply has to clip the coupon to get $0.50 off his or her next purchase. Why do companies offer these coupons? Why don't they just cut the price of the product by $0.50?

The answer is that coupons allow companies to price discriminate. Companies know that not all customers are willing to spend the time to clip coupons. Moreover, the willingness to clip coupons is related to the customer's willingness to pay for the good. A rich and busy executive is unlikely to spend her time clipping discount coupons out of the newspaper, and she is probably willing to pay a higher price for many goods. A person who is unemployed is more likely to clip coupons and to have a lower willingness to pay. Thus, by charging a lower price only to those customers who clip coupons, firms can successfully price discriminate.

ity of the seats—orchestra, mezzanine, balcony and so on—while other price differences were a result of various forms of discounting.

The combination of quality variation and discounts led to widely varying ticket prices. The average difference of two tickets chosen at random on a given night was about 40 percent of the average price. This is comparable to the price variation in airline tickets. . . .

The ticket promotions also varied over the 199 performances of the show. Targeted direct mail was used early on, while two-for-one tickets were not introduced until about halfway through the run.

The tickets offered for sale at the TKTS booth in Times Square are typically orchestra seats, the best category of seats available. But the discounted tickets at TKTS tend to be the lower-quality orchestra seats. They sell at a fixed discount of 50 percent, but are offered only for performances that day.

Mr. Leslie's goal was primarily to model the behavior of the theatergoer. The audience for Broadway shows is highly diverse. About 10 percent, according to a 1991 survey conducted by Broadway producers, had household incomes of $25,000 or $35,000 while an equal number had incomes over $150,000 (in 1990 dollars).

The prices and discounting policy set by the producers of Broadway shows try to use this heterogeneity to get people to sort themselves by their willingness to pay for tickets.

You probably will not see Donald Trump waiting in line at TKTS; presumably, those in his income class do not mind paying full price. But a lot of students, unemployed actors and tourists do use TKTS.

Yes, it is inconvenient to wait in line at TKTS. But that is the point. If it weren't inconvenient, everyone would do it, and this would result in substantially lower revenues for Broadway shows.

Mr. Leslie uses some advanced econometric techniques to estimate the values that different income groups put on the various categories of tickets. He finds that Broadway producers do a pretty good job, in general, at maximizing revenue. . . .

We are likely to see more and more goods and services sold using the same sort of differential pricing. As more and more transactions become computer-mediated, it becomes easier for sellers to collect data, to experiment with pricing and to analyze the results of those experiments.

This, of course, makes life more complicated for us consumers. The flip side is that pricing variations make those good deals more likely.

Last time I was in New York, I was pleased that I managed to get a ticket to "The Producers" for half price. It almost made up for the fact that I had to book my airline ticket two weeks in advance and stay over a Saturday night.

Source: *New York Times*, January 13, 2005.

Financial Aid Many colleges and universities give financial aid to needy students. One can view this policy as a type of price discrimination. Wealthy students have greater financial resources and, therefore, a higher willingness to pay than needy students. By charging high tuition and selectively offering financial aid, schools in effect charge prices to customers based on the value they place on going to that school. This behavior is similar to that of any price-discriminating monopolist.

Quantity Discounts So far in our examples of price discrimination, the monopolist charges different prices to different customers. Sometimes, however, monopolists price discriminate by charging different prices to the same customer for different units that the customer buys. For example, many firms offer lower prices to customers who buy large quantities. A bakery might charge $0.50 for each donut but $5 for a dozen. This is a form of price discrimination because the customer pays a higher price for the first unit bought than for the twelfth. Quantity discounts are often a successful way of price discriminating because a customer's willingness to pay for an additional unit declines as the customer buys more units.

QUICK QUIZ   Give two examples of price discrimination. • How does perfect price discrimination affect consumer surplus, producer surplus, and total surplus?

PUBLIC POLICY TOWARD MONOPOLIES

We have seen that monopolies, in contrast to competitive markets, fail to allocate resources efficiently. Monopolies produce less than the socially desirable quantity of output and, as a result, charge prices above marginal cost. Policymakers in the government can respond to the problem of monopoly in one of four ways:

*   By trying to make monopolized industries more competitive
*   By regulating the behavior of the monopolies
*   By turning some private monopolies into public enterprises
*   By doing nothing at all

INCREASING COMPETITION WITH ANTITRUST LAWS

If Coca-Cola and PepsiCo wanted to merge, the deal would be closely examined by the federal government before it went into effect. The lawyers and economists in the Department of Justice might well decide that a merger between these two large soft drink companies would make the U.S. soft drink market substantially less competitive and, as a result, would reduce the economic well-being of the country as a whole. If so, the Department of Justice would challenge the merger in court, and if the judge agreed, the two companies would not be allowed to merge. It is precisely this kind of challenge that prevented software giant Microsoft from buying Intuit in 1994.

The government derives this power over private industry from the antitrust laws, a collection of statutes aimed at curbing monopoly power. The first and most important of these laws was the Sherman Antitrust Act, which Congress passed in 1890 to reduce the market power of the large and powerful "trusts" that were viewed as dominating the economy at the time. The Clayton Antitrust Act, passed in 1914, strengthened the government's powers and authorized private lawsuits. As the U.S. Supreme Court once put it, the antitrust laws are "a comprehensive charter of economic liberty aimed at preserving free and unfettered competition as the rule of trade."

The antitrust laws give the government various ways to promote competition. They allow the government to prevent mergers, such as our hypothetical merger between Coca-Cola and PepsiCo. They also allow the government to break up companies. For example, in 1984, the government split up AT&T, the large telecommunications company, into eight smaller companies. Finally, the antitrust laws prevent companies from coordinating their activities in ways that make markets less competitive.

Antitrust laws have costs as well as benefits. Sometimes companies merge not to reduce competition but to lower costs through more efficient joint production. These benefits from mergers are sometimes called *synergies*. For example, many U.S. banks have merged in recent years and, by combining operations, have been able to reduce administrative staff. If antitrust laws are to raise social welfare, the government must be able to determine which mergers are desirable and which are not. That is, it must be able to measure and compare the social benefit from

"BUT IF WE DO MERGE WITH AMALGAMATED, WE'LL HAVE ENOUGH RESOURCES TO FIGHT THE ANTI-TRUST VIOLATION CAUSED BY THE MERGER."

CARTOON: © 2003 BY SIDNEY HARRIS

In The News

Airline Mergers

When firms consider merging, executives keep one eye on business fundamentals and another eye on regulatory policy and politics.

Delta's Merger Buzz May Stir the Industry

Delta Air Lines Inc. is seriously considering a merger with either Northwest Airlines Corp. or United Airlines parent UAL Corp., according to people close to the situation, a move that could spur a new round of industry matchmaking as rising fuel costs hurt airline stocks.

At a meeting today, Delta's board is expected to act on a proposal to give Chief Executive Officer Richard Anderson a green light to pursue formal merger discussions with both Northwest and United. . . .

The market reacted enthusiastically yesterday after the news of a prospective deal was reported by *The Wall Street Journal.* Delta shares rose $2.46, or 18%. . . .

Any big U.S. airline merger is sure to draw heavy regulatory scrutiny because of the impact on fares and competition. United and Delta are the second- and third-largest carriers by traffic behind AMR Corp.'s American Airlines. Continental is No. 4, and Northwest is No. 5.

Still, a new round of industry consolidation would help airlines reduce excess capacity, raise fares and boost profit margins battered by oil's rise to nearly $100 a barrel, though it likely would lead to more grumbling from stressed passengers.

Merged airlines could save money by combining computer systems, reducing corporate costs and closing some hubs. Also, bigger airlines may have an edge in winning corporate accounts because they have broader route networks.

Consolidation has taken on new urgency because carriers believe the chances of getting one or two big deals approved by antitrust authorities are better under the current Republican administration. Airline executives and investors believe deals need to be forged in the next 30 to 45 days to allow enough time for scrutiny before the new administration takes office a year from now.

Source: *The Wall Street Journal,* January 11, 2008.

synergies to the social costs of reduced competition. Critics of the antitrust laws are skeptical that the government can perform the necessary cost–benefit analysis with sufficient accuracy.

REGULATION

Another way the government deals with the problem of monopoly is by regulating the behavior of monopolists. This solution is common in the case of natural monopolies, such as water and electric companies. These companies are not allowed to charge any price they want. Instead, government agencies regulate their prices.

What price should the government set for a natural monopoly? This question is not as easy as it might at first appear. One might conclude that the price should equal the monopolist's marginal cost. If price equals marginal cost, customers will buy the quantity of the monopolist's output that maximizes total surplus, and the allocation of resources will be efficient.

In The News

Public Transport and Private Enterprise

In many cities, the mass transit system of buses and subways is a monopoly run by the local government. But is this the best system?

Man with a Van
By John Tierney

Vincent Cummins looks out from his van with the wary eyes of a hardened criminal. It is quiet this evening in downtown Brooklyn . . . too quiet. "Watch my back for me!" he barks into the microphone of his C.B. radio, addressing a fellow outlaw in a van who just drove by him on Livingston Street. He looks left and right. No police cars in sight. None of the usual unmarked cars, either. Cummins pauses for a second—he has heard on the C.B. that cops have just busted two other drivers—but he can't stop himself. "Watch my back!" he repeats into the radio as he ruthlessly pulls over to the curb.

Five seconds later, evil triumphs. *A middle-aged woman with a shopping bag climbs into the van . . . and Cummins drives off with impunity!* His new victim and the other passengers laugh when asked why they're riding this illegal jitney. What fool would pay $1.50 to stand on the bus or sub-

VINCENT CUMMINS: OUTLAW ENTREPRENEUR

way when you're guaranteed a seat here for $1? Unlike bus drivers, the van drivers make change and accept bills, and the vans run

more frequently at every hour of the day. "It takes me an hour to get home if I use the bus," explains Cynthia Peters, a nurse born in Trinidad. "When I'm working late, it's very scary waiting in the dark for the bus and then walking the three blocks home. With Vincent's van, I get home in less than half an hour. He takes me right to the door and waits until I get inside."

Cummins would prefer not to be an outlaw. A native of Barbados, he has been driving his van full time ever since an injury forced him to give up his job as a machinist. "I could be collecting disability," he says, "but it's better to work." He met Federal requirements to run an interstate van service, then spent years trying to get approval to operate in the city. His application, which included more than 900 supporting statements from riders, business groups, and church leaders, was approved by the City Taxi and Limousine Commission as well as by the Department of Transportation. Mayor Giuliani supported him. But this summer the City

There are, however, two practical problems with marginal-cost pricing as a regulatory system. The first arises from the logic of cost curves. By definition, natural monopolies have declining average total cost. As we first discussed in Chapter 13, when average total cost is declining, marginal cost is less than average total cost. This situation is illustrated in Figure 10, which shows a firm with a large fixed cost and then constant marginal cost thereafter. If regulators were to set price equal to marginal cost, that price must be less than the firm's average total cost, and the firm would lose money. Instead of charging such a low price, the monopoly firm would just exit the industry.

Regulators can respond to this problem in various ways, none of which is perfect. One way is to subsidize the monopolist. In essence, the government picks

Council rejected his application for a license, as it has rejected most applications over the past four years, which is why thousands of illegal drivers in Brooklyn and Queens are dodging the police.

Council members claim they're trying to prevent vans from causing accidents and traffic problems, although no one who rides the vans takes these protestations seriously. Vans with accredited and insured drivers like Cummins are no more dangerous or disruptive than taxis. The only danger they pose is to the public transit monopoly, whose union leaders have successfully led the campaign against them.

The van drivers have refuted two modern urban myths: that mass transit must lose money and that it must be a public enterprise. Entrepreneurs like Cummins are thriving today in other cities—Seoul and Buenos Aires rely entirely on private, profitable bus companies—and they once made New York the world leader in mass transit. The first horsecars and elevated trains were developed here by private companies. The first subway was partly financed with a loan from the city, but it was otherwise a private operation, built and run quite profitably with the fare set at a nickel—the equivalent of less than a dollar today.

Eventually though, New York's politicians drove most private transit companies out of business by refusing to adjust the fare for inflation. When the enterprises lost money in the 1920's, Mayor John Hylan offered to teach them efficient management. If the city ran the subway, he promised, it would make money while preserving the nickel fare and freeing New Yorkers from "serfdom" and "dictatorship" of the "grasping transportation monopolies." But expenses soared as soon as government merged the private systems into a true monopoly. The fare, which remained a nickel through seven decades of private transit, has risen 2,900 percent under public management—and today the Metropolitan Transportation Authority still manages to lose about $2 per ride. Meanwhile, a jitney driver can provide better service at lower prices and still make a profit.

"Transit could be profitable again if entrepreneurs are given a chance," says Daniel B. Klein, an economist at Santa Clara University in California and the co-author of *Curb Rights*, a new book from the Brookings Institution on mass transit. "Government has demonstrated that it has no more business producing transit than producing cornflakes. It should concentrate instead on establishing new rules to foster competition." To encour-age private operators to make a long-term investment in regular service along a route, the Brookings researchers recommend selling them exclusive "curb rights" to pick up passengers waiting at certain stops along the route. That way part-time opportunists couldn't swoop in to steal regular customers from a long-term operator. But to encourage competition, at other corners along the route there should also be common stops where passengers could be picked up by any licensed jitney or bus.

Elements of this system already exist where jitneys have informally established their own stops separate from the regular buses, but the City Council is trying to eliminate these competitors. Besides denying licenses to new drivers like Cummins, the Council has forbidden veteran drivers with licenses to operate on bus routes. Unless these restrictions are overturned in court—a suit on the drivers' behalf has been filed by the Institute for Justice, a public-interest law firm in Washington—the vans can compete only by breaking the law. At this very moment, despite the best efforts of the police and the Transport Workers Union, somewhere in New York a serial predator like Cummins is luring another unsuspecting victim. He may even be making change for a $5 bill.

up the losses inherent in marginal-cost pricing. Yet to pay for the subsidy, the government needs to raise money through taxation, which involves its own deadweight losses. Alternatively, the regulators can allow the monopolist to charge a price higher than marginal cost. If the regulated price equals average total cost, the monopolist earns exactly zero economic profit. Yet average-cost pricing leads to deadweight losses because the monopolist's price no longer reflects the marginal cost of producing the good. In essence, average-cost pricing is like a tax on the good the monopolist is selling.

The second problem with marginal-cost pricing as a regulatory system (and with average-cost pricing as well) is that it gives the monopolist no incentive to reduce costs. Each firm in a competitive market tries to reduce its costs because

10 FIGURE

Marginal-Cost Pricing for a Natural Monopoly
Because a natural monopoly has declining average total cost, marginal cost is less than average total cost. Therefore, if regulators require a natural monopoly to charge a price equal to marginal cost, price will be below average total cost, and the monopoly will lose money.

lower costs mean higher profits. But if a regulated monopolist knows that regulators will reduce prices whenever costs fall, the monopolist will not benefit from lower costs. In practice, regulators deal with this problem by allowing monopolists to keep some of the benefits from lower costs in the form of higher profit, a practice that requires some departure from marginal-cost pricing.

PUBLIC OWNERSHIP

The third policy used by the government to deal with monopoly is public ownership. That is, rather than regulating a natural monopoly that is run by a private firm, the government can run the monopoly itself. This solution is common in many European countries, where the government owns and operates utilities such as telephone, water, and electric companies. In the United States, the government runs the Postal Service. The delivery of ordinary first-class mail is often thought to be a natural monopoly.

Economists usually prefer private to public ownership of natural monopolies. The key issue is how the ownership of the firm affects the costs of production. Private owners have an incentive to minimize costs as long as they reap part of the benefit in the form of higher profit. If the firm's managers are doing a bad job of keeping costs down, the firm's owners will fire them. By contrast, if the government bureaucrats who run a monopoly do a bad job, the losers are the customers and taxpayers, whose only recourse is the political system. The bureaucrats may become a special-interest group and attempt to block cost-reducing reforms. Put simply, as a way of ensuring that firms are well run, the voting booth is less reliable than the profit motive.

DOING NOTHING

Each of the foregoing policies aimed at reducing the problem of monopoly has drawbacks. As a result, some economists argue that it is often best for the government not to try to remedy the inefficiencies of monopoly pricing. Here is the assessment of economist George Stigler, who won the Nobel Prize for his work in industrial organization:

> A famous theorem in economics states that a competitive enterprise economy will produce the largest possible income from a given stock of resources. No real economy meets the exact conditions of the theorem, and all real economies will fall short of the ideal economy—a difference called "market failure." In my view, however, the degree of "market failure" for the American economy is much smaller than the "political failure" arising from the imperfections of economic policies found in real political systems.

As this quotation makes clear, determining the proper role of the government in the economy requires judgments about politics as well as economics.

QUICK QUIZ Describe the ways policymakers can respond to the inefficiencies caused by monopolies. List a potential problem with each of these policy responses.

CONCLUSION: THE PREVALENCE OF MONOPOLIES

This chapter has discussed the behavior of firms that have control over the prices they charge. We have seen that these firms behave very differently from the competitive firms studied in the previous chapter. Table 2 summarizes some of the key similarities and differences between competitive and monopoly markets.

From the standpoint of public policy, a crucial result is that a monopolist produces less than the socially efficient quantity and charges a price above marginal cost. As a result, a monopoly causes deadweight losses. In some cases, these

	Competition	Monopoly	
			TABLE 2
Similarities			**Competition versus Monopoly: A Summary Comparison**
Goal of firms	Maximize profits	Maximize profits	
Rule for maximizing	$MR = MC$	$MR = MC$	
Can earn economic profits in the short run?	Yes	Yes	
Differences			
Number of firms	Many	One	
Marginal revenue	$MR = P$	$MR < P$	
Price	$P = MC$	$P > MC$	
Produces welfare-maximizing level of output?	Yes	No	
Entry in long run?	Yes	No	
Can earn economic profits in long run?	No	Yes	
Price discrimination possible?	No	Yes	

inefficiencies can be mitigated through price discrimination by the monopolist, but other times, they call for policymakers to take an active role.

How prevalent are the problems of monopoly? There are two answers to this question.

In one sense, monopolies are common. Most firms have some control over the prices they charge. They are not forced to charge the market price for their goods because their goods are not exactly the same as those offered by other firms. A Ford Taurus is not the same as a Toyota Camry. Ben and Jerry's ice cream is not the same as Breyer's. Each of these goods has a downward-sloping demand curve, which gives each producer some degree of monopoly power.

Yet firms with substantial monopoly power are rare. Few goods are truly unique. Most have substitutes that, even if not exactly the same, are similar. Ben and Jerry can raise the price of their ice cream a little without losing all their sales, but if they raise it very much, sales will fall substantially as their customers switch to another brand.

In the end, monopoly power is a matter of degree. It is true that many firms have some monopoly power. It is also true that their monopoly power is usually limited. In such a situation, we will not go far wrong assuming that firms operate in competitive markets, even if that is not precisely the case.

SUMMARY

- A monopoly is a firm that is the sole seller in its market. A monopoly arises when a single firm owns a key resource, when the government gives a firm the exclusive right to produce a good, or when a single firm can supply the entire market at a smaller cost than many firms could.

- Because a monopoly is the sole producer in its market, it faces a downward-sloping demand curve for its product. When a monopoly increases production by 1 unit, it causes the price of its good to fall, which reduces the amount of revenue earned on all units produced. As a result, a monopoly's marginal revenue is always below the price of its good.

- Like a competitive firm, a monopoly firm maximizes profit by producing the quantity at which marginal revenue equals marginal cost. The monopoly then chooses the price at which that quantity is demanded. Unlike a competitive firm, a monopoly firm's price exceeds its marginal revenue, so its price exceeds marginal cost.

- A monopolist's profit-maximizing level of output is below the level that maximizes the sum of consumer and producer surplus. That is, when the monopoly charges a price above marginal cost, some consumers who value the good more than its cost of production do not buy it. As a result, monopoly causes deadweight losses similar to the deadweight losses caused by taxes.

- A monopolist often can raise its profits by charging different prices for the same good based on a buyer's willingness to pay. This practice of price discrimination can raise economic welfare by getting the good to some consumers who otherwise would not buy it. In the extreme case of perfect price discrimination, the deadweight loss of monopoly is completely eliminated, and all the surplus in the market goes to the monopoly producer. More generally, when price discrimination is imperfect, it can either raise or lower welfare compared to the outcome with a single monopoly price.

- Policymakers can respond to the inefficiency of monopoly behavior in four ways. They can use the antitrust laws to try to make the industry more competitive. They can regulate the prices that the monopoly charges. They can turn the monopolist into a government-run enterprise. Or if the market failure is deemed small compared to the inevitable imperfections of policies, they can do nothing at all.

KEY CONCEPTS

monopoly, *p. 312*   natural monopoly, *p. 314*   price discrimination, *p. 326*

QUESTIONS FOR REVIEW

1. Give an example of a government-created monopoly. Is creating this monopoly necessarily bad public policy? Explain.
2. Define *natural monopoly*. What does the size of a market have to do with whether an industry is a natural monopoly?
3. Why is a monopolist's marginal revenue less than the price of its good? Can marginal revenue ever be negative? Explain.
4. Draw the demand, marginal-revenue, average-total-cost, and marginal-cost curves for a monopolist. Show the profit-maximizing level of output, the profit-maximizing price, and the amount of profit.
5. In your diagram from the previous question, show the level of output that maximizes total surplus. Show the deadweight loss from the monopoly. Explain your answer.
6. Give two examples of price discrimination. In each case, explain why the monopolist chooses to follow this business strategy.
7. What gives the government the power to regulate mergers between firms? From the standpoint of the welfare of society, give a good reason and a bad reason that two firms might want to merge.
8. Describe the two problems that arise when regulators tell a natural monopoly that it must set a price equal to marginal cost.

PROBLEMS AND APPLICATIONS

1. A publisher faces the following demand schedule for the next novel of one of its popular authors:

Price	Quantity Demanded
$100	0 novels
90	100,000
80	200,000
70	300,000
60	400,000
50	500,000
40	600,000
30	700,000
20	800,000
10	900,000
0	1,000,000

The author is paid $2 million to write the book, and the marginal cost of publishing the book is a constant $10 per book.

a. Compute total revenue, total cost, and profit at each quantity. What quantity would a profit-maximizing publisher choose? What price would it charge?

b. Compute marginal revenue. (Recall that $MR = \Delta TR\ /\ \Delta Q$.) How does marginal revenue compare to the price? Explain.

c. Graph the marginal-revenue, marginal-cost, and demand curves. At what quantity do the marginal-revenue and marginal-cost curves cross? What does this signify?

d. In your graph, shade in the deadweight loss. Explain in words what this means.

e. If the author were paid $3 million instead of $2 million to write the book, how would this affect the publisher's decision regarding the price to charge? Explain.

f. Suppose the publisher was not profit-maximizing but was concerned with maximizing economic efficiency. What price would it charge for the book? How much profit would it make at this price?

2. Suppose that a natural monopolist was required by law to charge average total cost. On a diagram, label the price charged and the deadweight loss to society relative to marginal-cost pricing.

3. Suppose the Clean Springs Water Company has a monopoly on bottled water sales in California. If the price of tap water increases, what is the change in Clean Springs' profit-maximizing levels of output, price, and profit? Explain in words and with a graph.

4. A small town is served by many competing supermarkets, which have constant marginal cost.

a. Using a diagram of the market for groceries, show the consumer surplus, producer surplus, and total surplus.

b. Now suppose that the independent supermarkets combine into one chain. Using a new diagram, show the new consumer surplus, producer surplus, and total surplus. Relative to the competitive market, what is the transfer from consumers to producers? What is the deadweight loss?

5. Johnny Rockabilly has just finished recording his latest CD. His record company's marketing department determines that the demand for the CD is as follows:

Price	Number of CDs
$24	10,000
22	20,000
20	30,000
18	40,000
16	50,000
14	60,000

The company can produce the CD with no fixed cost and a variable cost of $5 per CD.

a. Find total revenue for quantity equal to 10,000, 20,000, and so on. What is the marginal revenue for each 10,000 increase in the quantity sold?

b. What quantity of CDs would maximize profit? What would the price be? What would the profit be?

c. If you were Johnny's agent, what recording fee would you advise Johnny to demand from the record company? Why?

6. A company is considering building a bridge across a river. The bridge would cost $2 million to build and nothing to maintain. The following table shows the company's anticipated demand over the lifetime of the bridge:

Price per Crossing	Number of Crossings, in Thousands
$8	0
7	100
6	200
5	300
4	400
3	500
2	600
1	700
0	800

a. If the company were to build the bridge, what would be its profit-maximizing price? Would that be the efficient level of output? Why or why not?

b. If the company is interested in maximizing profit, should it build the bridge? What would be its profit or loss?

c. If the government were to build the bridge, what price should it charge?

d. Should the government build the bridge? Explain.

7. Larry, Curly, and Moe run the only saloon in town. Larry wants to sell as many drinks as possible without losing money. Curly wants the saloon to bring in as much revenue as possible. Moe wants to make the largest possible profits. Using a single diagram of the saloon's demand curve and its cost curves, show the price and quantity combinations favored by each of the three partners. Explain.

8. For many years, AT&T was a regulated monopoly, providing both local and long-distance telephone service.

a. Explain why long-distance phone service was originally a natural monopoly.

b. Over the past two decades, many companies have launched communication satellites, each of which can transmit a limited number of calls. How did the growing role of satellites change the cost structure of long-distance phone service?

After a lengthy legal battle with the government, AT&T agreed to compete with other companies in the long-distance market. It also agreed to spin off its local phone service into the "Baby Bells," which remain highly regulated.

c. Why might it be efficient to have competition in long-distance phone service and regulated monopolies in local phone service?

9. Consider the relationship between monopoly pricing and price elasticity of demand:

a. Explain why a monopolist will never produce a quantity at which the demand curve is inelastic. (Hint: If demand is inelastic and the firm raises its price, what happens to total revenue and total costs?)

b. Draw a diagram for a monopolist, precisely labeling the portion of the demand curve that is inelastic. (Hint: The answer is related to the marginal-revenue curve.)

c. On your diagram, show the quantity and price that maximizes total revenue.

10. If the government wanted to encourage a monopoly to produce the socially efficient quantity, should it use a per-unit tax or a per-unit subsidy? Explain how this tax or subsidy would achieve the socially efficient level of output. Among the various interested parties—the monopoly firm, the monopoly's consumers, and other taxpayers—who would support the policy and who would oppose it?

11. You live in a town with 300 adults and 200 children, and you are thinking about putting on a play to entertain your neighbors and make some money. A play has a fixed cost of $2,000, but selling an extra ticket has zero marginal cost. Here are the demand schedules for your two types of customer:

Price	Adults	Children
$10	0	0
9	100	0
8	200	0
7	300	0
6	300	0
5	300	100
4	300	200
3	300	200
2	300	200
1	300	200
0	300	200

a. To maximize profit, what price would you charge for an adult ticket? For a child's ticket? How much profit do you make?

b. The city council passes a law prohibiting you from charging different prices to different customers. What price do you set for a ticket now? How much profit do you make?

c. Who is worse off because of the law prohibiting price discrimination? Who is better off? (If you can, quantify the changes in welfare.)

d. If the fixed cost of the play were $2,500 rather than $2,000, how would your answers to parts (a), (b), and (c) change?

12. Based on market research, a recording company obtains the following information about the demand and production costs of its new CD:

$$Price = 1{,}000 - 10Q$$
$$Total\ Revenue = 1{,}000Q - 10Q^2$$
$$Marginal\ Revenue = 1{,}000 - 20Q$$
$$Marginal\ Cost = 100 + 10Q$$

where Q indicates the number of copies sold and P is the price in cents.

a. Find the price and quantity that maximizes the company's profit.

b. Find the price and quantity that would maximize social welfare.

c. Calculate the deadweight loss from monopoly.

d. Suppose, in addition to the costs above, the musician on the album has to be paid. The company is considering four options:
   i.   A flat fee of 2,000 cents
   ii. 50 percent of the profits
   iii. 150 cents per unit sold
   iv. 50 percent of the revenue
   For each option, calculate the profit-maximizing price and quantity. Which, if any, of these compensation schemes would alter the deadweight loss from monopoly? Explain.

13. Many schemes for price discriminating involve some cost. For example, discount coupons take up the time and resources of both the buyer and the seller. This question considers the implications of costly price discrimination. To keep things simple, let's assume that our monopolist's production costs are simply proportional to output so that average total cost and marginal cost are constant and equal to each other.

a. Draw the cost, demand, and marginal-revenue curves for the monopolist. Show the price the monopolist would charge without price discrimination.

b. In your diagram, mark the area equal to the monopolist's profit and call it X. Mark the area equal to consumer surplus and call it Y. Mark the area equal to the deadweight loss and call it Z.

c. Now suppose that the monopolist can perfectly price discriminate. What is the monopolist's profit? (Give your answer in terms of X, Y, and Z.)

d. What is the change in the monopolist's profit from price discrimination? What is the change in total surplus from price discrimination? Which change is larger? Explain. (Give your answer in terms of X, Y, and Z.)

e. Now suppose that there is some cost of price discrimination. To model this cost, let's assume that the monopolist has to pay a fixed cost C to price discriminate. How would a monopolist make the decision whether to pay this fixed cost? (Give your answer in terms of X, Y, Z, and C.)

f. How would a benevolent social planner, who cares about total surplus, decide whether the monopolist should price discriminate? (Give your answer in terms of X, Y, Z, and C.)

g. Compare your answers to parts (e) and (f). How does the monopolist's incentive to price discriminate differ from the social planner's? Is it possible that the monopolist will price discriminate even though it is not socially desirable?

Monopolistic Competition

Y ou walk into a bookstore to buy a book to read during your next vacation. On the store's shelves you find a Sue Grafton mystery, a Stephen King thriller, a Danielle Steel romance, a David McCullough history, and many other choices. When you pick out a book and buy it, what kind of market are you participating in?

On the one hand, the market for books seems competitive. As you look over the shelves at your bookstore, you find many authors and many publishers vying for your attention. A buyer in this market has thousands of competing products from which to choose. And because anyone can enter the industry by writing and publishing a book, the book business is not very profitable. For every highly paid novelist, there are hundreds of struggling ones.

On the other hand, the market for books seems monopolistic. Because each book is unique, publishers have some latitude in choosing what price to charge. The sellers in this market are price makers rather than price takers. And indeed, the price of books greatly exceeds marginal cost. The price of a typical hardcover novel, for instance, is about $25, whereas the cost of printing one additional copy of the novel is less than $5.

The market for novels fits neither the competitive nor the monopoly model. Instead, it is best described by the model of *monopolistic competition*, the subject of this chapter. The term "monopolistic competition" might at first seem to be an oxymoron, like "jumbo shrimp." But as we will see, monopolistically competitive industries are monopolistic in some ways and competitive in others. The model describes not only the publishing industry but also the market for many other goods and services.

BETWEEN MONOPOLY AND PERFECT COMPETITION

The previous two chapters analyzed markets with many competitive firms and markets with a single monopoly firm. In Chapter 14, we saw that the price in a perfectly competitive market always equals the marginal cost of production. We also saw that, in the long run, entry and exit drive economic profit to zero, so the price also equals average total cost. In Chapter 15, we saw how monopoly firms can use their market power to keep prices above marginal cost, leading to a positive economic profit for the firm and a deadweight loss for society. Competition and monopoly are extreme forms of market structure. Competition occurs when there are many firms in a market offering essentially identical products; monopoly occurs when there is only one firm in a market.

Although the cases of perfect competition and monopoly illustrate some important ideas about how markets work, most markets in the economy include elements of both these cases and, therefore, are not completely described by either of them. The typical firm in the economy faces competition, but the competition is not so rigorous as to make the firm a price taker like the firms analyzed in Chapter 14. The typical firm also has some degree of market power, but its market power is not so great that the firm can be described exactly by the monopoly model presented in Chapter 15. In other words, many industries fall somewhere between the polar cases of perfect competition and monopoly. Economists call this situation *imperfect competition.*

oligopoly
a market structure in which only a few sellers offer similar or identical products

One type of imperfectly competitive market is an **oligopoly**, which is a market with only a few sellers, each offering a product that is similar or identical to the products offered by other sellers. Economists measure a market's domination by a small number of firms with a statistic called the *concentration ratio*, which is the percentage of total output in the market supplied by the four largest firms. In the U.S. economy, most industries have a four-firm concentration ratio under 50 percent, but in some industries, the biggest firms play a more dominant role. Highly concentrated industries include breakfast cereal (which has a concentration ratio of 83 percent), aircraft manufacturing (85 percent), electric lamp bulbs (89 percent), household laundry equipment (90 percent), and cigarettes (99 percent). These industries are best described as oligopolies.

monopolistic competition
a market structure in which many firms sell products that are similar but not identical

A second type of imperfectly competitive market is called **monopolistic competition**. This describes a market structure in which there are many firms selling products that are similar but not identical. In a monopolistically competitive market, each firm has a monopoly over the product it makes, but many other firms make similar products that compete for the same customers.

To be more precise, monopolistic competition describes a market with the following attributes:

- *Many sellers:* There are many firms competing for the same group of customers.
- *Product differentiation:* Each firm produces a product that is at least slightly different from those of other firms. Thus, rather than being a price taker, each firm faces a downward-sloping demand curve.

- *Free entry and exit:* Firms can enter or exit the market without restriction. Thus, the number of firms in the market adjusts until economic profits are driven to zero.

A moment's thought reveals a long list of markets with these attributes: books, music CDs, movies, computer games, restaurants, piano lessons, cookies, furniture, and so on.

Monopolistic competition, like oligopoly, is a market structure that lies between the extreme cases of competition and monopoly. But oligopoly and monopolistic competition are quite different. Oligopoly departs from the perfectly competitive ideal of Chapter 14 because there are only a few sellers in the market. The small number of sellers makes rigorous competition less likely and strategic interactions among them vitally important. By contrast, under monopolistic competition, there are many sellers, each of which is small compared to the market. A monopolistically competitive market departs from the perfectly competitive ideal because each of the sellers offers a somewhat different product.

Figure 1 summarizes the four types of market structure. The first question to ask about any market is how many firms there are. If there is only one firm, the market is a monopoly. If there are only a few firms, the market is an oligopoly. If there are many firms, we need to ask another question: Do the firms sell identical or differentiated products? If the many firms sell differentiated products, the market is monopolistically competitive. If the many firms sell identical products, the market is perfectly competitive.

Because reality is never as clear-cut as theory, at times you may find it hard to decide what structure best describes a market. There is, for instance, no magic number that separates "few" from "many" when counting the number of firms. (Do the approximately dozen companies that now sell cars in the United States make this market an oligopoly or more competitive? The answer is open to debate.)

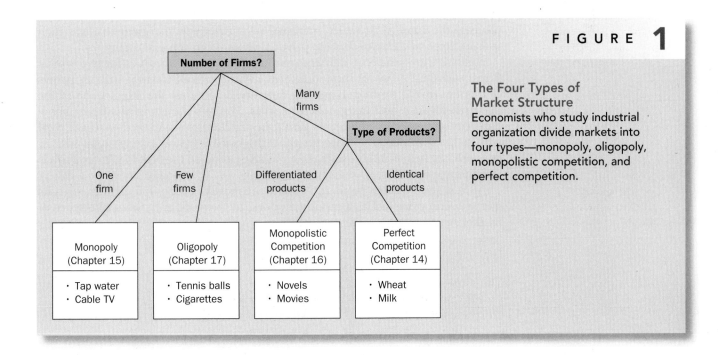

FIGURE 1

The Four Types of Market Structure
Economists who study industrial organization divide markets into four types—monopoly, oligopoly, monopolistic competition, and perfect competition.

Similarly, there is no sure way to determine when products are differentiated and when they are identical. (Are different brands of milk really the same? Again, the answer is debatable.) When analyzing actual markets, economists have to keep in mind the lessons learned from studying all types of market structure and then apply each lesson as it seems appropriate.

Now that we understand how economists define the various types of market structure, we can continue our analysis of them. In the next chapter we analyze oligopoly. In this chapter we examine monopolistic competition.

QUICK QUIZ   Define *oligopoly* and *monopolistic competition* and give an example of each.

COMPETITION WITH DIFFERENTIATED PRODUCTS

To understand monopolistically competitive markets, we first consider the decisions facing an individual firm. We then examine what happens in the long run as firms enter and exit the industry. Next, we compare the equilibrium under monopolistic competition to the equilibrium under perfect competition that we examined in Chapter 14. Finally, we consider whether the outcome in a monopolistically competitive market is desirable from the standpoint of society as a whole.

THE MONOPOLISTICALLY COMPETITIVE FIRM IN THE SHORT RUN

Each firm in a monopolistically competitive market is, in many ways, like a monopoly. Because its product is different from those offered by other firms, it faces a downward-sloping demand curve. (By contrast, a perfectly competitive firm faces a horizontal demand curve at the market price.) Thus, the monopolistically competitive firm follows a monopolist's rule for profit maximization: It chooses to produce the quantity at which marginal revenue equals marginal cost and then uses its demand curve to find the price at which it can sell that quantity.

Figure 2 shows the cost, demand, and marginal-revenue curves for two typical firms, each in a different monopolistically competitive industry. In both panels of this figure, the profit-maximizing quantity is found at the intersection of the marginal-revenue and marginal-cost curves. The two panels in this figure show different outcomes for the firm's profit. In panel (a), price exceeds average total cost, so the firm makes a profit. In panel (b), price is below average total cost. In this case, the firm is unable to make a positive profit, so the best the firm can do is to minimize its losses.

All this should seem familiar. A monopolistically competitive firm chooses its quantity and price just as a monopoly does. In the short run, these two types of market structure are similar.

THE LONG-RUN EQUILIBRIUM

The situations depicted in Figure 2 do not last long. When firms are making profits, as in panel (a), new firms have an incentive to enter the market. This entry increases the number of products from which customers can choose and,

Monopolistic competitors, like monopolists, maximize profit by producing the quantity at which marginal revenue equals marginal cost. The firm in panel (a) makes a profit because, at this quantity, price is above average total cost. The firm in panel (b) makes losses because, at this quantity, price is less than average total cost.

Monopolistic Competitors in the Short Run

(a) Firm Makes Profit
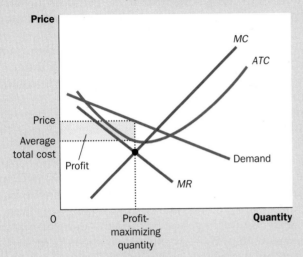

(b) Firm Makes Losses

"GIVEN THE DOWNWARD SLOPE OF OUR DEMAND CURVE, AND THE EASE WITH WHICH OTHER FIRMS CAN ENTER THE INDUSTRY, WE CAN STRENGTHEN OUR PROFIT POSITION ONLY BY EQUATING MARGINAL COST AND MARGINAL REVENUE. ORDER MORE JELLY BEANS."

therefore, reduces the demand faced by each firm already in the market. In other words, profit encourages entry, and entry shifts the demand curves faced by the incumbent firms to the left. As the demand for incumbent firms' products falls, these firms experience declining profit.

Conversely, when firms are making losses, as in panel (b), firms in the market have an incentive to exit. As firms exit, customers have fewer products from which to choose. This decrease in the number of firms expands the demand faced by those firms that stay in the market. In other words, losses encourage exit, and exit shifts the demand curves of the remaining firms to the right. As the demand for the remaining firms' products rises, these firms experience rising profit (that is, declining losses).

This process of entry and exit continues until the firms in the market are making exactly zero economic profit. Figure 3 depicts the long-run equilibrium. Once the market reaches this equilibrium, new firms have no incentive to enter, and existing firms have no incentive to exit.

Notice that the demand curve in this figure just barely touches the average-total-cost curve. Mathematically, we say the two curves are *tangent* to each other. These two curves must be tangent once entry and exit have driven profit to zero. Because profit per unit sold is the difference between price (found on the demand curve) and average total cost, the maximum profit is zero only if these two curves touch each other without crossing. Also note that this point of tangency occurs at the same quantity where marginal revenue equals marginal cost. That these two points line up is not a coincidence: It is required because this particular quantity maximizes profit and the maximum profit is exactly zero in the long run.

To sum up, two characteristics describe the long-run equilibrium in a monopolistically competitive market:

3 FIGURE

A Monopolistic Competitor in the Long Run
In a monopolistically competitive market, if firms are making profit, new firms enter, and the demand curves for the incumbent firms shift to the left. Similarly, if firms are making losses, old firms exit, and the demand curves of the remaining firms shift to the right. Because of these shifts in demand, a monopolistically competitive firm eventually finds itself in the long-run equilibrium shown here. In this long-run equilibrium, price equals average total cost, and the firm earns zero profit.

- As in a monopoly market, price exceeds marginal cost. This conclusion arises because profit maximization requires marginal revenue to equal marginal cost and because the downward-sloping demand curve makes marginal revenue less than the price.
- As in a competitive market, price equals average total cost. This conclusion arises because free entry and exit drive economic profit to zero.

The second characteristic shows how monopolistic competition differs from monopoly. Because a monopoly is the sole seller of a product without close substitutes, it can earn positive economic profit, even in the long run. By contrast, because there is free entry into a monopolistically competitive market, the economic profit of a firm in this type of market is driven to zero.

MONOPOLISTIC VERSUS PERFECT COMPETITION

Figure 4 compares the long-run equilibrium under monopolistic competition to the long-run equilibrium under perfect competition. (Chapter 14 discussed the equilibrium with perfect competition.) There are two noteworthy differences between monopolistic and perfect competition: excess capacity and the markup.

Panel (a) shows the long-run equilibrium in a monopolistically competitive market, and panel (b) shows the long-run equilibrium in a perfectly competitive market. Two differences are notable. (1) The perfectly competitive firm produces at the efficient scale, where average total cost is minimized. By contrast, the monopolistically competitive firm produces at less than the efficient scale. (2) Price equals marginal cost under perfect competition, but price is above marginal cost under monopolistic competition.

FIGURE 4

Monopolistic versus Perfect Competition

Excess Capacity   As we have just seen, entry and exit drive each firm in a monopolistically competitive market to a point of tangency between its demand and average-total-cost curves. Panel (a) of Figure 4 shows that the quantity of output at this point is smaller than the quantity that minimizes average total cost. Thus, under monopolistic competition, firms produce on the downward-sloping portion of their average-total-cost curves. In this way, monopolistic competition contrasts starkly with perfect competition. As panel (b) of Figure 4 shows, free entry in competitive markets drives firms to produce at the minimum of average total cost.

The quantity that minimizes average total cost is called the *efficient scale* of the firm. In the long run, perfectly competitive firms produce at the efficient scale, whereas monopolistically competitive firms produce below this level. Firms are said to have *excess capacity* under monopolistic competition. In other words, a monopolistically competitive firm, unlike a perfectly competitive firm, could increase the quantity it produces and lower the average total cost of production. The firm forgoes this opportunity because it would need to cut its price to sell the additional output. It is more profitable for a monopolistic competitor to continue operating with excess capacity.

Markup over Marginal Cost   A second difference between perfect competition and monopolistic competition is the relationship between price and marginal cost. For a competitive firm, such as that shown in panel (b) of Figure 4, price equals marginal cost. For a monopolistically competitive firm, such as that shown in panel (a), price exceeds marginal cost because the firm always has some market power.

How is this markup over marginal cost consistent with free entry and zero profit? The zero-profit condition ensures only that price equals average total cost. It does *not* ensure that price equals marginal cost. Indeed, in the long-run equilibrium, monopolistically competitive firms operate on the declining portion of their average-total-cost curves, so marginal cost is below average total cost. Thus, for price to equal average total cost, price must be above marginal cost.

In this relationship between price and marginal cost, we see a key behavioral difference between perfect competitors and monopolistic competitors. Imagine that you were to ask a firm the following question: "Would you like to see another customer come through your door ready to buy from you at your current price?" A perfectly competitive firm would answer that it didn't care. Because price exactly equals marginal cost, the profit from an extra unit sold is zero. By contrast, a monopolistically competitive firm is always eager to get another customer. Because its price exceeds marginal cost, an extra unit sold at the posted price means more profit.

According to an old quip, monopolistically competitive markets are those in which sellers send Christmas cards to the buyers. Trying to attract more customers makes sense only if price exceeds marginal cost.

MONOPOLISTIC COMPETITION AND THE WELFARE OF SOCIETY

Is the outcome in a monopolistically competitive market desirable from the standpoint of society as a whole? Can policymakers improve on the market outcome? In previous chapters we evaluated markets from the standpoint of efficiency—that is, whether society is getting the most it can out of its scarce resources. We learned that competitive markets lead to efficient outcomes, unless there are externalities, and that monopoly markets lead to deadweight losses. Monopolistically competitive markets are more complex than either of these polar cases, so evaluating welfare in these markets is a more subtle exercise.

One source of inefficiency is the markup of price over marginal cost. Because of the markup, some consumers who value the good at more than the marginal cost of production (but less than the price) will be deterred from buying it. Thus, a monopolistically competitive market has the normal deadweight loss of monopoly pricing.

Although this outcome is undesirable compared to the first-best outcome of price equal to marginal cost, there is no easy way for policymakers to fix the problem. To enforce marginal-cost pricing, policymakers would need to regulate all firms that produce differentiated products. Because such products are so common in the economy, the administrative burden of such regulation would be overwhelming.

Moreover, regulating monopolistic competitors would entail all the problems of regulating natural monopolies. In particular, because monopolistic competitors are making zero profits already, requiring them to lower their prices to equal marginal cost would cause them to make losses. To keep these firms in business, the government would need to help them cover these losses. Rather than raise taxes to pay for these subsidies, policymakers may decide it is better to live with the inefficiency of monopolistic pricing.

Another way in which monopolistic competition may be socially inefficient is that the number of firms in the market may not be "ideal." That is, there may be too much or too little entry. One way to think about this problem is in terms of the externalities associated with entry. Whenever a new firm considers entering the market with a new product, it considers only the profit it would make. Yet its entry would also have two effects that are external to the firm:

- *The product-variety externality:* Because consumers get some consumer surplus from the introduction of a new product, entry of a new firm conveys a positive externality on consumers.
- *The business-stealing externality:* Because other firms lose customers and profits from the entry of a new competitor, entry of a new firm imposes a negative externality on existing firms.

Thus, in a monopolistically competitive market, there are positive and negative externalities associated with the entry of new firms. Depending on which externality is larger, a monopolistically competitive market could have either too few or too many products.

Both of these externalities are closely related to the conditions for monopolistic competition. The product-variety externality arises because a new firm would offer a product different from those of the existing firms. The business-stealing externality arises because firms post a price above marginal cost and, therefore, are always eager to sell additional units. Conversely, because perfectly competitive firms produce identical goods and charge a price equal to marginal cost, neither of these externalities exists under perfect competition.

In The News

Insufficient Variety as a Market Failure

University of Pennsylvania economist Joel Waldfogel argues that, in the presence of large fixed costs, the market may insufficiently service customers with unusual preferences.

If the Shoe Doesn't Fit
By Joel Waldfogel

Last week, Nike unveiled a shoe designed specifically for American Indians. The sneaker has both a native-theme design and—more importantly—a wider shape to accommodate the distinctly shaped feet of American Indians. With diabetes and related conditions near epidemic levels in some tribes, American Indian leaders were happy to welcome this comfortable product. If anything, what seems odd is that it took so long. After all, free-market economists have told us for decades that we should rely on market decisions, not the government, to meet our needs, because it's the market that satisfies everyone's every desire.

And yet it turns out that it's the Indians' long wait for a good sneaker that's typical. For small groups with preferences outside the norm, the market often fails to deliver, as I argue in my new book, *The Tyranny of*

the Market: Why You Can't Always Get What You Want.

John Stuart Mill pointed out that voting gives rise to a tyranny of the majority. If we vote on what color shirts to make—or whether to make wide or narrow shoes—then the majority gets what it prefers, and the minority does not. The market, on the other hand, is supposed to work differ-

ently. As Milton Friedman eloquently put it in 1962, "the characteristic feature of action through political channels is that it tends to require or enforce substantial conformity. The great advantage of the market is that it permits wide diversity. Each man can vote, as it were, for the color of tie he wants and get it; he does not have to see what color the majority wants and then, if he is in the minority, submit." This is a wonderful argument. Except that for many products and for many people, it's wrong.

Two simple conditions that prevail in many markets mean that individual taste alone doesn't determine individual satisfaction. These conditions are (1) big setup costs and (2) preferences that differ across groups; when they're present, an individual's satisfaction is a function of how many people share his or her tastes. In other words, in these cases, markets share some of the objectionable features of government. They give bigger groups more and better options.

In the end, we can conclude only that monopolistically competitive markets do not have all the desirable welfare properties of perfectly competitive markets. That is, the invisible hand does not ensure that total surplus is maximized under monopolistic competition. Yet because the inefficiencies are subtle, hard to measure, and hard to fix, there is no easy way for public policy to improve the market outcome.

QUICK QUIZ List the three key attributes of monopolistic competition. • Draw and explain a diagram to show the long-run equilibrium in a monopolistically competitive market. How does this equilibrium differ from that in a perfectly competitive market?

In my research, I've discovered that this phenomenon is widespread. Ten years ago, I started studying radio-station listening patterns. I noticed that people listened to the radio more in metro areas of the United States with relatively large populations. This is not terribly surprising. In larger cities, more stations can attract enough listeners and advertising revenue to cover their costs and stay on the air. With more to choose from on the dial, residents tune in more. So, in this situation of high fixed costs (each station needs a following to keep broadcasting), people help one another by making more options viable.

But who benefits whom? When I looked at black and white listeners separately, I noticed something surprising. Blacks listen more in cities with larger black populations, and whites listen more in cities with larger white populations. Black listening does *not* increase where there's a higher white population, and white listening does not increase with a higher black population. Which means that while overall people help each other by increasing the number of stations on the dial, blacks do not help whites, and whites do not help blacks. Similar patterns arise for Hispanics and non-Hispanics.

A closer look at the data—necessary only because I'm a middle-aged white economist—showed why this was happening. Blacks and whites don't listen to the same radio stations. The black-targeted formats account for about two-thirds of black listening and only 3 percent of white listening. Similarly, the formats that attract the largest white audiences, like country, attract almost no blacks. This means that if you dropped Larry the Cable Guy and a few thousand of his friends from a helicopter (with parachutes) into a metro area, you'd create more demand for country and perhaps album-rock stations, which would be nice for white listeners. But the influx wouldn't help black listeners at all.

In this example, different population groups don't help each other, but they don't hurt each other, either. Sometimes, though, the effect that groups have on each other through the market is actually negative. Industries like daily newspapers offer essentially one product per market. Because the paper can be pitched to appeal to one group or another, the larger one group is, the less the product is tailored to anyone else. This is the tyranny of the majority translated almost literally from politics into markets.

This brings us back to Nike's new shoe. Foot Locker is full of options that fit me and most other Americans. But American Indians make up just 1.5 percent of the U.S. population, and with feet on average three sizes wider, they need different-sized shoes. If we had all voted in a national election on whether the Ministry of Shoes should make wide or typical-width shoes, we surely would have chosen the latter. That's why Friedman condemned government allocation. And yet the market made the same choice. If Nike's announcement looks like a solution to this problem of ignored minority preference, it really isn't. The company took too many years to bring the shoe on line, and according to the Associated Press, the new sneaker "represents less of a financial opportunity than a goodwill and branding effort."

The tyranny of the market arises elsewhere. With drug development costs near $1 billion, if you are going to be sick, hope that your disease is common enough to attract the interest of drug makers. If you want to fly from your town to Chicago, hope that your city is big enough to fill a plane every day.

When you're not so lucky, you benefit when the government steps in on your behalf, with subsidies for research on drugs for rare diseases or for air service to small locales. For a generation, influential economists have argued for letting the market decide a wide array of questions, to protect your freedom to choose whatever you want. This is true—if everyone agrees with you.

Source: *Slate*, Thursday, October 4, 2007.

ADVERTISING

It is nearly impossible to go through a typical day in a modern economy without being bombarded with advertising. Whether you are reading a newspaper, watching television, or driving down the highway, some firm will try to convince you to buy its product. Such behavior is a natural feature of monopolistic competition (as well as some oligopolistic industries). When firms sell differentiated products and charge prices above marginal cost, each firm has an incentive to advertise to attract more buyers to its particular product.

The amount of advertising varies substantially across products. Firms that sell highly differentiated consumer goods, such as over-the-counter drugs, perfumes, soft drinks, razor blades, breakfast cereals, and dog food, typically spend between 10 and 20 percent of revenue for advertising. Firms that sell industrial products, such as drill presses and communications satellites, typically spend very little on advertising. And firms that sell homogeneous products, such as wheat, peanuts, or crude oil, spend nothing at all.

For the economy as a whole, about 2 percent of total firm revenue is spent on advertising. This spending takes many forms, including commercials on television and radio, space in newspapers and magazines, direct mail, the yellow pages, billboards, and the Internet.

The Debate over Advertising

Is society wasting the resources it devotes to advertising? Or does advertising serve a valuable purpose? Assessing the social value of advertising is difficult and often generates heated argument among economists. Let's consider both sides of the debate.

The Critique of Advertising   Critics of advertising argue that firms advertise to manipulate people's tastes. Much advertising is psychological rather than informational. Consider, for example, the typical television commercial for some brand of soft drink. The commercial most likely does not tell the viewer about the product's price or quality. Instead, it might show a group of happy people at a party on a beach on a beautiful sunny day. In their hands are cans of the soft drink. The goal of the commercial is to convey a subconscious (if not subtle) message: "You too can have many friends and be happy, if only you drink our product." Critics of advertising argue that such a commercial creates a desire that otherwise might not exist.

Critics also argue that advertising impedes competition. Advertising often tries to convince consumers that products are more different than they truly are. By increasing the perception of product differentiation and fostering brand loyalty, advertising makes buyers less concerned with price differences among similar goods. With a less elastic demand curve, each firm charges a larger markup over marginal cost.

The Defense of Advertising   Defenders of advertising argue that firms use advertising to provide information to customers. Advertising conveys the prices of the goods offered for sale, the existence of new products, and the locations of retail outlets. This information allows customers to make better choices about what to buy and, thus, enhances the ability of markets to allocate resources efficiently.

Defenders also argue that advertising fosters competition. Because advertising allows customers to be more fully informed about all the firms in the market, customers can more easily take advantage of price differences. Thus, each firm has less market power. In addition, advertising allows new firms to enter more easily because it gives entrants a means to attract customers from existing firms.

Over time, policymakers have come to accept the view that advertising can make markets more competitive. One important example is the regulation of advertising for certain professions, such as lawyers, doctors, and pharmacists. In the past, these groups succeeded in getting state governments to prohibit advertising in their fields on the grounds that advertising was "unprofessional." In recent years, however, the courts have concluded that the primary effect of these restrictions on advertising was to curtail competition. They have, therefore, overturned many of the laws that prohibit advertising by members of these professions.

 ## ADVERTISING AND THE PRICE OF EYEGLASSES

What effect does advertising have on the price of a good? On the one hand, advertising might make consumers view products as being more different than they otherwise would. If so, it would make markets less competitive and firms' demand curves less elastic, and this would lead firms to charge higher prices. On the other hand, advertising might make it easier for consumers to find the firms offering the best prices. In this case, it would make markets more competitive and firms' demand curves more elastic, which would lead to lower prices.

In an article published in the *Journal of Law and Economics* in 1972, economist Lee Benham tested these two views of advertising. In the United States during the 1960s, the various state governments had vastly different rules about advertising by optometrists. Some states allowed advertising for eyeglasses and eye examinations. Many states, however, prohibited it. For example, the Florida law read as follows:

> It is unlawful for any person, firm, or corporation to . . . advertise either directly or indirectly by any means whatsoever any definite or indefinite price or credit terms on prescriptive or corrective lens, frames, complete prescriptive or corrective glasses, or any optometric service. . . . This section is passed in the interest of public health, safety, and welfare, and its provisions shall be liberally construed to carry out its objects and purposes.

Professional optometrists enthusiastically endorsed these restrictions on advertising.

Benham used the differences in state law as a natural experiment to test the two views of advertising. The results were striking. In those states that prohibited advertising, the average price paid for a pair of eyeglasses was $33. (This number is not as low as it seems, for this price is from 1963, when all prices were much lower than they are today. To convert 1963 prices into today's dollars, you can multiply them by about 7.) In states that did not restrict advertising, the average price was $26. Thus, advertising reduced average prices by more than 20 percent. In the market for eyeglasses, and probably in many other markets as well, advertising fosters competition and leads to lower prices for consumers.   ●

ADVERTISING AS A SIGNAL OF QUALITY

Many types of advertising contain little apparent information about the product being advertised. Consider a firm introducing a new breakfast cereal. A typical advertisement might have some highly paid actor eating the cereal and exclaiming how wonderful it tastes. How much information does the advertisement really provide?

The answer is more than you might think. Defenders of advertising argue that even advertising that appears to contain little hard information may in fact tell consumers something about product quality. The willingness of the firm to spend a large amount of money on advertising can itself be a *signal* to consumers about the quality of the product being offered.

FYI

Galbraith versus Hayek

Two great economists of the 20th century were John Kenneth Galbraith and Frederic Hayek. They held very different views about advertising, which reflected their views about the capitalist system more broadly.

John Kenneth Galbraith's most famous book was *The Affluent Society,* published in 1958. In it, he argued that corporations use advertising to create demand for products that people otherwise do not want or need. The market system should not be applauded, he believed, for satisfying desires that it has itself created. Galbraith was skeptical that economic growth was leading to higher levels of well-being, because people's aspirations were being made to keep pace with their increased material prosperity. He worried that as advertising and salesmanship artificially enhanced the desire for private goods, public spending on such items as better schools and better parks suffered. The result, according to Galbraith, was "private opulence and public squalor." Galbraith's policy recommendation was clear: Increase the size of government.

Frederic Hayek's most famous book was *The Road to Serfdom,* published in 1944. It argued that an expansive government inevitably means a sacrifice of personal freedoms. Hayek also wrote a

John Kenneth Galbraith

Frederic Hayek

well-known critique of Galbraith in 1961, addressing specifically Galbraith's view of advertising. Hayek observed that advertising was merely one example of a larger phenomenon: Our social environment creates many of our preferences. Literature, art, and music are all acquired tastes. A person's demand for hearing a Mozart concerto may have been created in a music appreciation class, but this fact does not make the desire less legitimate or the music professor a sinister influence. Hayek concluded, "It is because each individual producer thinks that the consumers can be persuaded to like his products that he endeavors to influence them. But though this effort is part of the influences which shape consumers' taste, no producer can in any real sense 'determine' them."

These two economists disagreed about the roles of advertising, markets, and government, but they did have one thing in common: great acclaim. In 1974, Hayek won the Nobel Prize in economics. In 2000, President Clinton awarded Galbraith the National Medal of Freedom. And even though their books are now many decades old, they are still well worth reading. The issues that Hayek and Galbraith addressed are timeless, and their insights apply as well to our economy as to their own.

Consider the problem facing two firms—Post and Kellogg. Each company has just come up with a recipe for a new cereal, which it would sell for $3 a box. To keep things simple, let's assume that the marginal cost of making cereal is zero, so the $3 is all profit. Each company knows that if it spends $10 million on advertising, it will get 1 million consumers to try its new cereal. And each company knows that if consumers like the cereal, they will buy it not once but many times.

First consider Post's decision. Based on market research, Post knows that its cereal is only mediocre. Although advertising would sell one box to each of 1 million consumers, the consumers would quickly learn that the cereal is not very good and stop buying it. Post decides it is not worth paying $10 million in advertising to get only $3 million in sales. So it does not bother to advertise. It sends its cooks back to the test kitchen to find another recipe.

Kellogg, on the other hand, knows that its cereal is great. Each person who tries it will buy a box a month for the next year. Thus, the $10 million in advertising will bring in $36 million in sales. Advertising is profitable here because Kellogg has a good product that consumers will buy repeatedly. Thus, Kellogg chooses to advertise.

Now that we have considered the behavior of the two firms, let's consider the behavior of consumers. We began by asserting that consumers are inclined to try a new cereal that they see advertised. But is this behavior rational? Should a consumer try a new cereal just because the seller has chosen to advertise it?

In fact, it may be completely rational for consumers to try new products that they see advertised. In our story, consumers decide to try Kellogg's new cereal because Kellogg advertises. Kellogg chooses to advertise because it knows that its cereal is quite good, while Post chooses not to advertise because it knows that its cereal is mediocre. By its willingness to spend money on advertising, Kellogg signals to consumers the quality of its cereal. Each consumer thinks, quite sensibly, "Boy, if the Kellogg Company is willing to spend so much money advertising this new cereal, it must be really good."

What is most surprising about this theory of advertising is that the content of the advertisement is irrelevant. Kellogg signals the quality of its product by its willingness to spend money on advertising. What the advertisements say is not as important as the fact that consumers know ads are expensive. By contrast, cheap advertising cannot be effective at signaling quality to consumers. In our example, if an advertising campaign cost less than $3 million, both Post and Kellogg would use it to market their new cereals. Because both good and mediocre cereals would be advertised, consumers could not infer the quality of a new cereal from the fact that it is advertised. Over time, consumers would learn to ignore such cheap advertising.

This theory can explain why firms pay famous actors large amounts of money to make advertisements that, on the surface, appear to convey no information at all. The information is not in the advertisement's content but simply in its existence and expense.

BRAND NAMES

Advertising is closely related to the existence of brand names. In many markets, there are two types of firms. Some firms sell products with widely recognized brand names, while other firms sell generic substitutes. For example, in a typical drugstore, you can find Bayer aspirin on the shelf next to generic aspirin. In a typical grocery store, you can find Pepsi next to less familiar colas. Most often, the firm with the brand name spends more on advertising and charges a higher price for its product.

Just as there is disagreement about the economics of advertising, there is disagreement about the economics of brand names. Let's consider both sides of the debate.

Critics argue that brand names cause consumers to perceive differences that do not really exist. In many cases, the generic good is almost indistinguishable from the brand-name good. Consumers' willingness to pay more for the brand-name good, these critics assert, is a form of irrationality fostered by advertising. Economist Edward Chamberlin, one of the early developers of the theory of monopolistic competition, concluded from this argument that brand names were bad for the economy. He proposed that the government discourage their use by refusing to enforce the exclusive trademarks that companies use to identify their products.

More recently, economists have defended brand names as a useful way for consumers to ensure that the goods they buy are of high quality. There are two related arguments. First, brand names provide consumers with *information* about quality when quality cannot be easily judged in advance of purchase. Second, brand names give firms an *incentive* to maintain high quality because firms have a financial stake in maintaining the reputation of their brand names.

To see how these arguments work in practice, consider a famous brand name: McDonald's hamburgers. Imagine that you are driving through an unfamiliar town and want to stop for lunch. You see a McDonald's and a local restaurant next to it. Which do you choose? The local restaurant may in fact offer better food at lower prices, but you have no way of knowing that. By contrast, McDonald's offers a consistent product across many cities. Its brand name is useful to you as a way of judging the quality of what you are about to buy.

The McDonald's brand name also ensures that the company has an incentive to maintain quality. For example, if some customers were to become ill from bad food sold at a McDonald's, the news would be disastrous for the company. McDonald's would lose much of the valuable reputation that it has built up with years of expensive advertising. As a result, it would lose sales and profit not just in the outlet that sold the bad food but in its many outlets throughout the country. By contrast, if some customers were to become ill from bad food at a local restaurant, that restaurant might have to close down, but the lost profits would be much smaller. Hence, McDonald's has a greater incentive to ensure that its food is safe.

The debate over brand names thus centers on the question of whether consumers are rational in preferring brand names to generic substitutes. Critics argue that brand names are the result of an irrational consumer response to advertising. Defenders argue that consumers have good reason to pay more for brand-name products because they can be more confident in the quality of these products.

QUICK QUIZ How might advertising make markets less competitive? How might it make markets more competitive? ● Give the arguments for and against brand names.

CONCLUSION

Monopolistic competition is true to its name: It is a hybrid of monopoly and competition. Like a monopoly, each monopolistic competitor faces a downward-sloping demand curve and, as a result, charges a price above marginal cost. As in a perfectly competitive market, there are many firms, and entry and exit drive the profit of each monopolistic competitor toward zero. Table 1 summarizes these lessons.

Because monopolistically competitive firms produce differentiated products, each firm advertises to attract customers to its own brand. To some extent, advertising manipulates consumers' tastes, promotes irrational brand loyalty, and impedes competition. To a larger extent, advertising provides information, establishes brand names of reliable quality, and fosters competition.

The theory of monopolistic competition seems to describe many markets in the economy. It is somewhat disappointing, therefore, that the theory does not yield simple and compelling advice for public policy. From the standpoint of the economic theorist, the allocation of resources in monopolistically competitive markets is not perfect. Yet from the standpoint of a practical policymaker, there may be little that can be done to improve it.

TABLE 1

Monopolistic Competition: Between Perfect Competition and Monopoly

	Market Structure		
	Perfect Competition	Monopolistic Competition	Monopoly
Features that all three market structures share			
Goal of firms	Maximize profits	Maximize profits	Maximize profits
Rule for maximizing	$MR = MC$	$MR = MC$	$MR = MC$
Can earn economic profits in the short run?	Yes	Yes	Yes
Features that monopolistic competition shares with monopoly			
Price taker?	Yes	No	No
Price	$P = MC$	$P > MC$	$P > MC$
Produces welfare-maximizing level of output?	Yes	No	No
Features that monopolistic competition shares with competition			
Number of firms	Many	Many	One
Entry in long run?	Yes	Yes	No
Can earn economic profits in long run?	No	No	Yes

SUMMARY

- A monopolistically competitive market is characterized by three attributes: many firms, differentiated products, and free entry.

- The equilibrium in a monopolistically competitive market differs from that in a perfectly competitive market in two related ways. First, each firm in a monopolistically competitive market has excess capacity. That is, it operates on the downward-sloping portion of the average-total-cost curve. Second, each firm charges a price above marginal cost.

- Monopolistic competition does not have all the desirable properties of perfect competition. There is the standard deadweight loss of monopoly caused by the markup of price over marginal cost. In addition, the number of firms (and thus the variety of products) can be too large or too small. In practice, the ability of policymakers to correct these inefficiencies is limited.

- The product differentiation inherent in monopolistic competition leads to the use of advertising and brand names. Critics of advertising and brand names argue that firms use them to manipulate consumers' tastes and to reduce competition. Defenders of advertising and brand names argue that firms use them to inform consumers and to compete more vigorously on price and product quality.

KEY CONCEPTS

oligopoly, *p. 346*   monopolistic competition, *p. 346*

QUESTIONS FOR REVIEW

1. Describe the three attributes of monopolistic competition. How is monopolistic competition like monopoly? How is it like perfect competition?
2. Draw a diagram depicting a firm that is making a profit in a monopolistically competitive market. Now show what happens to this firm as new firms enter the industry.
3. Draw a diagram of the long-run equilibrium in a monopolistically competitive market. How is price related to average total cost? How is price related to marginal cost?

4. Does a monopolistic competitor produce too much or too little output compared to the most efficient level? What practical considerations make it difficult for policymakers to solve this problem?
5. How might advertising reduce economic well-being? How might advertising increase economic well-being?
6. How might advertising with no apparent informational content in fact convey information to consumers?
7. Explain two benefits that might arise from the existence of brand names.

PROBLEMS AND APPLICATIONS

1. Among monopoly, oligopoly, monopolistic competition, and perfect competition, how would you classify the markets for each of the following drinks?
   a. tap water
   b. bottled water
   c. cola
   d. beer

2. Classify the following markets as perfectly competitive, monopolistic, or monopolistically competitive, and explain your answers.
   a. wooden no. 2 pencils
   b. copper
   c. local telephone service
   d. peanut butter
   e. lipstick

3. For each of the following characteristics, say whether it describes a perfectly competitive firm, a monopolistically competitive firm, both, or neither.
   a. Sells a product differentiated from that of its competitors
   b. Has marginal revenue less than price
   c. Earns economic profit in the long run
   d. Produces at minimum of average total cost in the long run
   e. Equates marginal revenue and marginal cost
   f. Charges a price above marginal cost

4. For each of the following characteristics, say whether it describes a monopoly firm, a monopolistically competitive firm, both, or neither.
   a. Faces a downward-sloping demand curve
   b. Has marginal revenue less than price
   c. Faces the entry of new firms selling similar products
   d. Earns economic profit in the long run
   e. Equates marginal revenue and marginal cost
   f. Produces the socially efficient quantity of output

5. You are hired as the consultant to a monopolistically competitive firm. The firm reports the following information about its price, marginal cost, and average total cost. Can the firm possibly be maximizing profit? If not, what should it do to increase profit? If the firm is profit maximizing, is the firm in a long-run equilibrium? If not, what will happen to restore long-run equilibrium?
   a. $P < MC, P > ATC$
   b. $P > MC, P < ATC$
   c. $P = MC, P > ATC$
   d. $P > MC, P = ATC$

6. Sparkle is one firm of many in the market for toothpaste, which is in long-run equilibrium.
   a. Draw a diagram showing Sparkle's demand curve, marginal-revenue curve, average-total-cost curve, and marginal-cost curve. Label Sparkle's profit-maximizing output and price.
   b. What is Sparkle's profit? Explain.
   c. On your diagram, show the consumer surplus derived from the purchase of Sparkle toothpaste. Also show the deadweight loss relative to the efficient level of output.
   d. If the government forced Sparkle to produce the efficient level of output, what would happen to the firm? What would happen to Sparkle's customers?

7. For each of the following pairs of firms, explain which firm would be more likely to engage in advertising:
   a. a family-owned farm or a family-owned restaurant
   b. a manufacturer of forklifts or a manufacturer of cars
   c. a company that invented a very comfortable razor or a company that invented a less comfortable razor

8. Sleek Sneakers Co. is one of many firms in the market for shoes.
   a. Assume that Sleek is currently earning short-run economic profits. On a correctly labeled diagram, show Sleek's profit-maximizing output and price, as well as the area representing profit.

   b. What happens to Sleek's price, output, and profit in the long run? Explain this change in words, and show it on a new diagram.

   c. Suppose that over time consumers become more focused on stylistic differences among shoe brands. How would this change in attitudes affect each firm's price elasticity of demand? In the long run, how will this change in demand affect Sleek's price, output, and profits?

   d. At the profit-maximizing price you identified in part (c), is Sleek's demand curve elastic or inelastic? Explain.

9. Thirty years ago, the market for chicken was perfectly competitive. Then Frank Perdue began marketing chicken under his name.

   a. How do you suppose Perdue created a brand name for chicken? What did he gain from doing so?

   b. What did society gain from having brand-name chicken? What did society lose?

10. The makers of Tylenol pain reliever do a lot of advertising and have loyal customers. In contrast, the makers of generic acetaminophen do no advertising, and their customers shop only for the lowest price. Assume that the marginal costs of Tylenol and generic acetaminophen are the same and constant.

   a. Draw a diagram showing Tylenol's demand, marginal-revenue, and marginal-cost curves. Label Tylenol's price and markup over marginal cost.

   b. Repeat part (a) for a producer of generic acetaminophen. How do the diagrams differ? Which company has the bigger markup? Explain.

   c. Which company has the bigger incentive for careful quality control? Why?

11. In a box in this chapter, economist Joel Waldfogel argues that a free market may fail to serve some customers in the presence of fixed costs. Let's analyze this claim with an example.

   a. Suppose that there are N people who might consume a product sold by a monopoly firm. Each person has demand of $q = 2 - P$, so total demand for this product is $Q = Nq = 2N - NP$, or $P = 2 - Q/N$. Graph this market demand curve.

   b. For this market demand curve, the equation for marginal revenue is $MR = 2 - 2Q/N$. Add this marginal revenue curve to your graph.

   c. To keep things simple, suppose that the marginal cost of producing this product is zero. What quantity would a profit-maximizing monopolist produce? What price would it charge? Show this price on your graph.

   d. Ignoring for the moment the fixed costs, calculate profits, consumer surplus, and total surplus at this profit-maximizing price. (These will be functions of N.)

   e. Suppose now that before making this product, the firm has to pay fixed costs of research and development equal to $3,000,000. How large does N need to be before the profit-maximizing firm chooses to pay the fixed cost and produce this product? How large does N need to be before it is socially efficient to pay the fixed cost?

   f. Discuss how this example relates to Waldfogel's arguments about the inefficiency of free markets.

Oligopoly

If you go to a store to buy tennis balls, you will probably come home with one of four brands: Wilson, Penn, Dunlop, or Spalding. These four companies make almost all the tennis balls sold in the United States. Together these firms determine the quantity of tennis balls produced and, given the market demand curve, the price at which tennis balls are sold.

The market for tennis balls is an example of an **oligopoly**. The essence of an oligopolistic market is that there are only a few sellers. As a result, the actions of any one seller in the market can have a large impact on the profits of all the other sellers. Oligopolistic firms are interdependent in a way that competitive firms are not. Our goal in this chapter is to see how this interdependence shapes the firms' behavior and what problems it raises for public policy.

The analysis of oligopoly offers an opportunity to introduce **game theory**, the study of how people behave in strategic situations. By "strategic" we mean a situation in which a person, when choosing among alternative courses of action, must consider how others might respond to the action he takes. Strategic thinking is crucial not only in checkers, chess, and tic-tac-toe but in many business decisions. Because oligopolistic markets have only a small number of firms, each firm must act strategically. Each firm knows that its profit depends not only on how much it produces but also on how much the other firms produce. In making its production decision, each firm in an oligopoly should consider how its decision might affect the production decisions of all the other firms.

oligopoly
a market structure in which only a few sellers offer similar or identical products

game theory
the study of how people behave in strategic situations

Game theory is not necessary for understanding competitive or monopoly markets. In a market that is either perfectly competitive or monopolistically competitive, each firm is so small compared to the market that strategic interactions with other firms are not important. In a monopolized market, strategic interactions are absent because the market has only one firm. But, as we will see, game theory is useful for understanding oligopolies and many other situations in which small numbers of players are interacting with one another. Game theory helps explain the strategies that people choose, whether they are playing tennis or selling tennis balls.

MARKETS WITH ONLY A FEW SELLERS

Because an oligopolistic market has only a small group of sellers, a key feature of oligopoly is the tension between cooperation and self-interest. The group of oligopolists is best off cooperating and acting like a monopolist—producing a small quantity of output and charging a price above marginal cost. Yet because each oligopolist cares only about its own profit, there are powerful incentives at work that hinder a group of firms from maintaining the monopoly outcome.

A Duopoly Example

To understand the behavior of oligopolies, let's consider an oligopoly with only two members, called a *duopoly*. Duopoly is the simplest type of oligopoly. Oligopolies with three or more members face the same problems as duopolies, so we do not lose much by starting with the simpler case.

Imagine a town in which only two residents—Jack and Jill—own wells that produce water safe for drinking. Each Saturday, Jack and Jill decide how many gallons of water to pump, bring the water to town, and sell it for whatever price the market will bear. To keep things simple, suppose that Jack and Jill can pump as much water as they want without cost. That is, the marginal cost of water equals zero.

Table 1 shows the town's demand schedule for water. The first column shows the total quantity demanded, and the second column shows the price. If the two well owners sell a total of 10 gallons of water, water goes for $110 a gallon. If they sell a total of 20 gallons, the price falls to $100 a gallon. And so on. If you graphed these two columns of numbers, you would get a standard downward-sloping demand curve.

The last column in Table 1 shows the total revenue from the sale of water. It equals the quantity sold times the price. Because there is no cost to pumping water, the total revenue of the two producers equals their total profit.

Let's now consider how the organization of the town's water industry affects the price of water and the quantity of water sold.

Competition, Monopolies, and Cartels

Before considering the price and quantity of water that would result from the duopoly of Jack and Jill, let's discuss briefly what the outcome would be if the water market were either perfectly competitive or monopolistic. These two polar cases are natural benchmarks.

Quantity	Price	Total Revenue (and total profit)
0 gallons	$120	$ 0
10	110	1,100
20	100	2,000
30	90	2,700
40	80	3,200
50	70	3,500
60	60	3,600
70	50	3,500
80	40	3,200
90	30	2,700
100	20	2,000
110	10	1,100
120	0	0

The Demand Schedule for Water

If the market for water were perfectly competitive, the production decisions of each firm would drive price equal to marginal cost. Because we have assumed that the marginal cost of pumping additional water is zero, the equilibrium price of water under perfect competition would be zero as well. The equilibrium quantity would be 120 gallons. The price of water would reflect the cost of producing it, and the efficient quantity of water would be produced and consumed.

Now consider how a monopoly would behave. Table 1 shows that total profit is maximized at a quantity of 60 gallons and a price of $60 a gallon. A profit-maximizing monopolist, therefore, would produce this quantity and charge this price. As is standard for monopolies, price would exceed marginal cost. The result would be inefficient, because the quantity of water produced and consumed would fall short of the socially efficient level of 120 gallons.

What outcome should we expect from our duopolists? One possibility is that Jack and Jill get together and agree on the quantity of water to produce and the price to charge for it. Such an agreement among firms over production and price is called **collusion**, and the group of firms acting in unison is called a **cartel**. Once a cartel is formed, the market is in effect served by a monopoly, and we can apply our analysis from Chapter 15. That is, if Jack and Jill were to collude, they would agree on the monopoly outcome because that outcome maximizes the total profit that the producers can get from the market. Our two producers would produce a total of 60 gallons, which would be sold at a price of $60 a gallon. Once again, price exceeds marginal cost, and the outcome is socially inefficient.

A cartel must agree not only on the total level of production but also on the amount produced by each member. In our case, Jack and Jill must agree on how to split between themselves the monopoly production of 60 gallons. Each member of the cartel will want a larger share of the market because a larger market share means larger profit. If Jack and Jill agreed to split the market equally, each would produce 30 gallons, the price would be $60 a gallon, and each would get a profit of $1,800.

collusion
an agreement among firms in a market about quantities to produce or prices to charge

cartel
a group of firms acting in unison

The Equilibrium for an Oligopoly

Oligopolists would like to form cartels and earn monopoly profits, but that is often impossible. Squabbling among cartel members over how to divide the profit in the market can make agreement among them difficult. In addition, antitrust laws prohibit explicit agreements among oligopolists as a matter of public policy. Even talking about pricing and production restrictions with competitors can be a criminal offense. Let's therefore consider what happens if Jack and Jill decide separately how much water to produce.

At first, one might expect Jack and Jill to reach the monopoly outcome on their own, because this outcome maximizes their joint profit. In the absence of a binding agreement, however, the monopoly outcome is unlikely. To see why, imagine that Jack expects Jill to produce only 30 gallons (half of the monopoly quantity). Jack would reason as follows:

"I could produce 30 gallons as well. In this case, a total of 60 gallons of water would be sold at a price of $60 a gallon. My profit would be $1,800 (30 gallons × $60 a gallon). Alternatively, I could produce 40 gallons. In this case, a total of 70 gallons of water would be sold at a price of $50 a gallon. My profit would be $2,000 (40 gallons × $50 a gallon). Even though total profit in the market would fall, my profit would be higher, because I would have a larger share of the market."

Of course, Jill might reason the same way. If so, Jack and Jill would each bring 40 gallons to town. Total sales would be 80 gallons, and the price would fall to $40. Thus, if the duopolists individually pursue their own self-interest when deciding how much to produce, they produce a total quantity greater than the monopoly quantity, charge a price lower than the monopoly price, and earn total profit less than the monopoly profit.

Although the logic of self-interest increases the duopoly's output above the monopoly level, it does not push the duopolists to reach the competitive allocation. Consider what happens when each duopolist is producing 40 gallons. The price is $40, and each duopolist makes a profit of $1,600. In this case, Jack's self-interested logic leads to a different conclusion:

"Right now, my profit is $1,600. Suppose I increase my production to 50 gallons. In this case, a total of 90 gallons of water would be sold, and the price would be $30 a gallon. Then my profit would be only $1,500. Rather than increasing production and driving down the price, I am better off keeping my production at 40 gallons."

The outcome in which Jack and Jill each produce 40 gallons looks like some sort of equilibrium. In fact, this outcome is called a Nash equilibrium. (It is named after economic theorist John Nash, whose life was portrayed in the book and movie *A Beautiful Mind*.) A **Nash equilibrium** is a situation in which economic actors interacting with one another each choose their best strategy given the strategies the others have chosen. In this case, given that Jill is producing 40 gallons, the best strategy for Jack is to produce 40 gallons. Similarly, given that Jack is producing 40 gallons, the best strategy for Jill is to produce 40 gallons. Once they reach this Nash equilibrium, neither Jack nor Jill has an incentive to make a different decision.

This example illustrates the tension between cooperation and self-interest. Oligopolists would be better off cooperating and reaching the monopoly outcome. Yet because they pursue their own self-interest, they do not end up reaching the monopoly outcome and maximizing their joint profit. Each oligopolist is tempted to raise production and capture a larger share of the market. As each of them tries to do this, total production rises, and the price falls.

Nash equilibrium
a situation in which economic actors interacting with one another each choose their best strategy given the strategies that all the other actors have chosen

CHAPTER 17 OLIGOPOLY 369

At the same time, self-interest does not drive the market all the way to the competitive outcome. Like monopolists, oligopolists are aware that increasing the amount they produce reduces the price of their product, which in turn affects profits. Therefore, they stop short of following the competitive firm's rule of producing up to the point where price equals marginal cost.

In summary, *when firms in an oligopoly individually choose production to maximize profit, they produce a quantity of output greater than the level produced by monopoly and less than the level produced by competition. The oligopoly price is less than the monopoly price but greater than the competitive price (which equals marginal cost).*

HOW THE SIZE OF AN OLIGOPOLY AFFECTS THE MARKET OUTCOME

We can use the insights from this analysis of duopoly to discuss how the size of an oligopoly is likely to affect the outcome in a market. Suppose, for instance, that John and Joan suddenly discover water sources on their property and join Jack and Jill in the water oligopoly. The demand schedule in Table 1 remains the same, but now more producers are available to satisfy this demand. How would an increase in the number of sellers from two to four affect the price and quantity of water in the town?

If the sellers of water could form a cartel, they would once again try to maximize total profit by producing the monopoly quantity and charging the monopoly price. Just as when there were only two sellers, the members of the cartel would need to agree on production levels for each member and find some way to enforce the agreement. As the cartel grows larger, however, this outcome is less likely. Reaching and enforcing an agreement becomes more difficult as the size of the group increases.

If the oligopolists do not form a cartel—perhaps because the antitrust laws prohibit it—they must each decide on their own how much water to produce. To see how the increase in the number of sellers affects the outcome, consider the decision facing each seller. At any time, each well owner has the option to raise production by 1 gallon. In making this decision, the well owner weighs two effects:

- *The output effect:* Because price is above marginal cost, selling 1 more gallon of water at the going price will raise profit.
- *The price effect:* Raising production will increase the total amount sold, which will lower the price of water and lower the profit on all the other gallons sold.

If the output effect is larger than the price effect, the well owner will increase production. If the price effect is larger than the output effect, the owner will not raise production. (In fact, in this case, it is profitable to reduce production.) Each oligopolist continues to increase production until these two marginal effects exactly balance, taking the other firms' production as given.

Now consider how the number of firms in the industry affects the marginal analysis of each oligopolist. The larger the number of sellers, the less each seller is concerned about its own impact on the market price. That is, as the oligopoly grows in size, the magnitude of the price effect falls. When the oligopoly grows very large, the price effect disappears altogether. That is, the production decision of an individual firm no longer affects the market price. In this extreme case, each firm takes the market price as given when deciding how much to produce. It increases production as long as price is above marginal cost.

We can now see that a large oligopoly is essentially a group of competitive firms. A competitive firm considers only the output effect when deciding how much to produce: Because a competitive firm is a price taker, the price effect is absent. Thus, *as the number of sellers in an oligopoly grows larger, an oligopolistic market looks more and more like a competitive market. The price approaches marginal cost, and the quantity produced approaches the socially efficient level.*

This analysis of oligopoly offers a new perspective on the effects of international trade. Imagine that Toyota and Honda are the only automakers in Japan, Volkswagen and BMW are the only automakers in Germany, and Ford and General Motors are the only automakers in the United States. If these nations prohibited international trade in autos, each would have an auto oligopoly with only two members, and the market outcome would likely depart substantially from the competitive ideal. With international trade, however, the car market is a world market, and the oligopoly in this example has six members. Allowing free trade increases the number of producers from which each consumer can choose, and this increased competition keeps prices closer to marginal cost. Thus, the theory of oligopoly provides another reason, in addition to the theory of comparative advantage discussed in Chapter 3, why all countries can benefit from free trade.

QUICK QUIZ If the members of an oligopoly could agree on a total quantity to produce, what quantity would they choose? ● If the oligopolists do not act together but instead make production decisions individually, do they produce a total quantity more or less than in your answer to the previous question? Why?

THE ECONOMICS OF COOPERATION

As we have seen, oligopolies would like to reach the monopoly outcome, but doing so requires cooperation, which at times is difficult to establish and maintain. In this section we look more closely at the problems that arise when cooperation among actors is desirable but difficult. To analyze the economics of cooperation, we need to learn a little about game theory.

In particular, we focus on an important "game" called the **prisoners' dilemma**. This game provides insight into why cooperation is difficult. Many times in life, people fail to cooperate with one another even when cooperation would make them all better off. An oligopoly is just one example. The story of the prisoners' dilemma contains a general lesson that applies to any group trying to maintain cooperation among its members.

prisoners' dilemma
a particular "game" between two captured prisoners that illustrates why cooperation is difficult to maintain even when it is mutually beneficial

THE PRISONERS' DILEMMA

The prisoners' dilemma is a story about two criminals who have been captured by the police. Let's call them Bonnie and Clyde. The police have enough evidence to convict Bonnie and Clyde of the minor crime of carrying an unregistered gun, so that each would spend a year in jail. The police also suspect that the two criminals have committed a bank robbery together, but they lack hard evidence to convict them of this major crime. The police question Bonnie and Clyde in separate rooms, and they offer each of them the following deal:

"Right now, we can lock you up for 1 year. If you confess to the bank robbery and implicate your partner, however, we'll give you immunity and you can go free. Your partner will get 20 years in jail. But if you both confess to the crime, we won't need your testimony and we can avoid the cost of a trial, so you will each get an intermediate sentence of 8 years."

If Bonnie and Clyde, heartless bank robbers that they are, care only about their own sentences, what would you expect them to do? Figure 1 shows their choices. Each prisoner has two strategies: confess or remain silent. The sentence each prisoner gets depends on the strategy he or she chooses and the strategy chosen by his or her partner in crime.

Consider first Bonnie's decision. She reasons as follows: "I don't know what Clyde is going to do. If he remains silent, my best strategy is to confess, since then I'll go free rather than spending a year in jail. If he confesses, my best strategy is still to confess, since then I'll spend 8 years in jail rather than 20. So, regardless of what Clyde does, I am better off confessing."

In the language of game theory, a strategy is called a **dominant strategy** if it is the best strategy for a player to follow regardless of the strategies pursued by other players. In this case, confessing is a dominant strategy for Bonnie. She spends less time in jail if she confesses, regardless of whether Clyde confesses or remains silent.

dominant strategy
a strategy that is best for a player in a game regardless of the strategies chosen by the other players

Now consider Clyde's decision. He faces the same choices as Bonnie, and he reasons in much the same way. Regardless of what Bonnie does, Clyde can reduce his jail time by confessing. In other words, confessing is also a dominant strategy for Clyde.

In the end, both Bonnie and Clyde confess, and both spend 8 years in jail. Yet, from their standpoint, this is a terrible outcome. If they had *both* remained silent, both of them would have been better off, spending only 1 year in jail on the gun charge. Because each pursues his or her own interests, the two prisoners together reach an outcome that is worse for each of them.

You might have thought that Bonnie and Clyde would have foreseen this situation and planned ahead. But even with advanced planning, they would still run into problems. Imagine that, before the police captured Bonnie and Clyde, the two criminals had made a pact not to confess. Clearly, this agreement would

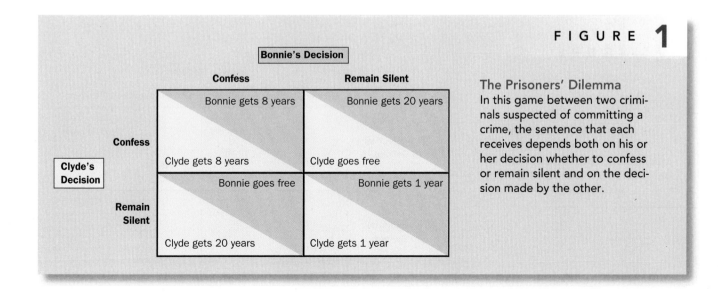

FIGURE 1

The Prisoners' Dilemma
In this game between two criminals suspected of committing a crime, the sentence that each receives depends both on his or her decision whether to confess or remain silent and on the decision made by the other.

make them both better off *if* they both lived up to it, because they would each spend only 1 year in jail. But would the two criminals in fact remain silent, simply because they had agreed to? Once they are being questioned separately, the logic of self-interest takes over and leads them to confess. Cooperation between the two prisoners is difficult to maintain, because cooperation is individually irrational.

OLIGOPOLIES AS A PRISONERS' DILEMMA

What does the prisoners' dilemma have to do with markets and imperfect competition? It turns out that the game oligopolists play in trying to reach the monopoly outcome is similar to the game that the two prisoners play in the prisoners' dilemma.

Consider again the choices facing Jack and Jill. After prolonged negotiation, the two suppliers of water agree to keep production at 30 gallons, so that the price will be kept high and together they will earn the maximum profit. After they agree on production levels, however, each of them must decide whether to cooperate and live up to this agreement or to ignore it and produce at a higher level. Figure 2 shows how the profits of the two producers depend on the strategies they choose.

Suppose you are Jack. You might reason as follows: "I could keep production low at 30 gallons as we agreed, or I could raise my production and sell 40 gallons. If Jill lives up to the agreement and keeps her production at 30 gallons, then I earn profit of $2,000 with high production and $1,800 with low production. In this case, I am better off with high production. If Jill fails to live up to the agreement and produces 40 gallons, then I earn $1,600 with high production and $1,500 with low production. Once again, I am better off with high production. So, regardless of what Jill chooses to do, I am better off reneging on our agreement and producing at a high level."

Producing 40 gallons is a dominant strategy for Jack. Of course, Jill reasons in exactly the same way, and so both produce at the higher level of 40 gallons. The result is the inferior outcome (from Jack and Jill's standpoint) with low profits for each of the two producers.

2 FIGURE

Jack and Jill's Oligopoly Game
In this game between Jack and Jill, the profit that each earns from selling water depends on both the quantity he or she chooses to sell and the quantity the other chooses to sell.

		Jack's Decision	
		High production: 40 Gallons	Low production: 30 Gallons
Jill's Decision	**High production: 40 Gallons**	Jack gets $1,600 profit / Jill gets $1,600 profit	Jack gets $1,500 profit / Jill gets $2,000 profit
	Low production: 30 Gallons	Jack gets $2,000 profit / Jill gets $1,500 profit	Jack gets $1,800 profit / Jill gets $1,800 profit

This example illustrates why oligopolies have trouble maintaining monopoly profits. The monopoly outcome is jointly rational for the oligopoly, but each oligopolist has an incentive to cheat. Just as self-interest drives the prisoners in the prisoners' dilemma to confess, self-interest makes it difficult for the oligopoly to maintain the cooperative outcome with low production, high prices, and monopoly profits.

 ## OPEC AND THE WORLD OIL MARKET

Our story about the town's market for water is fictional, but if we change water to crude oil, and Jack and Jill to Iran and Iraq, the story is close to being true. Much of the world's oil is produced by a few countries, mostly in the Middle East. These countries together make up an oligopoly. Their decisions about how much oil to pump are much the same as Jack and Jill's decisions about how much water to pump.

The countries that produce most of the world's oil have formed a cartel, called the Organization of Petroleum Exporting Countries (OPEC). As originally formed in 1960, OPEC included Iran, Iraq, Kuwait, Saudi Arabia, and Venezuela. By 1973, eight other nations had joined: Qatar, Indonesia, Libya, the United Arab Emirates, Algeria, Nigeria, Ecuador, and Gabon. These countries control about three-fourths of the world's oil reserves. Like any cartel, OPEC tries to raise the price of its product through a coordinated reduction in quantity produced. OPEC tries to set production levels for each of the member countries.

The problem that OPEC faces is much the same as the problem that Jack and Jill face in our story. The OPEC countries would like to maintain a high price of oil. But each member of the cartel is tempted to increase its production to get a larger share of the total profit. OPEC members frequently agree to reduce production but then cheat on their agreements.

OPEC was most successful at maintaining cooperation and high prices in the period from 1973 to 1985. The price of crude oil rose from $3 a barrel in 1972 to $11 in 1974 and then to $35 in 1981. But in the mid-1980s, member countries began arguing about production levels, and OPEC became ineffective at maintaining cooperation. By 1986 the price of crude oil had fallen back to $13 a barrel.

In recent years, the members of OPEC have continued to meet regularly, but the cartel has been less successful at reaching and enforcing agreements. Although the price of oil rose significantly in 2007 and 2008, the primary cause was increased demand in the world oil market, in part from a booming Chinese economy, rather than restricted supply. While this lack of cooperation among OPEC nations has reduced the profits of the oil-producing nations below what they might have been, it has benefited consumers around the world.   ●

OTHER EXAMPLES OF THE PRISONERS' DILEMMA

We have seen how the prisoners' dilemma can be used to understand the problem facing oligopolies. The same logic applies to many other situations as well. Here we consider two examples in which self-interest prevents cooperation and leads to an inferior outcome for the parties involved.

Arms Races   In the decades after World War II, the world's two superpowers— the United States and the Soviet Union—were engaged in a prolonged competition over military power. This topic motivated some of the early work on game theory. The game theorists pointed out that an arms race is much like the prisoners' dilemma.

To see this, consider the decisions of the United States and the Soviet Union about whether to build new weapons or to disarm. Each country prefers to have more arms than the other because a larger arsenal would give it more influence in world affairs. But each country also prefers to live in a world safe from the other country's weapons.

Figure 3 shows the deadly game. If the Soviet Union chooses to arm, the United States is better off doing the same to prevent the loss of power. If the Soviet Union chooses to disarm, the United States is better off arming because doing so would make it more powerful. For each country, arming is a dominant strategy. Thus, each country chooses to continue the arms race, resulting in the inferior outcome with both countries at risk.

Throughout the era of the Cold War, the United States and the Soviet Union attempted to solve this problem through negotiation and agreements over arms control. The problems that the two countries faced were similar to those that oligopolists encounter in trying to maintain a cartel. Just as oligopolists argue over production levels, the United States and the Soviet Union argued over the amount of arms that each country would be allowed. And just as cartels have trouble enforcing production levels, the United States and the Soviet Union each feared that the other country would cheat on any agreement. In both arms races and oligopolies, the relentless logic of self-interest drives the participants toward a noncooperative outcome that is worse for each party.

Common Resources In Chapter 11 we saw that people tend to overuse common resources. One can view this problem as an example of the prisoners' dilemma.

Imagine that two oil companies—Exxon and Texaco—own adjacent oil fields. Under the fields is a common pool of oil worth $12 million. Drilling a well to recover the oil costs $1 million. If each company drills one well, each will get half of the oil and earn a $5 million profit ($6 million in revenue minus $1 million in costs).

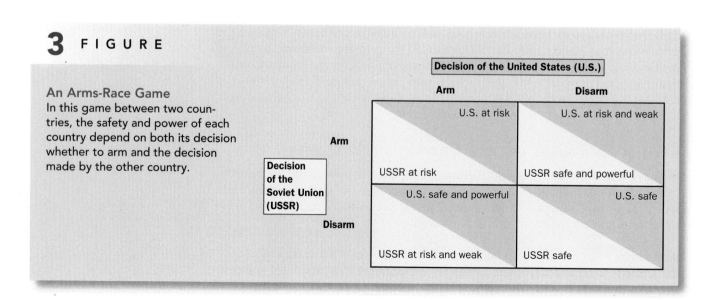

3 FIGURE

An Arms-Race Game
In this game between two countries, the safety and power of each country depend on both its decision whether to arm and the decision made by the other country.

	Decision of the United States (U.S.)	
	Arm	**Disarm**
Arm	U.S. at risk / USSR at risk	U.S. at risk and weak / USSR safe and powerful
Disarm	U.S. safe and powerful / USSR at risk and weak	U.S. safe / USSR safe

Decision of the Soviet Union (USSR)

Because the pool of oil is a common resource, the companies will not use it efficiently. Suppose that either company could drill a second well. If one company has two of the three wells, that company gets two-thirds of the oil, which yields a profit of $6 million. The other company gets one-third of the oil, for a profit of $3 million. Yet if each company drills a second well, the two companies again split the oil. In this case, each bears the cost of a second well, so profit is only $4 million for each company.

Figure 4 shows the game. Drilling two wells is a dominant strategy for each company. Once again, the self-interest of the two players leads them to an inferior outcome.

THE PRISONERS' DILEMMA AND THE WELFARE OF SOCIETY

The prisoners' dilemma describes many of life's situations, and it shows that cooperation can be difficult to maintain, even when cooperation would make both players in the game better off. Clearly, this lack of cooperation is a problem for those involved in these situations. But is lack of cooperation a problem from the standpoint of society as a whole? The answer depends on the circumstances.

In some cases, the noncooperative equilibrium is bad for society as well as the players. In the arms-race game in Figure 3, both the United States and the Soviet Union end up at risk. In the common-resources game in Figure 4, the extra wells dug by Texaco and Exxon are pure waste. In both cases, society would be better off if the two players could reach the cooperative outcome.

By contrast, in the case of oligopolists trying to maintain monopoly profits, lack of cooperation is desirable from the standpoint of society as a whole. The monopoly outcome is good for the oligopolists, but it is bad for the consumers of the product. As we first saw in Chapter 7, the competitive outcome is best for society because it maximizes total surplus. When oligopolists fail to cooperate, the quantity they produce is closer to this optimal level. Put differently, the invisible hand guides markets to allocate resources efficiently only when markets are

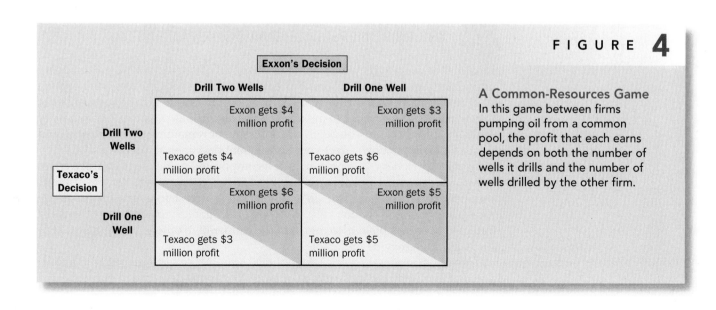

FIGURE 4

A Common-Resources Game
In this game between firms pumping oil from a common pool, the profit that each earns depends on both the number of wells it drills and the number of wells drilled by the other firm.

competitive, and markets are competitive only when firms in the market fail to cooperate with one another.

Similarly, consider the case of the police questioning two suspects. Lack of cooperation between the suspects is desirable, for it allows the police to convict more criminals. The prisoners' dilemma is a dilemma for the prisoners, but it can be a boon to everyone else.

WHY PEOPLE SOMETIMES COOPERATE

The prisoners' dilemma shows that cooperation is difficult. But is it impossible? Not all prisoners, when questioned by the police, decide to turn in their partners in crime. Cartels sometimes manage to maintain collusive arrangements, despite the incentive for individual members to defect. Very often, players can solve the prisoners' dilemma because they play the game not once but many times.

To see why cooperation is easier to enforce in repeated games, let's return to our duopolists, Jack and Jill, whose choices were given in Figure 2. Jack and Jill would like to agree to maintain the monopoly outcome in which each produces 30 gallons. Yet, if Jack and Jill are to play this game only once, neither has any incentive to live up to this agreement. Self-interest drives each of them to renege and choose the dominant strategy of 40 gallons.

Now suppose that Jack and Jill know that they will play the same game every week. When they make their initial agreement to keep production low, they can also specify what happens if one party reneges. They might agree, for instance, that once one of them reneges and produces 40 gallons, both of them will produce 40 gallons forever after. This penalty is easy to enforce, for if one party is producing at a high level, the other has every reason to do the same.

The threat of this penalty may be all that is needed to maintain cooperation. Each person knows that defecting would raise his or her profit from $1,800 to $2,000. But this benefit would last for only one week. Thereafter, profit would fall to $1,600 and stay there. As long as the players care enough about future profits, they will choose to forgo the one-time gain from defection. Thus, in a game of repeated prisoners' dilemma, the two players may well be able to reach the cooperative outcome.

 ## THE PRISONERS' DILEMMA TOURNAMENT

Imagine that you are playing a game of prisoners' dilemma with a person being "questioned" in a separate room. Moreover, imagine that you are going to play not once but many times. Your score at the end of the game is the total number of years in jail. You would like to make this score as small as possible. What strategy would you play? Would you begin by confessing or remaining silent? How would the other player's actions affect your subsequent decisions about confessing?

Repeated prisoners' dilemma is quite a complicated game. To encourage cooperation, players must penalize each other for not cooperating. Yet the strategy described earlier for Jack and Jill's water cartel—defect forever as soon as the other player defects—is not very forgiving. In a game repeated many times, a strategy that allows players to return to the cooperative outcome after a period of noncooperation may be preferable.

To see what strategies work best, political scientist Robert Axelrod held a tournament. People entered by sending computer programs designed to play repeated

In The News

Aumann and Schelling

In 2005, two prominent game theorists won the Nobel Prize.

Economic Work on "Game Theory" Wins Nobel Prize

By Jon E. Hilsenrath

The Cold War was a period of conflict management on a grand, frightening scale, and two researchers who explained how individuals negotiate such conflict won the Nobel Prize in economics for work that grew out of the period.

Thomas Schelling, an 84-year-old retired University of Maryland professor who served long stints as an adviser to the U.S. government, has written on managing the U.S.-Soviet buildup of nuclear arms and extended his theories to subjects such as drug addiction, racial segregation and global warming. Robert Aumann, 75, a mathematician by training and professor at Hebrew University in Jerusalem, added analytical rigor to the field that both professors helped to create, which has come to be known in economics as "game theory."

The two will share the 10 million kronor prize ($1.3 million) awarded by the Royal Swedish Academy of Sciences. Mr. Schelling is an American citizen, and Mr. Aumann is an American and Israeli citizen.

Game theory is the study of strategy and how people make decisions when interacting in conflict with one another. In a game of chess, two players act not only based on their own strategy, but also on expectations of how their opponent will behave and react. In the 1940s and 1950s, economists began to see their models of individual behavior needed to be less robotic and should reflect the kind of strategic dance found in games like chess.

The movement toward game theory was driven in part by mathematicians like Mr. Aumann and an associate from his days at the Massachusetts Institute of Technology named John Nash, whose life was portrayed in the movie "A Beautiful Mind." Mr. Nash won the economics prize with two others in 1994.

While Messrs. Nash and Aumann used math to give precise formulations to game theory, Prof. Schelling sought to give it practical meaning. He explained, for instance, how decision makers often find it advantageous to limit their own options to get concessions from an opponent. In some cases, for instance, it might be wise for a general to burn bridges behind his troops to send a credible and possibly game-changing message toward his enemy that he has no intention of retreating.

Economists have since applied this idea of "precommitment" to other areas, including business. Some companies, for example, might find it advantageous to build too much capacity, to alert would-be competitors that entering a market will lead them into a price war. . . .

Messrs. Schelling and Aumann both came of age during the Cold War, when fears of a nuclear confrontation between the Soviet Union and the U.S. led scholars to examine the motivations and decision-making of both sides. . . .

Prof. Schelling extended his research beyond the Cold War. For instance, his work has shown how even small differences in preferences between groups of people could lead to large-scale segregation in cities. It also has described drug addiction as a game against oneself. Someone who is trying to quit smoking, for instance, might flush cigarettes down the toilet because he realizes that "some time late at night he won't be able to resist them."

Source: *The Wall Street Journal*, October 11, 2005.

prisoners' dilemma. Each program then played the game against all the other programs. The "winner" was the program that received the fewest total years in jail.

The winner turned out to be a simple strategy called *tit-for-tat.* According to tit-for-tat, a player should start by cooperating and then do whatever the other player did last time. Thus, a tit-for-tat player cooperates until the other player defects; she then defects until the other player cooperates again. In other words, this strategy starts out friendly, penalizes unfriendly players, and forgives them if warranted. To Axelrod's surprise, this simple strategy did better than all the more complicated strategies that people had sent in.

The tit-for-tat strategy has a long history. It is essentially the biblical strategy of "an eye for an eye, a tooth for a tooth." The prisoners' dilemma tournament suggests that this may be a good rule of thumb for playing some of the games of life. ●

QUICK QUIZ Tell the story of the prisoners' dilemma. Write down a table showing the prisoners' choices and explain what outcome is likely. ● What does the prisoners' dilemma teach us about oligopolies?

PUBLIC POLICY TOWARD OLIGOPOLIES

One of the *Ten Principles of Economics* in Chapter 1 is that governments can sometimes improve market outcomes. This principle applies directly to oligopolistic markets. As we have seen, cooperation among oligopolists is undesirable from the standpoint of society as a whole, because it leads to production that is too low and prices that are too high. To move the allocation of resources closer to the social optimum, policymakers should try to induce firms in an oligopoly to compete rather than cooperate. Let's consider how policymakers do this and then examine the controversies that arise in this area of public policy.

RESTRAINT OF TRADE AND THE ANTITRUST LAWS

One way that policy discourages cooperation is through the common law. Normally, freedom of contract is an essential part of a market economy. Businesses and households use contracts to arrange mutually advantageous trades. In doing this, they rely on the court system to enforce contracts. Yet, for many centuries, judges in England and the United States have deemed agreements among competitors to reduce quantities and raise prices to be contrary to the public good. They have therefore refused to enforce such agreements.

The Sherman Antitrust Act of 1890 codified and reinforced this policy:

> Every contract, combination in the form of trust or otherwise, or conspiracy, in restraint of trade or commerce among the several States, or with foreign nations, is declared to be illegal. . . . Every person who shall monopolize, or attempt to monopolize, or combine or conspire with any person or persons to monopolize any part of the trade or commerce among the several States, or with foreign nations, shall be deemed guilty of a misdemeanor, and on conviction therefor, shall be punished by fine not exceeding fifty thousand dollars, or by imprisonment not exceeding one year, or by both said punishments, in the discretion of the court.

The Sherman Act elevated agreements among oligopolists from an unenforceable contract to a criminal conspiracy.

The Clayton Act of 1914 further strengthened the antitrust laws. According to this law, if a person could prove that he was damaged by an illegal arrangement to restrain trade, that person could sue and recover three times the damages he sustained. The purpose of this unusual rule of triple damages is to encourage private lawsuits against conspiring oligopolists.

Today, both the U.S. Justice Department and private parties have the authority to bring legal suits to enforce the antitrust laws. As we discussed in Chapter 15, these laws are used to prevent mergers that would lead to excessive market power in any single firm. In addition, these laws are used to prevent oligopolists from acting together in ways that would make their markets less competitive.

 ## AN ILLEGAL PHONE CALL

Firms in oligopolies have a strong incentive to collude in order to reduce production, raise price, and increase profit. The great 18th-century economist Adam Smith was well aware of this potential market failure. In *The Wealth of Nations* he wrote, "People of the same trade seldom meet together, but the conversation ends in a conspiracy against the public, or in some diversion to raise prices."

To see a modern example of Smith's observation, consider the following excerpt of a phone conversation between two airline executives in the early 1980s. The call was reported in the *New York Times* on February 24, 1983. Robert Crandall was president of American Airlines, and Howard Putnam was president of Braniff Airways.

CRANDALL: I think it's dumb as hell . . . to sit here and pound the @#$% out of each other and neither one of us making a #$%& dime.

PUTNAM: Do you have a suggestion for me?

CRANDALL: Yes, I have a suggestion for you. Raise your $%*& fares 20 percent. I'll raise mine the next morning.

PUTNAM: Robert, we . . .

CRANDALL: You'll make more money, and I will, too.

PUTNAM: We can't talk about pricing!

CRANDALL: Oh @#$%, Howard. We can talk about any &*#@ thing we want to talk about.

Putnam was right: The Sherman Antitrust Act prohibits competing executives from even talking about fixing prices. When Putnam gave a tape of this conversation to the Justice Department, the Justice Department filed suit against Crandall.

Two years later, Crandall and the Justice Department reached a settlement in which Crandall agreed to various restrictions on his business activities, including his contacts with officials at other airlines. The Justice Department said that the terms of settlement would "protect competition in the airline industry, by preventing American and Crandall from any further attempts to monopolize passenger airline service on any route through discussions with competitors about the prices of airline services." ●

CONTROVERSIES OVER ANTITRUST POLICY

Over time, much controversy has centered on what kinds of behavior the antitrust laws should prohibit. Most commentators agree that price-fixing agreements among competing firms should be illegal. Yet the antitrust laws have been used to condemn some business practices whose effects are not obvious. Here we consider three examples.

In The News

Public Price Fixing

If a group of producers coordinates their prices in secret meetings, they can be sent to jail for criminal violations of antitrust laws. But what if they discuss the same topic in public?

Market Talk

By Alistair Lindsay

Most companies have antitrust compliance policies. They typically—and quite rightly—identify a number of things that officers and employees should not do, on pain of criminal liability, eye-watering fines and unlimited damages actions. All make clear that companies must not agree with their competitors to fix prices. This is a bright-line rule. But it raises an important question: Can companies coordinate price increases without infringing the cartel rules?

In markets where competitors need to publish their prices to win business—for example, many retail markets—it is perfectly lawful to shadow a rival's increases, so long as each seller acts entirely independently in setting its charges. The very definition of an oligopoly is a market involving a small number of suppliers that set their own commercial strategies but take account of their competitors. One competitor may emerge as a leader, with others taking their cue on when to raise prices and by how much.

When prices are privately negotiated—as in many industrials markets—it is com-

mon for a customer to volunteer information about a rival's prices to obtain leverage: *"You've quoted £100 per ton, but X is offering £95 and I'm going to them unless you can do better."* A company that receives this information obtains valuable intelligence about what its rivals are charging, but it does not infringe cartel rules. . . .

Companies also sometimes signal to one another in their communications with investors, whether deliberately or not. A competitor which informs the markets, say, that it expects a price war to end in February is providing relevant information to actual and potential owners of its stock. But of course its rivals read the same reports and can change their strategies accordingly. So a statement to the market can serve as just as much of a signal to competitors as a statement made during a cartel meeting. . . .

Signaling through investor communications raises difficult questions for cartel enforcement. The enforcers want to protect consumers from the adverse effects of blatant signaling, but not at the price of losing transparency in financial markets. For example, it is highly relevant to an investor to know an airline's predicted growth of per-

mile passenger revenue for the next quarter. But a rival airline might use the announced figure as a benchmark when setting its own fares for the next quarter.

As things stand, cartel authorities have focused their efforts in such situations on blocking mergers in markets where signaling is prevalent, arguing that consolidation in such markets can further dampen competition by making coordination easier or more successful. However, they have not taken high-profile action alleging cartel infringements against companies for announcements made to investors.

If there is no justification for a particular announcement other than to signal to competitors, cartel authorities should seek to intervene. For in this case the public announcement is analytically the same as a private discussion directly with the rivals, and there is scope for consumers to be seriously harmed. But most announcements do serve legitimate purposes, such as keeping investors informed. In these cases, intervention by the cartel authorities seems too complex, given the disparate policy objectives in play.

Source: *The Wall Street Journal,* December 13, 2007.

Resale Price Maintenance   One example of a controversial business practice is *resale price maintenance,* also called *fair trade.* Imagine that Superduper Electronics sells DVD players to retail stores for $300. If Superduper requires the retailers to charge customers $350, it is said to engage in resale price maintenance. Any retailer that charged less than $350 would violate its contract with Superduper.

At first, resale price maintenance might seem anticompetitive and, therefore, detrimental to society. Like an agreement among members of a cartel, it prevents the retailers from competing on price. For this reason, the courts have often viewed resale price maintenance as a violation of the antitrust laws.

Yet some economists defend resale price maintenance on two grounds. First, they deny that it is aimed at reducing competition. To the extent that Superduper Electronics has any market power, it can exert that power through the wholesale price, rather than through resale price maintenance. Moreover, Superduper has no incentive to discourage competition among its retailers. Indeed, because a cartel of retailers sells less than a group of competitive retailers, Superduper would be worse off if its retailers were a cartel.

Second, economists believe that resale price maintenance has a legitimate goal. Superduper may want its retailers to provide customers a pleasant showroom and a knowledgeable sales force. Yet, without resale price maintenance, some customers would take advantage of one store's service to learn about the DVD player's special features and then buy the item at a discount retailer that does not provide this service. To some extent, good service is a public good among the retailers that sell Superduper products. As we discussed in Chapter 11, when one person provides a public good, others are able to enjoy it without paying for it. In this case, discount retailers would free ride on the service provided by other retailers, leading to less service than is desirable. Resale price maintenance is one way for Superduper to solve this free-rider problem.

The example of resale price maintenance illustrates an important principle: *Business practices that appear to reduce competition may in fact have legitimate purposes.* This principle makes the application of the antitrust laws all the more difficult. The economists, lawyers, and judges in charge of enforcing these laws must determine what kinds of behavior public policy should prohibit as impeding competition and reducing economic well-being. Often that job is not easy.

Predatory Pricing Firms with market power normally use that power to raise prices above the competitive level. But should policymakers ever be concerned that firms with market power might charge prices that are too low? This question is at the heart of a second debate over antitrust policy.

Imagine that a large airline, call it Coyote Air, has a monopoly on some route. Then Roadrunner Express enters and takes 20 percent of the market, leaving Coyote with 80 percent. In response to this competition, Coyote starts slashing its fares. Some antitrust analysts argue that Coyote's move could be anticompetitive: The price cuts may be intended to drive Roadrunner out of the market so Coyote can recapture its monopoly and raise prices again. Such behavior is called *predatory pricing*.

Although predatory pricing is a common claim in antitrust suits, some economists are skeptical of this argument and believe that predatory pricing is rarely, and perhaps never, a profitable business strategy. Why? For a price war to drive out a rival, prices have to be driven below cost. Yet if Coyote starts selling cheap tickets at a loss, it had better be ready to fly more planes, because low fares will attract more customers. Roadrunner, meanwhile, can respond to Coyote's predatory move by cutting back on flights. As a result, Coyote ends up bearing more than 80 percent of the losses, putting Roadrunner in a good position to survive the price war. As in the old Roadrunner-Coyote cartoons, the predator suffers more than the prey.

In The News

A Reversal of Policy

In 2007 the Supreme Court, by a slim majority, changed its view of retail price maintenance.

Century-Old Ban Lifted on Minimum Retail Pricing

By Stephen Labaton

WASHINGTON, June 28—Striking down an antitrust rule nearly a century old, the Supreme Court ruled on Thursday that it was not automatically unlawful for manufacturers and distributors to agree on minimum retail prices.

The decision will give producers significantly more, though not unlimited, power to dictate retail prices and to restrict the flexibility of discounters.

Five justices, agreeing with the nation's major manufacturers, said the new rule could in some instances lead to more competition and better service. But four dissenting justices agreed with 37 states and some consumer groups that abandoning the old rule could result in significantly higher prices and less competition for consumer and other goods.

The court struck down the 96-year-old rule that resale price maintenance agreements were an automatic, or per se, violation of the Sherman Antitrust Act. In its place, the court instructed judges considering such agreements for possible antitrust violations to apply a case-by-case approach, known as

a "rule of reason," to assess their impact on competition. The new rule is considerably more favorable to defendants.

The decision was handed down on the last day of the court's term, which has been notable for overturning precedents and for victories for big businesses and antitrust defendants. It was also the latest of a series of antitrust decisions in recent years rejecting per se rules that had prohibited various marketing agreements between companies.

The Bush administration, along with economists of the Chicago school, had argued that the blanket prohibition against resale price maintenance agreements was archaic and counterproductive because, they said, some resale price agreements actually promote competition.

For example, they said, such agreements can make it easier for a new producer by assuring retailers that they will be able to recoup their investments in helping to market the product. And some distributors would be unfairly harmed by others, like Internet-based retailers, which could offer discounts because they would not have the expense of product demonstrations or other specialized consumer services.

A majority of the court agreed that the flat ban on price agreements discouraged

these services and other marketing practices that could promote competition.

"In sum, it is a flawed antitrust doctrine that serves the interests of lawyers—by creating legal distinctions that operate as traps for the unaware—more than the interests of consumers—by requiring manufacturers to choose second-best options to achieve sound business objectives," the court said in an opinion written by Justice Anthony M. Kennedy and signed by Chief Justice John G. Roberts Jr. and Justices Antonin Scalia, Clarence Thomas and Samuel A. Alito Jr.

But in his dissent, portions of which he read from the bench, Justice Stephen G. Breyer said that there was no compelling reason to overturn a century's worth of Supreme Court decisions that had affirmed the prohibition on resale maintenance agreements.

"The only safe predictions to make about today's decision are that it will likely raise the price of goods at retail and that it will create considerable legal turbulence as lower courts seek to develop workable principles," he wrote. "I do not believe that the majority has shown new or changed conditions sufficient to warrant overruling a decision of such long standing."

Source: *New York Times*, June 29, 2007.

Economists continue to debate whether predatory pricing should be a concern for antitrust policymakers. Various questions remain unresolved. Is predatory pricing ever a profitable business strategy? If so, when? Are the courts capable of telling which price cuts are competitive and thus good for consumers and which are predatory? There are no simple answers.

Tying A third example of a controversial business practice is *tying*. Suppose that Makemoney Movies produces two new films—*Spiderman* and *Hamlet*. If Makemoney offers theaters the two films together at a single price, rather than separately, the studio is said to be tying its two products.

When the practice of tying movies was challenged in the courts, the Supreme Court banned it. The court reasoned as follows: Imagine that *Spiderman* is a blockbuster, whereas *Hamlet* is an unprofitable art film. Then the studio could use the high demand for *Spiderman* to force theaters to buy *Hamlet*. It seemed that the studio could use tying as a mechanism for expanding its market power.

Many economists are skeptical of this argument. Imagine that theaters are willing to pay $20,000 for *Spiderman* and nothing for *Hamlet*. Then the most that a theater would pay for the two movies together is $20,000—the same as it would pay for *Spiderman* by itself. Forcing the theater to accept a worthless movie as part of the deal does not increase the theater's willingness to pay. Makemoney cannot increase its market power simply by bundling the two movies together.

Why, then, does tying exist? One possibility is that it is a form of price discrimination. Suppose there are two theaters. City Theater is willing to pay $15,000 for *Spiderman* and $5,000 for *Hamlet*. Country Theater is just the opposite: It is willing to pay $5,000 for *Spiderman* and $15,000 for *Hamlet*. If Makemoney charges separate prices for the two films, its best strategy is to charge $15,000 for each film, and each theater chooses to show only one film. Yet if Makemoney offers the two movies as a bundle, it can charge each theater $20,000 for the movies. Thus, if different theaters value the films differently, tying may allow the studio to increase profit by charging a combined price closer to the buyers' total willingness to pay.

Tying remains a controversial business practice. The Supreme Court's argument that tying allows a firm to extend its market power to other goods is not well founded, at least in its simplest form. Yet economists have proposed more elaborate theories for how tying can impede competition. Given our current economic knowledge, it is unclear whether tying has adverse effects for society as a whole.

 ## THE MICROSOFT CASE

The most important and controversial antitrust case in recent years has been the U.S. government's suit against the Microsoft Corporation, filed in 1998. Certainly, the case did not lack drama. It pitted one of the world's richest men (Bill Gates) against one of the world's most powerful regulatory agencies (the U.S. Justice Department). Testifying for the government was a prominent economist (MIT professor Franklin Fisher). Testifying for Microsoft was an equally prominent economist (MIT professor Richard Schmalensee). At stake was the future of one of the world's most valuable companies (Microsoft) in one of the economy's fastest-growing industries (computer software).

A central issue in the Microsoft case involved tying—in particular, whether Microsoft should be allowed to integrate its Internet browser into its Windows operating system. The government claimed that Microsoft was bundling these two products together to expand its market power in computer operating systems into the unrelated market of Internet browsers. Allowing Microsoft to incorporate such products into its operating system, the government argued, would deter other software companies from entering the market and offering new products.

Microsoft responded by pointing out that putting new features into old products is a natural part of technological progress. Cars today include CD players and air conditioners, which were once sold separately, and cameras come with

"ME? A MONOPOLIST? NOW
JUST WAIT A MINUTE . . ."

built-in flashes. The same is true with operating systems. Over time, Microsoft has added many features to Windows that were previously stand-alone products. This has made computers more reliable and easier to use because consumers can be confident that the pieces work together. The integration of Internet technology, Microsoft argued, was the natural next step.

One point of disagreement concerned the extent of Microsoft's market power. Noting that more than 80 percent of new personal computers use a Microsoft operating system, the government argued that the company had substantial monopoly power, which it was trying to expand. Microsoft replied that the software market is always changing and that Microsoft's Windows was constantly being challenged by competitors, such as the Apple Mac and Linux operating systems. It also argued that the low price it charged for Windows—about $50, or only 3 percent of the price of a typical computer—was evidence that its market power was severely limited.

Like many large antitrust suits, the Microsoft case became a legal morass. In November 1999, after a long trial, Judge Penfield Jackson ruled that Microsoft had great monopoly power and that it had illegally abused that power. In June 2000, after hearings on possible remedies, he ordered that Microsoft be broken up into two companies—one that sold the operating system and one that sold applications software. A year later, an appeals court overturned Jackson's breakup order and handed the case to a new judge. In September 2001, the Justice Department announced that it no longer sought a breakup of the company and wanted to settle the case quickly.

A settlement was finally reached in November 2002. Microsoft accepted some restrictions on its business practices, and the government accepted that a browser would remain part of the Windows operating system. But the settlement did not end Microsoft's antitrust troubles. In recent years, the company has contended with several private antitrust suits, as well as suits brought by the European Union alleging a variety of anticompetitive behaviors. ●

QUICK QUIZ What kind of agreement is illegal for businesses to make? ● Why are the antitrust laws controversial?

CONCLUSION

Oligopolies would like to act like monopolies, but self-interest drives them toward competition. Where oligopolies end up on this spectrum depends on the number of firms in the oligopoly and how cooperative the firms are. The story of the prisoners' dilemma shows why oligopolies can fail to maintain cooperation, even when cooperation is in their best interest.

Policymakers regulate the behavior of oligopolists through the antitrust laws. The proper scope of these laws is the subject of ongoing controversy. Although price fixing among competing firms clearly reduces economic welfare and should be illegal, some business practices that appear to reduce competition may have legitimate if subtle purposes. As a result, policymakers need to be careful when they use the substantial powers of the antitrust laws to place limits on firm behavior.

SUMMARY

- Oligopolists maximize their total profits by forming a cartel and acting like a monopolist. Yet, if oligopolists make decisions about production levels individually, the result is a greater quantity and a lower price than under the monopoly outcome. The larger the number of firms in the oligopoly, the closer the quantity and price will be to the levels that would prevail under competition.

- The prisoners' dilemma shows that self-interest can prevent people from maintaining coopera-

tion, even when cooperation is in their mutual interest. The logic of the prisoners' dilemma applies in many situations, including arms races, common-resource problems, and oligopolies.

- Policymakers use the antitrust laws to prevent oligopolies from engaging in behavior that reduces competition. The application of these laws can be controversial, because some behavior that can appear to reduce competition may in fact have legitimate business purposes.

KEY CONCEPTS

oligopoly, *p. 365*
game theory, *p. 365*
collusion, *p. 367*

cartel, *p. 367*
Nash equilibrium, *p. 368*
prisoners' dilemma, *p. 370*

dominant strategy, *p. 371*

QUESTIONS FOR REVIEW

1. If a group of sellers could form a cartel, what quantity and price would they try to set?
2. Compare the quantity and price of an oligopoly to those of a monopoly.
3. Compare the quantity and price of an oligopoly to those of a competitive market.
4. How does the number of firms in an oligopoly affect the outcome in its market?

5. What is the prisoners' dilemma, and what does it have to do with oligopoly?
6. Give two examples other than oligopoly to show how the prisoners' dilemma helps to explain behavior.
7. What kinds of behavior do the antitrust laws prohibit?
8. What is resale price maintenance, and why is it controversial?

PROBLEMS AND APPLICATIONS

1. A large share of the world supply of diamonds comes from Russia and South Africa. Suppose that the marginal cost of mining diamonds is constant at $1,000 per diamond, and the demand for diamonds is described by the following schedule:

Price	Quantity
$8,000	5,000 diamonds
7,000	6,000
6,000	7,000
5,000	8,000
4,000	9,000
3,000	10,000
2,000	11,000
1,000	12,000

   a. If there were many suppliers of diamonds, what would be the price and quantity?
   b. If there were only one supplier of diamonds, what would be the price and quantity?
   c. If Russia and South Africa formed a cartel, what would be the price and quantity? If the countries split the market evenly, what would be South Africa's production and profit? What would happen to South Africa's profit if it increased its production by 1,000 while Russia stuck to the cartel agreement?
   d. Use your answers to part (c) to explain why cartel agreements are often not successful.

2. The *New York Times* (Nov. 30, 1993) reported that "the inability of OPEC to agree last week to cut production has sent the oil market into turmoil . . . [leading to] the lowest price for domestic crude oil since June 1990."
   a. Why were the members of OPEC trying to agree to cut production?
   b. Why do you suppose OPEC was unable to agree on cutting production? Why did the oil market go into "turmoil" as a result?
   c. The newspaper also noted OPEC's view "that producing nations outside the organization, like Norway and Britain, should do their share and cut production." What does the phrase "do their share" suggest about OPEC's desired relationship with Norway and Britain?

3. This chapter discusses companies that are oligopolists in the market for the goods they sell. Many of the same ideas apply to companies that are oligopolists in the market for the inputs they buy.
   a. If sellers who are oligopolists try to increase the price of goods they sell, what is the goal of buyers who are oligopolists?
   b. Major league baseball team owners have an oligopoly in the market for baseball players. What is the owners' goal regarding players' salaries? Why is this goal difficult to achieve?
   c. Baseball players went on strike in 1994 because they would not accept the salary cap that the owners wanted to impose. If the owners were already colluding over salaries, why did the owners feel the need for a salary cap?

4. Consider trade relations between the United States and Mexico. Assume that the leaders of the two countries believe the payoffs to alternative trade policies are as follows:

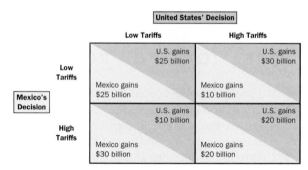

   a. What is the dominant strategy for the United States? For Mexico? Explain.
   b. Define *Nash equilibrium.* What is the Nash equilibrium for trade policy?
   c. In 1993 the U.S. Congress ratified the North American Free Trade Agreement, in which the United States and Mexico agreed to reduce trade barriers simultaneously. Do the perceived payoffs shown here justify this approach to trade policy? Explain.
   d. Based on your understanding of the gains from trade (discussed in Chapters 3 and 9), do you think that these payoffs actually

reflect a nation's welfare under the four possible outcomes?

5. Synergy and Dynaco are the only two firms in a specific high-tech industry. They face the following payoff matrix as they decide upon the size of their research budget:

Synergy Decision

		Large Budget	Small Budget
Dynaco's Decision	**Large Budget**	Synergy gains $20 million / Dynaco gains $30 million	Synergy gains zero / Dynaco gains $70 million
	Small Budget	Synergy gains $30 million / Dynaco gains zero	Synergy gains $40 million / Dynaco gains $50 million

a. Does Synergy have a dominant strategy? Explain.

b. Does Dynaco have a dominant strategy? Explain.

c. Is there a Nash equilibrium for this scenario? Explain. (Hint: Look closely at the definition of Nash equilibrium.)

6. You and a classmate are assigned a project on which you will receive one combined grade. You each want to receive a good grade, but you also want to avoid hard work. In particular, here is the situation:

- If both of you work hard, you both get an A, which gives each of you 40 units of happiness.
- If only one of you works hard, you both get a B, which gives each of you 30 units of happiness.
- If neither of you works hard, you both get a D, which gives each of you 10 units of happiness.
- Working hard costs 25 units of happiness.

a. Fill in the payoffs in the following decision box:

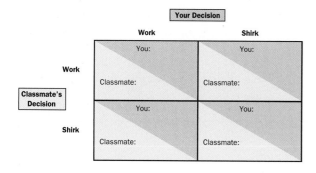

Your Decision

		Work	Shirk
Classmate's Decision	**Work**	You: / Classmate:	You: / Classmate:
	Shirk	You: / Classmate:	You: / Classmate:

b. What is the likely outcome? Explain your answer.

c. If you get this classmate as your partner on a series of projects throughout the year, rather than only once, how might that change the outcome you predicted in part (b)?

d. Another classmate cares more about good grades: He gets 50 units of happiness for a B, and 80 units of happiness from an A. If this classmate were your partner (but your preferences were unchanged), how would your answers to parts (a) and (b) change? Which of the two classmates would you prefer as a partner? Would he also want you as a partner?

7. A case study in the chapter describes a phone conversation between the presidents of American Airlines and Braniff Airways. Let's analyze the game between the two companies. Suppose that each company can charge either a high price for tickets or a low price. If one company charges $100, it earns low profits if the other company charges $100 also, and high profits if the other company charges $200. On the other hand, if the company charges $200, it earns very low profits if the other company charges $100, and medium profits if the other company charges $200 also.

a. Draw the decision box for this game.

b. What is the Nash equilibrium in this game? Explain.

c. Is there an outcome that would be better than the Nash equilibrium for both airlines? How could it be achieved? Who would lose if it were achieved?

8. Little Kona is a small coffee company that is considering entering a market dominated by Big Brew. Each company's profit depends on whether Little Kona enters and whether Big Brew sets a high price or a low price:

Big Brew

		High Price	Low Price
Little Kona	**Enter**	Brew makes $3 million / Kona makes $2 million	Brew makes $1 million / Kona loses $1 million
	Don't Enter	Brew makes $7 million / Kona makes zero	Brew makes $2 million / Kona makes zero

a. Does either player in this game have a dominant strategy?

b. Does your answer to part (a) help you figure out what the other player should do? What is the Nash equilibrium? Is there only one?

c. Big Brew threatens Little Kona by saying, "If you enter, we're going to set a low price, so you had better stay out." Do you think Little Kona should believe the threat? Why or why not?

d. If the two firms could collude and agree on how to split the total profits, what outcome would they pick?

9. Jeff and Steve are playing tennis. Every point comes down to whether Steve guesses correctly whether Jeff will hit the ball to Steve's left or right. The outcomes are:

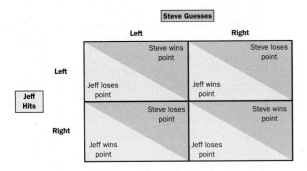

Does either player have a dominant strategy? If Jeff chooses a particular strategy (Left or Right) and sticks with it, what will Steve do? Can you think of a better strategy for Jeff to follow?

10. Let's return to the chapter's discussion of Jack and Jill's water duopoly. Suppose that Jack and Jill are at the duopoly's Nash equilibrium (80 gallons) when a third person, John, discovers a water source and joins the market as a third producer.

a. Jack and Jill propose that the three of them continue to produce a total of 80 gallons, splitting the market three ways. If John agrees to this, how much profit will he make?

b. After agreeing to the proposed deal, John is considering increasing his production by 10 gallons. If he does, and Jack and Jill stick to the agreement, how much profit will John make? What does this tell you about the proposed agreement?

c. What is the Nash equilibrium for this market with three producers? How does it compare to the Nash equilibrium with two producers?

The basic tools of supply and demand apply to goods and to labor services. Panel (a) shows how the supply and demand for apples determine the price of apples. Panel (b) shows how the supply and demand for apple pickers determine the wage of apple pickers.

FIGURE 1

The Versatility of Supply and Demand

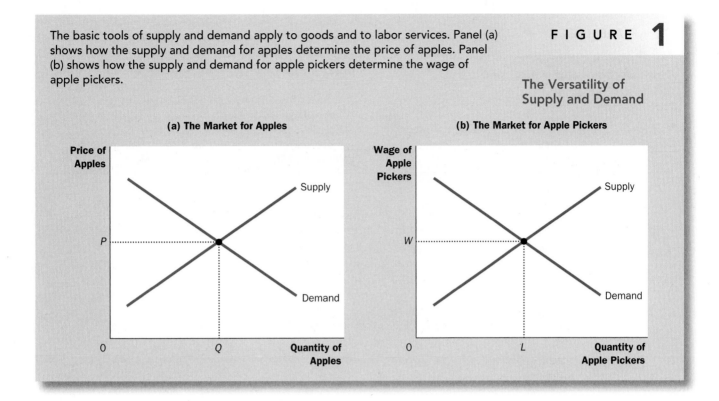

(a) The Market for Apples

(b) The Market for Apple Pickers

THE COMPETITIVE PROFIT-MAXIMIZING FIRM

Let's look at how a typical firm, such as an apple producer, decides the quantity of labor to demand. The firm owns an apple orchard and each week must decide how many apple pickers to hire to harvest its crop. After the firm makes its hiring decision, the workers pick as many apples as they can. The firm then sells the apples, pays the workers, and keeps what is left as profit.

We make two assumptions about our firm. First, we assume that our firm is *competitive* both in the market for apples (where the firm is a seller) and in the market for apple pickers (where the firm is a buyer). A competitive firm is a price taker. Because there are many other firms selling apples and hiring apple pickers, a single firm has little influence over the price it gets for apples or the wage it pays apple pickers. The firm takes the price and the wage as given by market conditions. It only has to decide how many apples to sell and how many workers to hire.

Second, we assume that the firm is *profit-maximizing*. Thus, the firm does not directly care about the number of workers it has or the number of apples it produces. It cares only about profit, which equals the total revenue from the sale of apples minus the total cost of producing them. The firm's supply of apples and its demand for workers are derived from its primary goal of maximizing profit.

THE PRODUCTION FUNCTION AND THE MARGINAL PRODUCT OF LABOR

To make its hiring decision, the firm must consider how the size of its workforce affects the amount of output produced. In other words, it must consider how the

1 TABLE

**How the Competitive Firm Decides
How Much Labor to Hire**

Labor L	Output Q	Marginal Product of Labor $MPL = \Delta Q / \Delta L$	Value of the Marginal Product of Labor $VMPL = P \times MPL$	Wage W	Marginal Profit $\Delta Profit = VMPL - W$
0 workers	0 bushels				
		100 bushels	$1,000	$500	$500
1	100				
		80	800	500	300
2	180				
		60	600	500	100
3	240				
		40	400	500	−100
4	280				
		20	200	500	−300
5	300				

number of apple pickers affects the quantity of apples it can harvest and sell. Table 1 gives a numerical example. In the first column is the number of workers. In the second column is the quantity of apples the workers harvest each week.

These two columns of numbers describe the firm's ability to produce. Recall that economists use the term **production function** to describe the relationship between the quantity of the inputs used in production and the quantity of output from production. Here the "input" is the apple pickers and the "output" is the apples. The other inputs—the trees themselves, the land, the firm's trucks and tractors, and so on—are held fixed for now. This firm's production function shows that if the firm hires 1 worker, that worker will pick 100 bushels of apples per week. If the firm hires 2 workers, the 2 workers together will pick 180 bushels per week. And so on.

Figure 2 graphs the data on labor and output presented in Table 1. The number of workers is on the horizontal axis, and the amount of output is on the vertical axis. This figure illustrates the production function.

One of the *Ten Principles of Economics* introduced in Chapter 1 is that rational people think at the margin. This idea is the key to understanding how firms decide what quantity of labor to hire. To take a step toward this decision, the third column in Table 1 gives the **marginal product of labor**, the increase in the amount of output from an additional unit of labor. When the firm increases the number of workers from 1 to 2, for example, the amount of apples produced rises from 100 to 180 bushels. Therefore, the marginal product of the second worker is 80 bushels.

Notice that as the number of workers increases, the marginal product of labor declines. That is, the production process exhibits **diminishing marginal product**. At first, when only a few workers are hired, they can pick the low-hanging fruit. As

production function
the relationship between the quantity of inputs used to make a good and the quantity of output of that good

marginal product of labor
the increase in the amount of output from an additional unit of labor

diminishing marginal product
the property whereby the marginal product of an input declines as the quantity of the input increases

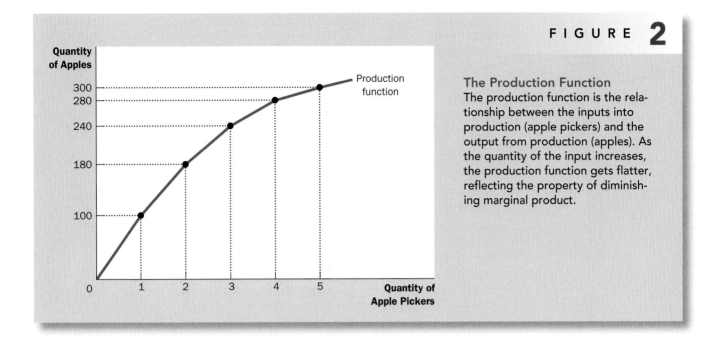

FIGURE **2**

The Production Function
The production function is the relationship between the inputs into production (apple pickers) and the output from production (apples). As the quantity of the input increases, the production function gets flatter, reflecting the property of diminishing marginal product.

the number of workers increases, additional workers have to climb higher up the ladders to find apples to pick. Hence, as more and more workers are hired, each additional worker contributes less to the production of apples. For this reason, the production function in Figure 2 becomes flatter as the number of workers rises.

THE VALUE OF THE MARGINAL PRODUCT AND THE DEMAND FOR LABOR

Our profit-maximizing firm is concerned more with money than with apples. As a result, when deciding how many workers to hire to pick apples, the firm considers how much profit each worker would bring in. Because profit is total revenue minus total cost, the profit from an additional worker is the worker's contribution to revenue minus the worker's wage.

To find the worker's contribution to revenue, we must convert the marginal product of labor (which is measured in bushels of apples) into the *value* of the marginal product (which is measured in dollars). We do this using the price of apples. To continue our example, if a bushel of apples sells for $10 and if an additional worker produces 80 bushels of apples, then the worker produces $800 of revenue.

The **value of the marginal product** of any input is the marginal product of that input multiplied by the market price of the output. The fourth column in Table 1 shows the value of the marginal product of labor in our example, assuming the price of apples is $10 per bushel. Because the market price is constant for a competitive firm while the marginal product declines with more workers, the value of the marginal product diminishes as the number of workers rises. Economists sometimes call this column of numbers the firm's *marginal revenue product:* It is the extra revenue the firm gets from hiring an additional unit of a factor of production.

value of the marginal product
the marginal product of an input times the price of the output

Now consider how many workers the firm will hire. Suppose that the market wage for apple pickers is $500 per week. In this case, as you can see in Table 1, the first worker that the firm hires is profitable: The first worker yields $1,000 in revenue, or $500 in profit. Similarly, the second worker yields $800 in additional revenue, or $300 in profit. The third worker produces $600 in additional revenue, or $100 in profit. After the third worker, however, hiring workers is unprofitable. The fourth worker would yield only $400 of additional revenue. Because the worker's wage is $500, hiring the fourth worker would mean a $100 reduction in profit. Thus, the firm hires only 3 workers.

It is instructive to consider the firm's decision graphically. Figure 3 graphs the value of the marginal product. This curve slopes downward because the marginal product of labor diminishes as the number of workers rises. The figure also includes a horizontal line at the market wage. To maximize profit, the firm hires workers up to the point where these two curves cross. Below this level of employment, the value of the marginal product exceeds the wage, so hiring another worker would increase profit. Above this level of employment, the value of the marginal product is less than the wage, so the marginal worker is unprofitable. Thus, *a competitive, profit-maximizing firm hires workers up to the point where the value of the marginal product of labor equals the wage.*

Having explained the profit-maximizing hiring strategy for a competitive firm, we can now offer a theory of labor demand. Recall that a firm's labor-demand curve tells us the quantity of labor that a firm demands at any given wage. We have just seen in Figure 3 that the firm makes that decision by choosing the quantity of labor at which the value of the marginal product equals the wage. As a result, *the value-of-marginal-product curve is the labor-demand curve for a competitive, profit-maximizing firm.*

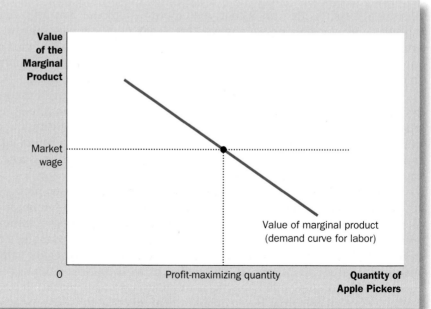

3 FIGURE

The Value of the Marginal Product of Labor
This figure shows how the value of the marginal product (the marginal product times the price of the output) depends on the number of workers. The curve slopes downward because of diminishing marginal product. For a competitive, profit-maximizing firm, this value-of-marginal-product curve is also the firm's labor-demand curve.

Value of the Marginal Product

Market wage

Value of marginal product (demand curve for labor)

0

Profit-maximizing quantity

Quantity of Apple Pickers

FYI

Input Demand and Output Supply: Two Sides of the Same Coin

In Chapter 14, we saw how a competitive, profit-maximizing firm decides how much of its output to sell: It chooses the quantity of output at which the price of the good equals the marginal cost of production. We have just seen how such a firm decides how much labor to hire: It chooses the quantity of labor at which the wage equals the value of the marginal product. Because the production function links the quantity of inputs to the quantity of output, you should not be surprised to learn that the firm's decision about input demand is closely linked to its decision about output supply. In fact, these two decisions are two sides of the same coin.

To see this relationship more fully, let's consider how the marginal product of labor (*MPL*) and marginal cost (*MC*) are related. Suppose an additional worker costs $500 and has a marginal product of 50 bushels of apples. In this case, producing 50 more bushels costs $500; the marginal cost of a bushel is $500 / 50, or $10. More generally, if *W* is the wage, and an extra unit of labor produces *MPL* units of output, then the marginal cost of a unit of output is $MC = W / MPL$.

This analysis shows that diminishing marginal product is closely related to increasing marginal cost. When our apple orchard grows crowded with workers, each additional worker adds less to the production of apples (*MPL* falls). Similarly, when the apple firm is producing a large quantity of apples, the orchard is already crowded with workers, so it is more costly to produce an additional bushel of apples (*MC* rises).

Now consider our criterion for profit maximization. We determined earlier that a profit-maximizing firm chooses the quantity of labor so that the value of the marginal product ($P \times MPL$) equals the wage (*W*). We can write this mathematically as

$$P \times MPL = W.$$

If we divide both sides of this equation by *MPL*, we obtain

$$P = W / MPL.$$

We just noted that W / MPL equals marginal cost, *MC*. Therefore, we can substitute to obtain

$$P = MC.$$

This equation states that the price of the firm's output is equal to the marginal cost of producing a unit of output. *Thus, when a competitive firm hires labor up to the point at which the value of the marginal product equals the wage, it also produces up to the point at which the price equals marginal cost.* Our analysis of labor demand in this chapter is just another way of looking at the production decision we first saw in Chapter 14.

WHAT CAUSES THE LABOR-DEMAND CURVE TO SHIFT?

We now understand the labor-demand curve: It reflects the value of the marginal product of labor. With this insight in mind, let's consider a few of the things that might cause the labor-demand curve to shift.

The Output Price   The value of the marginal product is marginal product times the price of the firm's output. Thus, when the output price changes, the value of the marginal product changes, and the labor-demand curve shifts. An increase in the price of apples, for instance, raises the value of the marginal product of each worker who picks apples and, therefore, increases labor demand from the firms that supply apples. Conversely, a decrease in the price of apples reduces the value of the marginal product and decreases labor demand.

Technological Change   Between 1960 and 2000, the amount of output a typical U.S. worker produced in an hour rose by 140 percent. Why? The most important

FYI

The Luddite Revolt

Over the long span of history, technological progress has been the worker's friend. It has increased productivity, labor demand, and wages. Yet there is no doubt that workers sometimes see technological progress as a threat to their standard of living.

One famous example occurred in England in the early 19th century, when skilled knitters saw their jobs threatened by the invention and spread of machines that could produce textiles using less skilled workers and at much lower cost. The displaced workers organized violent revolts against the new technology. They smashed the weaving machines used in the wool and cotton mills and, in some cases, set the homes of the mill owners on fire. Because the workers claimed to be led by General Ned Ludd (who may have been a legendary figure rather than a real person), they were called Luddites.

The Luddites wanted the British government to save their jobs by restricting the spread of the new technology. Instead, the Parliament took action to stop the Luddites. Thousands of troops were sent to suppress the Luddite riots, and the Parliament eventually made destroying machines a capital crime. After a trial in York in 1813, seventeen men were hanged for the offense. Many others were convicted and sent to Australia as prisoners.

The Luddites.

Today, the term *Luddite* refers to anyone who opposes technological progress.

reason is technological progress: Scientists and engineers are constantly figuring out new and better ways of doing things. This has profound implications for the labor market. Technological advance typically raises the marginal product of labor, which in turn increases the demand for labor and shifts the labor-demand curve to the right.

It is also possible for technological change to reduce labor demand. The invention of a cheap industrial robot, for instance, could conceivably reduce the marginal product of labor, shifting the labor-demand curve to the left. Economists call this *labor-saving* technological change. History suggests, however, that most technological progress is instead *labor-augmenting*. Such technological advance explains persistently rising employment in the face of rising wages: Even though wages (adjusted for inflation) increased by 131 percent during the last four decades of the 20th century, firms nonetheless increased by 80 percent the amount of labor they employed.

The Supply of Other Factors   The quantity available of one factor of production can affect the marginal product of other factors. A fall in the supply of ladders, for instance, will reduce the marginal product of apple pickers and thus the demand for apple pickers. We consider this linkage among the factors of production more fully later in the chapter.

QUICK QUIZ Define *marginal product of labor* and *value of the marginal product of labor*. • Describe how a competitive, profit-maximizing firm decides how many workers to hire.

THE SUPPLY OF LABOR

Having analyzed labor demand in detail, let's turn to the other side of the market and consider labor supply. A formal model of labor supply is included in Chapter 21, where we develop the theory of household decision making. Here we discuss briefly and informally the decisions that lie behind the labor-supply curve.

THE TRADE-OFF BETWEEN WORK AND LEISURE

One of the *Ten Principles of Economics* in Chapter 1 is that people face trade-offs. Probably no trade-off is more obvious or more important in a person's life than the trade-off between work and leisure. The more hours you spend working, the fewer hours you have to watch TV, enjoy dinner with friends, or pursue your favorite hobby. The trade-off between labor and leisure lies behind the labor-supply curve.

Another of the *Ten Principles of Economics* is that the cost of something is what you give up to get it. What do you give up to get an hour of leisure? You give up an hour of work, which in turn means an hour of wages. Thus, if your wage is $15 per hour, the opportunity cost of an hour of leisure is $15. And when you get a raise to $20 per hour, the opportunity cost of enjoying leisure goes up.

The labor-supply curve reflects how workers' decisions about the labor-leisure trade-off respond to a change in that opportunity cost. An upward-sloping labor-supply curve means that an increase in the wage induces workers to increase the quantity of labor they supply. Because time is limited, more hours of work mean that workers are enjoying less leisure. That is, workers respond to the increase in the opportunity cost of leisure by taking less of it.

It is worth noting that the labor-supply curve need not be upward sloping. Imagine you got that raise from $15 to $20 per hour. The opportunity cost of leisure is now greater, but you are also richer than you were before. You might decide that with your extra wealth you can now afford to enjoy more leisure. That is, at the higher wage, you might choose to work fewer hours. If so, your labor-supply curve would slope backward. In Chapter 21, we discuss this possibility in terms of conflicting effects on your labor-supply decision (called the income and substitution effects). For now, we ignore the possibility of backward-sloping labor supply and assume that the labor-supply curve is upward sloping.

"I REALLY DIDN'T ENJOY WORKING FIVE DAYS A WEEK, FIFTY WEEKS A YEAR FOR FORTY YEARS, BUT I NEEDED THE MONEY."

WHAT CAUSES THE LABOR-SUPPLY CURVE TO SHIFT?

The labor-supply curve shifts whenever people change the amount they want to work at a given wage. Let's now consider some of the events that might cause such a shift.

Changes in Tastes   In 1950, 34 percent of women were employed at paid jobs or looking for work. In 2000, the number had risen to 60 percent. There are many explanations for this development, but one of them is changing tastes, or attitudes toward work. A generation or two ago, it was the norm for women to stay at home while raising children. Today, family sizes are smaller, and more mothers choose to work. The result is an increase in the supply of labor.

Changes in Alternative Opportunities   The supply of labor in any one labor market depends on the opportunities available in other labor markets. If the wage earned by pear pickers suddenly rises, some apple pickers may choose to switch occupations, and the supply of labor in the market for apple pickers falls.

Immigration   Movement of workers from region to region, or country to country, is another important source of shifts in labor supply. When immigrants come to the United States, for instance, the supply of labor in the United States increases, and the supply of labor in the immigrants' home countries falls. In fact, much of the policy debate about immigration centers on its effect on labor supply and, thereby, equilibrium wages in the labor market.

QUICK QUIZ   Who has a greater opportunity cost of enjoying leisure—a janitor or a brain surgeon? Explain. Can this help explain why doctors work such long hours?

EQUILIBRIUM IN THE LABOR MARKET

So far we have established two facts about how wages are determined in competitive labor markets:

- The wage adjusts to balance the supply and demand for labor.
- The wage equals the value of the marginal product of labor.

At first, it might seem surprising that the wage can do both of these things at once. In fact, there is no real puzzle here, but understanding why there is no puzzle is an important step to understanding wage determination.

Figure 4 shows the labor market in equilibrium. The wage and the quantity of labor have adjusted to balance supply and demand. When the market is in this equilibrium, each firm has bought as much labor as it finds profitable at the equilibrium wage. That is, each firm has followed the rule for profit maximization: It has hired workers until the value of the marginal product equals the wage. Hence, the wage must equal the value of the marginal product of labor once it has brought supply and demand into equilibrium.

This brings us to an important lesson: *Any event that changes the supply or demand for labor must change the equilibrium wage and the value of the marginal product by the same amount because these must always be equal.* To see how this works, let's consider some events that shift these curves.

SHIFTS IN LABOR SUPPLY

Suppose that immigration increases the number of workers willing to pick apples. As Figure 5 shows, the supply of labor shifts to the right from S_1 to S_2. At the initial wage W_1, the quantity of labor supplied now exceeds the quantity demanded.

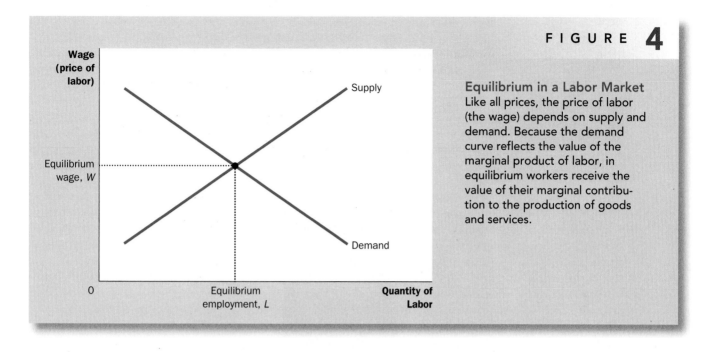

FIGURE **4**

Wage (price of labor)

Equilibrium wage, W

Supply

Demand

0   Equilibrium employment, L   Quantity of Labor

Equilibrium in a Labor Market
Like all prices, the price of labor (the wage) depends on supply and demand. Because the demand curve reflects the value of the marginal product of labor, in equilibrium workers receive the value of their marginal contribution to the production of goods and services.

This surplus of labor puts downward pressure on the wage of apple pickers, and the fall in the wage from W_1 to W_2 in turn makes it profitable for firms to hire more workers. As the number of workers employed in each apple orchard rises, the marginal product of a worker falls, and so does the value of the marginal product. In the new equilibrium, both the wage and the value of the marginal product of labor are lower than they were before the influx of new workers.

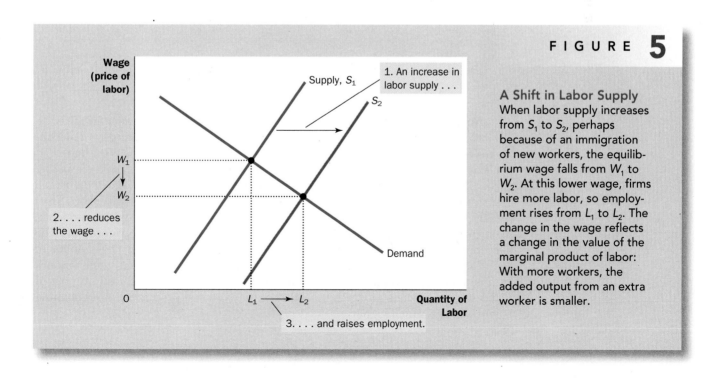

FIGURE **5**

Wage (price of labor)

Supply, S_1

S_2

1. An increase in labor supply . . .

W_1
W_2

2. . . . reduces the wage . . .

Demand

0   L_1 L_2 Quantity of Labor

3. . . . and raises employment.

A Shift in Labor Supply
When labor supply increases from S_1 to S_2, perhaps because of an immigration of new workers, the equilibrium wage falls from W_1 to W_2. At this lower wage, firms hire more labor, so employment rises from L_1 to L_2. The change in the wage reflects a change in the value of the marginal product of labor: With more workers, the added output from an extra worker is smaller.

In The News

The Economics of Immigration

Here is an interview with Pia Orrenius, an economist at the Federal Reserve Bank of Dallas who studies immigration.

Pia Orrenius

Q: What can you tell us about the size of the immigrant population in the United States?

A: Immigrants make up about 12 percent of the overall population, which means about 36 million foreign-born live in the United States. The commonly accepted estimate for the undocumented portion of the foreign-born population is 11 million. Immigrants come from all parts of the world, but we've seen big changes in their origins. In the 1950s and 1960s, 75 percent of immigrants were from Europe. Today, about 75 percent are from Latin America and Asia. Inflows are also much larger today, with 1 million to 2 million newcomers entering each year.

What's interesting about the United States is how our economy has been able to absorb immigrants and put them to work. U.S. immigrants have high employ-ment rates compared with other developed countries. This is partly because we don't set high entry-level wages or have strict hiring and firing rules. In this type of flexible system, you have more job openings. You have more opportunities. You also have lower entry-level wages, but immigrants at least get their foot in the door.

Being in the workforce allows immigrants to interact with the rest of society. They learn the language faster, pay taxes and become stakeholders.

Q: Where do immigrants fit into the U.S. economy?

A: Our immigrants are diverse in economic terms. We rely on immigrants for both high- and low-skilled jobs. Some immigrants do medium-skilled work, but more than anything else they're found on the low and the high ends of the education distribution.

The economic effects are different depending on which group you're talking about. We have an extremely important group of high-skilled immigrants. We rely on them to fill important, high-level jobs in technology, science and research. About 40 percent of our Ph.D. scientists and engi-

An episode from Israel illustrates how a shift in labor supply can alter the equilibrium in a labor market. During most of the 1980s, many thousands of Palestinians regularly commuted from their homes in the Israeli-occupied West Bank and Gaza Strip to jobs in Israel, primarily in the construction and agriculture industries. In 1988, however, political unrest in these occupied areas induced the Israeli government to take steps that, as a by-product, reduced this supply of workers. Curfews were imposed, work permits were checked more thoroughly, and a ban on overnight stays of Palestinians in Israel was enforced more rigorously. The economic impact of these steps was exactly as theory predicts: The number of Palestinians with jobs in Israel fell by half, while those who continued to work in Israel enjoyed wage increases of about 50 percent. With a reduced number of Palestinian workers in Israel, the value of the marginal product of the remaining workers was much higher.

neers were born in another country. We also employ many high-skilled immigrants in the health sector.

High-skilled immigration has good economic effects—it adds to GDP growth. It also has beneficial fiscal effects—the impact on government finances is large and positive. People tend to focus on illegal or low-skilled immigration when discussing immigrants and often do not recognize the tremendous contribution of high-skilled immigrants.

Q: What about the low-skilled immigration?

A: With low-skilled immigration, the economic benefits are there as well but have to be balanced against the fiscal impact, which is likely negative.

What makes the fiscal issue more difficult is the distribution of the burden. The federal government reaps much of the revenue from immigrants who work and pay employment taxes. State and local governments realize less of that benefit and have to pay more of the costs associated with low-skilled immigration—usually health care and educational expenses.

Q: Does it matter whether the immigration is legal or not?

A: If you're making value judgments about immigrants, or if you're discussing national security, you probably need to distinguish between those who come legally and those who don't. From an economic perspective, however, it makes more sense to differentiate among immigrants of various skill levels than it does to focus on legal status.

The economic benefits of low-skilled immigrants aren't typically going to depend on how they entered the United States. Illegal immigrants may pay less in taxes, but they're also eligible for fewer benefits. So being illegal doesn't mean these immigrants have a worse fiscal impact. In fact, a low-skilled illegal immigrant can create less fiscal burden than a low-skilled legal immigrant because the undocumented don't qualify for most benefits.

Q: How does immigration affect jobs and earnings for the native-born population?

A: We focus a lot on that—for example, exactly how immigration has affected the

wages of Americans, particularly the low-skilled who lack a high school degree. The reason we worry about this is that real wages have been falling for low-skilled U.S. workers over the past 25 years or so.

The studies tend to show that not much of the decline is due to inflows of immigrants. The consensus seems to be that wages are about 1 to 3 percent lower today as a result of immigration. Some scholars find larger effects for low-skilled workers. Still, labor economists think it's a bit of a puzzle that they haven't been able to systematically identify larger adverse wage effects.

The reason may be the way the economy is constantly adjusting to the inflow of immigrants. On a geographical basis, for example, a large influx of immigrants into an area tends to encourage an inflow of capital to put them to use. So you have a shift out in labor supply, but you also have a shift out in labor demand, and the wage effects are ameliorated.

Source: *Southwest Economy*, March/April 2006.

SHIFTS IN LABOR DEMAND

Now suppose that an increase in the popularity of apples causes their price to rise. This price increase does not change the marginal product of labor for any given number of workers, but it does raise the *value* of the marginal product. With a higher price of apples, hiring more apple pickers is now profitable. As Figure 6 shows, when the demand for labor shifts to the right from D_1 to D_2, the equilibrium wage rises from W_1 to W_2, and equilibrium employment rises from L_1 to L_2. Once again, the wage and the value of the marginal product of labor move together.

This analysis shows that prosperity for firms in an industry is often linked to prosperity for workers in that industry. When the price of apples rises, apple producers make greater profit, and apple pickers earn higher wages. When the price

6 FIGURE

A Shift in Labor Demand
When labor demand increases from D_1 to D_2, perhaps because of an increase in the price of the firm's output, the equilibrium wage rises from W_1 to W_2, and employment rises from L_1 to L_2. Again, the change in the wage reflects a change in the value of the marginal product of labor: With a higher output price, the added output from an extra worker is more valuable.

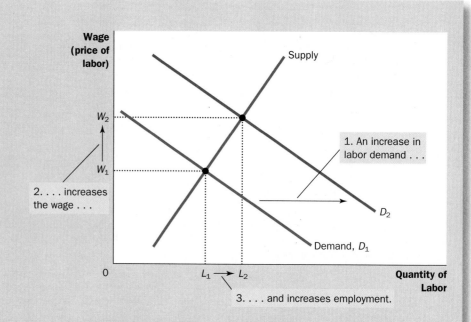

of apples falls, apple producers earn smaller profit, and apple pickers earn lower wages. This lesson is well known to workers in industries with highly volatile prices. Workers in oil fields, for instance, know from experience that their earnings are closely linked to the world price of crude oil.

From these examples, you should now have a good understanding of how wages are set in competitive labor markets. Labor supply and labor demand together determine the equilibrium wage, and shifts in the supply or demand curve for labor cause the equilibrium wage to change. At the same time, profit maximization by the firms that demand labor ensures that the equilibrium wage always equals the value of the marginal product of labor.

PRODUCTIVITY AND WAGES

One of the *Ten Principles of Economics* in Chapter 1 is that our standard of living depends on our ability to produce goods and services. We can now see how this principle works in the market for labor. In particular, our analysis of labor demand shows that wages equal productivity as measured by the value of the marginal product of labor. Put simply, highly productive workers are highly paid, and less productive workers are less highly paid.

This lesson is key to understanding why workers today are better off than workers in previous generations. Table 2 presents some data on growth in productivity and growth in real wages (that is, wages adjusted for inflation). From 1959 to 2006, productivity as measured by output per hour of work grew about 2.1 percent per year. Real wages grew at 2.0 percent—almost exactly the same rate. With a growth rate of 2 percent per year, productivity and real wages double about every 35 years.

Time Period	Growth Rate of Productivity	Growth Rate of Real Wages
1959–2006	2.1%	2.0%
1959–1973	2.8	2.8
1973–1995	1.4	1.2
1995–2006	2.6	2.5

TABLE 2

Productivity and Wage Growth in the United States

Source: Economic Report of the President 2008, Table B-49. Growth in productivity is measured here as the annualized rate of change in output per hour in the nonfarm business sector. Growth in real wages is measured as the annualized change in compensation per hour in the nonfarm business sector divided by the implicit price deflator for that sector. These productivity data measure average productivity—the quantity of output divided by the quantity of labor—rather than marginal productivity, but average and marginal productivity are thought to move closely together.

Productivity growth varies over time. Table 2 also shows the data for three shorter periods that economists have identified as having very different productivity experiences. Around 1973, the U.S. economy experienced a significant slowdown in productivity growth that lasted until 1995. The cause of the productivity slowdown is not well understood, but the link between productivity and real wages is exactly as standard theory predicts. The slowdown in productivity growth from 2.8 to 1.4 percent per year coincided with a slowdown in real wage growth from 2.8 to 1.2 percent per year.

Productivity growth picked up again around 1995, and many observers hailed the arrival of the "new economy." This productivity acceleration is most often attributed to the spread of computers and information technology. As theory predicts, growth in real wages picked up as well. From 1995 to 2006, productivity grew by 2.6 percent per year, and real wages grew by 2.5 percent per year.

The bottom line: Both theory and history confirm the close connection between productivity and real wages. ●

QUICK QUIZ How does an immigration of workers affect labor supply, labor demand, the marginal product of labor, and the equilibrium wage?

THE OTHER FACTORS OF PRODUCTION: LAND AND CAPITAL

We have seen how firms decide how much labor to hire and how these decisions determine workers' wages. At the same time that firms are hiring workers, they are also deciding about other inputs to production. For example, our apple-producing firm might have to choose the size of its apple orchard and the number of ladders for its apple pickers. We can think of the firm's factors of production as falling into three categories: labor, land, and capital.

FYI

Monopsony

On the preceding pages, we built our analysis of the labor market with the tools of supply and demand. In doing so, we assumed that the labor market was competitive. That is, we assumed that there were many buyers and sellers of labor, so each buyer or seller had a negligible effect on the wage.

Yet imagine the labor market in a small town dominated by a single large employer. That employer can exert a large influence on the going wage, and it may well use that market power to alter the outcome. Such a market in which there is a single buyer is called a *monopsony*.

A monopsony (a market with one buyer) is in many ways similar to a monopoly (a market with one seller). Recall from Chapter 15 that a monopoly firm produces less of the good than would a competitive firm; by reducing the quantity offered for sale, the monopoly firm moves along the product's demand curve, raising the price and also its profits. Similarly, a monopsony firm in a labor market hires fewer workers than would a competitive firm; by reducing the number of jobs available, the monopsony firm moves along the labor supply curve, reducing the wage it pays and raising its profits. Thus, both monopolists and monopsonists reduce economic activity in a market below the socially optimal level. In both cases, the existence of market power distorts the outcome and causes deadweight losses.

This book does not present the formal model of monopsony because, in the world, monopsonies are rare. In most labor markets, workers have many possible employers, and firms compete with one another to attract workers. In this case, the model of supply and demand is the best one to use.

---

capital
the equipment and structures used to produce goods and services

The meaning of the terms *labor* and *land* is clear, but the definition of *capital* is somewhat tricky. Economists use the term **capital** to refer to the stock of equipment and structures used for production. That is, the economy's capital represents the accumulation of goods produced in the past that are being used in the present to produce new goods and services. For our apple firm, the capital stock includes the ladders used to climb the trees, the trucks used to transport the apples, the buildings used to store the apples, and even the trees themselves.

EQUILIBRIUM IN THE MARKETS FOR LAND AND CAPITAL

What determines how much the owners of land and capital earn for their contribution to the production process? Before answering this question, we need to distinguish between two prices: the purchase price and the rental price. The *purchase price* of land or capital is the price a person pays to own that factor of production indefinitely. The *rental price* is the price a person pays to use that factor for a limited period of time. It is important to keep this distinction in mind because, as we will see, these prices are determined by somewhat different economic forces.

Having defined these terms, we can now apply the theory of factor demand that we developed for the labor market to the markets for land and capital. Because the wage is the rental price of labor, much of what we have learned about wage determination applies also to the rental prices of land and capital. As Figure 7 illustrates, the rental price of land, shown in panel (a), and the rental price of capital, shown in panel (b), are determined by supply and demand. Moreover, the

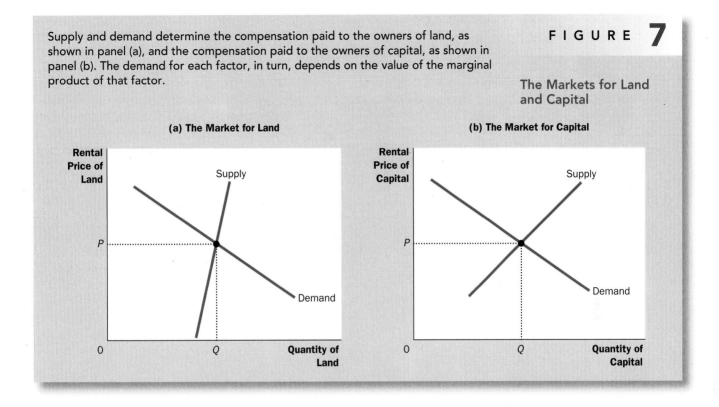

Supply and demand determine the compensation paid to the owners of land, as shown in panel (a), and the compensation paid to the owners of capital, as shown in panel (b). The demand for each factor, in turn, depends on the value of the marginal product of that factor.

FIGURE **7**

The Markets for Land and Capital

demand for land and capital is determined just like the demand for labor. That is, when our apple-producing firm is deciding how much land and how many ladders to rent, it follows the same logic as when deciding how many workers to hire. For both land and capital, the firm increases the quantity hired until the value of the factor's marginal product equals the factor's price. Thus, the demand curve for each factor reflects the marginal productivity of that factor.

We can now explain how much income goes to labor, how much goes to landowners, and how much goes to the owners of capital. As long as the firms using the factors of production are competitive and profit-maximizing, each factor's rental price must equal the value of the marginal product for that factor. *Labor, land, and capital each earn the value of their marginal contribution to the production process.*

Now consider the purchase price of land and capital. The rental price and the purchase price are related: Buyers are willing to pay more for a piece of land or capital if it produces a valuable stream of rental income. And as we have just seen, the equilibrium rental income at any point in time equals the value of that factor's marginal product. Therefore, the equilibrium purchase price of a piece of land or capital depends on both the current value of the marginal product and the value of the marginal product expected to prevail in the future.

LINKAGES AMONG THE FACTORS OF PRODUCTION

We have seen that the price paid to any factor of production—labor, land, or capital—equals the value of the marginal product of that factor. The marginal product of any factor, in turn, depends on the quantity of that factor that is available. Because of diminishing marginal product, a factor in abundant supply has

FYI

What Is Capital Income?

Labor income is an easy concept to understand: It is the paycheck that workers get from their employers. The income earned by capital, however, is less obvious.

In our analysis, we have been implicitly assuming that households own the economy's stock of capital—ladders, drill presses, warehouses, and so on—and rent it to the firms that use it. Capital income, in this case, is the rent that households receive for the use of their capital. This assumption simplified our analysis of how capital owners are compensated, but it is not entirely realistic. In fact, firms usually own the capital they use, and, therefore, they receive the earnings from this capital.

These earnings from capital, however, eventually are paid to households. Some of the earnings are paid in the form of interest to those households who have lent money to firms. Bondholders and bank depositors are two examples of recipients of interest. Thus, when you receive interest on your bank account, that income is part of the economy's capital income.

In addition, some of the earnings from capital are paid to households in the form of dividends. Dividends are payments by a firm to the firm's stockholders. A stockholder is a person who has bought a share in the ownership of the firm and, therefore, is entitled to share in the firm's profits.

A firm does not have to pay out all its earnings to households in the form of interest and dividends. Instead, it can retain some earnings within the firm and use these earnings to buy additional capital. Although these retained earnings are not paid to the firm's stockholders, the stockholders benefit from them nonetheless. Because retained earnings increase the amount of capital the firm owns, they tend to increase future earnings and, thereby, the value of the firm's stock.

These institutional details are interesting and important, but they do not alter our conclusion about the income earned by the owners of capital. Capital is paid according to the value of its marginal product, regardless of whether this income is transmitted to households in the form of interest or dividends or whether it is kept within firms as retained earnings.

a low marginal product and thus a low price, and a factor in scarce supply has a high marginal product and a high price. As a result, when the supply of a factor falls, its equilibrium factor price rises.

When the supply of any factor changes, however, the effects are not limited to the market for that factor. In most situations, factors of production are used together in a way that makes the productivity of each factor dependent on the quantities of the other factors available for use in the production process. As a result, a change in the supply of any one factor alters the earnings of all the factors.

For example, suppose a hurricane destroys many of the ladders that workers use to pick apples from the orchards. What happens to the earnings of the various factors of production? Most obviously, the supply of ladders falls, and, therefore, the equilibrium rental price of ladders rises. Those owners who were lucky enough to avoid damage to their ladders now earn a higher return when they rent out their ladders to the firms that produce apples.

Yet the effects of this event do not stop at the ladder market. Because there are fewer ladders with which to work, the workers who pick apples have a smaller marginal product. Thus, the reduction in the supply of ladders reduces the demand for the labor of apple pickers, and this causes the equilibrium wage to fall.

This story shows a general lesson: An event that changes the supply of any factor of production can alter the earnings of all the factors. The change in earnings of any factor can be found by analyzing the impact of the event on the value of the marginal product of that factor.

CASE STUDY   THE ECONOMICS OF THE BLACK DEATH

In 14th-century Europe, the bubonic plague wiped out about one-third of the population within a few years. This event, called the *Black Death*, provides a grisly natural experiment to test the theory of factor markets that we have just developed. Consider the effects of the Black Death on those who were lucky enough to survive. What do you think happened to the wages earned by workers and the rents earned by landowners?

To answer this question, let's examine the effects of a reduced population on the marginal product of labor and the marginal product of land. With a smaller supply of workers, the marginal product of labor rises. (This is diminishing marginal product working in reverse.) Thus, we would expect the Black Death to raise wages.

Because land and labor are used together in production, a smaller supply of workers also affects the market for land, the other major factor of production in medieval Europe. With fewer workers available to farm the land, an additional unit of land produced less additional output. In other words, the marginal product of land fell. Thus, we would expect the Black Death to lower rents.

In fact, both predictions are consistent with the historical evidence. Wages approximately doubled during this period, and rents declined 50 percent or more. The Black Death led to economic prosperity for the peasant classes and reduced incomes for the landed classes. ●

WORKERS WHO SURVIVED THE PLAGUE WERE LUCKY IN MORE WAYS THAN ONE.

QUICK QUIZ What determines the income of the owners of land and capital? ● How would an increase in the quantity of capital affect the incomes of those who already own capital? How would it affect the incomes of workers?

CONCLUSION

This chapter explained how labor, land, and capital are compensated for the roles they play in the production process. The theory developed here is called the *neoclassical theory of distribution*. According to the neoclassical theory, the amount paid to each factor of production depends on the supply and demand for that factor. The demand, in turn, depends on that particular factor's marginal productivity. In equilibrium, each factor of production earns the value of its marginal contribution to the production of goods and services.

The neoclassical theory of distribution is widely accepted. Most economists begin with the neoclassical theory when trying to explain how the U.S. economy's $14 trillion of income is distributed among the economy's various members. In the following two chapters, we consider the distribution of income in more detail. As you will see, the neoclassical theory provides the framework for this discussion.

Even at this point, you can use the theory to answer the question that began this chapter: Why are computer programmers paid more than gas station attendants?

It is because programmers can produce a good of greater market value than can gas station attendants. People are willing to pay dearly for a good computer game, but they are willing to pay little to have their gas pumped and their windshield washed. The wages of these workers reflect the market prices of the goods they produce. If people suddenly got tired of using computers and decided to spend more time driving, the prices of these goods would change, and so would the equilibrium wages of these two groups of workers.

SUMMARY

- The economy's income is distributed in the markets for the factors of production. The three most important factors of production are labor, land, and capital.

- The demand for factors, such as labor, is a derived demand that comes from firms that use the factors to produce goods and services. Competitive, profit-maximizing firms hire each factor up to the point at which the value of the marginal product of the factor equals its price.

- The supply of labor arises from individuals' trade-off between work and leisure. An upward-sloping labor-supply curve means that people respond to an increase in the wage by working more hours and enjoying less leisure.

- The price paid to each factor adjusts to balance the supply and demand for that factor. Because factor demand reflects the value of the marginal product of that factor, in equilibrium each factor is compensated according to its marginal contribution to the production of goods and services.

- Because factors of production are used together, the marginal product of any one factor depends on the quantities of all factors that are available. As a result, a change in the supply of one factor alters the equilibrium earnings of all the factors.

KEY CONCEPTS

factors of production, *p. 392*
production function, *p. 394*
marginal product of labor, *p. 394*

diminishing marginal
product, *p. 394*

value of the marginal
product, *p. 395*
capital, *p. 406*

QUESTIONS FOR REVIEW

1. Explain how a firm's production function is related to its marginal product of labor, how a firm's marginal product of labor is related to the value of its marginal product, and how a firm's value of marginal product is related to its demand for labor.

2. Give two examples of events that could shift the demand for labor, and explain why they do so.

3. Give two examples of events that could shift the supply of labor, and explain why they do so.

4. Explain how the wage can adjust to balance the supply and demand for labor while simultaneously equaling the value of the marginal product of labor.

5. If the population of the United States suddenly grew because of a large immigration, what would happen to wages? What would happen to the rents earned by the owners of land and capital?

PROBLEMS AND APPLICATIONS

1. Suppose that the president proposes a new law aimed at reducing healthcare costs: All Americans are required to eat one apple daily.
   a. How would this apple-a-day law affect the demand and equilibrium price of apples?
   b. How would the law affect the marginal product and the value of the marginal product of apple pickers?
   c. How would the law affect the demand and equilibrium wage for apple pickers?
2. Show the effect of each of the following events on the market for labor in the computer manufacturing industry.
   a. Congress buys personal computers for all U.S. college students.
   b. More college students major in engineering and computer science.
   c. Computer firms build new manufacturing plants.
3. Suppose that labor is the only input used by a perfectly competitive firm. The firm's production function is as follows:

Days of Labor	Units of Output
0 days	0 units
1	7
2	13
3	19
4	25
5	28
6	29
7	29

   a. Calculate the marginal product for each additional worker.
   b. Each unit of output sells for $10. Calculate the value of the marginal product of each worker.
   c. Compute the demand schedule showing the number of workers hired for all wages from zero to $100 a day.
   d. Graph the firm's demand curve.
   e. What happens to this demand curve if the price of output rises from $10 to $12 per unit?
4. Smiling Cow Dairy can sell all the milk it wants for $4 a gallon, and it can rent all the robots it wants to milk the cows at a capital rental price of $100 a day. It faces the following production schedule:

Number of Robots	Total Product
0	0 gallons
1	50
2	85
3	115
4	140
5	150
6	155

   a. In what kind of market structure does the firm sell its output? How can you tell?
   b. In what kind of market structure does the firm rent robots? How can you tell?
   c. Calculate the marginal product and the value of the marginal product for each additional robot.
   d. How many robots should the firm rent? Explain.
5. Your enterprising uncle opens a sandwich shop that employs 7 people. The employees are paid $6 per hour, and a sandwich sells for $3. If your uncle is maximizing his profit, what is the value of the marginal product of the last worker he hired? What is that worker's marginal product?
6. Suppose a freeze destroys part of the Florida orange crop.
   a. Explain what happens to the price of oranges and the marginal product of orange pickers as a result of the freeze. Can you say what happens to the demand for orange pickers? Why or why not?
   b. Suppose the price of oranges doubles and the marginal product falls by 30 percent. What happens to the equilibrium wage of orange pickers?
   c. Suppose the price of oranges rises by 30 percent and the marginal product falls by 50 percent. What happens to the equilibrium wage of orange pickers?
7. Leadbelly Co. sells pencils in a perfectly competitive product market and hires workers in a perfectly competitive labor market. Assume that the market wage rate for workers is $150 per day.
   a. What rule should Leadbelly follow to hire the profit-maximizing amount of labor?

b. At the profit-maximizing level of output, the marginal product of the last worker hired is 30 boxes of pencils per day. Calculate the price of a box of pencils.

c. Draw a diagram of the labor market for pencil workers (as in Figure 4 of this chapter) next to a diagram of the labor supply and demand for Leadbelly Co. (as in Figure 3). Label the equilibrium wage and quantity of labor for both the market and the firm. How are these diagrams related?

d. Suppose some pencil workers switch to jobs in the growing computer industry. On the side-by-side diagrams from part (c), show how this change affects the equilibrium wage and quantity of labor for both the pencil market and for Leadbelly. How does this change affect the marginal product of labor at Leadbelly?

8. During the 1980s, 1990s, and the first decade of the 21st century, the United States experienced a significant inflow of capital from abroad. For example, Toyota, BMW, and other foreign car companies built auto plants in the United States.

a. Using a diagram of the U.S. capital market, show the effect of this inflow on the rental price of capital in the United States and on the quantity of capital in use.

b. Using a diagram of the U.S. labor market, show the effect of the capital inflow on the average wage paid to U.S. workers.

9. In recent years, some policymakers have proposed requiring firms to give workers certain fringe benefits, such as health insurance. Let's consider the effects of such a policy on the labor market.

a. Suppose that a law required firms to give each worker $3 of fringe benefits for every hour that the worker is employed by the firm. How does this law affect the marginal profit that a firm earns from each worker? How does the law affect the demand curve for labor? Draw your answer on a graph with the cash wage on the vertical axis.

b. If there is no change in labor supply, how would this law affect employment and wages?

c. Why might the labor-supply curve shift in response to this law? Would this shift in labor supply raise or lower the impact of the law on wages and employment?

d. As Chapter 6 discussed, the wages of some workers, particularly the unskilled and inexperienced, are kept above the equilibrium level by minimum-wage laws. What effect would a fringe-benefit mandate have for these workers?

10. This chapter has assumed that labor is supplied by individual workers acting competitively. In some markets, however, the supply of labor is determined by a union of workers.

a. Explain why the situation faced by a labor union may resemble the situation faced by a monopoly firm.

b. The goal of a monopoly firm is to maximize profits. Is there an analogous goal for labor unions?

c. Now extend the analogy between monopoly firms and unions. How do you suppose that the wage set by a union compares to the wage in a competitive market? How do you suppose employment differs in the two cases?

d. What other goals might unions have that make unions different from monopoly firms?

Earnings and Discrimination

In the United States today, the typical physician earns about $200,000 a year, the typical police officer about $50,000, and the typical farmworker about $20,000. These examples illustrate the large differences in earnings that are so common in our economy. The differences explain why some people live in mansions, ride in limousines, and vacation on the French Riviera, while other people live in small apartments, ride a bus, and vacation in their own backyards.

Why do earnings vary so much from person to person? Chapter 18, which developed the basic neoclassical theory of the labor market, offers an answer to this question. There we saw that wages are governed by labor supply and labor demand. Labor demand, in turn, reflects the marginal productivity of labor. In equilibrium, each worker is paid the value of his or her marginal contribution to the economy's production of goods and services.

This theory of the labor market, though widely accepted by economists, is only the beginning of the story. To understand the wide variation in earnings that we observe, we must go beyond this general framework and examine more precisely what determines the supply and demand for different types of labor. That is our goal in this chapter.

SOME DETERMINANTS OF EQUILIBRIUM WAGES

Workers differ from one another in many ways. Jobs also have differing characteristics—both in terms of the wage they pay and in terms of their nonmonetary attributes. In this section, we consider how the characteristics of jobs and workers affect labor supply, labor demand, and equilibrium wages.

COMPENSATING DIFFERENTIALS

When a worker is deciding whether to take a job, the wage is only one of many job attributes that the worker takes into account. Some jobs are easy, fun, and safe, while others are hard, dull, and dangerous. The better the job as gauged by these nonmonetary characteristics, the more people there are who are willing to do the job at any given wage. In other words, the supply of labor for easy, fun, and safe jobs is greater than the supply of labor for hard, dull, and dangerous jobs. As a result, "good" jobs will tend to have lower equilibrium wages than "bad" jobs.

For example, imagine you are looking for a summer job in a local beach community. Two kinds of jobs are available. You can take a job as a beach-badge checker, or you can take a job as a garbage collector. The beach-badge checkers take leisurely strolls along the beach during the day and check to make sure the tourists have bought the required beach permits. The garbage collectors wake up before dawn to drive dirty, noisy trucks around town to pick up garbage. Which job would you want? Most people would prefer the beach job if the wages were the same. To induce people to become garbage collectors, the town has to offer higher wages to garbage collectors than to beach-badge checkers.

Economists use the term **compensating differential** to refer to a difference in wages that arises from nonmonetary characteristics of different jobs. Compensating differentials are prevalent in the economy. Here are some examples:

compensating differential
a difference in wages that arises to offset the nonmonetary characteristics of different jobs

- Coal miners are paid more than other workers with similar levels of education. Their higher wage compensates them for the dirty and dangerous nature of coal mining, as well as the long-term health problems that coal miners experience.
- Workers who work the night shift at factories are paid more than similar workers who work the day shift. The higher wage compensates them for having to work at night and sleep during the day, a lifestyle that most people find undesirable.
- Professors are paid less than lawyers and doctors, who have similar amounts of education. Professors' lower wages compensate them for the great intellectual and personal satisfaction that their jobs offer. (Indeed, teaching economics is so much fun that it is surprising that economics professors are paid anything at all!)

"ON THE ONE HAND, I KNOW I COULD MAKE MORE MONEY IF I LEFT PUBLIC SERVICE FOR THE PRIVATE SECTOR, BUT, ON THE OTHER HAND, I COULDN'T CHOP OFF HEADS."

HUMAN CAPITAL

As we discussed in the previous chapter, the word *capital* usually refers to the economy's stock of equipment and structures. The capital stock includes the farmer's tractor, the manufacturer's factory, and the teacher's chalkboard. The essence of capital is that it is a factor of production that itself has been produced.

There is another type of capital that, while less tangible than physical capital, is just as important to the economy's production. **Human capital** is the accumulation of investments in people. The most important type of human capital is education. Like all forms of capital, education represents an expenditure of resources at one time to raise productivity in the future. But unlike an investment in other forms of capital, an investment in education is tied to a specific person, and this linkage is what makes it human capital.

Not surprisingly, workers with more human capital on average earn more than those with less human capital. College graduates in the United States, for example, earn almost twice as much as those workers who end their education with a high school diploma. This large difference has been documented in many countries around the world. It tends to be even larger in less developed countries, where educated workers are in scarce supply.

It is easy to see why education raises wages from the perspective of supply and demand. Firms—the demanders of labor—are willing to pay more for the highly educated because highly educated workers have higher marginal products. Workers—the suppliers of labor—are willing to pay the cost of becoming educated only if there is a reward for doing so. In essence, the difference in wages between highly educated workers and less educated workers may be considered a compensating differential for the cost of becoming educated.

human capital
the accumulation of investments in people, such as education and on-the-job training

THE INCREASING VALUE OF SKILLS

"The rich get richer, and the poor get poorer." Like many adages, this one is not always true, but recently it has been. Many studies have documented that the earnings gap between workers with high skills and workers with low skills has increased over the past two decades.

Table 1 presents data on the average earnings of college graduates and of high school graduates without any additional education. These data show the increase in the financial reward from education. In 1980, a man on average earned 44 percent more with a college degree than without one; by 2005, this figure had risen to 87 percent. For a woman, the reward for attending college rose from a 35 percent increase in earnings to a 72 percent increase. The incentive to stay in school is as great today as it has ever been.

Why has the gap in earnings between skilled and unskilled workers widened in recent years? No one knows for sure, but economists have proposed two hypotheses to explain this trend. Both hypotheses suggest that the demand for skilled labor has risen over time relative to the demand for unskilled labor. The shift in demand has led to a corresponding change in wages, which in turn has led to greater inequality.

The first hypothesis is that international trade has altered the relative demand for skilled and unskilled labor. In recent years, the amount of trade with other countries has increased substantially. As a percentage of total U.S. production of goods and services, imports have risen from 5 percent in 1970 to 16 percent in 2005, and exports have risen from 6 percent in 1970 to 11 percent in 2005. Because unskilled labor is plentiful and cheap in many foreign countries, the United States tends to import goods produced with unskilled labor and export goods produced

1 **TABLE**

Average Annual Earnings by Educational Attainment
College graduates have always earned more than workers without the benefit of college, but the salary gap has grown even larger over the past few decades.

	1980	2005
Men		
High school, no college	$41,083	$40,112
College graduates	$59,196	$75,130
Percent extra for college grads	+44%	+87%
Women		
High school, no college	$24,775	$28,657
College graduates	$33,452	$49,326
Percent extra for college grads	+35%	+72%

Note: Earnings data are adjusted for inflation and are expressed in 2005 dollars. Data apply to full-time, year-round workers age 18 and over. Data for college graduates exclude workers with additional schooling beyond college, such as a master's degree or PhD.

Source: U.S. Census Bureau and author's calculations.

with skilled labor. Thus, when international trade expands, the domestic demand for skilled labor rises, and the domestic demand for unskilled labor falls.

The second hypothesis is that changes in technology have altered the relative demand for skilled and unskilled labor. Consider, for instance, the introduction of computers. Computers raise the demand for skilled workers who can use the new machines and reduce the demand for the unskilled workers whose jobs are replaced by the computers. For example, many companies now rely more on computer databases, and less on filing cabinets, to keep business records. This change raises the demand for computer programmers and reduces the demand for filing clerks. Thus, as more firms use computers, the demand for skilled labor rises, and the demand for unskilled labor falls.

Economists have found it difficult to gauge the validity of these two hypotheses. It is possible that both are true: Increasing international trade and technological change may share responsibility for the increasing income inequality we have observed in recent decades.   ●

ABILITY, EFFORT, AND CHANCE

Why do major league baseball players get paid more than minor league players? Certainly, the higher wage is not a compensating differential. Playing in the major leagues is not a less pleasant job than playing in the minor leagues; in fact, the opposite is true. The major leagues do not require more years of schooling or more experience. To a large extent, players in the major leagues earn more just because they have greater natural ability.

Natural ability is important for workers in all occupations. Because of heredity and upbringing, people differ in their physical and mental attributes. Some people are strong, others weak. Some people are smart, others less so. Some people

In The News

The Loss of Manufacturing Jobs

In the early 1940s, about one in three American workers worked in manufacturing. Today, that figure is about one in ten. According to former Secretary of Labor Robert Reich, the loss of manufacturing jobs is not a reason to worry. But it is a reason to study hard.

Nice Work If You Can Get It

By Robert B. Reich

It's hard to listen to a politician or pundit these days without hearing that America is "losing jobs" to poorer nations—manufacturing jobs to China, back-office work to India, just about every job to Latin America. This lament distracts our attention from the larger challenge of preparing more Americans for better jobs. . . .

It's true that U.S. manufacturing employment has been dropping for many years, but that's not primarily due to foreigners taking these jobs. Factory jobs are vanishing all over the world. . . . I recently toured a U.S. factory containing two employees and 400 computerized robots. The two live people sat in front of computer screens and instructed the robots. In a few years this factory won't have a single employee on site, except for an occasional visiting technician who repairs and upgrades the robots, like the gas man changing your meter.

Manufacturing is following the same trend as agriculture. As productivity rises, employment falls because fewer people are needed. In 1910, a third of Americans worked on farms. Now, fewer than 3 percent do. Since 1995, even as manufacturing employment has dropped around the world, global industrial output has risen more than 30 percent. . . .

Want to blame something? Blame new knowledge. Knowledge created the electronic gadgets and software that can now do almost any routine task. This goes well beyond the factory floor. America also used to have lots of elevator operators, telephone operators, bank tellers, and service-station attendants. Most have been replaced by technology. . . .

Any job that's even slightly routine is disappearing from the United States. But this doesn't mean we are left with fewer jobs. It means only that we have fewer routine jobs. . . .

Look closely at the economy today and you find two growing categories of work—but only the first is commanding better pay and benefits. This category involves identifying and solving new problems. Here, workers do R&D, design, and engineering. Or they are responsible for high-level sales, marketing, and advertising. They're composers, writers, and producers. They're lawyers, bankers, financiers, journalists, doctors, and management consultants. I call this "symbolic analysis" work because most of it has to do with analyzing, manipulating, and communicating through numbers, shapes, words, ideas. This kind of work usually requires a college degree. . . .

A second growing category of work in America involves personal services. Computers and robots can't do these jobs because they require care and attentiveness. Workers in other nations can't do them because they must be done in person. Some personal-service workers need education beyond high school—nurses, physical therapists, and medical technicians. But most don't, such as restaurant workers, cabbies, retail workers, security guards, and hospital attendants. In contrast to that of symbolic analysts, the pay of most personal-service workers in the United States is stagnant or declining. That's because the supply of personal-service workers is growing quickly, as more and more people who'd otherwise have factory or routine service jobs join their ranks. Legal and undocumented immigrants are also pouring into this sector.

But America's long-term problem isn't too few jobs. It's the widening income gap between personal-service workers and symbolic analysts. The long-term solution is to help spur upward mobility by getting more Americans a good education, including access to college.

Source: *The Wall Street Journal,* December 26, 2003.

are outgoing, others awkward in social situations. These and many other personal characteristics determine how productive workers are and, therefore, play a role in determining the wages they earn.

Closely related to ability is effort. Some people work hard, others are lazy. We should not be surprised to find that those who work hard are more productive and earn higher wages. To some extent, firms reward workers directly by paying people based on what they produce. Salespeople, for instance, are often paid a percentage of the sales they make. At other times, hard work is rewarded less directly in the form of a higher annual salary or a bonus.

Chance also plays a role in determining wages. If a person attended a trade school to learn how to repair televisions with vacuum tubes and then found this skill made obsolete by the invention of solid-state electronics, he or she would end up earning a low wage compared to others with similar years of training. The low wage of this worker is due to chance—a phenomenon that economists recognize but do not shed much light on.

How important are ability, effort, and chance in determining wages? It is hard to say because these factors are difficult to measure. But indirect evidence suggests that they are very important. When labor economists study wages, they relate a worker's wage to those variables that can be measured, such as years of schooling, years of experience, age, and job characteristics. All these measured variables affect a worker's wage as theory predicts, but they account for less than half of the variation in wages in our economy. Because so much of the variation in wages is left unexplained, omitted variables, including ability, effort, and chance, must play an important role.

THE BENEFITS OF BEAUTY

People differ in many ways. One difference is in how attractive they are. The actress Keira Knightley, for instance, is a beautiful woman. In part for this reason, her movies attract large audiences. Not surprisingly, the large audiences mean a large income for Ms. Knightley.

How prevalent are the economic benefits of beauty? Labor economists Daniel Hamermesh and Jeff Biddle tried to answer this question in a study published in the December 1994 issue of the *American Economic Review*. Hamermesh and Biddle examined data from surveys of individuals in the United States and Canada. The interviewers who conducted the survey were asked to rate each respondent's physical appearance. Hamermesh and Biddle then examined how much the wages of the respondents depended on the standard determinants—education, experience, and so on—and how much they depended on physical appearance.

Hamermesh and Biddle found that beauty pays. People who are deemed more attractive than average earn 5 percent more than people of average looks, and people of average looks earn 5 to 10 percent more than people considered less attractive than average. Similar results were found for men and women.

What explains these differences in wages? There are several ways to interpret the "beauty premium."

One interpretation is that good looks are themselves a type of innate ability determining productivity and wages. Some people are born with the physical attributes of a movie star; other people are not. Good looks are useful in any job in which workers present themselves to the public—such as acting, sales, and waiting on tables. In this case, an attractive worker is more valuable to the firm than

GOOD LOOKS PAY.

an unattractive worker. The firm's willingness to pay more to attractive workers reflects its customers' preferences.

A second interpretation is that reported beauty is an indirect measure of other types of ability. How attractive a person appears depends on more than just heredity. It also depends on dress, hairstyle, personal demeanor, and other attributes that a person can control. Perhaps a person who successfully projects an attractive image in a survey interview is more likely to be an intelligent person who succeeds at other tasks as well.

A third interpretation is that the beauty premium is a type of discrimination, a topic to which we return later. ●

AN ALTERNATIVE VIEW OF EDUCATION: SIGNALING

Earlier we discussed the human-capital view of education, according to which schooling raises workers' wages because it makes them more productive. Although this view is widely accepted, some economists have proposed an alternative theory, which emphasizes that firms use educational attainment as a way of sorting between high-ability and low-ability workers. According to this alternative view, when people earn a college degree, for instance, they do not become more productive, but they do *signal* their high ability to prospective employers. Because it is easier for high-ability people to earn a college degree than it is for low-ability people, more high-ability people get college degrees. As a result, it is rational for firms to interpret a college degree as a signal of ability.

The signaling theory of education is similar to the signaling theory of advertising discussed in Chapter 16. In the signaling theory of advertising, the advertisement itself contains no real information, but the firm signals the quality of its product to consumers by its willingness to spend money on advertising. In the signaling theory of education, schooling has no real productivity benefit, but the worker signals his innate productivity to employers by his willingness to spend years at school. In both cases, an action is being taken not for its intrinsic benefit but because the willingness to take that action conveys private information to someone observing it.

Thus, we now have two views of education: the human-capital theory and the signaling theory. Both views can explain why more educated workers tend to earn more than less educated workers. According to the human-capital view, education makes workers more productive; according to the signaling view, education is correlated with natural ability. But the two views have radically different predictions for the effects of policies that aim to increase educational attainment. According to the human-capital view, increasing educational levels for all workers would raise all workers' productivity and thereby their wages. According to the signaling view, education does not enhance productivity, so raising all workers' educational levels would not affect wages.

Most likely, truth lies somewhere between these two extremes. The benefits to education are probably a combination of the productivity-enhancing effects of human capital and the productivity-revealing effects of signaling. The open question is the relative size of these two effects.

THE SUPERSTAR PHENOMENON

Although most actors earn little and often take jobs as waiters to support themselves, Johnny Depp earns millions of dollars for each film he makes. Similarly,

In The News

The Human Capital of Terrorists

Workers with more education are better at all kinds of tasks, even those aimed at destruction.

Even for Shoe Bombers, Education and Success Are Linked

By Austan Goolsbee

The fifth anniversary of 9/11 passed with a great deal of hand-wringing over all the people who want to kill Americans. Especially worrisome is the apparent rise of terrorists whose origins seem far from fanatical.

These terrorists are not desperately poor uneducated people from the Middle East. A surprisingly large share of them have college and even graduate degrees. Increasingly, they seem to be from Britain, like the shoe bomber Richard C. Reid and most of the suspects in the London Underground bombings and the liquid explosives plot.

This has left the public wondering, Why are some educated people from Western countries so prone to fanaticism?

Before trying to answer that question, though, some economists argue that we need to think about what makes a successful terrorist and they warn against extrapolating from the terrorists we catch. It is a problem economists typically refer to as "selection bias."

In their new study, "Attack Assignments in Terror Organizations and the Productivity of Suicide Bombers," two economists, Efraim Benmelech of Harvard University and Claude Berrebi of the RAND Corporation, set out to analyze the productivity of terrorists

in the same way they might analyze the auto industry. But they defined the "success" of terrorists by their ability to kill.

They gathered data on Palestinian suicide bombers in Israel from 2000 to 2005 and found that for terrorists, just like for regular workers, experience and education improve productivity. Suicide bombers who are older—in their late 20's and early 30's—and better educated are less likely to be caught on their missions and are more likely to kill large numbers of people at bigger, more difficult targets than younger and more poorly educated bombers.

Professor Benmelech and Dr. Berrebi compare a Who's Who of the biggest suicide bombers to more typical bombers. Whereas typical bombers were younger than 21 and about 18 percent of them had at least some college education, the average age of the most successful bombers was almost 26 and 60 percent of them were college educated.

Experience and education also affect the chances of being caught. Every additional year of age reduces the chance by 12 percent. Having more than a high school education cuts the chance by more than half.

There are many examples where young or uneducated terrorists made stupid mistakes that foiled them. Professor Benmelech recounts the case last April of a teenager from Nablus apprehended by Israeli soldiers before carrying out his bombing because he was wearing an overcoat on a 95-degree

day. Mr. Reid, the failed shoe bomber, had only a high school degree. Would an older terrorist with more education have tried to light a match on his shoe (as Mr. Reid did) in plain view of the flight attendant and other passengers who proceeded to thwart his plan? Would a better-educated terrorist have been more discreet? We will never know.

The research suggests, however, that there may be a reason that the average age of the 9/11 hijackers (at least the ones for whom we have a birth date) was close to 26 and that the supposed leader, Mohammed Atta, was 33 with a graduate degree.

As Professor Benmelech put it in an interview: "It's clear that there are some terrorist missions that require a certain level of skill to accomplish. The older terrorists with better educations seem to be less likely to fail them. Perhaps it is not surprising, then, that terrorist organizers assign them to these more difficult missions."

Among Palestinian suicide bombers, the older and better-educated bombers are assigned to targets in bigger cities where they can potentially kill greater numbers of people. That same idea means that the terrorists assigned to attack the United States are probably different from the typical terrorist. They will be drawn from people whose skills make them better at evading security.

Source: *New York Times,* September 14, 2006.

while most people who play tennis do it for free as a hobby, Lindsay Davenport earns millions on the pro tour. Depp and Davenport are superstars in their fields, and their great public appeal is reflected in astronomical incomes.

Why do Depp and Davenport earn so much? It is not surprising that incomes differ within occupations. Good carpenters earn more than mediocre carpenters, and good plumbers earn more than mediocre plumbers. People vary in ability and effort, and these differences lead to differences in income. Yet the best carpenters and plumbers do not earn the many millions that are common among the best actors and athletes. What explains the difference?

To understand the tremendous incomes of Depp and Davenport, we must examine the special features of the markets in which they sell their services. Superstars arise in markets that have two characteristics:

- Every customer in the market wants to enjoy the good supplied by the best producer.
- The good is produced with a technology that makes it possible for the best producer to supply every customer at low cost.

If Johnny Depp is the best actor around, then everyone will want to see his next movie; seeing twice as many movies by an actor half as talented is not a good substitute. Moreover, it is *possible* for everyone to enjoy a performance by Johnny Depp. Because it is easy to make multiple copies of a film, Depp can provide his service to millions of people simultaneously. Similarly, because tennis games are broadcast on television, millions of fans can enjoy the extraordinary athletic skills of Lindsay Davenport.

We can now see why there are no superstar carpenters and plumbers. Other things equal, everyone prefers to employ the best carpenter, but a carpenter, unlike a movie actor, can provide his services to only a limited number of customers. Although the best carpenter will be able to command a somewhat higher wage than the average carpenter, the average carpenter will still be able to earn a good living.

ABOVE-EQUILIBRIUM WAGES: MINIMUM-WAGE LAWS, UNIONS, AND EFFICIENCY WAGES

Most analyses of wage differences among workers are based on the equilibrium model of the labor market—that is, wages are assumed to adjust to balance labor supply and labor demand. But this assumption does not always apply. For some workers, wages are set above the level that brings supply and demand into equilibrium. Let's consider three reasons this might be so.

One reason for above-equilibrium wages is minimum-wage laws, as we first saw in Chapter 6. Most workers in the economy are not affected by these laws because their equilibrium wages are well above the legal minimum. But for some workers, especially the least skilled and experienced, minimum-wage laws raise wages above the level they would earn in an unregulated labor market.

A second reason that wages might rise above their equilibrium level is the market power of labor unions. A **union** is a worker association that bargains with employers over wages and working conditions. Unions often raise wages above the level that would prevail without a union, perhaps because they can threaten to withhold labor from the firm by calling a **strike**. Studies suggest that union workers earn about 10 to 20 percent more than similar nonunion workers.

union
a worker association that bargains with employers over wages and working conditions

strike
the organized withdrawal of labor from a firm by a union

efficiency wages
above-equilibrium wages
paid by firms to increase
worker productivity

A third reason for above-equilibrium wages is suggested by the theory of **efficiency wages**. This theory holds that a firm can find it profitable to pay high wages because doing so increases the productivity of its workers. In particular, high wages may reduce worker turnover, increase worker effort, and raise the quality of workers who apply for jobs at the firm. If this theory is correct, then some firms may choose to pay their workers more than they would normally earn.

Above-equilibrium wages, whether caused by minimum-wage laws, unions, or efficiency wages, have similar effects on the labor market. In particular, pushing a wage above the equilibrium level raises the quantity of labor supplied and reduces the quantity of labor demanded. The result is a surplus of labor, or unemployment. The study of unemployment and the public policies aimed to deal with it is usually considered a topic within macroeconomics, so it goes beyond the scope of this chapter. But it would be a mistake to ignore these issues completely when analyzing earnings. Although most wage differences can be understood while maintaining the assumption of equilibrium in the labor market, above-equilibrium wages play a role in some cases.

QUICK QUIZ   Define *compensating differential* and give an example. ● Give two reasons more educated workers earn more than less educated workers.

THE ECONOMICS OF DISCRIMINATION

discrimination
the offering of different
opportunities to similar
individuals who differ
only by race, ethnic
group, sex, age, or other
personal characteristics

Another source of differences in wages is discrimination. **Discrimination** occurs when the marketplace offers different opportunities to similar individuals who differ only by race, ethnic group, sex, age, or other personal characteristics. Discrimination reflects some people's prejudice against certain groups in society. Discrimination is an emotionally charged topic that often generates heated debate, but economists try to study the topic objectively to separate myth from reality.

MEASURING LABOR-MARKET DISCRIMINATION

How much does discrimination in labor markets affect the earnings of different groups of workers? This question is important, but answering it is not easy.

There is no doubt that different groups of workers earn substantially different wages, as Table 2 demonstrates. The median black man in the United States is paid 21 percent less than the median white man, and the median black woman is paid 8 percent less than the median white woman. The differences by sex are also significant. The median white woman is paid 23 percent less than the median white man, and the median black woman is paid 10 percent less than the median black man. Taken at face value, these differentials look like evidence that employers discriminate against blacks and women.

Yet there is a potential problem with this inference. Even in a labor market free of discrimination, different people have different wages. People differ in the amount of human capital they have and in the kinds of work they are able and willing to do. The wage differences we observe in the economy are, to some extent, attributable to the determinants of equilibrium wages we discussed in the preceding section. Simply observing differences in wages among broad groups—whites and blacks, men and women—does not prove that employers discriminate.

TABLE **2**

Median Annual Earnings by Race and Sex

	White	Black	Percent Earnings Are Lower for Black Workers
Men	$41,982	$32,976	21%
Women	$32,173	$29,680	8%
Percent Earnings Are Lower for Women Workers	23%	10%	

Note: Earnings data are for the year 2005 and apply to full-time, year-round workers over age 14.

Source: U.S. Census Bureau.

Consider, for example, the role of human capital. Among male workers, whites are about 75 percent more likely to have a college degree than blacks. Thus, at least some of the difference between the wages of whites and the wages of blacks can be traced to differences in educational attainment. Among white workers, men and women are now about equally likely to have a college degree, but men are about 11 percent more likely to earn a graduate or professional degree after college, indicating that some of the wage differential between men and women is also attributable to educational attainment.

Moreover, human capital may be more important in explaining wage differentials than measures of years of schooling suggest. Historically, public schools in predominantly black areas have been of lower quality—as measured by expenditure, class size, and so on—than public schools in predominantly white areas. Similarly, for many years, schools directed girls away from science and math courses, even though these subjects may have had greater value in the marketplace than some of the alternatives. If we could measure the quality as well as the quantity of education, the differences in human capital among these groups would seem even larger.

Human capital acquired in the form of job experience can also help explain wage differences. In particular, women tend to have less job experience on average than men. One reason is that female labor-force participation has increased over the past several decades. Because of this historic change, the average female worker today is younger than the average male worker. In addition, women are more likely to interrupt their careers to raise children. For both reasons, the experience of the average female worker is less than the experience of the average male worker.

Yet another source of wage differences is compensating differentials. Men and women do not always choose the same type of work, and this fact may help explain some of the earnings differential between men and women. For example, women are more likely to be secretaries, and men are more likely to be truck drivers. The relative wages of secretaries and truck drivers depend in part on the working conditions of each job. Because these nonmonetary aspects are hard to measure, it is difficult to gauge the practical importance of compensating differentials in explaining the wage differences that we observe.

In the end, the study of wage differences among groups does not establish any clear conclusion about the prevalence of discrimination in U.S. labor markets. Most economists believe that some of the observed wage differentials are attributable to discrimination, but there is no consensus about how much. The only conclusion about which economists are in consensus is a negative one: Because the differences in average wages among groups in part reflect differences in human capital and job characteristics, they do not by themselves say anything about how much discrimination there is in the labor market.

Of course, differences in human capital among groups of workers may themselves reflect discrimination. The less rigorous curriculums historically offered to female students, for instance, can be considered a discriminatory practice. Similarly, the inferior schools historically available to black students may be traced to prejudice on the part of city councils and school boards. But this kind of discrimination occurs long before the worker enters the labor market. In this case, the disease is political, even if the symptom is economic.

 ## IS EMILY MORE EMPLOYABLE THAN LAKISHA?

Although measuring the extent of discrimination from labor-market outcomes is hard, some compelling evidence for the existence of such discrimination comes from a creative "field experiment." Economists Marianne Bertrand and Sendhil Mullainathan answered more than 1,300 help-wanted ads run in Boston and Chicago newspapers by sending in nearly 5,000 fake résumés. Half of the résumés had names that were common in the African American community, such as Lakisha Washington or Jamal Jones. The other half had names that were more common among the white population, such as Emily Walsh and Greg Baker. Otherwise, the résumés were similar. The results of this experiment were published in the *American Economic Review* in September 2004.

The researchers found large differences in how employers responded to the two groups of résumés. Job applicants with white names received about 50 percent more calls from interested employers than applicants with African American names. The study found that this discrimination occurred for all types of employers, including those who claimed to be an "Equal Opportunity Employer" in their help-wanted ads. The researchers concluded that "racial discrimination is still a prominent feature of the labor market." ●

DISCRIMINATION BY EMPLOYERS

Let's now turn from measurement to the economic forces that lie behind discrimination in labor markets. If one group in society receives a lower wage than another group, even after controlling for human capital and job characteristics, who is to blame for this differential?

The answer is not obvious. It might seem natural to blame employers for discriminatory wage differences. After all, employers make the hiring decisions that determine labor demand and wages. If some groups of workers earn lower wages than they should, then it seems that employers are responsible. Yet many economists are skeptical of this easy answer. They believe that competitive, market economies provide a natural antidote to employer discrimination. That antidote is called the profit motive.

Imagine an economy in which workers are differentiated by their hair color. Blondes and brunettes have the same skills, experience, and work ethic. Yet because of discrimination, employers prefer not to hire workers with blonde hair. Thus, the demand for blondes is lower than it otherwise would be. As a result, blondes earn a lower wage than brunettes.

How long can this wage differential persist? In this economy, there is an easy way for a firm to beat out its competitors: It can hire blonde workers. By hiring blondes, a firm pays lower wages and thus has lower costs than firms that hire brunettes. Over time, more and more "blonde" firms enter the market to take advantage of this cost advantage. The existing "brunette" firms have higher costs and, therefore, begin to lose money when faced with the new competitors. These losses induce the brunette firms to go out of business. Eventually, the entry of blonde firms and the exit of brunette firms cause the demand for blonde workers to rise and the demand for brunette workers to fall. This process continues until the wage differential disappears.

Put simply, business owners who care only about making money are at an advantage when competing against those who also care about discriminating. As a result, firms that do not discriminate tend to replace those that do. In this way, competitive markets have a natural remedy for employer discrimination.

 ## SEGREGATED STREETCARS AND THE PROFIT MOTIVE

In the early 20th century, streetcars in many southern cities were segregated by race. White passengers sat in the front of the streetcars, and black passengers sat in the back. What do you suppose caused and maintained this discriminatory practice? And how was this practice viewed by the firms that ran the streetcars?

In a 1986 article in the *Journal of Economic History*, economic historian Jennifer Roback looked at these questions. Roback found that the segregation of races on streetcars was the result of laws that required such segregation. Before these laws were passed, racial discrimination in seating was rare. It was far more common to segregate smokers and nonsmokers.

Moreover, the firms that ran the streetcars often opposed the laws requiring racial segregation. Providing separate seating for different races raised the firms' costs and reduced their profit. One railroad company manager complained to the city council that, under the segregation laws, "the company has to haul around a good deal of empty space."

Here is how Roback describes the situation in one southern city:

> The railroad company did not initiate the segregation policy and was not at all eager to abide by it. State legislation, public agitation, and a threat to arrest the president of the railroad were all required to induce them to separate the races on their cars. . . . There is no indication that the management was motivated by belief in civil rights or racial equality. The evidence indicates their primary motives were economic; separation was costly. . . . Officials of the company may or may not have disliked blacks, but they were not willing to forgo the profits necessary to indulge such prejudice.

The story of southern streetcars illustrates a general lesson: Business owners are usually more interested in making profit than in discriminating against a particular group. When firms engage in discriminatory practices, the ultimate source

In The News

Gender Differences

Recent economic research is shedding light on why men and women choose different career paths.

The Difference between Men and Women, Revisited: It's About Competition

By Hal R. Varian

Gender differences are a topic of endless discussion for parents, teachers and social scientists. . . . A noteworthy case in point is a recent National Bureau of Economic Research working paper by a Stanford economist, Muriel Niederle, and Lise Vesterlund, a University of Pittsburgh economist, titled, "Do Women Shy Away From Competition? Do Men Compete Too Much?"

It is widely noted that women are not well represented in high-paying corporate jobs, or in mathematics, science and engi-neering jobs. As the authors observe, the "standard economic explanations for such occupational differences include prefer-ences, ability and discrimination."

To this list the authors add a new factor: attitudes toward competitive environments. If men prefer more competitive environ-ments than women, then there will be more men represented in areas where competi-tion is intense.

Of course, discussions of gender differ-ences of any sort can only be statements about averages; it is clear that there are women who thrive in competitive envi-ronments and men who do not. Further-more, attitudes toward competition may be ingrained or a result of factors like social stereotyping.

Is there any evidence that the hypoth-esis is true? Do men really prefer more com-petitive environments than women? One could cite anecdote after anecdote, but the authors took a much more direct approach: they ran an experiment.

By using an experiment, the authors were able to determine not only whether men and women differ in their willingness to compete, but more important, whether they differ in their willingness to compete conditioned on their actual performance.

The economists asked 80 subjects, divided into groups of two women and two men, to add up sets of five two-digit numbers for five minutes. The subjects per-formed the task first on a piece-rate basis (50 cents for each correct answer) and then

of the discrimination often lies not with the firms themselves but elsewhere. In this particular case, the streetcar companies segregated whites and blacks because discriminatory laws, which the companies opposed, required them to do so. ●

DISCRIMINATION BY CUSTOMERS AND GOVERNMENTS

The profit motive is a strong force acting to eliminate discriminatory wage dif-ferentials, but there are limits to its corrective abilities. Two important limiting factors are customer preferences and government policies.

To see how customer preferences for discrimination can affect wages, consider again our imaginary economy with blondes and brunettes. Suppose that restau-rant owners discriminate against blondes when hiring waiters. As a result, blonde waiters earn lower wages than brunette waiters. In this case, a restaurant can open up with blonde waiters and charge lower prices. If customers care only about the quality and price of their meals, the discriminatory firms will be driven out of business, and the wage differential will disappear.

as a tournament (the person with the most correct answers in each group received $2 per correct answer, while other participants received nothing). Note that a subject with a 25 percent chance of being a winner in the tournament received the same average payment as in the piece-rate system.

All participants were told how many problems they got right, but not their relative performance. After completing the two tasks, the subjects were asked to choose whether they preferred a piece-rate system or a tournament for the third set of problems.

There were several interesting findings in this experiment. First, there were no differences between men and women in their performance under either compensation system. Despite this, twice as many men selected the tournament as women (75 percent versus 35 percent).

Even if one accounts for performance by comparing only men and women with the same number of correct answers, the women have a 38 percent lower probability of choosing the tournament compensation.

Why were the men much more likely to choose the tournament? Perhaps it was because they felt more confident about their abilities. The data support this hypothesis, with 75 percent of the men believing that they won their four-player tournament, while 43 percent of the women thought they were best in their group.

Though both groups were overconfident about their performance, the men were much more so. . . . The results of this experiment are consistent with the finding by a Berkeley finance professor, Terry Odean, that men trade stocks excessively, apparently because they (wrongly) feel that they have exceptional ability to pick winners. Women trade less, but do better on average, because they are more likely to follow a buy-and-hold strategy.

The authors summarized their experimental results by saying, "From a payoff-maximizing perspective, high-performing women enter the tournament too rarely, and low-performing men enter the tournament too often." The low-performing men and the high-performing women are both hurt by this behavior but, in this experiment at least, the costs to the women who did not choose the tournament when they should have exceeded the costs to the men who should have avoided the tournament.

One should not read too much into one study. But if it is really true that women choose occupations that involve less competition, then one may well ask why. Sociobiologists may suggest that such differences come from genetic propensities; sociologists may argue for differences in social roles and expectations; developmental psychologists may emphasize child-rearing practices. Whatever the cause, Ms. Niederle and Ms. Vesterlund have certainly raised a host of interesting and important questions.

Source: *New York Times,* March 9, 2006.

On the other hand, it is possible that customers prefer being served by brunette waiters. If this preference for discrimination is strong, the entry of blonde restaurants need not succeed in eliminating the wage differential between brunettes and blondes. That is, if customers have discriminatory preferences, a competitive market is consistent with a discriminatory wage differential. An economy with such discrimination would contain two types of restaurants. Blonde restaurants hire blondes, have lower costs, and charge lower prices. Brunette restaurants hire brunettes, have higher costs, and charge higher prices. Customers who did not care about the hair color of their waiters would be attracted to the lower prices at the blonde restaurants. Bigoted customers would go to the brunette restaurants and would pay for their discriminatory preference in the form of higher prices.

Another way for discrimination to persist in competitive markets is for the government to mandate discriminatory practices. If, for instance, the government passed a law stating that blondes could wash dishes in restaurants but could not work as waiters, then a wage differential could persist in a competitive market. The example of segregated streetcars in the foregoing case study is one example of government-mandated discrimination. More recently, before South Africa abandoned its system of apartheid, blacks were prohibited from working in some jobs. Discriminatory governments pass such laws to suppress the normal equalizing force of free and competitive markets.

To sum up: *Competitive markets contain a natural remedy for employer discrimination. The entry into the market of firms that care only about profit tends to eliminate discriminatory wage differentials. These wage differentials persist in competitive markets only when customers are willing to pay to maintain the discriminatory practice or when the government mandates it.*

 ## DISCRIMINATION IN SPORTS

As we have seen, measuring discrimination is often difficult. To determine whether one group of workers is discriminated against, a researcher must correct for differences in the productivity between that group and other workers in the economy. Yet in most firms, it is difficult to measure a particular worker's contribution to the production of goods and services.

One type of firm in which such corrections are easier is the sports team. Professional teams have many objective measures of productivity. In baseball, for instance, we can measure a player's batting average, the frequency of home runs, the number of stolen bases, and so on.

Studies of sports teams suggest that racial discrimination is, in fact, common and that much of the blame lies with customers. One study, published in the *Journal of Labor Economics* in 1988, examined the salaries of basketball players and found that black players earned 20 percent less than white players of comparable ability. The study also found that attendance at basketball games was larger for teams with a greater proportion of white players. One interpretation of these facts is that, at least at the time of the study, customer discrimination made black players less profitable than white players for team owners. In the presence of such customer discrimination, a discriminatory wage gap can persist, even if team owners care only about profit.

A similar situation once existed for baseball players. A study using data from the late 1960s showed that black players earned less than comparable white players. Moreover, fewer fans attended games pitched by blacks than games pitched by whites, even though black pitchers had better records than white pitchers. Studies of more recent salaries in baseball, however, have found no evidence of discriminatory wage differentials.

Another study, published in the *Quarterly Journal of Economics* in 1990, examined the market prices of old baseball cards. This study found similar evidence of discrimination. The cards of black hitters sold for 10 percent less than the cards of comparable white hitters, and the cards of black pitchers sold for 13 percent less than the cards of comparable white pitchers. These results suggest customer discrimination among baseball fans.   ●

QUICK QUIZ Why is it hard to establish whether a group of workers is being discriminated against? ● Explain how profit-maximizing firms tend to eliminate discriminatory wage differentials. ● How might a discriminatory wage differential persist?

CONCLUSION

In competitive markets, workers earn a wage equal to the value of their marginal contribution to the production of goods and services. There are, however, many things that affect the value of the marginal product. Firms pay more for workers who are more talented, more diligent, more experienced, and more educated because these workers are more productive. Firms pay less to those workers against whom customers discriminate because these workers contribute less to revenue.

The theory of the labor market we have developed in the last two chapters explains why some workers earn higher wages than other workers. The theory does not say that the resulting distribution of income is equal, fair, or desirable in any way. That is the topic we take up in Chapter 20.

SUMMARY

- Workers earn different wages for many reasons. To some extent, wage differentials compensate workers for job attributes. Other things equal, workers in hard, unpleasant jobs are paid more than workers in easy, pleasant jobs.

- Workers with more human capital are paid more than workers with less human capital. The return to accumulating human capital is high and has increased over the past two decades.

- Although years of education, experience, and job characteristics affect earnings as theory predicts, there is much variation in earnings that cannot be explained by things that economists can measure. The unexplained variation in earnings is largely attributable to natural ability, effort, and chance.

- Some economists have suggested that more educated workers earn higher wages not because education raises productivity but because workers with high natural ability use education as a way to signal their high ability to employers. If this signaling theory is correct, then increasing the educational attainment of all workers would not raise the overall level of wages.

- Wages are sometimes pushed above the level that brings supply and demand into balance. Three reasons for above-equilibrium wages are minimum-wage laws, unions, and efficiency wages.

- Some differences in earnings are attributable to discrimination based on race, sex, or other factors. Measuring the amount of discrimination is difficult, however, because one must correct for differences in human capital and job characteristics.

- Competitive markets tend to limit the impact of discrimination on wages. If the wages of a group of workers are lower than those of another group for reasons not related to marginal productivity, then nondiscriminatory firms will be more profitable than discriminatory firms. Profit-maximizing behavior, therefore, can reduce discriminatory wage differentials. Discrimination persists in competitive markets, however, if customers are willing to pay more to discriminatory firms or if the government passes laws requiring firms to discriminate.

KEY CONCEPTS

compensating differential, *p. 414*

human capital, *p. 415*

union, *p. 421*

strike, *p. 421*

efficiency wages, *p. 422*

discrimination, *p. 422*

QUESTIONS FOR REVIEW

1. Why are coal miners paid more than other workers with similar amounts of education?
2. In what sense is education a type of capital?
3. How might education raise a worker's wage without raising the worker's productivity?
4. What conditions lead to economic superstars? Would you expect to see superstars in dentistry? In music? Explain.
5. Give three reasons a worker's wage might be above the level that balances supply and demand.

6. What difficulties arise in deciding whether a group of workers has a lower wage because of discrimination?
7. Do the forces of economic competition tend to exacerbate or ameliorate discrimination based on race?
8. Give an example of how discrimination might persist in a competitive market.

PROBLEMS AND APPLICATIONS

1. College students sometimes work as summer interns for private firms or the government. Many of these positions pay little or nothing.
   a. What is the opportunity cost of taking such a job?
   b. Explain why students are willing to take these jobs.
   c. If you were to compare the earnings later in life of workers who had worked as interns and those who had taken summer jobs that paid more, what would you expect to find?
2. As explained in Chapter 6, a minimum-wage law distorts the market for low-wage labor. To reduce this distortion, some economists advocate a two-tiered minimum-wage system, with a regular minimum wage for adult workers and a lower, "subminimum" wage for teenage workers. Give two reasons a single minimum wage might distort the labor market for teenage workers more than it would the market for adult workers.
3. A basic finding of labor economics is that workers who have more experience in the labor force are paid more than workers who have less experience (holding constant the amount of formal

education). Why might this be so? Some studies have also found that experience at the same job (called *job tenure*) has an extra positive influence on wages. Explain.
4. At some colleges and universities, economics professors receive higher salaries than professors in some other fields.
   a. Why might this be true?
   b. Some other colleges and universities have a policy of paying equal salaries to professors in all fields. At some of these schools, economics professors have lighter teaching loads than professors in some other fields. What role do the differences in teaching loads play?
5. Imagine that someone were to offer you a choice: You could spend 4 years studying at the world's best university, but you would have to keep your attendance there a secret. Or you could be awarded an official degree from the world's best university, but you couldn't actually attend. Which choice do you think would enhance your future earnings more? What does your answer say about the debate over signaling versus human capital in the role of education?

6. When recording devices were first invented almost 100 years ago, musicians could suddenly supply their music to large audiences at low cost. How do you suppose this development affected the income of the best musicians? How do you suppose it affected the income of average musicians?

7. A current debate in education is whether teachers should be paid on a standard pay scale based solely upon their years of training and teaching experience, or whether part of their salary should be based upon their performance (called "merit pay").
   a. Why might merit pay be desirable?
   b. Who might be opposed to a system of merit pay?
   c. What is a potential challenge of merit pay?
   d. A related issue: Why might a school district decide to pay teachers significantly more than the salaries offered by surrounding districts?

8. When Alan Greenspan (who would later become chairman of the Federal Reserve) ran an economic consulting firm in the 1960s, he primarily hired female economists. He once told the *New York Times*, "I always valued men and women equally, and I found that because others did not, good women economists were cheaper than men." Is Greenspan's behavior profit-maximizing? Is it admirable or despicable? If more employers were like Greenspan, what would happen to the wage differential between men and women? Why might other economic consulting firms at the time not have followed Greenspan's business strategy?

9. Suppose that all young women were channeled into careers as secretaries, nurses, and teachers; at the same time, young men were encouraged to consider these three careers and many others as well.
   a. Draw a diagram showing the combined labor market for secretaries, nurses, and teachers. Draw a diagram showing the combined labor market for all other fields. In which market is the wage higher? Do men or women receive higher wages on average?
   b. Now suppose that society changed and encouraged both young women and young men to consider a wide range of careers. Over time, what effect would this change have on the wages in the two markets you illustrated in part (a)? What effect would the change have on the average wages of men and women?

10. Economist June O'Neill has argued that "until family roles are more equal, women are not likely to have the same pattern of market work and earnings as men." What does she mean by the "pattern" of market work? How do these characteristics of jobs and careers affect earnings?

11. This chapter considers the economics of discrimination by employers, customers, and governments. Now consider discrimination by workers. Suppose that some brunette workers did not like working with blonde workers. Do you think this worker discrimination could explain lower wages for blonde workers? If such a wage differential existed, what would a profit-maximizing entrepreneur do? If there were many such entrepreneurs, what would happen over time?

Income Inequality
and Poverty

"The only difference between the rich and other people," Mary Colum once said to Ernest Hemingway, "is that the rich have more money." Maybe so. But this claim leaves many questions unanswered. The gap between rich and poor is a fascinating and important topic of study—for the comfortable rich, for the struggling poor, and for the aspiring and worried middle class.

From the previous two chapters, you should have some understanding about why different people have different incomes. A person's earnings depend on the supply and demand for that person's labor, which in turn depend on natural ability, human capital, compensating differentials, discrimination, and so on. Because labor earnings make up about three-fourths of the total income in the U.S. economy, the factors that determine wages are also largely responsible for determining how the economy's total income is distributed among the various members of society. In other words, they determine who is rich and who is poor.

In this chapter, we discuss the distribution of income—a topic that raises some fundamental questions about the role of economic policy. One of the *Ten Principles of Economics* in Chapter 1 is that governments can sometimes improve market outcomes. This possibility is particularly important when considering the distribution of income. The invisible hand of the marketplace acts to allocate resources efficiently, but it does not necessarily ensure that resources are allocated fairly. As a result, many economists—though not all—believe that the government should redistribute income to achieve greater equality. In doing so, however, the government runs into another of the *Ten Principles of Economics:* People face trade-offs. When the government enacts policies to make the distribution of income more equal, it distorts incentives, alters behavior, and makes the allocation of resources less efficient.

Our discussion of the distribution of income proceeds in three steps. First, we assess how much inequality there is in our society. Second, we consider some different views about what role the government should play in altering the distribution of income. Third, we discuss various public policies aimed at helping society's poorest members.

THE MEASUREMENT OF INEQUALITY

We begin our study of the distribution of income by addressing four questions of measurement:

- How much inequality is there in our society?
- How many people live in poverty?
- What problems arise in measuring the amount of inequality?
- How often do people move among income classes?

These measurement questions are the natural starting point from which to discuss public policies aimed at changing the distribution of income.

U.S. INCOME INEQUALITY

Imagine that you lined up all the families in the economy according to their annual income. Then you divided the families into five equal groups: the bottom fifth, the second fifth, the middle fifth, the fourth fifth, and the top fifth. Table 1 shows the income ranges for each of these groups, as well as for the top 5 percent. You can use this table to find where your family lies in the income distribution.

For examining differences in the income distribution over time, economists find it useful to present the income data as in Table 2. This table shows the share

"AS FAR AS I'M CONCERNED, THEY CAN DO WHAT THEY WANT WITH THE MINIMUM WAGE, JUST AS LONG AS THEY KEEP THEIR HANDS OFF THE MAXIMUM WAGE."

1 TABLE

The Distribution of Income in the United States: 2005

Group	Annual Family Income
Bottom Fifth	Under $25,616
Second Fifth	$25,616–$45,021
Middle Fifth	$45,021–$68,304
Fourth Fifth	$68,304–$103,100
Top Fifth	$103,100 and over
Top 5 percent	$184,500 and over

Source: U.S. Bureau of the Census.

TABLE 2

Year	Bottom Fifth	Second Fifth	Middle Fifth	Fourth Fifth	Top Fifth	Top 5%
2005	4.0%	9.6%	15.3%	22.9%	48.1%	21.1%
2000	4.3	9.8	15.5	22.8	47.4	20.8
1990	4.6	10.8	16.6	23.8	44.3	17.4
1980	5.2	11.5	17.5	24.3	41.5	15.3
1970	5.5	12.2	17.6	23.8	40.9	15.6
1960	4.8	12.2	17.8	24.0	41.3	15.9
1950	4.5	12.0	17.4	23.4	42.7	17.3
1935	4.1	9.2	14.1	20.9	51.7	26.5

Source: U.S. Bureau of the Census.

Income Inequality in the United States
This table shows the percentage of total before-tax income received by families in each fifth of the income distribution and by those families in the top 5 percent.

of total income that each group of families received in selected years. In 2005, the bottom fifth of all families received 4.0 percent of all income, and the top fifth of all families received 48.1 percent of all income. In other words, even though the top and bottom fifths include the same number of families, the top fifth has about twelve times as much income as the bottom fifth.

The last column in the table shows the share of total income received by the very richest families. In 2005, the top 5 percent of families received 21.1 percent of total income, which was greater than the total income of the poorest 40 percent.

Table 2 also shows the distribution of income in various years beginning in 1935. At first glance, the distribution of income appears to have been remarkably stable over time. Throughout the past several decades, the bottom fifth of families has received about 4 to 5 percent of income, while the top fifth has received about 40 to 50 percent of income. Closer inspection of the table reveals some trends in the degree of inequality. From 1935 to 1970, the distribution gradually became more equal. The share of the bottom fifth rose from 4.1 to 5.5 percent, and the share of the top fifth fell from 51.7 percent to 40.9 percent. In more recent years, this trend has reversed itself. From 1970 to 2005, the share of the bottom fifth fell from 5.5 percent to 4.0 percent, and the share of the top fifth rose from 40.9 to 48.1 percent.

In Chapter 19, we discussed some explanations for this recent rise in inequality. Increases in international trade with low-wage countries and changes in technology have tended to reduce the demand for unskilled labor and raise the demand for skilled labor. As a result, the wages of unskilled workers have fallen relative to the wages of skilled workers, and this change in relative wages has increased inequality in family incomes.

INEQUALITY AROUND THE WORLD

How does the amount of inequality in the United States compare to that in other countries? This question is interesting, but answering it is problematic. For some countries, data are not available. Even when they are, not every country collects data in the same way; for example, some countries collect data on individual incomes, whereas other countries collect data on family incomes, and still others collect data on expenditure rather than income. As a result, whenever we find a difference between two countries, we can never be sure whether it reflects a true difference in the economies or merely a difference in the way data are collected.

With this warning in mind, consider Figure 1, which compares inequality in twelve countries. The inequality measure is the ratio of the income received by the richest tenth of the population to the income of the poorest tenth. The most equality is found in Japan, where the top tenth receives 4.5 times as much income as the bottom tenth. The least equality is found in Brazil, where the top group receives 51.3 times as much income as the bottom group. Although all countries have significant disparities between rich and poor, the degree of inequality varies substantially around the world.

When countries are ranked by inequality, the United States ends up around the middle of the pack. The United States has more income inequality than other economically advanced countries, such as Japan, Germany, and Canada. But the United States has a more equal income distribution than many developing countries, such as South Africa, Brazil, and Mexico.

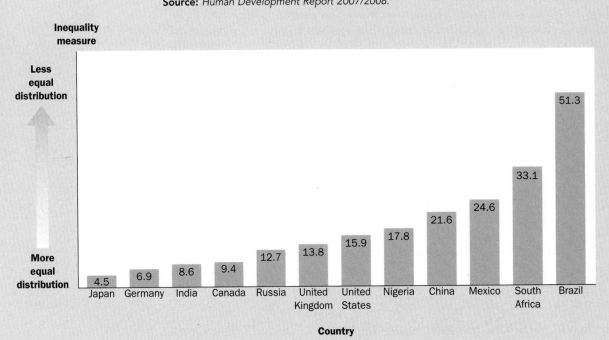

1 FIGURE

Inequality around the World

This figure shows a measure of inequality: the income (or expenditure) that goes to the richest 10 percent of the population divided by the income (or expenditure) that goes to the poorest 10 percent. Among these nations, Japan and Germany have the most equal distribution of economic well-being, while South Africa and Brazil have the least equal.

Source: *Human Development Report 2007/2008.*

THE POVERTY RATE

A commonly used gauge of the distribution of income is the poverty rate. The **poverty rate** is the percentage of the population whose family income falls below an absolute level called the **poverty line**. The poverty line is set by the federal government at roughly three times the cost of providing an adequate diet. This line is adjusted every year to account for changes in the level of prices, and it depends on family size.

To get some idea about what the poverty rate tells us, consider the data for 2005. In that year, the median family had an income of $56,194, and the poverty line for a family of four was $19,971. The poverty rate was 12.6 percent. In other words, 12.6 percent of the population were members of families with incomes below the poverty line for their family size.

Figure 2 shows the poverty rate since 1959, when the official data begin. You can see that the poverty rate fell from 22.4 percent in 1959 to a low of 11.1 percent in 1973. This decline is not surprising, because average income in the economy (adjusted for inflation) rose more than 50 percent during this period. Because the poverty line is an absolute rather than a relative standard, more families are pushed above the poverty line as economic growth pushes the entire income distribution upward. As John F. Kennedy once put it, a rising tide lifts all boats.

Since the early 1970s, however, the economy's rising tide has left some boats behind. Despite continued growth in average income, the poverty rate has not declined below the level reached in 1973. This lack of progress in reducing poverty in recent decades is closely related to the increasing inequality we saw in Table 2. Although economic growth has raised the income of the typical family, the increase in inequality has prevented the poorest families from sharing in this greater economic prosperity.

poverty rate
the percentage of the population whose family income falls below an absolute level called the poverty line

poverty line
an absolute level of income set by the federal government for each family size below which a family is deemed to be in poverty

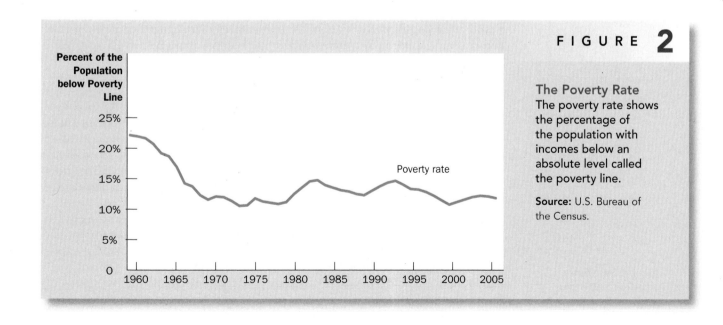

FIGURE **2**

The Poverty Rate
The poverty rate shows the percentage of the population with incomes below an absolute level called the poverty line.

Source: U.S. Bureau of the Census.

3 TABLE

Who Is Poor?
This table shows that the poverty rate varies greatly among different groups within the population.

Group	Poverty Rate
All persons	12.6%
White, not Hispanic	8.3
Black	24.9
Hispanic	21.8
Asian	11.1
Children (under age 18)	17.6
Elderly (over age 64)	10.1
Married-couple families	5.9
Female household, no spouse present	31.1

Source: U.S. Bureau of the Census. Data are for 2005.

Poverty is an economic malady that affects all groups within the population, but it does not affect all groups with equal frequency. Table 3 shows the poverty rates for several groups, and it reveals three striking facts:

- Poverty is correlated with race. Blacks and Hispanics are about three times more likely to live in poverty than are whites.
- Poverty is correlated with age. Children are more likely than average to be members of poor families, and the elderly are less likely than average to be poor.
- Poverty is correlated with family composition. Families headed by a female adult and without a spouse present are about five times as likely to live in poverty as a family headed by a married couple.

These three facts have described U.S. society for many years, and they show which people are most likely to be poor. These effects also work together: Among black and Hispanic children in female-headed households, about half live in poverty.

PROBLEMS IN MEASURING INEQUALITY

Although data on the income distribution and the poverty rate help to give us some idea about the degree of inequality in our society, interpreting these data is not always straightforward. The data are based on households' annual incomes. What people care about, however, is not their incomes but their ability to maintain a good standard of living. For at least three reasons, data on the income distribution and the poverty rate give an incomplete picture of inequality in living standards.

In-Kind Transfers   Measurements of the distribution of income and the poverty rate are based on families' *money* income. Through various government programs, however, the poor receive many nonmonetary items, including food stamps, housing vouchers, and medical services. Transfers to the poor given in the form of goods and services rather than cash are called **in-kind transfers**. Standard measurements of the degree of inequality do not take account of these in-kind transfers.

Because in-kind transfers are received mostly by the poorest members of society, the failure to include in-kind transfers as part of income greatly affects the

in-kind transfers
transfers to the poor given in the form of goods and services rather than cash

measured poverty rate. According to a study by the Census Bureau, if in-kind transfers were included in income at their market value, the number of families in poverty would be about 10 percent lower than the standard data indicate.

The Economic Life Cycle   Incomes vary predictably over people's lives. A young worker, especially one in school, has a low income. Income rises as the worker gains maturity and experience, peaks at around age 50, and then falls sharply when the worker retires at around age 65. This regular pattern of income variation is called the **life cycle**.

Because people can borrow and save to smooth out life cycle changes in income, their standard of living in any year depends more on lifetime income than on that year's income. The young often borrow, perhaps to go to school or to buy a house, and then repay these loans later when their incomes rise. People have their highest saving rates when they are middle-aged. Because people can save in anticipation of retirement, the large declines in incomes at retirement need not lead to similar declines in the standard of living. This normal life cycle pattern causes inequality in the distribution of annual income, but it does not necessarily represent true inequality in living standards.

Transitory versus Permanent Income   Incomes vary over people's lives not only because of predictable life cycle variation but also because of random and transitory forces. One year a frost kills off the Florida orange crop, and Florida orange growers see their incomes fall temporarily. At the same time, the Florida frost drives up the price of oranges, and California orange growers see their incomes temporarily rise. The next year the reverse might happen.

Just as people can borrow and lend to smooth out life cycle variation in income, they can also borrow and lend to smooth out transitory variation in income. To the extent that a family saves in good years and borrows (or depletes its savings) in bad years, transitory changes in income need not affect its standard of living. A family's ability to buy goods and services depends largely on its **permanent income**, which is its normal, or average, income.

To gauge inequality of living standards, the distribution of permanent income is more relevant than the distribution of annual income. Many economists believe that people base their consumption on their permanent income; as a result, inequality in consumption is one gauge of inequality of permanent income. Because permanent income and consumption are less affected by transitory changes in income, they are more equally distributed than is current income.

> **life cycle**
> the regular pattern of income variation over a person's life

> **permanent income**
> a person's normal income

ALTERNATIVE MEASURES OF INEQUALITY

A recent study by Michael Cox and Richard Alm of the Federal Reserve Bank of Dallas shows how different measures of inequality lead to dramatically different results. Cox and Alm compared American households in the top fifth of the income distribution to those in the bottom fifth to see how far apart they are. They used data from 2006 and reported some of their results in an article in the *New York Times* on February 10, 2008.

According to Cox and Alm, the richest fifth of U.S. households has an average income of $149,963, while the poorest fifth has an average income of $9,974. Thus, the top group has about 15 times as much income as the bottom group.

The gap between rich and poor shrinks a bit if taxes are taken into account. Because the tax system is progressive, the top group pays a higher percentage of its income in taxes than does the bottom group. Cox and Alm find that the richest fifth has 14 times as much after-tax income as the poorest fifth.

The gap shrinks more substantially if one looks at consumption rather than income. Households having an unusually good year are more likely to be in the top group and are likely to save a high fraction out of their incomes. Households having an unusually bad year are more likely to be in the bottom group and are more likely to consume out of their savings. According to Cox and Alms, the consumption of the richest fifth is only 3.9 times as much as the consumption of the poorest fifth.

The consumption gap becomes smaller still if one corrects for differences in the number of people in the household. Because larger families are more likely to have two earners, they are more likely to find themselves near the top of the income distribution. But they also have more mouths to feed. Cox and Alms report that households in the top fifth have an average of 3.1 people, while those in the bottom fifth have an average of 1.7 people. As a result, consumption per person in the richest fifth of households is only 2.1 times as much as consumption per person in the poorest fifth.

These data show that inequality in material standards of living is much smaller than inequality in annual income.   ●

ECONOMIC MOBILITY

People sometimes speak of "the rich" and "the poor" as if these groups consisted of the same families year after year. In fact, this is not at all the case. Economic mobility, the movement of people among income classes, is substantial in the U.S. economy. Movements up the income ladder can be due to good luck or hard work, and movements down the ladder can be due to bad luck or laziness. Some of this mobility reflects transitory variation in income, while some reflects more persistent changes in income.

Because economic mobility is so great, many of those below the poverty line are there only temporarily. Poverty is a long-term problem for relatively few families. In a typical 10-year period, about one in four families falls below the poverty line in at least 1 year. Yet fewer than 3 percent of families are poor for 8 or more years. Because it is likely that the temporarily poor and the persistently poor face different problems, policies that aim to combat poverty need to distinguish between these groups.

Another way to gauge economic mobility is the persistence of economic success from generation to generation. Economists who have studied this topic find that having an above-average income carries over from parents to children, but the persistence is far from perfect, indicating substantial mobility among income classes. If a father earns 20 percent above his generation's average income, his son will most likely earn 8 percent above his generation's average income. There is only a small correlation between the income of a grandfather and the income of a grandson.

One result of this great economic mobility is that the U.S. economy is filled with self-made millionaires (as well as with heirs who squandered the fortunes they inherited). According to one study, about four of five millionaires made their money on their own, often by starting and building a business or by climbing the corporate ladder. Only one in five millionaires inherited their fortunes.

In The News

What to Make of Rising Inequality

An economist offers his perspective on the rise in U.S. income inequality.

Incomes and Inequality: What the Numbers Don't Tell Us

By Tyler Cowen

The growing inequality in wealth and income has led many people to question whether the contemporary American economy is rigged in favor of the rich. While there is little doubt that the gap between the wealthy and everybody else has widened in recent years, the situation is not as unfair as some of the numbers seem to imply.

Much of the measured growth in income inequality has resulted from natural demographic trends. In general, there is more income inequality among older populations than among younger populations, if only because older people have had more time to experience rising or falling fortunes.

Furthermore, more-educated groups show greater income inequality than less-educated groups. Uneducated people are more likely to be clustered in a tight range of relatively low incomes. But the educated will include a greater range of highly motivated breadwinners and relaxed bohemians, and a greater range of winning and losing investors. A result is a greater variety of incomes. Since the United States is growing older and also more educated, income inequality will naturally rise.

Thomas Lemieux, professor of economics at the University of British Columbia, estimates that these demographic effects account for about three-quarters of the observed rise in income inequality for men and 69 to 95 percent of the observed rise in income inequality for women ("Increasing Residual Wage Inequality: Composition Effects, Noisy Data, or Rising Demand for Skill?" *The American Economic Review,* June 2006). In other words, rising income inequality is not just a result of unfairness or bad public policy. . . .

In any case, income is not the only—or even the most—important measure of inequality. For instance, inequality of consumption—the difference between what the poor consume and what the rich consume—does not show a significant upward trend (Dirk Krueger and Fabrizio Perri, "Does Income Inequality Lead to Consumption Inequality?" *The Review of Economic Studies,* January 2006). Consumption, of course, is not an ideal indicator of well-being; a high or steady level of purchases may reflect growing debt, and the ease of buying a big-screen TV does not reflect a comparable ease in buying good health care.

Happiness, possibly the most relevant variable for a study of inequality, is also the hardest to measure. Nonetheless, inequality of happiness is usually less marked than inequality of income, at least in wealthy societies. A man earning $500,000 a year is not usually 10 times as happy as a man earning $50,000 a year. The $50,000 earner still enjoys most of the conveniences of the modern world. Even if more money makes people happier, it appears to do so at a declining rate, which places a natural check on the inequality of happiness.

Studies of personal happiness, based on questionnaires and self-reporting, indicate that the inequality of happiness is not growing over time in the United States. Furthermore, the United States has an inequality of happiness roughly comparable to that of Sweden or Denmark, two nations with strongly egalitarian reputations. (See the symposium in *Journal of Happiness Studies,* December 2005.) American society offers good opportunities for people to be happy, even if not everyone becomes rich.

If we look at leisure, from 1965 to 2003, less-educated groups experienced a bigger boost in free time than more-educated groups (Mark Aguiar and Erik Hurst, "Measuring Trends in Leisure: The Allocation of Time Over Five Decades," Federal Reserve Bank of Boston Working Paper). In other words, the high earners are working hard for their money and perhaps they are having less fun. . . .

The broader philosophical question is why we should worry about inequality—of any kind—much at all. Life is not a race against fellow human beings. . . . We should continue to improve opportunities for lower-income people, but inequality as a major and chronic American problem has been overstated.

Source: *New York Times,* January 25, 2007.

QUICK QUIZ What does the poverty rate measure? • Describe three potential problems in interpreting the measured poverty rate.

THE POLITICAL PHILOSOPHY OF REDISTRIBUTING INCOME

We have just seen how the economy's income is distributed and have considered some of the problems in interpreting measured inequality. This discussion was *positive* in the sense that it merely described the world as it is. We now turn to the *normative* question facing policymakers: What should the government do about economic inequality?

This question is not just about economics. Economic analysis alone cannot tell us whether policymakers should try to make our society more egalitarian. Our views on this question are, to a large extent, a matter of political philosophy. Yet because the government's role in redistributing income is central to so many debates over economic policy, here we digress from economic science to consider a bit of political philosophy.

UTILITARIANISM

utilitarianism
the political philosophy according to which the government should choose policies to maximize the total utility of everyone in society

utility
a measure of happiness or satisfaction

A prominent school of thought in political philosophy is **utilitarianism**. The founders of utilitarianism are the English philosophers Jeremy Bentham (1748–1832) and John Stuart Mill (1806–1873). To a large extent, the goal of utilitarians is to apply the logic of individual decision making to questions concerning morality and public policy.

The starting point of utilitarianism is the notion of **utility**—the level of happiness or satisfaction that a person receives from his or her circumstances. Utility is a measure of well-being and, according to utilitarians, is the ultimate objective of all public and private actions. The proper goal of the government, they claim, is to maximize the sum of utility achieved by everyone in society.

The utilitarian case for redistributing income is based on the assumption of *diminishing marginal utility*. It seems reasonable that an extra dollar of income provides a poor person with more additional utility than an extra dollar would provide to a rich person. In other words, as a person's income rises, the extra well-being derived from an additional dollar of income falls. This plausible assumption, together with the utilitarian goal of maximizing total utility, implies that the government should try to achieve a more equal distribution of income.

The argument is simple. Imagine that Peter and Paul are the same, except that Peter earns $80,000 and Paul earns $20,000. In this case, taking a dollar from Peter to pay Paul will reduce Peter's utility and raise Paul's utility. But because of diminishing marginal utility, Peter's utility falls by less than Paul's utility rises. Thus, this redistribution of income raises total utility, which is the utilitarian's objective.

At first, this utilitarian argument might seem to imply that the government should continue to redistribute income until everyone in society has exactly the same income. Indeed, that would be the case if the total amount of income—$100,000 in our example—were fixed. But in fact, it is not. Utilitarians reject complete equalization of incomes because they accept one of the *Ten Principles of Economics* presented in Chapter 1: People respond to incentives.

To take from Peter to pay Paul, the government must pursue policies that redistribute income. The U.S. federal income tax and welfare system are examples. Under these policies, people with high incomes pay high taxes, and people with low incomes receive income transfers. Yet if the government takes away additional income a person might earn through higher income taxes or reduced transfers, both Peter and Paul have less incentive to work hard. As they work less, society's income falls, and so does total utility. The utilitarian government has to balance the gains from greater equality against the losses from distorted incentives. To maximize total utility, therefore, the government stops short of making society fully egalitarian.

A famous parable sheds light on the utilitarian's logic. Imagine that Peter and Paul are thirsty travelers trapped at different places in the desert. Peter's oasis has much water; Paul's has little. If the government could transfer water from one oasis to the other without cost, it would maximize total utility from water by equalizing the amount in the two places. But suppose that the government has only a leaky bucket. As it tries to move water from one place to the other, some of the water is lost in transit. In this case, a utilitarian government might still try to move some water from Peter to Paul, depending on the size of Paul's thirst and the size of the bucket's leak. But with only a leaky bucket at its disposal, a utilitarian government will stop short of trying to reach complete equality.

LIBERALISM

A second way of thinking about inequality might be called **liberalism**. Philosopher John Rawls develops this view in his book *A Theory of Justice*. This book was first published in 1971, and it quickly became a classic in political philosophy.

Rawls begins with the premise that a society's institutions, laws, and policies should be just. He then takes up the natural question: How can we, the members of society, ever agree on what justice means? It might seem that every person's point of view is inevitably based on his or her particular circumstances—whether he or she is talented or less talented, diligent or lazy, educated or less educated, born to a wealthy family or a poor one. Could we ever *objectively* determine what a just society would be?

To answer this question, Rawls proposes the following thought experiment. Imagine that before any of us is born, we all get together for a meeting to design the rules that govern society. At this point, we are all ignorant about the station in life each of us will end up filling. In Rawls's words, we are sitting in an "original position" behind a "veil of ignorance." In this original position, Rawls argues, we can choose a just set of rules for society because we must consider how those rules will affect every person. As Rawls puts it, "Since all are similarly situated and no one is able to design principles to favor his particular conditions, the principles of justice are the result of fair agreement or bargain." Designing public policies and institutions in this way allows us to be objective about what policies are just.

Rawls then considers what public policy designed behind this veil of ignorance would try to achieve. In particular, he considers what income distribution a person would consider fair if that person did not know whether he or she would end up at the top, bottom, or middle of the distribution. Rawls argues that a person in the original position would be especially concerned about the possibility of being at the *bottom* of the income distribution. In designing public policies, therefore, we should aim to raise the welfare of the worst-off person in society. That is, rather than maximizing the sum of everyone's utility, as a utilitarian would do,

liberalism
the political philosophy according to which the government should choose policies deemed just, as evaluated by an impartial observer behind a "veil of ignorance"

maximin criterion
the claim that the government should aim to maximize the well-being of the worst-off person in society

Rawls would maximize the minimum utility. Rawls's rule is called the **maximin criterion**.

Because the maximin criterion emphasizes the least fortunate person in society, it justifies public policies aimed at equalizing the distribution of income. By transferring income from the rich to the poor, society raises the well-being of the least fortunate. The maximin criterion would not, however, lead to a completely egalitarian society. If the government promised to equalize incomes completely, people would have no incentive to work hard, society's total income would fall substantially, and the least fortunate person would be worse off. Thus, the maximin criterion still allows disparities in income because such disparities can improve incentives and thereby raise society's ability to help the poor. Nonetheless, because Rawls's philosophy puts weight on only the least fortunate members of society, it calls for more income redistribution than does utilitarianism.

Rawls's views are controversial, but the thought experiment he proposes has much appeal. In particular, this thought experiment allows us to consider the redistribution of income as a form of **social insurance**. That is, from the perspective of the original position behind the veil of ignorance, income redistribution is like an insurance policy. Homeowners buy fire insurance to protect themselves from the risk of their house burning down. Similarly, when we as a society choose policies that tax the rich to supplement the incomes of the poor, we are all insuring ourselves against the possibility that we might have been a member of a poor family. Because people dislike risk, we should be happy to have been born into a society that provides us this insurance.

social insurance
government policy aimed at protecting people against the risk of adverse events

It is not at all clear, however, that rational people behind the veil of ignorance would truly be so averse to risk as to follow the maximin criterion. Indeed, because a person in the original position might end up anywhere in the distribution of outcomes, he or she might treat all possible outcomes equally when designing public policies. In this case, the best policy behind the veil of ignorance would be to maximize the average utility of members of society, and the resulting notion of justice would be more utilitarian than Rawlsian.

LIBERTARIANISM

libertarianism
the political philosophy according to which the government should punish crimes and enforce voluntary agreements but not redistribute income

A third view of inequality is called **libertarianism**. The two views we have considered so far—utilitarianism and liberalism—both view the total income of society as a shared resource that a social planner can freely redistribute to achieve some social goal. By contrast, libertarians argue that society itself earns no income—only individual members of society earn income. According to libertarians, the government should not take from some individuals and give to others to achieve any particular distribution of income.

For instance, philosopher Robert Nozick writes the following in his famous 1974 book *Anarchy, State, and Utopia*:

> We are not in the position of children who have been given portions of pie by someone who now makes last minute adjustments to rectify careless cutting. There is no *central* distribution, no person or group entitled to control all the resources, jointly deciding how they are to be doled out. What each person gets, he gets from others who give to him in exchange for something, or as a gift. In a free society, diverse persons control different resources, and new holdings arise out of the voluntary exchanges and actions of persons.

Whereas utilitarians and liberals try to judge what amount of inequality is desirable in a society, Nozick denies the validity of this very question.

The libertarian alternative to evaluating economic *outcomes* is to evaluate the *process* by which these outcomes arise. When the distribution of income is achieved unfairly—for instance, when one person steals from another—the government has the right and duty to remedy the problem. But as long as the process determining the distribution of income is just, the resulting distribution is fair, no matter how unequal.

Nozick criticizes Rawls's liberalism by drawing an analogy between the distribution of income in society and the distribution of grades in a course. Suppose you were asked to judge the fairness of the grades in the economics course you are now taking. Would you imagine yourself behind a veil of ignorance and choose a grade distribution without knowing the talents and efforts of each student? Or would you ensure that the process of assigning grades to students is fair without regard for whether the resulting distribution is equal or unequal? For the case of grades at least, the libertarian emphasis on process over outcomes is compelling.

Libertarians conclude that equality of opportunities is more important than equality of incomes. They believe that the government should enforce individual rights to ensure that everyone has the same opportunity to use his or her talents and achieve success. Once these rules of the game are established, the government has no reason to alter the resulting distribution of income.

QUICK QUIZ Pam earns more than Pauline. Someone proposes taxing Pam to supplement Pauline's income. How would a utilitarian, a liberal, and a libertarian evaluate this proposal?

POLICIES TO REDUCE POVERTY

As we have just seen, political philosophers hold various views about what role the government should take in altering the distribution of income. Political debate among the larger population of voters reflects a similar disagreement. Despite these continuing debates, most people believe that, at the very least, the government should try to help those most in need. According to a popular metaphor, the government should provide a "safety net" to prevent any citizen from falling too far.

Poverty is one of the most difficult problems that policymakers face. Poor families are more likely than the overall population to experience homelessness, drug dependence, health problems, teenage pregnancy, illiteracy, unemployment, and low educational attainment. Members of poor families are both more likely to commit crimes and more likely to be victims of crimes. Although it is hard to separate the causes of poverty from the effects, there is no doubt that poverty is associated with various economic and social ills.

Suppose that you were a policymaker in the government, and your goal was to reduce the number of people living in poverty. How would you achieve this goal? Here we examine some of the policy options that you might consider. Each of these options helps some people escape poverty, but none of them is perfect, and deciding upon the best combination to use is not easy.

Minimum-Wage Laws

Laws setting a minimum wage that employers can pay workers are a perennial source of debate. Advocates view the minimum wage as a way of helping the working poor without any cost to the government. Critics view it as hurting those it is intended to help.

The minimum wage is easily understood using the tools of supply and demand, as we first saw in Chapter 6. For workers with low levels of skill and experience, a high minimum wage forces the wage above the level that balances supply and demand. It therefore raises the cost of labor to firms and reduces the quantity of labor that those firms demand. The result is higher unemployment among those groups of workers affected by the minimum wage. Although those workers who remain employed benefit from a higher wage, those who might have been employed at a lower wage are worse off.

The magnitude of these effects depends crucially on the elasticity of demand. Advocates of a high minimum wage argue that the demand for unskilled labor is relatively inelastic so that a high minimum wage depresses employment only slightly. Critics of the minimum wage argue that labor demand is more elastic, especially in the long run when firms can adjust employment and production more fully. They also note that many minimum-wage workers are teenagers from middle-class families so that a high minimum wage is imperfectly targeted as a policy for helping the poor.

Welfare

welfare
government programs that supplement the incomes of the needy

One way to raise the living standards of the poor is for the government to supplement their incomes. The primary way the government does this is through the welfare system. **Welfare** is a broad term that encompasses various government programs. Temporary Assistance for Needy Families (TANF) is a program that assists families with children and no adult able to support the family. In a typical family receiving such assistance, the father is absent, and the mother is at home raising small children. Another welfare program is Supplemental Security Income (SSI), which provides assistance to the poor who are sick or disabled. Note that for both of these welfare programs, a poor person cannot qualify for assistance simply by having a low income. He or she must also establish some additional "need," such as small children or a disability.

A common criticism of welfare programs is that they create incentives for people to become "needy." For example, these programs may encourage families to break up, for many families qualify for financial assistance only if the father is absent. The programs may also encourage illegitimate births, for many poor, single women qualify for assistance only if they have children. Because poor, single mothers are such a large part of the poverty problem and because welfare programs seem to raise the number of poor, single mothers, critics of the welfare system assert that these policies exacerbate the very problems they are supposed to cure. As a result of these arguments, the welfare system was revised in a 1996 law that limited the amount of time recipients could stay on welfare.

How severe are these potential problems with the welfare system? No one knows for sure. Proponents of the welfare system point out that being a poor, single mother on welfare is a difficult existence at best, and they are skeptical that many people would be encouraged to pursue such a life if it were not thrust upon them. Moreover, trends over time do not support the view that the decline of the two-parent family is largely a symptom of the welfare system, as the system's critics sometimes claim. Since the early 1970s, welfare benefits (adjusted for inflation) have declined, yet the percentage of children living with only one parent has risen.

Negative Income Tax

Whenever the government chooses a system to collect taxes, it affects the distribution of income. This is clearly true in the case of a progressive income tax, whereby high-income families pay a larger percentage of their income in taxes than do low-income families. As we discussed in Chapter 12, equity across income groups is an important criterion in the design of a tax system.

Many economists have advocated supplementing the income of the poor using a **negative income tax**. According to this policy, every family would report its income to the government. High-income families would pay a tax based on their incomes. Low-income families would receive a subsidy. In other words, they would "pay" a "negative tax."

negative income tax
a tax system that collects revenue from high-income households and gives subsidies to low-income households

For example, suppose the government used the following formula to compute a family's tax liability:

$$\text{Taxes owed} = (\tfrac{1}{3} \text{ of income}) - \$10,000.$$

In this case, a family that earned $60,000 would pay $10,000 in taxes, and a family that earned $90,000 would pay $20,000 in taxes. A family that earned $30,000 would owe nothing. And a family that earned $15,000 would "owe" –$5,000. In other words, the government would send this family a check for $5,000.

Under a negative income tax, poor families would receive financial assistance without having to demonstrate need. The only qualification required to receive assistance would be a low income. Depending on one's point of view, this feature can be either an advantage or a disadvantage. On the one hand, a negative income tax does not encourage illegitimate births and the breakup of families, as critics of the welfare system believe current policy does. On the other hand, a negative income tax would subsidize not only the unfortunate but also those who are simply lazy and, in some people's eyes, undeserving of government support.

One actual tax provision that works much like a negative income tax is the Earned Income Tax Credit (EITC). This credit allows poor working families to receive income tax refunds greater than the taxes they paid during the year. Because the Earned Income Tax Credit applies only to the working poor, it does not discourage recipients from working, as other antipoverty programs are claimed to do. For the same reason, however, it also does not help alleviate poverty due to unemployment, sickness, or other inability to work.

In-Kind Transfers

Another way to help the poor is to provide them directly with some of the goods and services they need to raise their living standards. For example, charities provide the needy with food, shelter, and toys at Christmas. The government gives

In The News

Child Labor

What is the best way to reduce the use of child labor around the world?

Research Changes Ideas about Children and Work
By Virginia Postrel

When Americans think about child labor in poor countries, they rarely picture girls fetching water or boys tending livestock. Yet most of the 211 million children, ages 5 to 14, who work worldwide are not in factories. They are working in agriculture—from 92 percent in Vietnam to 63 percent in Guatemala—and most are not paid directly.

"Contrary to popular perception in high-income countries, most working children are employed by their parents rather than in manufacturing establishments or other forms of wage employment," two Dartmouth economists, Eric V. Edmonds and Nina Pavcnik, wrote in "Child Labor in the

Global Economy," published in the Winter 2005 *Journal of Economic Perspectives*.

Their article surveys what is known about child labor. Research over the past several years, by these economists and others, has begun to erode some popular beliefs about why children work, what they do and when they are likely to leave work for school.

When he started working on child labor issues six years ago, Professor Edmonds said in an interview, "[T]he conventional view was that child labor really wasn't about poverty." Children's work, many policy makers believed, "reflected perhaps parental callousness or a lack of education for parents about the benefits of educating your child." So policies to curb child labor focused on educating parents about why their children should not work and banning children's employment to remove the temptation.

Recent research, however, casts doubt on the cultural explanation. "In every context that I've looked at things, child labor seems to be almost entirely about poverty. I wouldn't say it's only about poverty, but it's got a lot to do with poverty," Professor Edmonds said.

poor families *food stamps*, which are government vouchers that can be used to buy food at stores; the stores then redeem the vouchers for money. The government also gives many poor people healthcare through a program called *Medicaid*.

Is it better to help the poor with these in-kind transfers or with direct cash payments? There is no clear answer.

Advocates of in-kind transfers argue that such transfers ensure that the poor get what they need most. Among the poorest members of society, alcohol and drug addiction is more common than it is in society as a whole. By providing the poor with food and shelter, society can be more confident that it is not helping to support such addictions. This is one reason in-kind transfers are more politically popular than cash payments to the poor.

Advocates of cash payments, on the other hand, argue that in-kind transfers are inefficient and disrespectful. The government does not know what goods and services the poor need most. Many of the poor are ordinary people down on their luck. Despite their misfortune, they are in the best position to decide how to raise their own living standards. Rather than giving the poor in-kind transfers of goods

As families' incomes increase, children tend to stop working and, where schools are available, they go to school. If family incomes drop, children are more likely to return to work.

Some of the best data, and the most noteworthy results, come from Vietnam, which tracked about 3,000 households from 1993 to 1998. This was a period of rapid economic growth, in which gross domestic product rose about 9 percent a year.

In a paper published in the Winter 2005 *Journal of Human Resources*, "Does Child Labor Decline With Improving Economic Status?" Professor Edmonds found that child labor dropped by nearly 30 percent over this five-year period. Rising incomes explain about 60 percent of that shift.

The effects were greatest for families escaping poverty. For those who crossed the official poverty line, earning enough to pay for adequate food and basic necessities, higher incomes accounted for 80 percent of the drop in child labor. In 1993, 58 percent of the population fell below the poverty line, compared with 33 percent five years later.

"Child labor does not appear to vary with per capita expenditure until households can meet their food needs, and it then declines dramatically," Professor Edmonds wrote.

During this same period, Vietnam repealed its policy against exporting rice. That opened a big new market for Vietnamese farmers—the country went from almost no exports to being one of the world's top rice exporters—and significantly raised the price of rice.

This change, along with the family survey data, allowed Professors Edmonds and Pavcnik to examine what happens when household incomes rise but children's labor also becomes more valuable. Their paper, "The Effect of Trade Liberalization on Child Labor," was published in the March 2005 *Journal of International Economics*.

In the interview, Professor Edmonds said he expected that the booming market for rice would lead more children to work in agriculture, if only on their own families' farms, because the value of their labor had risen substantially. But that was not what happened.

"Instead, it looks like what households did was, with rising income, they purchased substitutes for child labor. They used more fertilizers. There was more mechanization, more purchasing of tools," he said, adding, "It was the opposite of what I expected to find coming in." . . .

The results from Vietnam suggest that families do not want their children to work. Parents pull their children out of work when they can afford to, even when the wages children could earn are rising: Poverty, not culture, appears to be the fundamental problem. . . .

"Most child labor policy even today is directed at trying to get kids into unemployment—to limit working opportunities for kids," he said in the interview. But, "if households are already in a situation where they don't want their children to be working, but they're forced to because of their circumstance, taking additional steps to prevent the kids from working is punishing the poorest for being poor."

Source: *New York Times*, July 14, 2005.

and services that they may not want, it may be better to give them cash and allow them to buy what they think they need most.

ANTIPOVERTY PROGRAMS AND WORK INCENTIVES

Many policies aimed at helping the poor can have the unintended effect of discouraging the poor from escaping poverty on their own. To see why, consider the following example. Suppose that a family needs an income of $15,000 to maintain a reasonable standard of living. And suppose that, out of concern for the poor, the government promises to guarantee every family that income. Whatever a family earns, the government makes up the difference between that income and $15,000. What effect would you expect this policy to have?

The incentive effects of this policy are obvious: Any person who would make under $15,000 by working has little incentive to find and keep a job. For every dollar that the person would earn, the government would reduce the income supplement by a dollar. In effect, the government taxes 100 percent of additional earnings. An effective marginal tax rate of 100 percent is surely a policy with a large deadweight loss.

The adverse effects of this high effective tax rate can persist over time. A person discouraged from working loses the on-the-job training that a job might offer. In addition, his or her children miss the lessons learned by observing a parent with a full-time job, and this may adversely affect their own ability to find and hold a job.

Although the antipoverty program we have been discussing is hypothetical, it is not as unrealistic as might first appear. Welfare, Medicaid, food stamps, and the Earned Income Tax Credit are all programs aimed at helping the poor, and they are all tied to family income. As a family's income rises, the family becomes ineligible for these programs. When all these programs are taken together, it is common for families to face effective marginal tax rates that are very high. Sometimes the effective marginal tax rates even exceed 100 percent so that poor families are worse off when they earn more. By trying to help the poor, the government discourages those families from working. According to critics of antipoverty programs, these programs alter work attitudes and create a "culture of poverty."

It might seem that there is an easy solution to this problem: Reduce benefits to poor families more gradually as their incomes rise. For example, if a poor family loses 30 cents of benefits for every dollar it earns, then it faces an effective marginal tax rate of 30 percent. Although this effective tax reduces work effort to some extent, it does not eliminate the incentive to work completely.

The problem with this solution is that it greatly increases the cost of programs to combat poverty. If benefits are phased out gradually as a poor family's income rises, then families just above the poverty level will also be eligible for substantial benefits. The more gradual the phase-out, the more families are eligible, and the more the program costs. Thus, policymakers face a trade-off between burdening the poor with high effective marginal tax rates and burdening taxpayers with costly programs to reduce poverty.

There are various other ways to reduce the work disincentive of antipoverty programs. One is to require any person collecting benefits to accept a government-provided job—a system sometimes called *workfare*. Another possibility is to provide benefits for only a limited period of time. This route was taken in the 1996 welfare reform bill, which imposed a 5-year lifetime limit on welfare recipients. When President Clinton signed the bill, he explained his policy as follows: "Welfare should be a second chance, not a way of life."

How has the reform worked? The debate over the bill persists to this day, but there is no doubt that its passage was followed by a large decrease in the welfare rolls and a large increase in employment among those groups traditionally on welfare. In a 2003 study, economist Rebecca Blank, a prominent expert on the welfare system, summarized the experience as follows:

> This nation transformed its assistance programs to poor families with children from cash-assistance oriented programs aimed at providing income support, to work-assistance programs aimed at encouraging and supporting work. Critics can argue that the changes have left us with an inadequate safety net, in which an increasing number of families will be unable to return for assistance due to time limits, past sanctions, and limited state funds. Meanwhile, work requirements force women into unstable, difficult work situations with low wages and inadequate support for child care, healthcare or other family needs. Supporters

can argue that the system has now worked for seven years. Due to a mix of economic good fortune and well-designed policies, a substantial number of women who would previously have been receiving welfare are now in employment building a record of experience and demonstrating to their children the importance of work preparation. Dire predictions about deep poverty and greatly increased homelessness have not come to pass. Even if the work-support system is far from perfect, it may be preferable to the poorly-functioning AFDC [Aid to Families with Dependent Children] welfare system of the past.

QUICK QUIZ   List three policies aimed at helping the poor, and discuss the pros and cons of each.

CONCLUSION

People have long reflected on the distribution of income in society. Plato, the ancient Greek philosopher, concluded that in an ideal society the income of the richest person would be no more than four times the income of the poorest person. Although the measurement of inequality is difficult, it is clear that our society has much more inequality than Plato recommended.

One of the *Ten Principles of Economics* discussed in Chapter 1 is that governments can sometimes improve market outcomes. There is little consensus, however, about how this principle should be applied to the distribution of income. Philosophers and policymakers today do not agree on how much income inequality is desirable, or even whether public policy should aim to alter the distribution of income. Much of public debate reflects this disagreement. Whenever taxes are raised, for instance, lawmakers argue over how much of the tax hike should fall on the rich, the middle class, and the poor.

Another of the *Ten Principles of Economics* is that people face trade-offs. This principle is important to keep in mind when thinking about economic inequality. Policies that penalize the successful and reward the unsuccessful reduce the incentive to succeed. Thus, policymakers face a trade-off between equality and efficiency. The more equally the pie is divided, the smaller the pie becomes. This is the one lesson concerning the distribution of income about which almost everyone agrees.

SUMMARY

- Data on the distribution of income show a wide disparity in our society. The richest fifth of families earns more than ten times as much income as the poorest fifth.

- Because in-kind transfers, the economic life cycle, transitory income, and economic mobility are so important for understanding variation in income, it is difficult to gauge the degree of inequality in our society using data on the distribution of income in a single year. When these other factors are taken into account, they tend to suggest that economic well-being is more equally distributed than is annual income.

- Political philosophers differ in their views about the role of government in altering the distribution of income. Utilitarians (such as John Stuart Mill) would choose the distribution of income to maximize the sum of utility of everyone in soci-

ety. Liberals (such as John Rawls) would determine the distribution of income as if we were behind a "veil of ignorance" that prevented us from knowing our own stations in life. Libertarians (such as Robert Nozick) would have the government enforce individual rights to ensure a fair process but then not be concerned about inequality in the resulting distribution of income.

- Various policies aim to help the poor—minimum-wage laws, welfare, negative income taxes, and in-kind transfers. While these policies help some families escape poverty, they also have unintended side effects. Because financial assistance declines as income rises, the poor often face very high effective marginal tax rates, which discourage poor families from escaping poverty on their own.

KEY CONCEPTS

poverty rate, *p. 437*
poverty line, *p. 437*
in-kind transfers, *p. 438*
life cycle, *p. 439*
permanent income, *p. 439*

utilitarianism, *p. 442*
utility, *p. 442*
liberalism, *p. 443*
maximin criterion, *p. 444*
social insurance, *p. 444*

libertarianism, *p. 444*
welfare, *p. 446*
negative income tax, *p. 447*

QUESTIONS FOR REVIEW

1. Does the richest fifth of the U.S. population earn closer to two, four, or ten times the income of the poorest fifth?
2. How does the extent of income inequality in the United States compare to that of other nations around the world?
3. What groups in the U.S. population are most likely to live in poverty?
4. When gauging the amount of inequality, why do transitory and life cycle variations in income cause difficulties?
5. How would a utilitarian, a liberal, and a libertarian determine how much income inequality is permissible?
6. What are the pros and cons of in-kind (rather than cash) transfers to the poor?
7. Describe how antipoverty programs can discourage the poor from working. How might you reduce this disincentive? What are the disadvantages of your proposed policy?

PROBLEMS AND APPLICATIONS

1. Table 2 shows that income inequality in the United States has increased since 1970. Some factors contributing to this increase were discussed in Chapter 19. What are they?

2. Table 3 shows that the percentage of children in families with income below the poverty line far exceeds the percentage of the elderly in such families. How might the allocation of government money across different social programs have contributed to this phenomenon? (Hint: See Chapter 12.)

3. Economists often view life cycle variation in income as one form of transitory variation in income around people's lifetime, or permanent, income. In this sense, how does your current income compare to your permanent income? Do you think your current income accurately reflects your standard of living?

4. The chapter discusses the importance of economic mobility.
   a. What policies might the government pursue to increase economic mobility *within* a generation?
   b. What policies might the government pursue to increase economic mobility *across* generations?
   c. Do you think we should reduce spending on current welfare programs to increase spending on programs that enhance economic mobility? What are some of the advantages and disadvantages of doing so?

5. Consider two communities. In one community, ten families have incomes of $100,000 each and ten families have incomes of $20,000 each. In the other community, ten families have incomes of $200,000 each and ten families have incomes of $22,000 each.
   a. In which community is the distribution of income more unequal? In which community is the problem of poverty likely to be worse?
   b. Which distribution of income would Rawls prefer? Explain.
   c. Which distribution of income do you prefer? Explain.
   d. Why might someone have the opposite preference?

6. The chapter uses the analogy of a "leaky bucket" to explain one constraint on the redistribution of income.
   a. What elements of the U.S. system for redistributing income create the leaks in the bucket? Be specific.
   b. Do you think that Republicans or Democrats generally believe that the bucket used for redistributing income is leakier? How does that belief affect their views about the amount of income redistribution that the government should undertake?

7. Suppose there are two possible income distributions in a society of ten people. In the first distribution, nine people have incomes of $30,000 and one person has an income of $10,000. In the second distribution, all ten people have incomes of $25,000.
   a. If the society had the first income distribution, what would be the utilitarian argument for redistributing income?
   b. Which income distribution would Rawls consider more equitable? Explain.
   c. Which income distribution would Nozick consider more equitable? Explain.

8. The poverty rate would be substantially lower if the market value of in-kind transfers were added to family income. The largest in-kind transfer is Medicaid, the government health program for the poor. Let's say the program costs $7,000 per recipient family.
   a. If the government gave each recipient family a $7,000 check instead of enrolling them in the Medicaid program, do you think that most of these families would spend that money to purchase health insurance? Why? (Recall that the poverty level for a family of four is about $20,000.)
   b. How does your answer to part (a) affect your view about whether we should determine the poverty rate by valuing in-kind transfers at the price the government pays for them? Explain.
   c. How does your answer to part (a) affect your view about whether we should provide assistance to the poor in the form of cash transfers or in-kind transfers? Explain.

9. Consider two of the income security programs in the United States: Temporary Assistance for Needy Families (TANF) and the Earned Income Tax Credit (EITC).

   a. When a woman with children and very low income earns an extra dollar, she receives less in TANF benefits. What do you think is the effect of this feature of TANF on the labor supply of low-income women? Explain.

   b. The EITC provides greater benefits as low-income workers earn more income (up to a point). What do you think is the effect of this program on the labor supply of low-income individuals? Explain.

   c. What are the disadvantages of eliminating TANF and allocating the savings to the EITC?

10. John and Jeremy are utilitarians. John believes that labor supply is highly elastic, whereas Jeremy believes that labor supply is quite inelastic. How do you suppose their views about income redistribution differ?

PART VII
Topics for Further Study

The Theory of Consumer Choice

When you walk into a store, you are confronted with thousands of goods that you might buy. Because your financial resources are limited, however, you cannot buy everything that you want. You therefore consider the prices of the various goods offered for sale and buy a bundle of goods that, given your resources, best suits your needs and desires.

In this chapter, we develop a theory that describes how consumers make decisions about what to buy. Thus far in this book, we have summarized consumers' decisions with the demand curve. As we have seen, the demand curve for a good reflects consumers' willingness to pay for it. When the price of a good rises, consumers are willing to pay for fewer units, so the quantity demanded falls. We now look more deeply at the decisions that lie behind the demand curve. The theory of consumer choice presented in this chapter provides a more complete understanding of demand, just as the theory of the competitive firm in Chapter 14 provides a more complete understanding of supply.

One of the *Ten Principles of Economics* discussed in Chapter 1 is that people face trade-offs. The theory of consumer choice examines the trade-offs that people face in their role as consumers. When a consumer buys more of one good, he can afford less of other goods. When he spends more time enjoying leisure and less time working, he has lower income and can afford less consumption. When he spends more of his income in the present and saves less of it, he must accept a lower level of consumption in the future. The theory of consumer choice examines how consumers facing these trade-offs make decisions and how they respond to changes in their environment.

After developing the basic theory of consumer choice, we apply it to three questions about household decisions. In particular, we ask:

- Do all demand curves slope downward?
- How do wages affect labor supply?
- How do interest rates affect household saving?

At first, these questions might seem unrelated. But as we will see, we can use the theory of consumer choice to address each of them.

THE BUDGET CONSTRAINT: WHAT THE CONSUMER CAN AFFORD

Most people would like to increase the quantity or quality of the goods they consume—to take longer vacations, drive fancier cars, or eat at better restaurants. People consume less than they desire because their spending is *constrained*, or limited, by their income. We begin our study of consumer choice by examining this link between income and spending.

To keep things simple, we examine the decision facing a consumer who buys only two goods: pizza and Pepsi. Of course, real people buy thousands of different kinds of goods. Assuming there are only two goods greatly simplifies the problem without altering the basic insights about consumer choice.

We first consider how the consumer's income constrains the amount he spends on pizza and Pepsi. Suppose the consumer has an income of $1,000 per month and he spends his entire income on pizza and Pepsi. The price of a pizza is $10, and the price of a pint of Pepsi is $2.

The table in Figure 1 shows some of the many combinations of pizza and Pepsi that the consumer can buy. The first row in the table shows that if the consumer spends all his income on pizza, he can eat 100 pizzas during the month, but he would not be able to buy any Pepsi at all. The second row shows another possible consumption bundle: 90 pizzas and 50 pints of Pepsi. And so on. Each consumption bundle in the table costs exactly $1,000.

The graph in Figure 1 illustrates the consumption bundles that the consumer can choose. The vertical axis measures the number of pints of Pepsi, and the horizontal axis measures the number of pizzas. Three points are marked on this figure. At point A, the consumer buys no Pepsi and consumes 100 pizzas. At point B, the consumer buys no pizza and consumes 500 pints of Pepsi. At point C, the consumer buys 50 pizzas and 250 pints of Pepsi. Point C, which is exactly at the middle of the line from A to B, is the point at which the consumer spends an equal amount ($500) on pizza and Pepsi. These are only three of the many combinations of pizza and Pepsi that the consumer can choose. All the points on the line from A to B are possible. This line, called the **budget constraint**, shows the consumption bundles that the consumer can afford. In this case, it shows the trade-off between pizza and Pepsi that the consumer faces.

budget constraint
the limit on the consumption bundles that a consumer can afford

The slope of the budget constraint measures the rate at which the consumer can trade one good for the other. Recall that the slope between two points is calculated

The budget constraint shows the various bundles of goods that the consumer can buy for a given income. Here the consumer buys bundles of pizza and Pepsi. The table and graph show what the consumer can afford if his income is $1,000, the price of pizza is $10, and the price of Pepsi is $2.

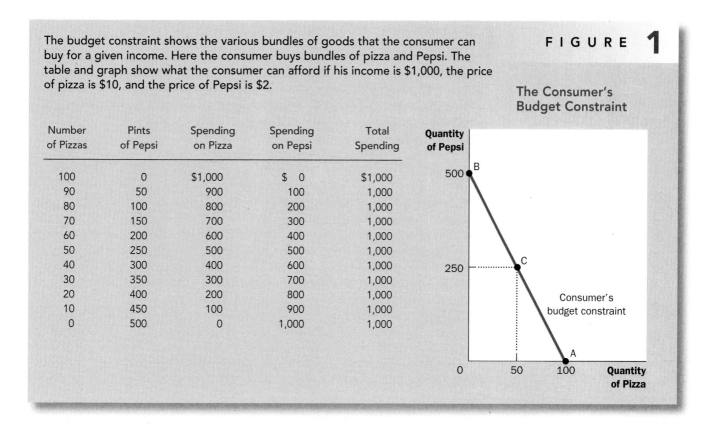

FIGURE 1

The Consumer's Budget Constraint

Number of Pizzas	Pints of Pepsi	Spending on Pizza	Spending on Pepsi	Total Spending
100	0	$1,000	$ 0	$1,000
90	50	900	100	1,000
80	100	800	200	1,000
70	150	700	300	1,000
60	200	600	400	1,000
50	250	500	500	1,000
40	300	400	600	1,000
30	350	300	700	1,000
20	400	200	800	1,000
10	450	100	900	1,000
0	500	0	1,000	1,000

as the change in the vertical distance divided by the change in the horizontal distance ("rise over run"). From point A to point B, the vertical distance is 500 pints, and the horizontal distance is 100 pizzas. Thus, the slope is 5 pints per pizza. (Actually, because the budget constraint slopes downward, the slope is a negative number. But for our purposes, we can ignore the minus sign.)

Notice that the slope of the budget constraint equals the *relative price* of the two goods—the price of one good compared to the price of the other. A pizza costs 5 times as much as a pint of Pepsi, so the opportunity cost of a pizza is 5 pints of Pepsi. The budget constraint's slope of 5 reflects the trade-off the market is offering the consumer: 1 pizza for 5 pints of Pepsi.

QUICK QUIZ   Draw the budget constraint for a person with income of $1,000 if the price of Pepsi is $5 and the price of pizza is $10. What is the slope of this budget constraint?

PREFERENCES: WHAT THE CONSUMER WANTS

Our goal in this chapter is to see how consumers make choices. The budget constraint is one piece of the analysis: It shows the combinations of goods the consumer can afford given his income and the prices of the goods. The consumer's choices, however, depend not only on his budget constraint but also on his preferences regarding the two goods. Therefore, the consumer's preferences are the next piece of our analysis.

REPRESENTING PREFERENCES WITH INDIFFERENCE CURVES

The consumer's preferences allow him to choose among different bundles of pizza and Pepsi. If you offer the consumer two different bundles, he chooses the bundle that best suits his tastes. If the two bundles suit his tastes equally well, we say that the consumer is *indifferent* between the two bundles.

Just as we have represented the consumer's budget constraint graphically, we can also represent his preferences graphically. We do this with indifference curves. An **indifference curve** shows the bundles of consumption that make the consumer equally happy. In this case, the indifference curves show the combinations of pizza and Pepsi with which the consumer is equally satisfied.

Figure 2 shows two of the consumer's many indifference curves. The consumer is indifferent among combinations A, B, and C because they are all on the same curve. Not surprisingly, if the consumer's consumption of pizza is reduced, say, from point A to point B, consumption of Pepsi must increase to keep him equally happy. If consumption of pizza is reduced again, from point B to point C, the amount of Pepsi consumed must increase yet again.

The slope at any point on an indifference curve equals the rate at which the consumer is willing to substitute one good for the other. This rate is called the **marginal rate of substitution** (*MRS*). In this case, the marginal rate of substitution measures how much Pepsi the consumer requires to be compensated for a one-unit reduction in pizza consumption. Notice that because the indifference curves are not straight lines, the marginal rate of substitution is not the same at all points on a given indifference curve. The rate at which a consumer is willing to trade one good for the other depends on the amounts of the goods he is already consuming. That is, the rate at which a consumer is willing to trade pizza for Pepsi depends on whether he is hungrier or thirstier, which in turn depends on how much pizza and Pepsi he is consuming.

The consumer is equally happy at all points on any given indifference curve, but he prefers some indifference curves to others. Because he prefers more consumption to less, higher indifference curves are preferred to lower ones. In Figure 2, any point on curve I_2 is preferred to any point on curve I_1.

indifference curve
a curve that shows consumption bundles that give the consumer the same level of satisfaction

marginal rate of substitution
the rate at which a consumer is willing to trade one good for another

2 FIGURE

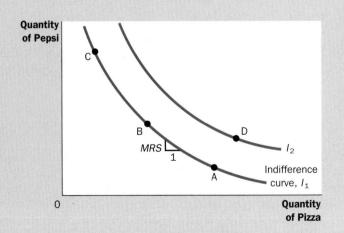

The Consumer's Preferences
The consumer's preferences are represented with indifference curves, which show the combinations of pizza and Pepsi that make the consumer equally satisfied. Because the consumer prefers more of a good, points on a higher indifference curve (I_2 here) are preferred to points on a lower indifference curve (I_1). The marginal rate of substitution (*MRS*) shows the rate at which the consumer is willing to trade Pepsi for pizza. It measures the quantity of Pepsi the consumer must be given in exchange for 1 pizza.

A consumer's set of indifference curves gives a complete ranking of the consumer's preferences. That is, we can use the indifference curves to rank any two bundles of goods. For example, the indifference curves tell us that point D is preferred to point A because point D is on a higher indifference curve than point A. (That conclusion may be obvious, however, because point D offers the consumer both more pizza and more Pepsi.) The indifference curves also tell us that point D is preferred to point C because point D is on a higher indifference curve. Even though point D has less Pepsi than point C, it has more than enough extra pizza to make the consumer prefer it. By seeing which point is on the higher indifference curve, we can use the set of indifference curves to rank any combination of pizza and Pepsi.

FOUR PROPERTIES OF INDIFFERENCE CURVES

Because indifference curves represent a consumer's preferences, they have certain properties that reflect those preferences. Here we consider four properties that describe most indifference curves:

- *Property 1: Higher indifference curves are preferred to lower ones.* People usually prefer to consume more goods rather than less. This preference for greater quantities is reflected in the indifference curves. As Figure 2 shows, higher indifference curves represent larger quantities of goods than lower indifference curves. Thus, the consumer prefers being on higher indifference curves.

- *Property 2: Indifference curves are downward sloping.* The slope of an indifference curve reflects the rate at which the consumer is willing to substitute one good for the other. In most cases, the consumer likes both goods. Therefore, if the quantity of one good is reduced, the quantity of the other good must increase for the consumer to be equally happy. For this reason, most indifference curves slope downward.

- *Property 3: Indifference curves do not cross.* To see why this is true, suppose that two indifference curves did cross, as in Figure 3. Then, because point A is on the same indifference curve as point B, the two points would make the consumer equally happy. In addition, because point B is on the same indifference curve as point C, these two points would make the consumer equally

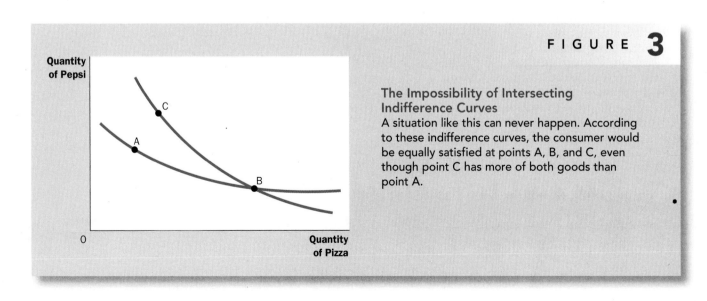

FIGURE **3**

The Impossibility of Intersecting Indifference Curves
A situation like this can never happen. According to these indifference curves, the consumer would be equally satisfied at points A, B, and C, even though point C has more of both goods than point A.

happy. But these conclusions imply that points A and C would also make the consumer equally happy, even though point C has more of both goods. This contradicts our assumption that the consumer always prefers more of both goods to less. Thus, indifference curves cannot cross.

- *Property 4: Indifference curves are bowed inward.* The slope of an indifference curve is the marginal rate of substitution—the rate at which the consumer is willing to trade off one good for the other. The marginal rate of substitution (*MRS*) usually depends on the amount of each good the consumer is currently consuming. In particular, because people are more willing to trade away goods that they have in abundance and less willing to trade away goods of which they have little, the indifference curves are bowed inward. As an example, consider Figure 4. At point A, because the consumer has a lot of Pepsi and only a little pizza, he is very hungry but not very thirsty. To induce the consumer to give up 1 pizza, he has to be given 6 pints of Pepsi: The marginal rate of substitution is 6 pints per pizza. By contrast, at point B, the consumer has little Pepsi and a lot of pizza, so he is very thirsty but not very hungry. At this point, he would be willing to give up 1 pizza to get 1 pint of Pepsi: The marginal rate of substitution is 1 pint per pizza. Thus, the bowed shape of the indifference curve reflects the consumer's greater willingness to give up a good that he already has in large quantity.

TWO EXTREME EXAMPLES OF INDIFFERENCE CURVES

The shape of an indifference curve tells us about the consumer's willingness to trade one good for the other. When the goods are easy to substitute for each other, the indifference curves are less bowed; when the goods are hard to substitute,

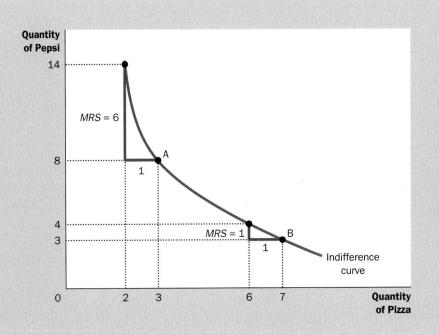

4 FIGURE

Bowed Indifference Curves Indifference curves are usually bowed inward. This shape implies that the marginal rate of substitution (*MRS*) depends on the quantity of the two goods the consumer is consuming. At point A, the consumer has little pizza and much Pepsi, so he requires a lot of extra Pepsi to induce him to give up one of the pizzas: The marginal rate of substitution is 6 pints of Pepsi per pizza. At point B, the consumer has much pizza and little Pepsi, so he requires only a little extra Pepsi to induce him to give up one of the pizzas: The marginal rate of substitution is 1 pint of Pepsi per pizza.

the indifference curves are very bowed. To see why this is true, let's consider the extreme cases.

Perfect Substitutes   Suppose that someone offered you bundles of nickels and dimes. How would you rank the different bundles?

Most likely, you would care only about the total monetary value of each bundle. If so, you would always be willing to trade 2 nickels for 1 dime, regardless of the number of nickels and dimes in the bundle. Your marginal rate of substitution between nickels and dimes would be a fixed number—2.

We can represent your preferences over nickels and dimes with the indifference curves in panel (a) of Figure 5. Because the marginal rate of substitution is constant, the indifference curves are straight lines. In this extreme case of straight indifference curves, we say that the two goods are **perfect substitutes**.

perfect substitutes
two goods with straight-line indifference curves

Perfect Complements   Suppose now that someone offered you bundles of shoes. Some of the shoes fit your left foot, others your right foot. How would you rank these different bundles?

In this case, you might care only about the number of pairs of shoes. In other words, you would judge a bundle based on the number of pairs you could assemble from it. A bundle of 5 left shoes and 7 right shoes yields only 5 pairs. Getting 1 more right shoe has no value if there is no left shoe to go with it.

We can represent your preferences for right and left shoes with the indifference curves in panel (b) of Figure 5. In this case, a bundle with 5 left shoes and 5 right shoes is just as good as a bundle with 5 left shoes and 7 right shoes. It is also just as good as a bundle with 7 left shoes and 5 right shoes. The indifference curves,

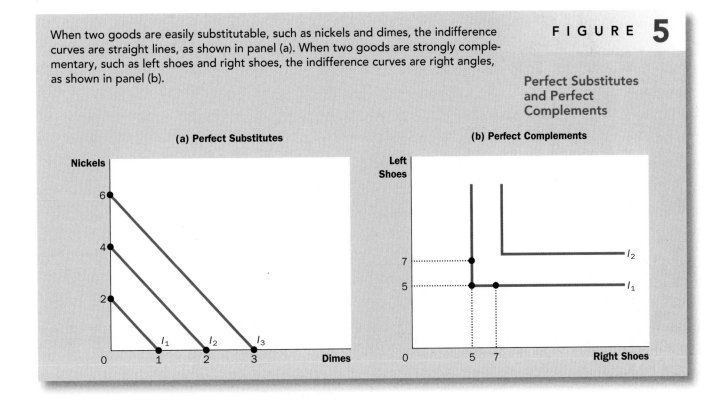

When two goods are easily substitutable, such as nickels and dimes, the indifference curves are straight lines, as shown in panel (a). When two goods are strongly complementary, such as left shoes and right shoes, the indifference curves are right angles, as shown in panel (b).

FIGURE **5**

Perfect Substitutes and Perfect Complements

perfect complements
two goods with right-angle indifference curves

therefore, are right angles. In this extreme case of right-angle indifference curves, we say that the two goods are **perfect complements**.

In the real world, of course, most goods are neither perfect substitutes (like nickels and dimes) nor perfect complements (like right shoes and left shoes). More typically, the indifference curves are bowed inward, but not so bowed as to become right angles.

QUICK QUIZ Draw some indifference curves for pizza and Pepsi. Explain the four properties of these indifference curves.

OPTIMIZATION: WHAT THE CONSUMER CHOOSES

The goal of this chapter is to understand how a consumer makes choices. We have the two pieces necessary for this analysis: the consumer's budget constraint (how much he can afford to spend) and the consumer's preferences (what he wants to spend it on). Now we put these two pieces together and consider the consumer's decision about what to buy.

THE CONSUMER'S OPTIMAL CHOICES

Consider once again our pizza and Pepsi example. The consumer would like to end up with the best possible combination of pizza and Pepsi for him—that is, the combination on his highest possible indifference curve. But the consumer must also end up on or below his budget constraint, which measures the total resources available to him.

Figure 6 shows the consumer's budget constraint and three of his many indifference curves. The highest indifference curve that the consumer can reach (I_2 in the figure) is the one that just barely touches his budget constraint. The point at

6 FIGURE

The Consumer's Optimum
The consumer chooses the point on his budget constraint that lies on the highest indifference curve. At this point, called the optimum, the marginal rate of substitution equals the relative price of the two goods. Here the highest indifference curve the consumer can reach is I_2. The consumer prefers point A, which lies on indifference curve I_3, but the consumer cannot afford this bundle of pizza and Pepsi. By contrast, point B is affordable, but because it lies on a lower indifference curve, the consumer does not prefer it.

FYI

Utility: An Alternative Way to Describe Preferences and Optimization

We have used indifference curves to represent the consumer's preferences. Another common way to represent preferences is with the concept of *utility*. Utility is an abstract measure of the satisfaction or happiness that a consumer receives from a bundle of goods. Economists say that a consumer prefers one bundle of goods to another if one provides more utility than the other.

Indifference curves and utility are closely related. Because the consumer prefers points on higher indifference curves, bundles of goods on higher indifference curves provide higher utility. Because the consumer is equally happy with all points on the same indifference curve, all these bundles provide the same utility. You can think of an indifference curve as an "equal-utility" curve.

The *marginal utility* of any good is the increase in utility that the consumer gets from an additional unit of that good. Most goods are assumed to exhibit *diminishing marginal utility:* The more of the good the consumer already has, the lower the marginal utility provided by an extra unit of that good.

The marginal rate of substitution between two goods depends on their marginal utilities. For example, if the marginal utility of good X is twice the marginal utility of good Y, then a person would need 2 units of good Y to compensate for losing 1 unit of good X, and the marginal rate of substitution equals 2. More generally, the marginal rate of substitution (and thus the slope of the indifference curve) equals the marginal utility of one good divided by the marginal utility of the other good.

Utility analysis provides another way to describe consumer optimization. Recall that at the consumer's optimum, the marginal rate of substitution equals the ratio of prices. That is,

$$MRS = P_X / P_Y.$$

Because the marginal rate of substitution equals the ratio of marginal utilities, we can write this condition for optimization as

$$MU_X / MU_Y = P_X / P_Y.$$

Now rearrange this expression to become

$$MU_X / P_X = MU_Y / P_Y.$$

This equation has a simple interpretation: At the optimum, the marginal utility per dollar spent on good X equals the marginal utility per dollar spent on good Y. (Why? If this equality did not hold, the consumer could increase utility by spending less on the good that provided lower marginal utility per dollar and more on the good that provided higher marginal utility per dollar.)

When economists discuss the theory of consumer choice, they might express the theory using different words. One economist might say that the goal of the consumer is to maximize utility. Another economist might say that the goal of the consumer is to end up on the highest possible indifference curve. The first economist would conclude that at the consumer's optimum, the marginal utility per dollar is the same for all goods, whereas the second would conclude that the indifference curve is tangent to the budget constraint. In essence, these are two ways of saying the same thing.

which this indifference curve and the budget constraint touch is called the *optimum*. The consumer would prefer point A, but he cannot afford that point because it lies above his budget constraint. The consumer can afford point B, but that point is on a lower indifference curve and, therefore, provides the consumer less satisfaction. The optimum represents the best combination of pizza and Pepsi available to the consumer.

Notice that, at the optimum, the slope of the indifference curve equals the slope of the budget constraint. We say that the indifference curve is tangent to the budget constraint. The slope of the indifference curve is the marginal rate of substitution between pizza and Pepsi, and the slope of the budget constraint is the relative price of pizza and Pepsi. Thus, *the consumer chooses consumption of the two goods so that the marginal rate of substitution equals the relative price.*

In Chapter 7, we saw how market prices reflect the marginal value that consumers place on goods. This analysis of consumer choice shows the same result in another way. In making his consumption choices, the consumer takes as given the relative price of the two goods and then chooses an optimum at which his marginal rate of substitution equals this relative price. The relative price is the rate at which the *market* is willing to trade one good for the other, whereas the marginal rate of substitution is the rate at which the *consumer* is willing to trade one good for the other. At the consumer's optimum, the consumer's valuation of the two goods (as measured by the marginal rate of substitution) equals the market's valuation (as measured by the relative price). As a result of this consumer optimization, market prices of different goods reflect the value that consumers place on those goods.

HOW CHANGES IN INCOME AFFECT THE CONSUMER'S CHOICES

Now that we have seen how the consumer makes a consumption decision, let's examine how this decision responds to changes in the consumer's income. To be specific, suppose that income increases. With higher income, the consumer can afford more of both goods. The increase in income, therefore, shifts the budget constraint outward, as in Figure 7. Because the relative price of the two goods has not changed, the slope of the new budget constraint is the same as the slope of the initial budget constraint. That is, an increase in income leads to a parallel shift in the budget constraint.

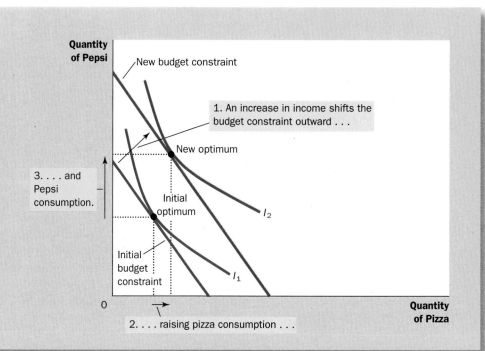

7 FIGURE

An Increase in Income
When the consumer's income rises, the budget constraint shifts out. If both goods are normal goods, the consumer responds to the increase in income by buying more of both of them. Here the consumer buys more pizza and more Pepsi.

The expanded budget constraint allows the consumer to choose a better combination of pizza and Pepsi, one that is on a higher indifference curve. Given the shift in the budget constraint and the consumer's preferences as represented by his indifference curves, the consumer's optimum moves from the point labeled "initial optimum" to the point labeled "new optimum."

Notice that, in Figure 7, the consumer chooses to consume more Pepsi and more pizza. Although the logic of the model does not require increased consumption of both goods in response to increased income, this situation is the most common one. As you may recall from Chapter 4, if a consumer wants more of a good when his income rises, economists call it a **normal good**. The indifference curves in Figure 7 are drawn under the assumption that both pizza and Pepsi are normal goods.

Figure 8 shows an example in which an increase in income induces the consumer to buy more pizza but less Pepsi. If a consumer buys less of a good when his income rises, economists call it an **inferior good**. Figure 8 is drawn under the assumption that pizza is a normal good and Pepsi is an inferior good.

Although most goods are normal goods, there are some inferior goods in the world. One example is bus rides. As income increases, consumers are more likely to own cars or take a taxi and less likely to ride a bus. Bus rides, therefore, are an inferior good.

normal good
a good for which an increase in income raises the quantity demanded

inferior good
a good for which an increase in income reduces the quantity demanded

How Changes in Prices Affect the Consumer's Choices

Let's now use this model of consumer choice to consider how a change in the price of one of the goods alters the consumer's choices. Suppose, in particular, that the

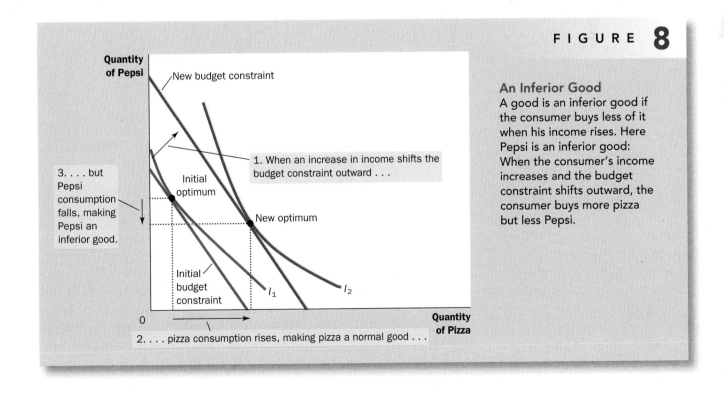

FIGURE 8

An Inferior Good
A good is an inferior good if the consumer buys less of it when his income rises. Here Pepsi is an inferior good: When the consumer's income increases and the budget constraint shifts outward, the consumer buys more pizza but less Pepsi.

Quantity of Pepsi

New budget constraint

3. . . . but Pepsi consumption falls, making Pepsi an inferior good.

Initial optimum

1. When an increase in income shifts the budget constraint outward . . .

New optimum

Initial budget constraint

I_1 I_2

0

Quantity of Pizza

2. . . . pizza consumption rises, making pizza a normal good . . .

price of Pepsi falls from $2 to $1 per pint. It is no surprise that the lower price expands the consumer's set of buying opportunities. In other words, a fall in the price of any good shifts the budget constraint outward.

Figure 9 considers more specifically how the fall in price affects the budget constraint. If the consumer spends his entire $1,000 income on pizza, then the price of Pepsi is irrelevant. Thus, point A in the figure stays the same. Yet if the consumer spends his entire income of $1,000 on Pepsi, he can now buy 1,000 rather than only 500 pints. Thus, the end point of the budget constraint moves from point B to point D.

Notice that in this case the outward shift in the budget constraint changes its slope. (This differs from what happened previously when prices stayed the same but the consumer's income changed.) As we have discussed, the slope of the budget constraint reflects the relative price of pizza and Pepsi. Because the price of Pepsi has fallen to $1 from $2, while the price of pizza has remained $10, the consumer can now trade a pizza for 10 rather than 5 pints of Pepsi. As a result, the new budget constraint has a steeper slope.

How such a change in the budget constraint alters the consumption of both goods depends on the consumer's preferences. For the indifference curves drawn in this figure, the consumer buys more Pepsi and less pizza.

income effect
the change in consumption that results when a price change moves the consumer to a higher or lower indifference curve

substitution effect
the change in consumption that results when a price change moves the consumer along a given indifference curve to a point with a new marginal rate of substitution

INCOME AND SUBSTITUTION EFFECTS

The impact of a change in the price of a good on consumption can be decomposed into two effects: an **income effect** and a **substitution effect**. To see what these two effects are, consider how our consumer might respond when he learns that the price of Pepsi has fallen. He might reason in the following ways:

9 FIGURE

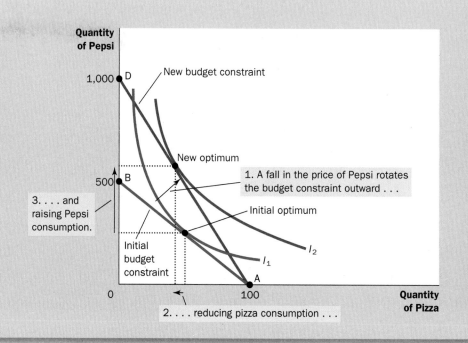

A Change in Price
When the price of Pepsi falls, the consumer's budget constraint shifts outward and changes slope. The consumer moves from the initial optimum to the new optimum, which changes his purchases of both pizza and Pepsi. In this case, the quantity of Pepsi consumed rises, and the quantity of pizza consumed falls.

- "Great news! Now that Pepsi is cheaper, my income has greater purchasing power. I am, in effect, richer than I was. Because I am richer, I can buy both more pizza and more Pepsi." (This is the income effect.)
- "Now that the price of Pepsi has fallen, I get more pints of Pepsi for every pizza that I give up. Because pizza is now relatively more expensive, I should buy less pizza and more Pepsi." (This is the substitution effect.)

Which statement do you find more compelling?

In fact, both of these statements make sense. The decrease in the price of Pepsi makes the consumer better off. If pizza and Pepsi are both normal goods, the consumer will want to spread this improvement in his purchasing power over both goods. This income effect tends to make the consumer buy more pizza and more Pepsi. Yet at the same time, consumption of Pepsi has become less expensive relative to consumption of pizza. This substitution effect tends to make the consumer choose less pizza and more Pepsi.

Now consider the result of these two effects working at the same time. The consumer certainly buys more Pepsi because the income and substitution effects both act to raise purchases of Pepsi. But it is ambiguous whether the consumer buys more pizza because the income and substitution effects work in opposite directions. This conclusion is summarized in Table 1.

We can interpret the income and substitution effects using indifference curves. *The income effect is the change in consumption that results from the movement to a higher indifference curve. The substitution effect is the change in consumption that results from being at a point on an indifference curve with a different marginal rate of substitution.*

Figure 10 shows graphically how to decompose the change in the consumer's decision into the income effect and the substitution effect. When the price of Pepsi falls, the consumer moves from the initial optimum, point A, to the new optimum, point C. We can view this change as occurring in two steps. First, the consumer moves *along* the initial indifference curve, I_1, from point A to point B. The consumer is equally happy at these two points, but at point B, the marginal rate of substitution reflects the new relative price. (The dashed line through point B reflects the new relative price by being parallel to the new budget constraint.) Next, the

Good	Income Effect	Substitution Effect	Total Effect
Pepsi	Consumer is richer, so he buys more Pepsi.	Pepsi is relatively cheaper, so consumer buys more Pepsi.	Income and substitution effects act in same direction, so consumer buys more Pepsi.
Pizza	Consumer is richer, so he buys more pizza.	Pizza is relatively more expensive, so consumer buys less pizza.	Income and substitution effects act in opposite directions, so the total effect on pizza consumption is ambiguous.

TABLE 1

Income and Substitution Effects When the Price of Pepsi Falls

10 FIGURE

Income and Substitution Effects
The effect of a change in price can be broken down into an income effect and a substitution effect. The substitution effect—the movement along an indifference curve to a point with a different marginal rate of substitution—is shown here as the change from point A to point B along indifference curve I_1. The income effect—the shift to a higher indifference curve—is shown here as the change from point B on indifference curve I_1 to point C on indifference curve I_2.

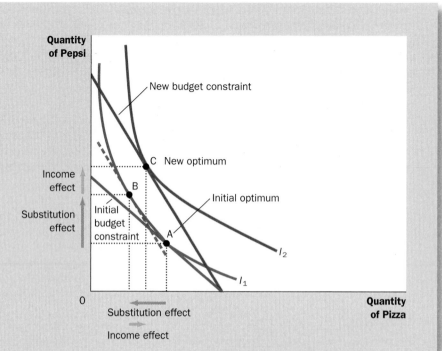

consumer *shifts* to the higher indifference curve, I_2, by moving from point B to point C. Even though point B and point C are on different indifference curves, they have the same marginal rate of substitution. That is, the slope of the indifference curve I_1 at point B equals the slope of the indifference curve I_2 at point C.

Although the consumer never actually chooses point B, this hypothetical point is useful to clarify the two effects that determine the consumer's decision. Notice that the change from point A to point B represents a pure change in the marginal rate of substitution without any change in the consumer's welfare. Similarly, the change from point B to point C represents a pure change in welfare without any change in the marginal rate of substitution. Thus, the movement from A to B shows the substitution effect, and the movement from B to C shows the income effect.

DERIVING THE DEMAND CURVE

We have just seen how changes in the price of a good alter the consumer's budget constraint and, therefore, the quantities of the two goods that he chooses to buy. The demand curve for any good reflects these consumption decisions. Recall that a demand curve shows the quantity demanded of a good for any given price. We can view a consumer's demand curve as a summary of the optimal decisions that arise from his budget constraint and indifference curves.

For example, Figure 11 considers the demand for Pepsi. Panel (a) shows that when the price of a pint falls from $2 to $1, the consumer's budget constraint shifts outward. Because of both income and substitution effects, the consumer increases

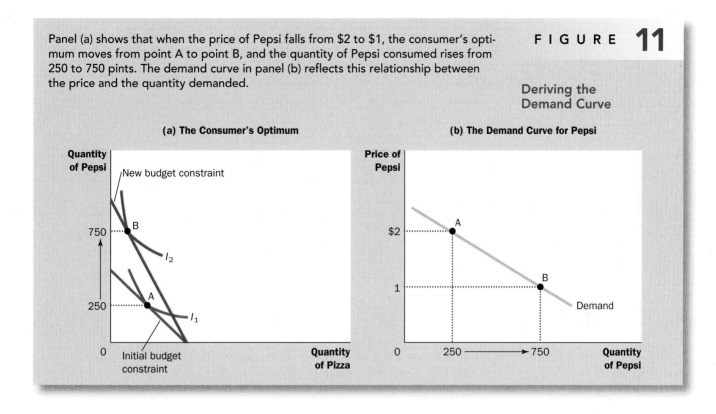

FIGURE **11**

Deriving the
Demand Curve

Panel (a) shows that when the price of Pepsi falls from $2 to $1, the consumer's optimum moves from point A to point B, and the quantity of Pepsi consumed rises from 250 to 750 pints. The demand curve in panel (b) reflects this relationship between the price and the quantity demanded.

(a) The Consumer's Optimum

(b) The Demand Curve for Pepsi

his purchases of Pepsi from 250 to 750 pints. Panel (b) shows the demand curve that results from this consumer's decisions. In this way, the theory of consumer choice provides the theoretical foundation for the consumer's demand curve.

It may be comforting to know that the demand curve arises naturally from the theory of consumer choice, but this exercise by itself does not justify developing the theory. There is no need for a rigorous, analytic framework just to establish that people respond to changes in prices. The theory of consumer choice is, however, useful in studying various decisions that people make as they go about their lives, as we see in the next section.

QUICK QUIZ Draw a budget constraint and indifference curves for pizza and Pepsi. Show what happens to the budget constraint and the consumer's optimum when the price of pizza rises. In your diagram, decompose the change into an income effect and a substitution effect.

THREE APPLICATIONS

Now that we have developed the basic theory of consumer choice, let's use it to shed light on three questions about how the economy works. These three questions might at first seem unrelated. But because each question involves household decision making, we can address it with the model of consumer behavior we have just developed.

Do All Demand Curves Slope Downward?

Normally, when the price of a good rises, people buy less of it. This usual behavior, called the *law of demand*, is reflected in the downward slope of the demand curve.

As a matter of economic theory, however, demand curves can sometimes slope upward. In other words, consumers can sometimes violate the law of demand and buy *more* of a good when the price rises. To see how this can happen, consider Figure 12. In this example, the consumer buys two goods—meat and potatoes. Initially, the consumer's budget constraint is the line from point A to point B. The optimum is point C. When the price of potatoes rises, the budget constraint shifts inward and is now the line from point A to point D. The optimum is now point E. Notice that a rise in the price of potatoes has led the consumer to buy a larger quantity of potatoes.

Why is the consumer responding in a seemingly perverse way? In this example, potatoes are a strongly inferior good. When the price of potatoes rises, the consumer is poorer. The income effect makes the consumer want to buy less meat and more potatoes. At the same time, because the potatoes have become more expensive relative to meat, the substitution effect makes the consumer want to buy more meat and less potatoes. In this particular case, however, the income effect is so strong that it exceeds the substitution effect. In the end, the consumer responds to the higher price of potatoes by buying less meat and more potatoes.

Economists use the term **Giffen good** to describe a good that violates the law of demand. (The term is named for economist Robert Giffen, who first noted this possibility.) In this example, potatoes are a Giffen good. Giffen goods are inferior goods for which the income effect dominates the substitution effect. Therefore, they have demand curves that slope upward.

Giffen good
a good for which an increase in the price raises the quantity demanded

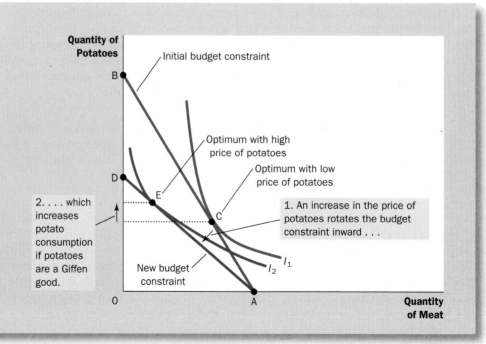

12   **FIGURE**

A Giffen Good
In this example, when the price of potatoes rises, the consumer's optimum shifts from point C to point E. In this case, the consumer responds to a higher price of potatoes by buying less meat and more potatoes.

THE SEARCH FOR GIFFEN GOODS

Have any actual Giffen goods ever been observed? Some historians suggest that potatoes were a Giffen good during the Irish potato famine of the 19th century. Potatoes were such a large part of people's diet that when the price of potatoes rose, it had a large income effect. People responded to their reduced living standard by cutting back on the luxury of meat and buying more of the staple food of potatoes. Thus, it is argued that a higher price of potatoes actually raised the quantity of potatoes demanded.

A recent study by Robert Jensen and Nolan Miller has produced similar but more concrete evidence for the existence of Giffen goods. These two economists conducted a field experiment for 5 months in the Chinese province of Hunan. They gave randomly selected households vouchers that subsidized the purchase of rice, a staple in local diets, and used surveys to measure how consumption of rice responded to changes in the price. They found strong evidence that poor households exhibited Giffen behavior. Lowering the price of rice with the subsidy voucher caused households to reduce their consumption of rice, and removing the subsidy had the opposite effect. Jensen and Miller wrote, "To the best of our knowledge, this is the first rigorous empirical evidence of Giffen behavior."

Thus, the theory of consumer choice allows demand curves to slope upward, and sometimes that strange phenomenon actually occurs. As a result, the law of demand we first saw in Chapter 4 is not completely reliable. It is safe to say, however, that Giffen goods are very rare. ●

How Do Wages Affect Labor Supply?

So far, we have used the theory of consumer choice to analyze how a person allocates income between two goods. We can use the same theory to analyze how a person allocates time. People spend some of their time enjoying leisure and some of it working so they can afford to buy consumption goods. The essence of the time-allocation problem is the trade-off between leisure and consumption.

Consider the decision facing Sally, a freelance software designer. Sally is awake for 100 hours per week. She spends some of this time enjoying leisure—riding her bike, watching television, and studying economics. She spends the rest of this time developing software at her computer. For every hour she works developing software, she earns $50, which she spends on consumption goods—food, clothing, and music downloads. Her wage ($50) reflects the trade-off Sally faces between leisure and consumption. For every hour of leisure she gives up, she works one more hour and gets $50 of consumption.

Figure 13 shows Sally's budget constraint. If she spends all 100 hours enjoying leisure, she has no consumption. If she spends all 100 hours working, she earns a weekly consumption of $5,000 but has no time for leisure. If she works a normal 40-hour week, she enjoys 60 hours of leisure and has weekly consumption of $2,000.

Figure 13 uses indifference curves to represent Sally's preferences for consumption and leisure. Here consumption and leisure are the two "goods" between which Sally is choosing. Because Sally always prefers more leisure and more consumption, she prefers points on higher indifference curves to points on lower ones. At a wage of $50 per hour, Sally chooses a combination of consumption and leisure represented by the point labeled "optimum." This is the point on the budget constraint that is on the highest possible indifference curve, I_2.

13 FIGURE

The Work-Leisure Decision
This figure shows Sally's budget constraint for deciding how much to work, her indifference curves for consumption and leisure, and her optimum.

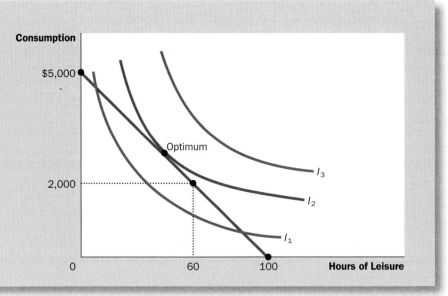

Now consider what happens when Sally's wage increases from $50 to $60 per hour. Figure 14 shows two possible outcomes. In each case, the budget constraint, shown in the left graphs, shifts outward from BC_1 to BC_2. In the process, the budget constraint becomes steeper, reflecting the change in relative price: At the higher wage, Sally earns more consumption for every hour of leisure that she gives up.

Sally's preferences, as represented by her indifference curves, determine how her choice regarding consumption and leisure responds to the higher wage. In both panels, consumption rises. Yet the response of leisure to the change in the wage is different in the two cases. In panel (a), Sally responds to the higher wage by enjoying less leisure. In panel (b), Sally responds by enjoying more leisure.

Sally's decision between leisure and consumption determines her supply of labor because the more leisure she enjoys, the less time she has left to work. In each panel of Figure 14, the right graph shows the labor-supply curve implied by Sally's decision. In panel (a), a higher wage induces Sally to enjoy less leisure and work more, so the labor-supply curve slopes upward. In panel (b), a higher wage induces Sally to enjoy more leisure and work less, so the labor-supply curve slopes "backward."

At first, the backward-sloping labor-supply curve is puzzling. Why would a person respond to a higher wage by working less? The answer comes from considering the income and substitution effects of a higher wage.

Consider first the substitution effect. When Sally's wage rises, leisure becomes more costly relative to consumption, and this encourages Sally to substitute away from leisure and toward consumption. In other words, the substitution effect induces Sally to work harder in response to higher wages, which tends to make the labor-supply curve slope upward.

Now consider the income effect. When Sally's wage rises, she moves to a higher indifference curve. She is now better off than she was. As long as consumption and leisure are both normal goods, she tends to want to use this increase in well-being to enjoy both higher consumption and greater leisure. In other words, the

The two panels of this figure show how a person might respond to an increase in the wage. The graphs on the left show the consumer's initial budget constraint, BC_1, and new budget constraint, BC_2, as well as the consumer's optimal choices over consumption and leisure. The graphs on the right show the resulting labor-supply curve. Because hours worked equal total hours available minus hours of leisure, any change in leisure implies an opposite change in the quantity of labor supplied. In panel (a), when the wage rises, consumption rises and leisure falls, resulting in a labor-supply curve that slopes upward. In panel (b), when the wage rises, both consumption and leisure rise, resulting in a labor-supply curve that slopes backward.

F I G U R E **14**

An Increase
in the Wage

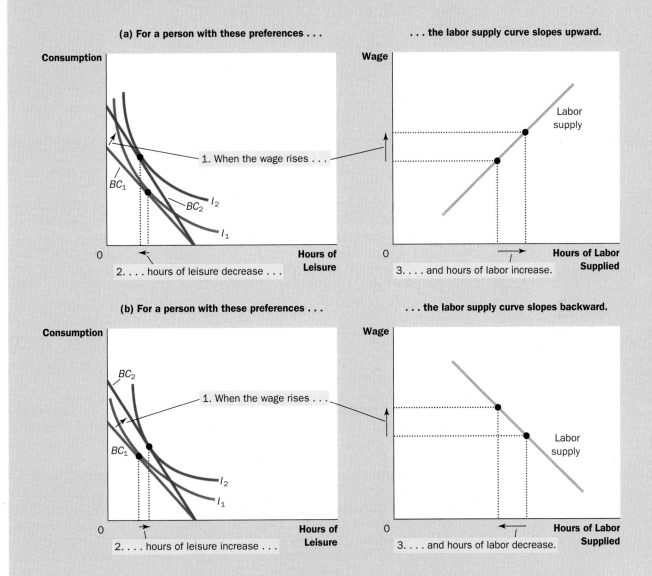

income effect induces her to work less, which tends to make the labor-supply curve slope backward.

In the end, economic theory does not give a clear prediction about whether an increase in the wage induces Sally to work more or less. If the substitution effect is greater than the income effect for Sally, she works more. If the income effect is greater than the substitution effect, she works less. The labor-supply curve, therefore, could be either upward or backward sloping.

CASE STUDY

INCOME EFFECTS ON LABOR SUPPLY: HISTORICAL TRENDS, LOTTERY WINNERS, AND THE CARNEGIE CONJECTURE

The idea of a backward-sloping labor-supply curve might at first seem like a mere theoretical curiosity, but in fact, it is not. Evidence indicates that the labor-supply curve, considered over long periods, does in fact slope backward. A hundred years ago, many people worked six days a week. Today, five-day workweeks are the norm. At the same time that the length of the workweek has been falling, the wage of the typical worker (adjusted for inflation) has been rising.

Here is how economists explain this historical pattern: Over time, advances in technology raise workers' productivity and, thereby, the demand for labor. The increase in labor demand raises equilibrium wages. As wages rise, so does the reward for working. Yet rather than responding to this increased incentive by working more, most workers choose to take part of their greater prosperity in the form of more leisure. In other words, the income effect of higher wages dominates the substitution effect.

"No more 9 to 5 for me."

Further evidence that the income effect on labor supply is strong comes from a very different kind of data: winners of lotteries. Winners of large prizes in the lottery see large increases in their incomes and, as a result, large outward shifts in their budget constraints. Because the winners' wages have not changed, however, the *slopes* of their budget constraints remain the same. There is, therefore, no substitution effect. By examining the behavior of lottery winners, we can isolate the income effect on labor supply.

The results from studies of lottery winners are striking. Of those winners who win more than $50,000, almost 25 percent quit working within a year, and another 9 percent reduce the number of hours they work. Of those winners who win more than $1 million, almost 40 percent stop working. The income effect on labor supply of winning such a large prize is substantial.

Similar results were found in a 1993 study, published in the *Quarterly Journal of Economics,* of how receiving a bequest affects a person's labor supply. The study found that a single person who inherits more than $150,000 is four times as likely to stop working as a single person who inherits less than $25,000. This finding would not have surprised the 19th-century industrialist Andrew Carnegie. Carnegie warned that "the parent who leaves his son enormous wealth generally deadens the talents and energies of the son, and tempts him to lead a less useful and less worthy life than he otherwise would." That is, Carnegie viewed the income effect on labor supply to be substantial and, from his paternalistic perspective, regrettable. During his life and at his death, Carnegie gave much of his vast fortune to charity. ●

How Do Interest Rates Affect Household Saving?

An important decision that every person faces is how much income to consume today and how much to save for the future. We can use the theory of consumer choice to analyze how people make this decision and how the amount they save depends on the interest rate their savings will earn.

Consider the decision facing Sam, a worker planning for retirement. To keep things simple, let's divide Sam's life into two periods. In the first period, Sam is young and working. In the second period, he is old and retired. When young, Sam earns $100,000. He divides this income between current consumption and saving. When he is old, Sam will consume what he has saved, including the interest that his savings have earned.

Suppose the interest rate is 10 percent. Then for every dollar that Sam saves when young, he can consume $1.10 when old. We can view "consumption when young" and "consumption when old" as the two goods that Sam must choose between. The interest rate determines the relative price of these two goods.

Figure 15 shows Sam's budget constraint. If he saves nothing, he consumes $100,000 when young and nothing when old. If he saves everything, he consumes nothing when young and $110,000 when old. The budget constraint shows these and all the intermediate possibilities.

Figure 15 uses indifference curves to represent Sam's preferences for consumption in the two periods. Because Sam prefers more consumption in both periods, he prefers points on higher indifference curves to points on lower ones. Given his preferences, Sam chooses the optimal combination of consumption in both periods of life, which is the point on the budget constraint that is on the highest possible indifference curve. At this optimum, Sam consumes $50,000 when young and $55,000 when old.

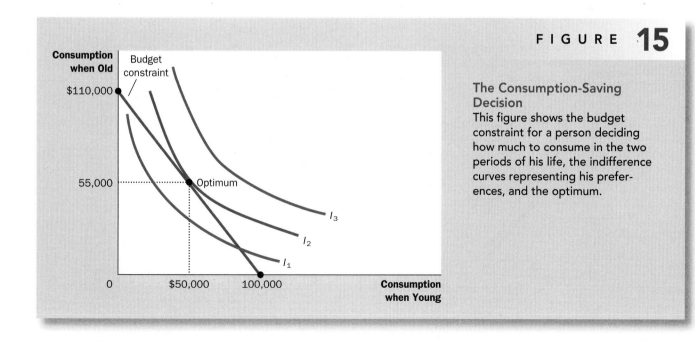

FIGURE **15**

The Consumption-Saving Decision
This figure shows the budget constraint for a person deciding how much to consume in the two periods of his life, the indifference curves representing his preferences, and the optimum.

Now consider what happens when the interest rate increases from 10 percent to 20 percent. Figure 16 shows two possible outcomes. In both cases, the budget constraint shifts outward and becomes steeper. At the new higher interest rate, Sam gets more consumption when old for every dollar of consumption that he gives up when young.

The two panels show the results given different preferences by Sam. In both cases, consumption when old rises. Yet the response of consumption when young to the change in the interest rate is different in the two cases. In panel (a), Sam responds to the higher interest rate by consuming less when young. In panel (b), Sam responds by consuming more when young.

Sam's saving is his income when young minus the amount he consumes when young. In panel (a), consumption when young falls when the interest rate rises, so saving must rise. In panel (b), Sam consumes more when young, so saving must fall.

The case shown in panel (b) might at first seem odd: Sam responds to an increase in the return to saving by saving less. Yet this behavior is not as peculiar as it might seem. We can understand it by considering the income and substitution effects of a higher interest rate.

Consider first the substitution effect. When the interest rate rises, consumption when old becomes less costly relative to consumption when young. Therefore, the substitution effect induces Sam to consume more when old and less when young. In other words, the substitution effect induces Sam to save more.

Now consider the income effect. When the interest rate rises, Sam moves to a higher indifference curve. He is now better off than he was. As long as consump-

16 FIGURE

An Increase in the Interest Rate

In both panels, an increase in the interest rate shifts the budget constraint outward. In panel (a), consumption when young falls, and consumption when old rises. The result is an increase in saving when young. In panel (b), consumption in both periods rises. The result is a decrease in saving when young.

tion in both periods consists of normal goods, he tends to want to use this increase in well-being to enjoy higher consumption in both periods. In other words, the income effect induces him to save less.

The result depends on both the income and substitution effects. If the substitution effect of a higher interest rate is greater than the income effect, Sam saves more. If the income effect is greater than the substitution effect, Sam saves less. Thus, the theory of consumer choice says that an increase in the interest rate could either encourage or discourage saving.

Although this ambiguous result is interesting from the standpoint of economic theory, it is disappointing from the standpoint of economic policy. It turns out that an important issue in tax policy hinges in part on how saving responds to interest rates. Some economists have advocated reducing the taxation of interest and other capital income, arguing that such a policy change would raise the after-tax interest rate that savers can earn and would thereby encourage people to save more. Other economists have argued that because of offsetting income and substitution effects, such a tax change might not increase saving and could even reduce it. Unfortunately, research has not led to a consensus about how interest rates affect saving. As a result, there remains disagreement among economists about whether changes in tax policy aimed to encourage saving would, in fact, have the intended effect.

QUICK QUIZ Explain how an increase in the wage can potentially decrease the amount that a person wants to work.

CONCLUSION: DO PEOPLE REALLY THINK THIS WAY?

The theory of consumer choice describes how people make decisions. As we have seen, it has broad applicability. It can explain how a person chooses between pizza and Pepsi, work and leisure, consumption and saving, and on and on.

At this point, however, you might be tempted to treat the theory of consumer choice with some skepticism. After all, you are a consumer. You decide what to buy every time you walk into a store. And you know that you do not decide by writing down budget constraints and indifference curves. Doesn't this knowledge about your own decision making provide evidence against the theory?

The answer is no. The theory of consumer choice does not try to present a literal account of how people make decisions. It is a model. And as we first discussed in Chapter 2, models are not intended to be completely realistic.

The best way to view the theory of consumer choice is as a metaphor for how consumers make decisions. No consumer (except an occasional economist) goes through the explicit optimization envisioned in the theory. Yet consumers are aware that their choices are constrained by their financial resources. And given those constraints, they do the best they can to achieve the highest level of satisfaction. The theory of consumer choice tries to describe this implicit, psychological process in a way that permits explicit, economic analysis.

Just as the proof of the pudding is in the eating, the test of a theory is in its applications. In the last section of this chapter, we applied the theory of consumer choice to three practical issues about the economy. If you take more advanced courses in economics, you will see that this theory provides the framework for much additional analysis.

SUMMARY

- A consumer's budget constraint shows the possible combinations of different goods he can buy given his income and the prices of the goods. The slope of the budget constraint equals the relative price of the goods.

- The consumer's indifference curves represent his preferences. An indifference curve shows the various bundles of goods that make the consumer equally happy. Points on higher indifference curves are preferred to points on lower indifference curves. The slope of an indifference curve at any point is the consumer's marginal rate of substitution—the rate at which the consumer is willing to trade one good for the other.

- The consumer optimizes by choosing the point on his budget constraint that lies on the highest indifference curve. At this point, the slope of the indifference curve (the marginal rate of substitution between the goods) equals the slope of the budget constraint (the relative price of the goods).

- When the price of a good falls, the impact on the consumer's choices can be broken down into an income effect and a substitution effect. The income effect is the change in consumption that arises because a lower price makes the consumer better off. The substitution effect is the change in consumption that arises because a price change encourages greater consumption of the good that has become relatively cheaper. The income effect is reflected in the movement from a lower to a higher indifference curve, whereas the substitution effect is reflected by a movement along an indifference curve to a point with a different slope.

- The theory of consumer choice can be applied in many situations. It explains why demand curves can potentially slope upward, why higher wages could either increase or decrease the quantity of labor supplied, and why higher interest rates could either increase or decrease saving.

KEY CONCEPTS

budget constraint, *p. 458*
indifference curve, *p. 460*
marginal rate of
   substitution, *p. 460*

perfect substitutes, *p. 463*
perfect complements, *p. 464*
normal good, *p. 467*
inferior good, *p. 467*

income effect, *p. 468*
substitution effect, *p. 468*
Giffen good, *p. 472*

QUESTIONS FOR REVIEW

1. A consumer has income of $3,000. Wine costs $3 per glass, and cheese costs $6 per pound. Draw the consumer's budget constraint. What is the slope of this budget constraint?
2. Draw a consumer's indifference curves for wine and cheese. Describe and explain four properties of these indifference curves.
3. Pick a point on an indifference curve for wine and cheese and show the marginal rate of sub-

stitution. What does the marginal rate of substitution tell us?
4. Show a consumer's budget constraint and indifference curves for wine and cheese. Show the optimal consumption choice. If the price of wine is $3 per glass and the price of cheese is $6 per pound, what is the marginal rate of substitution at this optimum?

5. A person who consumes wine and cheese gets a raise, so his income increases from $3,000 to $4,000. Show what happens if both wine and cheese are normal goods. Now show what happens if cheese is an inferior good.

6. The price of cheese rises from $6 to $10 per pound, while the price of wine remains $3 per glass. For a consumer with a constant income of $3,000, show what happens to consumption of wine and cheese. Decompose the change into income and substitution effects.

7. Can an increase in the price of cheese possibly induce a consumer to buy more cheese? Explain.

PROBLEMS AND APPLICATIONS

1. Jennifer divides her income between coffee and croissants (both of which are normal goods). An early frost in Brazil causes a large increase in the price of coffee in the United States.
   a. Show the effect of the frost on Jennifer's budget constraint.
   b. Show the effect of the frost on Jennifer's optimal consumption bundle assuming that the substitution effect outweighs the income effect for croissants.
   c. Show the effect of the frost on Jennifer's optimal consumption bundle assuming that the income effect outweighs the substitution effect for croissants.

2. Compare the following two pairs of goods:
   • Coke and Pepsi
   • Skis and ski bindings
   a. In which case are the two goods complements? In which case are they substitutes?
   b. In which case do you expect the indifference curves to be fairly straight? In which case do you expect the indifference curves to be very bowed?
   c. In which case will the consumer respond more to a change in the relative price of the two goods?

3. Mario consumes only cheese and crackers.
   a. Could cheese and crackers both be inferior goods for Mario? Explain.
   b. Suppose that cheese is a normal good for Mario while crackers are an inferior good. If the price of cheese falls, what happens to Mario's consumption of crackers? What happens to his consumption of cheese? Explain.

4. Jim buys only milk and cookies.
   a. In year 1, Jim earns $100, milk costs $2 per quart, and cookies cost $4 per dozen. Draw Jim's budget constraint.
   b. Now suppose that all prices increase by 10 percent in year 2 and that Jim's salary increases by 10 percent as well. Draw Jim's new budget constraint. How would Jim's optimal combination of milk and cookies in year 2 compare to his optimal combination in year 1?

5. A college student has two options for meals: eating at the dining hall for $6 per meal, or eating a Cup O' Soup for $1.50 per meal. His weekly food budget is $60.
   a. Draw the budget constraint showing the trade-off between dining hall meals and Cups O' Soup. Assuming that he spends equal amounts on both goods, draw an indifference curve showing the optimum choice. Label the optimum as point A.
   b. Suppose the price of a Cup O' Soup now rises to $2. Using your diagram from part (a), show the consequences of this change in price. Assume that our student now spends only 30 percent of his income on dining hall meals. Label the new optimum as point B.
   c. What happened to the quantity of Cups O' Soup consumed as a result of this price change? What does this result say about the income and substitution effects? Explain.
   d. Use points A and B to draw a demand curve for Cup O' Soup. What is this type of good called?

6. Consider your decision about how many hours to work.
   a. Draw your budget constraint assuming that you pay no taxes on your income. On the same diagram, draw another budget constraint assuming that you pay 15 percent tax.
   b. Show how the tax might lead to more hours of work, fewer hours, or the same number of hours. Explain.

7. Sarah is awake for 100 hours per week. Using one diagram, show Sarah's budget constraints if she earns $6 per hour, $8 per hour, and $10 per hour. Now draw indifference curves such that Sarah's labor-supply curve is upward sloping when the wage is between $6 and $8 per hour, and backward sloping when the wage is between $8 and $10 per hour.

8. Draw the indifference curve for someone deciding how to allocate time between work and leisure. Suppose the wage increases. Is it possible that the person's consumption would fall? Is this plausible? Discuss. (Hint: Think about income and substitution effects.)

9. Suppose you take a job that pays $30,000 and set some of this income aside in a savings account that pays an annual interest rate of 5 percent. Use a diagram with a budget constraint and indifference curves to show how your consumption changes in each of the following situations. To keep things simple, assume that you pay no taxes on your income.
   a. Your salary increases to $40,000.
   b. The interest rate on your bank account rises to 8 percent.

10. As discussed in the text, we can divide an individual's life into two hypothetical periods: "young" and "old." Suppose the individual earns income only when young and saves some of that income to consume when old. If the interest rate on savings falls, can you tell what happens to consumption when young? Can you tell what happens to consumption when old? Explain.

11. Consider a couple's decision about how many children to have. Assume that over a lifetime a couple has 200,000 hours of time to either work or raise children. The wage is $10 per hour. Raising a child takes 20,000 hours of time.
   a. Draw the budget constraint showing the trade-off between lifetime consumption and number of children. (Ignore the fact that children come only in whole numbers!) Show indifference curves and an optimum choice.
   b. Suppose the wage increases to $12 per hour. Show how the budget constraint shifts. Using income and substitution effects, discuss the impact of the change on number of children and lifetime consumption.

   c. We observe that, as societies get richer and wages rise, people typically have fewer children. Is this fact consistent with this model? Explain.

12. Economist George Stigler once wrote that, according to consumer theory, "if consumers do not buy less of a commodity when their incomes rise, they will surely buy less when the price of the commodity rises." Explain this statement using the concepts of income and substitution effects.

13. The welfare system provides income to some needy families. Typically, the maximum payment goes to families that earn no income; then, as families begin to earn income, the welfare payment declines gradually and eventually disappears. Let's consider the possible effects of this program on a family's labor supply.
   a. Draw a budget constraint for a family assuming that the welfare system did not exist. On the same diagram, draw a budget constraint that reflects the existence of the welfare system.
   b. Adding indifference curves to your diagram, show how the welfare system could reduce the number of hours worked by the family. Explain, with reference to both the income and substitution effects.
   c. Using your diagram from part (b), show the effect of the welfare system on the well-being of the family.

14. Five consumers have the following marginal utility of apples and pears:

	Marginal Utility of Apples	Marginal Utility of Pears
Jerry	12	6
George	6	6
Elaine	6	3
Kramer	3	6
Newman	12	3

The price of an apple is $2, and the price of a pear is $1. Which, if any, of these consumers are optimizing over their choice of fruit? For those who are not, how should they change their spending?

Frontiers of Microeconomics

conomics is a study of the choices that people make and the resulting interactions they have with one another. This study has many facets, as we have
seen in the preceding chapters. Yet it would be a mistake to think that all
the facets we have seen make up a finished jewel, perfect and unchanging. Like
all scientists, economists are always on the lookout for new areas to study and
new phenomena to explain. This final chapter on microeconomics offers an assort-
ment of three topics at the discipline's frontier to see how economists are trying to
expand their understanding of human behavior and society.

The first topic is the economics of *asymmetric information*. Many times in life,
some people are better informed than others, and this difference in information
can affect the choices they make and how they deal with one another. Thinking
about this asymmetry can shed light on many aspects of the world, from the market for used cars to the custom of gift giving.

The second topic we examine in this chapter is *political economy*. Throughout
this book, we have seen many examples where markets fail and government
policy can potentially improve matters. But "potentially" is a needed qualifier:
Whether this potential is realized depends on how well our political institutions
work. The field of political economy uses the tools of economics to understand the
functioning of government.

The third topic in this chapter is *behavioral economics*. This field brings some of
the insights from psychology into the study of economic issues. It offers a view of

human behavior that is more subtle and complex than that found in conventional economic theory, but this view may also be more realistic.

This chapter covers a lot of ground. To do so, it offers not a full helping of these three topics but, instead, a taste of each. One goal is to show a few of the directions economists are heading in their effort to expand knowledge of how the economy works. Another goal is to whet your appetite for more courses in economics.

ASYMMETRIC INFORMATION

"I know something you don't know." This statement is a common taunt among children, but it also conveys a deep truth about how people sometimes interact with one another. Many times in life, one person knows more about what is going on than another. A difference in access to relevant knowledge is called an *information asymmetry.*

Examples abound. A worker knows more than his employer about how much effort he puts into his job. A seller of a used car knows more than the buyer about the car's condition. The first is an example of a *hidden action,* whereas the second is an example of a *hidden characteristic.* In each case, the uninformed party (the employer, the car buyer) would like to know the relevant information, but the informed party (the worker, the car seller) may have an incentive to conceal it.

Because asymmetric information is so prevalent, economists have devoted much effort in recent decades to studying its effects. And indeed, the 2001 Nobel Prize in Economics was awarded to three economists (George Akerlof, Michael Spence, and Joseph Stiglitz) for their pioneering work on this topic. Let's discuss some of the insights that this study has revealed.

Hidden Actions: Principals, Agents, and Moral Hazard

moral hazard
the tendency of a person who is imperfectly monitored to engage in dishonest or otherwise undesirable behavior

agent
a person who is performing an act for another person, called the principal

principal
a person for whom another person, called the agent, is performing some act

Moral hazard is a problem that arises when one person, called the **agent**, is performing some task on behalf of another person, called the **principal**. If the principal cannot perfectly monitor the agent's behavior, the agent tends to undertake less effort than the principal considers desirable. The phrase *moral hazard* refers to the risk, or "hazard," of inappropriate or otherwise "immoral" behavior by the agent. In such a situation, the principal tries various ways to encourage the agent to act more responsibly.

The employment relationship is the classic example. The employer is the principal, and the worker is the agent. The moral-hazard problem is the temptation of imperfectly monitored workers to shirk their responsibilities. Employers can respond to this problem in various ways:

- *Better monitoring.* Parents hiring nannies have been known to plant hidden video cameras in their homes to record the nanny's behavior when the parents are away. The aim is to catch irresponsible behavior.
- *High wages.* According to *efficiency-wage theories* (discussed in Chapter 19), some employers may choose to pay their workers a wage above the level that equilibrates supply and demand in the labor market. A worker who earns an above-equilibrium wage is less likely to shirk because, if he is caught and fired, he might not be able to find another high-paying job.

- *Delayed payment.* Firms can delay part of a worker's compensation, so if the worker is caught shirking and is fired, he suffers a larger penalty. One example of delayed compensation is the year-end bonus. Similarly, a firm may choose to pay its workers more later in their lives. Thus, the wage increases that workers get as they age may reflect not just the benefits of experience but also a response to moral hazard.

Employers can use any combination of these various mechanisms to reduce the problem of moral hazard.

There are also many examples of moral hazard beyond the workplace. A homeowner with fire insurance will likely buy too few fire extinguishers because the homeowner bears the cost of the extinguisher while the insurance company receives much of the benefit. A family may live near a river with a high risk of flooding because the family enjoys the scenic views, while the government bears the cost of disaster relief after a flood. Many regulations are aimed at addressing the problem: An insurance company may require homeowners to buy fire extinguishers, and the government may prohibit building homes on land with high risk of flooding. But the insurance company does not have perfect information about how cautious homeowners are, and the government does not have perfect information about the risk that families undertake when choosing where to live. As a result, the problem of moral hazard persists.

HIDDEN CHARACTERISTICS: ADVERSE SELECTION AND THE LEMONS PROBLEM

Adverse selection is a problem that arises in markets in which the seller knows more about the attributes of the good being sold than the buyer does. In such a situation, the buyer runs the risk of being sold a good of low quality. That is, the "selection" of goods sold may be "adverse" from the standpoint of the uninformed buyer.

adverse selection
the tendency for the mix of unobserved attributes to become undesirable from the standpoint of an uninformed party

The classic example of adverse selection is the market for used cars. Sellers of used cars know their vehicles' defects while buyers often do not. Because owners of the worst cars are more likely to sell them than are the owners of the best cars, buyers are apprehensive about getting a "lemon." As a result, many people avoid buying vehicles in the used car market. This lemons problem can explain why a used car only a few weeks old sells for thousands of dollars less than a new car of the same type. A buyer of the used car might surmise that the seller is getting rid of the car quickly because the seller knows something about it that the buyer does not.

A second example of adverse selection occurs in the labor market. According to another efficiency-wage theory, workers vary in their abilities, and they may know their own abilities better than do the firms that hire them. When a firm cuts the wage it pays, the more talented workers are more likely to quit, knowing they are better able to find other employment. Conversely, a firm may choose to pay an above-equilibrium wage to attract a better mix of workers.

A third example of adverse selection occurs in markets for insurance. For example, buyers of health insurance know more about their own health problems than do insurance companies. Because people with greater hidden health problems are more likely to buy health insurance than are other people, the price of health insurance reflects the costs of a sicker-than-average person. As a result, people

FYI

Corporate Management

Much production in the modern economy takes place within corporations. Like other firms, corporations buy inputs in markets for the factors of production and sell their output in markets for goods and services. Also like other firms, they are guided in their decisions by the objective of profit maximization. But a large corporation has to deal with some issues that do not arise in, say, a small family-owned business.

What is distinctive about a corporation? From a legal standpoint, a corporation is an organization that is granted a charter recognizing it as a separate legal entity, with its own rights and responsibilities distinct from those of its owners and employees. From an economic standpoint, the most important feature of the corporate form of organization is the separation of ownership and control. One group of people, called the shareholders, own the corporation and share in its profits. Another group of people, called the managers, are employed by the corporation to make decisions about how to deploy the corporation's resources.

The separation of ownership and control creates a principal-agent problem. In this case, the shareholders are the principals, and the managers are the agents. The chief executive officer and other managers, who are in the best position to know the available business opportunities, are charged with the task of maximizing profits for the shareholders. But ensuring that they carry out this task is not always easy. The managers may have goals of their own, such as taking life easy, having a plush office and a private jet, throwing lavish parties, or presiding over a large business empire. The managers' goals may not always coincide with the goal of profit maximization.

The corporation's board of directors is responsible for hiring and firing the top management. The board monitors the managers' performance, and it designs their compensation packages. These packages often include incentives aimed at aligning the interest of shareholders with the interest of management. Managers might be given bonuses based on performance or options to buy the company's stock, which are more valuable if the company performs well.

Note, however, that the directors are themselves agents of the shareholders. The existence of a board overseeing management only shifts the principal-agent problem. The issue then becomes how to ensure that the board of directors fulfills its own legal obligation of acting in the best interest of the shareholders. If the directors become too friendly with management, they may not provide the required oversight.

The corporation's principal-agent problem became big news around 2005. The top managers of several prominent companies, such as Enron, Tyco, and WorldCom, were found to be engaging in activities that enriched themselves at the expense of their shareholders. In these cases, the actions were so extreme as to be criminal, and the corporate managers were not just fired but also sent to prison. Some shareholders sued directors for failing to monitor management sufficiently.

Fortunately, criminal activity by corporate managers is rare. But in some ways, it is only the tip of the iceberg. Whenever ownership and control are separated, as they are in most large corporations, there is an inevitable tension between the interests of shareholders and the interests of management.

in average health may be discouraged from buying health insurance by the high price.

When markets suffer from adverse selection, the invisible hand does not necessarily work its magic. In the used car market, owners of good cars may choose to keep them rather than sell them at the low price that skeptical buyers are willing to pay. In the labor market, wages may be stuck above the level that balances supply and demand, resulting in unemployment. In insurance markets, buyers with low risk may choose to remain uninsured because the policies they are offered fail to reflect their true characteristics. Advocates of government-provided health insurance sometimes point to the problem of adverse selection as one reason not to trust the private market to provide the right amount of health insurance on its own.

SIGNALING TO CONVEY PRIVATE INFORMATION

Although asymmetric information is sometimes a motivation for public policy, it also motivates some individual behavior that otherwise might be hard to explain. Markets respond to problems of asymmetric information in many ways. One of them is **signaling**, which refers to actions taken by an informed party for the sole purpose of credibly revealing his private information.

signaling
an action taken by an informed party to reveal private information to an uninformed party

We have seen examples of signaling in previous chapters. As we saw in Chapter 16, firms may spend money on advertising to signal to potential customers that they have high-quality products. As we saw in Chapter 20, students may earn college degrees to signal to potential employers that they are high-ability individuals. Recall that the signaling theory of education contrasts with the human-capital theory, which asserts that education increases a person's productivity, rather than merely conveying information about innate talent. These two examples of signaling (advertising, education) may seem very different, but below the surface, they are much the same: In both cases, the informed party (the firm, the student) is using the signal to convince the uninformed party (the customer, the employer) that the informed party is offering something of high quality.

What does it take for an action to be an effective signal? Obviously, it must be costly. If a signal were free, everyone would use it, and it would convey no information. For the same reason, there is another requirement: The signal must be less costly, or more beneficial, to the person with the higher-quality product. Otherwise, everyone would have the same incentive to use the signal, and the signal would reveal nothing.

Consider again our two examples. In the advertising case, a firm with a good product reaps a larger benefit from advertising because customers who try the product once are more likely to become repeat customers. Thus, it is rational for the firm with a good product to pay for the cost of the signal (advertising), and it is rational for the customer to use the signal as a piece of information about the product's quality. In the education case, a talented person can get through school more easily than a less talented one. Thus, it is rational for the talented person to pay for the cost of the signal (education), and it is rational for the employer to use the signal as a piece of information about the person's talent.

The world is replete with instances of signaling. Magazine ads sometimes include the phrase "as seen on TV." Why does a firm selling a product in a magazine choose to stress this fact? One possibility is that the firm is trying to convey its willingness to pay for an expensive signal (a spot on television) in the hope that you will infer that its product is of high quality. For the same reason, graduates of elite schools are always sure to put that fact on their résumés.

 ## GIFTS AS SIGNALS

A man is debating what to give his girlfriend for her birthday. "I know," he says to himself, "I'll give her cash. After all, I don't know her tastes as well as she does, and with cash, she can buy anything she wants." But when he hands her the money, she is offended. Convinced he doesn't really love her, she breaks off the relationship.

What's the economics behind this story?

In some ways, gift giving is a strange custom. As the man in our story suggests, people typically know their own preferences better than others do, so we might expect everyone to prefer cash to in-kind transfers. If your employer substituted merchandise of his choosing for your paycheck, you would likely object to this means of payment. But your reaction is very different when someone who (you hope) loves you does the same thing.

One interpretation of gift giving is that it reflects asymmetric information and signaling. The man in our story has private information that the girlfriend would like to know: Does he really love her? Choosing a good gift for her is a signal of his love. Certainly, the act of picking out a gift, rather than giving cash, has the right characteristics to be a signal. It is costly (it takes time), and its cost depends on private information (how much he loves her). If he really loves her, choosing a good gift is easy because he is thinking about her all the time. If he doesn't love her, finding the right gift is more difficult. Thus, giving a gift that suits the girlfriend is one way for him to convey the private information of his love for her. Giving cash shows that he isn't even bothering to try.

The signaling theory of gift giving is consistent with another observation: People care most about the custom when the strength of affection is most in question. Thus, giving cash to a girlfriend or boyfriend is usually a bad move. But when college students receive a check from their parents, they are less often offended. The parents' love is less likely to be in doubt, so the recipient probably won't interpret the cash gift as a signal of lack of affection. ●

SCREENING TO INDUCE INFORMATION REVELATION

When an informed party takes actions to reveal his private information, the phenomenon is called signaling. When an uninformed party takes actions to induce the informed party to reveal private information, the phenomenon is called **screening**.

Some screening is common sense. A person buying a used car may ask that it be checked by an auto mechanic before the sale. A seller who refuses this request reveals his private information that the car is a lemon. The buyer may decide to offer a lower price or to look for another car.

Other examples of screening are more subtle. For example, consider a firm that sells car insurance. The firm would like to charge a low premium to safe drivers and a high premium to risky drivers. But how can it tell them apart? Drivers know whether they are safe or risky, but the risky ones won't admit it. A driver's history is one piece of information (which insurance companies in fact use), but because of the intrinsic randomness of car accidents, history is an imperfect indicator of future risks.

The insurance company might be able to sort out the two kinds of drivers by offering different insurance policies that would induce them to separate themselves. One policy would have a high premium and cover the full cost of any accidents that occur. Another policy would have low premiums but would have, say, a $1,000 deductible. (That is, the driver would be responsible for the first $1,000 of damage, and the insurance company would cover the remaining risk.) Notice that the deductible is more of a burden for risky drivers because they are more likely to have an accident. Thus, with a large enough deductible, the low-premium policy with a deductible would attract the safe drivers, while the high-premium policy without a deductible would attract the risky drivers. Faced with these two policies, the two kinds of drivers would reveal their private information by choosing different insurance policies.

"NOW WE'LL SEE HOW MUCH HE LOVES ME."

screening
an action taken by an uninformed party to induce an informed party to reveal information

ASYMMETRIC INFORMATION AND PUBLIC POLICY

We have examined two kinds of asymmetric information: moral hazard and adverse selection. And we have seen how individuals may respond to the problem with signaling or screening. Now let's consider what the study of asymmetric information suggests about the proper scope of public policy.

The tension between market success and market failure is central in microeconomics. We learned in Chapter 7 that the equilibrium of supply and demand is efficient in the sense that it maximizes the total surplus that society can obtain in a market. Adam Smith's invisible hand seemed to reign supreme. This conclusion was then tempered with the study of externalities (Chapter 10), public goods (Chapter 11), imperfect competition (Chapters 15 through 17), and poverty (Chapter 20). These examples of market failure showed that government can sometimes improve market outcomes.

The study of asymmetric information gives us a new reason to be wary of markets. When some people know more than others, the market may fail to put resources to their best use. People with high-quality used cars may have trouble selling them because buyers will be afraid of getting a lemon. People with few health problems may have trouble getting low-cost health insurance because insurance companies lump them together with those who have significant (but hidden) health problems.

Although asymmetric information may call for government action in some cases, three facts complicate the issue. First, as we have seen, the private market can sometimes deal with information asymmetries on its own using a combination of signaling and screening. Second, the government rarely has more information than the private parties. Even if the market's allocation of resources is not first-best, it may be second-best. That is, when there are information asymmetries, policymakers may find it hard to improve upon the market's admittedly imperfect outcome. Third, the government is itself an imperfect institution—a topic we take up in the next section.

QUICK QUIZ A person who buys a life insurance policy pays a certain amount per year and receives for his family a much larger payment in the event of his death. Would you expect buyers of life insurance to have higher or lower death rates than the average person? How might this be an example of moral hazard? Of adverse selection? How might a life insurance company deal with these problems?

POLITICAL ECONOMY

As we have seen, markets left on their own do not always reach a desirable allocation of resources. When we judge the market's outcome to be either inefficient or inequitable, there may be a role for the government to step in and improve the situation. Yet before we embrace an activist government, we need to consider one more fact: The government is also an imperfect institution. The field of **political economy** (sometimes called the field of *public choice*) applies the methods of economics to study how government works.

political economy
the study of government using the analytic methods of economics

THE CONDORCET VOTING PARADOX

Most advanced societies rely on democratic principles to set government policy. When a city is deciding between two locations to build a new park, for example, we have a simple way to choose: The majority gets its way. Yet for most policy issues, the number of possible outcomes far exceeds two. A new park, for instance, could be placed in many possible locations. In this case, as the 18th-century French political theorist Marquis de Condorcet famously noted, democracy might run into some problems trying to choose the best outcome.

For example, suppose there are three possible outcomes, labeled A, B, and C, and there are three voter types with the preferences shown in Table 1. The mayor of our town wants to aggregate these individual preferences into preferences for society as a whole. How should she do it?

At first, she might try some pairwise votes. If she asks voters to choose first between B and C, voter types 1 and 2 will vote for B, giving B the majority. If she then asks voters to choose between A and B, voter types 1 and 3 will vote for A, giving A the majority. Observing that A beats B, and B beats C, the mayor might conclude that A is the voters' clear choice.

But wait: Suppose the mayor then asks voters to choose between A and C. In this case, voter types 2 and 3 vote for C, giving C the majority. That is, under pairwise majority voting, A beats B, B beats C, and C beats A. Normally, we expect preferences to exhibit a property called *transitivity:* If A is preferred to B, and B is preferred to C, then we would expect A to be preferred to C. The **Condorcet paradox** is that democratic outcomes do not always obey this property. Pairwise voting might produce transitive preferences for society in some cases, but as our example in the table shows, it cannot be counted on to do so.

One implication of the Condorcet paradox is that the order which things are voted on can affect the result. If the mayor suggests choosing first between A and B and then comparing the winner to C, the town ends up choosing C. But if the voters choose first between B and C and then compare the winner to A, the town ends up with A. And if the voters choose first between A and C and then compare the winner to B, the town ends up with B.

The Condorcet paradox teaches two lessons. The narrow lesson is that when there are more than two options, setting the agenda (that is, deciding the order which items are voted on) can have a powerful influence over the outcome of a democratic election. The broad lesson is that majority voting by itself does not tell us what outcome a society really wants.

Condorcet paradox
the failure of majority rule to produce transitive preferences for society

1 TABLE

The Condorcet Paradox
If voters have these preferences over outcomes A, B, and C, then in pairwise majority voting, A beats B, B beats C, and C beats A.

	Voter Type		
	Type 1	Type 2	Type 3
Percent of Electorate	35	45	20
First choice	A	B	C
Second choice	B	C	A
Third choice	C	A	B

ARROW'S IMPOSSIBILITY THEOREM

Since political theorists first noticed Condorcet's paradox, they have spent much energy studying existing voting systems and proposing new ones. For example, as an alternative to pairwise majority voting, the mayor of our town could ask each voter to rank the possible outcomes. For each voter, we could give 1 point for last place, 2 points for second to last, 3 points for third to last, and so on. The outcome that receives the most total points wins. With the preferences in Table 1, outcome B is the winner. (You can do the arithmetic yourself.) This voting method is called a *Borda count* for the 18th-century French mathematician and political theorist who devised it. It is often used in polls that rank sports teams.

Is there a perfect voting system? Economist Kenneth Arrow took up this question in his 1951 book *Social Choice and Individual Values.* Arrow started by defining what a perfect voting system would be. He assumes that individuals in society have preferences over the various possible outcomes: A, B, C, and so on. He then assumes that society wants a voting system to choose among these outcomes that satisfies several properties:

- *Unanimity:* If everyone prefers A to B, then A should beat B.
- *Transitivity:* If A beats B, and B beats C, then A should beat C.
- *Independence of irrelevant alternatives:* The ranking between any two outcomes A and B should not depend on whether some third outcome C is also available.
- *No dictators:* There is no person who always gets his way, regardless of everyone else's preferences.

These all seem like desirable properties of a voting system. Yet Arrow proved, mathematically and incontrovertibly, that *no voting system can satisfy all these properties.* This amazing result is called **Arrow's impossibility theorem**.

The mathematics needed to prove Arrow's theorem is beyond the scope of this book, but we can get some sense of why the theorem is true from a couple of examples. We have already seen the problem with the method of majority rule. The Condorcet paradox shows that majority rule fails to produce a ranking of outcomes that always satisfies transitivity.

As another example, the Borda count fails to satisfy the independence of irrelevant alternatives. Recall that, using the preferences in Table 1, outcome B wins with a Borda count. But suppose that suddenly C disappears as an alternative. If the Borda count method is applied only to outcomes A and B, then A wins. (Once again, you can do the arithmetic on your own.) Thus, eliminating alternative C changes the ranking between A and B. This change occurs because the result of the Borda count depends on the number of points that A and B receive, and the number of points depends on whether the irrelevant alternative, C, is also available.

Arrow's impossibility theorem is a deep and disturbing result. It doesn't say that we should abandon democracy as a form of government. But it does say that, no matter what voting system society adopts for aggregating the preferences of its members, in some way it will be flawed as a mechanism for social choice.

Arrow's impossibility theorem
a mathematical result showing that, under certain assumed conditions, there is no scheme for aggregating individual preferences into a valid set of social preferences

THE MEDIAN VOTER IS KING

Despite Arrow's theorem, voting is how most societies choose their leaders and public policies, often by majority rule. The next step in studying government is to examine how governments run by majority rule work. That is, in a democratic society, who determines what policy is chosen? In some cases, the theory of democratic government yields a surprisingly simple answer.

Let's consider an example. Imagine that society is deciding how much money to spend on some public good, such as the army or the national parks. Each voter has his own most preferred budget, and he always prefers outcomes closer to his most preferred value to outcomes farther away. Thus, we can line up voters from those who prefer the smallest budget to those who prefer the largest. Figure 1 is an example. Here there are 100 voters, and the budget size varies from zero to $20 billion. Given these preferences, what outcome would you expect democracy to produce?

According to a famous result called the **median voter theorem**, majority rule will produce the outcome most preferred by the median voter. The *median voter* is the voter exactly in the middle of the distribution. In this example, if you take the line of voters ordered by their preferred budgets and count 50 voters from either end of the line, you will find that the median voter wants a budget of $10 billion. By contrast, the average preferred outcome (calculated by adding the preferred outcomes and dividing by the number of voters) is $9 billion, and the modal outcome (the one preferred by the greatest number of voters) is $15 billion.

The median voter rules the day because his preferred outcome beats any other proposal in a two-way race. In our example, more than half the voters want $10 billion or more, and more than half want $10 billion or less. If someone proposes, say, $8 billion instead of $10 billion, everyone who prefers $10 billion or more will vote with the median voter. Similarly, if someone proposes $12 billion instead of $10 billion, everyone who wants $10 billion or less will vote with the median voter. In either case, the median voter has more than half the voters on his side.

median voter theorem
a mathematical result showing that if voters are choosing a point along a line and each voter wants the point closest to his most preferred point, then majority rule will pick the most preferred point of the median voter

1 FIGURE

The Median Voter Theorem: An Example
This bar chart shows how 100 voters' most preferred budgets are distributed over five options, ranging from zero to $20 billion. If society makes its choice by majority rule, the median voter (who here prefers $10 billion) determines the outcome.

What about the Condorcet voting paradox? It turns out that when the voters are picking a point along a line and each voter aims for his own most preferred point, the Condorcet paradox cannot arise. The median voter's most preferred outcome beats all comers.

One implication of the median voter theorem is that if two political parties are each trying to maximize their chance of election, they will both move their positions toward the median voter. Suppose, for example, that the Democratic Party advocates a budget of $15 billion, while the Republican Party advocates a budget of $10 billion. The Democratic position is more popular in the sense that $15 billion has more proponents than any other single choice. Nonetheless, the Republicans get more than 50 percent of the vote: They will attract the 20 voters who want $10 billion, the 15 voters who want $5 billion, and the 25 voters who want zero. If the Democrats want to win, they will move their platform toward the median voter. Thus, this theory can explain why the parties in a two-party system are similar to each other: They are both moving toward the median voter.

Another implication of the median voter theorem is that minority views are not given much weight. Imagine that 40 percent of the population want a lot of money spent on the national parks, and 60 percent want nothing spent. In this case, the median voter's preference is zero, regardless of the intensity of the minority's view. Such is the logic of democracy. Rather than reaching a compromise that takes into account everyone's preferences, majority rule looks only to the person in the exact middle of the distribution.

POLITICIANS ARE PEOPLE TOO

When economists study consumer behavior, they assume that consumers buy the bundle of goods and services that gives them the greatest level of satisfaction. When economists study firm behavior, they assume that firms produce the quantity of goods and services that yields the greatest level of profits. What should they assume when they study people involved in the practice of politics?

Politicians also have objectives. It would be nice to assume that political leaders are always looking out for the well-being of society as a whole, that they are aiming for an optimal combination of efficiency and equality. Nice, perhaps, but not realistic. Self-interest is as powerful a motive for political actors as it is for consumers and firm owners. Some politicians are motivated by a desire for reelection and are willing to sacrifice the national interest when doing so solidifies their base of voters. Other politicians are motivated by simple greed. If you have any doubt, you should look at the world's poor nations, where corruption among government officials is a common impediment to economic development.

This book is not the place to develop a theory of political behavior. But when thinking about economic policy, remember that this policy is made not by a benevolent king but by real people with their own all-too-human desires. Sometimes they are motivated to further the national interest, but sometimes they are motivated by their own political and financial ambitions. We shouldn't be surprised when economic policy fails to resemble the ideals derived in economics textbooks.

"Isn't that the real genius of democracy?...The VOTERS are ultimately to blame."

QUICK QUIZ A public school district is voting on the school budget and the resulting student-teacher ratio. A poll finds that 20 percent of the voters want a ratio of 9:1, 25 percent want a ratio of 10:1, 15 percent want a ratio of 11:1, and 40 percent want a ratio of 12:1. What outcome would you expect the district to end up with? Explain.

In The News

Farm Policy and Politics

What motivates politicians? Humorist Dave Barry offers an answer with his analysis of the Farm Security Act of 2002.

Farmer on the Dole
By Dave Barry

If you're like most American taxpayers, you often wake up in the middle of the night in a cold sweat and ask yourself: "Am I doing enough to support mohair producers?"

I am pleased to report that you are, thanks to bold action taken recently by the United States Congress (motto: "Hey, it's not OUR money!"). I am referring to the 2002 Farm Security Act, which recently emerged from the legislative process very much the way a steaming wad of processed vegetation emerges from the digestive tract of a cow.

The purpose of the Farm Security Act is to provide farmers with "price stability." What do we mean by "price stability"? We mean: your money. You have already been very generous about this: Last year alone, you gave more than $20 billion worth of price stability to farmers. Since 1996, you've given more than a million dollars apiece to more than 1,000 lucky recipients, many of which are actually big agribusinesses. Some of the "farmers" you've sent your money to are billionaires, such as Ted Turner and Charles Schwab, as well as major corporations, such as Chevron, DuPont and John Hancock Mutual Life Insurance.

But that is NOTHING compared with how generous you're about to get, taxpayers! Thanks to the Farm Security Act, over the next 10 years, you'll be providing farmers with 70 percent MORE stability, for a total of $180 billion. At this rate, in a few years farmers will be so stable that they'll have to huddle in their root cellars for fear of being struck by bales of taxpayer-supplied cash raining down on the Heartland states from Air Force bombers.

Perhaps you are asking yourself: "Wait a minute! Isn't this kind of like, I don't know . . . *welfare?*"

No, it is not. Welfare is when the government gives money to people who produce

BEHAVIORAL ECONOMICS

behavioral economics
the subfield of economics that integrates the insights of psychology

Economics is a study of human behavior, but it is not the only field that can make that claim. The social science of psychology also sheds light on the choices that people make in their lives. The fields of economics and psychology usually proceed independently, in part because they address a different range of questions. But recently, a field called **behavioral economics** has emerged in which economists are making use of basic psychological insights. Let's consider some of these insights here.

PEOPLE AREN'T ALWAYS RATIONAL

Economic theory is populated by a particular species of organism, sometimes called *Homo economicus*. Members of this species are always rational. As firm managers, they maximize profits. As consumers, they maximize utility (or equivalently, pick the point on the highest indifference curve). Given the constraints they face, they rationally weigh all the costs and benefits and always choose the best possible course of action.

nothing. Whereas the farm-money recipients produce something that is critical to our nation: votes. Powerful congresspersons from both parties, as well as President Bush, believe that if they dump enough of your money on farm states, the farm states will re-elect them, thus enabling them to continue the vital work of dumping your money on the farm states. So as we see, it's not welfare at all! It's bribery.

But let us not forget the element of National Security. This is where your mohair comes in. As you know, "mohair" is the hair of any animal whose name begins with "mo," such as moose, mouse, mongoose or moray eel.

No, wait, sorry. "Mohair" is actually wool made from the hair of a goat. During WWII, mohair was used to make military uniforms, so it was considered to be a strategic material, and Congress decided that you, the taxpayer, should pay people to produce it. But of course today mohair has no vital mili-

tary purpose, and so . . . you are STILL paying people to produce it! And thanks to the Farm Security Act, you will continue to pay millions and millions of dollars, every year, to mohair producers!

As I say, this is for National Security. If terrorists, God forbid, ever manage to construct a giant time machine and transport the United States back to 1941, and we have to fight World War II again, WE WILL BE READY.

You will also be thrilled, as a taxpayer, to learn that the Farm Security Act provides new subsidies for producers of lentils and chickpeas. And not a moment too soon. This nation has become far too dependent on imported lentils and chickpeas. Try to picture the horror of living in a world in which foreigners, in foreign countries, suddenly cut off our lentil and chickpea supply. Imagine how you would feel if you had to look your small child in the eye and say, "I'm sorry, little Billy or Suzy as the case may

be, but there will be no lentils or chickpeas tonight, and all because we taxpayers were too shortsighted to fork over millions of dollars in support for domestic lentil and chickpea producers, who thus were forced to compete in the market like everybody else, and . . . HEY, COME BACK HERE!"

Yes, that would be a horrible world, all right. And that is why I totally support the Farm Security Act. I hope you agree with me, though I realize that some of you may not; in fact, some of you may be so angry about this column that you've decided to never read anything by me again.

Well, guess what: I don't care! Thanks to the Humor Security Act recently passed by Congress, I'll be getting huge sums of money from the federal government to continue grinding out these columns, year after year, even if nobody wants to read them!

No, that would be stupid.

Source: *Boston Globe Magazine*, June 30, 2002.

Real people, however, are *Homo sapiens*. Although in many ways they resemble the rational, calculating people assumed in economic theory, they are far more complex. They can be forgetful, impulsive, confused, emotional, and shortsighted. These imperfections of human reasoning are the bread and butter of psychologists, but until recently, economists have neglected them.

Herbert Simon, one of the first social scientists to work at the boundary of economics and psychology, suggested that humans should be viewed not as rational maximizers but as *satisficers*. Rather than always choosing the best course of action, they make decisions that are merely good enough. Similarly, other economists have suggested that humans are only "near rational" or that they exhibit "bounded rationality."

Studies of human decision making have tried to detect systematic mistakes that people make. Here are a few of the findings:

- *People are overconfident.* Imagine that you were asked some numerical questions, such as the number of African countries in the United Nations, the height of the tallest mountain in North America, and so on. Instead of being asked for a single estimate, however, you were asked to give a 90 percent confidence interval—a range such that you were 90 percent confident the true number falls within it. When psychologists run experiments like this, they find that most people give ranges that are too small: The true number falls within their intervals far less than 90 percent of the time. That is, most people are too sure of their own abilities.

- *People give too much weight to a small number of vivid observations.* Imagine that you are thinking about buying a car of brand X. To learn about its reliability, you read *Consumer Reports,* which has surveyed 1,000 owners of car X. Then you run into a friend who owns car X, and she tells you that her car is a lemon. How do you treat your friend's observation? If you think rationally, you will realize that she has only increased your sample size from 1,000 to 1,001, which does not provide much new information. But because your friend's story is so vivid, you may be tempted to give it more weight in your decision making than you should.

- *People are reluctant to change their minds.* People tend to interpret evidence to confirm beliefs they already hold. In one study, subjects were asked to read and evaluate a research report on whether capital punishment deters crime. After reading the report, those who initially favored the death penalty said they were surer in their view, and those who initially opposed the death penalty also said they were surer in their view. The two groups interpreted the same evidence in exactly opposite ways.

Think about decisions you have made in your own life. Do you exhibit some of these traits?

A hotly debated issue is whether deviations from rationality are important for understanding economic phenomena. An intriguing example arises in the study of 401(k) plans, the tax-advantaged retirement savings accounts that some firms offer their workers. In some firms, workers can choose to participate in the plan by filling out a simple form. In other firms, workers are automatically enrolled and can opt out of the plan by filling out a simple form. It turns out many more workers participate in the second case than in the first. If workers were perfectly rational maximizers, they would choose the optimal amount of retirement saving, regardless of the default offered by their employer. In fact, workers' behavior appears to exhibit substantial inertia. Understanding their behavior seems easier once we abandon the model of rational man.

Why, you might ask, is economics built on the rationality assumption when psychology and common sense cast doubt on it? One answer is that the assumption, even if not exactly true, may be true enough that it yields reasonably accurate models of behavior. For example, when we studied the differences between competitive and monopoly firms, the assumption that firms rationally maximize profit yielded many important and valid insights. Incorporating complex psychological deviations from rationality into the story might have added realism, but it also would have muddied the waters and made those insights harder to find. Recall from Chapter 2 that economic models are not meant to replicate reality but are supposed to show the essence of the problem at hand as an aid to understanding.

Another reason economists so often assume rationality may be that economists are themselves not rational maximizers. Like most people, they are overconfident, and they are reluctant to change their minds. Their choice among alternative theories of human behavior may exhibit excessive inertia. Moreover, economists may be content with a theory that is not perfect but is good enough. The model of rational man may be the theory of choice for a satisficing social scientist.

PEOPLE CARE ABOUT FAIRNESS

Another insight about human behavior is best illustrated with an experiment called the *ultimatum game.* The game works like this: Two volunteers (who are otherwise strangers to each other) are told that they are going to play a game and could win a total of $100. Before they play, they learn the rules. The game begins with a coin toss, which is used to assign the volunteers to the roles of player A and player B. Player A's job is to propose a division of the $100 prize between himself and the other player. After player A makes his proposal, player B decides whether to accept or reject it. If he accepts it, both players are paid according to the proposal. If player B rejects the proposal, both players walk away with nothing. In either case, the game then ends.

Before proceeding, stop and think about what you would do in this situation. If you were player A, what division of the $100 would you propose? If you were player B, what proposals would you accept?

Conventional economic theory assumes in this situation that people are rational wealth-maximizers. This assumption leads to a simple prediction: Player A should propose that he gets $99 and player B gets $1, and player B should accept the proposal. After all, once the proposal is made, player B is better off accepting it as long as he gets something out of it. Moreover, because player A knows that accepting the proposal is in player B's interest, player A has no reason to offer him more than $1. In the language of game theory (discussed in Chapter 17), the 99-1 split is the Nash equilibrium.

Yet when experimental economists ask real people to play the ultimatum game, the results differ from this prediction. People in player B's role usually reject proposals that give them only $1 or a similarly small amount. Anticipating this, people in the role of player A usually propose giving player B much more than $1. Some people will offer a 50-50 split, but it is more common for player A to propose giving player B an amount such as $30 or $40, keeping the larger share for himself. In this case, player B usually accepts the proposal.

What's going on here? The natural interpretation is that people are driven in part by some innate sense of fairness. A 99-1 split seems so wildly unfair to many people that they reject it, even to their own detriment. By contrast, a 70-30 split is still unfair, but it is not so unfair that it induces people to abandon their normal self-interest.

Throughout our study of household and firm behavior, the innate sense of fairness has not played any role. But the results of the ultimatum game suggest that perhaps it should. For example, in Chapters 18 and 19, we discussed how wages were determined by labor supply and labor demand. Some economists have suggested that the perceived fairness of what a firm pays its workers should also enter the picture. Thus, when a firm has an especially profitable year, workers (like player B) may expect to be paid a fair share of the prize, even if the standard equilibrium does not dictate it. The firm (like player A) might well decide to give workers more than the equilibrium wage for fear that the workers might otherwise try to punish the firm with reduced effort, strikes, or even vandalism.

PEOPLE ARE INCONSISTENT OVER TIME

Imagine some dreary task, such as doing your laundry, shoveling snow off your driveway, or filling out your income tax forms. Now consider the following questions:

In The News

This Is Your Brain on Economics

Research is increasingly focused on the intersection of economics and neuroscience.

Enter the Neuro-Economists: Why Do Investors Do What They Do?

By Tyler Cowen

Las Vegas uses flashing lights and ringing bells to create an illusion of reward and to encourage risk taking. Insurance company offices present a more somber mood to remind us of our mortality. Every marketer knows that context and presentation influence our decisions.

For the first time, economists are studying these phenomena scientifically. The economists are using a new technology that allows them to trace the activity of neurons inside the brain and thereby study how emotions influence our choices, including economic choices like gambles and investments.

For instance, when humans are in a "positive arousal state," they think about

prospective benefits and enjoy the feeling of risk. All of us are familiar with the giddy excitement that accompanies a triumph. Camelia Kuhnen and Brian Knutson, two researchers at Stanford University, have found that people are more likely to take a foolish risk when their brains show this kind of activation.

But when people think about costs, they use different brain modules and become more anxious. They play it too safe, at least

in the laboratory. Furthermore, people are especially afraid of ambiguous risks with unknown odds. This may help explain why so many investors are reluctant to seek out foreign stock markets, even when they could diversify their portfolios at low cost.

If one truth shines through, it is that people are not consistent or fully rational decision makers. Peter L. Bossaerts, an economics professor at the California Institute of Technology, has found that brains assess risk and return separately, rather than making a single calculation of what economists call expected utility.

Researchers can see on the screen how people compartmentalize their choices into different parts of their brains. This may not always sound like economics but neuro-economists start with the insight—borrowed from the economist Friedrich Hayek—that resources are scarce within the brain and must be allocated to competing uses. Whether in economies or brains,

1. Would you prefer (A) to spend 50 minutes doing the task right now or (B) to spend 60 minutes doing the task tomorrow?
2. Would you prefer (A) to spend 50 minutes doing the task in 90 days or (B) to spend 60 minutes doing the task in 91 days?

When asked questions like these, many people choose B to question 1 and A to question 2. When looking ahead to the future (as in question 2), they minimize the amount of time spent on the dreary task. But faced with the prospect of doing the task immediately (as in question 1), they choose to put it off.

In some ways, this behavior is not surprising: Everyone procrastinates from time to time. But from the standpoint of the theory of rational man, it is puzzling. Suppose that, in response to question 2, a person chooses to spend 50 minutes in well-functioning systems should not be expected to exhibit centralized command and control.

Neuro-economics is just getting started. The first major empirical paper was published in 2001 by Kevin McCabe, Daniel Houser, Lee Ryan, Vernon Smith and Theodore Trouard, all economics professors. A neuro-economics laboratory at Cal Tech, led by Colin F. Camerer, a math prodigy and now an economics professor, has assembled the foremost group of interdisciplinary researchers. Many of the early entrants, who have learned neurology as well as economics, continue to dominate the field.

Investors are becoming interested in the money-making potential of these ideas. Imagine training traders to set their emotions aside or testing their objectivity in advance with brain scans. Futuristic devices might monitor their emotions on the trading floor or in a bargaining session and instruct them how to compensate for possible mistakes.

Are the best traders most adept at reading the minds of others? Or is trading skill correlated with traits like the ability to calculate and ignore the surrounding caldron of human emotions?

More ambitiously, future research may try to determine when a short-term price bubble will collapse. Does the market tide turn when people stop smiling, adjust to their adrenalin levels or make different kinds of eye contact?

Not all of neuro-economics uses brain scans. Andrew W. Lo, a professor at the Sloan School of Management at the Massachusetts Institute of Technology, applied polygraph-like techniques to securities traders to show that anxiety and fear affect market behavior. Measuring eye movements, which is easy and cheap, helps the researcher ascertain what is on a subject's mind. Other researchers have opened up monkey skulls to measure individual neurons; monkey neurons fire in proportion to the amount and probability of rewards. But do most economists care? Are phrases like "nucleus accumbens"—referring to a subcortical nucleus of the brain associated with reward—welcome in a profession caught up in interest rates and money supply? Skeptics question whether neuro-economics explains real-world phenomena.

The neuro-economists admit that their endeavor is in its infancy. It is difficult to identify brain modules and their roles. Even if one part of the brain is active at a particular moment, how is that incorporated into a person's broader method for making decisions?

The number of people scanned in any study is typically small, if only because the hookups cost about $500 an hour and require access to an expensive machine. Furthermore, the setting may matter. Perhaps we cannot equate choices made on the New York Stock Exchange trading floor with choices made under a hospital scanner, where the subject must lie on his back, remain motionless and endure a loud whirring, all the while calculating a trading strategy.

That said, neuro-economics will make huge strides as technology allows researchers to identify more brain regions and read brains more accurately and at lower cost. It is a growth area in a profession that knows human feelings matter, but does not always know what to do with them.

What is the next step? Perhaps neuro-economics should turn its attention to political economy. Do people use the same part of their brains to vote as to trade? Is voting governed by fear, disgust or perhaps the desire to gain something new and exciting?

Source: *New York Times*, April 20, 2006.

90 days. Then, when the 90th day arrives, we allow him to change his mind. In effect, he then faces question 1, so he opts for doing the task the next day. But why should the mere passage of time affect the choices he makes?

Many times in life, people make plans for themselves, but then they fail to follow through. A smoker promises himself that he will quit, but within a few hours of smoking his last cigarette, he craves another and breaks his promise. A person trying to lose weight promises that he will stop eating dessert, but when the waiter brings the dessert cart, the promise is forgotten. In both cases, the desire for instant gratification induces the decision maker to abandon his past plans.

Some economists believe that the consumption-saving decision is an important instance in which people exhibit this inconsistency over time. For many people, spending provides a type of instant gratification. Saving, like passing up the cigarette or the dessert, requires a sacrifice in the present for a reward in the distant future. And just as many smokers wish they could quit and many overweight individuals wish they ate less, many consumers wish they saved more of their income. According to one survey, 76 percent of Americans said they were not saving enough for retirement.

An implication of this inconsistency over time is that people should try to find ways to commit their future selves to following through on their plans. A smoker trying to quit may throw away his cigarettes, and a person on a diet may put a lock on the refrigerator. What can a person who saves too little do? He should find some way to lock up his money before he spends it. Some retirement accounts, such as 401(k) plans, do exactly that. A worker can agree to have some money taken out of his paycheck before he ever sees it. The money is deposited in an account that can be used before retirement only with a penalty. Perhaps that is one reason these retirement accounts are so popular: They protect people from their own desires for instant gratification.

QUICK QUIZ Describe at least three ways in which human decision making differs from that of the rational individual of conventional economic theory.

CONCLUSION

This chapter has examined the frontier of microeconomics. You may have noticed that we have sketched out ideas rather than fully developing them. This is no accident. One reason is that you might study these topics in more detail in advanced courses. Another reason is that these topics remain active areas of research and, therefore, are still being fleshed out.

To see how these topics fit into the broader picture, recall the *Ten Principles of Economics* from Chapter 1. One principle states that markets are usually a good way to organize economic activity. Another principle states that governments can sometimes improve market outcomes. As you study economics, you can more fully appreciate the truth of these principles as well as the caveats that go with them. The study of asymmetric information should make you more wary of market outcomes. The study of political economy should make you more wary of government solutions. And the study of behavioral economics should make you wary of any institution that relies on human decision making, including both the market and the government.

If there is a unifying theme to these topics, it is that life is messy. Information is imperfect, government is imperfect, and people are imperfect. Of course, you knew this long before you started studying economics, but economists need to understand these imperfections as precisely as they can if they are to explain, and perhaps even improve, the world around them.

SUMMARY

- In many economic transactions, information is asymmetric. When there are hidden actions, principals may be concerned that agents suffer from the problem of moral hazard. When there are hidden characteristics, buyers may be concerned about the problem of adverse selection among the sellers. Private markets sometimes deal with asymmetric information with signaling and screening.

- Although government policy can sometimes improve market outcomes, governments are themselves imperfect institutions. The Condorcet paradox shows that majority rule fails to produce transitive preferences for society, and Arrow's impossibility theorem shows that no voting system will be perfect. In many situations, democratic institutions will produce the outcome desired by the median voter, regardless of the preferences of the rest of the electorate. Moreover, the individuals who set government policy may be motivated by self-interest rather than the national interest.

- The study of psychology and economics reveals that human decision making is more complex than is assumed in conventional economic theory. People are not always rational, they care about the fairness of economic outcomes (even to their own detriment), and they can be inconsistent over time.

KEY CONCEPTS

moral hazard, *p. 484*
agent, *p. 484*
principal, *p. 484*
adverse selection, *p. 485*
signaling, *p. 487*

screening, *p. 488*
political economy, *p. 489*
Condorcet paradox, *p. 490*
Arrow's impossibility
    theorem, *p. 491*

median voter theorem, *p. 492*
behavioral economics, *p. 494*

QUESTIONS FOR REVIEW

1. What is moral hazard? List three things an employer might do to reduce the severity of this problem.
2. What is adverse selection? Give an example of a market in which adverse selection might be a problem.
3. Define *signaling* and *screening* and give an example of each.
4. What unusual property of voting did Condorcet notice?
5. Explain why majority rule respects the preferences of the median voter rather than the average voter.
6. Describe the ultimatum game. What outcome from this game would conventional economic theory predict? Do experiments confirm this prediction? Explain.

PROBLEMS AND APPLICATIONS

1. Each of the following situations involves moral hazard. In each case, identify the principal and the agent, and explain why there is asymmetric information. How does the action described reduce the problem of moral hazard?
   a. Landlords require tenants to pay security deposits.
   b. Firms compensate top executives with options to buy company stock at a given price in the future.
   c. Car insurance companies offer discounts to customers who install antitheft devices in their cars.

2. Suppose that the Live-Long-and-Prosper Health Insurance Company charges $5,000 annually for a family insurance policy. The company's president suggests that the company raise the annual price to $6,000 to increase its profits. If the firm followed this suggestion, what economic problem might arise? Would the firm's pool of customers tend to become more or less healthy on average? Would the company's profits necessarily increase?

3. A case study in this chapter describes how a boyfriend can signal to a girlfriend that he loves her by giving an appropriate gift. Do you think saying "I love you" can also serve as a signal? Why or why not?

4. Some AIDS activists believe that health insurance companies should not be allowed to ask applicants if they are infected with the HIV virus that causes AIDS. Would this rule help or hurt those who are HIV-positive? Would it help or hurt those who are not HIV-positive? Would it exacerbate or mitigate the problem of adverse selection in the market for health insurance? Do you think it would increase or decrease the number of people without health insurance? In your opinion, would this be a good policy? Explain your answers to each question.

5. The government is considering two ways to help the needy: giving them cash or giving them free meals at soup kitchens. Give an argument for giving cash. Give an argument, based on asymmetric information, for why the soup kitchen may be better than the cash handout.

6. Ken walks into an ice-cream parlor.

   WAITER: "We have vanilla and chocolate today."
   KEN: "I'll take vanilla."
   WAITER: "I almost forgot. We also have strawberry."
   KEN: "In that case, I'll take chocolate."

   What standard property of decision making is Ken violating? (Hint: Reread the section on Arrow's impossibility theorem.)

7. Three friends are choosing a restaurant for dinner. Here are their preferences:

	Rachel	Ross	Joey
First choice	Italian	Italian	Chinese
Second choice	Chinese	Chinese	Mexican
Third choice	Mexican	Mexican	French
Fourth choice	French	French	Italian

   a. If the three friends use a Borda count to make their decision, where do they go to eat?
   b. On their way to their chosen restaurant, they see that the Mexican and French restaurants are closed, so they use a Borda count again to decide between the remaining two restaurants. Where do they decide to go now?
   c. How do your answers to parts (a) and (b) relate to Arrow's impossibility theorem?

8. Three friends are choosing a TV show to watch. Here are their preferences:

	Chandler	Phoebe	Monica
First choice	Lost	Heroes	Scrubs
Second choice	Heroes	Scrubs	Lost
Third choice	Scrubs	Lost	Heroes

   a. If the three friends try using a Borda count to make their choice, what would happen?
   b. Monica suggests a vote by majority rule. She proposes that first they choose between *Lost* and *Heroes,* and then they choose between the winner of the first vote and *Scrubs.* If they all vote their preferences honestly, what outcome would occur?
   c. Should Chandler agree to Monica's suggestion? What voting system would he prefer?

d. Phoebe and Monica convince Chandler to go along with Monica's proposal. In round one, Chandler dishonestly says he prefers *Heroes* over *Lost.* Why might he do this?

9. Five roommates are planning to spend the weekend in their dorm room watching movies, and they are debating how many movies to watch. Here is their willingness to pay:

	Quentin	Spike	Ridley	Martin	Steven
First film	$7	$5	$4	$2	$1
Second film	6	4	2	1	0
Third film	5	3	1	0	0
Fourth film	3	1	0	0	0
Fifth film	1	0	0	0	0

A video costs $8 to rent, which the roommates split equally, so each pays $1.60 per movie.

a. What is the efficient number of movies to watch (that is, the number that maximizes total surplus)?

b. From the standpoint of each roommate, what is the preferred number of movies?

c. What is the preference of the median roommate?

d. If the roommates held a vote on the efficient outcome versus the median voter's preference, how would each person vote? Which outcome would get a majority?

e. If one of the roommates proposed a different number of movies, could his proposal beat the winner from part (d) in a vote?

f. Can majority rule be counted on to reach efficient outcomes in the provision of public goods?

10. A group of athletes are competing in a multi-day triathlon. They have a running race on day one, a swimming race on day two, and a biking race on day three. You know the order in which the athletes finish each of the three components. From this information, you are asked to rank the athletes in the overall competition. You are given the following conditions:

- The ordering of athletes should be transitive: If athlete A is ranked above athlete B, and athlete B is ranked above athlete C, then athlete A must rank above athlete C.
- If athlete A beats athlete B in all three races, athlete A should rank higher than athlete B.
- The rank ordering of any two athletes should not depend on whether a third athlete drops out of the competition just before the final ranking.

According to Arrow's theorem, there are only three ways to rank the athletes that satisfy these properties. What are they? Are these desirable? Why or why not? Can you think of a better ranking scheme? Which of the three properties above does your scheme not satisfy?

11. Why might a political party in a two-party system choose not to move toward the median voter? (Hint: Think about abstentions from voting and political contributions.)

12. Two ice-cream stands are deciding where to locate along a 1-mile beach. The people are uniformly located along the beach, and each person sitting on the beach buys exactly 1 ice-cream cone per day from the nearest stand. Each ice-cream seller wants the maximum number of customers. Where along the beach will the two stands locate?

13. Explain why the following reactions might reflect some deviation from rationality.

a. After a widely reported earthquake in California, many people call their insurance company to apply for earthquake insurance.

b. In January, many fitness clubs offer special annual membership fees to attract customers who have made New Year's resolutions to exercise more. Even when these memberships are costly, many of these new customers seldom visit the gym to work out.

SUGGESTIONS *for* SUMMER READING

IF YOU ENJOYED THE ECONOMICS COURSE THAT YOU
HAVE JUST FINISHED, YOU MIGHT LIKE TO READ MORE ABOUT
ECONOMIC ISSUES IN THE FOLLOWING BOOKS.

· · ·

WILLIAM BREIT AND BARRY T. HIRSCH

Lives of the Laureates

(Cambridge, MA: MIT Press, 2004)

Eighteen winners of the Nobel Prize in Economics
offer autobiographical essays about their lives
and work.

· · ·

PAUL COLLIER

*The Bottom Billion: Why the Poorest Countries
Are Failing and What Can Be Done About It*

(New York: Oxford University Press, 2007)

A former research director at the World Bank offers
his insights into how to help the world's poor.

· · ·

AVINASH DIXIT AND BARRY NALEBUFF

*Thinking Strategically: A Competitive Edge
in Business, Politics, and Everyday Life*

(New York: Norton, 1991)

This introduction to game theory discusses how
all people—from corporate executives to criminals
under arrest—should and do make strategic
decisions.

· · ·

WILLIAM EASTERLY

*The Elusive Quest for Growth: Economists'
Adventures and Misadventures in the Tropics*

(Cambridge, MA: MIT Press, 2001)

A former World Bank economist examines the many
attempts to help the world's poorest nations and
why these attempts have so often failed.

· · ·

MILTON FRIEDMAN

Capitalism and Freedom

(Chicago: University of Chicago Press, 1962)

In this classic book, one of the most important economists of the 20th century argues that society should
rely less on the government and more on
the free market.

· · ·

ALAN GREENSPAN

*The Age of Turbulence: Adventures
in a New World*

(New York: Penguin Press, 2007)

An economist, former Fed chairman, and
Washington insider looks back on his fascinating
life and offers insights on the world economy.

Glossary

ability-to-pay principle the idea that taxes should be levied on a person according to how well that person can shoulder the burden

absolute advantage the ability to produce a good using fewer inputs than another producer

accounting profit total revenue minus total explicit cost

adverse selection the tendency for the mix of unobserved attributes to become undesirable from the standpoint of an uninformed party

agent a person who is performing an act for another person, called the principal

Arrow's impossibility theorem a mathematical result showing that, under certain assumed conditions, there is no scheme for aggregating individual preferences into a valid set of social preferences

average fixed cost fixed cost divided by the quantity of output

average revenue total revenue divided by the quantity sold

average tax rate total taxes paid divided by total income

average total cost total cost divided by the quantity of output

average variable cost variable cost divided by the quantity of output

behavioral economics the subfield of economics that integrates the insights of psychology

benefits principle the idea that people should pay taxes based on the benefits they receive from government services

budget constraint the limit on the consumption bundles that a consumer can afford

budget deficit an excess of government spending over government receipts

budget surplus an excess of government receipts over government spending

business cycle fluctuations in economic activity, such as employment and production

capital the equipment and structures used to produce goods and services

cartel a group of firms acting in unison

circular-flow diagram a visual model of the economy that shows how dollars flow through markets among households and firms

Coase theorem the proposition that if private parties can bargain without cost over the allocation of resources, they can solve the problem of externalities on their own

collusion an agreement among firms in a market about quantities to produce or prices to charge

common resources goods that are rival in consumption but not excludable

comparative advantage the ability to produce a good at a lower opportunity cost than another producer

compensating differential a difference in wages that arises to offset the nonmonetary characteristics of different jobs

competitive market a market with many buyers and sellers trading identical products so that each buyer and seller is a price taker

complements two goods for which an increase in the price of one leads to a decrease in the demand for the other

Condorcet paradox the failure of majority rule to produce transitive preferences for society

constant returns to scale the property whereby long-run average total cost stays the same as the quantity of output changes

consumer surplus the amount a buyer is willing to pay for a good minus the amount the buyer actually pays for it

corrective tax a tax designed to induce private decision makers to take account of the social costs that arise from a negative externality

cost the value of everything a seller must give up to produce a good

cost–benefit analysis a study that compares the costs and benefits to society of providing a public good

cross-price elasticity of demand a measure of how much the quantity demanded of one good responds to a change in the price of another good, computed as the percentage change in quantity demanded of the first good divided by the percentage change in the price of the second good

deadweight loss the fall in total surplus that results from a market distortion, such as a tax

demand curve   a graph of the relationship between the price of a good and the quantity demanded

demand schedule   a table that shows the relationship between the price of a good and the quantity demanded

diminishing marginal product   the property whereby the marginal product of an input declines as the quantity of the input increases

discrimination   the offering of different opportunities to similar individuals who differ only by race, ethnic group, sex, age, or other personal characteristics

diseconomies of scale   the property whereby long-run average total cost rises as the quantity of output increases

dominant strategy   a strategy that is best for a player in a game regardless of the strategies chosen by the other players

economic profit   total revenue minus total cost, including both explicit and implicit costs

economics   the study of how society manages its scarce resources

economies of scale   the property whereby long-run average total cost falls as the quantity of output increases

efficiency   the property of society getting the most it can from its scarce resources

efficiency wages   above-equilibrium wages paid by firms to increase worker productivity

efficient scale   the quantity of output that minimizes average total cost

elasticity   a measure of the responsiveness of quantity demanded or quantity supplied to one of its determinants

equality   the property of distributing economic prosperity uniformly among the members of society

equilibrium   a situation in which the market price has reached the level at which quantity supplied equals quantity demanded

equilibrium price   the price that balances quantity supplied and quantity demanded

equilibrium quantity   the quantity supplied and the quantity demanded at the equilibrium price

excludability   the property of a good whereby a person can be prevented from using it

explicit costs   input costs that require an outlay of money by the firm

exports   goods produced domestically and sold abroad

externality   the uncompensated impact of one person's actions on the well-being of a bystander

factors of production   the inputs used to produce goods and services

fixed costs   costs that do not vary with the quantity of output produced

free rider   a person who receives the benefit of a good but avoids paying for it

game theory   the study of how people behave in strategic situations

Giffen good   a good for which an increase in the price raises the quantity demanded

horizontal equity   the idea that taxpayers with similar abilities to pay taxes should pay the same amount

human capital   the knowledge and skills that workers acquire through education, training, and experience

implicit costs   input costs that do not require an outlay of money by the firm

imports   goods produced abroad and sold domestically

incentive   something that induces a person to act

income effect   the change in consumption that results when a price change moves the consumer to a higher or lower indifference curve

income elasticity of demand   a measure of how much the quantity demanded of a good responds to a change in consumers' income, computed as the percentage change in quantity demanded divided by the percentage change in income

indifference curve   a curve that shows consumption bundles that give the consumer the same level of satisfaction

inferior good   a good for which, other things equal, an increase in income leads to a decrease in demand

inflation   an increase in the overall level of prices in the economy

in-kind transfers   transfers to the poor given in the form of goods and services rather than cash

internalizing the externality   altering incentives so that people take account of the external effects of their actions

law of demand   the claim that, other things equal, the quantity demanded of a good falls when the price of the good rises

law of supply   the claim that, other things equal, the quantity supplied of a good rises when the price of the good rises

law of supply and demand   the claim that the price of any good adjusts to bring the quantity supplied and the quantity demanded for that good into balance

liberalism   the political philosophy according to which the government should choose policies deemed just, as evaluated by an impartial observer behind a "veil of ignorance"

libertarianism   the political philosophy according to which the government should punish crimes and enforce voluntary agreements but not redistribute income

life cycle   the regular pattern of income variation over a person's life

lump-sum tax   a tax that is the same amount for every person

macroeconomics the study of economy-wide phenomena, including inflation, unemployment, and economic growth

marginal changes small incremental adjustments to a plan of action

marginal cost the increase in total cost that arises from an extra unit of production

marginal product the increase in output that arises from an additional unit of input

marginal product of labor the increase in the amount of output from an additional unit of labor

marginal rate of substitution the rate at which a consumer is willing to trade one good for another

marginal revenue the change in total revenue from an additional unit sold

marginal tax rate the extra taxes paid on an additional dollar of income

market a group of buyers and sellers of a particular good or service

market economy an economy that allocates resources through the decentralized decisions of many firms and households as they interact in markets for goods and services

market failure a situation in which a market left on its own fails to allocate resources efficiently

market power the ability of a single economic actor (or small group of actors) to have a substantial influence on market prices

maximin criterion the claim that the government should aim to maximize the well-being of the worst-off person in society

median voter theorem a mathematical result showing that if voters are choosing a point along a line and each voter wants the point closest to his most preferred point, then majority rule will pick the most preferred point of the median voter

microeconomics the study of how households and firms make decisions and how they interact in markets

monopolistic competition a market structure in which many firms sell products that are similar but not identical

monopoly a firm that is the sole seller of a product without close substitutes

moral hazard the tendency of a person who is imperfectly monitored to engage in dishonest or otherwise undesirable behavior

Nash equilibrium a situation in which economic factors interacting with one another each choose their best strategy given the strategies that all the other factors have chosen

natural monopoly a monopoly that arises because a single firm can supply a good or service to an entire market at a smaller cost than could two or more firms

negative income tax a tax system that collects revenue from high-income households and gives subsidies to low-income households

normal good a good for which, other things equal, an increase in income leads to an increase in demand

normative statements claims that attempt to prescribe how the world should be

oligopoly a market structure in which only a few sellers offer similar or identical products

opportunity cost whatever must be given up to obtain some item

perfect complements two goods with right-angle indifference curves

perfect substitutes two goods with straight-line indifference curves

permanent income a person's normal income

political economy the study of government using the analytic methods of economics

positive statements claims that attempt to describe the world as it is

poverty line an absolute level of income set by the federal government for each family size below which a family is deemed to be in poverty

poverty rate the percentage of the population whose family income falls below an absolute level called the poverty line

price ceiling a legal maximum on the price at which a good can be sold

price discrimination the business practice of selling the same good at different prices to different customers

price elasticity of demand a measure of how much the quantity demanded of a good responds to a change in the price of that good, computed as the percentage change in quantity demanded divided by the percentage change in price

price elasticity of supply a measure of how much the quantity supplied of a good responds to a change in the price of that good, computed as the percentage change in quantity supplied divided by the percentage change in price

price floor a legal minimum on the price at which a good can be sold

principal a person for whom another person, called the agent, is performing some act

prisoners' dilemma a particular "game" between two captured prisoners that illustrates why cooperation is difficult to maintain even when it is mutually beneficial

private goods goods that are both excludable and rival in consumption

producer surplus the amount a seller is paid for a good minus the seller's cost of providing it

production function the relationship between the quantity of inputs used to make a good and the quantity of output of that good

production possibilities frontier a graph that shows the combinations of output that the economy can possibly produce given the available factors of production and the available production technology

productivity   the quantity of goods and services produced from each unit of labor input

profit   total revenue minus total cost

progressive tax   a tax for which high-income taxpayers pay a larger fraction of their income than do low-income taxpayers

property rights   the ability of an individual to own and exercise control over scarce resources

proportional tax   a tax for which high-income and low-income taxpayers pay the same fraction of income

public goods   goods that are neither excludable nor rival in consumption

quantity demanded   the amount of a good that buyers are willing and able to purchase

quantity supplied   the amount of a good that sellers are willing and able to sell

rational people   people who systematically and purposefully do the best they can to achieve their objectives

regressive tax   a tax for which high-income taxpayers pay a smaller fraction of their income than do low-income taxpayers

rivalry in consumption   the property of a good whereby one person's use diminishes other people's use

scarcity   the limited nature of society's resources

screening   an action taken by an uninformed party to induce an informed party to reveal information

shortage   a situation in which quantity demanded is greater than quantity supplied

signaling   an action taken by an informed party to reveal private information to an uninformed party

social insurance   government policy aimed at protecting people against the risk of adverse events

strike   the organized withdrawal of labor from a firm by a union

substitutes   two goods for which an increase in the price of one leads to an increase in the demand for the other

substitution effect   the change in consumption that results when a price change moves the consumer along a given indifference curve to a point with a new marginal rate of substitution

sunk cost   a cost that has already been committed and cannot be recovered

supply curve   a graph of the relationship between the price of a good and the quantity supplied

supply schedule   a table that shows the relationship between the price of a good and the quantity supplied

surplus   a situation in which quantity supplied is greater than quantity demanded

tariff   a tax on goods produced abroad and sold domestically

tax incidence   the manner in which the burden of a tax is shared among participants in a market

total cost   the market value of the inputs a firm uses in production

total revenue (for firm)   the amount a firm receives for the sale of its output

total revenue (in a market)   the amount paid by buyers and received by sellers of a good, computed as the price of the good times the quantity sold

Tragedy of the Commons   a parable that illustrates why common resources are used more than is desirable from the standpoint of society as a whole

transaction costs   the costs that parties incur in the process of agreeing to and following through on a bargain

union   a worker association that bargains with employers over wages, benefits, and working conditions

utilitarianism   the political philosophy according to which the government should choose policies to maximize the total utility of everyone in society

utility   a measure of happiness or satisfaction

value of the marginal product   the marginal product of an input times the price of the output

variable costs   costs that vary with the quantity of output produced

vertical equity   the idea that taxpayers with a greater ability to pay taxes should pay larger amounts

welfare   government programs that supplement the incomes of the needy

welfare economics   the study of how the allocation of resources affects economic well-being

willingness to pay   the maximum amount that a buyer will pay for a good

world price   the price of a good that prevails in the world market for that good

Index

Note: Page numbers in **boldface** refer to pages where key terms are defined.